THE ULTIMATE
FLYING WINGS

OF THE

LUFTWAFFE

THE ULTIMATE FLYING WINGS OF THE LUFTWAFFE

JUSTO MIRANDA

FONTHILL

Fonthill Media Language Policy

Fonthill Media publishes in the international English language market. One language edition is published worldwide. As there are minor differences in spelling and presentation, especially with regard to American English and British English, a policy is necessary to define which form of English to use. The Fonthill Policy is to use the form of English native to the author. Justo Miranda was born and educated in Spain and now lives at Madrid therefore British English has been adopted in this publication.

Fonthill Media Limited
Fonthill Media LLC
www.fonthillmedia.com
office@fonthillmedia.com

First published in the United Kingdom
and the United States of America 2015

British Library Cataloguing in Publication Data:
A catalogue record for this book is available from the British Library

ISBN 978-1-78155-372-5

Typeset in Mrs Eaves XL Serif Narrow 11pt on 13.5pt
Printed by CPI Group (UK) Ltd, Croydon, CR0 4YY

Contents

Stealth

The dream of Icarus reflects one of the noblest aspirations of humankind: to fly like a bird. It is considered something positive in all cultures—a synonym of power, liberty, and the ascent to a superior plane of existence. Loki is the opposite character. He is considered a master of deceit in Nordic mythology for his capacity to adopt different appearances or become invisible under a magical cape. According to the values of western Christians, Loki was a negative character that cowardly attacked his enemies without taking any risk. But in German mythology, he is considered cunning and efficient; the Germanic hero Siegfried imitated him using the invisibility cape, *Tarnkappe*. There are similar theories in Japan that oppose the nobility of the samurai to the night ambushes of ninjas, contributing to the universal debate between medieval ideals of chivalry and the advantages of military efficiency. Icarus and Loki are antagonistic characters like the ying and the yang, but their combined capacities create an invincible weapon; the dream of any warrior is to fly over their enemy and strike without being detected.

In 1911, the fabric-covered wings of the Italian Rumpler Taube monoplanes, which carried bomber missions over Libya, were painted with clear nitrate dope over linen. Pilots soon discovered that it was much more difficult to get a sight of this aircraft from the ground against a clear sunny sky.

In May 1912, a German Taube was experimentally coated with a transparent cellulosic sheet named 'Emaillite'. During the flight tests conducted by Lieutenant Edouard Nitter in Wiener-Neustadt, it was established that an Emaillite-coated aircraft became practically invisible over an altitude of 1000 feet.

In 1913, the French presented a monoplane Moreau with transparent wings at the Salon de l'Aviation. The coating consisted of two 0.5-mm layers of 'Emaillite', with a sheet of tulle between each layer to increase its resistance to tearing.

In 1914, Russian engineer Ledebeff tried a new cellulosic cladding on the structure of a Farman biplane, but the material had an excessive elasticity that affected the lifting capacity of the wings.

In the summer of 1913, German engineer Anton Knubel conducted experiments in Münster, coating a Taube with a transparent material named 'Aeroid' to increase the invisibility effect. The aircraft structure was itself painted sky blue. In 1915, Knubel started using 'Cellon', an acetyl cellulosic acid compound made by Rheinisch-Westfälischen

Sprengstoff AG (Rhine-Westfalian Explosives Ltd) in Cologne. The 'Cellon' was transparent, slightly flammable, and could be sewn or glued, though it may not have been very resistant to tearing since the inventor killed himself in an Albatros B.II with transparent wings on 8 September.

On 9 July 1916, another almost invisible aircraft, marked with red crosses, was seen during a test flight in the Somme area by the B.E. 2C of No. 16 Squadron RFC, and was unsuccessfully chased by French fighters. It was one of the three Fokker E.IIIs (*Werknummer* 616, 627, 639) that had been clad with 'Cellon' in June.

The invisibility tests continued during the war, using Aviatik C-1 reconnaissance airplanes and bombers Linke-Hoffman R.I and Gotha VGO in 1917. In dry weather the 'Cellon' was as transparent and as smooth as glass, but it degraded with humidity, losing its aerodynamic properties. One of the Fokker *Eindecker* was coated with the material at 0.4 mm thickness; it weighed 25 kg more than the usual fabric and required much maintenance.

The Central Powers finally had to give up the magic *Tarnkappe* of Siegfried, in favour of a more vulgar material that was more resistant to heat, rain, and tearing. Since 1916, a new fabric had come into usage on the Western Front; it was patterned with polygons of different colours, which reduced the visibility of airplanes by creating the illusion of ground tones.

The new camouflage system was named *Lozenge-Tarnung* on account of its design, based on the Impressionist painters' technique. It produced a distortional optical effect during combat manoeuvres that made accurate aim very difficult for the enemy.

The end of the nineteeth century had seen zoologists discover that tiger stripes mimic the vertical shadows in the reed beds where they hide for hunting. This is a good example of static camouflage. Conversely, zebra stripes seemed to have evolved to increase visibility, although surprisingly five out of six attacks from lions fail. The physical explanation is that the undulation of the zebra stripes whilst the animal is in motion produces 'akinetopsia', an optical distortion that affects the brain mechanism to calculate distances.

The Royal Navy was the first to apply this principle to warfare, and towards 1915, almost every warship was painted with white, black, grey, and blue diagonal stripes to disorientate the telemeters of enemy artillery.

In the air, the Albatros D.V fighters of the Jasta 37 were the first to use optical distortion techniques, with its tailplane painted in black and white diagonal stripes. In combat, violent turns of the airplane achieved the 'zebra effect', thus disrupting the aim of the British pilots. Certainly, the latter had the additional resource of the Iron Crosses painted on the upper wing as a point of reference, but the *Lozenge* camouflage and the aircraft vibration during tight turns made the distance estimation very difficult in deflection shooting. The Fokker DR.I of the Jasta 6 also used the 'zebra effect', and its tailplane, fuselage, and even the interplane struts were painted with stripes.

The system produced results, so that by 1917, almost every German reconnaissance two-seater airplane operating on the Western Front had a rectangular patch of diagonal stripes on its fuselage.

The Royal Flying Corps began to imitate these tactics, and in 1918 it was common to see the Bristol F-2B and Sopwith Camel emblazoned with a series of white bands over their khaki rear fuselage. The technique reached its peak of refinement during the summer of 1918 when the Albatros D.V flown by Lt Fritz Rumey was assigned to the Jasta 5, an elite squadron. On this airplane the diagonal stripes had four different widths and had been painted in spirals along the fuselage, giving it the appearance of a striped candy cane.

The Austrians had their own opinion on the subject. They started painting small spirals on the upper surfaces of the Phönix fighters, and later, in around 1917, they camouflaged the Aviatiks with a special scheme of hexagons. The colours of these hexagons varied in intensity, with lighter shades on the wing tips and tail surfaces intended to blur the characteristic shape of the airplane.

The British had a problem with the colour of their airplanes. After 1915, all were painted brown, and both fighter pilots and the anti-aircraft artillery had the tendency to open fire on anything of a different colour—French airplanes included. Consequently, British experiments were more conservative, even if the roundels on the upper wing of some airplanes were latterly painted in an asymmetric position to confuse the enemy, using a tactic similar to the false eye some tropical fishes have near the tail. They also used additional, more blurred roundels, painted on unusual spots of the airplane, like the tailplane, the back of the fuselage, or the central section of the upper wing.

In 1918, limited attempts were made at skewed-perspective box-grids, diminishing overlapping rectangles and high visibility but misleading geometrical designs. These experiments were shaped by the advice of painters of the 'Vorticist School'—the British version of the Futurism Movement—such as Wyndham Lewis. Their ultimate objective was to create in the enemy pilot that second of doubt or confusion that was frequently the key to escape.

These practices did not end with the First World War. In 1923, the Finnish Fokker D.VII was painted in a 'splinter' scheme in dark blue, light grey, purple, and light green. During the '30s, the new Luftwaffe started to use the 'splinter' in two or three different shades, although some Heinkel 45 light bombers, seen during the Spanish Civil War, still kept their *Lozenge* camouflage.

In 1935, the Hawker Demon fighters of No. 74 Squadron of the RAF, based in Malta, tried a new type of camouflage in ochre, yellow, grey, green, and brick red, with just one roundel starboard of the upper wing and the opposite aileron painted in aluminium. The general idea, apparently not very successful, was not to make the plane hard to see, but rather, hard to be aimed at by enemy pilots.

During the early 1930s, French chemists created a new transparent material similar to cellophane, named 'Rodoid' or organic glass. In 1935, the Russian engineer S. G. Kozlov launched new experiments, replacing the fabric coating of a Yakovlev AIR-4 trainer with 'Rodoid' sheets. To reinforce the optical effect, the inner structure of the airplane had been painted in aluminium colour. The flight test was conducted by two airplanes of the AIR-4 model (one standard and the other with transparent cladding) flying in parallel to test the difference of visibility from the ground. A reduction of visibility by 75 per cent was recorded. However, the test also revealed that the 'Rodoid' had electrostatic properties that caused it to accumulate the dust generated during take off, thus losing much of its transparency. The invisible airplane project, named 'Nyeridimyi Samolyet', was cancelled in 1935.

The Munich crisis of September 1938 proved, among other things, how unprepared the French and British air forces were for battle. At that time, London was defended by biplanes that were slower than the 'postal' Heinkel He 111. Allied fighters Hawker Fury and the Dewoitine 510 lost their aluminized painting of peace time and were hastily covered with a dark green layer.

Despite their theoretical initial neutrality, North American airplanes also lost the chrome yellow on their wings. In 1940, the US Army Air Corps performed low-visibility camouflage tests with the Curtiss P.36 and Northrop A-17 A. The US Navy reproduced the British experiments of the 'Vorticist School' with the Brewster F2A and Northrop BT-1 in North Island, California. Finally, mass production prevailed—the Seversky and Curtiss were painted in olive drab, and the Brewster and Grumman in naval grey.

In 1939, the colour of European aviation came to match the darkness of its future. The Germans used a splinter pattern in two shades of dark green. The British used dark green and dark earth on the upper surfaces, and black and white on the undersides. The French used earth, ash, and dark green. Over the Franco-German border, all airplanes looked the same, so much so that the German Bf 109 shot down Belgian Hurricanes on neutrality patrols, mistaking them for British fighters. The authentic Hurricanes of the British Expeditionary Force (BEF) in turn shot down French recce Potez 630 airplanes, confusing them with German heavy fighters Bf 110, and were attacked by Morane fighters that took them for Luftwaffe airplanes.

Only the Poles showed some creativity. Upon entering war with Germany, most Polish fighters were well positioned in auxiliary aerodromes; square-shaped national markings were painted on the wings in asymmetric positions, and some PZL P.11C fighters of No. 161 Squadron had schemes of optical distortion painted in zig-zags over the wings, though this was not nearly enough to overcome the technical and numeric superiority of the Luftwaffe.

Once airplanes came to be manufactured in tens of thousands in the Second World War, the dynamic of their assembly lines did not allow for any experimentation with complex camouflages. There was not even the time or manpower to paint the airplanes, so many Mustangs, Fortresses, and Thunderbolts were delivered with a naked aluminium coating, while nationality roundels were replaced with big decals.

In a global battlefield that stretched from the jungle to the sea and from the Arctic to the desert, airplanes were given every kind of conceivable camouflage to avoid observation. Some missions, like stratospheric combat, photographic reconnaissance, or night-fighting, required specially modified airplanes with camouflage schemes adapted to the environment in which they operated.

The Ju 86P, Bf 109 G-6/AS, Spitfire HF Mk VIII, Westland Welkin, and D. H. Mosquito NF.XV—all intended for high-altitude combat—were painted light grey. The Lockheed P-38 F-5s that photographed the Ruhr at medium height were painted a bluish fog-grey; the Spitfire P.R. Mk IV and Mosquito P.R. Mk XVI were painted a deep blue colour to eliminate their visibility against the sky at high altitude; while the Spitfire P.R. Mk VII of No. 541 Squadron, operating at dawn in clear weather, was painted a pink colour. For combat in darkness, the RAF painted the under surfaces of all its bombers black, thus making them less visible to the reflectors.

Until 1943, all night-fighters were painted in black. Germany used the Arado Ar 68E, Bf 109 E-4, Bf 110 C-6 and E-2, Do 17 Z-10, Do 215 B-5, and Do 217 J and N. The British used the Defiant Mk II, Hurricane Mk II, Beaufighter Mk II, Mosquito NF. Mk II, and even some Spitfire Mk VBs of No. 111 Squadron. At the beginning they used an extra-matt anti-reflective paint, but it became apparent that it produced drag, limiting the airplanes' speed. The Americans operated in Europe and the Pacific with the Northrop P-61 and Douglas Havoc II, the Japanese with the Nakajima J1N1-S *Gekko*, the Italians with the Caproni Vizzola F-5, and the French with the Potez 631. Black paint seemed to be the most logical solution, but it was far from an infallible technique, since black aircraft were very vulnerable to observation from above when flying over clouds that were illuminated by reflectors from the ground.

The Germans started to use this to their advantage in August 1943, using conventional fighters Bf 109 and Fw 190 in the *Wilde Sau* night operations. In the winter of 1942, some Do 215 B-5 and Do 217 J night fighters were experimentally painted in light grey, to make them less visible to the gunners of the Lancaster and pilots of the Mosquito NF. II escort. The results were good and it was ordered that all night fighters be fully painted with RLM 76 *Hellblau* (light blue).

Harking back to experiments that applied 'night' *Lozenge* to Gotha bombers in the First World War, hazing effects were improved by patches or 'worm' schemes of RLM 75 *Hell Violett-Grau* (light grey–violet), which blurred the outline of aircraft. These schemes worked better on bigger airplanes—the Ju 88 G-6, Do 217 N, and Bf 110 G-4—while fighters Bf 109 G-5 and G-6 and Fw 190 A-6 were painted in RLM 02 *Grüngrau* (light green-grey). Some had the underside starboard wing painted in black to facilitate spotting by their own flak.

After 1943, the idea was adopted for Mosquito night fighters, and their overall black camouflage was changed to the standard daylight dark green and ocean grey on the upper surfaces. Undersurfaces were kept black because the RAF considered it more effective in hiding from reflectors, provided that the Mosquitos flew over a layer of clouds.

The accuracy and volume of fire from flak increased daily. Among British fighters making strafing missions over occupied France, the number of casualties grew without interruption until 1945.

In 1942, Captain Paul Hexter designed a black and white dazzle camouflage scheme for the underside of ground attack airplanes. A test on a Mustang Mk IA suggested that, as it had done with the warships of the First World War, black and white dazzle camouflage distorted the distance calculation of German telemeters during flights at low altitude—the so-called 'zebra effect'. Its use was never generalized due to its difficult maintenance.

Since time immemorial, magicians have hidden objects by distracting the attention of their audience, and the same principle applies here. In May 1940, the gunners of the BEF defending the French aerodrome at Vitry were preparing to aim fire at two Messerschmitts headed towards them at an altitude of 600 feet. Focused on their objective, the gunners were caught unawares by the second pair of the *Schwarm* that surged from a cluster of trees at ground level and destroyed several Hurricanes of No. 56 Squadron. In the Pacific, the *Betty* torpedo bombers of the Japanese Imperial Navy used the same technique, operating in groups of three airplanes, of which a single one flew at medium altitude.

In the Mediterranean, the Sicilian-style camouflage of the Savoia 79 of the Regia Aeronautica rendered the airplane too visible over the sea. Some machines specialising in torpedo attacks were painted with a layer of light grey in the front of the fuselage and on the leading edges of wings to diminish frontal visibility.

In the Atlantic, anti-submarine aircraft of the US Navy had the same problem: the U-boat immersed at the slightest hint of a sighting. In 1943, an experiment under the code name 'Yehudi' was performed with a view to reducing frontal visibility against the luminous background of the sky. It consisted of ten sealed-beam lights being installed along the leading edges of the wings and the rim of the engine cowling of an Avenger TBM-3D bomber. The tests proved that the airplane with the 'Yehudi' could only be detected from 2 miles distance; without the 'Yehudi' the airplane could be detected from 12 miles and the submarine therefore had time to escape.

The entry into service of new centimetric radars, which the Kriegsmarine's *Metox* detectors could not trace, disrupted the previous balance in the Battle of the Atlantic by rendering the 'Yehudi' useless. But the experiments continued on Liberators, and were only declassified in the 1980s.

During the Vietnam War, the idea was resumed under the 'Compass-Ghost' code name and tests were pursued on a blue and white F-4 Phantom, to which nine high-intensity lamps were attached on the wings and fuselage, reducing its detection range by 30 per cent.

In the mid-1990s, progress achieved in Computer Generated Holography, wavelength computation with the Fourier transform method, and Point Source Holograms, allowed the creation of holographic images in 3D around an object in order to hide it. But the system only functioned with static objects and the phased array optics required a considerable amount of electronic equipment.

In 2003, researchers at the University of Tokyo developed an active camouflage system with video cameras that registered backgrounds around the object that should be camouflaged. This background was then projected in front of the object to render it invisible.

In 2004, the discovery of graphene made possible to manufacture curved video screens and adapt them to any surface. An aircraft sheathed in graphene screens and equipped with video cameras registering background from every angle, and then projecting the images onto the screens at the other side of the aircraft, may become practically invisible.

Layers of graphene are extremely thin so that several with different properties may be superimposed. Thanks to the 'Adaptiv' system developed by BAE Systems in 2011, under the optical screen it is possible to select a layer of hexagonal graphene elements to be heated or cooled down. This layer very efficiently acts as infra-red camouflage.

INFRA-RED (IR)

In the first year of the Second World War, an attempt was made to improve the detection capabilities of night fighters with the help of searchlights installed onboard aircraft.

Italians used a night version of the Fiat CR-42 with searchlights in gondolas under the wings and a prolonged engine exhaust. The system was inefficient due to the limited power of the searchlights.

In 1942 there were ten British 'Turbinlite' operational squadrons of Douglas Havoc bombers fitted with a powerful searchlight on the nose. Guided by radar until the intruder came into proximity, the bombers would light up suddenly, giving the accompanying Hurricane Mk II fighters the opportunity to visually locate the target. The system had a weakness in the difficulty inherent in coordinating attacks in darkness and the easy targets that searchlights made for German gunners; it was left to one side by mid-1943.

In order to level the playing field, the Luftwaffe started using infra-red searchlights with a diameter of 30 cm installed under the nose of some Bf 110 D-3 and E-1 versions. The radiation reflected on the target was made visible for the human eye through an IR telescope named *Q-Rohr*, installed in front of the pilot.

The system was developed by Allgemeine Elektrizitätsgesellschaft (AEG) in Berlin and Zeiss in Jena under the name *Spanner Anlage I*, and entered into service in 1941 with some Messerschmitts of 4./NJG1 Squadron and ten Dornier 17 Z-7 and Z-10 of I./NJG2 Squadron. The latest were equipped with a more powerful searchlight with a diameter of 60 cm, installed in the nose cone. Later on, the system was experimentally installed in the Do 215 B-5 of the 4./NJG1. In all cases, *Spanner I* proved to be inadequate, unable to distinguish friend from foe, and with a range of only 200 m.

In February 1942, a Do 217 E-2 was modified with the installation of a FuG 202 radar with a minimum detection range of 200 m and an IR active *Spanner III* seeker for short distances. It was an improved version of larger scope, with a searchlight of 60 cm diameter, manufactured by AEG. It was useful for an approximation amid the clouds, although in most cases, a target within 200 m was visible without electronic assistance.

The *Spanner II* was an IR passive device developed by AEG–Zeiss for its use in single-engine fighters, detecting only IR emitting targets such as exhaust flames. It was tested on an Fw 190 A on 10 December 1941, with poor results.

The development of the IR devices was difficult and slow. Until the Zeiss FuG 280 *Kiel Z* appeared in 1945, the results of tests were disappointing. It was a passive seeker, with a 4,000-m range and a 25-cm-diameter scanning mirror with 20-degree side-to-side forward view that displayed the indications on a cathode ray tube. It was tested on the Ju 88 G-6 (3C + AB) of I./NJG4 on 12 March 1945—too late to be useful.

The main shortfall of the first *Spanner* was the reduced field of vision of its telescope. The image also suffered interferences from the moon, the stars, flares, and explosions of flak.

In 1944, the Luftwaffe started using *Verbandsflug* tactics, with a great number of night fighters operating in the same sector. To avoid confusion, the airplanes identified themselves using the infra-red lamp named *Gänsebrust*.

British bombers used IR navigation lights from 1944 onwards. To locate them, the Germans developed the IR seeker named *Falter*, which was difficult to use, with just 15 degrees of field vision.

Another system, called *Mücke*, was being tested at the end of the war in Europe. Although the Allies preferred to use their advanced centimetric radars, the Luftwaffe ordered the firms AEG and Siemens to develop the airborne warning devices *Froschauge* and *Katze*—the latest based on the *Spanner II*—and an IR jamming system named *Wärmebold* that were never used in combat.

RADAR

German scientists of the Gesellschaft für Elektroakustische und Mechanische Apparate mbH (GEMA) obtained their first practical radar in 1934. The prototype operated at a wavelength of 50 cm. It was followed by the naval radio telemeter *Seetakt* in autumn 1936, the early warning radar *Freya* at the beginning of 1937, and the flak director *Würzburg* in mid-1939.

Military men and politicians who were in on the secret thought that only Germany had radio detection technology, but scientists with professional contacts outside of the Reich had their doubts. In an effort to clarify this important issue, the Chief of Communication Affairs of the Luftwaffe, General Wolfgang Martini, obtained permission from Göring to transform the obsolete *Graf Zeppelin II* (LZ 130) airship into a sophisticated ELINT platform, with the objective of spying on the military radio emissions of potentially hostile countries.

A week before the Munich Agreement to annex the Sudetenland, the LZ 130—with a group of thirty radio operators onboard—made a reconnaissance flight of 11 hours along the Czech frontier while its crew scanned the ether for unusual signals, without any results. During the flight it was established that the structure of LZ 130 considerably impinged on the effectiveness of the receptors, which were equipped with simple non-directional dipole aerials. The problem was solved by installing some directional aerials in a spy gondola that could be lowered as much as 4,000 feet below the airship.

On 13 April and 15 June 1939, LZ 130 made two secret flights of 30 hours, possibly along the French, Belgian, and Dutch border. On 12 July, the Electronic Intelligence (ELINT) mission was directed to the coast of Belgium and Holland, going up to 140 miles from the east coast of Britain. Four days later, the airship looked for radio signals over Polish borders. The flight was repeated on 22 July.

The start of the Second World War was imminent and Martini could not find any signs of enemy radars. On 2 August, it was the turn of the British. LZ 130 scanned the Dutch and Belgian coasts once again, before turning northwards to the UK's North Sea coast, again without any results. During the return flight, it pretended to suffer a failure, to get within visual distance of the coast, near Aberdeen, in order to investigate a strange antenna mast that was emitting strong radio impulses in several frequencies. The only British answer was the visit of a Miles Magister trainer from No. 612 Squadron that had come to investigate the giant.

The next day, there was a diplomatic protest without major consequences. That seemed to put an end to the matter in as much as the Oberkommando der Luftwaffe (OKL) reached the conclusion that British antennas were only being used to study long distance radio transmissions by way of the layers of ionized air in the atmosphere. In fact, during its 48-hour flight, the Zeppelin had been located by twelve radar stations of the British 'Chain Home' which operated in the 25-Mhz band. The emissions went undetected by the Germans who mainly focused their search on the radio spectrum above 100 Mhz, the *Freya* frequency.

Such a demonstration of ethnocentrism is hardly unique to the proud Nazi military men. For fifty years, researchers of the Search for Extraterrestrial Intelligence (SETI) project have been looking for radio emissions that would prove the existence of extraterrestrial intelligence within hydrogen (1.2 Ghz) and OH (1.64 Ghz) frequencies, following the logic that intelligence goes hand in hand with the presence of water.

The fact is that in 1940 the Germans captured two mobile radar stations abandoned by the British in Dunkirk, finally finding out that they operated in 4-m wavelength. The British also measured the emissions of the antennas of the 'Chain Home' in Dover in 12 m. General Martini concluded that German equipment was superior to the British (*Freya* worked in 2.40 m, *Seetakt* in 80 cm and *Würzburg* in 53 cm). This excess of confidence would cost the Luftwaffe the loss of 1,887 airplanes that summer, thanks to British radar.

General Martini also ignored that France had already built an anti-iceberg radar in 1934 for the SS *Normandie* liner. It functioned with two emitters, each in 80 cm and 16 cm, and was installed in Sannois in 1939, supporting the defence of Paris without being detected by the ELINT German services. Neither did the latter suspect the existence of the 70-cm Dutch radar, the only prototype built by the Delft and Leiden scientists, which was dismantled after the May 1940 tests to avoid capture.

On 18 December 1939, the *Freya* station of Wangerooge directed the Bf 109 fighters of the 10./JG 26 and II./JG 77 in the daylight interception of twenty-two Wellington bombers of No. 3 Group, which had tried to attack the Kriegsmarine base of Heligoland. The casualties surpassed 50 per cent, and the RAF was forced to bomb by night for the rest of the war. At the beginning of May 1940, German flak shot down British aircraft for the first time—a bomber dropping propaganda leaflets—with the help of a *Würzburg*.

The RAF continued its nightly offensives until a photographic survey made at the end of 1940 showed that only a quarter of the bombings hit their objectives. The only resource left was to attack cities, the only target that could be identified from the air in darkness.

But to achieve this aim, British bombers would have to go through the German air defence system, the *Kammhuber* Line, which extended from Denmark to Paris. It was divided into sectors, named *Himmelbett* cells, each of which was equipped with a pair of *Würzburg* and an interception control that guided the night fighter towards any bomber that made its way into its surveillance area. German fighters did not have Identification Friend or Foe (IFF) until 1942 and only one could operate for every sector for the sake of avoiding confusion.

German fighters also lacked airborne radar, therefore they used the *Würzburg* system to guide the fighters near enough to the intruder to visually locate it by its blue exhaust flames. This was a recurring concern for the British Bomber Command, which went to great lengths to reduce luminosity. From the beginning of 1941, the Technical Office of the Boscombe Down test centre worked fervently on the design of flame damping, tailored to each type of engine and aircraft, performing optical test flights and laboratory simulations at different altitudes. Towards 1944, different Infra-red (IR) measurement techniques were also employed.

In 1939, Telefunken manufactured a radio telemeter that operated on a 60-cm wavelength and proposed—without success—the design to be manufactured as a radio altimeter for the Luftwaffe. In February 1940, research went on, this time tilting the beam towards the horizontal, with a view to exploring its potential to locate aircraft. The project was delayed until April 1941 due to disagreements within the Technical Office of the Luftwaffe on the position of the antennae.

The telemeter was put into service in 1942 as FuG 202 *Lichtenstein BC*. It operated on 490 Mhz, generating a narrow beam that made following the target difficult. Its *Matratzen* antenna, with four double pairs of 27.5-cm dipoles mounted on the aircraft nose, reduced speed by 40.2 kph. This was not much of a problem for a Bf 110, but it excessively reduced the performance of heavy fighters such as the Dornier Do 217, which was ultimately used to test the new IR *Spanner* detectors.

The Lichtenstein fed only primary information through the cathodic tubes, which would have registered in the following way: 'there is something ahead and a little to the left' and 'there is something in front of and slightly above you'. Based on this information, the radar operator gave instructions to the pilot until he could see the exhaust flames: eight meant a Lancaster, four a Halifax, and two a Wellington.

Once the British started to use 'Window' countermeasures at the end of 1943, the FuG 202 was replaced by the FuG 220 Lichtenstein SN-2. The new radar used the huge *Hirschgeweih* antenna with dipoles of 1.15 m, but was immune to Window and had a range of 4,000 m. Besides the considerable drag produced by the antenna, its main fault was that its minimum range of 400 m did not allow for visual target acquisition. Any target closer than that could not be detected because the echo returned while the receiver was still switched off. Until the problem was resolved in the form of the SN-2c, one of the *Matratzen* dipoles of the FuG 202 was provisionally installed between the antennae to be used at short distance. The speed reduction to a Ju 88 was excessive, but not to a Bf 110 G-4 or He 119 A-0.

Even after visually identifying the target, the task of a fighter was not easy. Upon examination of Allied bomber wreckages, few were hit fewer than twenty times by 20-mm rounds. A statistical study of the Luftwaffe established that to achieve twenty hits with an Ikaria MGFF cannon from a range of 400 m, it was necessary to shoot 352 rounds of fire; the issue was that the weapon was fed by ammunition drums that contained only sixty shells.

The Do 217 night fighters needed to get away after each attack to manually recharge their cannons; consequently, they occasionally lost track of their targets. The same study stated that 450 *g* of HE were required to destroy a four-engine bomber, that is, the equivalent of a 55-mm hit or five 30-mm hits. The 30-mm cannon available was the Rheinmetall-Borsig Mk 108. With this weapon, according to the statistics, it would be necessary to shoot eighty-eight rounds of fire to make five hits—a low effective range. For this reason, the Mk 108 was not very popular among the crews of night fighters, especially because the explosion triggered by its potent *Minengeschoss* ammunition frequently triggered the explosion of the bomber at close range. The impact angle of these cannons was problematic; in a conventional attack from the rear, their blunt-nosed projectiles struck the wings and fuselage of their target at a very sharp angle and frequently bounced off instead of drilling the surface.

The belt-fed Mauser MG 151/20 cannon was mainly consigned to the production of the Bf 109 F-4 and not available in sufficient quantity until 1943. The same can be said of the 55-mm and 270-kg Mk 112 until 1945.

The solution, based on British concepts from the First World War, received the strange name of *Schräge Musik* and consisted of positioning the fighter itself underneath the bomber and to shoot from below, with cannons in vertical position.

The main advantage of this strategy was that, from this angle, the bomber offered a bigger target and it was easier to shoot at the fuel tanks located in its wings. It was also easier to make the bomber explode if shots reached the bomb bay. *Schräge Musik* came into usage by the end of 1943, and as soon as 1945, the Technical Office of the Luftwaffe considered it standard equipment for the *Nachtjagd*.

This tactic was felt to be further warranted by the tenacity of British heavy bombers, who had the 'disgusting' habit of defending themselves with their own two rear turrets, which had a compounded fire power equivalent to one 1940 Spitfire. Tail gunners increased their chances of survival by removing the Plexiglas panel in front of their eyes, which gave them a visibility advantage over the night-fighter pilots who saw the world through a 10-cm-thick armoured windshield.

By the end of 1943, the Mosquito NF.II of No. 100 Group started to perform 'Mahmoud' missions, escorting the bomber stream up to Berlin. They had an AI Mk IV radar that worked either in frontal search or in tail warning mode and was already superior to the *Lichtenstein*—an advantage that only increased throughout the rest of the war. German casualties grew by the day, making it necessary to install either the *Lichtenstein SN-2d* or the *Neptun-R* tail warning radar. However, the Mosquito's wooden airframe made detection very difficult for this radar at medium range.

British bombers also started using the 'Monica' tail warning radar in the summer of 1943. When the presence of an aggressor was detected, pilots made a brusque turn or 'corkscrew' manoeuvre to break contact and escape—in the event of bombers—or positioned themselves behind the attacker—in the event of fighters. Were this fighting sequence to occur in the darkness, the advantage was on the side whose radar had the widest angle. For this reason, some Bf 110 and Ju 88 night fighters carried additional *Flensburg* passive receiver antennae in the wings to supplement the main radar function. By 1945, both sides were using steerable parabolic antennae.

The *Neptun* series of radars was designed to replace the *Lichtenstein*, which by 1944 was no longer immune to either the new Window or British electronic countermeasures. But *Neptun* still had detection problems at a range below 300 m due to a returning echo. Shorter centimetric wavelengths would resolve many of these issues because they could be accurately focused and directed by a reflector small enough to be carried internally. In August 1942, the Germans estimated that the equipment able to operate on centimetric wavelengths could not be built until 1944. In December 1942, the Mosquito made the first accurate attack with the 'Oboe' system (an application of their IFF); soon afterwards, the Germans learnt how to interfere with it when emitting on 1.25 m.

On 15 January 1943, the Technical Office of the Luftwaffe concluded that centimetric wavelengths did not represent a military advantage significant enough to justify the effort required to obtain them. Conversion to centimetric wavelengths would have meant retiring all available radio technicians from the war front, modifying the production lines to manufacture new types of radio lamps, obtaining bigger quantities of wolfram from the Allied countries, and delaying the series production of the *Neptun*.

On 2 February, a Stirling bomber of the Pathfinder Force that marked targets for an incursion against Hamburg was shot down by flak over Rotterdam. Examination of the wreckage disclosed that part of its electronic equipment operated on a 9-cm wavelength. Its self-destruction mechanism had failed to work, and this was the first 'H2S' cartographic radar to be recovered by the Germans almost intact.

This type of radar was based on cavity magnetron technology, a casual discovery made by J. T. Randall and A. H. Boot in 1940. When German technicians were able to apply this technology to their radar sets, they were astonished by the quality of the images received through its small parabolic mirror. The geography of the landscape and even the shape of ships and airplanes could be clearly distinguished, and at a time when the *Lichtenstein SN-2* still operated on 3.30 m.

German manufacturing systems still took some time to adapt to the new technology, and the already overburdened electronics industry was only able to produce ten copies, denominated *Berlin N-1*, before the end of the war in Europe.

Meanwhile, the Allies had managed to regain the upper hand over the waves: U-boats were located and destroyed in the darkness, without any reaction from their *Metox* to the 9-cm emissions. When the new *Naxos* radars were installed, the Allies started to emit on 3-cm wavelengths and the slaughter of U-boats carried on. In the air, *Lichtenstein* emissions were detected by the 'Serrate' radar devices of the Beaufighter and Mosquito, and the German IFF was efficiently interfered with by the 'Perfectos' system.

Oboe incursions resumed with the help of 9-cm transmissions because it was impossible to interfere with the German equipment of the time. On 24 July 1943, Bomber Command launched a massive attack on the heart of the Reich using Window, interference equipment installed in the aircraft, electronic decoys, and long-range escort fighters Mosquito N.F. XII and N.F. XIII. The latest was equipped with a nitrous-oxide boost that had also aided the successful hunting of the Fw 190 and Me 410 night intruders in the *Steinbock Operation*.

In May 1944, the new N.F. XIX was authorised to perform missions of free fighting over Germany, trying to attract enemy night fighters by emitting the same signals as British bombers equipped with Monica radar. By the beginning of 1945, the N.F. 30 came into operation with engines equipped with exhaust shrouds, designed for minimum IR emission and almost invisible in darkness. They were fast enough to hunt the Me 262 B-1a/U1 and the Fi 103 flying bombs.

Germany had lost its offensive lead and was forced to adopt a survivor strategy based on anti-radar techniques and equipment. The old Matratzen and Hirschgeweih antennae were replaced by *Panorama* swivelling mountings and *Parabolspiegel* (parabolic mirrors). Every detection set was improved with the addition of filters, Doppler devices, frequency-switching devices—*Bernhard, Eidechse, Feuerzange, Goldhammer, K-Laus, Kurmark, Laus, Mosaik, Nürnberg, Reiss-Laus, Riese-Gustav, Schliebelaus , Stendhal, Tastlaus, Taunus, Urechse, Wismar, Würzlaus* (named *Flammen*)—and complementary IR detectors and sound locators.

Airplanes and missiles were equipped with passive receivers of the types *Naxos, Fishpond, Kleiner Heidelberg, Postklystron*, and *Radieschen* that served to detect the emissions of the Allied radars. The U-boats and surface vessels of the Kriegsmarine were supplied with the naval equivalents of these devices—*Metox, Bali, Zypern, Palau, Sumatra*, and *Timor*.

Aluminium bands were also used to jam Allied radars, in imitation of the British Window strategy (under the German name *Düppelstreifen*). Besides being launched from bombers in the classic way, 86-mm launch rockets (similar to the current Chaff) were designed for the Kriegsmarine under the name Spgr.L/4.8 *Kurhessen*. They surrounded the ship in a cloud of metallic strips when detected by enemy radar. U-boats had been using the *Aphrodite IV* system (Fu MT1) since June 1943. Radar decoy balloons coated with metallic paint, anchored to a floating plate, rose a few metres above the water surface, producing a strong radar echo similar to that of the U-boat conning tower on British radar screens.

Another anti-radar technique developed was *Netzhemdsabsorption durch*, which involved the manufacturing of radar-absorbent materials (RAM). Its first practical application consisted of coating the U-boat snorkels with a special compound of rubber and carbon named *Sumpf* that almost obliterated the radar profile. It was first employed in May 1944, with a pressure and water resistant plastic *Zelligelit* coating.

Anti-sonar coatings *Tarnmatte* and *Wesch* were developed shortly afterwards for other parts of the submarine, like the deck and conning tower. The first one was a thick sheet of *Buna* synthetic rubber that contained iron oxide powder, and was used to deter the 9.7-cm wavelength of the H2S British radar. The second one was a rubber sheet containing carbonyl iron powder, about 7.62 mm thick, with a resonant frequency at 3 Ghz. The rest of the submarine hull was covered with *Alberich* anechoic coating, a 4-mm-thick rubber called *Oppanol* that deterred 'ASDIC' sonar pulses.

Anti-radar coating also existed for airplanes, for instance the *Schornsteinfeger*, developed in the Hochfrequenzinstitut (BHF) in Travemünde. This radar camouflage consisted of a thick bituminous paint, heavily loaded with carbon. When applied in thickness—carefully calculated in relation to the radar frequency—the arriving signal would be trapped within the dielectric material and its return energy damped out and transformed into heat. This paint was more efficient when applied to the non-metallic structures that anticipated later composite materials.

The most efficient device was the *IG-Jaumann*, developed by IG Farben. It consisted of 8-cm-thick panels formed by seven layers of conductive plastic carbon material separated by layers of dielectric *Igelit* polyvinylchloride. It was employed against wavelengths between 2 and 50 cm, effectively reducing the reflectivity of -20 dB over 2.15 Ghz. However, it could only be manufactured in curved or straight panels, which made its use on aircraft very difficult.

At least three aircraft manufacturers were experimenting with anti-radar materials during the last months of the war. The designer Kurt Tank of the Focke Wulf firm built the night fighter Ta 154 with wood to make it less easily detectable to Allied radars. The structure was of plywood *Lignofol L90*, and was coated with a new plastic, *Dynal Z5*, manufactured by Dynamit Nobel Troisdorf.

The wing elasticity modules were assembled with a synthetic glue named *Tego-Film* (equivalent to the 'Araldite' used on the British Mosquito). The *Tego-Film* was made of phenolic resin glues. Unfortunately, it could not be used for the mass production of the Ta 154 because the manufacturing plant that synthesised it, the Goldmann Company, was destroyed during the bombing of Wuppertal. The substitution of the *Tego Film* with the *Kaurit* adhesive, manufactured by Dynamit Nobel Troisdorf AG in Leverkausen, was rendered impossible due to its high levels of acidity, which eventually destroyed the wood.

The Ta 154 was not the only airplane to have suffered from the lack of *Tego-Film* in the 'stealth' project. The construction of the prototype Lippisch P.11, a *Schnellbomber* flying wing equipped with two HeS 011 turbojets, was also halted. It was a fast bomber able to fly at high altitude by means of radio navigation devices. It incorporated different anti-radar technologies, and had a plywood structure and a coating of *Dynal Z5*. It was expected that the high-altitude, stealth configuration of its flying wing and Schorn-steinfeger painting would make this bomber impossible to detect, so much so that plans were drawn up to create its night fighter equivalent. However, by the end of the war, only the central section of the wing had been built.

For their own part, the Gotha/Horten team created several designs of a flying wing fitted with excellent anti-radar features, such as a tailfin-free outer shape, *Formholz*—a moulded wooden coating (a 15-mm plywood/carbon/ sawdust/plywood composition)—and *Tronal* plastic. By the end of the war, the construction of a derivative of the Horten Ho VIII, named Ho XVIII, had begun in Göttingen. It was a prototype of an *Amerikabomber*, propelled by six Jumo 004 B turbojets, with a flying wing without tailfins and enough range to attack New York. Mass production was expected to commence in the under-ground workshops of the Kahla-Thuringia complex in 1945.

It seems odd that the little orthodox designs of the Horten brothers, a couple of enthu-siastic amateurs, attracted the attention of Göring. One might speculate that Germans only discovered the stealth effect associated with flying wing airframes by chance. It might have been as a consequence of an unusual Freya contact, or after reading the conclusions reached by a Dynamit Nobel Troisdorf confidential report on the inner structure of the Horten Va, a flying wing that was entirely built of synthetic material. Perhaps Göring saw in this technology an opportunity for greater negotiating power to achieve an honourable peace, as in 1918. Here was the possibility of a game-changer, comparable to the Stuka in 1939 or Window in 1943.

Amerikabomber was just one of the three secret programmes for the manufacturing of stealth bombers promoted by Göring. The first was the twin engine that Horten referred to in this book as *HVII Schnellkampflugzeug*, a weapon specially designed to cross the British defences of the Chain Home. Projects Arado Ar.I, Focke Wulf 1000 x 1000 x 1000, and Lippisch P.11, could also be considered within the limits of this specification. The second programme was the Horten XVIII (21 February 1945), a four-engine aircraft of the *Uralbomber* category with a flying wing configuration like in the Arado E-555, BMW *Strahlbomber Projekt II*, Junkers EF-130, and Messerschmitt P.1108 projects. The Horten XVIII (25 February 1945), described in the specialised literature as Horten XVIII B-1, was the third programme. It featured another flying wing with a span of 40 m, powered by six Jumo turbojets and designed to launch a bomb of 1,000 kg over New York or Washington while operating from bases in Germany.

After a lengthy study of the subject, this author cannot fail to understand the strategic and political advantages that might have derived from these projects. The Luftwaffe already had the capacity to bomb London in 1940, Moscow in 1941, and New York in 1943. To that end, it would have been able to deploy several Ju 390 bombers equipped with new in-flight refuelling devices, developed by Deutsche Forschungsanstalt für Segelflug (DFS), or the gigantic BV 222 flying boats that were able to land in the sea and refuel from U-boats stationed along their route. The long-range artillery of the German Army bombed London with V-2 rockets on a daily basis from mid-1944 onwards. A winged version of the V-2 was tested in Peenemünde and judged capable of reaching Moscow. In 1945, the von Braun team worked on the design of another two rockets destined to reach New York: the *Test Stand XII* project of the Kriegsmarine—basically a version of the V-2 with non-cryogenic propellants to be launched from U-boats—and the gigantic two-stage *Projektil Amerika* rocket.

Why then initiate the development of an intercontinental jet bomber? Why stealth? What could be launched from a Ho XVIII over New York that frightened the Americans enough to sign a separate peace treaty with Germany?

These questions create fertile ground for Nazi esotericism and conspiracy theorists who have described apocalyptic weapons able to change the course of the war. How much death may a green cylinder of 1,000 kg contain? Yet a comfortable majority of historians agree that the Germans had neither the uranium nor the money, nor even the belief in quantum theory, to manufacture a single nuclear bomb. Members of the Führer's staff also lacked the courage to suggest to him at this late stage that resources being used to manufacture the V-weapons should be reassigned to a project that might not work as expected.

What about a dirty bomb? Let us assume that the Oberkommando der Luftwaffe (OKL) was planning to send a Horten XVIII across the Atlantic Ocean by night and launches an AB-1000 container with radioactive dust over a city on the American east coast. Certainly such a strike would have ensured that, for the next twenty years, a number of American citizens would have died or become seriously ill. But what strategic or propagandistic advantage would that situation have offered the Germans at the war's close? Why would the OKL have bought into such a scheme? We must bear in mind that moral conventionalism of the time was very different and that hundreds of people died by the minute during the Second World War. The idea would not sell well if it did not produce terrible explosions and flames with massive instant destruction. Hollywood has been aware of that for a long time.

And what about non-conventional explosives? Tests performed in Rügener might have well been on a fuel-air bomb designed to disable the Allies' 'boxes' of bombers. The spray was formed by different combinations of coal powder, hydrogen, ethylene, petrol, Butan-Propane 50/50, and the *Myrol* compound based on vinylic ethers and aluminium powder. Some authors have suggested that the gases derived from the combustion were toxic and violated the Geneva Convention agreements; however, it is improbable that the Germans would have risked going to such lengths in 1945, while their cities were exposed to daily bombardment.

The same logic extends to the non-application of 50 tons of *N-Stoff*, the inextinguishable fire of the SS—manufactured in Europe by the end of the war—and of nerve-gases (15,000 tons of *Tabun* and over 100,000 aircraft bombs of *Soman*) that were never used against the Allies. Had they been, the phosphor bombs that the Lancasters dropped every night over German towns are likely to have been replaced with anthrax.

Although some communist scientists of the Manhattan project candidly informed the Soviets of their advances, the German scientists did not know that the Allies were building the atomic bomb. Hiroshima was a huge surprise to Reich scientists when they heard the news while being held prisoners in England.

As for the biologic war, although it may be conceivable to want to exchange peace terms with the antidote of a terrible disease, it is equally true that the Germans would not have needed a high-technology bomber to disseminate a virus. On the other hand, the work of a stealth bomber could be performed by fifty conventional bombers. Even accepting a high level of losses, some would have been able to pass through the enemy defences. Unless the bomb was something so special that it would require anti-radar technology to guarantee its delivery.

The question as to why these bombers were designed remains, as yet, without an answer. Like every new technology, the stealth programmes created more problems than it solved. It was fortuitously uncovered by the Americans in 1947 during the unexplained disappearance from a radar screen of a gigantic bomber Northrop YB-49; politicians and military staff alike seriously feared that the Soviets might use the knowledge of Dr Günther Bock—captured in Germany, together with some Horten prototypes—to build large fleets of flying wing bombers. Such an initiative would render useless the expensive LASHUP system, a chain of radar stations for air defence which the USA had already started to install.

The solution consisted of ordering the destruction of all the Northrop flying wings and the dissemination of the myth of a new circular design 'Flying Saucers' a type of wing that had never worked. The Soviets fell into the trap. They made some disappointing tests with Sukhanov circular wings and finally decided to copy the American bomber B-29. This airplane was an ideal vehicle to transport their huge A-bombs, which were each the size of a minivan.

These were the events that led humankind to the loss of a fascinating technology and the arrival of another pseudo-religion.

Justo Miranda
March 2014

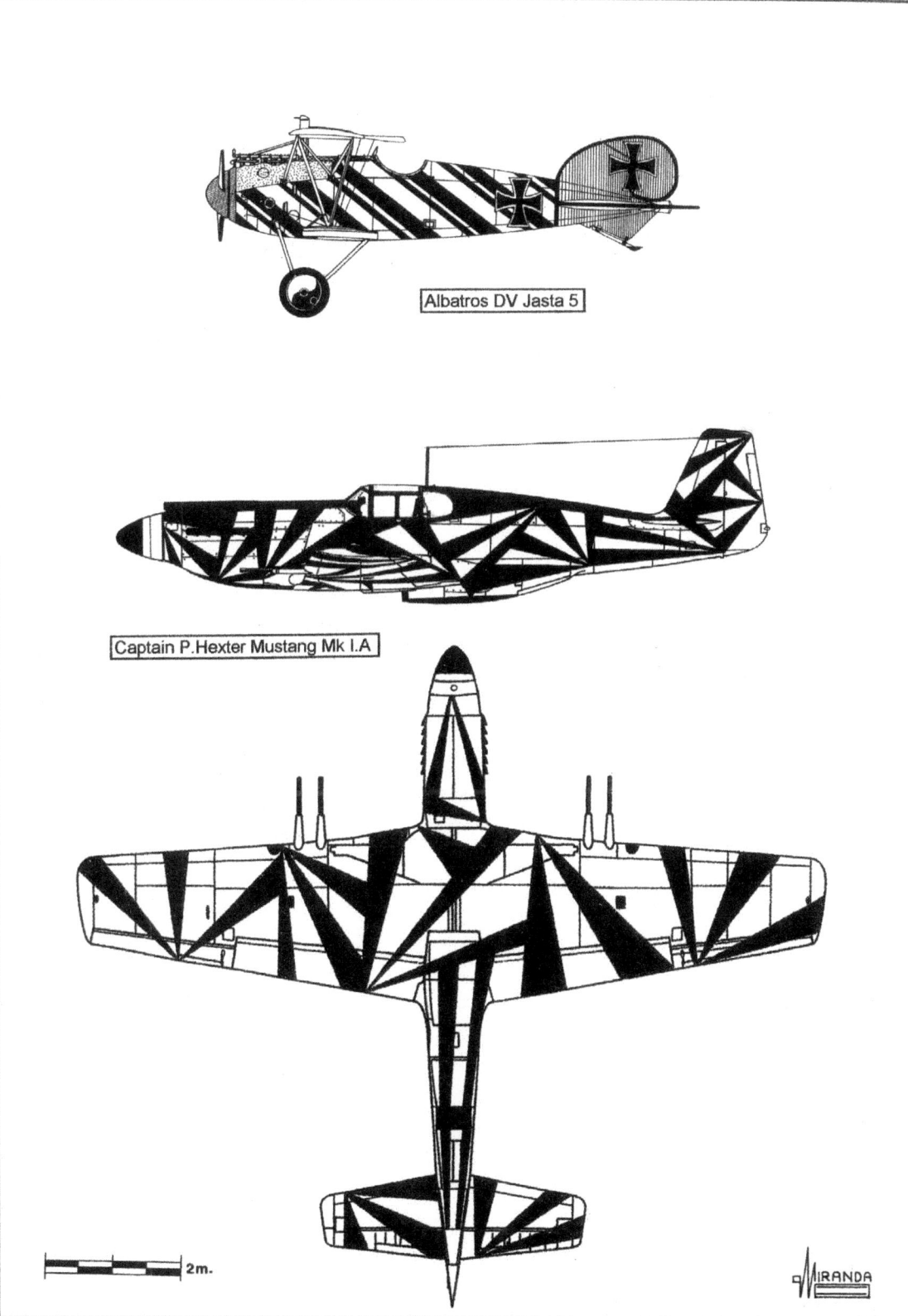

Albatros DV Jasta 5

Captain P.Hexter Mustang Mk I.A

2m.

MIRANDA

Brewster F2A , North Island , California . 1940

2m.

P.Z.L. P.11c of the 161 Sqn. Poland 1939

Chapter 1

Arado Ar.I

After the exhausting war of attrition of 1914–18, the Germans in the Second World War were determined to invest all their future strategy in the launch of a single, devastating strike at the right place and time—*Schwerpunkt*—to quickly defeat their enemies. After the initial successes in 1939, they reluctantly found themselves immersed in another long-lasting war with multiple enemies from distant countries, with administrative centres and weapons factories beyond the range of German bombers.

The Luftwaffe was an almost perfect tactical organisation. It had been designed to work in close coordination with the army, in short-duration blitzkrieg operations not far from its bases. Nevertheless, it was not ready for strategic missions, and did not even possess four-engine bombers capable of attacking the Soviet factories beyond the Urals. It also lacked a bomber fast enough to penetrate the British defences. The Messerschmitt Me 210 proved a very expensive failure and a national scandal. Meanwhile, the Ju 88 Junkers was the victim of a modification, ordered by Ernst Udet, to convert it into a dive bomber, thus cancelling out the advantages of speed and lightness in the original design.

The Luftwaffe was forced to use the single-engine fighter Bf 109 E to launch bombs over London in 1940, while the Fw 190 was used as bomber against the British air force bases for the remainder of the war in Europe. The attempt to transform the Me 262 into a bomber to counteract the planned invasion of D-Day, only served to ruin its career as an interceptor at a critical time during the bombing offensive waged against Germany.

Confidence in the *Himmelbett* night defence system—which had at its disposal old airplanes converted for this purpose—was very costly to the German people. The Technical Office of the Luftwaffe showed a great lack of vision in blocking all the night fighter projects proposed by German industry. They considered that the manufacturing of specialized airplanes was a waste of resources, and demanded additional capacity to carry bombs in day missions of ground attack. It was this military conservatism that delayed for years the manufacturing of the He 219, the only one of the seventeen twin-engine Luftwaffe airplanes that measured up to the Mosquitos of the Pathfinder Force in their nocturnal missions.

Given that the available Bf 110, Do 217, and Ju 88 lacked the required power and speed, some single-seat fighters—the Bf 109 and Fw 190—were equipped with radar. But the drag generated by the antennae and their limited pilot visibility and high landing speed, made them of little use for night operations.

On 15 August 1944, the Oberkommando der Luftwaffe proposed to activate two programmes for the manufacturing of night fighters. The first one, the *Sofortprogramm*, was published in October and was no more than an interim solution that consisted of fitting the three fastest models of airplanes available with radars and a second crew. The Me 262 B-1 was transformed into the Me 262 B-1a/U1, the Ar 234 B-2 into the Ar 234 B-2/N, and the Dornier Do 335 A-6 into the Do 335 B-6. This way out was ill-conceived because the *Hirschgeweih* antennae penalised the planes' performances, and the inclusion of the radar operator diminished fuel capacity. In actual fact, what the Luftwaffe needed was two types of night fighters: one light and fast to hunt Mosquitos, and another of great endurance to harass stream bombers along their entire route. These had to be big airplanes, with a crew of three and a great capacity for fuel, armament, and electronics.

In spite of Göring's threats, the German industry—slowed down as a result of the constant interference of the Technical Office of the Luftwaffe—had not yet solved any of these vital problems by January 1945, including the *Schnellbomber* (fast bomber) specification of 1942.

Besides Messerschmitt, there was just one German manufacturer with access to the scarce supply of turbojets: the Arado firm, which used them for the hugely disparaged Ar 234. Conceived during the autumn of 1940 as the ideal reconnaissance airplane, the Arado was converted into a bomber in November 1943 in an attempt to dissuade the Führer from using the Me 262 as a *Schnellbomber*. On 12 September 1944, the OKL repeated the process, ordering the Ar 234 rather than the Me 262 to be converted into a night fighter to avoid interrupting production of the latter.

After rejecting the heavy bomber programme Arado E 555, the *Volksjäger* (people's fighter), the Arado E 580 and the *Jägernotprogramm* (emergency fighter programme) Arado E 581 interceptor, the Luftwaffe authorised the manufacture of the Ar 234 C-3 (fighter, bomber, and recce multi-purpose airplane) as opposed to its two specialised versions, C-1 and C-2.

Those were the rules of the game when the OKL decided to publish specification number 12376/45 *Vorrückenprogramm* for the manufacturing of a *Hochleistung Nachtjäger* (high-performance night fighter) on 27 January 1945. Arado decided to present three designs of the flying wing type, with two vertical fins and rudders under the provisional denomination of E 583, conceived from the beginning with criteria of polyvalence and maximum operational flexibility.

The E 583 had a triangular wing of great surface area, able to quickly raise a lot of weight to a great altitude. It also had an impressive fuel capacity. Its forward fuselage could house parabolic antennae, armament, electronic equipment, and a crew of three. The engines were located outside and in a configuration that could adapt to all the types of available or projected turbojets, for easier maintenance.

Its first design, dated January 1945, was a very fast single-seat *Moskitojäger* with radar of fixed parabolic antenna that limited its night fighter capacity. The second, probably developed in February, was a two-seat *Schnellbomber* with internal capacity for carrying either 1,000 kg of bombs or two Rb 50/30 cameras for reconnaissance duties. The third, presented on 15 March, was a three-seat heavy *Nachtjäger* equipped with FuG 244 and FuG 218 (rear) radars, different combinations of armament—main, defensive and *Schräge*

Musik—and R100 or R4M rockets. To adapt to the changes to the specification of 2 March and 2 April, endurance was increased to 3½ hours with one stopped engine.

The E 583 meant a radical change of mentality for the Arado design team. Besides adopting advanced aerodynamic solutions, they had to adapt their whole production system to the wood and plastic working techniques made by artisans in a myriad of widely dispersed workshops. They also had to compete against Gotha and Focke Wulf for the procurement of new HeS 011 turbojets, and against Dornier for FuG 244 radars. In recognition of the prototype's transformation, the E 583 'Batwing' was renamed Arado Ar.I.

As a precaution against the traditionally minded OKL—who had, after all, rejected the Blohm und Voss P.215 night fighter on the grounds of it being too radical—a multi-task airplane version was designed with the same engines, radar, armament, and crew, but with conventional fuselage and arrowed wings and tail surfaces. It was named Arado Ar.II.

Technical data E 583 (27 January 1945)

Type	single-seat, all-weather interceptor fighter.
Wings	built of wood and plastic, 40-degree swept at the leading edge and 4-degree swept at the trailing edge, housing four fuel tanks and the main undercarriage legs, retracting inwards.
Fuselage	built of light alloy, housing the radar, the armament, the undercarriage nose leg (retractable to the rear) the cockpit—pressurised with control heating and frontal armour protecting against 12.7-mm shelling and 20 mm at the rear—and three fuel tanks.
Tailfins	built of wood.
Engines	two Heinkel HeS 011 turbojets, rated at 1,300-kp static thrust.
Armament	four Mk 108/30 cannons in the nose.
Wingspan	16.92 m
Length	11.77 m
Wing area	66 sq. m

Technical data E 583 (February 1945?)

Type	two-seat fast bomber and reconnaissance airplane.
Wings	built of wood and plastic, 40-degree swept at the leading edge and 7-degree swept at the trailing edge, housing six fuel tanks and the main undercarriage legs, retracting forwards.
Fuselage	built of light alloy, housing the armament, the undercarriage nose leg (retractable to the rear), the cockpit—pressurised with control heating—one weapons bay and one fuel tank.
Tailfins	built of wood.
Engines	two Heinkel HeS 011 turbojets, rated at 1,300-kp static thrust
Armament	four Mk 108/30 cannons in the nose, one Mk 213/20 in tail barbette, and 1,000 kg of bombs.
Wingspan	18.43 m
Length	12.95 m
Wing area	75 sq. m

Technical data E 583 (15 March 1945)	
Type	three-seat heavy night fighter.
Wings	built of wood and plastic, 40-degree swept at the leading edge and 13-degree swept at the trailing edge, housing six fuel tanks and the main undercarriage legs, retracting forwards.
Fuselage	built of light alloy, housing the radar, armament, the undercarriage nose leg (retractable to the rear), the cockpit—pressurised with control heating and frontal armour protecting against 12.7-mm shelling and from the rear against 20-mm—and two fuel tanks.
Tailfins	built of wood.
Engines	two Heinkel HeS 011 turbojets, rated at 1,300-kp static thrust.
Armament	six firing Mk 108/30 cannons in the nose, two Mk 108/30 cannons in Schräge Musik configuration (over the air intakes of engines), and two Mk 213/20 cannons in tail barbette.
Wingspan	18.43 m
Length	13.17 m
Height	3.80 m
Wing area	75 sq. m
Aspect ratio	4.5:1
Max. speed	810 kph
Ceiling	41,300 feet
Range	(with 6,600 litres of fuel) 1,600 km
Max. weight	15,700 kg

ELECTRONIC DEVICES (ALL-WEATHER FIGHTER)

EZ 42 *Adler* gyroscopic gunsight *Zielgerät* developed by Askania/Zeiss. It automatically computed the deflection angle required to hit a target when both aircraft were manoeuvring.

FuG 222 *Pauke S* fire control radar with fixed *Parabolspiegel* of 45 cm diameter and operation frequencies between 3250 and 3330 Mhz. Range 300–10,000 m. Weight of 220 kg.

FuG 16 VHF *Funksprechgerät* R/T device developed by Lorenz for air-to-ground and air-to-air communications. Frequencies between 38.5 and 42.3 Mhz. Wire aerial or Morane mast. There were four modes:
Y-Verfahren superimposed signal for fighter control position;
Gruppenbefehlswelle communication between aircraft;
Nachsicherung und Flugssicherung communication between the aircraft and the ground system;
Reichsjägerwelle continuous running commentary.

The FuG 16 ZY combined the 'homing' and *Y-Verfahren* functions and operated on a wavelength of 7 m.

FuG 25a *Erstling* IFF device *Kenngerät* was manufactured by GEMA and Brinkler. Emission frequency of 160 Mhz, reception frequency of 125 Mhz. Range of 100 km. Power of 600 W. Rod antenna under the fuselage (300 mm long), 10 degrees rear swept. Responded to *Freya*, *Würzburg*, and *Gemse* ground control radars. It could be used to calculate the distance of an airplane from the ground radar. The need to operate in several frequencies between 0.53 and 2.40 m considerably delayed its entry into service in the Luftwaffe. It was used in combination with the EGON (*Erstling- Gemse-Offensive-Navigation*) for radio navigation of bombers in combination with the FuMG 401A *Freya LZ* radar, as an alternative to the *Y-Gerät*. Weight of 12 kg.

FuG 101a *Feinhöhermesser* of 1.5 Kw, radioaltimeter developed by Siemens/LG. Operation frequencies between 337 and 400 MHz in continuous wave and frequency modulation (CW–FM with a 2-m error). Power 1.5 W. Weight of 16 kg. Range of between 150 and 1,500 m. It used two *Sender S101* and *Empfänger E 101* dipoles to transmit and receive.

FuG 125a *Hermine* radio-beacon receiver was developed by Lorenz. It operated in frequencies between 30 and 33.3 Mhz with a precision of 5 degrees. Weight of 10 kg. Range of 200 at 250 km. It operated in combination with the FuG 16 ZY *Zypresse* direction finder and the FuG 16 R/T device using the antenna and the D/F loop and Morane mast of these devices.

FuG 139 *Barbarossa Kommando Übertragungsgerät* (command relay equipment) used its antenna in combination with the IFF FuG 25a. Data was presented by the *Hellschreiber* teleprinter.

ELECTRONIC DEVICES (FAST BOMBER)

EZ 42 *Adler* gyroscopic gunsight *Zielgerät* developed by Askania/Zeiss. It automatically computed the deflection angle required to hit a target when both aircraft were manoeuvring.

FuG 16 VHF *Funksprechgerät* R/T device developed by Lorenz for air-to-ground and air-to-air communications. Frequencies between 38.5 and 42.3 Mhz. Wire aerial or Morane mast. There were four modes:
Y-Verfahren superimposed signal for fighter control position;
Gruppenbefehlswelle communication between aircraft;
Nachsicherung und Flugssicherung communication between the aircraft and the ground system;
Reichsjägerwelle continuous running commentary.

The FuG 16 ZY combined the homing and *Y-Verfahren* functions and operated on a wavelength of 7 m.

BZA-1 EGON bombing computer developed by GEMA for automatic blind bomb release in combination with the FuG 25a system and *Freya* ground radar stations.

Lofte 7K tachometric bombsight for level bombing operations.

Patin LKS 7D-15 three-axis autopilot.

RF2 C periscope.

FuG 25a *Erstling* IFF device *Kenngerät* was manufactured by GEMA and Brinkler. Emission frequency of 160 Mhz, reception frequency of 125 Mhz. Range of 100 km. Power of 600 W. Rod antenna under the fuselage (300 mm long), 10 degrees rear swept. Responded to *Freya*, *Würzburg*, and *Gemse* ground control radars. It could be used to calculate the distance of an airplane from the ground radar. The need to operate in several frequencies between 0.53 and 2.40 m considerably delayed its entry into service in the Luftwaffe. It was used in combination with the EGON (*Erstling- Gemse-Offensive-Navigation*) for radio navigation of bombers in combination with the FuMG 401A *Freya LZ* radar, as an alternative to the *Y-Gerät*. Weight of 12 kg.

FuG 101a *Feinhöhermesser* of 1.5 Kw, radioaltimeter developed by Siemens/LG. Operation frequencies between 337 and 400 MHz in continuous wave and frequency modulation (CW–FM with a 2-m error). Power 1.5 W. Weight of 16 kg. Range of between 150 and 1,500 m. It used two *Sender S101* and *Empfänger E 101* dipoles to transmit and receive.

FuG 123 *Truhe* cartographic radar *Leitstrahlverfahren* based on captured units of the British 'Gee' radar. Frequencies from 35 to 100 Mhz. It worked in combination with the ground stations of the FuS An 728 *Boden Truhe*.

ELECTRONIC DEVICES (HEAVY NIGHT FIGHTER)

EZ 42 *Adler* gyroscopic gunsight *Zielgerät* developed by Askania/Zeiss. It automatically computed the deflection angle required to hit a target when both aircraft were manoeu-vring. It could be connected to the *Oberon* system developed by Arado to fire the R100 rockets. *Oberon* is a clock device and the distance could be given by the FuG 218 *Neptun V* radar or specialised radar for launching the FuG 248 *Eule* type. The ignition mechanism was the EG3 *Elfe 3*. The EZ 42 could be used in combination with the *Gnom* automatic weapon-triggering and with the FuG 244 radar to fire R4M rockets.

EZ 42 + FuG 218 *Neptun* + EG3 *Elfe 3* = *Oberon* à R100
EZ 42 + FuG 248 *Eule* + EG3 *Elfe 3* = *Oberon* à R100
EZ 42 + FuG 244 + *Gnom* = *Faun* R4M or Mk 108/30
EZ 42 + FuG 217/218 *Neptun* + MZ1 *Hexe* = *Faun* à R4M
Oberon + *Faun* = *Oberon–Uhr*

EiV 125 crew intercom developed by FFO.

Peil G6 Ludwig with APZ6 manufactured by Telefunken. Long wave/medium wave (LW/MW) radiogoniometer that used its own EZ6 receiver (200–1200 Khz) or could be associated with the FuG 10 system. Compatible with the FuG 350Zc *Naxos*. Flat antenna with radial ribs. Incorporates APZ6 automatic radiogoniometer *Automatische Peilzusatz*. Weight of 24 kg.

FuBl 3E with AWG *Funklandegerät* blind landing device developed by Lorenz in combination with the FuG 130, the FuG 101a, and the FuG 10/FuG 17(EB4). The AWG 1 *Auswertergerät* was an angle and speed calculator developed by F&H in 1944. It used the same comb-shaped antenna as the FuBl2, sometimes covered by a fairing. Weight of 10 kg.

FuG 24 SE VHF *Funksprechgerät* R/T device developed by Lorenz for single-seat fighters. Operation frequencies between 37.8 and 47.75 Mhz. It was used in combination with the ZVG *Zielflugrorsatzgerät* direction finder device. Power of 5 Kw, VHF wave. Whip antenna. Weight of 18 kg.

FuG 25a *Erstling* IFF device *Kenngerät* was manufactured by GEMA and Brinkler. Emission frequency of 160 Mhz, reception frequency of 125 Mhz. Range of 100 km. Power of 600 W. Rod antenna under the fuselage (300 mm long), 10 degrees rear swept. Responded to *Freya*, *Würzburg*, and *Gemse* ground control radars. It could be used to calculate the distance of an airplane from the ground radar. The need to operate in several frequencies between 0.53 and 2.40 m considerably delayed its entry into service in the Luftwaffe. It was used in combination with the EGON (*Erstling- Gemse-Offensive-Navigation*) for radio navigation of bombers in combination with the FuMG 401A *Freya LZ* radar, as an alternative to the *Y-Gerät*. Weight of 12 kg.

FuG 29 *Reportage* ground-to-air control and airborne situation report receiver. It weighed 8 kg.

FuG 101a *Feinhöhermesser* of 1.5 Kw, radioaltimeter developed by Siemens/LG. Operation frequencies between 337 and 400 MHz in continuous wave and frequency modulation (CW–FM with a 2-m error). Power 1.5 W. Weight of 16 kg. Range of between 150 and 1,500 m. It used two *Sender S101* and *Empfänger E 101* dipoles to transmit and receive.

FuG 218 *Neptun R-3* of 30-100 Kw developed by Siemens/FFO as *Rückwärtswarngerät* tail warning radar. Operation frequencies between 162 and 187 Mhz. Range of between 120 and 5,000 m. Vision angle of 60 degrees horizontally and vertically. *Stachel* antenna of two elements on a small curved mast that was also used for the FuG 350 Z *Naxos* passive receiver. Weight of 46 kg. Thrust of 30 at 100 Kw.

FuG 244 *Bremen 0* air-to-air radar developed by Telefunken. Operation frequency between 3,250 and 3,330 Mhz. Range between 200 and 5,000 m. *Parabolspiegel* of 70 cm diameter with searching range of 100 degrees to either side and 20 degrees downwards. Wavelength from 9 to 9.3 cm. Power of 20 Kw. Weight of 100 kg. It was a pre-production device derived from the FuG 240/3 with higher definition capacity and less weight. The series version FuG 245 *Bremen* was meant to be manufactured in 1946.

FuG 280 *Kiel Z* passive IR homer developed by Zeiss as *U-R Suchgerät* using lead-sulphite photo-cells. Opening angle of 20 degrees that could be manually operated with
corrections of 35 degrees to either side by means of a mobile mirror. Range of 4,000
m. Weight of 42 kg. The presentation of data was made over a screen named *Q-Rohr*. It
was sometimes used in combination with the FuG 218 *Neptun R-3* rear warning radar.

Zeiss *Revi* C16 A-N auxiliary gunsight to aim the *Schräge Musik* cannons.

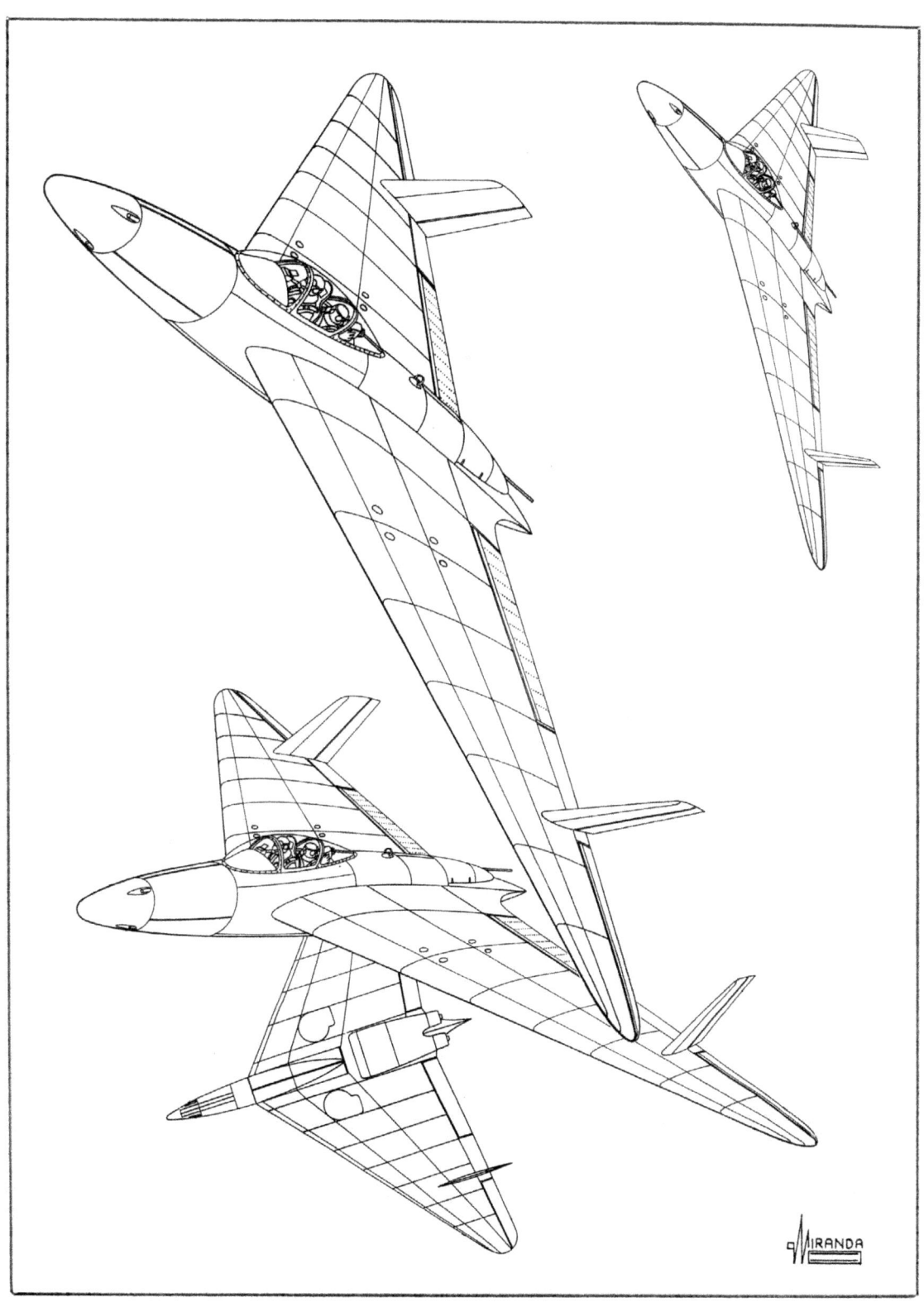

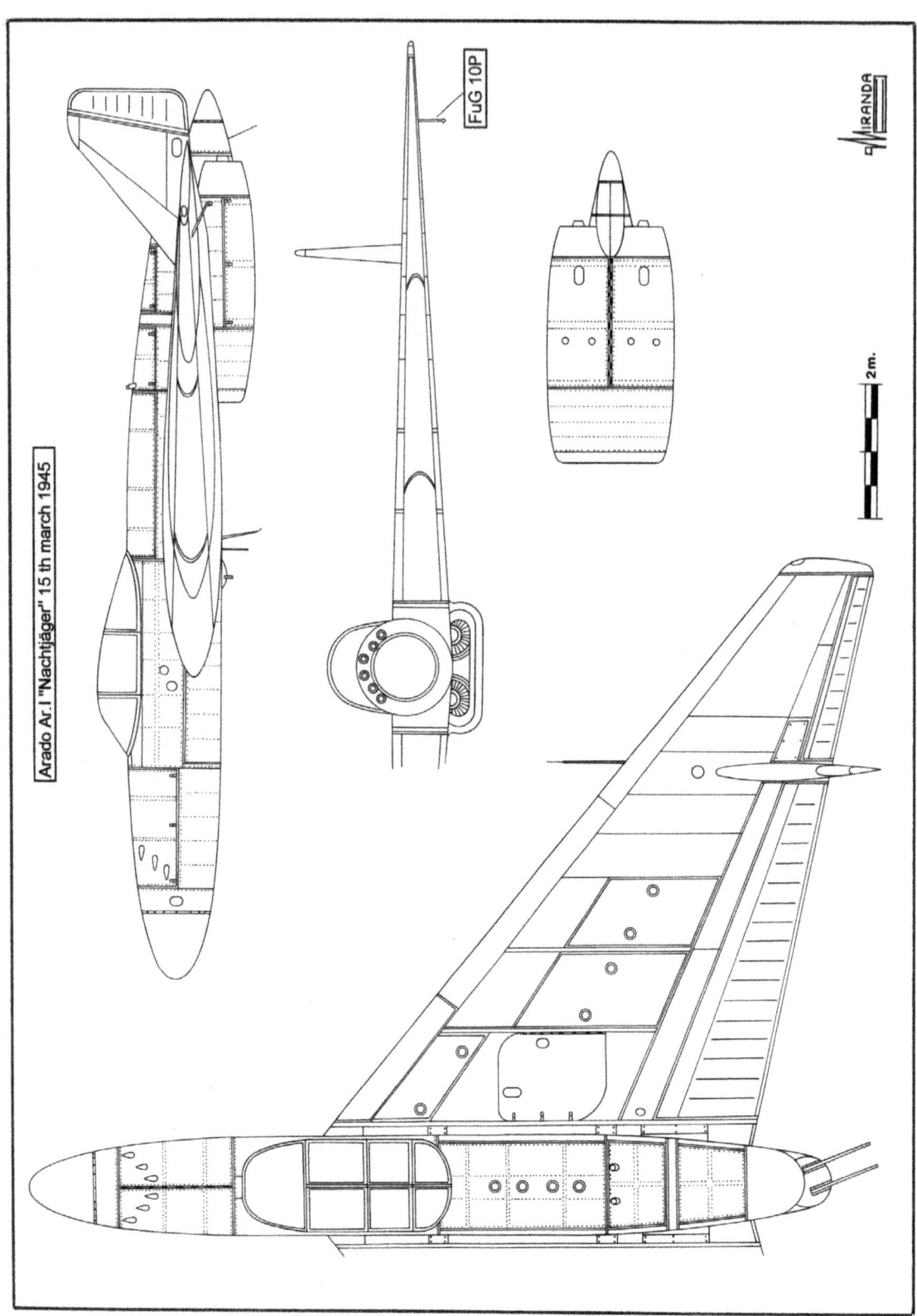

Arado Ar. I "Nachtjäger" 15 th march 1945

FuG 10P

2 m.

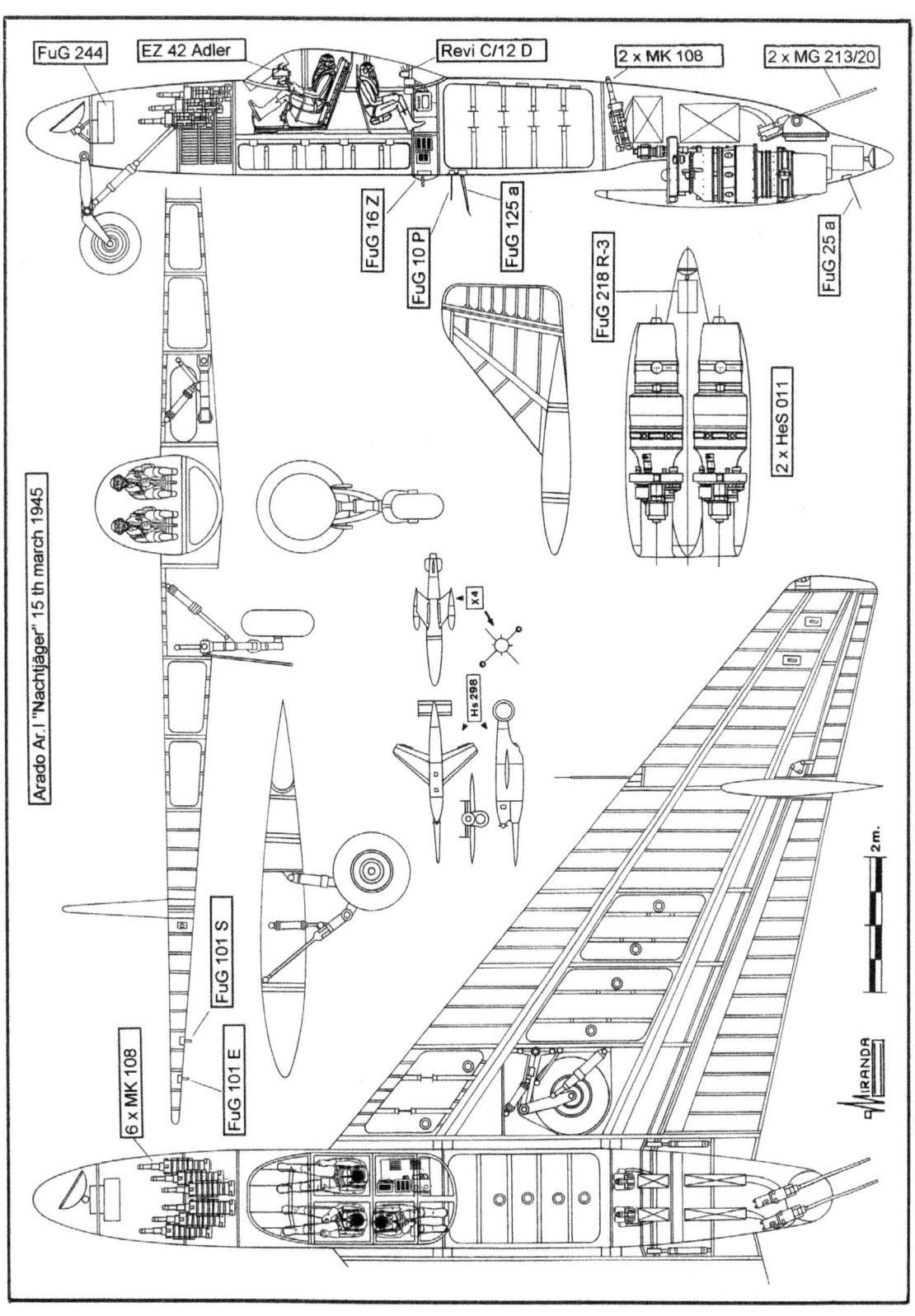

FuG 244
EZ 42 Adler
Revi C/12 D
2 x MK 108
2 x MG 213/20
FuG 16 Z
FuG 10 P
FuG 125 a
FuG 218 R-3
FuG 25 a
2 x HeS 011
Arado Ar.I "Nachtjäger" 15 th march 1945
FuG 101 S
FuG 101 E
6 x MK 108
2 m.
MIRANDA

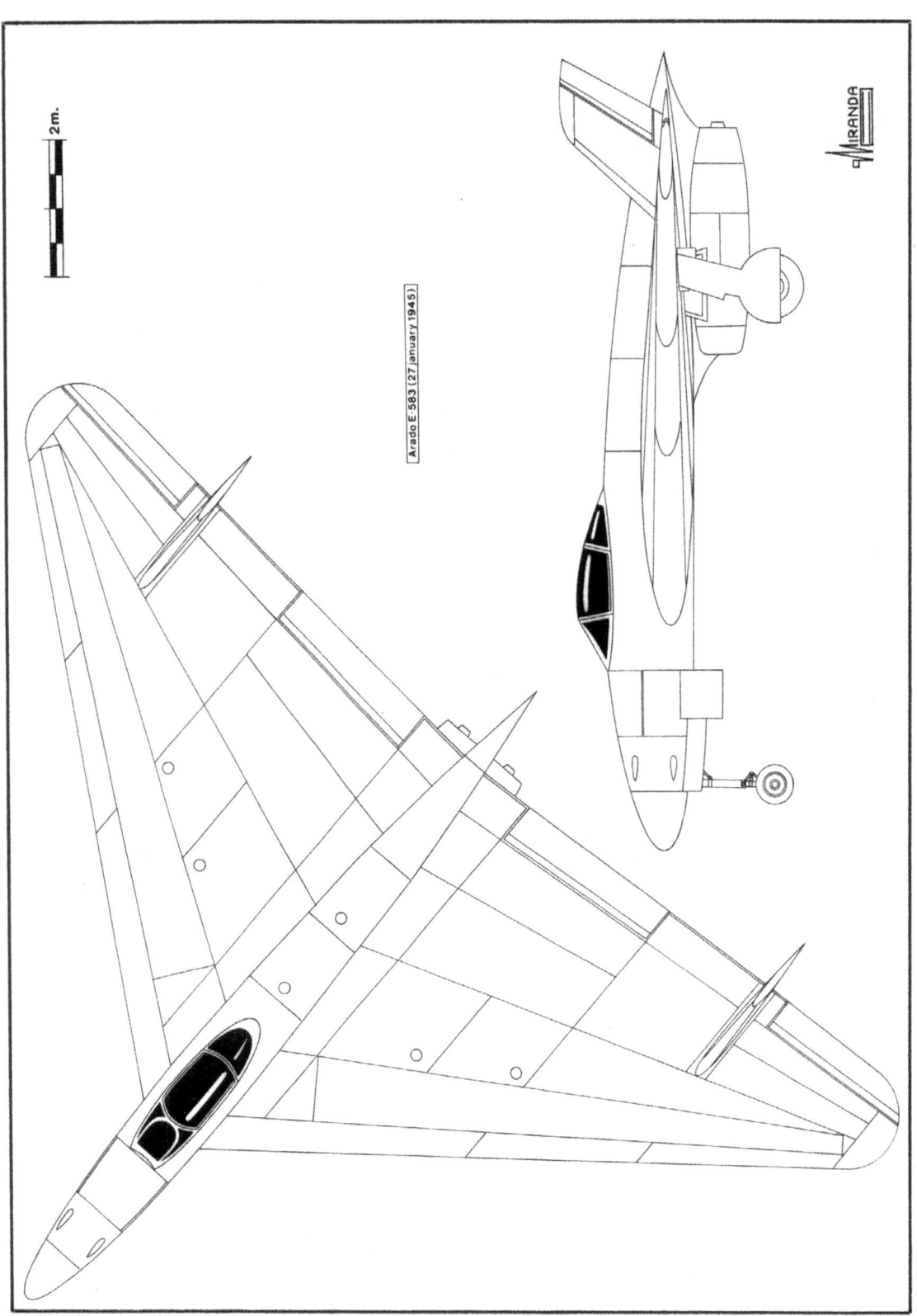

2 m.

Arado E.583 (27 January 1945)

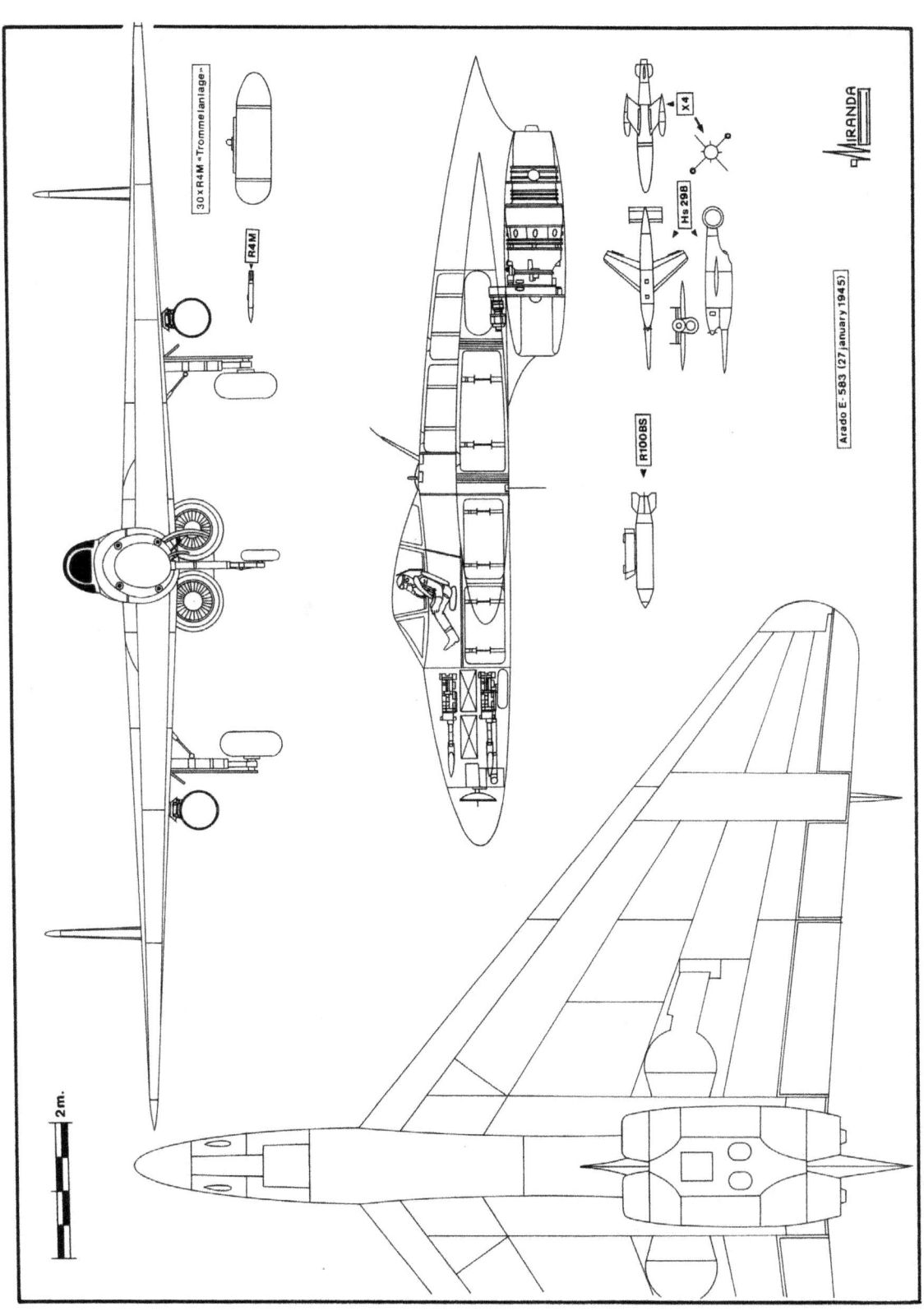

30 x R4M «Trommellanlage»

R4M

Arado E-583 (27 january 1945)

X4

Hs 298

R100 BS

MIRANDA

2 m.

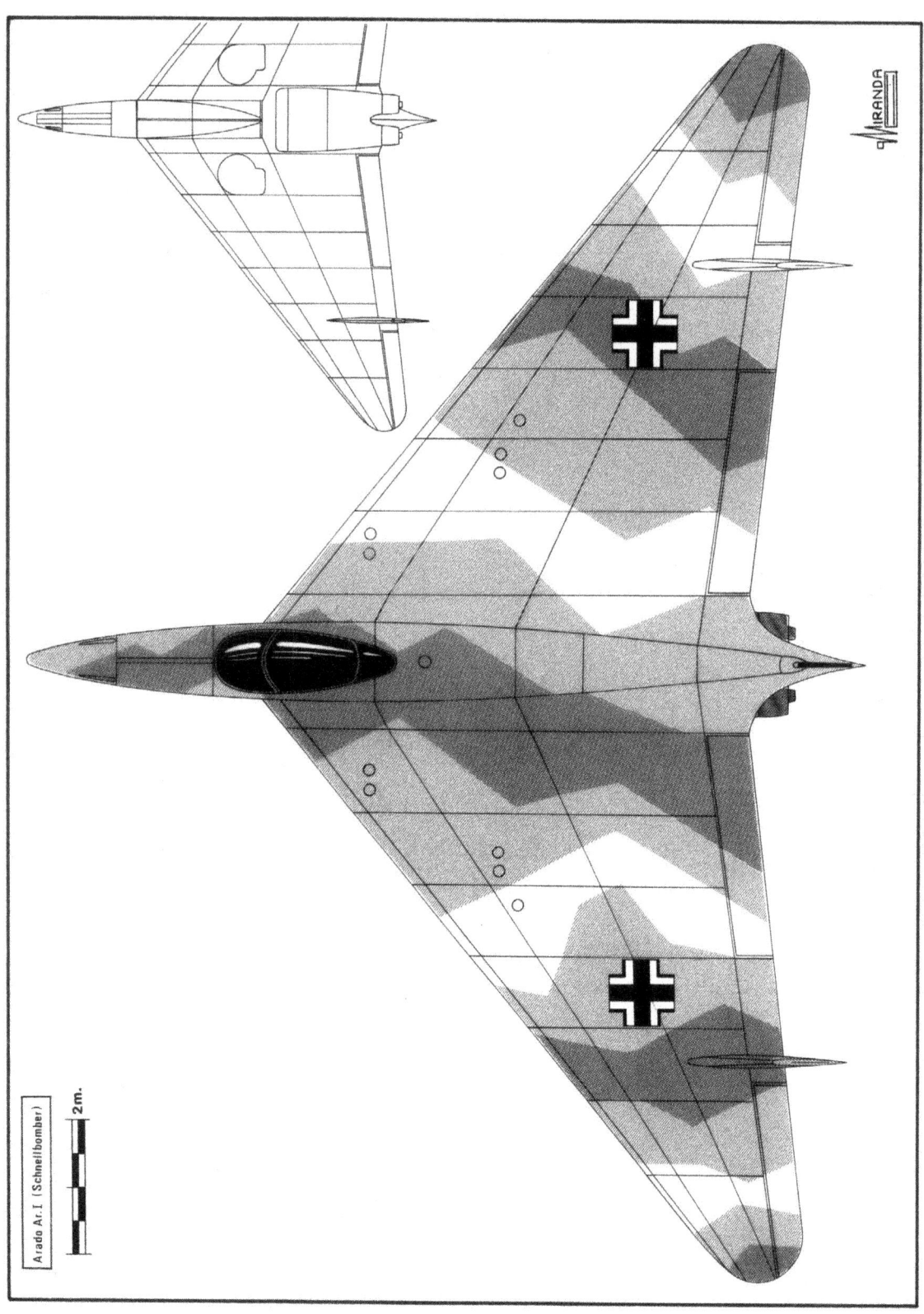

Arado Ar.I (Schnellbomber)

2 m.

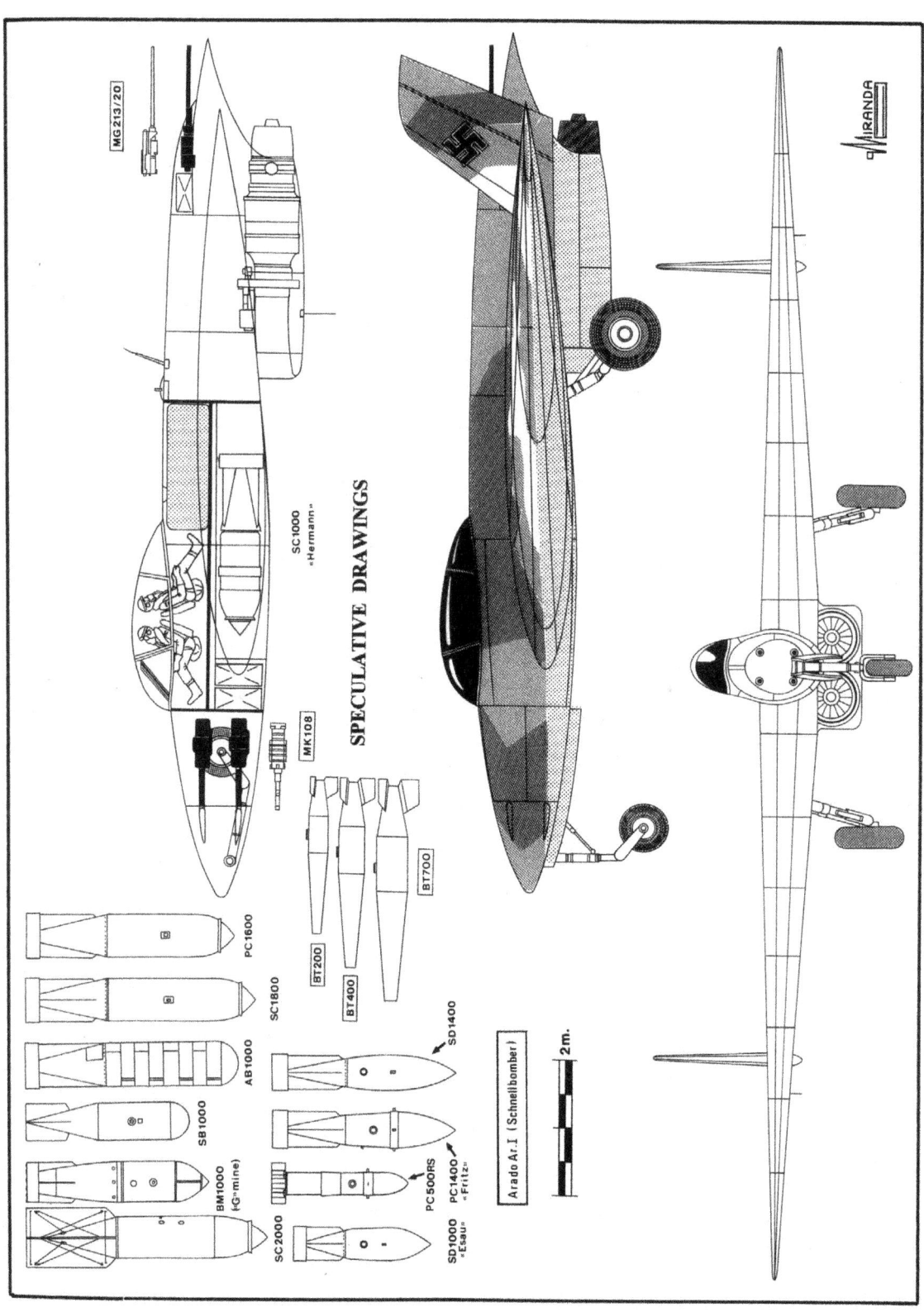

MG 213/20

SC1000
«Hermann»

MK108

SPECULATIVE DRAWINGS

BT700

BT400

BT200

PC1600

SC1800

AB1000

SB1000

SD1400

BM1000
(G-mine)

SC2000

PC1400
«Fritz»

PC500RS

SD1000
«Esau»

Arado Ar.I (Schnellbomber)

2 m.

Chapter 2

Arado E-581

During the Second World War only two airplane manufacturers had access to the scarce number of Jumo 004 and BMW 003 turbojet engines. One of them was Messerschmitt, who used them to power the Me 262, and the other was Arado, for the Ar 234.

The OKL tried to rationalise production by assigning to Messerschmitt the manufacturing of jet fighters, and to Arado that of the jet bombers.

The Ar 234 received every type of criticism due to its conservative aerodynamics, and the firm focused its energies on experimenting with swept wings to improve the performance of future models of the 234. By mid-1944, it was decided to use the V16 prototype as a test bed for the new wings. It was equipped with two BMW 003 TLR engines and Walter rockets to achieve high altitude.

The first type of crescent wing designed, *Versuchsflügel I* (experimental wing configuration), was fitted with movable leading edges and was tested in the wind tunnel using scale models with two and four engines, as well as two different types of swept-back tailplanes. The *Versuchsflügel II* was its simplified version, whereas the *Versuchsflügel III* had a straight wing similar to that of the Ar 234 C and with the same type of coupled engines within each gondola. It was different from the standard wing in that it had a laminar-flow aerofoil. The *Versuchsflügel IV* was an adaptation of Type II, installed in a high position over the fuselage and able to carry more fuel. *Versuchsflügel V* was a pure 35-degree swept-back wing.

The results obtained in the wind tunnel were not satisfactory. Therefore, the design team of Professor Walter Blume decided to gain experience with delta wings by building eleven 1/10 scale models that represented all possible combinations of wings, tailfins, and turbojets. He was looking for the ideal shape for the future fast bomber.

The aerodynamic research programme Arado E.555 was cancelled in November 1944 due to the lack of resources available for the manufacture of big bombers and the urgent demand for fighters. Arado's response to this new situation was the Arado E-581 fighter project, a 42-per-cent scaled-down version of the E-555-3. The turbojets of the time were not very powerful, and the best formula to maximize their performance was to build the lightest and smallest possible airplane. In essence, the E-581 was a turbojet suspended under a triangular wing of 22.5 sq. m, with a pilot sitting over the air duct.

Its two first designs were conceived by Dr Laute in the second half of 1944. It was expected that the E-581-1 would be powered by a Jumo 004 and the E-581-2 by a BMW 003. The E-581-3 was an improved model with self-sealing fuel tanks and an armoured cockpit.

The E-581-4 was supposed to be powered by a new HeS 011 turbojet, and to make more efficient use of the excess power, the wing surface was expanded to 24.5 sq. m. However, wind tunnel tests proved that the bifurcated air intake, designed for a longer engine, generated undesired turbulences in the air duct, so that the latter would need redesigning.

The final model, E-581-5, was presented to the OKL on 8 January 1945, but its manufacture was rejected in favour of the Focke Wulf Ta 183/I, winner of the *Jägernotprogramm* contest.

Technical data (E-581-5)

Type	single-seat interceptor fighter.
Wings	built of wood and plywood, 45-degree swept at the leading edge and 37- and 4-degree swept at the trailing edge, containing the armament, the fuel tanks, the main undercarriage members, flaps, elevators, ailerons, and tailfins.
Fuselage	built of light alloy, housing the nose leg, the cockpit, and the engine.
Armament	two Mk 108 cannons in the wing roots.
Fuel tanks	three of 1,250-litre total capacity in the wing.
Engine	one Heinkel HeS 011 turbojet, rated at 1,300-kp static thrust.
Wingspan	8.95 m
Length	5.65 m
Height	2.60 m
Wing area	24.50 sq. m
Aspect ratio	3.27:1
Max. weight	3,734 kg

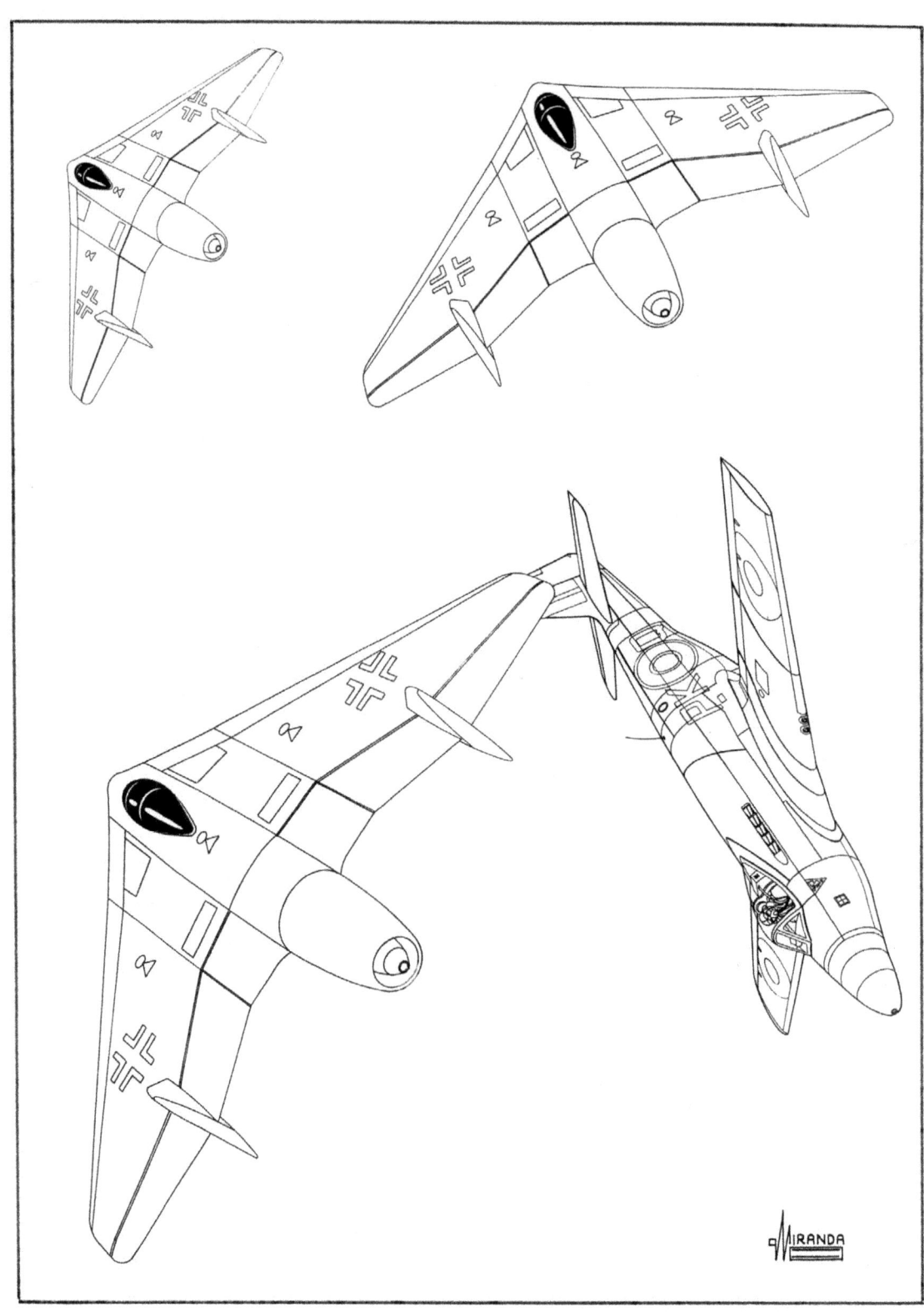

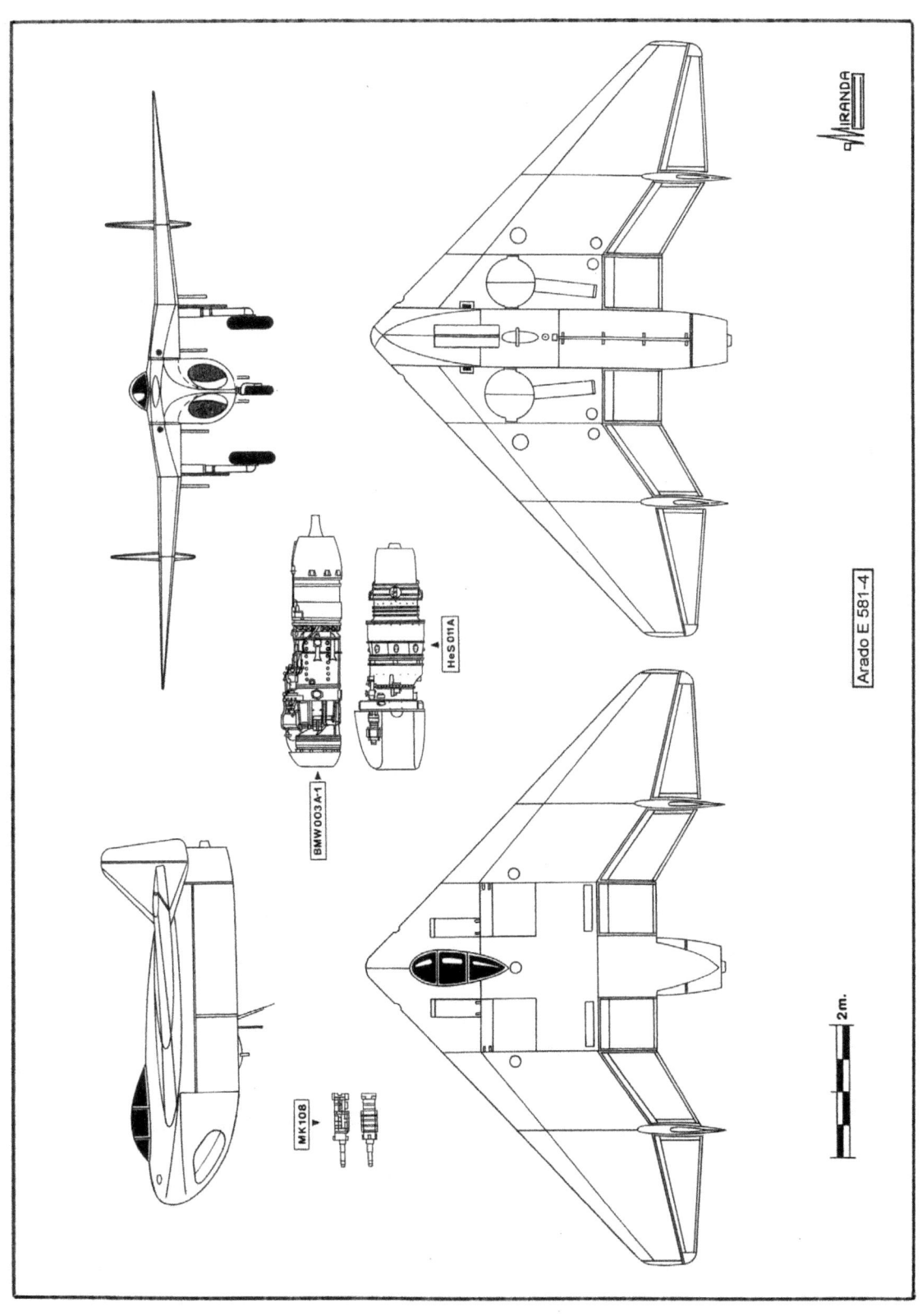

MIRANDA

Arado E 581-4

HeS 011A

BMW 003A-1

MK 108

2 m.

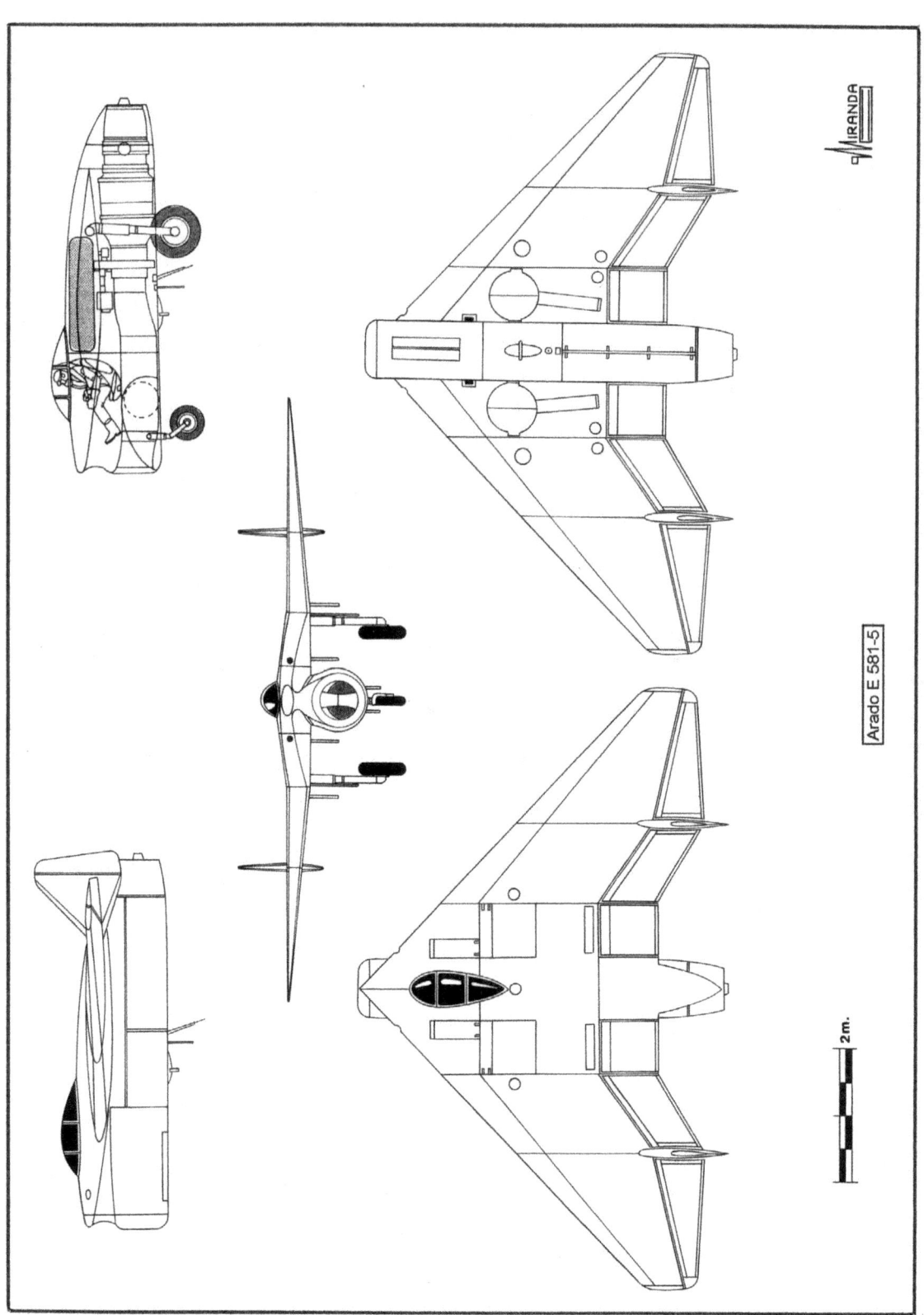

Arado E 581-5

2m.

Chapter 3

Blohm und Voss P.217 (5 February 1945)

The ingenious 'Batwing' configuration used on the firm's fighter projects since July 1944 was too advanced for its time, and the Luftwaffe technicians criticised the lateral stability of the designs. Therefore the advanced Batwing P.208 fighter was presented to the Oberkommando der Luftwaffe, together with the P.207, an alternative design with a straight wing and conventional tail surfaces. The same happened with the P.211 swept wing, winner of the *Volksjäger* contest on 19 September 1944, which was nevertheless presented together with the conventional P.210.

When the OKL published the *Jägernotprogramm* specification, the answer from Blohm und Voss was the P.212 Batwing fitted with a double tailfin to improve lateral stability. The P.217, the conservative version with a delta wing, was presented as an alternative.

One of the main objections to the Batwing configuration was its high wing loading, which required large landing strips for take off at a time when fighters were forced to use stretches of autobahn instead. So the P.217 was designed with a great surface wing, similar to the one in the Arado E.581, with forward swept canard winglets to improve take off, performance, and low speed control. Non-strategic materials and some already existent mechanical components, like the undercarriage and canopy, would have been mainly used in its manufacture. To avoid losing power in the turbojet, the air duct was made completely straight and cleared of obstacles, which in turn meant that the cockpit was placed in an asymmetric position.

Visibility during take off and landing was practically non-existent, so one might speculate as to whether a ventral window might eventually have been installed to facilitate these manoeuvres.

Technical data	
Type	single-seat jet fighter.
Wings	built of wood and plywood, aspect ratio 2.46:1, 65- and 57-degree swept at the leading edge, 60- and 27-degree swept at the trailing edge and 15-degree anhedral wingtips. With elevators, ailerons, and flaps.
Fuselage	steel-tube structure and light alloy cladding, housing the armament, the undercarriage, the cockpit, a fuel tank, the turbojet, the tailfin (built of wood), and the -45-degree forward-swept winglets.

Engine	one HeS 011 turbojet rated at 1,300-kp static thrust.
Armament	three Mk 108/30 cannons in the nose.
Undercarriage	from a Bf 109 G-6 standard.
Wingspan	8 m
Length	7.05 m
Height	3.09 m
Wing	area 26 sq. m
Max. weight	4,200 kg

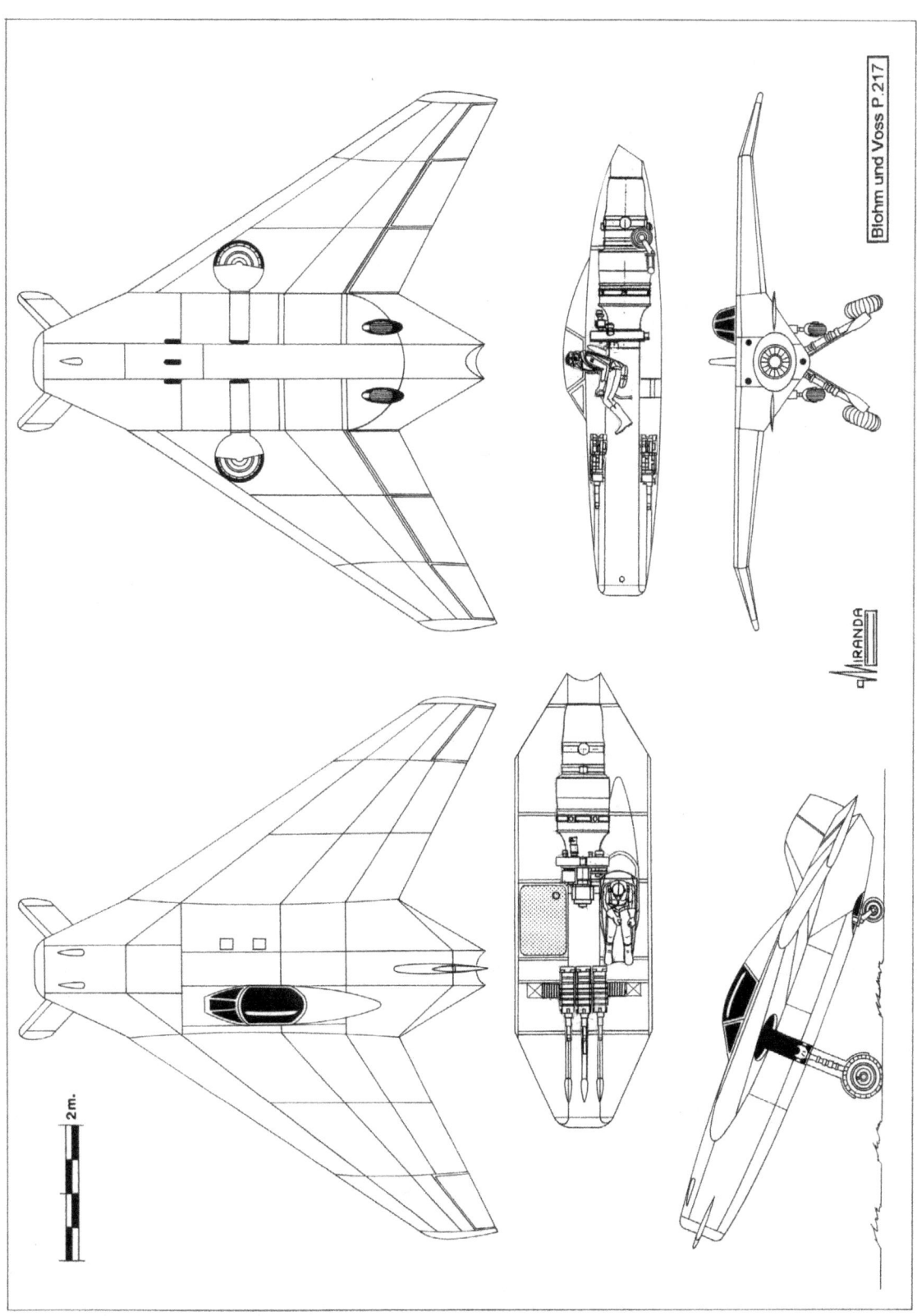

Chapter 4

BMW *Strahljäger Projekt V* (3 November 1944)

With the exception of the Heinkel AG and Junkers AG, the rest of German manufacturers of aircraft engines lacked the necessary infrastructure to build airframes. However, the airplane projects designed by BMW and Daimler Benz at that time have been documented. They were mainly simple ideas to promote engines that were less in demand.

It became evident in 1943 that Germany did not have the required resources to manufacture big fleets of strategic bombers. Therefore, the projected heavy engines that fighter designers tended to ignore needed to be adapted or die.

Daimler Benz had developed the technology to integrate two V-12 engines coupled together to drive a single control shaft able to power the bomber Heinkel He 177, but this turned into a fiasco. When production was cancelled, another version was being tested—the DB 613—a more powerful model with two DB 603 and contra-rotating airscrews.

On 21 January 1944, Daimler published the report *Konstruktionsbericht K.21*. It included a study on the different possibilities of combining an Mk 412/55 cannon with the DB 613 engine of 3,800 hp, to be used in heavy fighters in the Blackburn Firecrest or Douglas Skyraider range. But the engine was so heavy that it could only be adopted by Henschel for its P.75, a project of canard/pusher propellers with great problems in terms of stability, cooling, and undercarriage design.

The BMW company had developed the powerful turbojet, BMW 109-018—a monster of 4.95 m in length, 1.25 m in diameter, and 3,400-kp static thrust—to power the *Strahlbomber Projekt II* (jet bomber project II), a flying wing able to fly at 985 kph with 5,000 kg of bombs. However, this was a luxury that Germany could not afford. By the time *Projekt II* was cancelled at the end of 1944, there were few airplane projects under study able to house such a huge engine.

Blohm und Voss designed a 125-per-cent scaled-up version of the P.202 fighter, named P.198. It was a high-altitude interceptor with a BMW 018 suspended under the fuselage.

In 1945, Daimler Benz worked on several types of suicidal bombers. The most advanced of them all, the DB *Projekt F*, looked like a gigantic V1 bomb with swept wings and a BMW 018 replacing the traditional pulsejet.

In November 1944, BMW's EZS design team, led by the engineer Dr Huber, proposed a 65-per-cent scaled-down version of the *Strahlbomber* Projekt II powered by a single BMW 018. It was a flying wing of 23-m span, able to fly at 1,040 kph carrying heavy armament, either as a fast bomber or as a heavy fighter, and able to destroy a B-29 with a single shot of its four 55-mm cannons. It was a design with huge potential, and was known as TL BMW *Strahljäger* (jet fighter) *Projekt V*.

The drawings of the time do not appear to show flaps or slats in the wing structure of the *Strahlbomber* or *Strahljäger*. Therefore, it is only possible to speculate on its flying performance at low speed.

Technical data	
Type	single-seat heavy fighter.
Wings	built of wood and plywood, with 50- and 35-degree swept at the leading edge and 20-degree swept at the trailing edge, housing ten fuel tanks with a total capacity of 4,200 litres, the main undercarriage legs, armament, elevators, and ailerons.
Fuselage	light alloy structure housing nose leg, the pressurised cockpit, and the engine.
Armament	four Rheinmetall-Borsig Mk 112/55 cannons in the nose.
Wingspan	23 m
Length	10.80 m
Height	2.84 m
Wing area	96 sq. m
Max. weight	10,600 kg
Max. speed	1,040 kph
Climb rate	28 m/s
Ceiling	46,000 feet

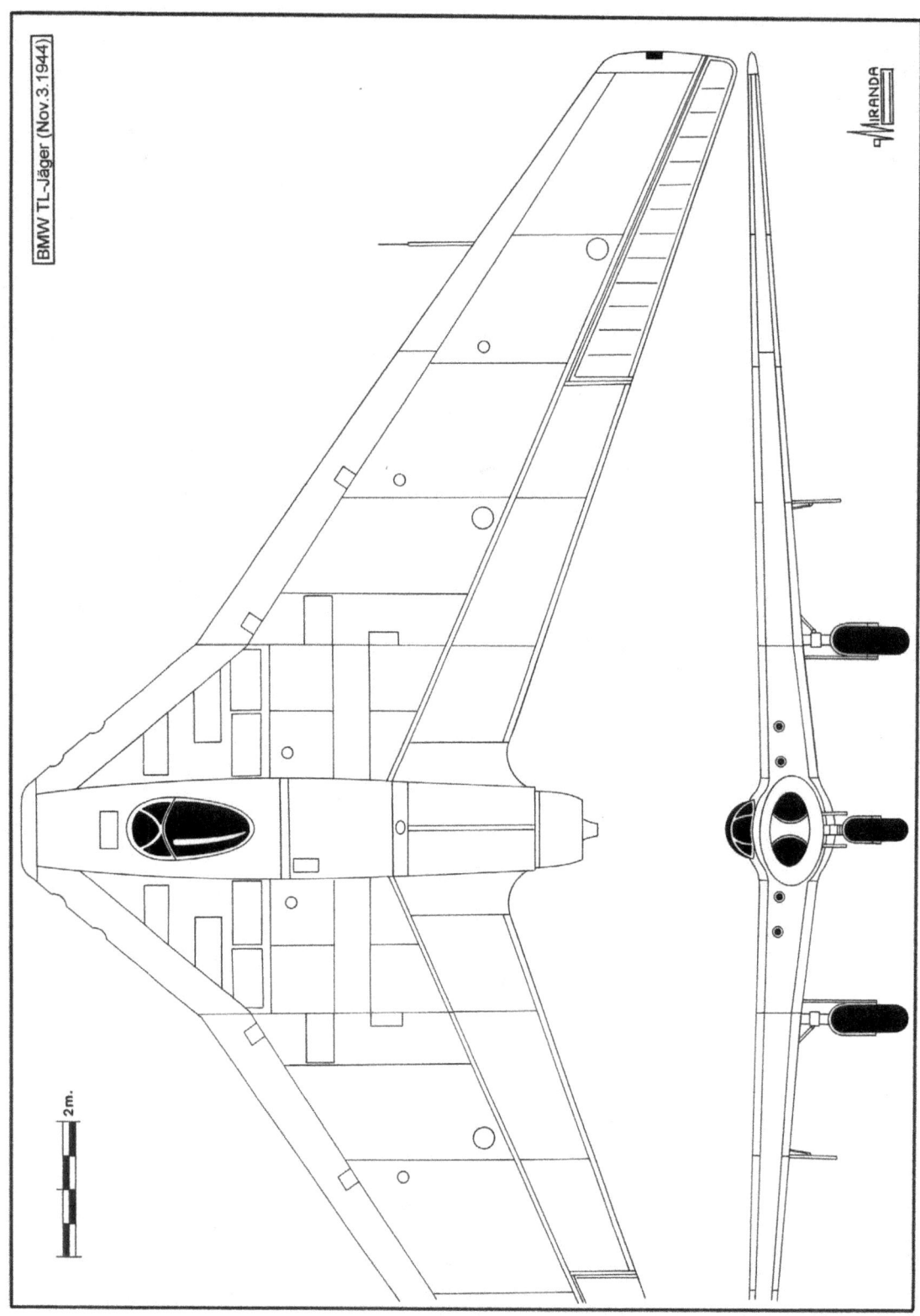

BMW TL-Jäger (Nov.3.1944)

2m.

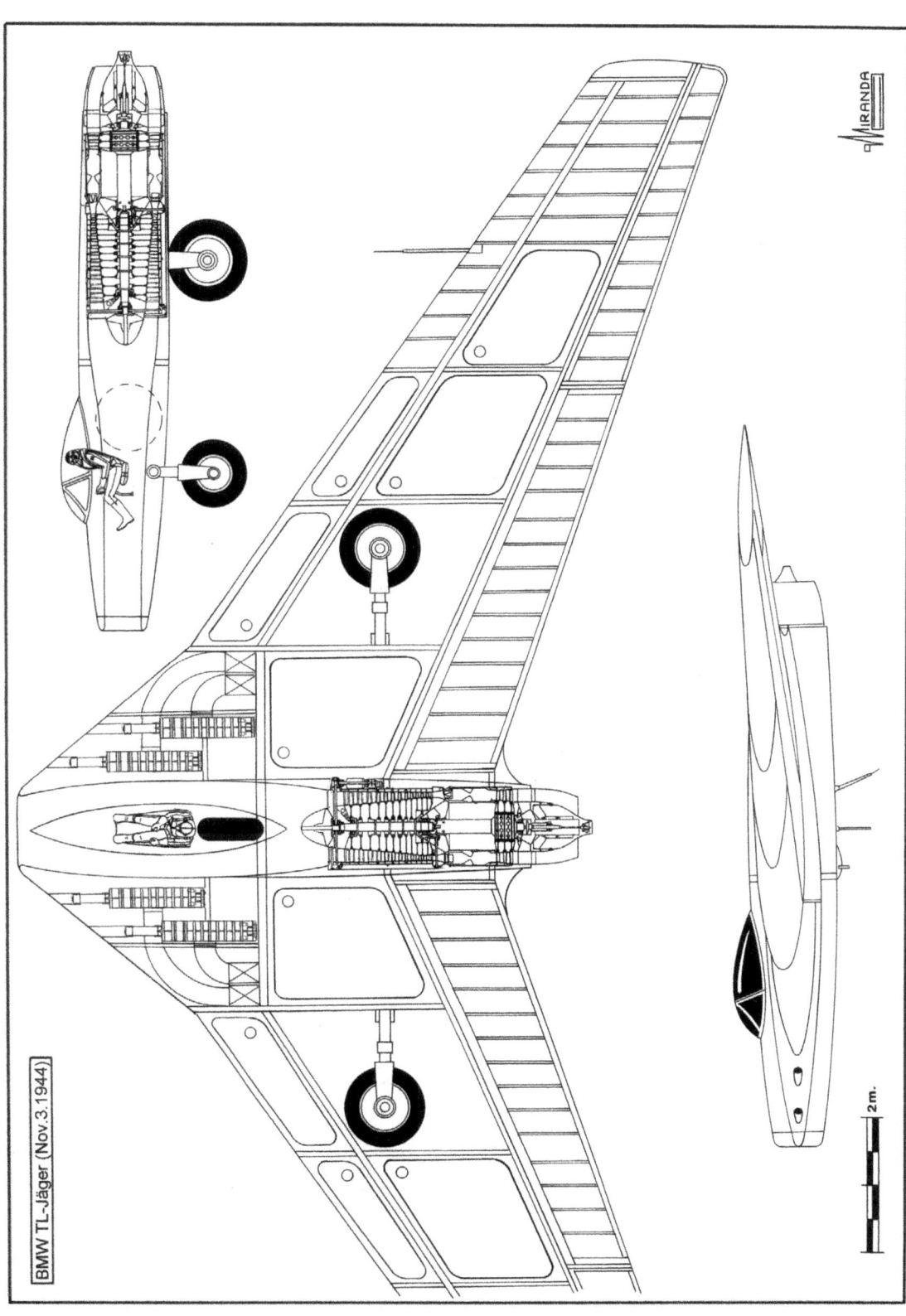

BMW TL-Jäger (Nov.3.1944)

2 m.

Chapter 5

Focke Wulf 1000 x 1000 x 1000

On 20 October 1942, the *Reichsluftfahrtministerium* (RLM) published a specification through its Technical Department for a fast bomber with 1,000 kg of payload, a penetration depth of 1,046 km (one third of the operational range), and a maximum speed of 700 kph, later on increased to 1,000 kph, at operational altitude.

In January 1943, the American bombers based in England embarked on daylight incursions over the Reich. Simultaneously, the RAF started to use the H2S cartographic radar that greatly improved the accuracy of night bombing. In spite of their sophisticated early warning network, German defences could not stop the attacks.

The British launched 600 tons of bombs over Berlin on 1 March. German retaliation meant the loss of fifty-seven bombers for the Luftwaffe, with the mediocre result of 100 tons dropped on London's outskirts. After the failure of the Me 210 and the He 177, the Germans did not have anything that could compete with the Mosquito and the Lancaster.

During a conference in Karinhall on 18 March, Göring warned the representatives of the aeronautical industry that he would not approve any new project until the requirements of the 1942 specification were met.

The Horten brothers decided to update its HVII *Schnellkampflugzeug* design of 26 March 1942, unifying it with one of the first versions of the Ho IX jet fighter (September 1942) to create a machine that fulfilled the wishes of the Reichsmarschall.

The Technisches Amt (Technical Office of the Luftwaffe) had already rejected the construction of the Lippisch P.11 *Schnellbomber* in May 1943, recommending its conversion into *Zerstörer* (Destroyer) in August.

The Horten bomber received official approval on 28 September, but an order to transform it into a high-altitude *Jägernotprogramm* fighter arrived in April 1944. In August of the same year, Focke Wulf proposed to build the *Schnellbomber* P.310239-10, a tailless delta similar in performance to the Lippisch model. This was an extremely advanced design for its time, known in specialised literature today as *Projekt 1000 x 1000 x 1000*.

This was a flying wing with a combat ceiling and maximum speed superior to any Allied fighter, designed for horizontal bombing at high altitude using the technology developed for the Ar 234. Given its virtual invulnerability, *Projekt 1000 x 1000 x 1000* may be considered a retaliation weapon specifically conceived to bomb London as a political target. The project received official approval as a V-weapon class by the end of the year, under the provisional designation of *Focke Wulf 1000 x 1000 x 1000 Entwurf B* (B configuration).

This was a remarkably versatile airplane, able to dive bomb and transport anti-ship missiles, capable of operating as *Nachtjäger*, *Mosquitojäger* or *Aufklärer* (reconnaissance airplane), and fitted with two Zeiss Rb 50/30 aerial cameras in the bomb bay.

In 'level bomb' mode, the airplane flew by radio navigation at 46,000 feet until 30 km from its target, at which point the pilot connected the three-axis *Patin PKS* autopilot and the *Lofte* tachometric bombsight. These two devices acted together, driving the airplane according to the pilot's movement of the bombsight. The bomb was automatically released when the plane reached the point predicted by the computer.

The 'blind bomb' mode used the EGON automatic bomb release system (integrated by the following electronic devices: FuG 16 Zy, FuG 101 radioaltimeter and FuG 123 cartographic radar), controlled by a pair of *Freya* ground radar stations.

In 'dive bomb' mode, the airplane flew into a shallow 30-degree dive attack, starting at 16,400 feet and using the *Bombenzielanlage für Sturzflug* (BZA) bomb-aiming computer with an RF2C periscope and PV1B sighting head. The bomb release was made at 5,000 feet. The split flaps could act as airbrakes.

The conversion of the *Focke Wulf 1000 x 1000 x 1000 Entwurf B* into *Mosquitojäger* was relatively simple: it only required the installation of an FuG 218 fire control radar with the fixed parabolic antenna of an FuG 222 in the nose and the replacement of inward fuel tanks with four Mk 108 cannons.

The flying wing configuration allowed the increase of load at higher altitude. Considering that the turbojets consumed at 32,800 feet a third of the fuel that they consumed at sea level, the *Schnellbomber* could be smaller and transport less fuel and more payload.

The problem with flying wing bombers was rotation during take off, due to their short length. Both the Focke Wulf and the Lippisch were equipped with jet deflection flaps, located behind the jet nozzles and detachable Rocket Assisted Take off (RATO) rockets. The wing construction was based on the technology developed by Focke Wulf for the Ta 154 night fighter.

The structure was of *Lignofol L90* plywood and the coating was of *Dynal Z5* new plastic, manufactured by Dynamit Nobel Troisdorf. The elasticity modules had to be assembled with synthetic glue, made of *Tego-Film* phenolic resin, equivalent to the Araldite used in the British Mosquito.

Some believe that this type of structure might have had certain 'stealth' qualities suited to avoid the radars of the time. The pressurised cockpit for extreme altitude was made of light alloy with extensively braced canopy, as was the rest of the forward fuselage, which absorbed the shock of the nose leg during landing.

As a precaution against the spin that a stopped engine or Flak near the airplane might cause, two vertical surfaces, fitted with small rudders, were installed in the wingtips.

Technical data

Type	high-altitude fast bomber.
Wings	built of plywood and plastic with 45-degree swept at the leading edge and 21-degree swept at the trailing edge, laminar profile with ailerons/elevators, split flaps and jet deflection flaps. Wingtips fins with rudders. They housed the main undercarriage legs, retracting inboards, the bomb bay, and four self-sealing fuel tanks.
Fuselage	built of light alloy, housing the nose leg, retracting forward, and the cockpit, pressurised with control heating, frontal and rear armoured, and ejector seat.
Engines	two Heinkel HeS 011 turbojets, each with 1,500-kg thrust and two Rheinmetall-Borsig 109-502 solid propellant RATO units with 771-kp peak thrust.
Armament	none
Bomb load	one SB 1000/410 Fallschirmbombe (parachute bomb) of 1,000 kg.
Wingspan	14 m
Length	10.26 m
Height	2.75 m
Wing area	55 sq. m
Max. weight	8,100 kg
Max. speed	1,060 kph
Range	2,500 km
Operational ratios	1,000 km
Service ceiling	46,000 feet

ELECTRONIC DEVICES

FuG 16 VHF *Funksprechgerät* R/T device, developed by Lorenz for air-to-ground and air-to-air communications. Frequencies between 38.5 and 42.3 Mhz. Wire aerial or Morane mast. There were four modes:
Y-Verfahren superimposed signal for fighter control position;
Gruppenbefehlswelle communication between aircraft;
Nachsicherung und Flugssicherung communication between the aircraft and the ground system;
Reichsjägerwelle continuous running commentary.

The FuG 16 ZY combined the homing and *Y-Verfahren* functions and operated on a wavelength of 7 m.

BZA-1 EGON bombing computer developed by GEMA for automatic blind bomb release in combination with the FuG 25a system and Freya ground radar stations.

Lofte 7K tachometric bombsight for level bombing operations.

Patin LKS 7D-15 three-axis autopilot.

RF2 C periscope made by Goerz.

Zeiss Rb 50/30 or Rb 75/30 aerial camera.

FuG 25a *Erstling* IFF device *Kenngerät* was manufactured by GEMA and Brinkler. Emission frequency of 160 Mhz, reception frequency of 125 Mhz. Range of 100 km. Power of 600 W. Rod antenna under the fuselage (300 mm long), 10 degrees rear swept. Responded to *Freya*, *Würzburg*, and *Gemse* ground control radars. It could be used to calculate the distance of an airplane from the ground radar. The need to operate in several frequencies between 0.53 and 2.40 m considerably delayed its entry into service in the Luftwaffe. It was used in combination with the EGON (*Erstling- Gemse-Offensive-Navigation*) for radio navigation of bombers in combination with the FuMG 401A *Freya LZ* radar, as an alternative to the *Y-Gerät*. Weight of 12 kg.

FuG 101a *Feinhöhermesser* of 1.5 Kw, radioaltimeter developed by Siemens/LG. Operation frequencies between 337 and 400 MHz in continuous wave and frequency modulation (CW–FM with a 2-m error). Power 1.5 W. Weight of 16 kg. Range of between 150 and 1,500 m. It used two *Sender S101* and *Empfänger E 101* dipoles to transmit and receive.

FuG 123 *Truhe* cartographic radar *Leitstrahlverfahren* based on captured units of the British 'Gee' radar. Frequencies from 35 to 100 Mhz. It worked in combination with the ground stations of the FuS An 728 *Boden Truhe*.

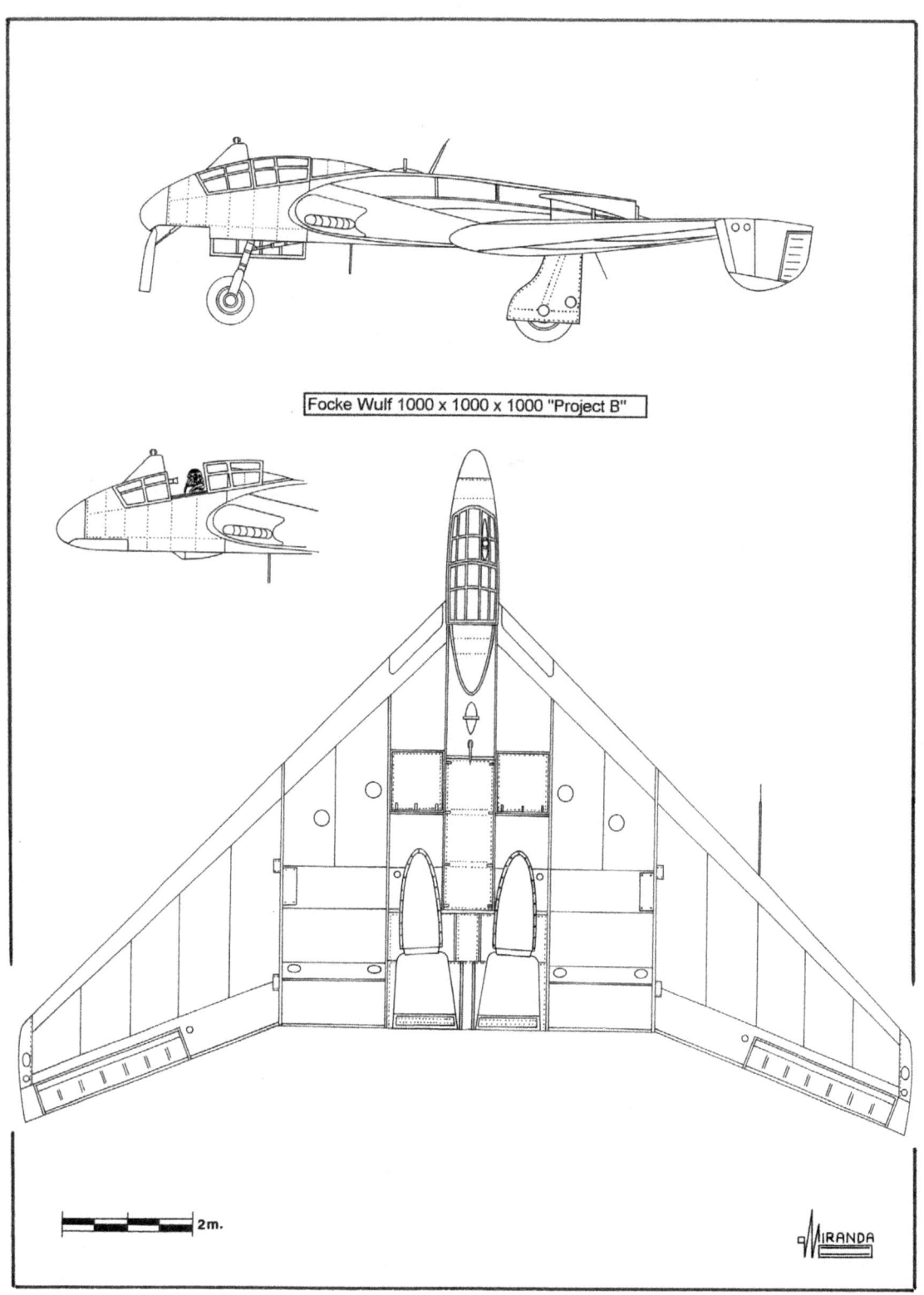

Focke Wulf 1000 x 1000 x 1000 "Project B"

2m.

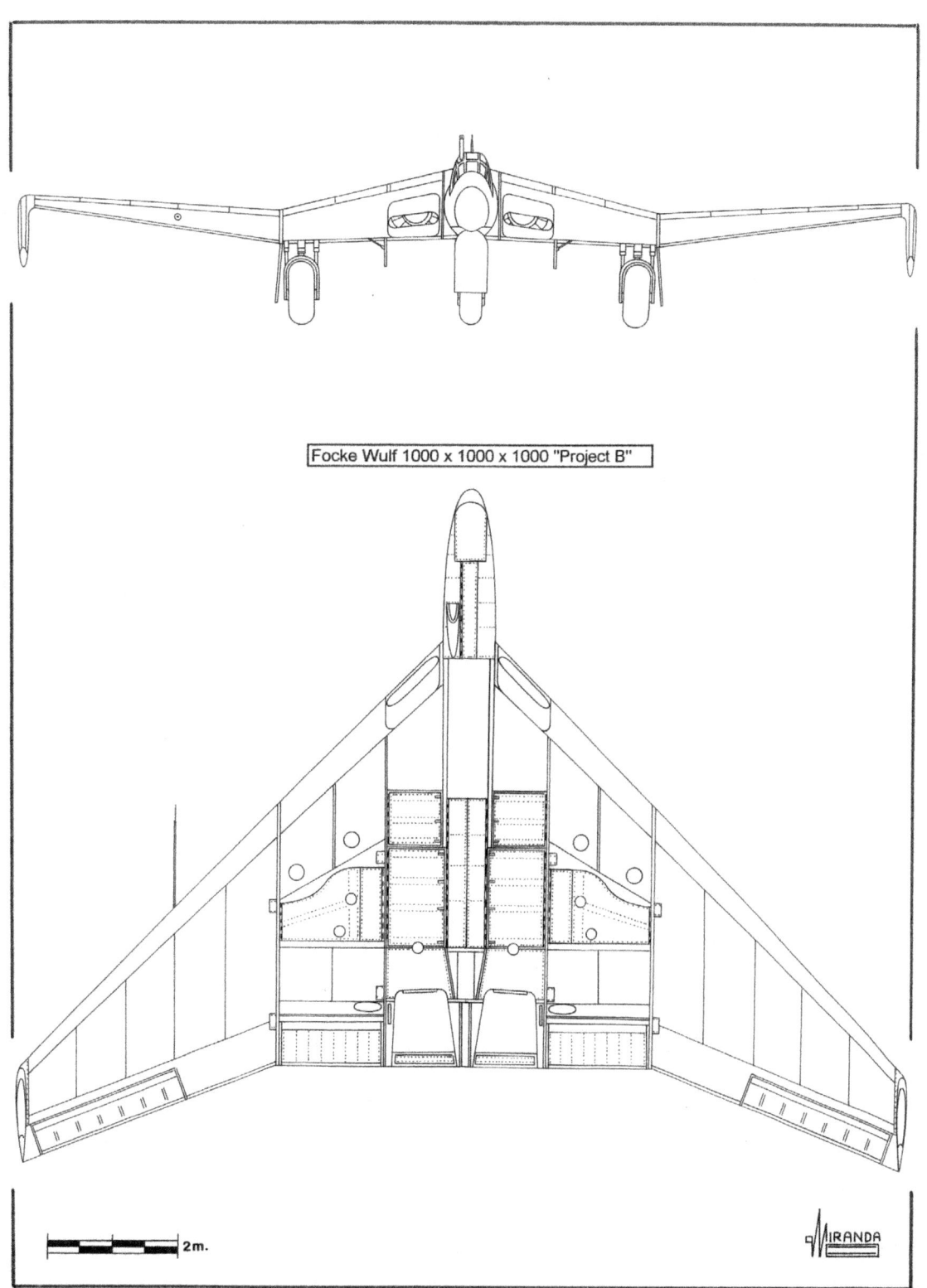

Focke Wulf 1000 x 1000 x 1000 "Project B"

2m.

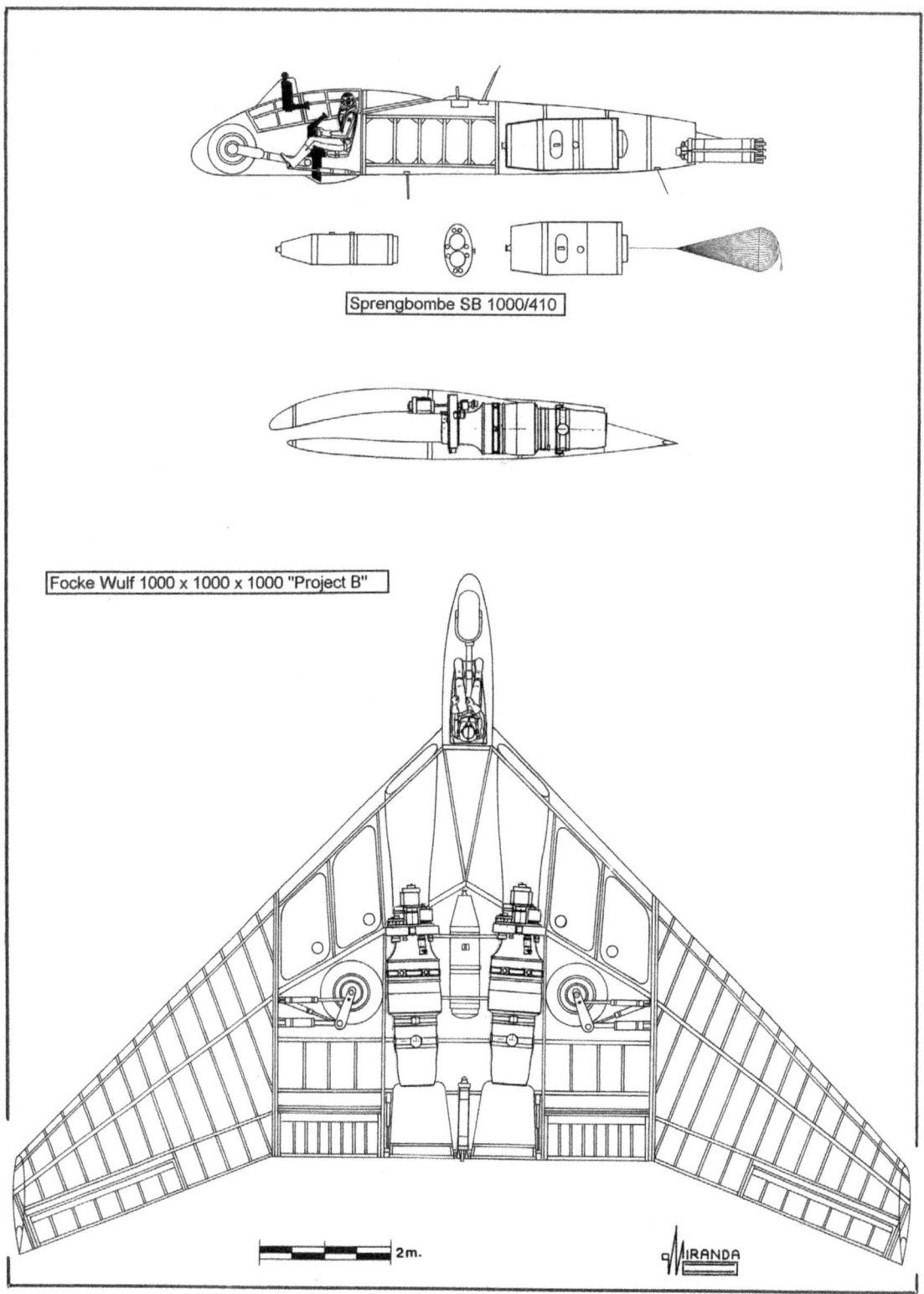

Sprengbombe SB 1000/410

Focke Wulf 1000 x 1000 x 1000 "Project B"

2m.

Chapter 6

Gotha P.60 A

In their quest for aerodynamic perfection, the Horten brothers designed the H IX interceptor in the spirit of a racer plane. Margins of longitudinal stability and available inner space were sacrificed to achieve a faster plane with a minimum frontal section. However, such a tight design would seriously hamper its potential for further development as a combat airplane when facing the realities of industrial production.

This was indeed the case when the RLM ordered the Gothaer Waggonfabrik AG to manufacture forty units (under the designation Ho 8-229) in May 1945. Upon examining the scale drawings of the project, the engineers of the company found a series of deficiencies that hindered the future development of more powerful versions of the airplane.

The Ho 8-229 lacked the required inner space to install new equipment or increase the number of crew members to convert it into training or night fighter versions. The only way to achieve this without creating any protuberances on the wing surface would be to enlarge the nose. However, this solution affected longitudinal stability and overloaded the nose oleo-leg, already at the limit of its structural resistance. The air intakes operation was also disturbed by the turbulence generated by the new frontal configuration. The Ho 229 V6 came under insurmountable difficulties when the integration of the new parabolic antennae radars *Berlin N-3* and *Bremen 0* was attempted.

There was also the structural problem of the central section of the wing. This had been designed to house two BMW 003 A-1 turbojets with a diameter of 69 cm. When it was decided to install the new Jumo 004 B engines of 80 cm diameter, the limit of the design was reached. It could not be modified again to house the future HeS 011 of 108 cm. To that end, it would have been necessary to redesign the central section of the wing and to perform a new series of aerodynamic tests for which no time was left.

In January 1945, the design team of the Gothaer Waggonfabrik AG led by Dr Ing. Hünerjäger proposed the construction of the P.60 to the RLM. It was a project for a high-altitude interceptor that used the same manufacturing methods as the Ho 8-229, but without some of its structural and aerodynamic limitations. The new model could use any type of German turbojet either already in service or still being developed. It was therefore decided to install them in the outer part of the wing in a dorsal and ventral position along the centerline, thus leaving room inside for fuel and equipment.

The pilot canopy was removed to counterbalance the increase of drag produced by the engines. The two members of the crew (in prone position) were located in a pressurised and armoured container in the forward area of the wing's central section. It was considered at the time that the prone position allowed the pilot to withstand high G values during the combat manoeuvres. A symmetrical profile wing with an increased sweep compared to the one in the Ho 8-229 (58 and 50 degrees at the leading edge) was also adopted.

To safeguard against stalling at landing, the leading edge was fitted with hydraulically activated slats. It also had conventional flaps in the ventral side of the wing central section. They were installed with a 15-degree forward sweep and could also act as airbrakes.

There were three types of control surfaces:

Elevators—located in the inner trailing edge and provided with auxiliary trim tabs.
Ailerons—located in the outer trailing edge with internally balanced control flaps.
Drag rudders—designed to avoid the need of an excessive physical effort from the pilot during high-speed manoeuvres.

The drag rudders were installed by pairs in the inner wingtips with an 18-degree slope in relation to the centreline. They twisted vertically over an axis, like the blades in a pair of scissors, sticking out from above and under the wing surface. The resulting drag delayed one wingtip in relation to the other (remaining in smooth configuration), thus achieving a very accurate directional control.

For small corrections of path—for example, to aim the guns—only the tips with 20-degree slope jutted out. Forty-five degrees were used for bigger adjustments—for example, to neutralise the crossed wing effect when landing—and 90 degrees only during combat manoeuvres. The system defaulted to zero-degree drag when the pilot pressure over the controls stopped. Compared to the Ho 8-229, where the nose oleo-leg held 45 per cent of the overall weight, the new weight distribution in the Gotha P.60 meant that the nose oleo-leg only held 15 per cent of the total weight, in an asymmetrical placement relative to the central axis of the airplane.

The armament was to be of four Mk 108 cannons for the *Höhenjäger* (High Altitude Interceptor) version, two Mk 103 cannons for the *Zerstörer* version, and two Mk 108 cannons and two RB 50/18 cameras for the *Aufklärer* version. It has also been planned to increase the ceiling and climb rate of the *Höhenjäger* with the installation of a bifuel HWK 509 B rocket in the space located between the engines. This version would have been denominated Gotha P.60 A/R.

During the project's lifespan, many criticized the difficulty for the crew to abandon the machine through the ventral hatch without being sucked in by the air intake of the lower engine. The same problem also existed in case of landing with the undercarriage in a folded position.

The pressurisation of the cockpit made the installation of another hatch in dorsal position difficult, and it did not eliminate the risk during bail-out. One solution—also adopted in the Arado E-583—consisted of installing both engines in ventral position and the access hatch in dorsal position. This version was denominated Gotha P.60 A-2.

The configuration did not remain because it diminished the rate of roll in combat, and further versions were to have ejector seats installed.

Technical data

Type	two-seat heavy fighter.
Phase	project
Wings	wood structure, plywood and Formholz cladding, each containing a fuel tank of 1,200 litres.
Fuselage	formed by the wing central section, welded steel-tube framework, plywood and Formholz cladding, including crew, frontal armour against 12.7-mm rounds and rear against 20-mm rounds, pressurisation system, electronic equipment, landing gear, a fuel tank of 1,200 litres, four cannons, and 650 cartridges.
Landing	gear the main wheels are stowed flat, with 90-degree rotation, in the mid portion of the centre section. The asymmetric nose oleo-leg was retractable to the rear and housed port of the cockpit.
Engines	two BMW 003 A-1 turbojets, each rated at 800-kp static thrust, mounted to the rear of the centre section, one above and one below.
Fuel tanks	two in the outer wings and one in the centre section with a total capacity of 3,600 litres. The P.60 A/R carried a tank of 620 litres of T-Stoff and one of 330 litres of C-Stoff in the central section—enough to last 6 minutes.
Armament	four Rheinmetall-Borsig Mk 108/30 cannons in the wing roots, with 150 rounds per outer gun and 175 rounds per inner gun. The Zerstörer version used two Rheinmetall-Borsig Mk 103/30 cannons with 175 rounds per gun.
Wingspan	12.2 m
Overall length	8.82 m
Fuselage length	7.63 m
Height	3.4 m
Wing area	46.8 sq. m
Overall area	110 sq. m
Max. weight	7,450 kg
Max. speed	915 kph
Ceiling	41,000 feet
Range	1,600 km

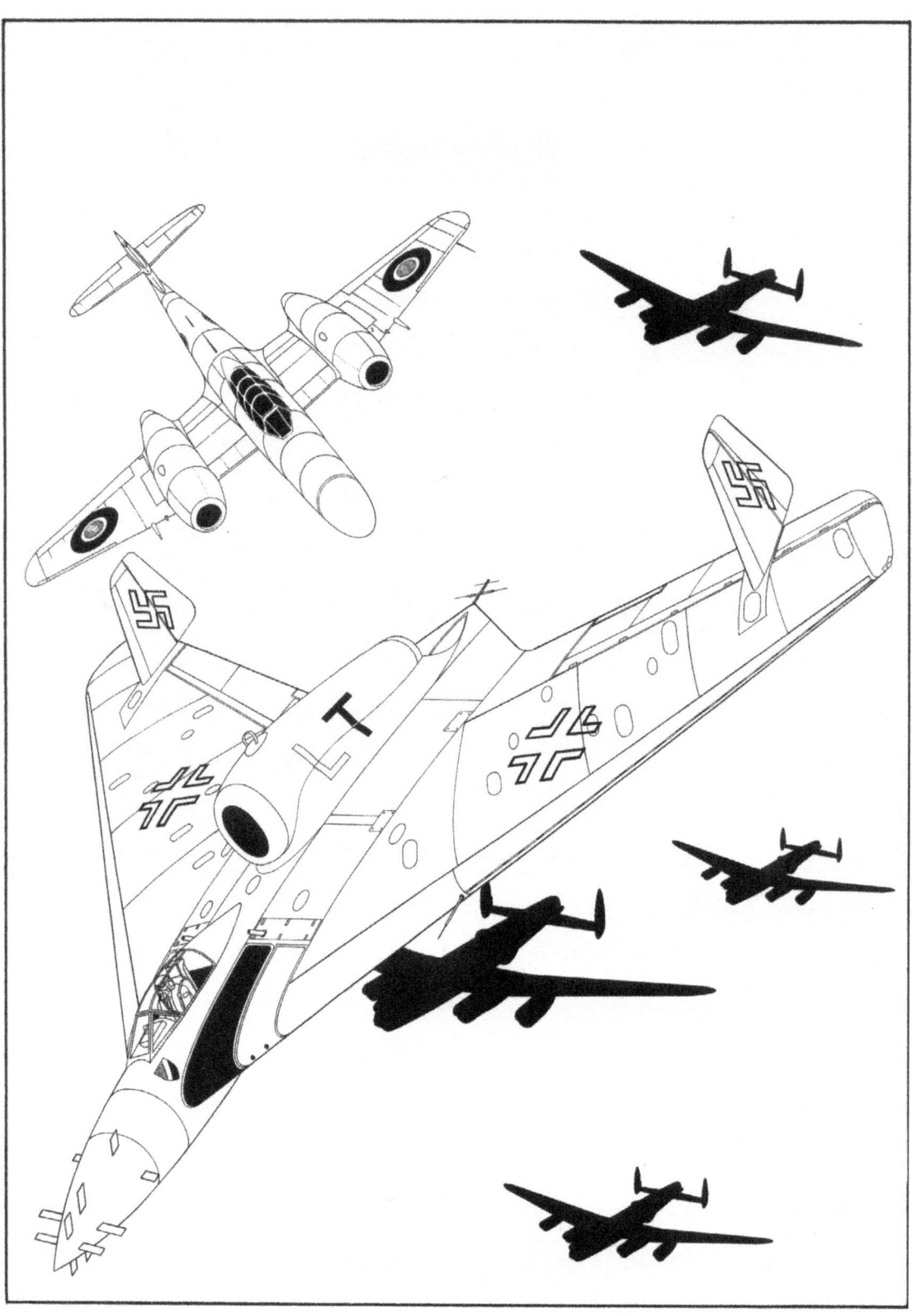

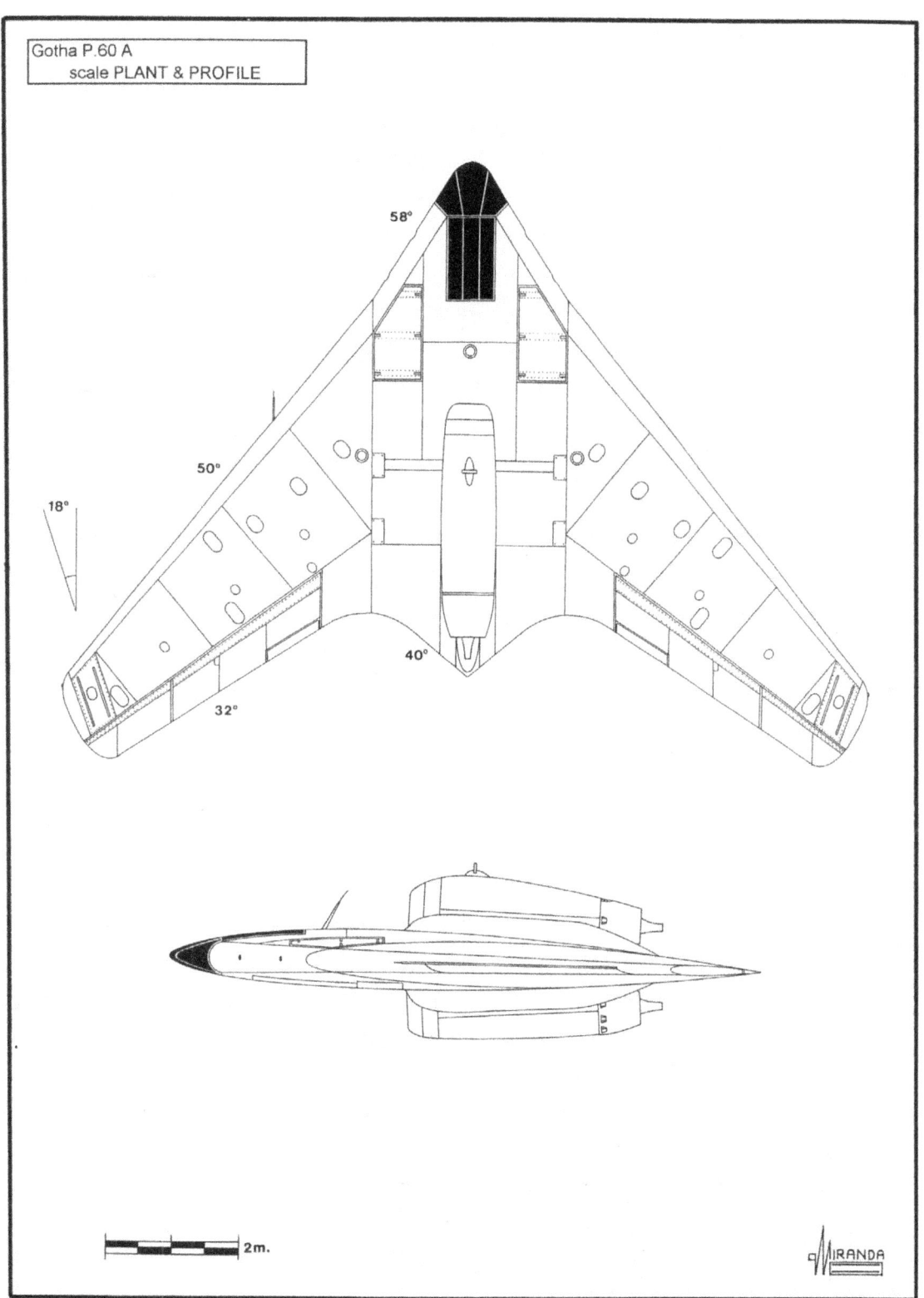

Gotha P.60 A
   scale PLANT & PROFILE

58°

50°

18°

40°

32°

2m.

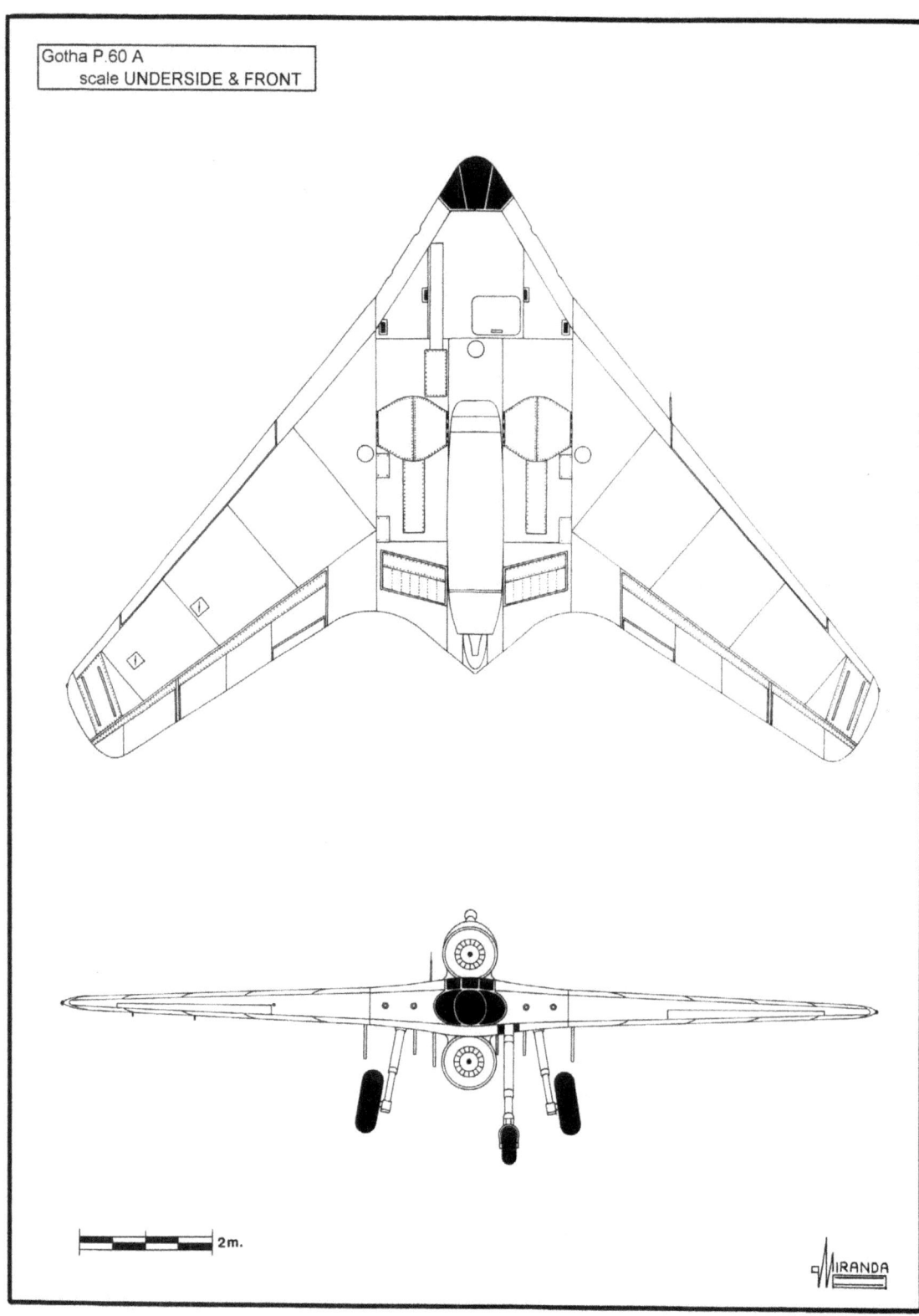

Gotha P.60 A
scale UNDERSIDE & FRONT

2m.

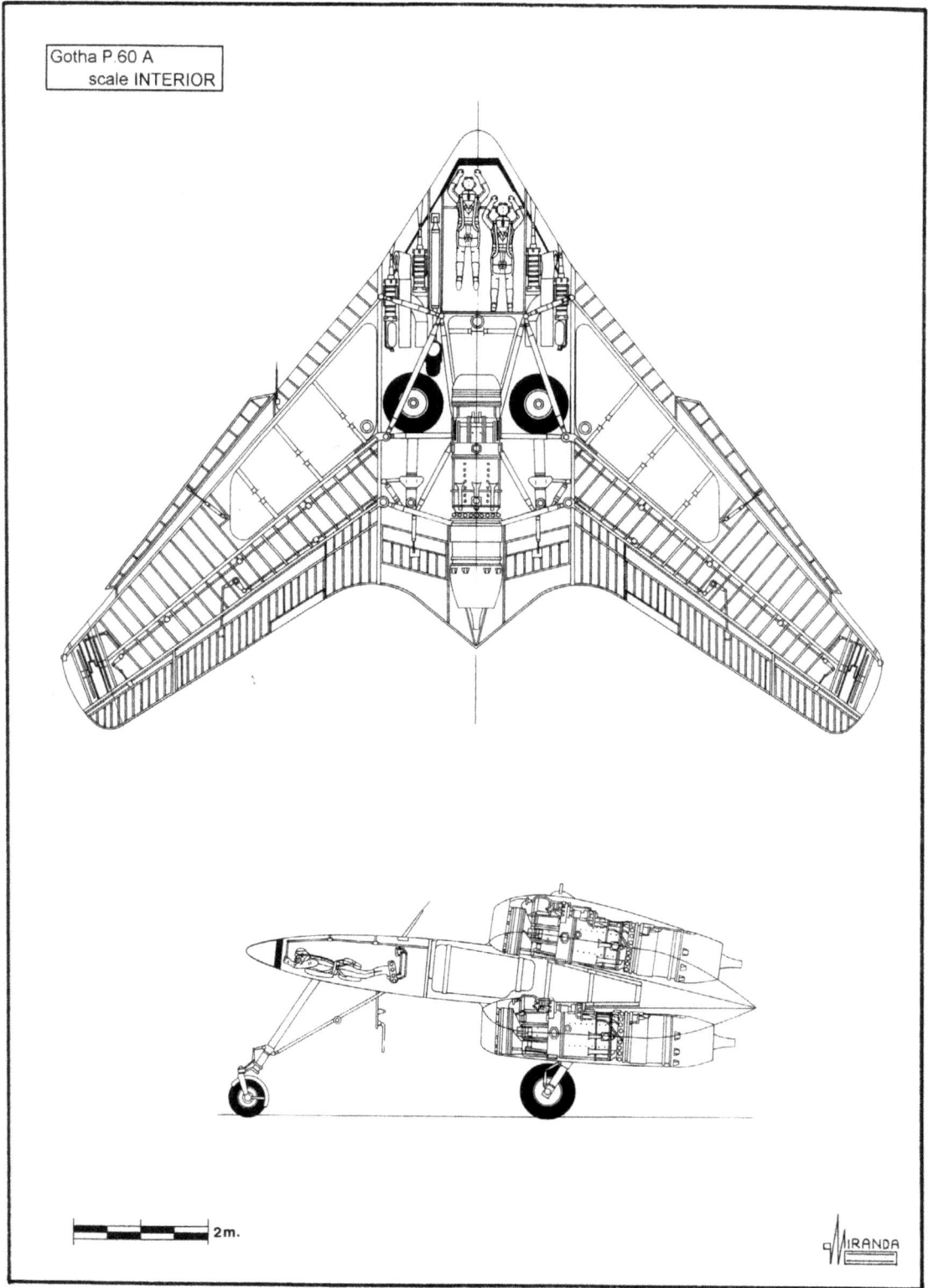

Gotha P.60 A
scale INTERIOR

2m.

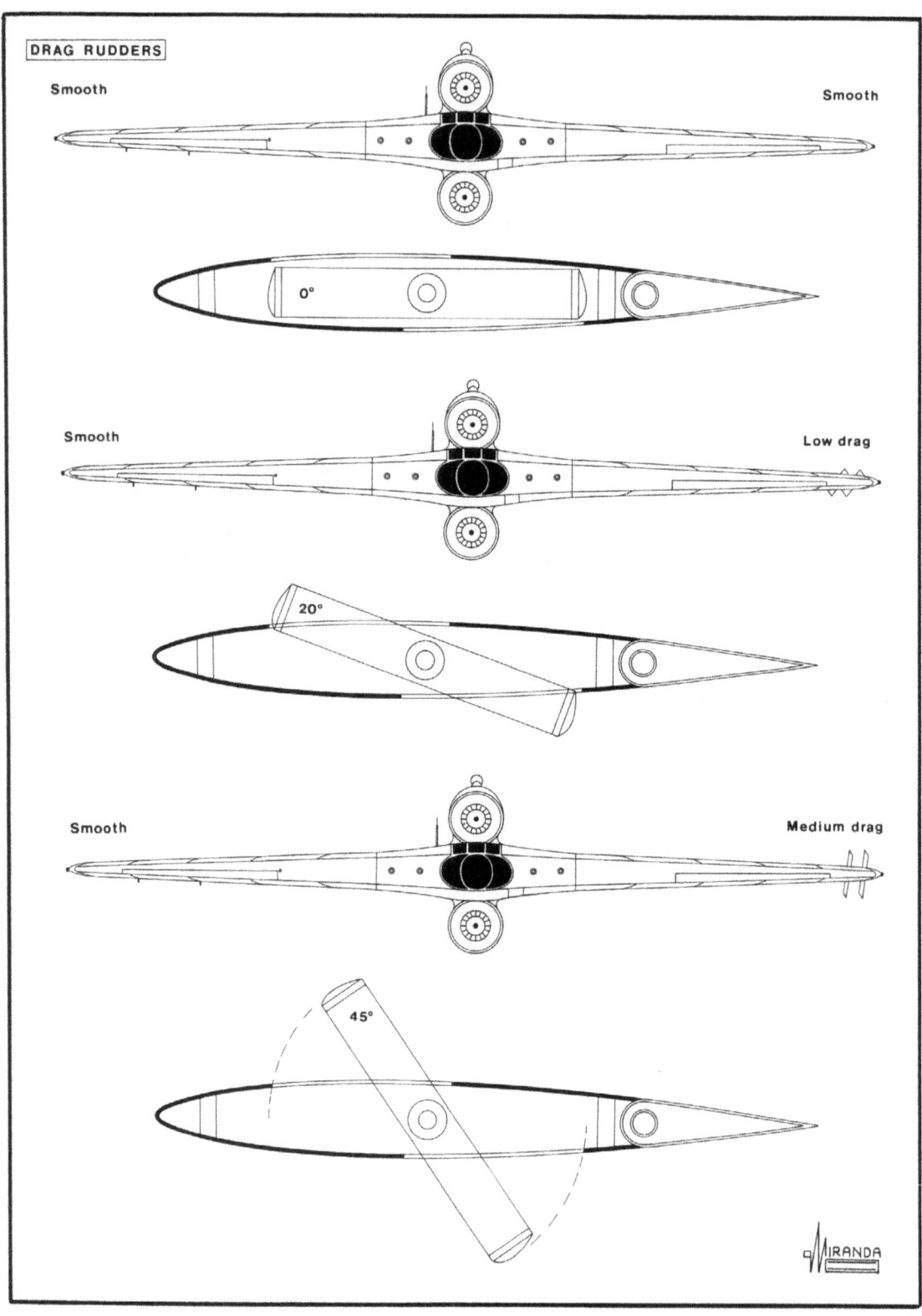

DRAG RUDDERS

Smooth   Smooth

0°

Smooth   Low drag

20°

Smooth   Medium drag

45°

MIRANDA

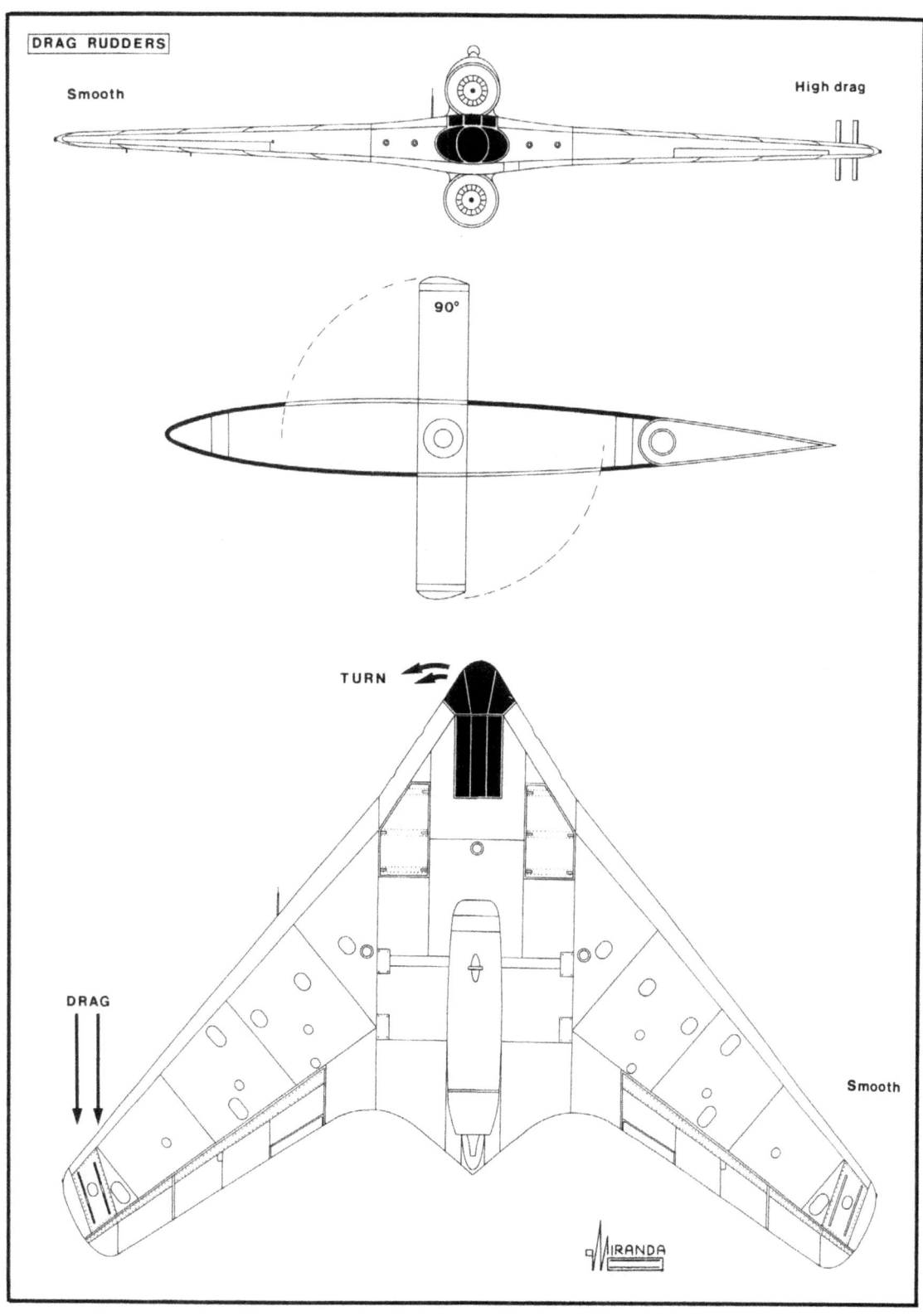

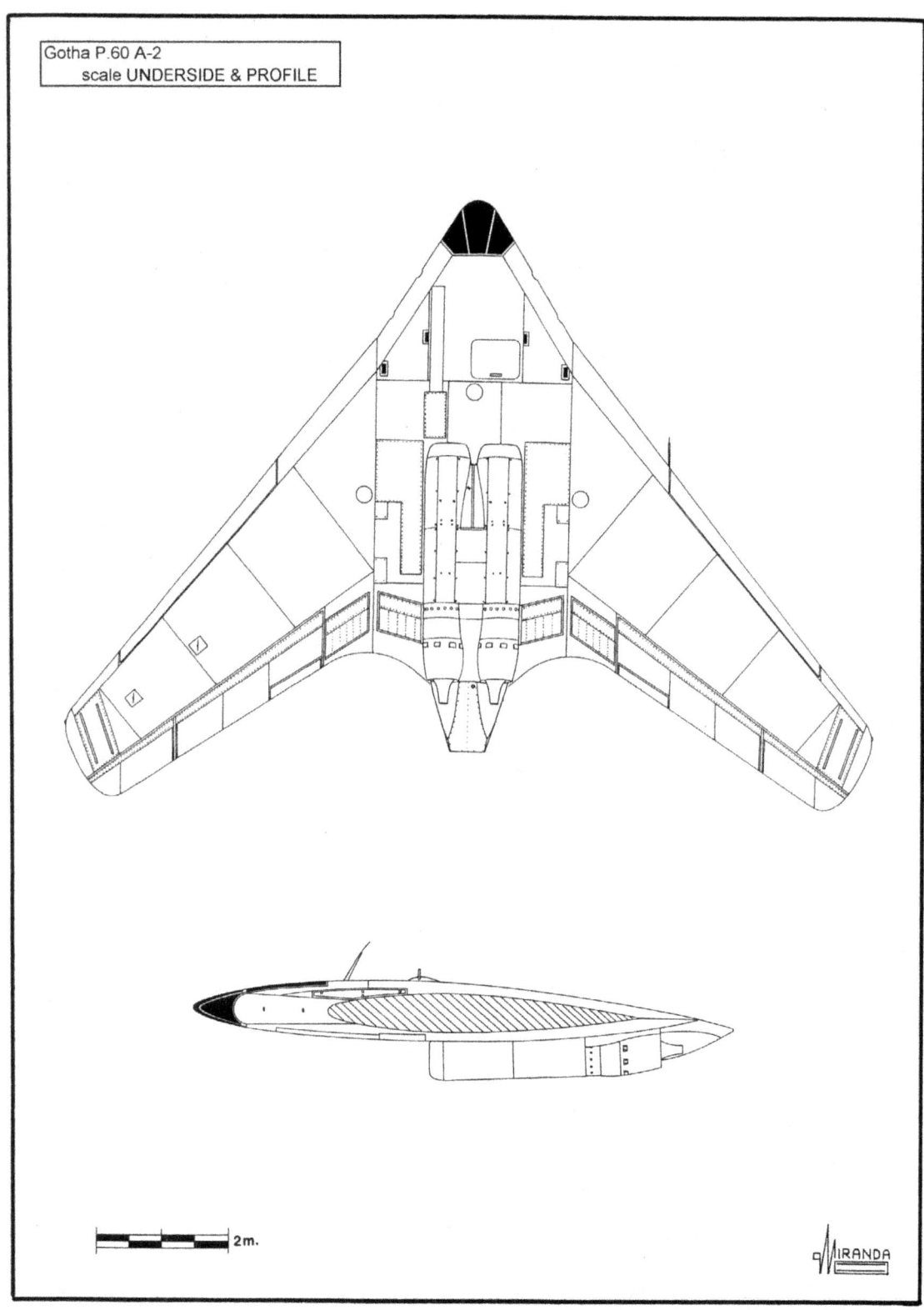

Gotha P.60 A-2
scale UNDERSIDE & PROFILE

2m.

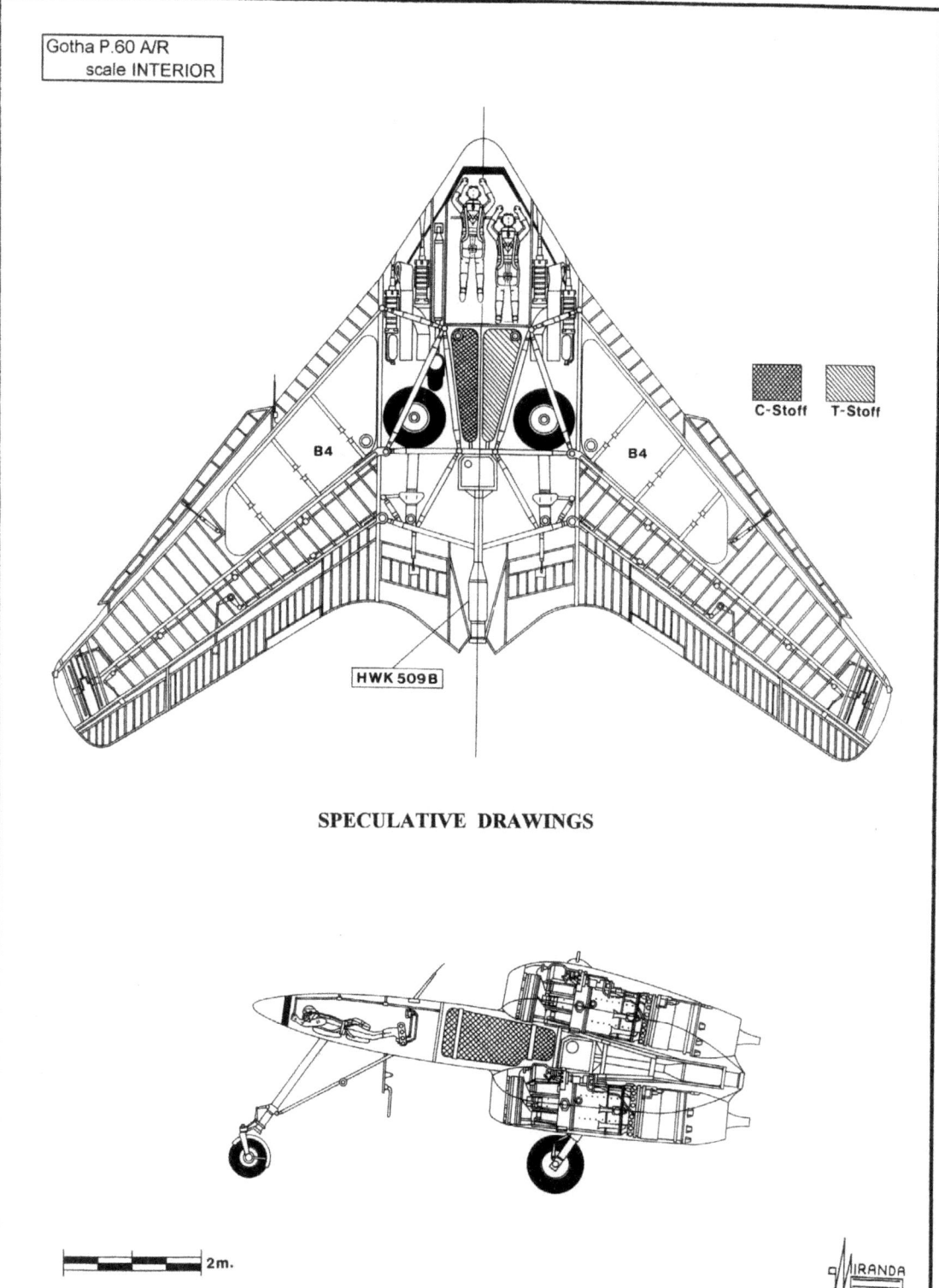

Gotha P.60 A/R
scale INTERIOR

C-Stoff   T-Stoff

B4   B4

HWK 509 B

SPECULATIVE DRAWINGS

2m.

Chapter 7

Gotha P.60 B

The possibility of having new HeS 011 engines in the short term allowed for the update of the P.60 A design. To achieve better performance from the higher level of power available, a bigger airplane was designed. It was almost a P.60 A, expanded by 110 per cent with small modifications.

The metallic bands offering structural resistance to the frontal section of the nose were removed to improve pilot visibility. The sweep of the leading edge was increased by one grade—thus lowering the trailing edge by two grades—and the separation between the trailing edge of the outer wing and the central section was less rounded than in the P.60 A, changing to a 28-degree forward sweep. Fuel capacity was increased to 4,300 litres. The maximum weight increased to 11,000 kg, and the main landing gear was redesigned.

It was planned to provide higher power with the installation of the B version of the HeS 011 with 1,500 kp of thrust and a Walter rocket of 2,000 kp, like the one in the P.60 A/R. The electronic equipment would consist of a Lorenz FuG 15 R/T communications system, a GEMA FuG 25, an *Erstling* IFF discriminator, and a Lorenz FuG 125 *Hermine* radio beacon receiver. Weapon racks to transport bombs and missiles could be installed at the wing roots.

Technical data	
Type	two-seat heavy fighter.
Phase	project
Wings	wood structure, plywood and Formholz cladding, each containing a fuel tank of 1,400 litres.
Fuselage	formed by the wing central section, welded steel-tube framework, plywood and Formholz cladding, including crew, frontal armour against 12.7-mm rounds and at the rear against against 20-mm rounds, pressurisation system, electronic equipment, landing gear, a fuel tank of 1,500 litres, four cannons, and 650 cartridges.
Landing gear	the main wheels are stowed flat, with 90-degree rotation, in the mid-portion of the centre section. The asymmetric nose oleo-leg was retractable to the rear and housed port of the cockpit.
Engines	two HeS 011 A-0 turbojets, each rated at 1,300-kp static thrust, were mounted to the rear of the centre section, one above and one below.

Fuel tanks	two in the outer wings and one in the centre section with a total capacity of 4,300 litres.
Armament	four Rheinmetall-Borsig Mk 108/30 cannons in the wing roots, with 150 rounds per outer gun and 175 rounds per inner gun. The Zerstörer version used two Rheinmetall-Borsig Mk 103/30 cannons with 175 rounds per gun. The Aufklärer version replaced two of the Mk 108 cannons by an Rb 50/18 and an Rb 30/18 cameras.
Wingspan	13.6 m
Overall length	9.79 m
Fuselage length	8.06 m
Height	3.6 m
Wing area	54.7 sq. m
Overall area	128 sq. m
Max. weight	11,000 kg
Max. speed	980 kph
Ceiling	46,000 feet
Range	2,800 km

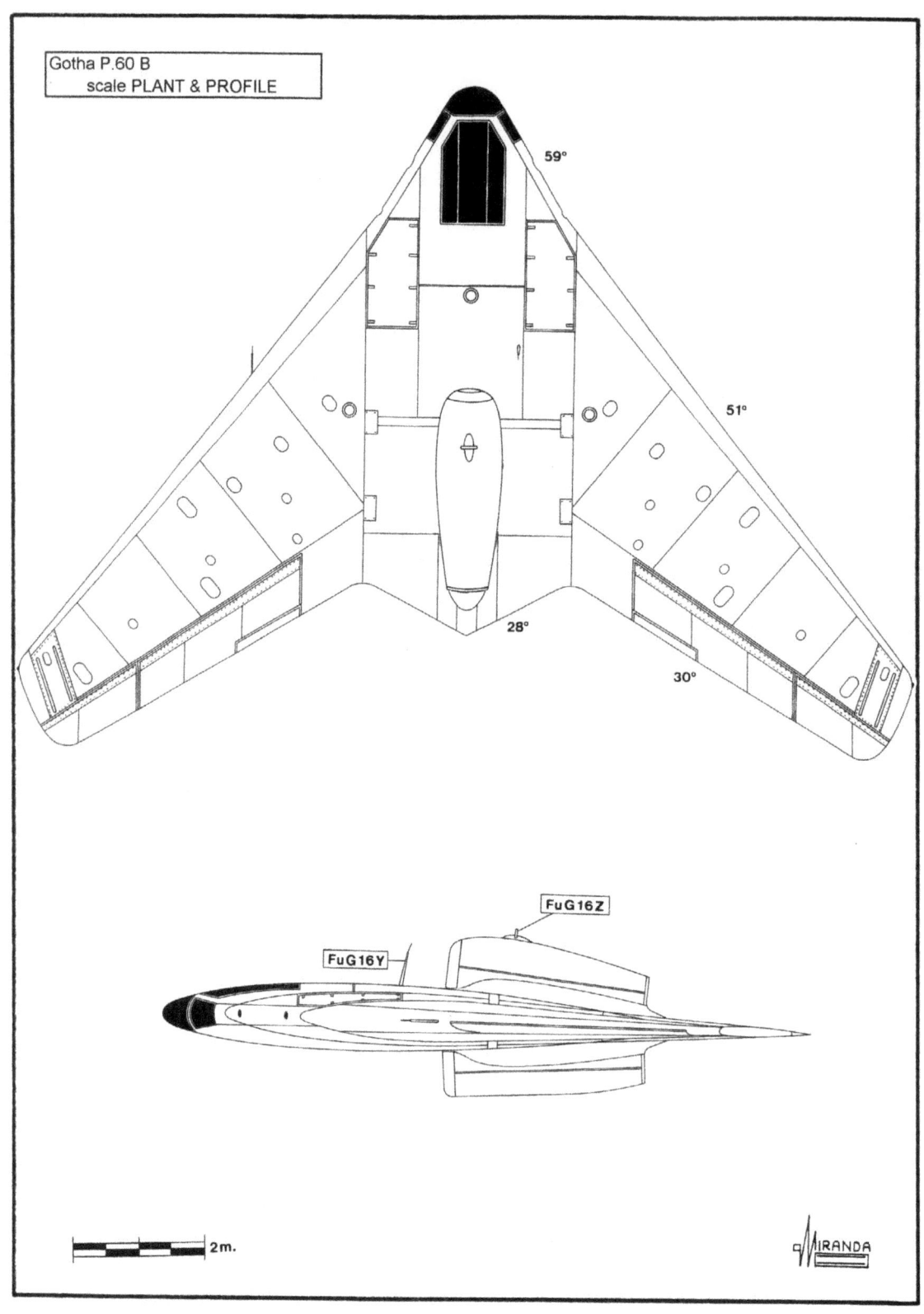

Gotha P.60 B
scale PLANT & PROFILE

59°

51°

28°

30°

FuG 16Z

FuG 16Y

2m.

MIRANDA

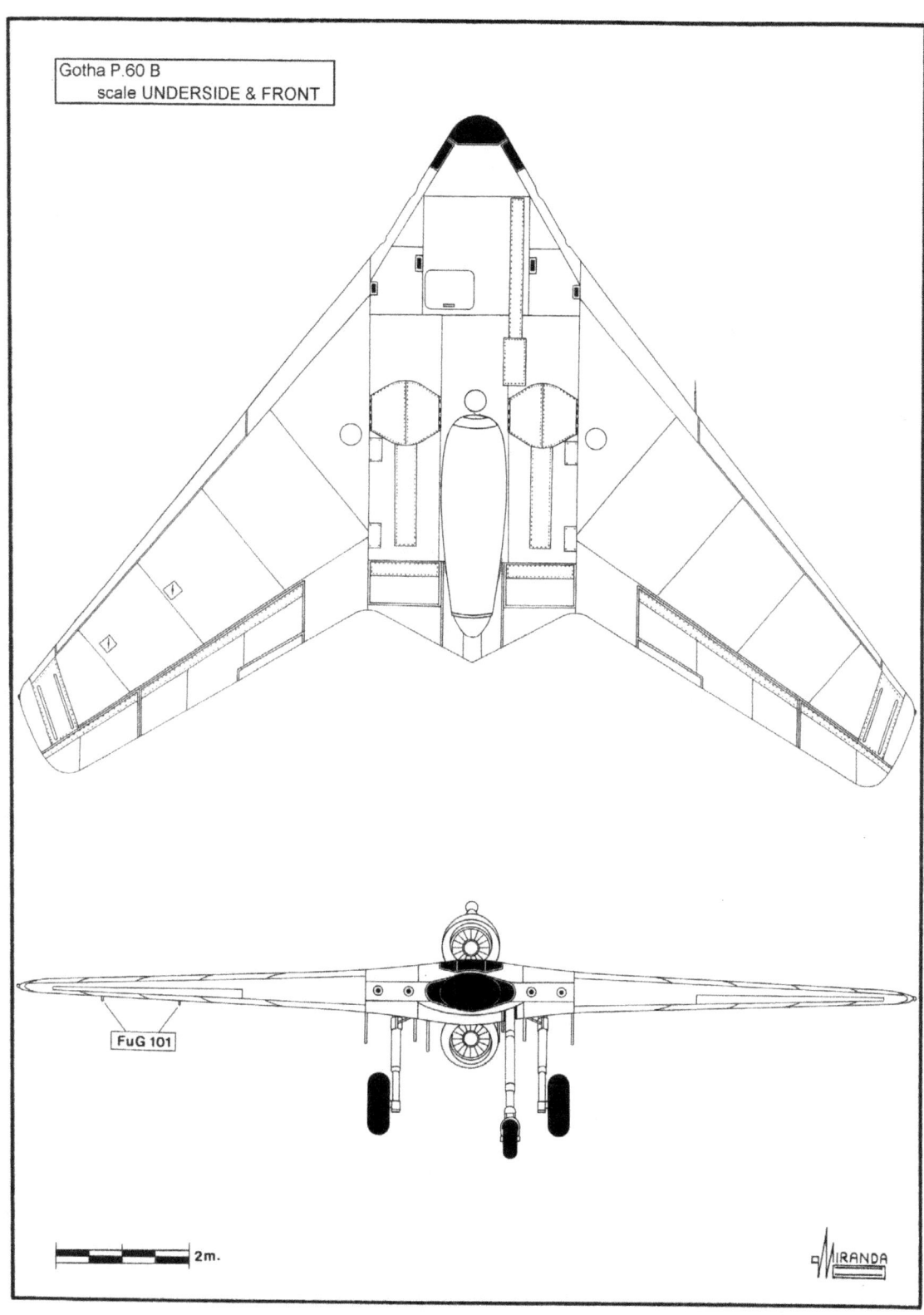

Gotha P.60 B
scale UNDERSIDE & FRONT

FuG 101

2m.

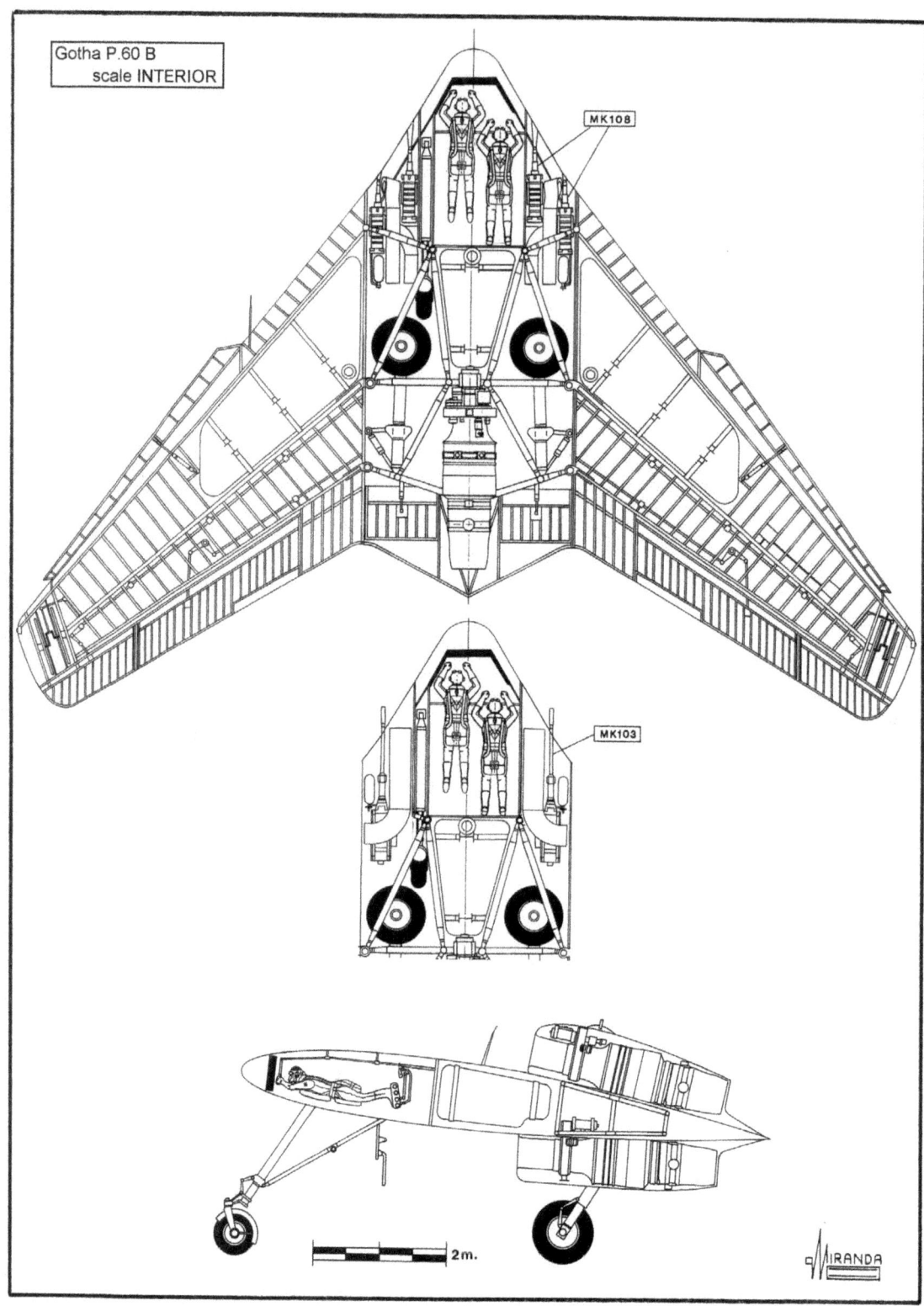

Gotha P.60 B
scale INTERIOR

MK108

MK103

2m.

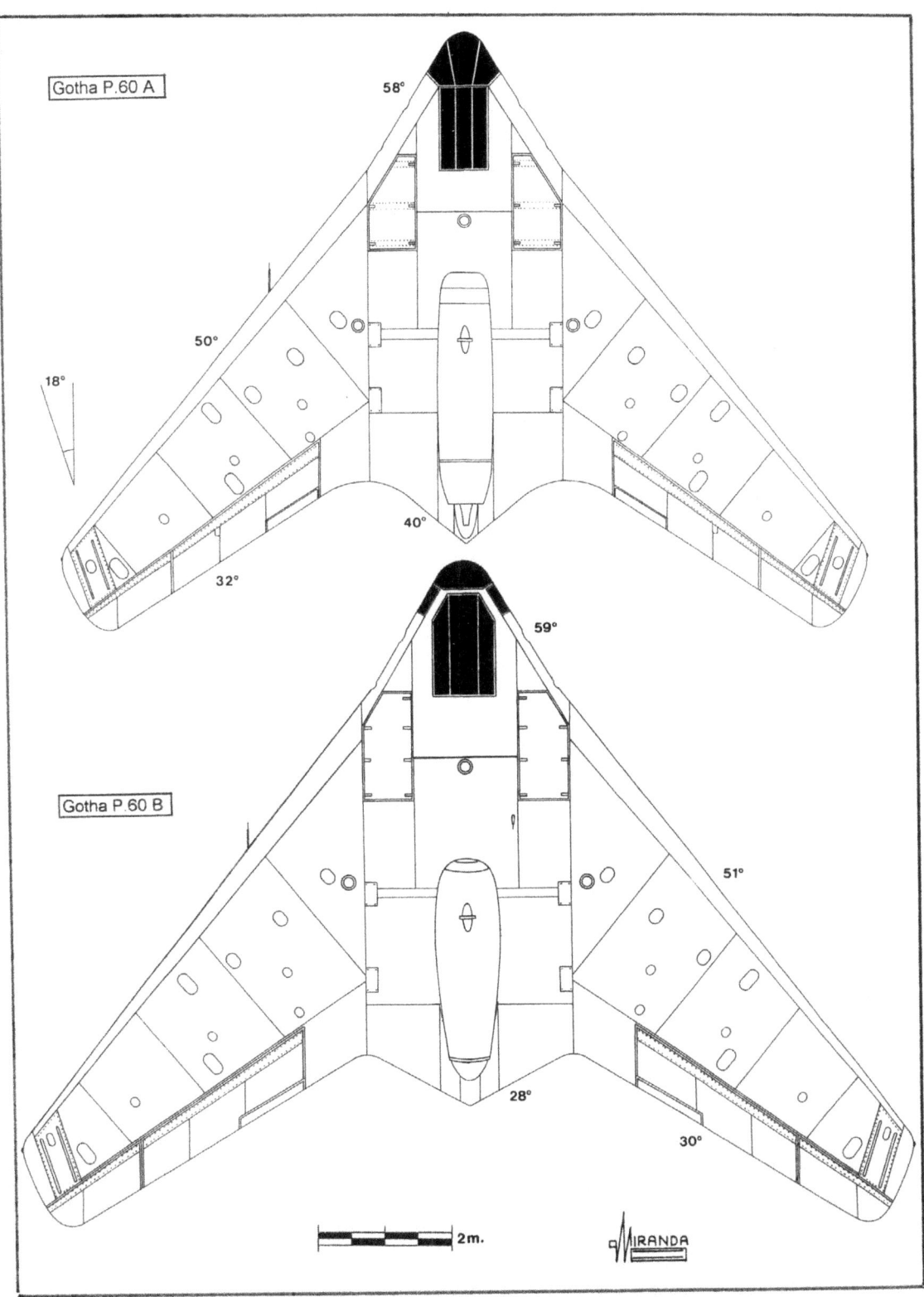

Gotha P.60 A

58°

50°

18°

32°

40°

Gotha P.60 B

59°

51°

28°

30°

2m.

MIRANDA

Chapter 8

Gotha P.60 C

By mid-1944, the Luftwaffe had to face an inconvenient truth: it did not have any night fighters capable of confronting the RAF Mosquito. The He 219 had good potential, but the aerodynamic drag produced by the external Hirschgeweih antennae, coupled with the weight of the first generation ejectable seats (activated by compressed air), reduced its speed and ceiling.

The Focke Wulf Ta 154, designed to hunt Mosquitos, was never mass produced. Its manufacturing was cancelled in July 1944 when the factory that manufactured *Tego-Film* glue (required for assembling subcomponents) was destroyed during a raid on Wuppertal. In August 1944, the Oberkommando der Luftwaffe proposed the transformation of available jet airplanes into new night fighters as an immediate solution.

Messerschmitt modified its trainer Me 262 B-1a, obtaining the night fighter Me 262 B-1a/U1; Arado transformed an Ar 234 B bomber into the Ar 234 B-2/N; and Horten proposed the Ho 229 V6, a two-seat radar equipped variant.

In spite of the powerful jet engines and advanced aerodynamics, these airplanes still had outer antennae that considerably hindered their performances. The appearance of the new centimetric radars of Telefunken FuG 240/3 *Berlin N-3* and FuG 244/245 *Bremen*—of which the parabolic antennae could be installed within the airplane—and the near availability of the HeS 011 turbojets, favoured the publication of 27 January 1945 specification. In the latter, the Technical Department of the RLM ordered the construction of a night fighter able to fly at 900 kph and reach a ceiling of 29,500 feet armed with four guns and an overall endurance of 4 hours.

By the end of February, an additional request was made regarding the new plane. It was required to use an oblique upward-firing *Schräge Musik* armament. Different options were presented to the contest: a variant of the Me 262 HG III (12 February 1945), a Focke Wulf with three turbojets, a jet version of the Dornier Do 335, and six flying wings—Arado E-583 (two-seat version of the E-581 heavy fighter), Blohm und Voss P.215 (scaled-up variant of P.212), Gotha P-60 C-1a (a modified P.60 B *Zerstörer*), Heinkel P.1079 B (without tailfin), Horten Ho 229 V6 (two-seat variant), and a two-seat version of the Junkers EF-128. Except for the Ho 229, all of these projects were to use the HeS 011 turbojet and, with the exception of the Go P-60 C-1a, the *Bremen 0* radar.

The P.60 B original design was adapted to the 27 January 1945 specification; namely, the nose was enlarged to install an FuG 240/3 radar with a parabolic antenna of 90 cm diameter in it. The lateral instability caused by this modification had to be corrected by installing two vertical surfaces at the wing trailing edges. The crew of two sat in tandem within a pressurised and armoured cockpit with a lateral opening canopy system very similar to the one in the Me 262 B-1a.

The design was modified by the end of February 1945 so that it could use the FuG 244 *Bremen 0* radar with an antenna of just 70 cm diameter. The diameter of the fuselage was reduced to produce a faster version (P.60 C-1b) equipped with *Schräge Musik*, ejector seats, and lighter electronic equipment based on the FuG 24 R/T system, originally designed for single-seat fighters. By the beginning of March 1945, the Luftwaffe did not need an all-weather interceptor *Moskitojäger*, but a heavy night fighter with a great amount of electronic equipment that required the inclusion of a third crew member. This left the Junkers, Heinkel, and Horten designs out of the contest as they could not increase crew room for structural reasons.

Messerschmitt was forced to enlarge the fuselage and redesign the wings of its Me 262 (17 March 1945 project) before finally being disqualified from the contest for three reasons: it used strategic material for its construction, it could not transport enough fuel, and the *Siemens antler* antenna of its radar was fixed. The Dornier was rejected on account of its full metallic construction and the Focke Wulf for consuming too much fuel.

The requirement of a third crew member for the Gotha P.60 posed a big problem: if its designers enlarged the nose, the airplane would become aerodynamically unstable; if the cockpit was extended rearwards, the upper engine air-intake would be left in the 'aerodynamic shadow' area.

The imaginative solution of installing both the navigator and radar operator in the wing roots was finally adopted, giving origin to the P.60 C-2 version. Because of the slow development of the FuG 244, the installation of other available radars was considered. The improved version of the FuG 228 *Lichtenstein SN-3,* provided with the new *Morgenstern* antenna of flat dipoles, could be installed in the nose of a P.60 within the ogival plywood fairing that also included a Naxos detector. The P.60 with *Lichstenstein* was named P.60 C-2a and was provided with an FuG 218 *Neptun R-3* tail warning radar and a wide range of electronic equipment compatible with the FuG 16 R/T system.

The C-2b variant was meant to use the FuG 240/3 *Berlin N-3* radar, the FuG 218 *Neptun R-3,* and electronic equipment compatible with the FuG 10P system with Peil G6 detector. By mid-March 1945, the only designs still in the competition were the Arado, Blohm und Voss, and Gotha. The three of them were flying wings with twin vertical fins.

The shape of the B&V P.215 was too radical for it to be seriously considered, and besides, it was being designed to use the FuG 244 only and without any possibility of moving the antenna. The Gotha, even in its heaviest version, was considerably faster than the Arado, but it was the latter that was finally chosen by the RLM, with the provision of a final modification (20 March 1945)—the use of defensive rear firing armament. The Arado, due to the location of its engines and crew, could carry a rearwards gun turret. Only a pair of fixed guns aimed by radar, like in the Ar 234 ones, could be installed in the Gotha.

The fact that the final designs were so similar to each other in shape is a curious case of convergent evolution that, common enough in the history of aviation, still causes surprise elsewhere. After the war, the Soviets, following the advice of Heinkel engineer Sigfried Günther, worked on an all-weather interceptor very similar to the Arado E-583. The fighter Vought F7U 'Cutlass' was built for the US Navy during the 1950s. It was based on the aerodynamic solutions used in the Junkers EF-128 and in the Blohm und Voss P.215, resulting in an unstable and dangerous design.

There was no successor to the Horten and Gotha designs and even the flying wing Northrop prototypes were destroyed to hide the secret of the 'stealth' shape. The solution to the superimposed turbojets was used by the British in the short Sperrin bomber of 1951 and in the English Electric P.1a fighter of 1954.

Chapter 9

Gotha P.60 C-1a

The original design, P.60 B, had to be modified to adapt to the 27 January 1945 specification. The wing, fuselage central section, and the main landing gear were kept. It was necessary to enlarge the nose to house the radar. The extended nose required the addition of two vertical tail surfaces at the wing trailing edges to keep the lateral stability.

The crew of two left the prone-position and were now sitting in tandem within a pressurised and armoured cockpit with lateral opening system very similar to the one in the Me 262 B-1a. This allowed the installation of the nose oleo-leg over the fuselage centreline. The leading-edge flaps were kept but the retractable drag-rudders were removed.

The armament was still the same as it had been in the P.60 B. The HeS 011 A engines were replaced by the HeS 011 A-0 version without any major consequence. Electronic equipment included the following elements: a Telefunken FuG 240/3 *Berlin N-3* radar weighing 180 kg and with a parabolic, remotely controlled swivelling antenna of 90 cm diameter; a Siemens FuG 101a radio altimeter with two inverted T dipolar antenna located under the right wing; a Lorenz FuG 10 K2 R/T long-range communications system with a 75-m-long electrically powered trailing-wire antenna under the left wing; a radio beacon Siemens FuG 120a teleprinter; an automatic Siemens FuG 130 radio landing system; an FFO EiV 125 crew intercom; and an Askania/Zeiss EZ 42 gyroscopic gunsight.

Technical data	
Type	two-seat night fighter.
Phase	project
Wings	wood structure, plywood and Formholz cladding, containing each a fuel tank of 1,275 litres.
Fuselage	welded steel-tube framework, plywood and Formholz cladding, including the electronic equipment, radar, crew, landing gear, two fuel tanks of 240 litres and 1,200 litres respectively, and four Mk 108/30 cannons with 480 cartridges.
Landing gear	the main wheels are stowed flat, with 90-degree rotation, in the mid-portion of the centre section, like in the P.60 B. The nose oleo-leg was retractable to the rear and housed under the crew seats.
Engines	two HeS 011 A-0 turbojets, each rated at 1,300-kp static thrust, were mounted to the rear of the centre section, one above and one below.

Fuel tanks	two in the wings and three in the fuselage with a total capacity of 4,230 litres.
Armament	four Rheinmetall-Borsig Mk 108/30 cannons in the wing roots with 120 rounds per gun.
Wingspan	13.5 m
Overall length	10.86 m
Fuselage length	9,072 m
Height	3.45 m
Wing area	54.7 sq. m
Max. weight	10,200 kg
Max. speed	950 kph
Ceiling	44,600 feet
Range	2,200 km

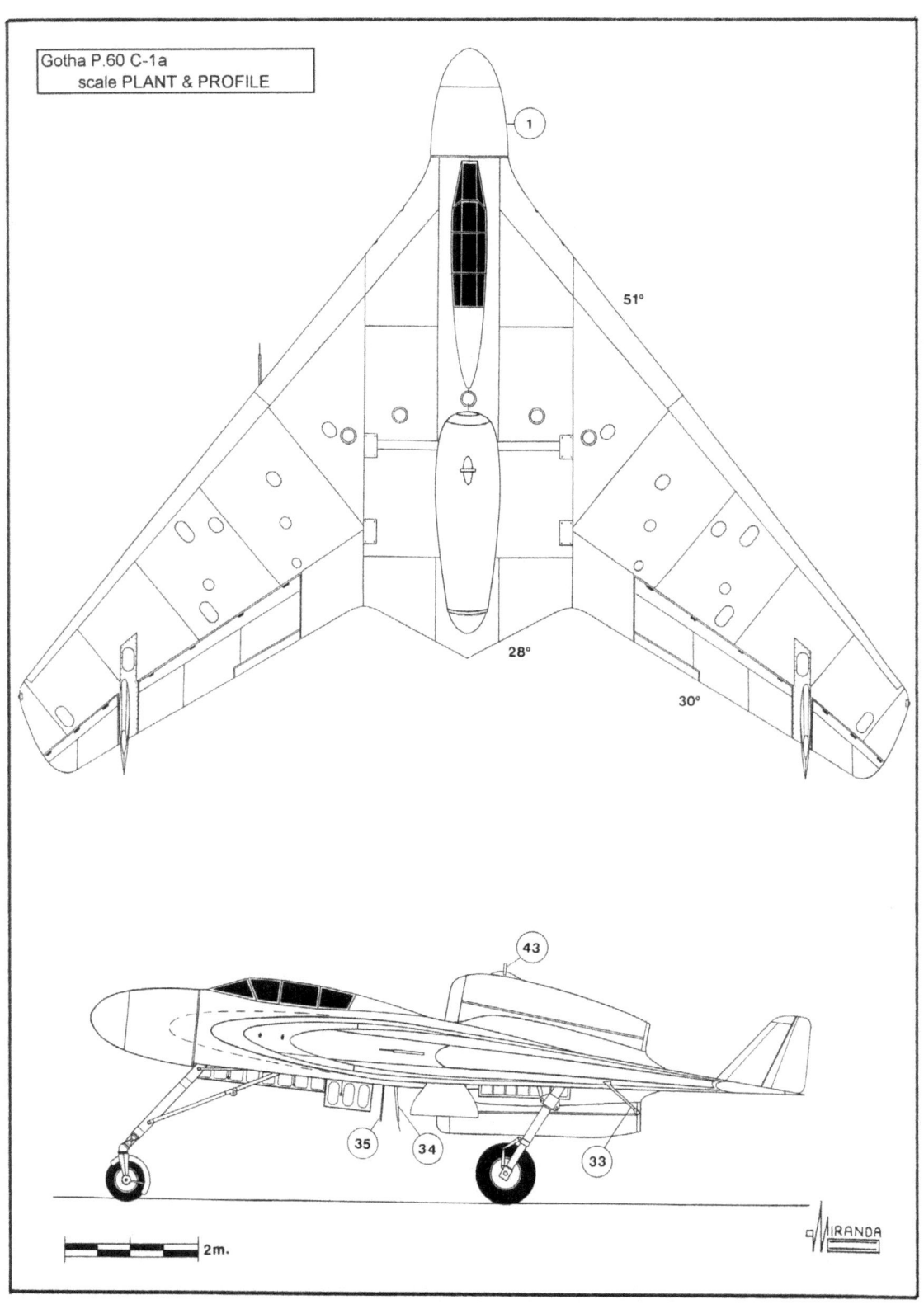

Gotha P.60 C-1a
  scale PLANT & PROFILE

51°

28°

30°

43

35   34

33

2m.

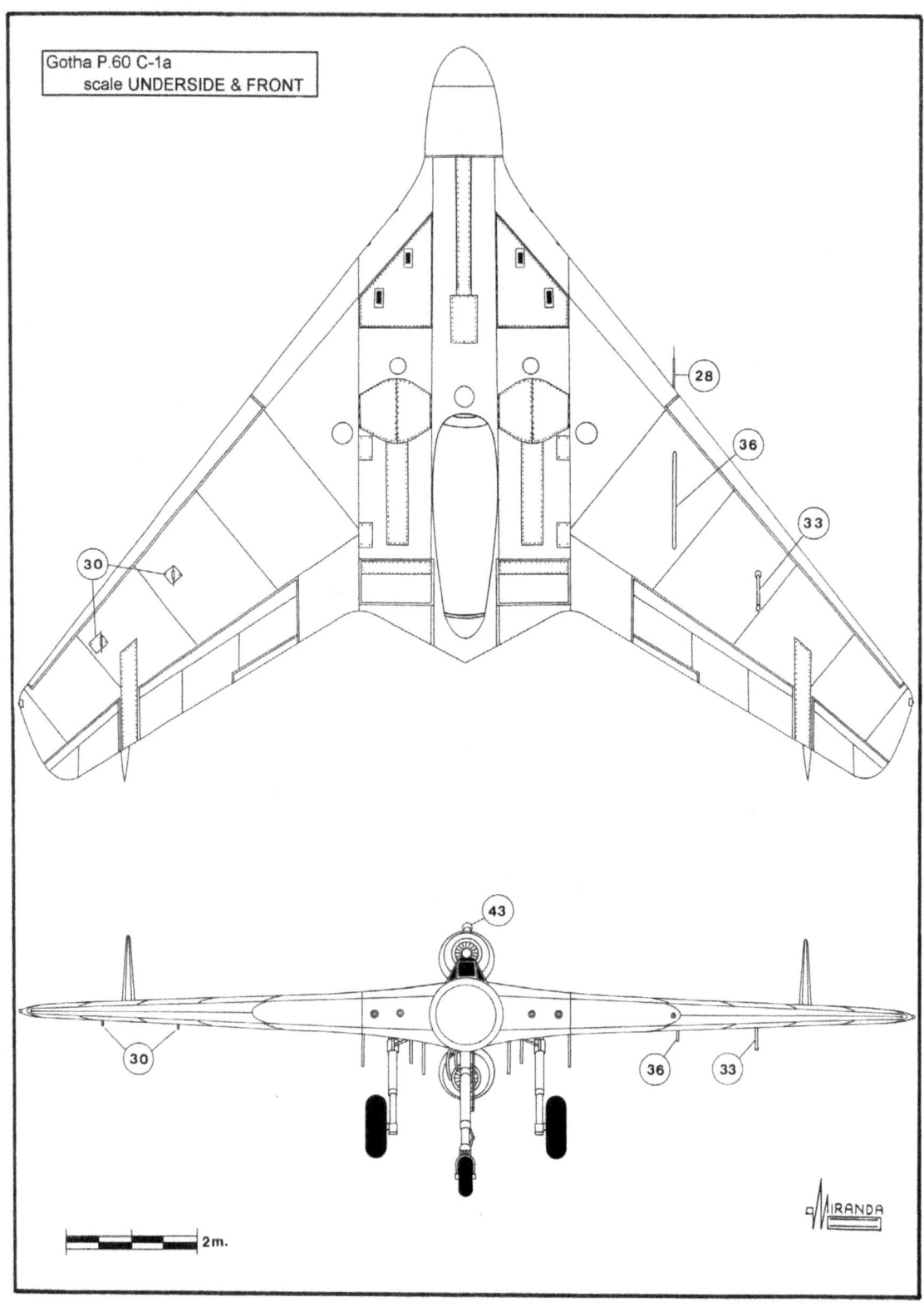

Gotha P.60 C-1a
scale UNDERSIDE & FRONT

2m.

Chapter 10

Gotha P.60 C-1b

One of the outcomes of the new Luftwaffe requirement to use *Schräge Musik* was that the C-1a had to be modified to include two Mk 108/30 (80 degrees upwards firing) cannons with 100 rounds per gun in the central section of the fuselage, behind the main armament.

The weight increase of 278 kg was partially balanced by adopting the new *Bremen* radar, which had a 70-cm-diameter antenna and was 80 kg lighter than the original *Berlin*. The smaller diameter of the antenna allowed a narrower fuselage design and a faster airplane. The increase of electronic equipment forced the redesign of the cockpit, equipped with a new one-piece detachable canopy to facilitate the use of ejectable seats *Schleudersitz Heinkel-Kartusche*, originally designed for the He-162; this posed similar ejection problems due to the dorsal engine position, behind the cockpit.

The Heinkel ejector seat was mounted on four rollers which moved in two parallel channels of 1.66 m length. The charge used was of 30 grams of powder in a catapult tube fixed to the upper end of the seat and at the lower end to the cockpit floor. Ejection velocity of 11 m/s and acceleration of 12 g were enough to save the upper engine. The electronic equipment assigned to this version seems to indicate that it was an all-weather interceptor based on the *Moskitojäger* formula.

The Telefunken FuG 244 *Bremen 0* radar pre-production series could aim its parabolic antenna up to 100 degrees in each direction. The communications equipment was based on the R/T Lorenz FuG 24 SE, a VHF device developed for single-seat fighters, with whip antenna in the lower section of the fuselage. The IFF was a GEMA FuG 25a with rod antenna (300 mm long, 10 degrees rear swept) in the lower section of the fuselage.

The location and identification from the ground stations was made by means of a Lorenz radio-beacon receiver FuG 125a that operated in combination with the FuG 16 ZY direction finder device using the Morane mast and D/F Loop of the FuG 16 R/T standard equipment. The command relay equipment was an FuG 139 Barbarossa operating in combination with the FuG 25a IFF and using its antenna. The radio altimeter was the standard FuG 101a equipment and the crew intercom was an FFO EiV 125.

The standard gyroscopic gunsight, EZ 42, did not serve for aiming the *Schräge Musik*, so an auxiliary Revi C16 A-N gunsight had to be installed in the upper section of the canopy, over the pilot's head.

Technical data

Type	two-seat, all-weather interceptor.
Phase	project
Wings	wood structure, plywood and Formholz cladding, each containing a fuel tank of 1,275 litres.
Fuselage	welded steel-tube framework, plywood and Formholz cladding, including the radar, electronic equipment, crew, ejector seats, landing gear, two fuel tanks of 240 litres each and one of 1,200 litres, six Mk 108 cannons, and 680 cartridges.
Landing	gear the main wheels are stowed flat, with 90-degree rotation, in the central section of the wing, like in the P.60 B. The nose oleo-leg was retractable to the rear and housed under the crew seats.
Engines	two HeS 011 A-0 turbojets, each rated at 1,300-kp static thrust, were mounted to the rear of the central section of the wing, one above and one below.
Fuel tanks	two in the wings and three in the fuselage with a total capacity of 4,230 litres.
Armament	four Rheinmetall-Borsig Mk 108/30 cannons in the wing roots with 120 rounds per gun and two Mk 108/30 cannons in 80-degree upwards Schräge Musik mounting with 100 rounds per gun.
Wingspan	13.5 m
Length	10.02 m
Fuselage length	8.7 m
Height	3.6 m
Wing area	54.7 sq. m
Empty weight	5,346 kg
Max. weight	10,470 kg
Max. speed	960 kph
Ceiling	44,300 feet
Range	2,200 km

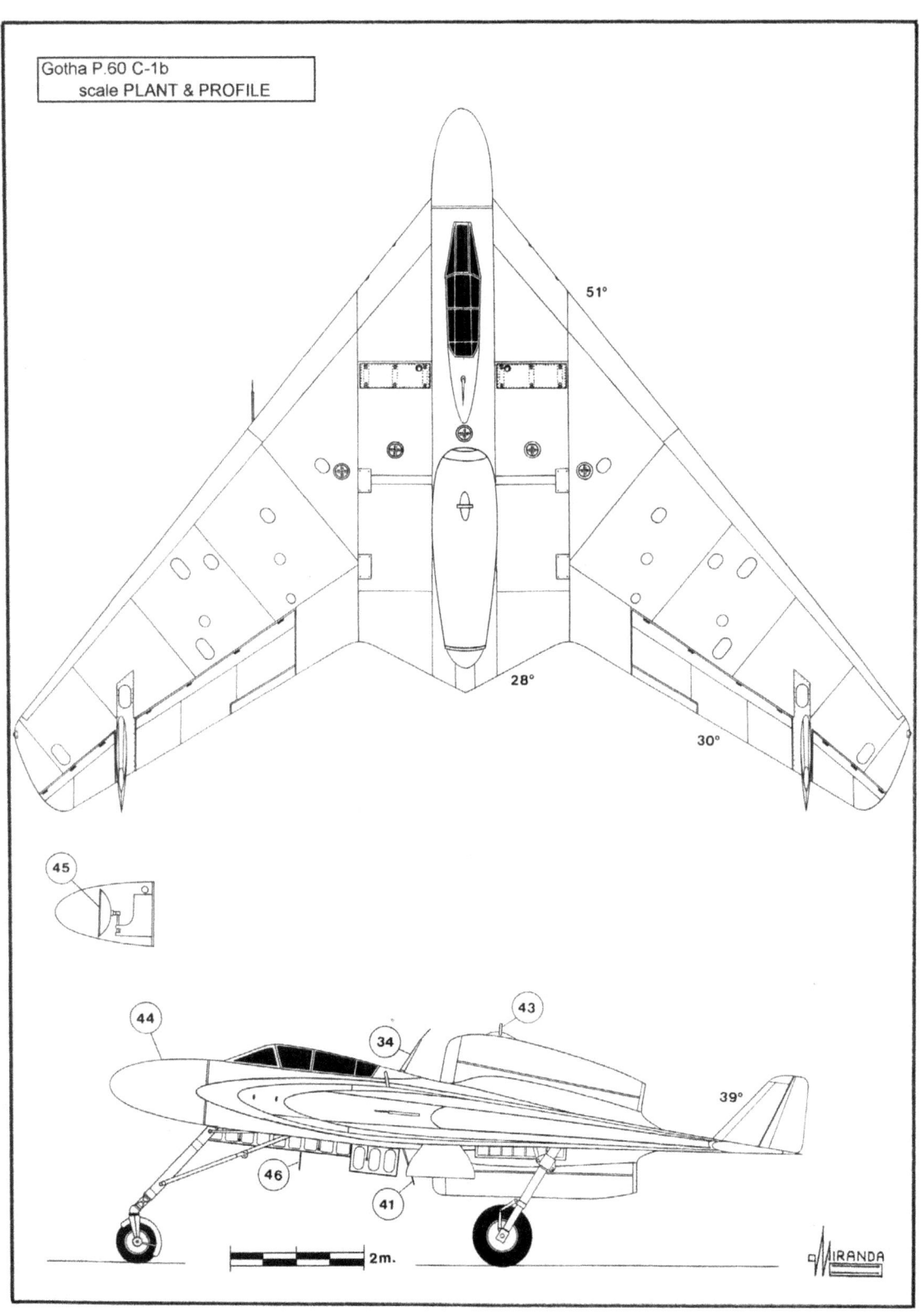

Gotha P.60 C-1b
scale PLANT & PROFILE

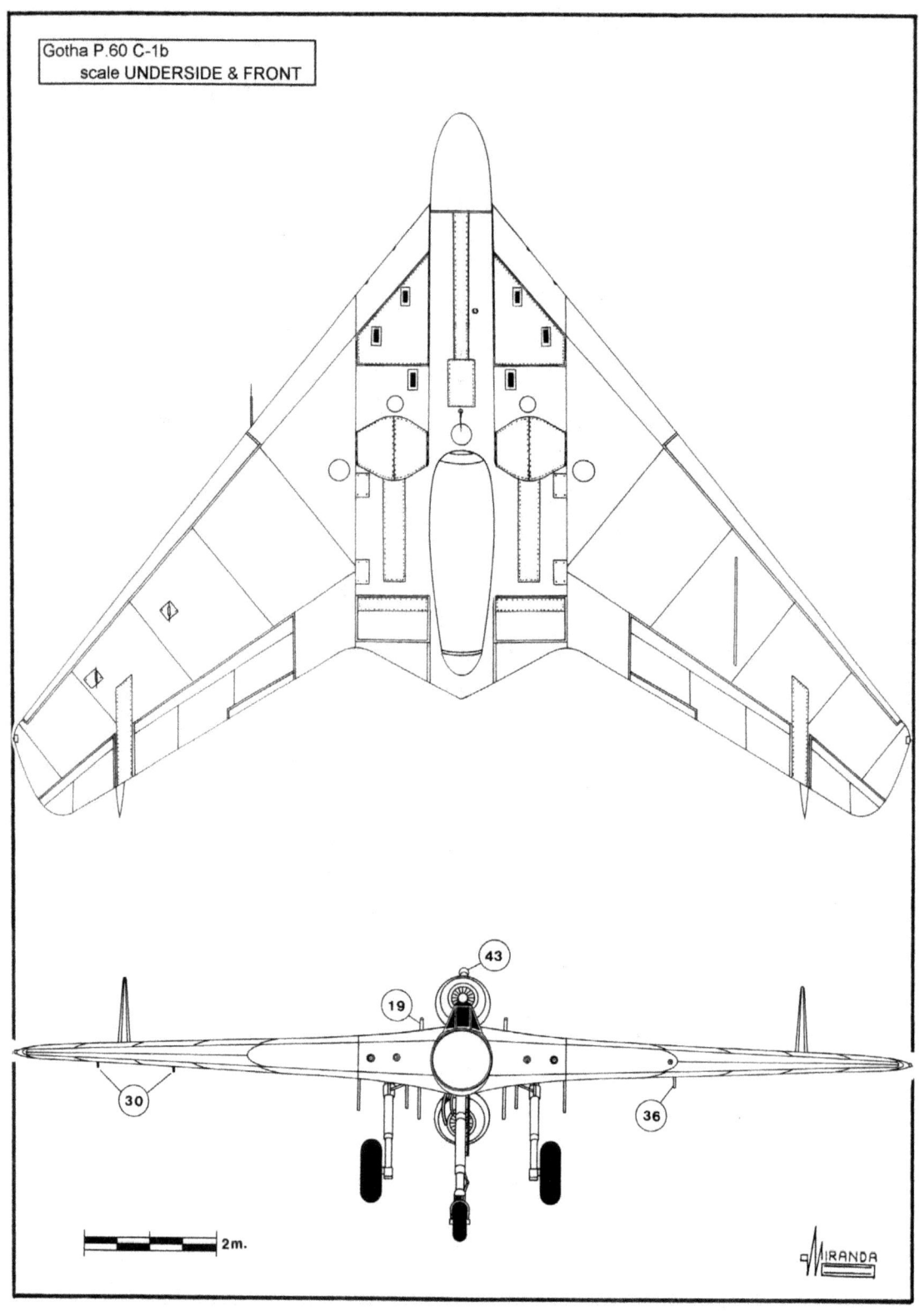

Gotha P.60 C-1b
scale UNDERSIDE & FRONT

43

19

30

36

2m.

MIRANDA

Chapter 11

Gotha P.60 C-2a

When the original specification was modified to include a third crew member by the beginning of 1945, the designers of the P.60 C had to face the problem caused by the enlargement of the cockpit that, in the style of the Me 262 B-2 (17 March 1945), would diminish the air flux into the upper engine. Enlarging the nose, with its heavy electronic equipment far from the airplane's centre of gravity, would produce longitudinal instability. Locating the navigator alongside the pilot, like in the Arado E-583 and Blohm & Voss P.215, would mean a considerable widening of the fuselage and a loss in performance.

The designers finally chose the imaginative solution of installing the navigator and radar operator in two reclining seats located within the wing roots, with a transparent cladding over their heads and an access hatch that could be ejected in emergencies, underneath their legs. The pilot sat normally in the central cockpit and was the only one with an ejector seat.

Due to the delay in the manufacturing of the *Bremen* radar, it was proposed that the FuG 228 *Lichtenstein SN-3*, developed by Telefunken as an improved variant of the FuG 220 *Lichtenstein SN-2*, should be a substitute. As an alternative to the parabolic antennae of Siemens, Telefunken had been working on a version of the *Hirschgeweih* that could be installed in a plywood cone, thus improving its aerodynamic performance. The new *Morgenstern* antenna consisted of a mast on which three pairs of flat section dipoles were mounted in a 90-degree cross configuration.

The radiator was located in a central position with lengths of one half to one quarter of a wavelength. Behind it the reflector was situated at one fifth to one quarter of a wavelength. The director was in front at one tenth to one eighth of a wavelength. The first *Morgenstern* antennae assigned to the FuG 220 equipment of the Ju 88 G-6 and Ju 388 J-3 heavy night fighters used the same dipoles in the shape of a circular section rod, as with in the *Hirschgeweih*.

The experiments performed at high speed with the Me 262 W.Nr. 170056 by the beginning of March proved that an antenna shaped like a sword blade (originally designed for the IFF FuG 226) produced less drag than the classic dipoles. The second generation of *Morgenstern* antennae assigned to the FuG 224 *Berlin A* had the radiator with dipoles in this sword blade shape, whilst the rest of the dipoles were pointed conic sticks.

The third generation assigned to the FuG 228 had all the dipoles of the *Breitbanddipolen* type. They were simple rectangular metallic plates of 63 cm x 8 cm that rendered good results during the tests performed with a Ju 88 in high aerodynamic drag *Hirschgeweih* configuration. The antenna designed for the P.60 C-2a (wavelength 2.6 to 2.03) had dipoles of 60.2 x 8 cm, 65 x 8 cm, and 66.8 x 8 cm separated from the radiator by 26 cm and 52 cm. It was housed within the ogival plywood fairing and included an FuG 350 Z *Naxos* detector fixed to the mast between the reflector and the FuG 228 container.

The airplane also carried a rear warning FuG 218 *Neptun R-3* radar with a *Stachel* antenna of two asymmetric horizontal dipoles located to the rear of the fuselage, between the engines. The rest of the electronic equipment was formed by FuG 101a, FuG 125a, FuG 16 ZY, FuG 16 R/T, FuG 25a, FuG 139, FuG 130, EiV 125, and EZ 42.

As for the manufacturing specification, an FuG 280 *Kiel Z* IR homer and new *Revi C-16 G Schräge Musik* gunsight reflector could also be installed. The rest of the equipment was very similar to that used in the C-1b version, with the exception of the fuel tanks in the wings, which were each enlarged to 1,560 litres.

Technical data

Type	three-seat heavy night fighter.
Phase	project
Wings	wood structure, plywood and Formholz cladding, each containing a fuel tank of 1,560 litres.
Fuselage	welded steel-tube framework, plywood and Formholz cladding, including the radar, electronic equipment, crew, ejector seat, landing gear, two fuel tanks of 240 litres and 1,200 litres respectively, six Mk 108 cannons, and 680 cartridges.
Landing	gear the main wheels are stowed flat, with 90-degree rotation, in the mid-portion of the centre section, like in the P.60 B. The nose oleo-leg was retractable to the rear and housed under the pilot seat.
Engines	two HeS 011 A-0 turbojets, each rated at 1,300-kp static thrust, were mounted to the rear of the central section, one above and one below.
Fuel tanks	two in the wings and three in the fuselage with a total capacity of 4,800 litres.
Armament	four Rheinmetall-Borsig Mk 108/30 cannons in the wing roots, with 120 rounds per gun and two Mk 108/30 cannons in 80-degree upwards Schräge Musik mounting with 100 rounds per gun.
Wingspan	3.5 m
Length	11.39 m
Fuselage length	9.65 m
Height	3.45 m
Wing area	54.7 sq. m
Empty weight	5,346 kg
Max. weight	10,380 kg
Max. speed	950 kph
Ceiling	44,000 feet
Range	2,500 km

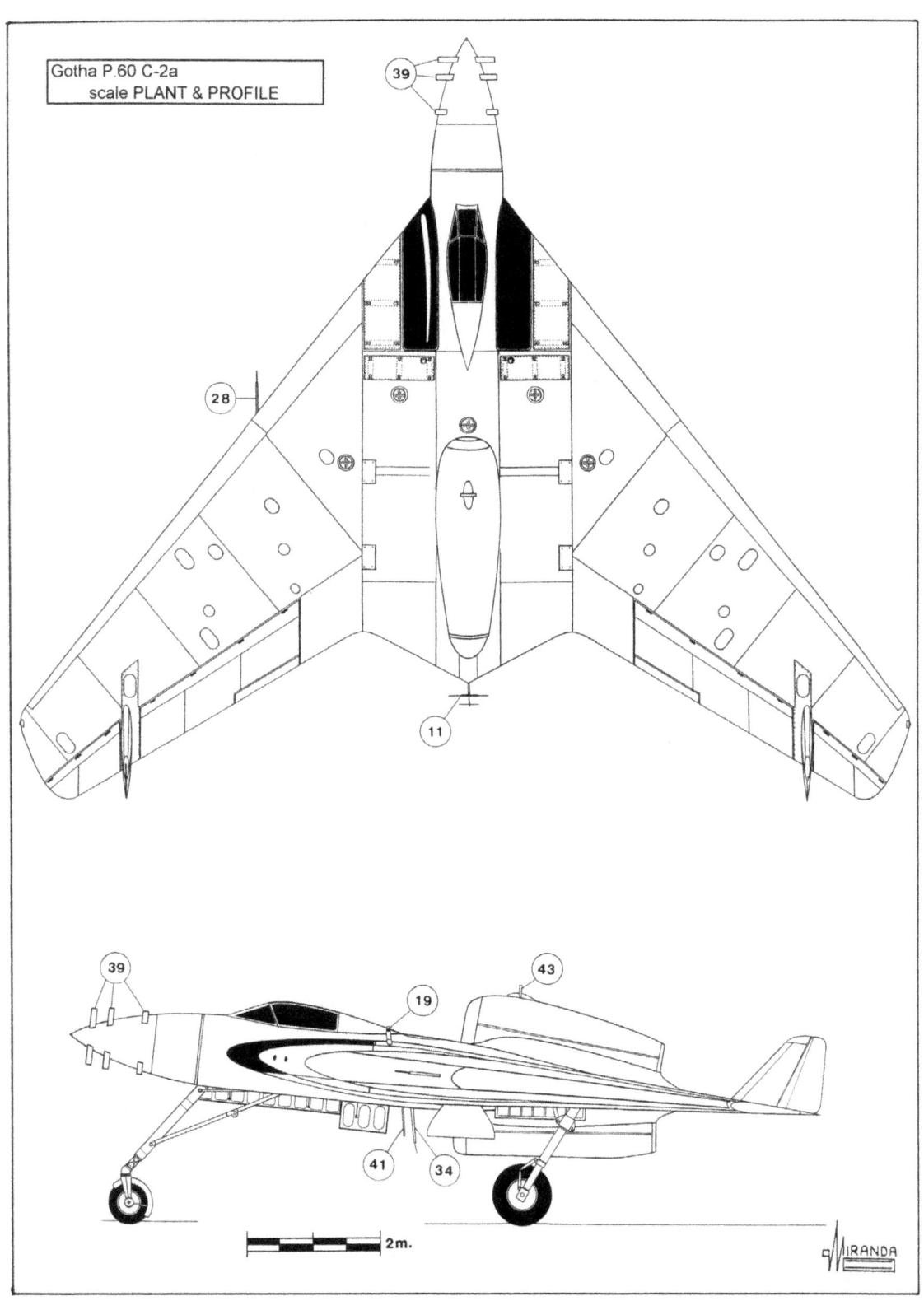

Gotha P.60 C-2a
scale PLANT & PROFILE

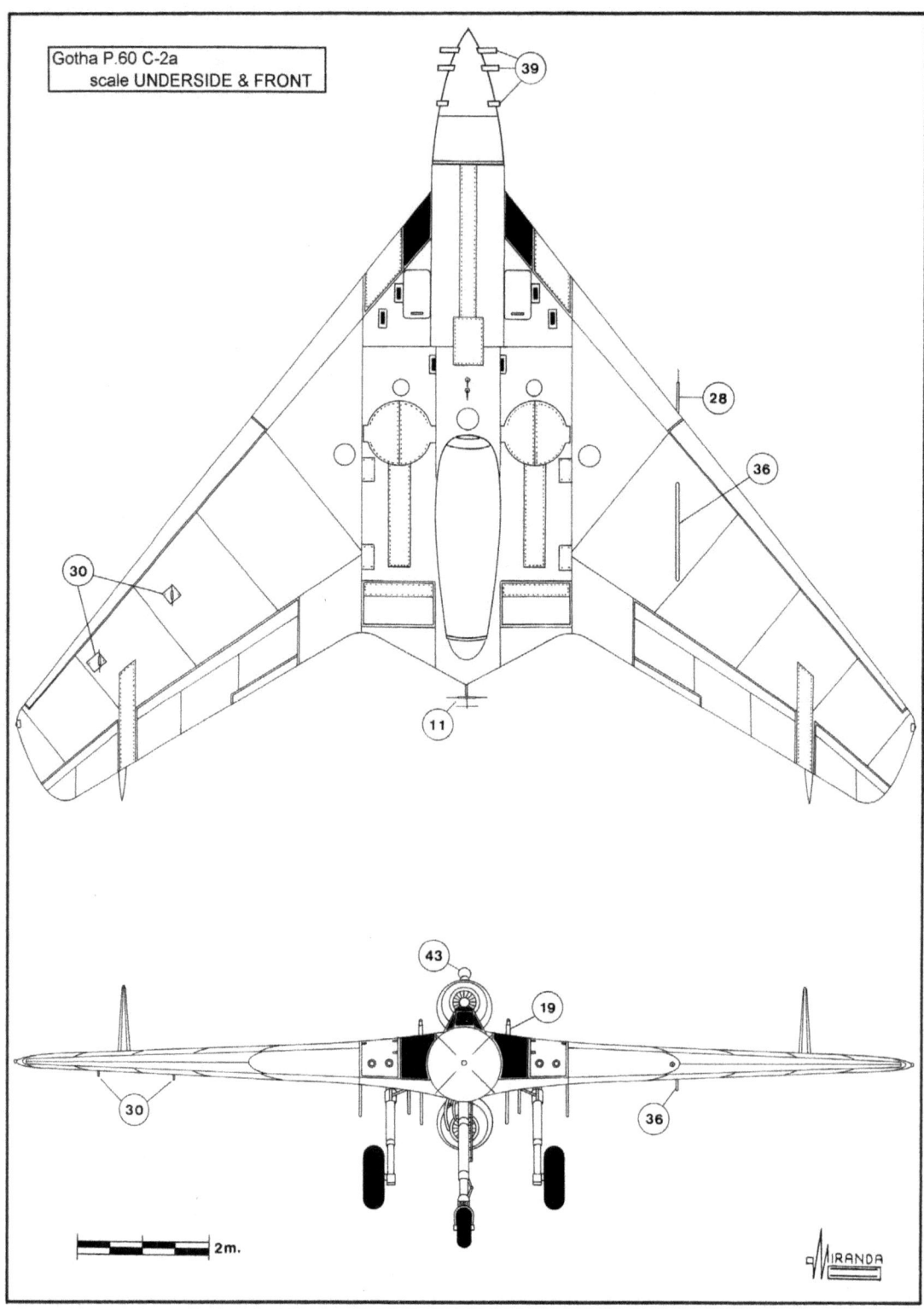

Gotha P.60 C-2a
scale UNDERSIDE & FRONT

2m.

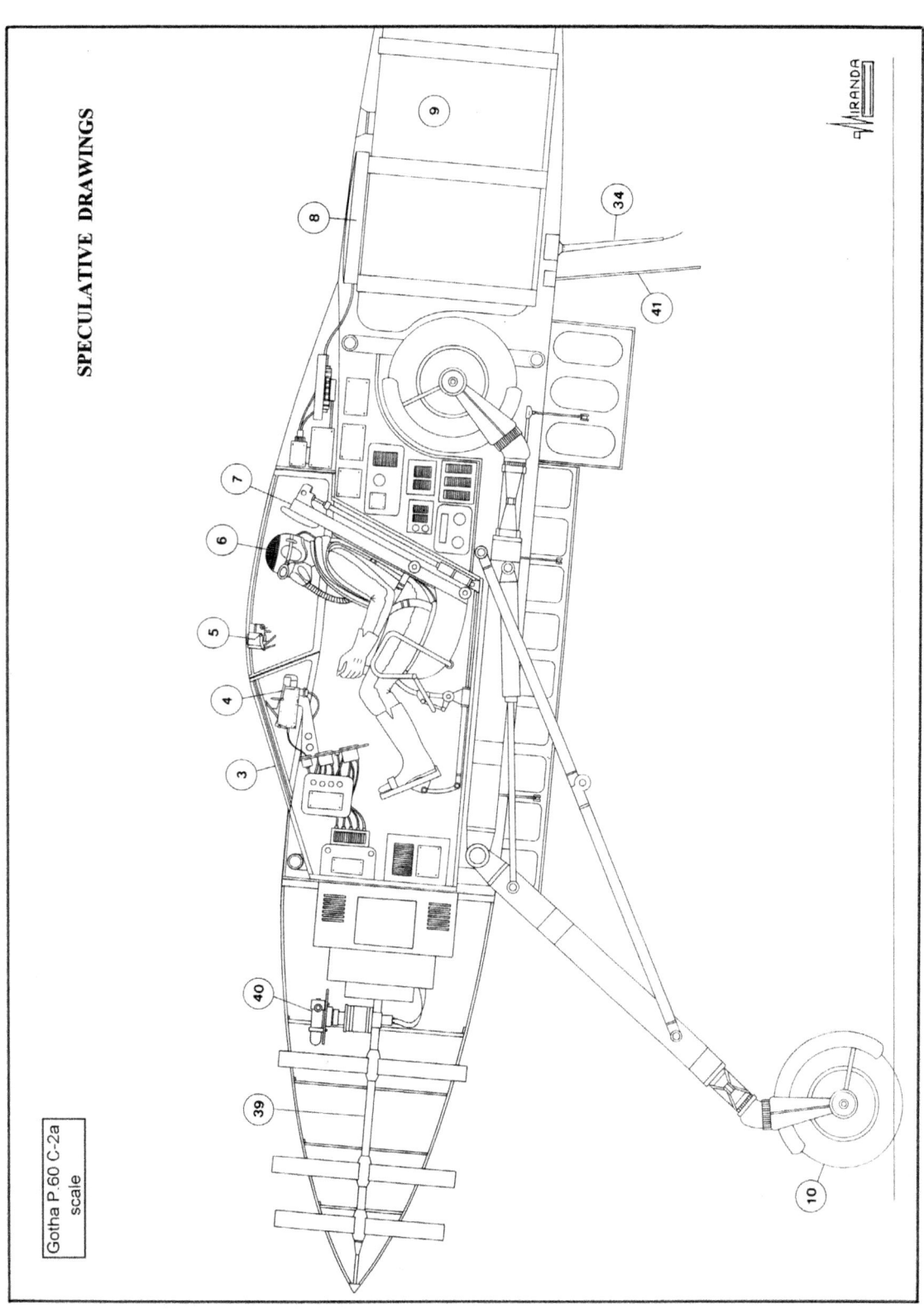

SPECULATIVE DRAWINGS

Gotha P.60 C-2a
scale

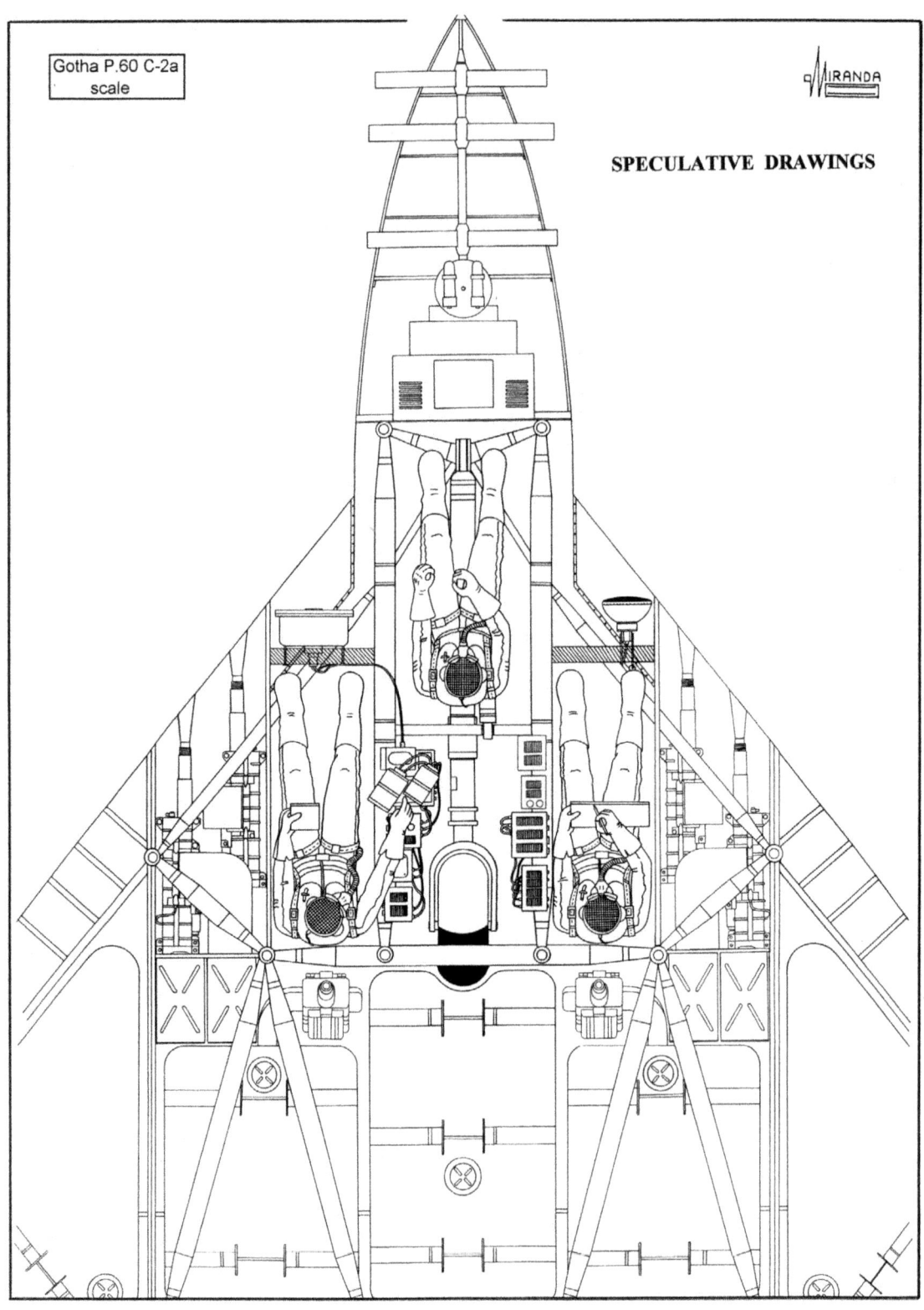

Gotha P.60 C-2a
scale

SPECULATIVE DRAWINGS

Chapter 12

Gotha P.60 C-2b

The Gotha P.60 C-2b was a variant of the P.60 C-2a, fitted with an FuG 240/3 *Berlin N-3* radar with *Parabolspiegel* antenna of 90 cm diameter, able to make a spiral search with 55-degree lateral opening. The rear warning radar was an FuG 218 *Neptun R-3*, able to detect the Serrate equipped Mosquito.

The electronic equipment was designed around the communications system FuG 10P, with MF and HF operating frequencies and two types of antennae; the rod-shaped antenna of the FuG 24 system was located under the fuselage, and an MF electrically powered trailing-wire of 75 m in length was located under the port wing. The IFF *Erstling* was replaced with the more advanced FuG 226 *Neuling* discriminator, which combined the identification and range finder functions and had two flat *Breitbandipolen* antennae located over the starboard wing.

The radio altimeter was an FuG 101a, with the two dipolar antennae in an inverted T, located beneath the starboard wing. The *Naxos* was replaced by a *Peil G6* radiogoniometer with an automatic APZ6 search system and flat antenna with radial ribs located over the fuselage, behind the pilot cabin. The autopilot was an FuG 130, connected to a blind landing device, FuBl 3E, with AWG1. Both systems shared a comb-shaped antenna covered by fairing located beneath the port wing.

The navigation system included an FuG 125a *Hermine* radio-beacon receiver and an FuG 120a *Bernhardine* teleprinter. Both of them used the Morane antenna of the FuG 16Y, located beneath the fuselage. The aiming system was composed of an FuG 280 *Kiel Z* passive IR homer, an EZ 42 gyroscopic gunsight (that could be combined with the FuG 240/3 radar and with the automatic EG3 *Elfe 3* trigger), and a *Revi C16 G* reflector gunsight for *Schräge Musik*.

The crew intercom was an EiV 125 and the armament consisted of four Rheinmetall-Borsig Mk 108/30 cannons in the wing roots with 120 rounds per gun, two Mk 108/30 cannons in 80-degree upwards *Schräge Musik* mounting and two MG 151/20 or MG 213/20 cannons with 250 cartridges each at the rear fuselage, aiming through the FuG 218 rear warning radar. They used conventional ammunition alternated with practice ammunition that was specially built for self-destruction at 800 m for deterrent purposes.

The crew was protected in the front part by armoured glass against 12.7-mm rounds from the bombers and in the rear part by metal plates against 20-mm rounds from the fighters. The passive anti-radar defences included the stealth shape and the moulded wood *Formholz* coating (15-mm plywood/carbon/ sawdust/plywood sandwich) coated by *Tronal* plastic and a *Schornsteinfeger* anti-radar paint coating.

Technical data	
Type	three-seat heavy night fighter.
Phase	project
Wings	wood structure, plywood and Formholz cladding, each containing a fuel tank of 1,560 litres.
Fuselage	welded steel-tube framework, plywood and Formholz cladding, including the radar, electronic equipment, armour, crew, ejector seat, landing gear, two fuel tanks of 240 litres each and one of 1,200 litres, six Mk 108/30 cannons, and 680 cartridges.
Landing gear	the main wheels are stowed flat, with 90-degree rotation, in the mid-portion of the central section of the wing, like in the P.60 B. The nose oleo-leg was retractable to the rear and housed under the pilot seat.
Engines	two HeS 011 A-0 turbojets, each rated at 1,300-kp static thrust, were mounted to the rear of the central section of the wing, one above and one below.
Fuel tanks	two in the external wings and three in the central section with a total capacity of 4,800 litres.
Armament	four Rheinmetall-Borsig Mk 108/30 cannons in the wing roots with 120 rounds per gun, two Mk 108/30 cannons in 80-degree upwards Schräge Musik mounting with 100 rounds per gun, and two MG 151/20 or MG 213/20 rear firing cannons in the rear part of the fuselage (to both sides of the engines) with 250 rounds per gun.
Wingspan	13.5 m
Length	10.87 m
Fuselage length	9.1 m
Heigh	3.45 m
Wing area	54.7 sq. m
Empty weight	5,520 kg
Max. weight	10,600 kg
Max. speed	930 kph
Ceiling	43,300 feet
Range	2,500 km

MISSION PROFILE

PILOT

Takes off, lands, and steers the airplane following the navigator and radio operator indications until reaching visual contact with the enemy bomber. To engage fire, he may choose the main armament by positioning himself at target level and using the EZ42 gyroscopic gunsight, or by positioning himself under the enemy bomber using the *Schräge Musik* and the C16 A-N gunsight. Once the target is hit, he performs an evasive manoeuvre. He does likewise when the radar operator detects a following airplane with the FuG 218 R-3 tail radar. The evasion manoeuvre consists of a twist to the left known as 'corkscrew'.

Pilot instruments
FuG 101 radioaltimeter
Airplane positioning indicators
Indicators of the state of the HeS 011 engines
Fuel and oil indicators
EiV 125 crew intercom
Fu Bl 3 blind landing device and FuG 130 autopilot

Navigator/radio operator
Steers the airplane from the base to the combat area using the FuG 125a *Hermine* radio-beacon receiver and FuG 120 *Bernhardine* radio-beacon teleprinter. Tunes into other airplanes' radio emissions, using the Peil G6 *Ludwig* radiogoniometer with APZ6 automatic detector, associated with the standard FuG 10P radio equipment.

Radio operator instruments
FuG 10 P, FuG 120a *Bernhardine*, EiV 125 Crew Intercom, Peil G6/APZ6, FuG 125a *Hermine*.

Radar operator
Once the airplane is in the combat area, the radar operator uses the FuG 240/3 search radar to detect airplanes up to 5,000 m away, moving the parabolic antenna in a spiral of up to 55 degrees in each direction. When a target appears on his screen, he uses the FuG 226 IFF to find out if it is an enemy airplane and indicates to the pilot how to get as close as possible. At 300 m, the radar cannot clearly distinguish the echoes reflected by the target. If the pilot has not yet located it visually, the FuG 280 IR equipment is used to refine the location of the fighter behind the bomber, thus enabling the pilot to fire at it without actually seeing it. If an enemy night fighter is detected by the FuG 218 R-3 tail warning radar, he gives instructions to the pilot to start an evasive action or to engage the rear firing armament.

Radar operator instruments
FuG 240/3 *Berlin N.3* search radar
FuG 218 R-3 tail warning radar
FuG 280 *Kiel Z* IR homer
FuG 226 *Neuling* IFF
EiV 125 crew intercom

To abandon the airplane in flight, the navigator and radar operator use an emergency mechanism to detach the access hatch and avoid the banging open door hitting them. When they have already bailed out, the pilot uses his Heinkel ejector seat, which has a 30-gram powder charge—enough to avoid the impact of the air-intake of the upper engine.

ELECTRONIC DEVICES

The EZ 42 *Adler* gyroscopic gunsight *Zielgerat* developed by Askania/Zeiss automatically computed the deflection angle required to hit a target when both aircraft were manoeuvring. It could be connected to the *Oberon* clock system developed by Arado to fire the R100 rockets. The distance could be given by the FuG 218 *Neptun V* radar or a specialised radar for launching of the FuG 248 *Eule* type. The ignition mechanism was the EG3 *Elfe 3*.

Adler could be used in combination with the *Gnom* automatic weapon-triggering and the FuG 244 radar to fire R4M rockets, in the following configurations:

EZ 42 + FuG 218 *Neptun* + EG3 *Elfe 3* = *Oberon* à R100
EZ 42 + FuG 248 *Eule* + EG3 Elfe 3 = *Oberon* à R100
EZ 42 + FuG 244 + *Gnom* = *Faun* à R4M or Mk 108/30
EZ 42 + FuG 217/218 *Neptun* + MZ1 *Hexe* = *Faun* à R4M
Oberon + *Faun* = *Oberon-Uhr*

EiV 125 crew intercom developed by FFO.

Peil G6 Ludwig with APZ6 manufactured by Telefunken. Long wave/medium wave (LW/MW) radiogoniometer that used its own EZ6 receiver (200–1200 Khz) or could be associated with the FuG 10 system. Compatible with the FuG 350Zc *Naxos*. Flat antenna with radial ribs. Incorporates APZ6 automatic radiogoniometer *Automatische Peilzusatz*. Weight of 24 kg.

FuBl 3E with AWG 1 *Funklandegerät* blind landing device developed by Lorenz in combination with the FuG 130, the FuG 101a, and the FuG 10/FuG 17(EB4). The AWG 1 (*Auswertergerät*) was an angle and speed calculator developed by F&H in 1944. It used the same comb-shaped antenna as the FuBl2, sometimes covered by a fairing. Weight of 10 kg.

FuG 10P MF and HF *Funksprechgerät* R/T device developed by Lorenz for a larger aircraft. Operation frequencies: MF 300–600 Khz, HF 3000–6000 Khz. Effective range: MF 200–500 km, HF 1000–2,000 km. RF power output: Telegraphy 70 W, Telephony 40 W. DC power input, maximum: 800 W. Two antennae: fixed or trailing, selectable remote control box, electrically powered trailing-wire antenna is 75 m long. It could be used for air-to-air and air-to-ground communication. It was used in combination with *Peil G6/APZ6* for navigation purposes. Weight of 100 kg.

FuG 16 VHF *Funksprechgerät* R/T device developed by Lorenz for air-to-ground and air-to-air communications. Frequencies between 38.5 and 42.3 Mhz. Wire aerial or Morane mast. There were four modes:
Y-Verfahren superimposed signal for fighter control position;
Gruppenbefehlswelle communication between aircraft;
Nachsicherung und Flugssicherung communication between the aircraft and the ground system;

Reichsjägerwelle continuous running commentary.

The FuG 16 ZY combined the homing and *Y-Verfahren* functions and operated on a wavelength of 7 m.

FuG 24 SE VHF *Funksprechgerät* R/T device developed by Lorenz for single-seat fighters. Operation frequencies between 37.8 and 47.75 Mhz. It was used in combination with the ZVG *Zielflugrorsatzgerät* direction finder device. Power of 5 Kw, VHF wave. Whip antenna. Weight of 18 kg.

FuG 25a *Erstling* IFF device manufactured by GEMA and Brinkler. Emission frequency of 160 Mhz, reception frequency of 125 Mhz. Range of 100 km. Power of 600 W. Rod antenna under the fuselage (300 mm long), 10 degrees rear swept. Responded to *Freya*, *Würzburg*, and *Gemse* ground control radars. It could be used to calculate the distance of an airplane from the ground radar. The need to operate in several frequencies between 0.53 and 2.40 m considerably delayed its entry into service in the Luftwaffe. It was used in combination with the EGON (*Erstling- Gemse-Offensive-Navigation*) for radio navigation of bombers in combination with the FuMG 401A *Freya LZ* radar, as an alternative to the *Y-Gerät*. Weight of 12 kg.

FuG 29 *Reportage*, ground-to-air control and airborne situation report receiver. Weight 8 kg.

FuG 101a *Feinhöhermesser* of 1.5 Kw, radioaltimeter developed by Siemens/LG. Operation frequencies between 337 and 400 MHz in continuous wave and frequency modulation (CW–FM with a 2-m error). Power 1.5 W. Weight of 16 kg. Range of between 150 and 1,500 m. It used two *Sender S101* and *Empfänger E 101* dipoles to transmit and receive.

FuG 120a *Bernhardine* radio beacon teleprinter developed by Siemens to receive the emissions from the FuS An 724/725 *Bernhard* (30-33.3 MHz) rotating beacon. The data was presented over a band of printed paper to diminish the efficiency of the enemy interference systems. The FuG 120k was a simplified version for single-seat fighters.

The FuG 120 could be used in combination with the FuG 10 K2 and FuG 16 R/T system and with the EBl3 receiver of the *Funklandegerät* FuBl2 blind landing system. Range of 5 to 400 km.

FuG 123 *Truhe* cartographic radar *Leitstrahlverfahren* based on captured units of the British 'Gee' radar. Frequencies from 35 to 100 Mhz. It worked in combination with the ground stations of the FuS An 728 *Boden Truhe*.

FuG 125a *Hermine* radio-beacon receiver was developed by Lorenz. It operated in frequencies between 30 and 33.3 Mhz with a precision of 5 degrees. Weight of 10 kg. Range of 200 at 250 km. It operated in combination with the FuG 16 ZY *Zypresse* direction finder and the FuG 16 R/T device using the antenna and the D/F loop and Morane mast of these devices. It receives the emissions from the FuS An 726 *Hermes*. It could be used in combination with the FuG 120 K *Bernhardine* to receive emissions from the FuS An 724/725 *Bernhard*. Combined with the EBl 3F system, it acted as a radio landing device. The presentation of data came via earphones.

FuG 130 automatic radio landing system *Funklandegerät* developed by Siemens/LGW in combination with the AWG1 calculator and the FuG 101a radioaltimeter. It used the same antenna as the FuBl 2.

FuG 135 *Uhu* device received continuous running commentary and airborne situation reports associated with the FuG 16 R/T device. Operation frequencies of 38.5 to 42.3 Mhz.

FuG 139 *Barbarossa* command relay equipment *Kommando Übertragungsgerät*. Used its antenna in combination with the IFF FuG 25a. The presentation of data was done by *Hellschreiber* teleprinter.

FuG 218 Neptun R-3 of 30-100 Kw developed by Siemens/FFO as *Rückwärtswarngerät* tail warning radar. Operation frequencies between 162 and 187 Mhz. Range of between 120 and 5,000 m. Vision angle of 60 degrees horizontally and vertically. *Stachel* antenna of two elements on a small curved mast that was also used for the FuG 350 Z *Naxos* passive receiver. Weight of 46 kg. Thrust of 30 at 100 Kw.

FuG 226 *Neuling* IFF discriminator developed by Lorenz. The two triangular antennae *Breitbanddipolen* of 850 x 100 mm were installed in parallel on the upper surface of the wing, separated by 70 mm from each other. The receiver operated at frequencies between 110–125 MHz and the emitter between 143 and 158 Mhz. Responded to by standard ground radars and airborne radars. Compatible with the FuS An 730/731 EGON radio navigation system. It also combined functions of aircraft identification *Kenn-und-Abfragegerät* and range finder.

FuG 228 *Lichtenstein SN-3* air-to-air radar developed by Telefunken. Operating frequencies 115 to 148 Mhz and 120 to 156 Mhz. Range of between 250 and 8,000 m. *Morgenstern* antenna with three flat dipole *Breitbanddipolen* systems in X formation, a radiator of one half to one quarter of one wavelength (2.6 to 2.03 m). The reflector of one fifth to one quarter of a wavelength was located behind the radiator; in front of it was a director of one tenth to one eighth of a wavelength. The presentation of data was made by two screens with lineal time bases. Weight of 95 kg. Power of 30 Kw. Vision angle of 120 degrees horizontally and 100 degrees vertically.

FuG 240/3 *Berlin N-3* air-to-air radar developed by Telefunken. Operation frequencies between 3250 and 3330 Mhz. Range of between 300 and 5,000 m. *Parabolspiegel* parabolic antenna of 90 cm diameter, able to make a spiral search with 55-degree lateral opening. Power of 15 Kw. Wavelength of 9.1 cm. Weight of 180 kg.

FuG 244 *Bremen 0* air-to-air radar developed by Telefunken. Operation frequency between 3,250 and 3,330 Mhz. Range between 200 and 5,000 m. *Parabolspiegel* of 70 cm diameter with searching range of 100 degrees to either side and 20 degrees downwards. Wavelength from 9 to 9.3 cm. Power of 20 Kw. Weight of 100 kg. It was a pre-production device derived from the FuG 240/3 with higher definition capacity and less weight. The series version FuG 245 *Bremen* was meant to be manufactured in 1946.

FuG 280 *Kiel Z* passive IR homer developed by Zeiss as *U-R Suchgerät* using lead-sulphite photo-cells. Opening angle of 20 degrees that could be manually operated with corrections of 35 degrees to either side by means of a mobile mirror. Range of 4,000 m. Weight of 42 kg. The presentation of data was made over a screen named *Q-Rohr*. It was sometimes used in combination with the FuG 218 *Neptun R-3* rear warning radar.

FuG 350 Zc *Naxos, Passive Ortungsgerät* (passive radar-receiver) of H2S, H2X, and AN APS 15 Allied radars developed by Telefunken. Weight of 24 kg. With EA 350Zb rotating antennae of 250 mm diameter and *SG* 350 Zc display unit. Frequency of 2500–3750 Mhz. Range of 100 km. Provided azimuth measurement only.

KEY TO ILLUSTRATIONS

1	FuG 240/3 *Berlin* N-3 search radar.
2	90-cm-diameter *Parabolspiegel* (parabolic antenna).
3	Armoured windshield.
4	Askania EZ 42 *Adler* gyroscopic gunsight.
5	Revi C16 A-N *Schräge Musik* gunsight.
6	Pilot.
7	Heinkel-*Kartusche* ejector seat.
8	*Peil G6 Ludwig* mit APZ6 automatic radiogoniometer.
9	1,200-litre fuel tank.
10	630 x 220-mm nose tyre.
11	FuG 218 R-3 tail warning radar *Stachel* antenna.
12	Landing light.
13	Armoured glass.
14	Navigator.
15	Ammunition containers for main Mk 108 guns.
16	FuG 280 *Kiel* Z Infra-red homer.
17	Two 30-mm MK 108 guns.
18	Radar operator.
19	Two 30-mm MK 108 guns (80 degree upwards firing for *Schräge Musik*).
20	240-litre fuel tank.
21	1,560-litre fuel tank.
22	Flaps.
23	Access hatch.
24	Leading edge flap.
25	Ammunition container for MK 108 *Schräge Musik* guns.
26	FuG 120 a *Bernhardine* radio beacon teleprinter.
27	900 x 200-mm main undercarriage tyre.
28	Pitot tube.
29	FuG 226 *Neuling* IFF.
30	FuG 101 antennae (S101 and E 101).
31	*Q-Rohr* for FuG 280.
32	Two 20-mm MG 213 guns (rearwards firing).
33	FuG 10P trailing wire antenna.
34	FuG 125a *Hermine*/FuG 120 Morane antenna.
35	FuG 10P rod antenna.
36	FuG 130/Fu Bl 3E comb antenna.
37	*Formholz* anti-radar coating.
38	Elevon.
39	*Morgenstern* antenna.
40	FuG 350 Zc *Naxos* passive radar-receiver.
41	FuG 25a *Erstling*/FuG 139 *Barbarossa* antenna.
42	FuG 228 *Lichtenstein* SN-3 search radar.
43	FuG 16 ZY *Zypresse*/FuG 125a *Hermine* D/F loop antenna.
44	FuG 244 *Bremen 0* search radar.
45	70-cm-diameter *Parabolspiegel* (parabolic antenna).
46	FuG 24 SE/VHF antenna.

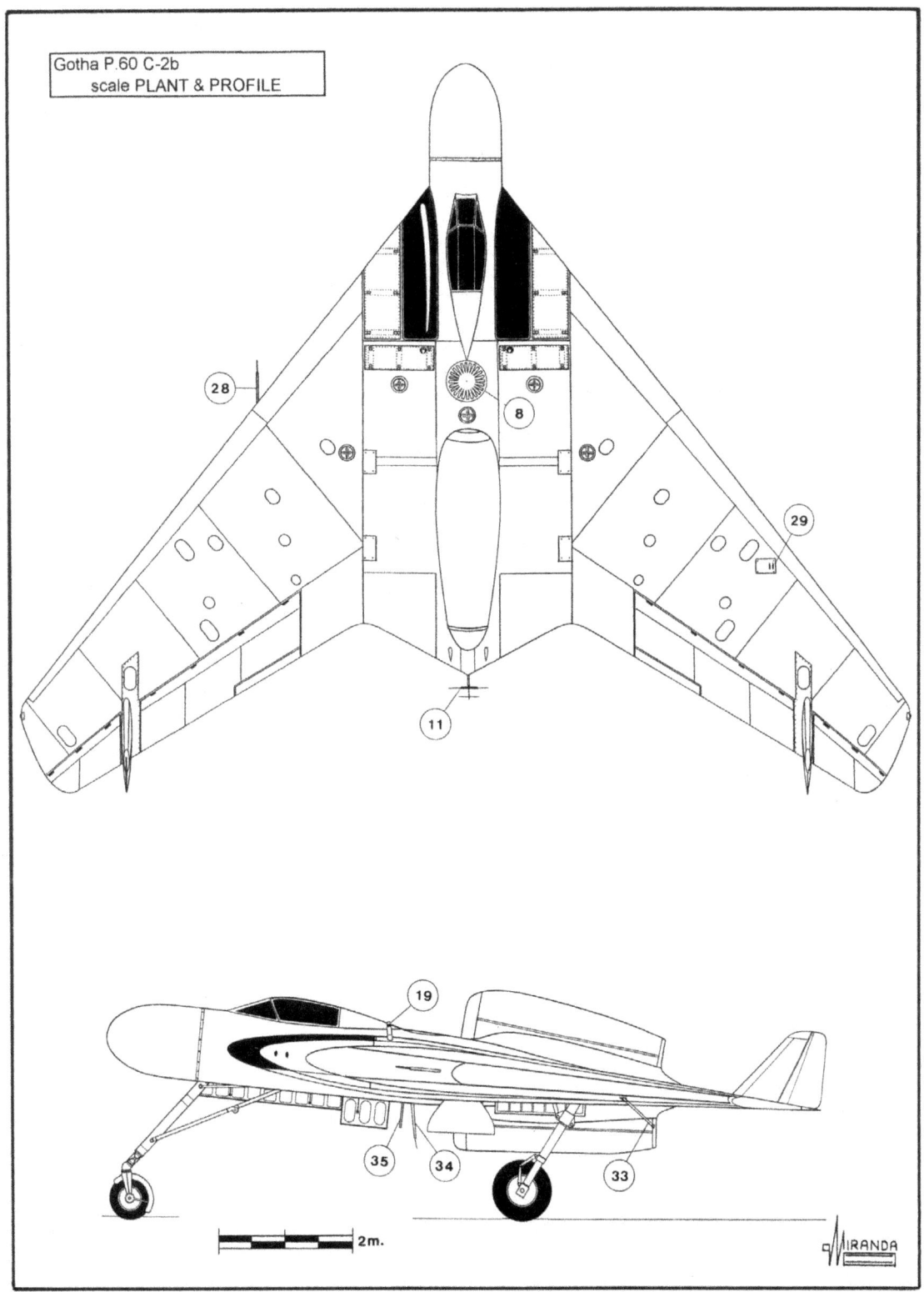

Gotha P.60 C-2b
scale PLANT & PROFILE

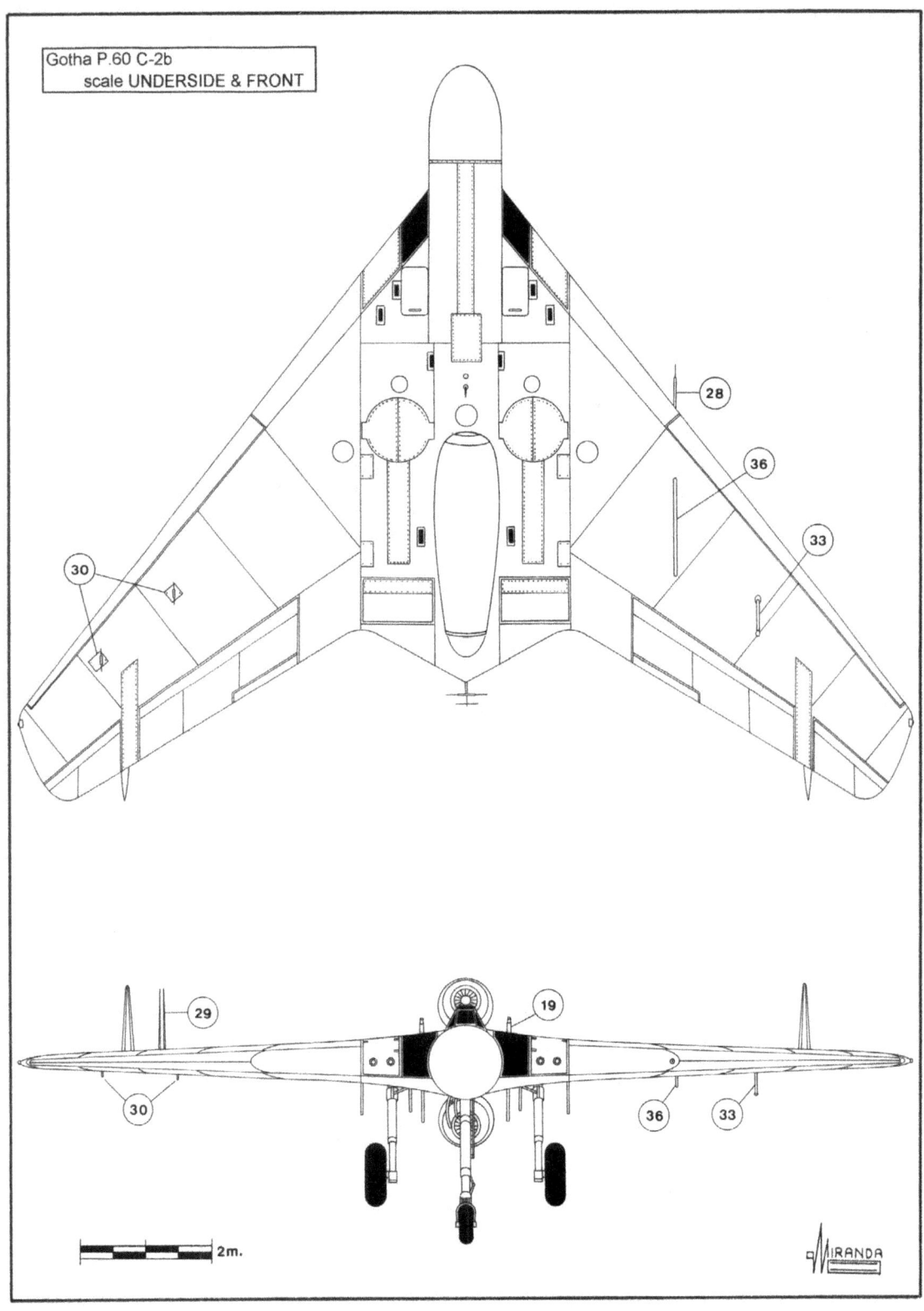

Gotha P.60 C-2b
scale UNDERSIDE & FRONT

2m.

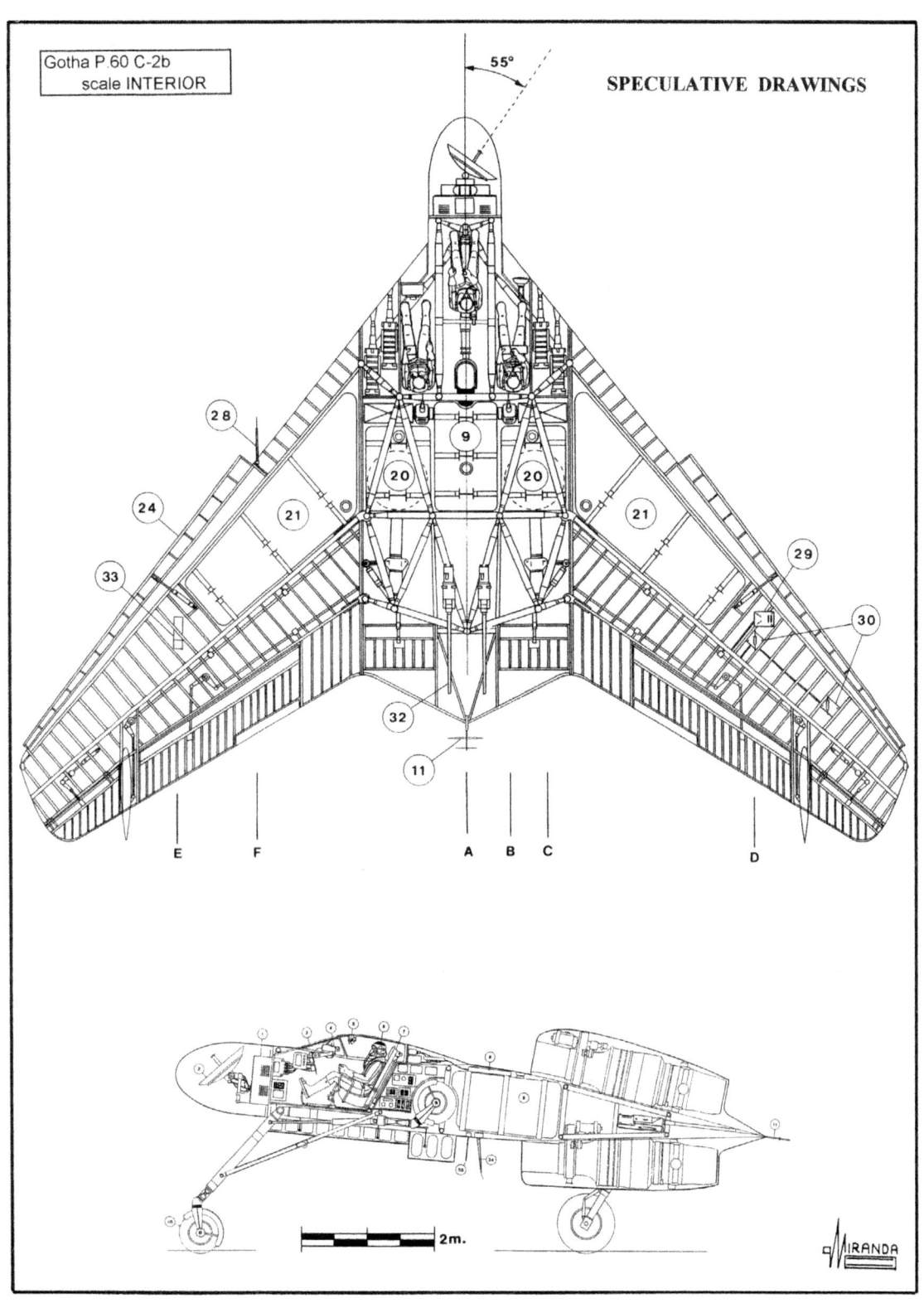

Gotha P.60 C-2b
scale INTERIOR

55°

SPECULATIVE DRAWINGS

2m.

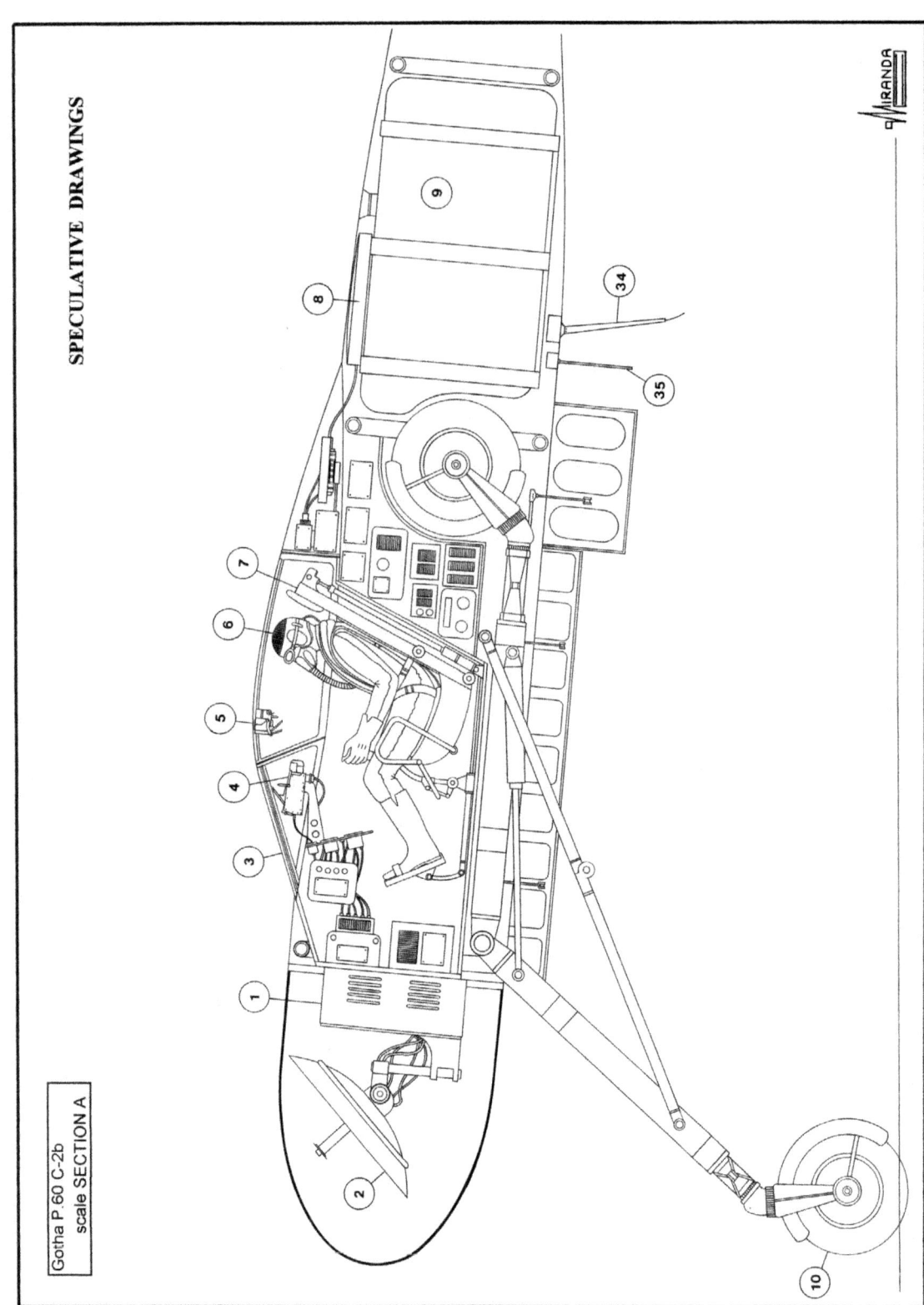

SPECULATIVE DRAWINGS

Gotha P.60 C-2b
scale SECTION A

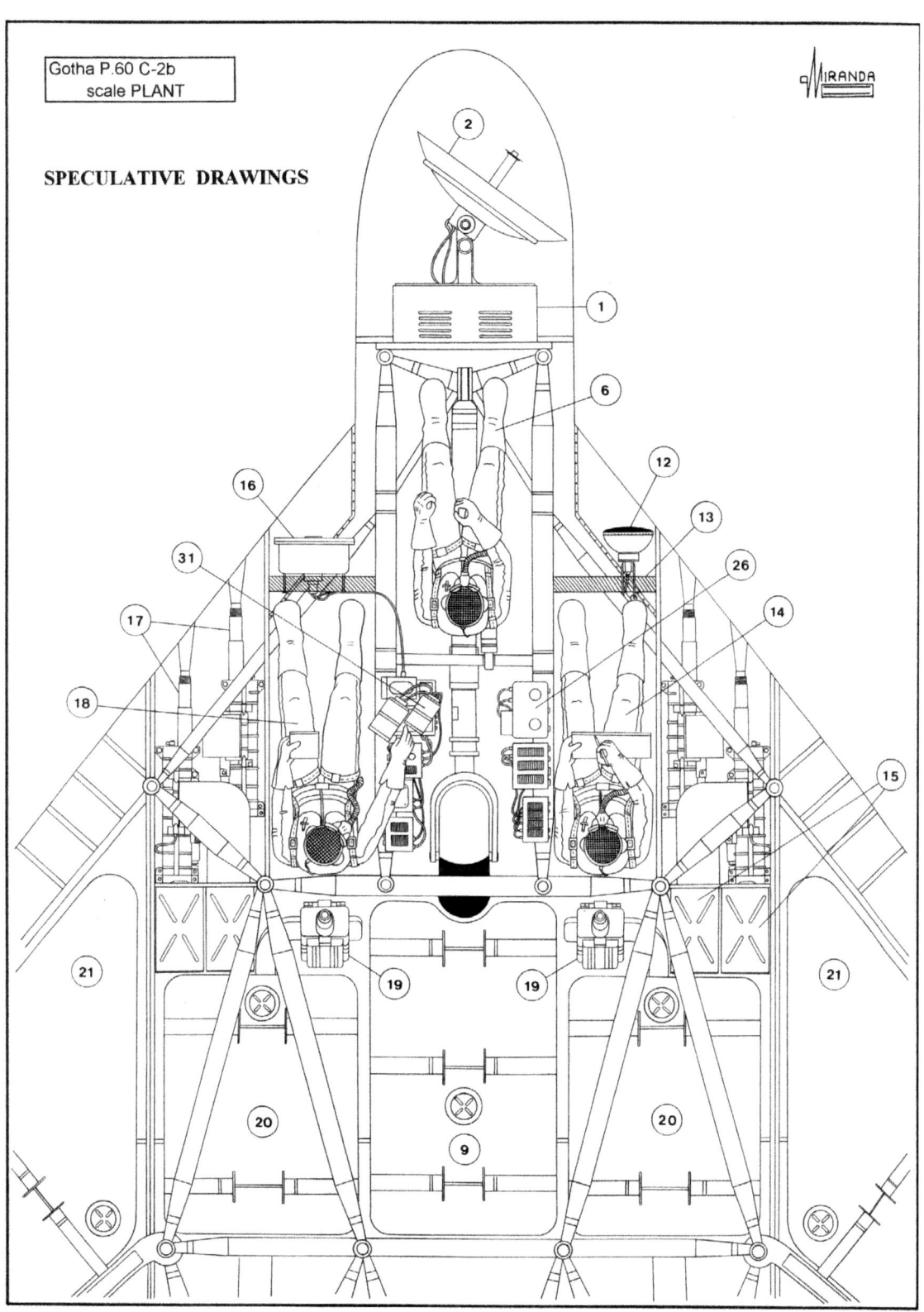

Gotha P.60 C-2b
scale PLANT

SPECULATIVE DRAWINGS

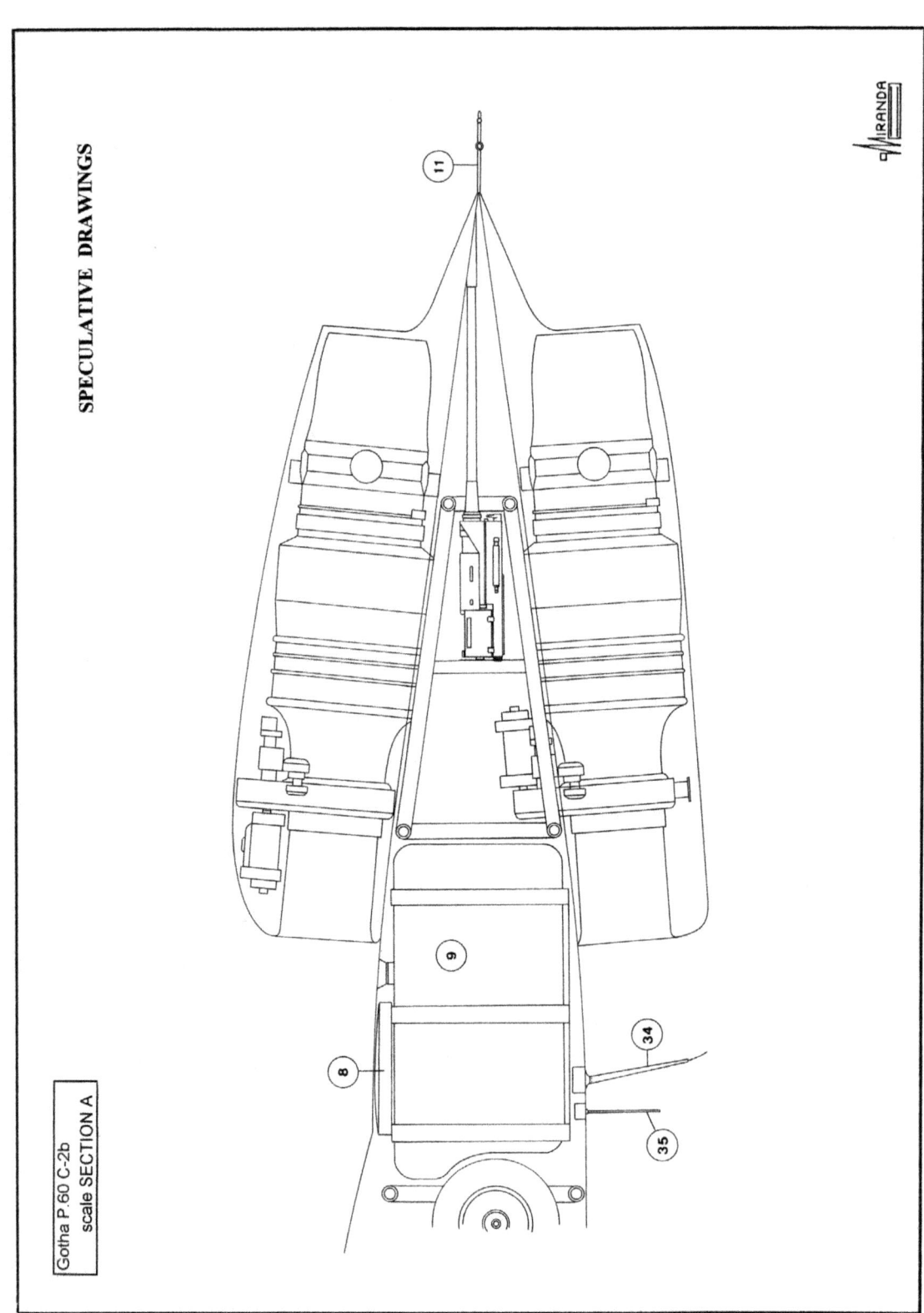

SPECULATIVE DRAWINGS

Gotha P.60 C-2b
scale SECTION A

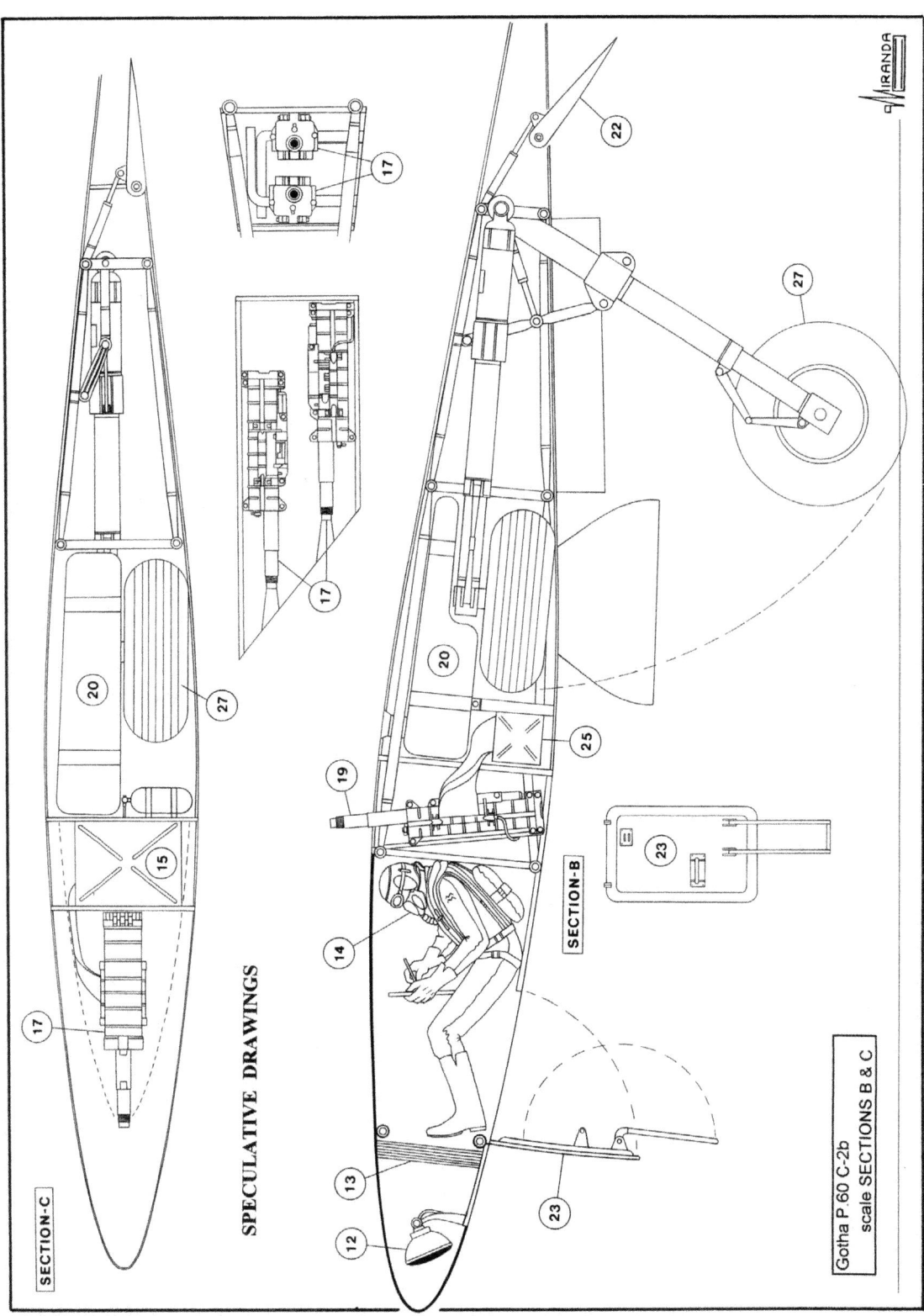

SPECULATIVE DRAWINGS

SECTION-C

SECTION-B

Gotha P.60 C-2b
scale SECTIONS B & C

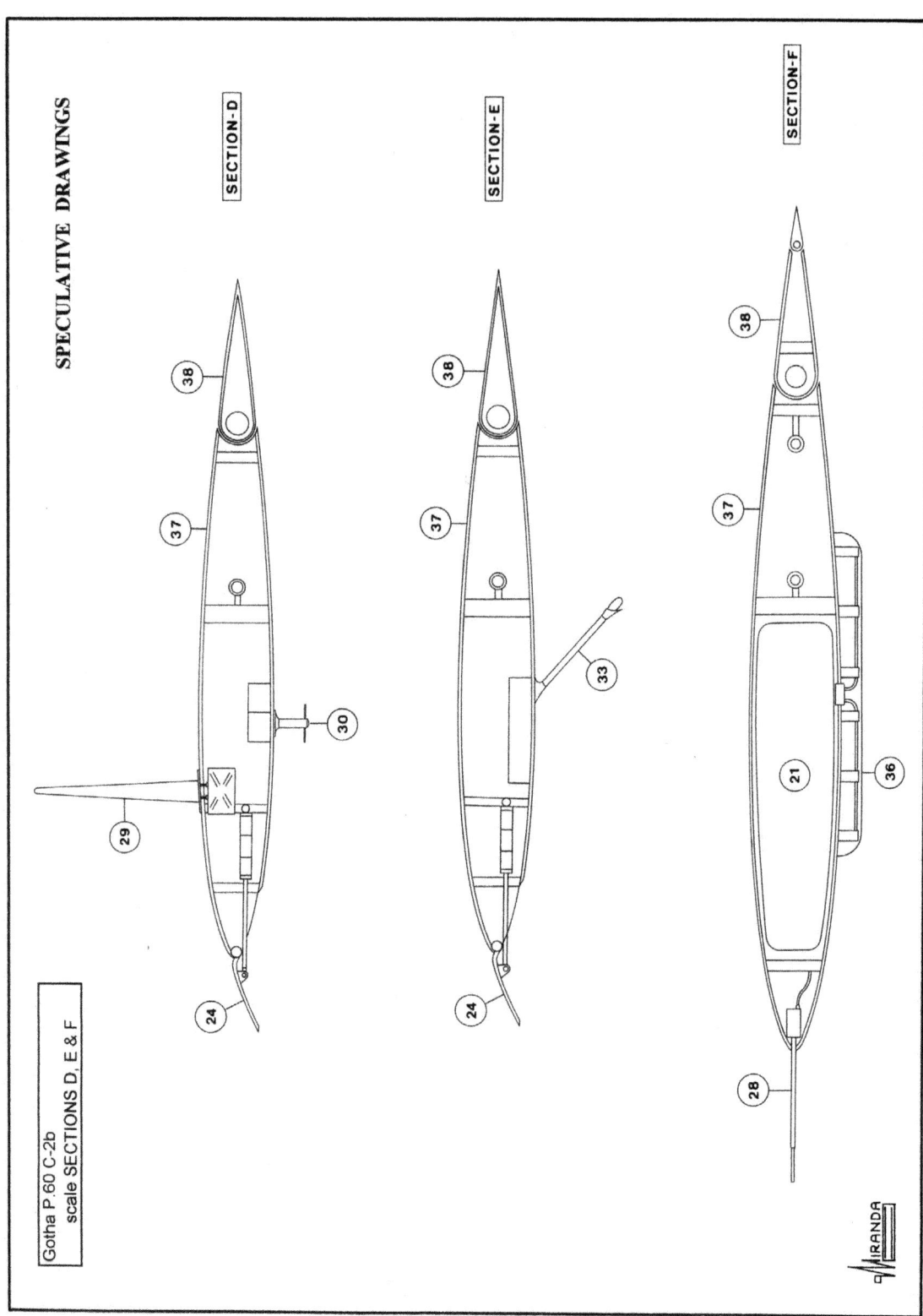

SPECULATIVE DRAWINGS

Gotha P.60 C-2b
scale SECTIONS D, E & F

SECTION-D

SECTION-E

SECTION-F

Chapter 13

Heinkel P.1078

By the end of 1944, Heinkel engineers had conceived an advanced system of automatic triggering weapons, combining the fire control radar FuG 222 *Pauke S* with the gyroscopic gunsight Askania EZ 42 *Adler*.

The 1078 project was created to prove that the system could be integrated into single-engined fighters, providing them with additional capacity to act as night fighters or *Moskitojägern* under ground control command (through the FuG 25a and FuG 125a devices installed onboard).

The P.1078 A was very similar to the Messerschmitt P.1101, with swept wings and tail surfaces. It had a small parabolic antenna fixed on the nose and two 30-mm cannons either side of the pilot.

The P.1078B had a 'Twin-boom' type fuselage and a 'Batwing' similar to that of the Blohm und Voss P.209.01, chosen to diminish the compressibility buffeting effect and the roll damping at high speed.

It was expected that the anhedral wingtips would perform the function of tailfins and tailplanes. The radar, the armament, and the nose leg were housed in the starboard fuselage and the cockpit—armoured but without an ejector seat—in the port fuselage.

The P.1078B received strong criticism from the Technisches Amt due to the lack of protection of the fuel tanks and the asymmetric nose leg. The batwing was also considered inefficient during combat turns and it was feared that the shockwaves generated by the twin nose cones would interfere with the operation of the air intake.

In an effort to dodge the objections that the Oberkommando der Luftwaffe might raise to the new aiming system, the design team of Heinkel removed the radar and installed a 'Single pod' with rectangular air intake. The wing type was kept, the inclination of the wingtips was increased, and the wing surface was reduced.

The new design was presented to the *Jägernotprogramm* as P.1078C at the end of 1944; it was rejected for having a lower ceiling than had been specified, a consequence of the changes applied to the wing. The project was cancelled on 27 February 1945.

Technical data P.1078 B

Type	single-seat, all-weather fighter.
Wings	built of wood/plywood with 45-degree swept at the leading edge and 25 degree at the trailing edge, with 46-degree anhedral wingtips, housing four fuel tanks, flaps, elevons and ailerons.
Fuselage	twin-boom type, built of light alloy, including the cockpit, the armament, the undercarriage, the radar, and the engine.
Armament	three Mk 108/30 cannons with 75 rpg in the starboard pod.
Engine	one Heinkel-Hirth HeS 109-011 turbojet rated at 1,300-kp static thrust.
Fuel tanks	four in the wings, with a total capacity of 1,190 litres.
Wingspan	9.40 m
Length	6.12 m
Height	2.44 m
Wing area	20 sq. m
Aspect ratio	4.35:1
Max. weight	3,882 kg
Max. speed	910 kph
Range	1,800 km
Ceiling	45,000 feet
Electronics	FuG 222 *Pauke S* fire control radar with automatic triggering of the weapons in combination with the EZ 42 gyroscopic gunsight, and one fixed *Parabolspiegel* of 45 cm diameter. FuG 16, FuG 25a, FuG 101a, FuG 125a, FuG 139.

Technical data P.1078 C

Type	single-seat interceptor fighter.
Wings	built of wood/plywood with 43-degree swept at the leading edge and 30-degree swept at the trailing edge, with 52-degree anhedral wingtips, housing four unprotected fuel tanks, flaps, elevons, and ailerons.
Fuselage	built of light alloy, including the cockpit, the armament, the undercarriage with tyres of (560 x 200, 660 x 190) and the engine.
Armament	four Mk 108/30 cannons in the nose with 100 rpg.
Engine	one Heinkel-Hirth HeS 109-011 turbojet rated at 1,300-kp static thrust.
Fuel tanks	four in the wings, with a total capacity of 1,210 litres.
Wingspan	9.28 m
Length	5.90 m
Height	2.55 m
Wing area	17.25 sq. m
Aspect ratio	4.55:1
Max. weight	3,915 kg
Max. speed.	1.050 kph
Ceiling	42,300 feet
Electronics	FuG 15, FuG 25a, FuG 125a, FuG 120, EZ 42.

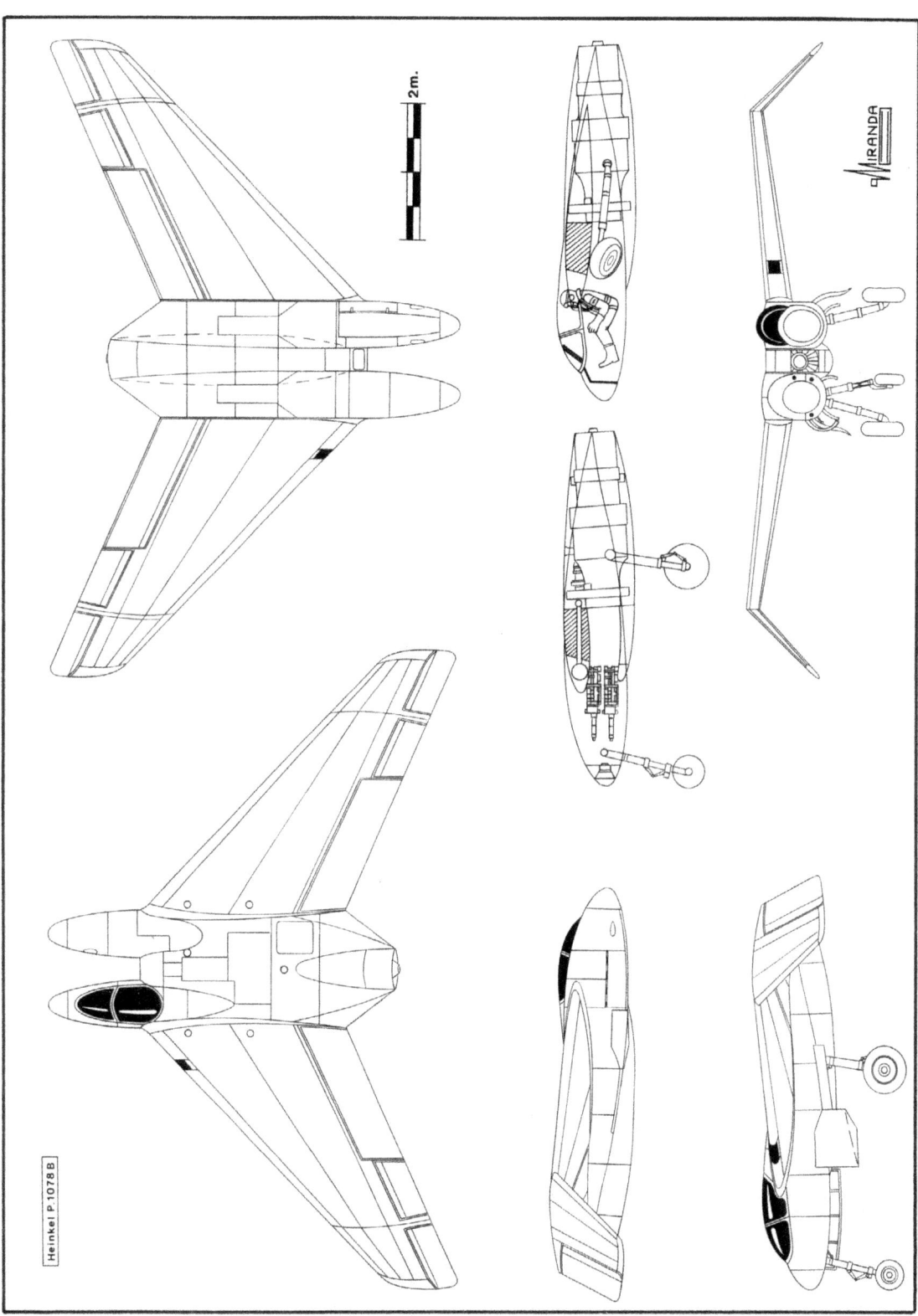

Heinkel P.1078 B

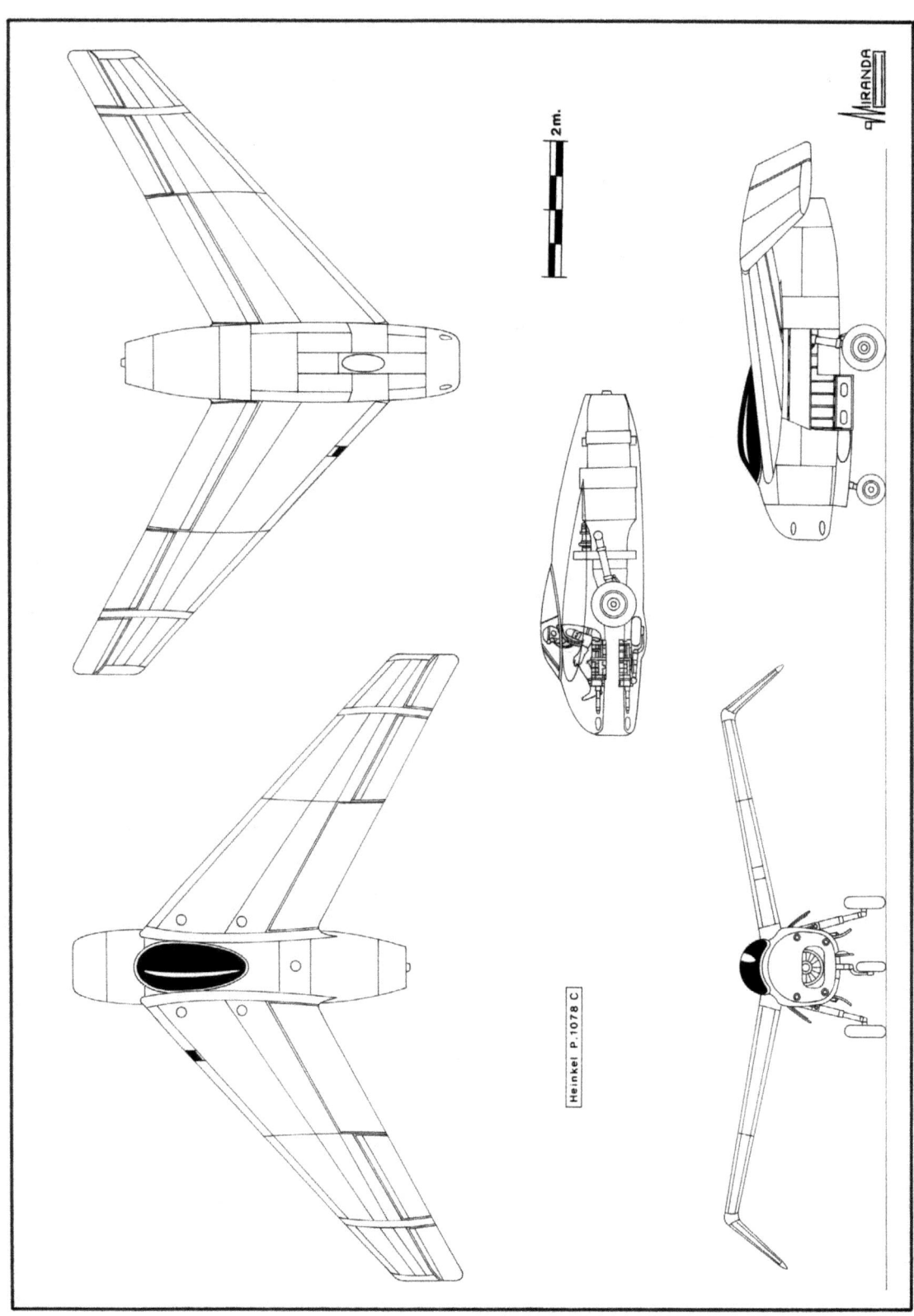

2 m.

Heinkel P.1078 C

Chapter 14

Heinkel P.1079

Originally conceived as the successor to the formidable He 219, the He P.1079 followed the same working scheme as the P.1078: a classical shaped version A and two flying wings with the same type of batwing as in the P.1078.

The Horten brothers proposed the construction of a two-seat version of the Ho 229 to adapt to the night fighter specification published by the Oberkommando der Luftwaffe in August 1944. At the same time, Heinkel started to work on the P.1079B with Jumo 004B engines and *Pauke* S radar.

On 27 January 1945, the specification was extended to request a maximum speed of 900 kph, a ceiling of 28,000 feet, and an endurance of 4 hours. There was no airplane with turbojets able to follow the last requirement. The P.1079 could only stay in the air for 2½ hours using detachable fuel tanks.

By the end of February, an additional requirement was formulated. The airplane had to use an oblique upwards firing *Schräge Musik* armament. Different contenders were put forward: a variant of the Me 262 HG III (12 February 1945), a Focke Wulf with three turbojets, a jet version of the Dornier Do 335, and six flying wings. These flying wings were the Arado E-583 (two-seat version of the E-581 heavy fighter), Blohm und Voss P.215 (scaled-up variant of P.212), Gotha P-60 C-1a (a modified P.60 B *Zerstörer*), Heinkel P.1079 B (without tailfin), Horten Ho 229 V6 (two-seat variant), and a two-seat version of the Junkers EF-128.

Also by the end of February, the OKL requested that the new fighter had to include the FuG 244 radar, together with *Schräge Musik* guns and ammunition, which would add 300 kg to the weight of the airplane.

Heinkel preferred to continue working on a lighter version *Entwurf II* without a tailfin, a *Moskitojäger* able to fly at more than 1,000 kph with a ceiling of 42,300 feet, thanks to the new Heinkel HeS 011 engines.

At the beginning of March, however, the Luftwaffe no longer needed all-weather interceptors; heavy night fighters with a third crew member, a great amount of electronic equipment, and maximum endurance to be able to harass the enemy bomber stream along its whole route, were the order of the day. Besides, after the fatal crash suffered by the Horten IX V2, the OKL strongly advised against the manufacturing of airplanes without tailfins, which was why the the Arado Ar.I ultimately won the contest.

The flight control of a batwing airplane at high speed was beyond technical expertise in 1945. It was not achieved until the Boeing computer-controlled 'Bird of Prey' in 1996.

Technical data (*Entwurf I*)

Type	two-seat, all-weather fighter.
Wings	built of wood/plywood, 30- and 43-degree swept at the leading edge and 25-degree swept at the trailing edge, housing the engines, elevators, ailerons, and six fuel tanks.
Fuselage	built of light alloy, housing the radar, the undercarriage, the armament, the cockpit, the tailfin, and two fuel tanks.
Engines	two Junkers-Jumo 004 B turbojets rated at 890-kp static thrust.
Fuel tanks	eight in the wings and fuselage, with a total capacity of 2,970 litres, and detachable tanks beneath the wings with an additional capacity of 980 litres.
Armament	four Mk 108/30 cannon in the nose.
Electronics	FuG 222 Pauke S radar with fixed 45-cm-diameter Parabolspiegel, FuG 24SE, FuG 25a IFF, FuG 125, FuG 16 R/T, FuG 139, FuG 101, EiV 25, EZ 42.
Wingspan	13 m
Length	9.10 m
Height	4.15 m
Wing area	38.70 sq. m
Max. weight	10,000 kg
Max. speed	907 kph
Ceiling	32,800 feet
Range	1,800 km

Technical data (*Entwurf II*)

Type	two-seat, all-weather fighter.
Wings	built of wood/plywood, 48-degree swept at the leading edge and 35-degree swept at the trailing edge, housing the engines, elevators, ailerons, and six fuel tanks.
Fuselage	built of light alloy, housing the radar, the undercarriage, the armament and two fuel tanks.
Engines	two Heinkel Hirth HeS 109-011 turbojets rated at 1,300-kp static thrust.
Fuel tanks	eight in the wings and fuselage, with a total capacity of 3,460 litres.
Armament	four Mk 108/30 cannons in the nose.
Electronics	FuG 222, FuG 24SE, FuG 25a, FuG 125, FuG 16 R/T, FuG 139, FuG 101, EiV 25, EZ 42.
Wingspan	13 m
Length	9.43 m
Height	2.78 m
Wing area	41.50 sq. m
Max. weight	10,967 kg
Max. speed	1,018 kph
Ceiling	42,300 feet
Range	3,000 km

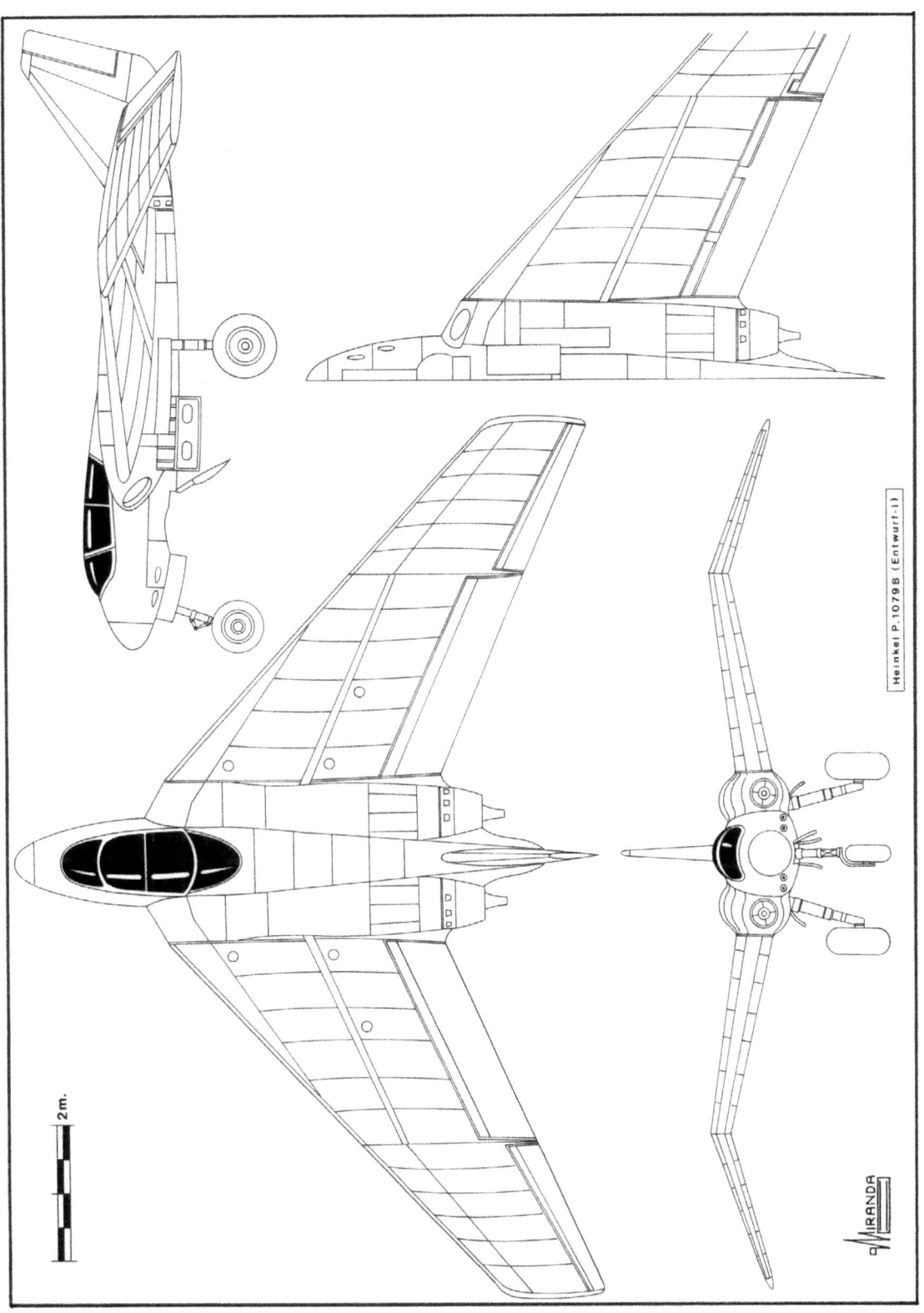

Heinkel P.1079 B (Entwurf-1)

2 m.

MIRANDA

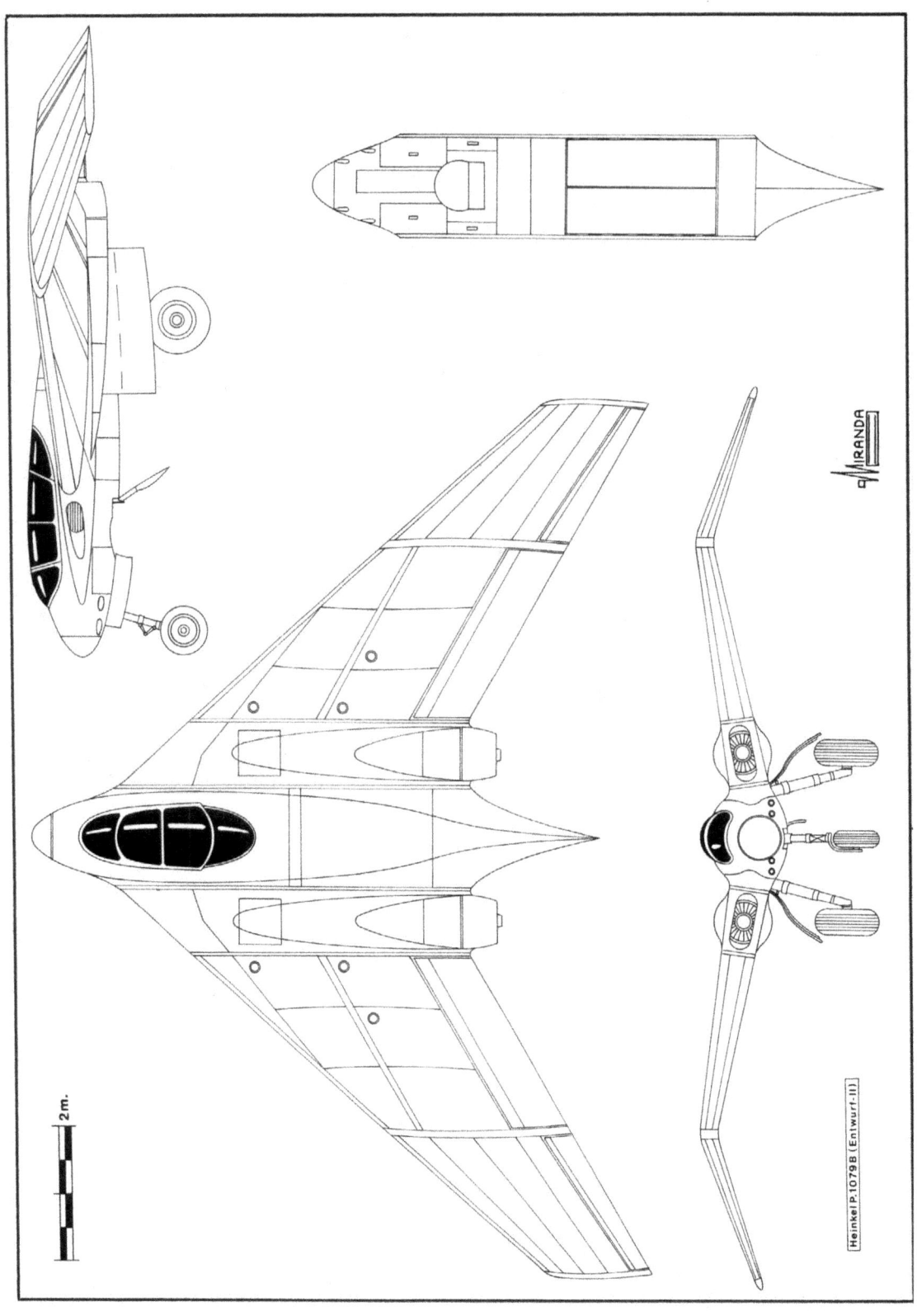

2 m.

Heinkel P.1079B (Entwurf-III)

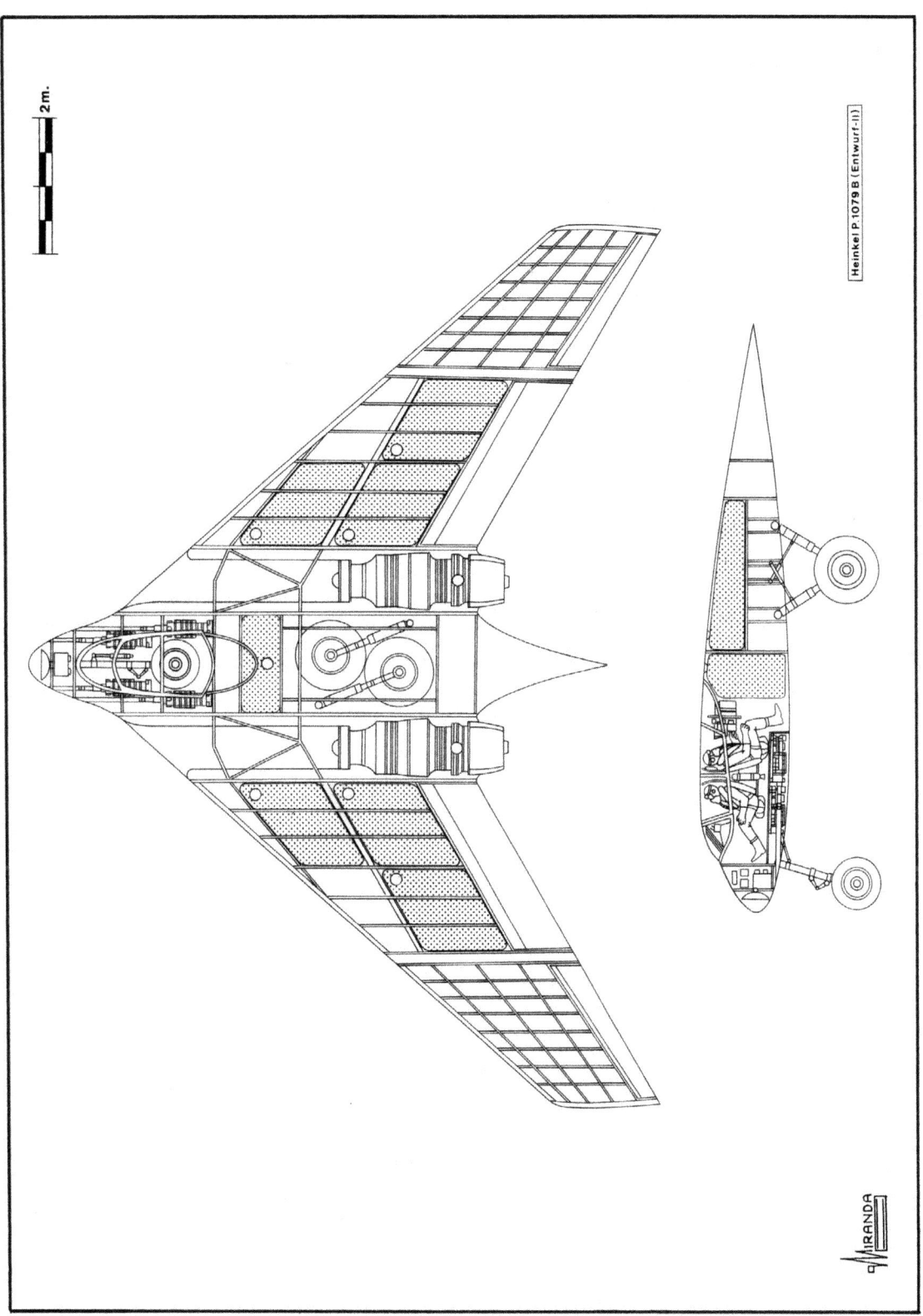

Heinkel P.1079 B (Entwurf-II)

2 m.

Chapter 15

Henschel P.130 Series

The interest of the Henschel firm in tailless airplanes began at the end of 1943, during their cooperation with Dr Alexander Lippisch on the design of the *Delta VI*.

In autumn 1944, the team led by Dipl. Ing. Friedrich Nicolaus proposed the building of the Henschel P.130, a tailless fighter powered by a Daimler Benz DB 603 piston engine with a pusher airscrew and double-cranked wing. The special design of the wing was expected to solve the problem of compressibility buffeting, and preserve the good features of low-speed flight.

On 15 September 1944, the Technischen Amt published the *Jägernotprogramm* specifications, requesting a high-performance emergency fighter powered by one of the new Heinkel HeS 011 turbojets from the German industry. The required maximum speed was of 1,000 kph at 23,000 feet and a ceiling of 46,000 feet with the same armament, electronics, and range as the Me 262.

Eight models initially competed in this contest: the Blohm und Voss P.213.03, Heinkel P.1078 C, Junkers EF 128, Messerschmitt P.1101, Messerschmitt P.1110/I, Messerschmitt P.1111, Focke Wulf Ta 183/I, and Focke Wulf Ta 183/II. In a second phase, they were joined by the Horten Ho 229, Junkers Ju 388, Messerschmitt P.1116, and Henschel P.135. The latter was a version of the P.130 powered by a HeS 011, on which the four guns had been moved to the wing roots and beneath the cockpit, displaced by the main fuel tank.

The declared winner was the Ta 183/I, of which 5,000 units per month were to be manufactured, which necessitated the whole production capability of the HeS 011. There was therefore a proposal to modify the P.135 so that it could use a less powerful BMW 003 turbojet or a bifuel Walter HWK 509 C rocket engine, with double combustion chamber, already manufactured to power the Messerschmitt Me 263.

The new version was named Henschel P.136.

Henschel P.130 technical data

Type	single-seat interceptor fighter.
Wings	built of wood, in five sections, with a double-cranked leading edge and 42 positive degree and 38 and 15 negative degree compound sweep. It had leading-edge slats to improve stall characteristics and split flaps ahead of the rudders. The inner

rudders acted as ailerons and the outboard rudders as elevons. Thickness of 12 per cent at the root and 10 per cent outboard.

Fuselage	light alloy structure, housing the armament, undercarriage, fuel tanks, and engine.
Cockpit	pressurised, control heating, frontal armour against 12.7-mm shelling and from the rear against 20-mm shelling. Heinkel-Kartusche ejector seat.
Tailfin	light alloy structure and cladding.
Undercarriage	tricycle type, nose wheel that would have retracted to the rear, rotating 90 degrees to lie flat in the wheel bay. The main wheels retracted forward into the fuselage.
Engine	a Daimler Benz DB 603 of 1,900 hp, twelve-cylinder, inverted Vee, liquid-cooled engine, driving a 3-m-diameter pusher propeller through an extension shaft.
Fuel tanks	two, located behind and under the cockpit.
Armament	four Mk 108/30 cannons in the nose.
Electronics	EZ 42 gyrogunsight, FuG 16 ZY VHF transmitter/receiver, FuG 25a IFF radio set.
Wingspan	9.20 m
Length	9 m
Height	4.30 m
Wing area	20.50 sq. m
Aspect ratio	4.13:1

Henschel P.135 technical data

Type	single-seat interceptor fighter.
Wings	built of wood, in five sections, with a double-cranked leading edge and and 42 positive degree and 38 and 15 negative degree compound sweep. It had leading-edge slats to improve stall characteristics and split flaps ahead of the rudders. The inner rudders acted as ailerons and the outboard rudders as elevons. Thickness of 12 per cent at the root and 10 per cent outboard.
Fuselage	light alloy structure, housing the armament, undercarriage, fuel tanks, and engine.
Cockpit	pressurised, control heating, frontal armour against 12.7-mm shelling and from the rear against 20 mm. Heinkel-Kartusche ejector seat.
Tailfin	light alloy structure and cladding.
Undercarriage	tricycle type, nose wheel that would have retracted to the rear, rotating 90 degrees to lie flat in the wheel bay. The main wheels retracted forward into the fuselage.
Engine	one Heinkel-Hirth HeS 011 turbojet rated at 1,300-kp static thrust.
Fuel tanks	two, located in front and behind the cockpit, with a total capacity of 1,920 litres.
Armament	two Mk 108/30 cannons beneath the cockpit and two Mk 108/30 in the wing roots.
Electronics	EZ 42 gyrogunsight, FuG 16 ZY VHF transmitter/receiver, FuG 25a IFF radio set.
Wingspan	9.20 m
Length	7.80 m
Height	4.10 m
Wing area	20.50 sq. m
Max. weight	5,500 kg

Henschel P.136 technical data

Type	single-seat interceptor fighter.
Wings	built of wood, in five sections, with a double-cranked leading edge and and 42 positive degree and 38 and 15 negative degree compound sweep. It had leading-edge slats to improve stall characteristics and split flaps ahead of the rudders. The inner rudders acted as ailerons and the outboard rudders as elevons. Thickness of 12 per cent at the root and 10 per cent outboard.
Fuselage	light alloy structure, housing the armament, undercarriage, fuel tanks, and engine.
Cockpit	pressurised, control heating, frontal armour against 12.7-mm shelling and from the rear against 20-mm shelling. Heinkel-Kartusche ejector seat.
Tailfin	light alloy structure and cladding.
Undercarriage	tricycle type, nose wheel that would have retracted to the rear, rotating 90 degrees to lie flat in the wheel bay. The main wheels retracted forward into the fuselage.
Engine	one Walter HWK 509 C bifuel rocket engine with two combustion chambers.
Propellants	tanks one of T-Stoff in front of the cockpit and one of C-Stoff behind.
Armament	two Mk 108/30 cannons under the cockpit and two Mk 108/30 in the wing roots.
Electronics	EZ 42 gyro-gunsight, FuG 16 ZY VHF transmitter/receiver, FuG 25a IFF radio set.
Wingspan	9.20 m
Length	8.40 m
Height	4.10 m
Wing area	20.50 sq. m
Aspect ratio	4.13:1

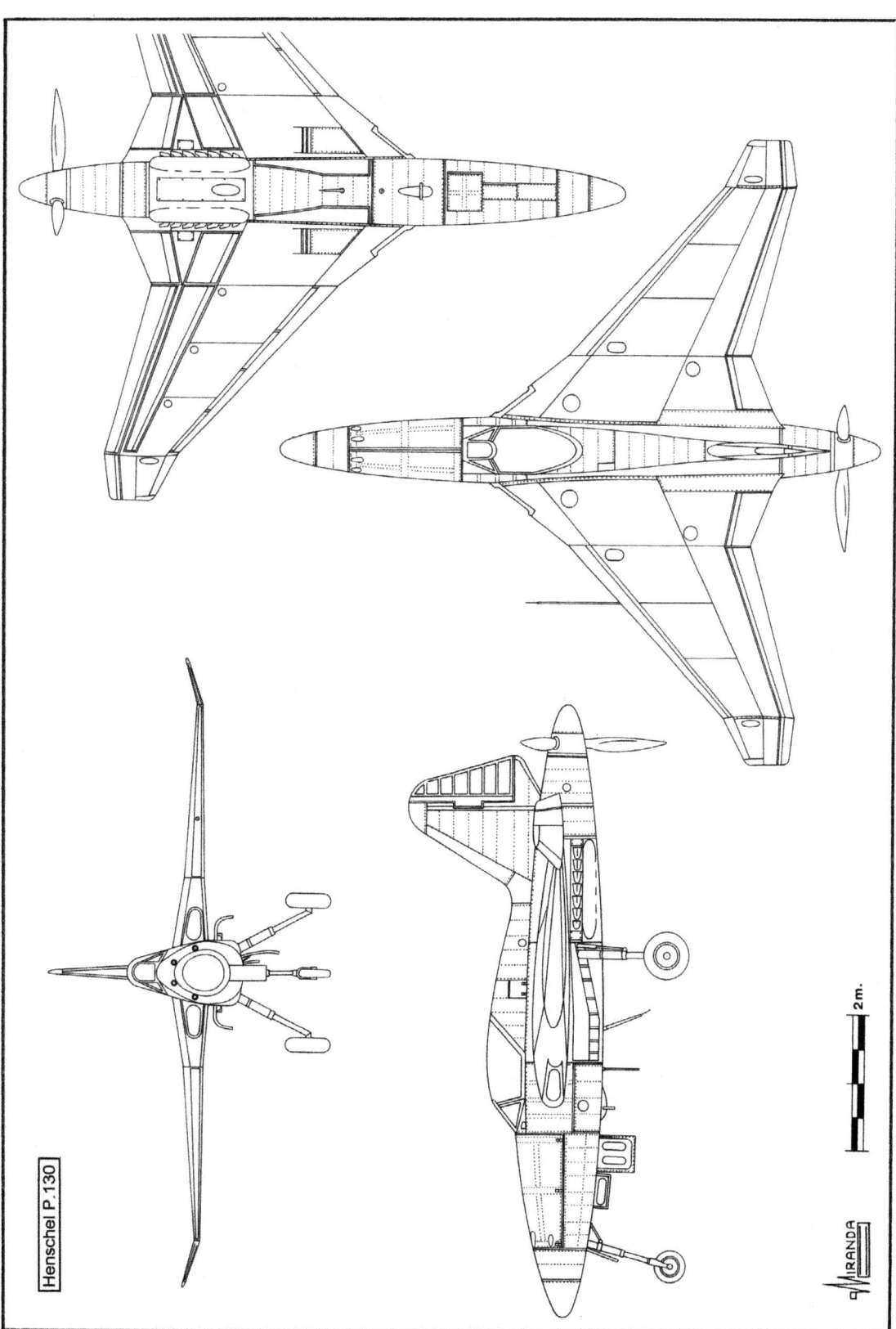

Henschel P.130

2 m.

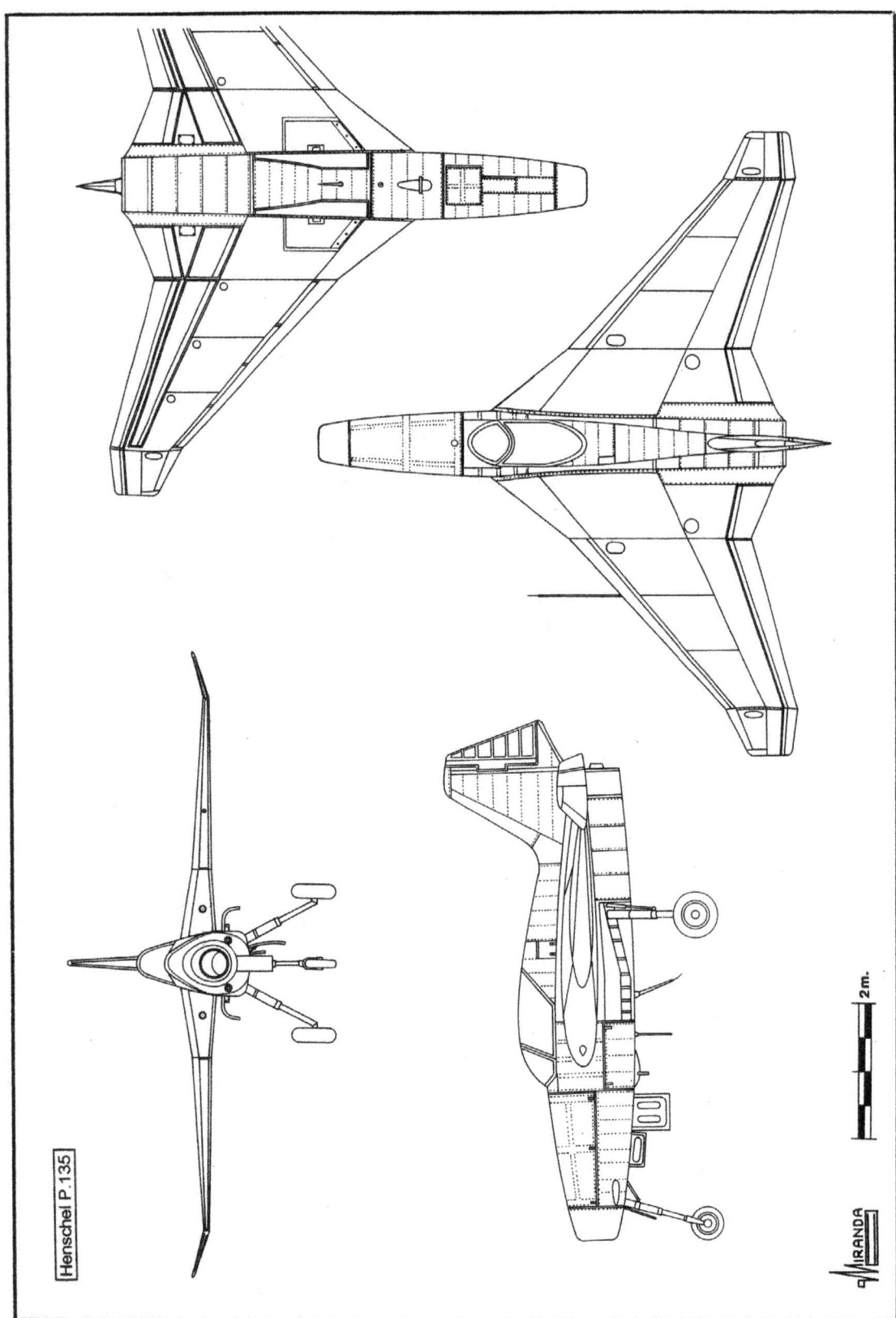

Henschel P.135

2 m.

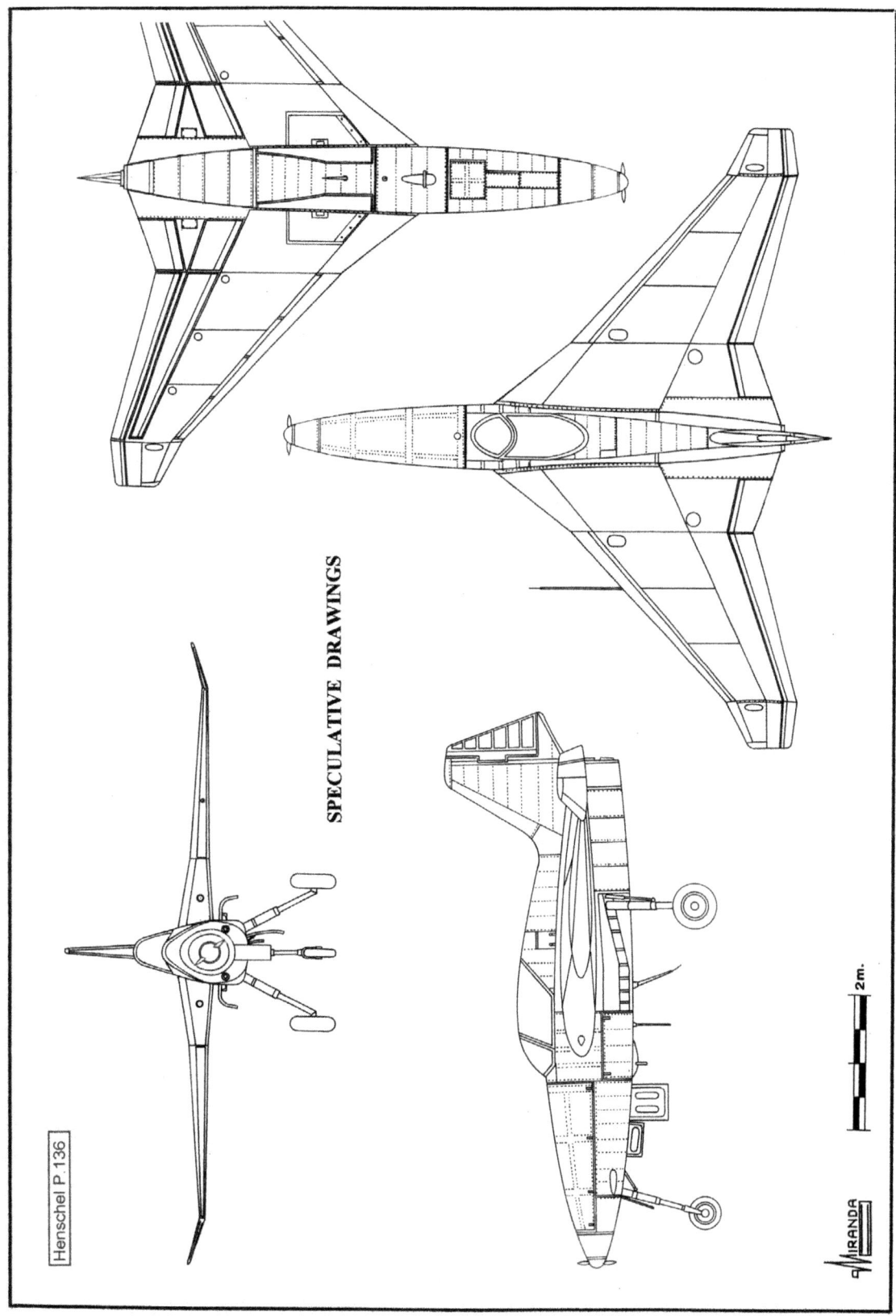

SPECULATIVE DRAWINGS

Henschel P.136

2m.

SPECULATIVE DRAWINGS

Henschel P.136

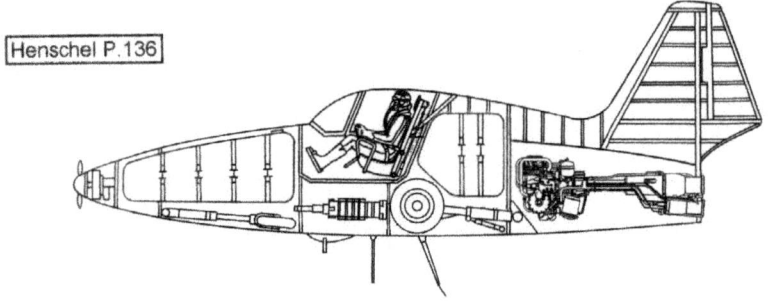

Henschel P.135

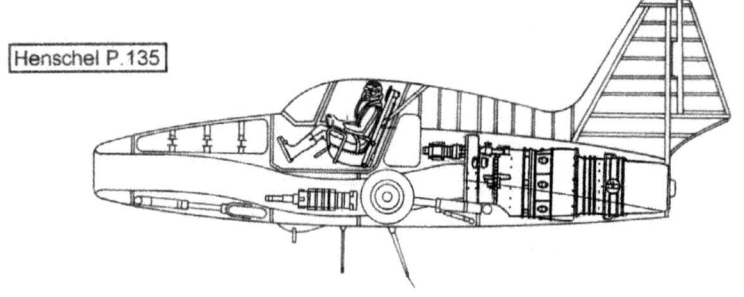

Henschel P.130

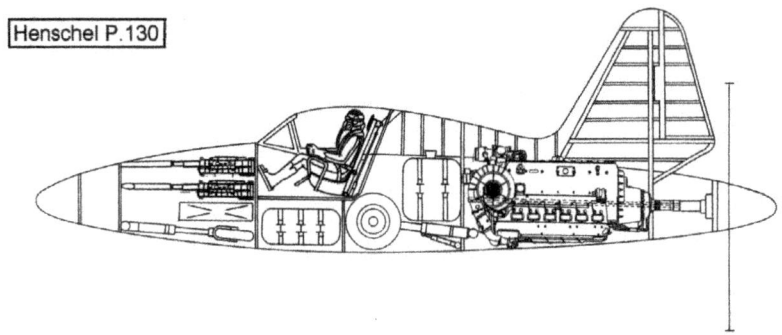

2 m.

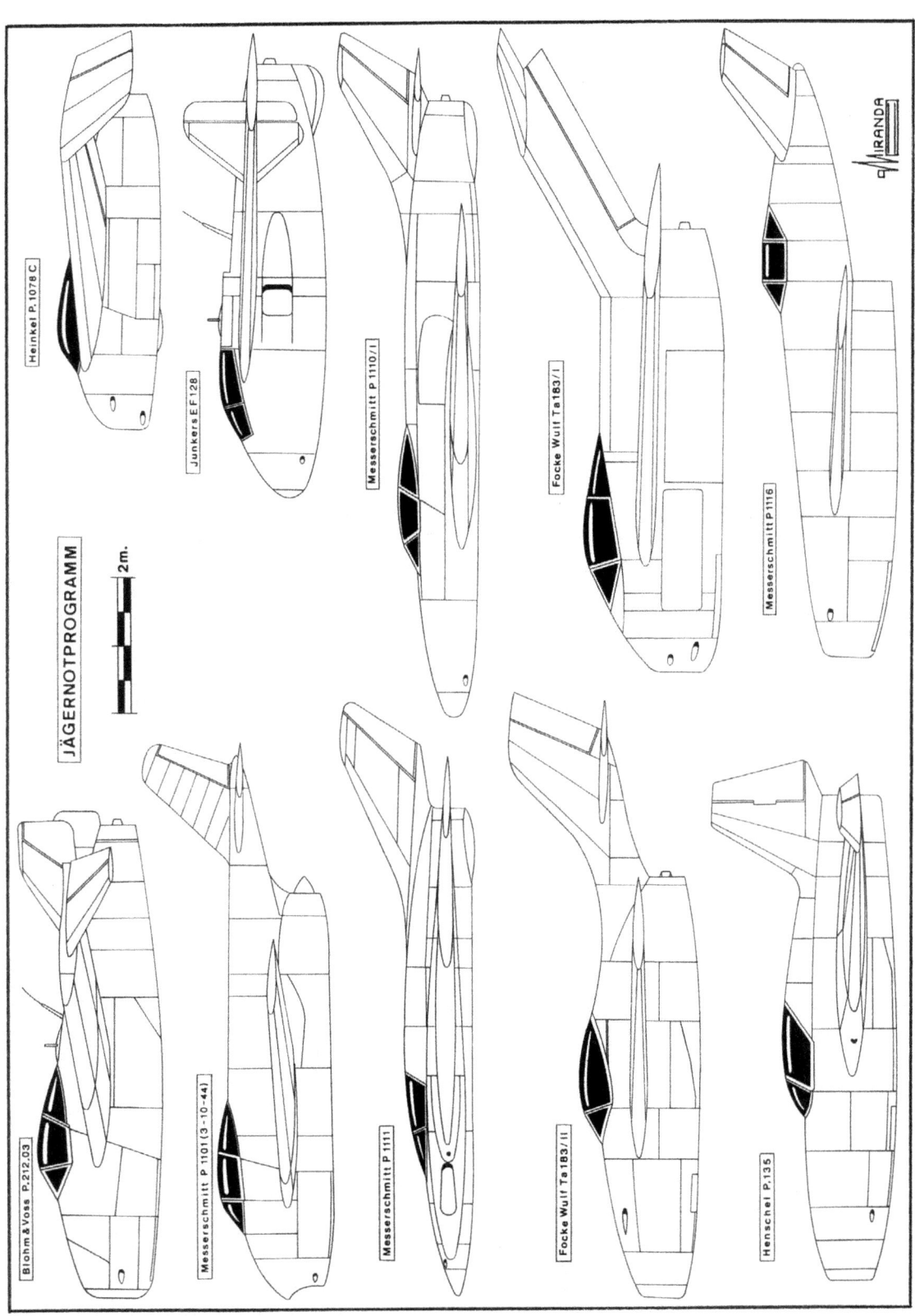

JÄGERNOTPROGRAMM

2m.

Heinkel P.1078 C

Junkers EF 128

Messerschmitt P 1110/I

Focke Wulf Ta 183/I

Messerschmitt P 1116

Blohm & Voss P.212.03

Messerschmitt P 1101 (3-10-44)

Messerschmitt P 111

Focke Wulf Ta 183/II

Henschel P.135

MIRANDA

16

Horten Ho 229 B-1

By mid-1944, the intensity of RAF night bombing offensive reached its peak. The Pathfinder Force airplanes had gained much experience in locating strategic targets at the heart of the Reich and identified them with light markers, so that the bomber stream that followed a few minutes later could accurately launch their loads.

Many bombers were equipped with the cartographic radar H2S, which was able to distinguish shorelines, rivers, and lakes, and very efficiently supported navigation.

But from the German perspective, the worst of all were the smaller attacks led by a dozen of Mosquitos, which misled the defences of the *Himmelbett* system over the chosen location for the bombing. In daylight they attacked U-boats in the Bay of Biscay and the small units of the Kriegsmarine in France and Norway with cannon fire; they bombed administrative centres and Gestapo headquarters and forced the cancellation of previously announced political meetings between Goebbels and Göring—all with accurate timing.

At night they bombed Berlin with impunity or identified targets with light markers to large formations of Lancasters and Halifaxes. At its highest point of provocation, the Pathfinder Force destroyed Ruhr factories with extremely accurate nightly bombings, even through fog and at 29,500 feet altitude. The Germans took months to find out that the Allies were being helped by the radar equipment of the 'Oboe' system, which was guiding them from the south-east of England.

The Reich's *Himmelbett* night system of defence, which covered five countries, dozens of radars—even from aboard specialised ships—thousands of cannons and searchlights, aerodromes, squadrons, control and command centres, and which extended through thousands of kilometres of cable, did not work. The night fighters obtained from the transformation of the veteran Bf 110, Do 217, Ju 88, Bf 109, and Fw 190 were not up to the task.

In October 1944, the Oberkommando der Luftwaffe ordered the conversion of the fastest available airplanes—Me 262, Ar 234, and Do 335—into emergency night fighters, following the *Sofortprogramm* directive. The modification consisted of installing a *Lichtenstein* radar and a second crew member to operate it.

After this adjustment, the Me 262 B-2/N and the Ar 234 B-2 went into service with some success in 1945. However, the air drag generated by the cumbersome *Hirschgeweih* antennae installed in the nose, and the removal of one of the fuel tanks to make room for the radar operator, penalised their maximum speed and endurance, partially annulling the advantage of their initial design.

The *Sofortprogramm* did not solve the problem. After dismissing the construction of dozens of night fighter projects and delaying the entry into service of the Heinkel He 219 for years, the Luftwaffe had to recognise its need for airplanes specifically designed for night combat.

Under these circumstances, the Horten brothers—who already had a very advanced design of a twin-seat version of the Ho229, originally projected for pilot training—proposed a night fighter based on the V6 prototype, already in the first manufacturing stages in the Gotha-Friedrichroda factory.

In accordance with the stalling *Sofortprogramm*, the V6 had the advantage of having been originally designed as a two-seater, with provision for additional fuel tanks in the wings. Initially they thought to install an FuG 218 *Neptun V/R* radar obtained from a Messerschmitt Bf 110 G4, with *Morgenstern* dipolar antennae in X configuration. It is safe to assume that the aesthetic implications of this instalment will not have been met with great enthusiasm by the Hortens.

On 27 January 1945, the OKL published the *Vorrückenprogramm* for high performance night fighters, to be equipped with Telefunken's FuG 244 *Bremen 0* radar with a parabolic antenna of 70 cm diameter. It was internally installed within an aerodynamic container of dielectric material and placed in the nose of the airplane.

The Hortens modified their project to adapt to the new *Hochleistung Nachtjäger* specification with the Ho 229 B-1 version, arming it with 30-mm cannons in forward firing *Schräge Musik* configuration, R4M and R 100 BS/MS rockets, detachable fuel tanks, ejector seats, gyroscopic gunsight, and additional tail warning radar *Neptun R-3*.

The Ho 229 B-1 was presented to the OKL on 1 March 1945. Had it reached manufacture, it would have surpassed anything the Allies had either in service or in development. It possessed powerful armament, versatile electronic equipment and unusual 'stealth' properties, due both to its aerodynamic features and the use of RAM materials in its construction.

A much-discussed experiment conducted by Northrop Grumman in 2008 proved that the radar signature of the Ho 229 was only 40 per cent of one Messserchmit Bf 109 fighter, meaning that it would have been practically undetectable to the radars used by the British Chain Home at the time.

Unfortunately for the Germans, the Hortens did not have the industrial capacity for the series production of the 229. The OKL assigned this task to the Gothaer Waggonfabrik in May 1945. Once there, the philosophy of the Hortens' design came into conflict with available production techniques. Finally, under direction of Dr. Ing. Hunerjäger, the Gotha design team reached the conclusion that the additional weight of the electronic equipment and extra crew member so penalised the longitudinal stability of the Ho 229 B-1 that take off would be impossible without the considerable ballast of about 500 kg at the rear of the airplane.

This was the last 'pure wing' design of Hortens. After the crash of the Ho 229 V2 on 18 February 1945, the OKL banned the manufacturing or airplanes without a tailfin.

Technical data

Type	two-seat night fighter.
Wings	wooden structure, plywood and *Formholz* cladding with 57- and 33-degree swept at the leading edge and 17-degree swept at the trailing edge, containing eight fuel tanks, elevators, flaps ailerons, and spoilers.
Fuselage	welded steel-tube framework, plywood and *Formholz* cladding, including the radar, electronic equipment, cockpit (pressurised, control heating, frontal armour, and ejector seats), landing gear, armament, engines, ventral airbrakes, and anti-spin parachute.
Engines	two Junkers Jumo 004 B-2 turbojets rated at 910-kp static thrust and two Schmidding 109-533 RATO solid fuel rockets with 1,000-kp peak thrust.
Fuel tanks	eight, in the wings, with a total capacity of 4,222 litres.
Armament	four Rheinmetall-Borsig Mk 108/30 forward firing cannon and two Mk 108/30 in upwards firing 80-degree *Schräge Musik* mounting, additional thirty-six R4M 55-mm unguided rockets in two detachable pods under the wing or four R 100 BS/MS heavy rockets which were released automatically by the *Oberon* system.
Wingspan	16.76 m
Length	(FuG 228) 10.40 m (FuG 240) 9.96 m (FuG 244)10 m
Height	3.05 m
Wing area	53.60 sq. m
Aspect ratio	5.2:1
Max. weight	10,500 kg
Max. speed	920 kph
Service ceiling	2,500 feet
Range	4,600 km
Electronics	any of the three Telefunken search radar that were available.
	FuG 228 *Lichtenstein SN-3* with *Morgenstern* antenna and X dipoles.
	FuG 240/3 *Berlin N-3* with a *Parabolspiegel* of 90 cm in diameter.
	FuG 244 *Bremen 0* with a *Parabolspiegel* of 70 cm in diameter.
	A Siemens FuG 218 *Neptun R-3* tail warning radar with *stachel* antenna.
	A passive radar receiver Telefunken FuG 350 Zc *Naxos*.
	A Lorenz FuG 125a *Hermine* radio-beacon receiver with FuG 120 Morane antenna.
	A GEMA FuG 25a *Erstling* IFF device with ventral rod antenna.
	A Lorenz FuG 24 SE VHF direction finder with ventral rod antenna.
	A Lorenz FuG 16 VHF R/T device with dorsal loop antenna.
	An FFO EiV 125 crew intercom.
	An Askania/Zeiss EZ 42 *Adler* gyroscopic gunsight.
	A *Revi C16 A-N Schräge Musik* gunsight.

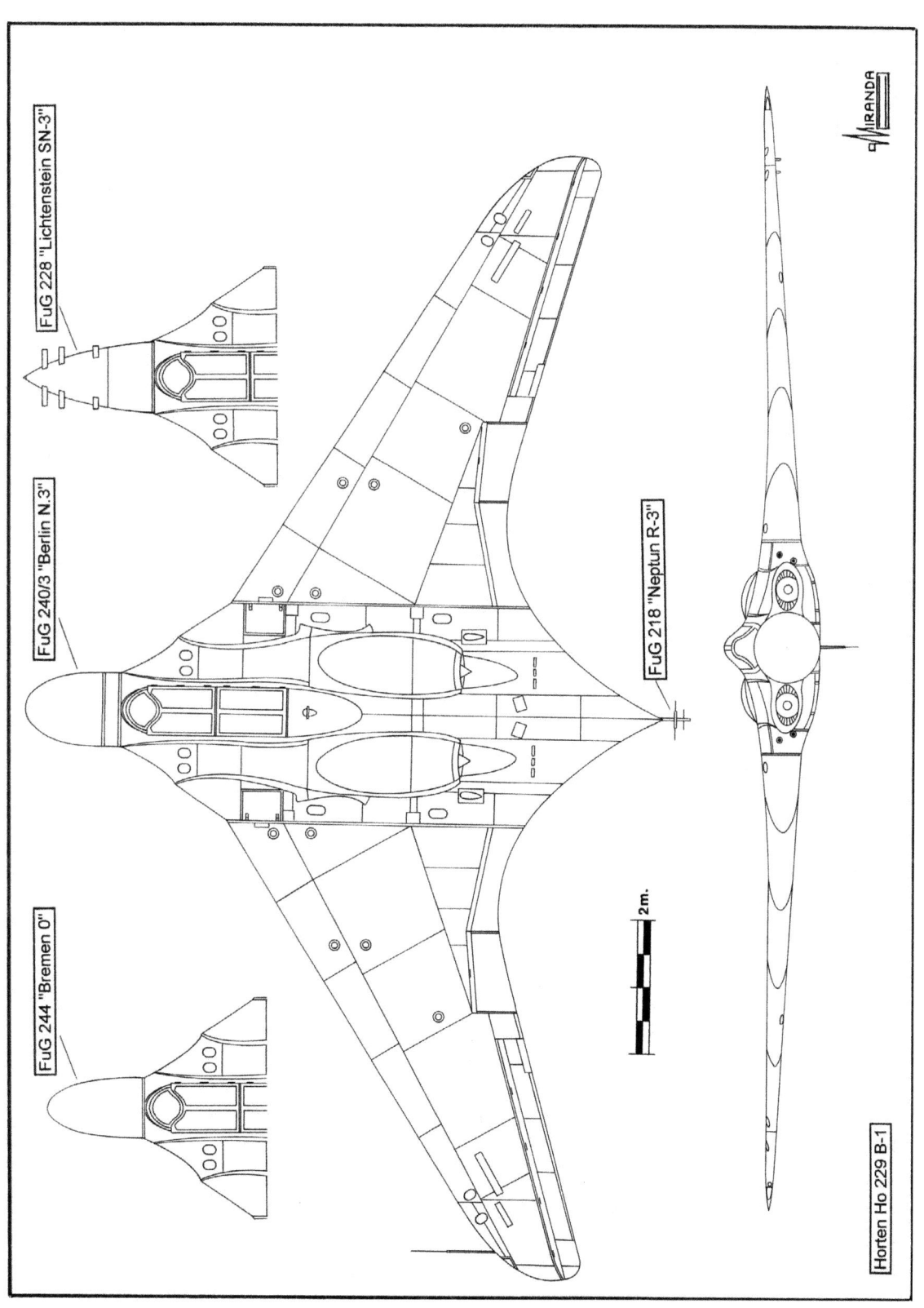

FuG 228 "Lichtenstein SN-3"

FuG 240/3 "Berlin N.3"

FuG 218 "Neptun R-3"

FuG 244 "Bremen 0"

2 m.

Horten Ho 229 B-1

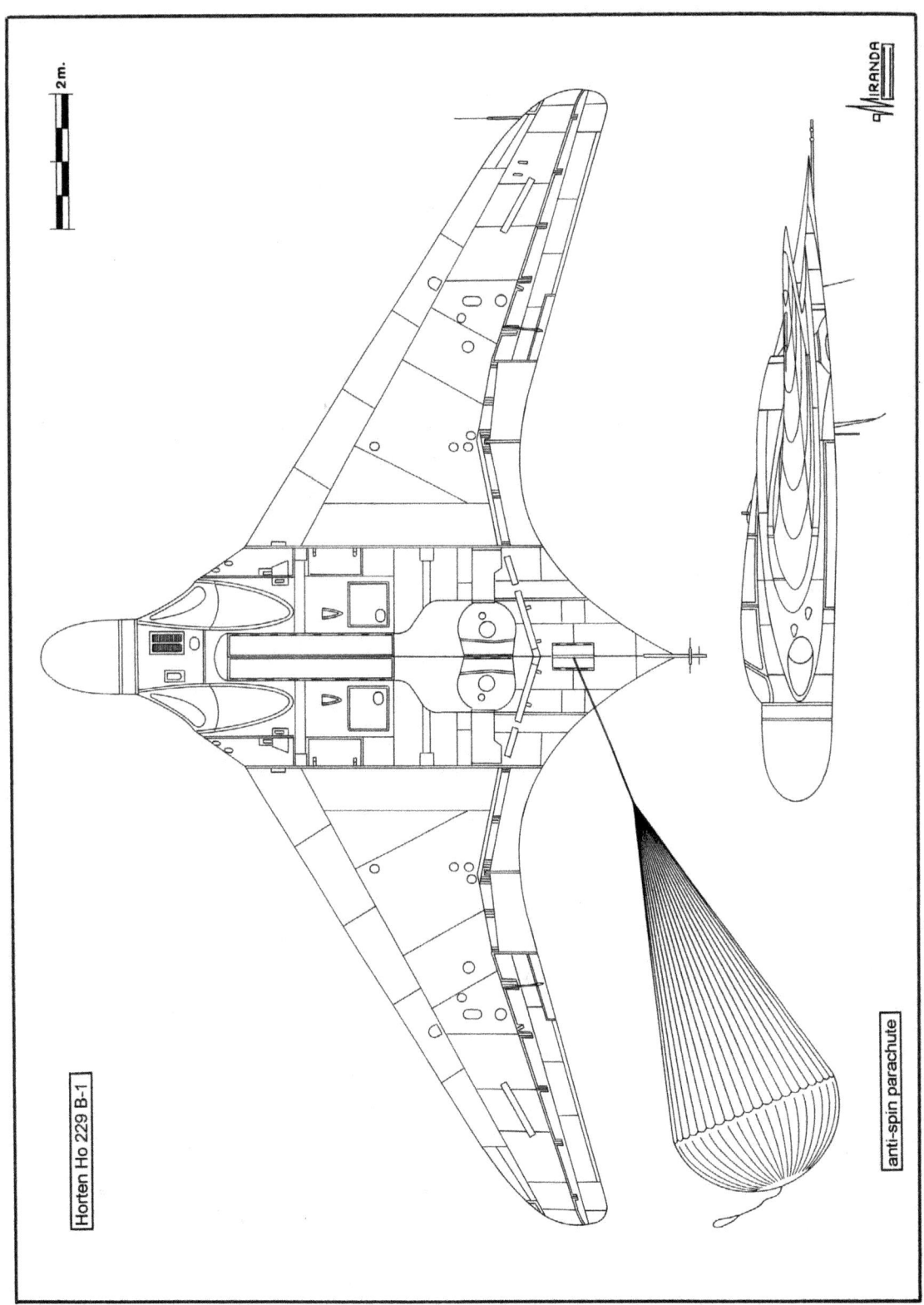

2m.

Horten Ho 229 B-1

anti-spin parachute

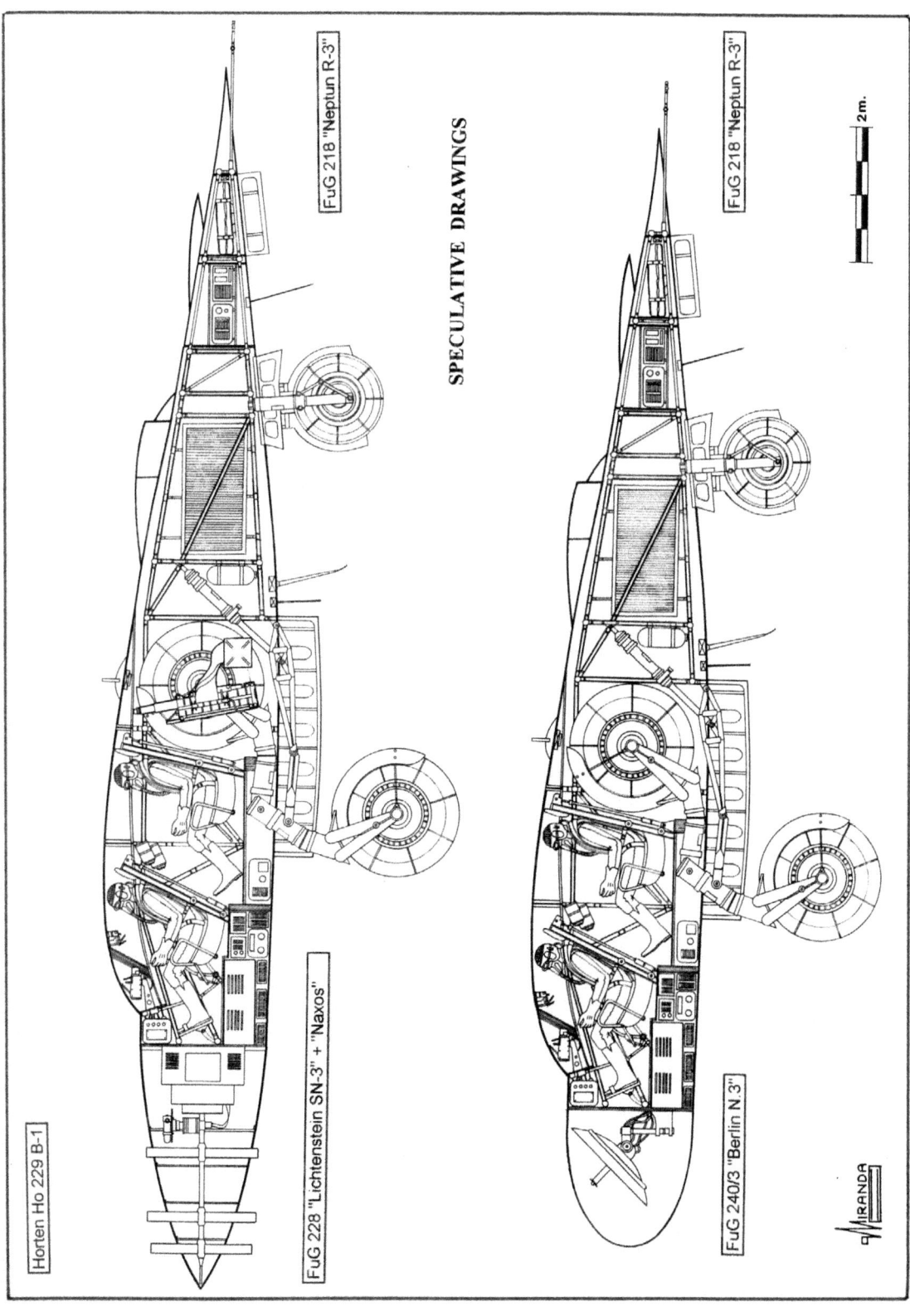

SPECULATIVE DRAWINGS

Horten Ho 229 B-1

FuG 218 "Neptun R-3"

FuG 228 "Lichtenstein SN-3" + "Naxos"

FuG 218 "Neptun R-3"

FuG 240/3 "Berlin N 3"

2m.

MIRANDA

17

Horten Ho 229 C *Schnellbomber*

After taking part in the Battle of Britain as technical officer of the JG26, Walter Horten reported to the *Jagdflugsinspektion* in May 1941.

Although very advanced for their time, the Luftwaffe was convinced that its fighters and bombers were not good enough to overcome British defences. Thanks to his new assignment, Walter had access to the new experimental DFS rocket airplanes and turbojet engines developed in secret by Bramo/BMW. He reached the conclusion that an airplane properly designed and with two turbojets could reach the speed of the DFS 194 and the flight endurance of the BF 110.

In September 1941, the Mosquito PR Mk I began to be used on photographic reconnaissance missions, flying with impunity over the Reich without being intercepted by any German fighter. The knowledge that both the DFS 194 and the Mosquito were built of wood, like the Horten sailplanes, was enough to make the two brothers start the design of their own 'German Mosquito'.

On 26 March 1942, this took the shape of a two-seat 40-degree swept flying wing of 19.09-m span, propelled by two Bramo/BMW 3302 turbojets of 600-kp thrust. It was able to carry two SC 1000 *Hermann* bombs to Scapa Flow or two SC 2500 *Max* bombs to London. It was armed with four MG 151/20 guns in the nose and a MG 81Z machine gun barbette, located at the rear of the fuselage that was remote-control aimed by the radio operator.

This design is known in specialized literature as the H VII *Schnellkampfflugzeug*. Together with the *Schnellbomber* (Fast Bomber), the Horten brothers designed a 1,000-kph single-seat fighter propelled by the same engines. It was a 40-degree swept flying wing of 19.09-m span, with the cockpit of a Ho Vc and 'trafficator type' drag rudders. This established it as a predecessor of the Horten 8-229.

There is no data about its planned armament but it seems reasonable to believe that four MG 151/20s would also have been installed into the nose. The two described projects potentially corresponded with the P.52 and P.53 designs of the *Gothaer Waggonfabrik Flugzeugbau* in Friedrichroda.

In September 1942, both projects were merged into one to make the most of the Herman Göring's *1000 x 1000 x 1000* proposal. The result was the Horten 8-229, a single-seat flying wing of 16.76-m span propelled by two BMW 003 turbojets of 800-kp thrust.

The diameter of this engine (0.69 m) was the same as that of the BMW 3302, but its length (3.56 m) did not allow its installation behind the wing spar as in the previous designs.

Two prototypes were built with the modified wing spar to house the forward section of the engine with a 2-degree slope, but when it was necessary to replace the BMW with two Jumo 004A engines of 0.96 m diameter at the beginning of 1944, the central section of the wing had to be modified again, thus preventing this airplane entering into production before the end of the war.

A design of such radical aerodynamics presented enormous problems with regards to the undercarriage, engines, armament, and flight stability, and after the loss of the Ho 229 V2 prototype and its pilot in February 1945, the Horten brothers determined to change the 'aerodynamics first' method of its design—which had previously made the Ho 229 B night fighter operationally unviable—and focus on further development capabilities and easy maintenance. The Ho 229 B night fighter could not use the new HeS 011 engines due to lack of inner room, nor could it use new radars with parabolic antennae due to the location of the air-intakes and the excess of weight that the second crew and electronic equipment exerted over the forward wheel that seriously compromised longitudinal stability.

The Ho 229 C *Schnellbomber*, a 45-degree swept wing with 16.6-m span, emerged as a result of the Hortens' changed mentality. Its tailfin and rudder provided longitudinal stability in case of malfunctioning in one of the turbojets, as well as the capacity to quickly recover control after going through a barrier of explosions produced by AA batteries. The single-seat cockpit located at the tailfin base, in a Lippisch style, could be easily converted into a twin seat for the night fighter version without having to increase the aircraft length.

The two Jumo 004B turbojets were suspended under the central section of the wing, allowing easy access for maintenance and eventual replacement in the future by others of wider diameter of the HeS 011 type. The new distribution of weights allowed the adoption of a better balanced landing gear, with a small forward wheel that folded under the pilot seat instead of it using the room reserved for the second crew, like in the Ho 229. The armament was increased to four Mk 108/30 cannons and two SC 500 bombs suspended under the outer wings. The location of the air intakes allowed the installation of voluminous radar in the nose, without any aerodynamic interference from the parabolic antenna fairing in the air flux, which was required by the engines.

The expectation was that all these advantages would outweigh the loss of performance produced by the extra drag.

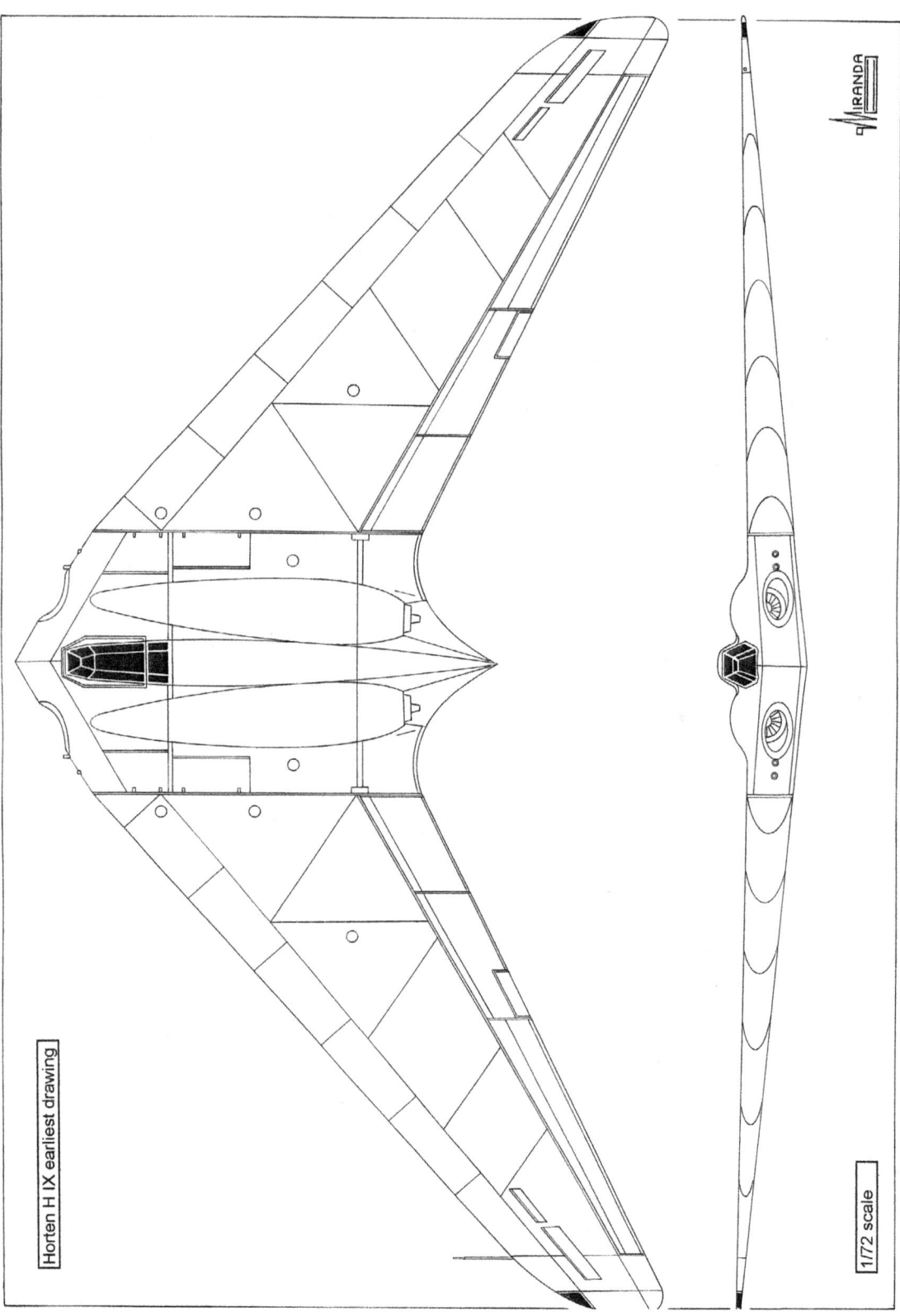

Horten H IX earliest drawing

1/72 scale

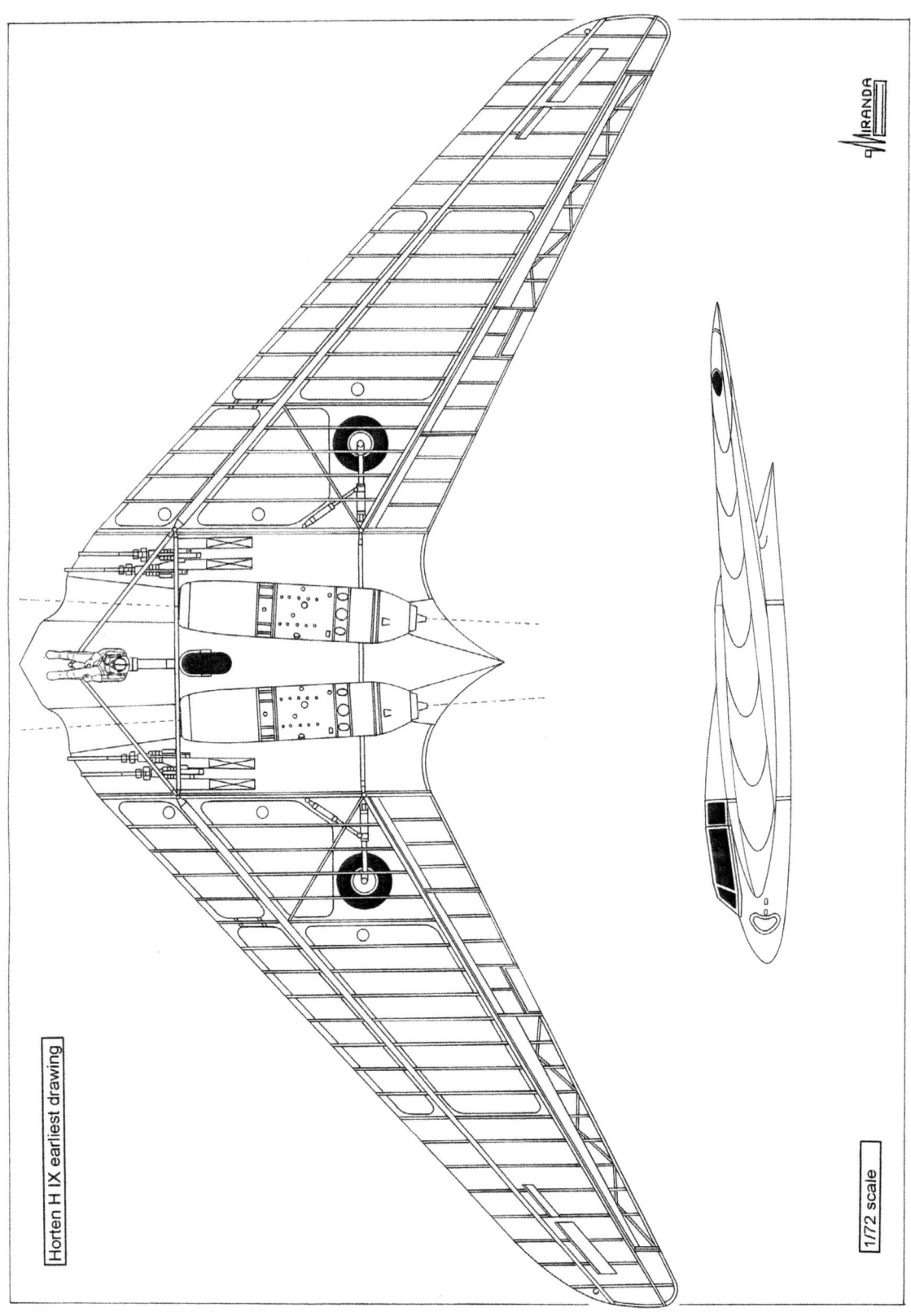

Horten H IX earliest drawing

1/72 scale

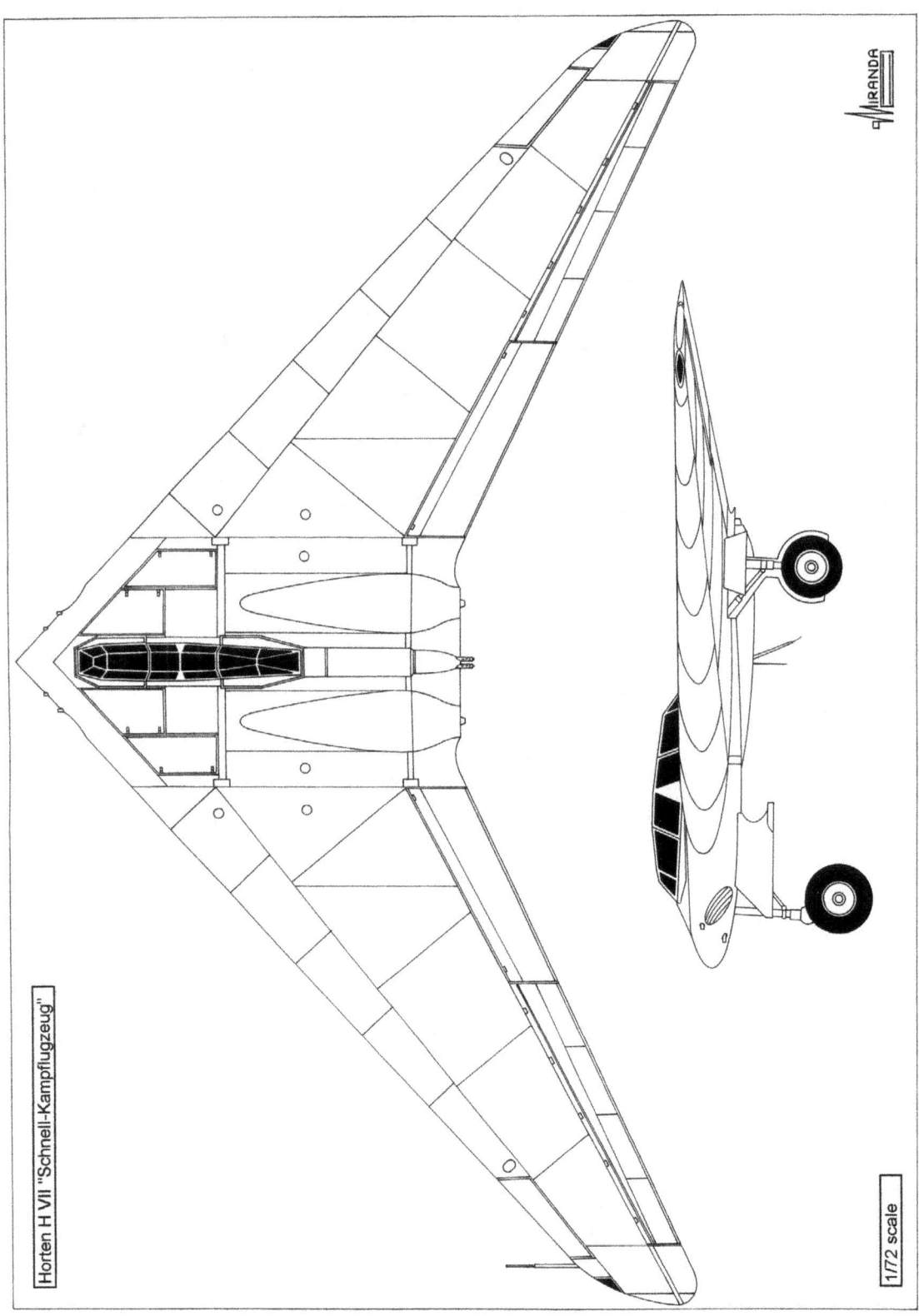

Horten H VII "Schnell-Kampflugzeug"

1/72 scale

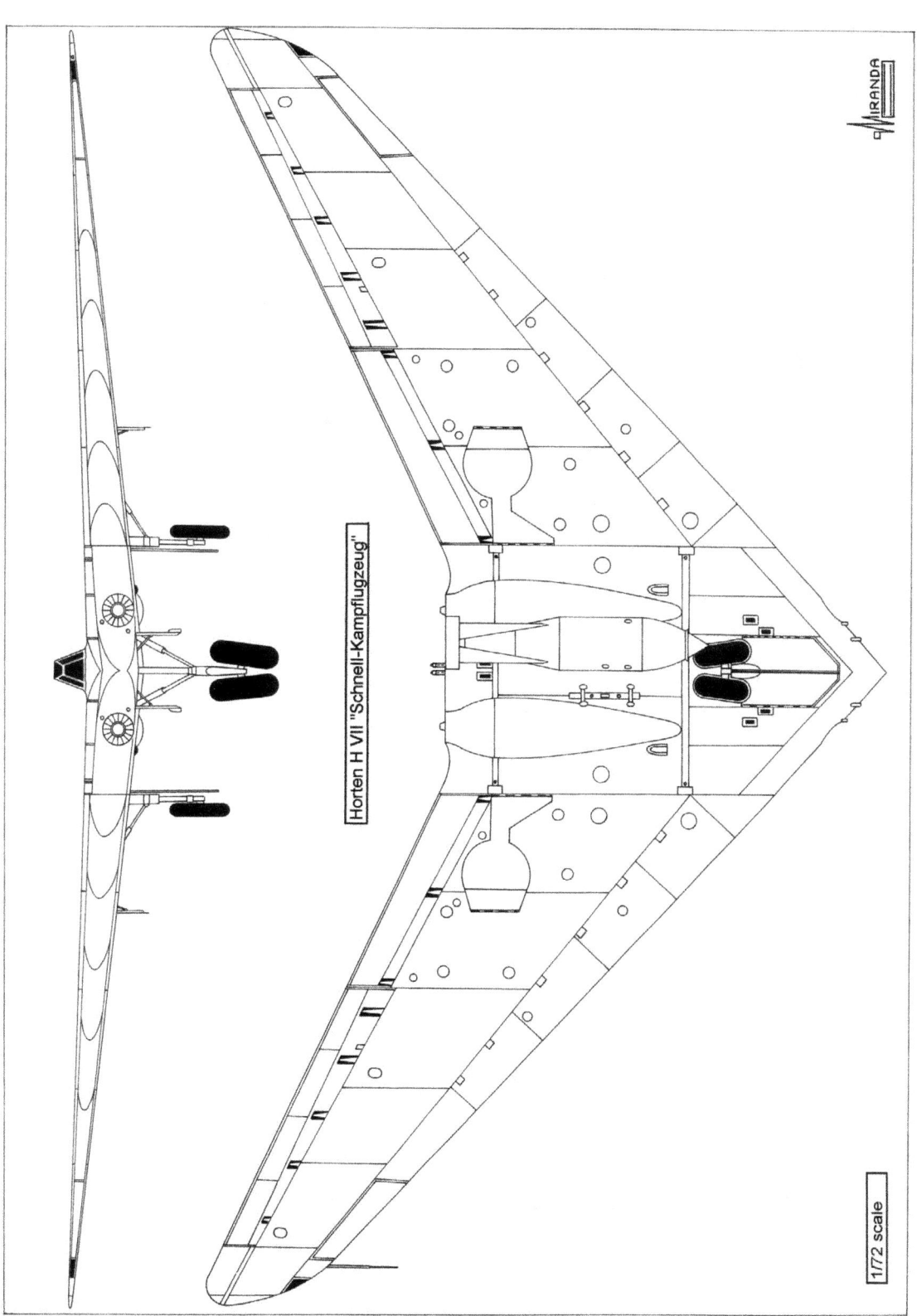

Horten H VII "Schnell-Kampflugzeug"

1/72 scale

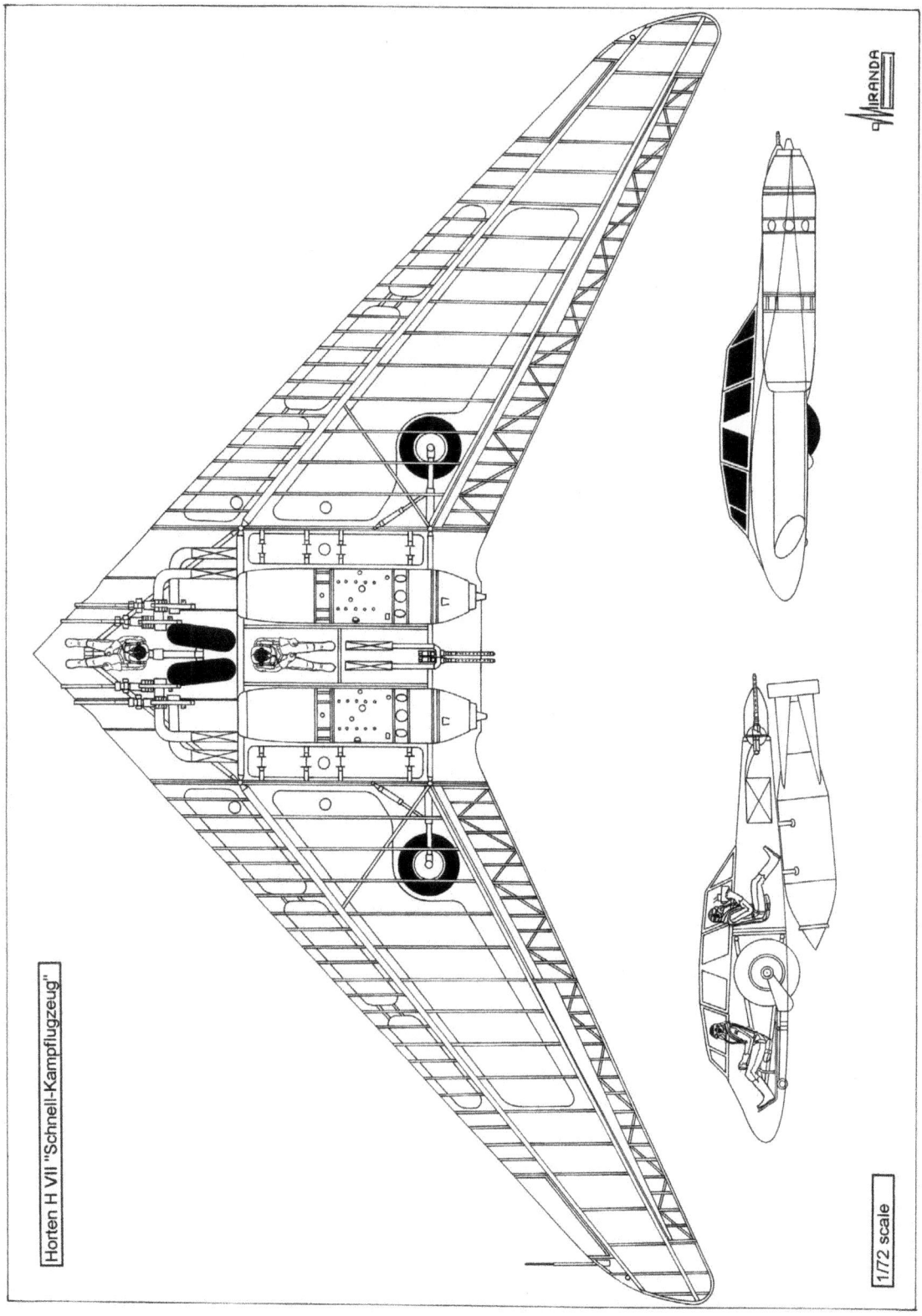

Horten H VII "Schnell-Kampflugzeug"

1/72 scale

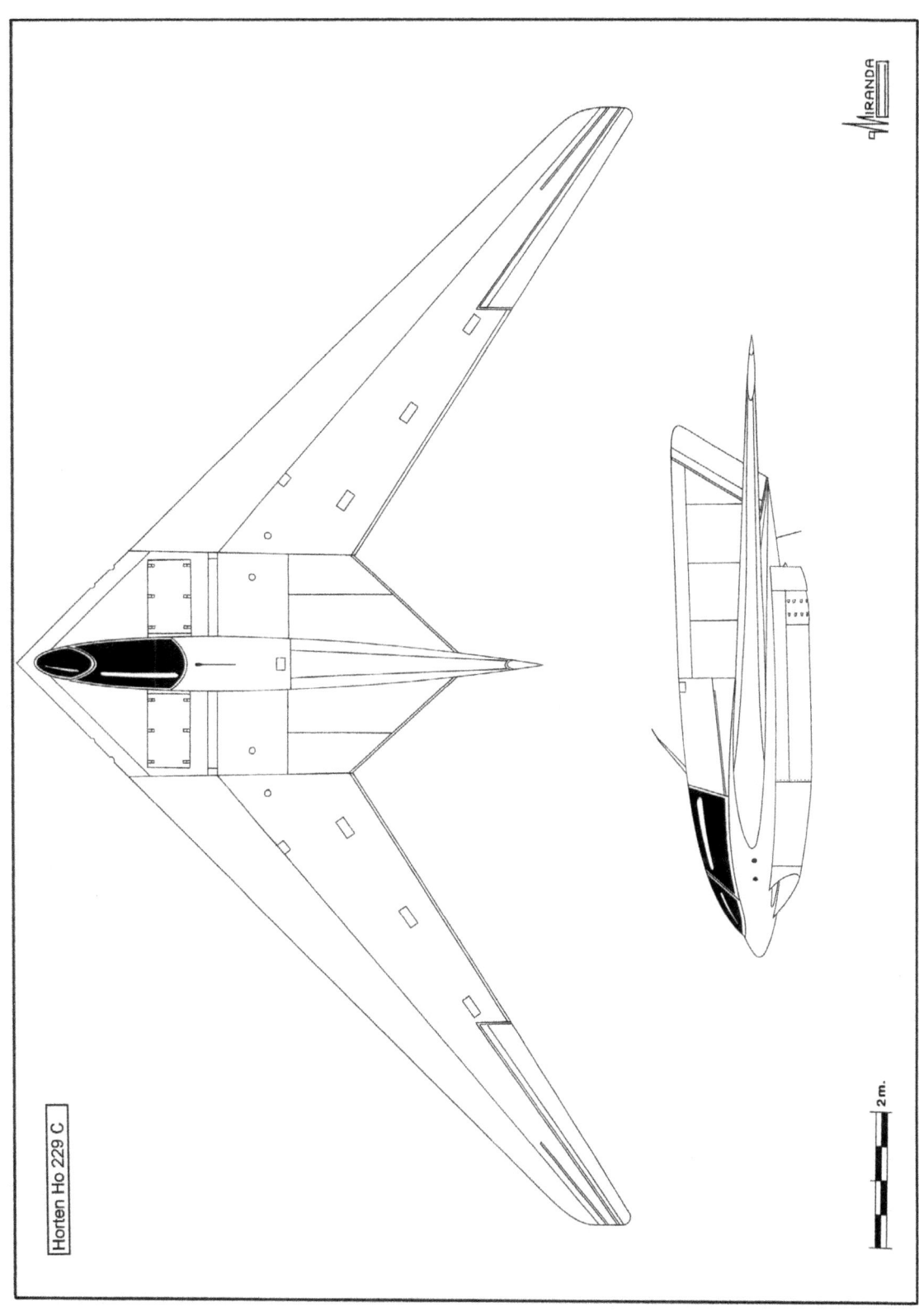

Horten Ho 229 C

2 m.

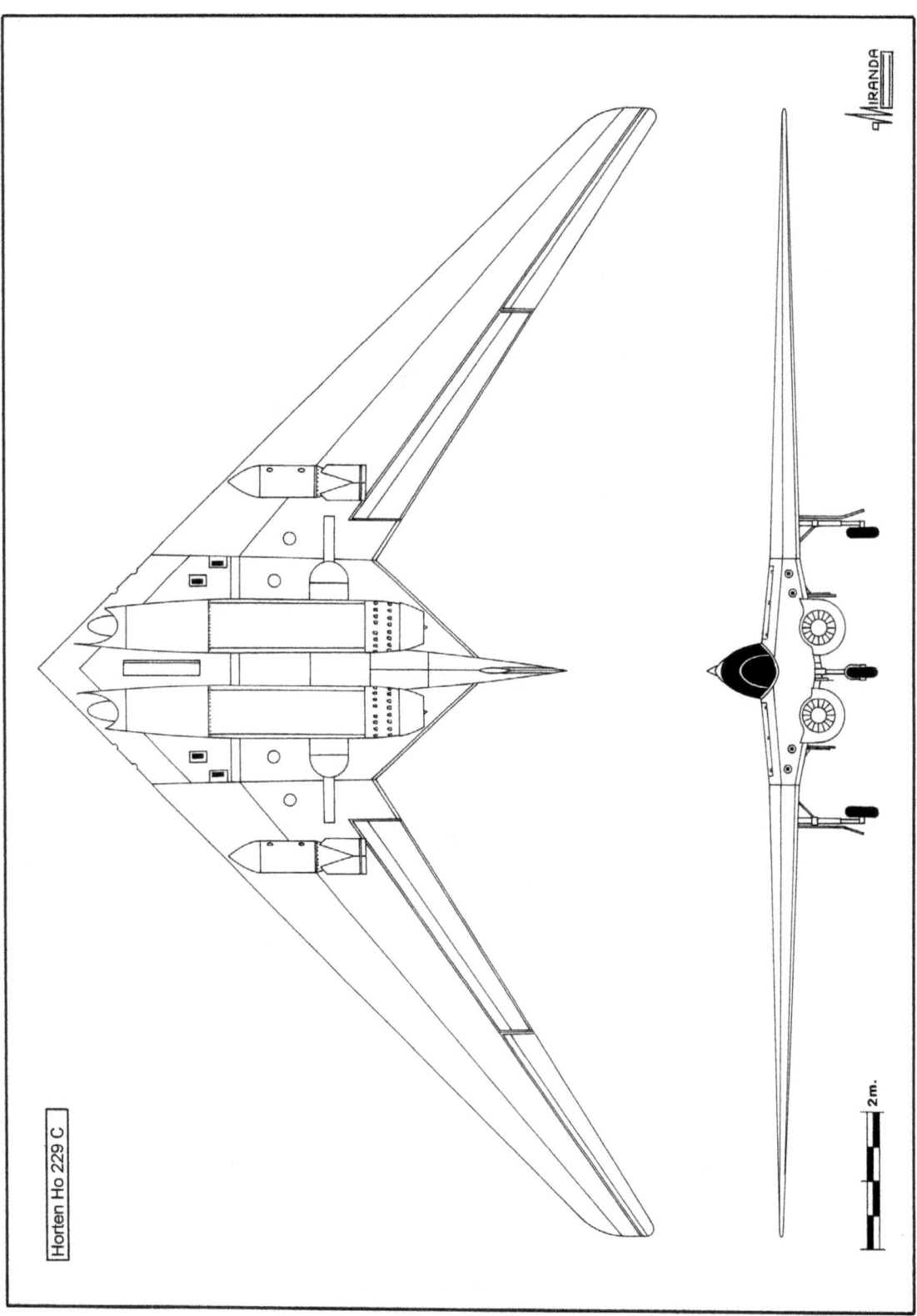

Horten Ho 229 C

2m.

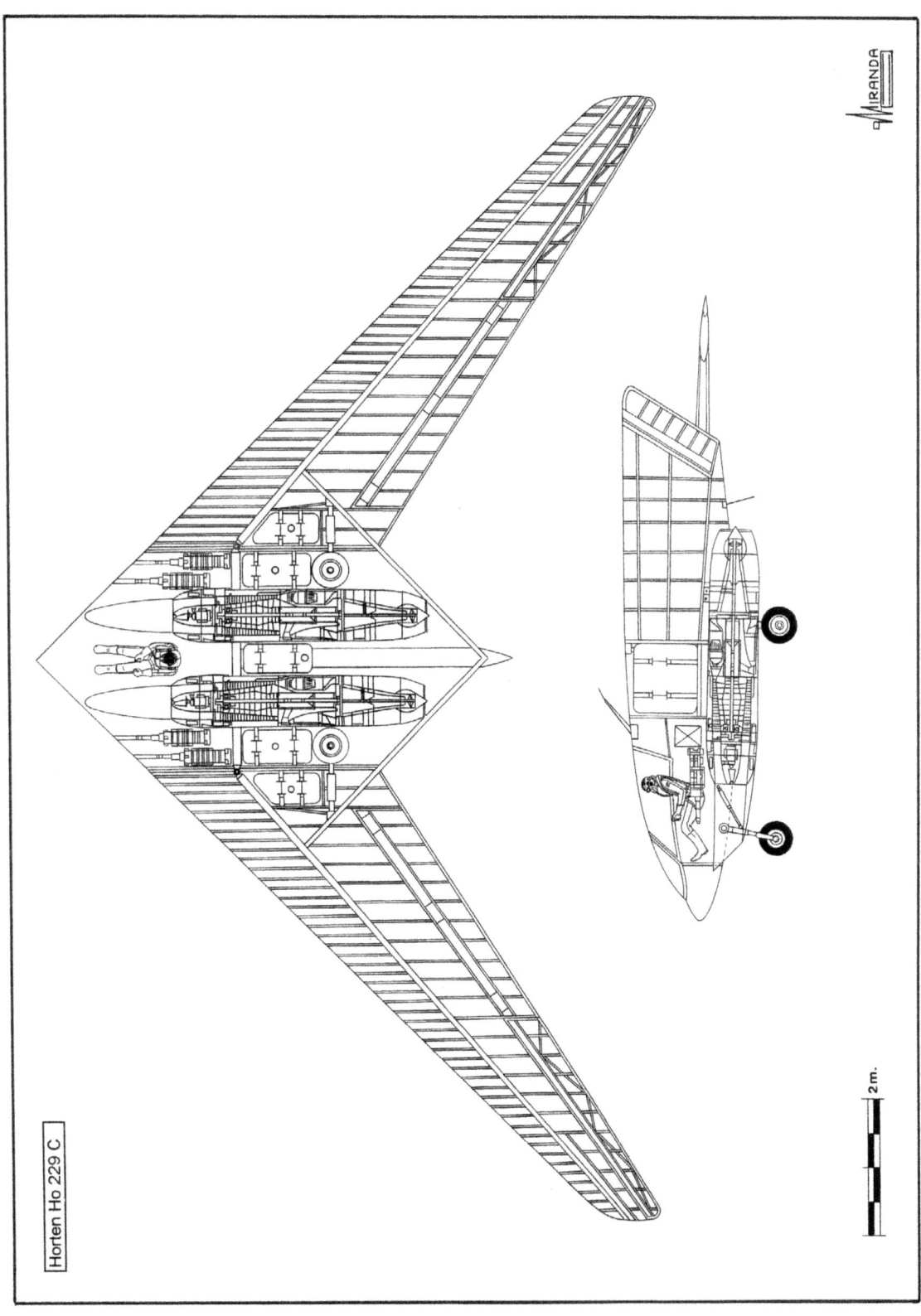

Horten Ho 229 C

2 m.

Chapter 18

Horten Ho X series

By mid-1944, the Oberkommando der Luftwaffe was forced to recognise that Messerschmitt's Me 262 heavy fighter, specifically designed to destroy bombers, left a lot to be desired when sent into close combat with conventional Allied fighters.

Below 7,000 rpm, the throttle had to be increased slowly to avoid the turbojets stopping without warning. Its service ceiling was insufficient, its manufacturing expensive, and its maintenance complex. Besides, like most heavy fighters designed in 1939, the Me 262 had serious problems concerning compressibility buffeting—an aerodynamic phenomenon unidentified until 1941—which caused the nacelles to generate a turbulent transonic flux during combat dives between 30,000 and 18,000 feet.

To overcome these deficiencies, the Technical Office of the Luftwaffe published the *Miniaturjäger* specification in November 1944, which looked for new jet fighter manufacturing techniques that utilized non-strategic materials and cheap pulsejet engines.

By mid-1944, the *Jägernotprogramm* contest was announced to build a high-altitude interceptor that was able to improve the performance of the Me 262 above 36,000 feet; on 8 September 1944, the *Volksjäger* specification was published. Its objective was to have a light jet fighter successor to the Bf 109 able to face the third generation of Allied fighters predicted for 1945.

The winner of the contest was the Blohm & Voss P.211 project, although its mass production was left aside in favour of the Heinkel P.1073 (later on known as He 162) as its construction required a lesser quantity of strategic materials. That was also the reason to reject the *Flitzer* and *Volksflugzeug* projects proposed by Focke Wulf. The Arado E-580 was also rejected due to poor visibility from its cockpit.

The Horten design team, having already presented their Ho IX as a candidate for the *Jägernotprogramm*, proposed a single-engine, scaled-down version of the Ho IX V6 as a *Volksjäger* solution under the designation Ho X. It was a very fast airplane that admitted the installation of either heavy or light armament and several types of turbojets. The Luftwaffe considered that it was not safe for use by inexperienced pilots due to its tendency to fall into a flat spin. This project is also referred to as Horten IX B in some publications, possibly referring to its initial design that included a BMW 003 turbojet.

During the two last years of the war, an ultra-secret research programme was developed in Germany under the name *Höchstgeschwindigkeit* (HG) with the objective of finding aerodynamic solutions to the compressibility buffeting issues. Messerschmitt proposed to refine the basic aerodynamic design of the Me 262 in a series of HG projects and prototypes. Moreover, new shapes of wings, fuselages and air intakes used in the air superiority fighters P.1106, 1110, 1111, and 1112 were attempted. The construction of a rocket airplane, specifically designed for transonic flight tests, was also proposed. It was a variant of the P.1106, named P.1106 R, which may be considered the equivalent to the American Bell X-1.

Alexander Lippisch proposed the construction of a delta ramjet plane named P.12 and two delta rocket planes—the DM-2, for transonic flight testing, and the DM-3, for supersonic flight testing. The DFS technical team started the construction of the DFS 346 in 1945. It was a swept-winged rocket transonic plane, able to explore transonic flight, which finally flew under Soviet supervision after the war.

All these airplanes were meant for very powerful engines—some ramjets produced up to 60,000 hp—to overcome the increasing air drag in their approach to the mythical sound barrier.

Themselves diverging from solutions favouring brute force, the Hortens believed that a small, aerodynamically perfect airplane, propelled by a single turbojet of 1,300 kp, could be built with non-strategic materials to obtain performance data on the transonic flow during a series of flights in gentle dive. This project was named Ho X to make Allied intelligence believe that it was a *Volksjäger* design. It had a 70-degree swept delta wing built of plywood and steel tubing, with the pilot in prone position and the turbojet installed within the central section with a dorsal air-intake.

To the Hortens, the transonic accident suffered on 6 July 1944 in the Me 163 V18 prototype during a test flight—in which almost the entire rudder of the aircraft was ripped away upon reaching 1,130 kph—suggested that tailfin vibrations and drag had to be prevented. Such yaw control was obtained in the Ho X by retractable drag rods located in the wingtips.

The small airplane, spanning just 7.2 m, needed to have a long runway and a great consumption of fuel to take off on its own. Therefore, it had to be transported in *Mistel* configuration by a specialized airplane. The launch had to be made at an altitude of 26,200 feet after which the Ho X would then climb up to 49,200 feet on its own. At that point, it would start a shallow dive, progressively increasing the speed until a theoretical limit of 1,195 kph (Mach 1.07) at 19,700 feet.

To protect the pilot from the highly destructive vibrations expected to be encountered during the transonic phase of the flight, the Hortens considered the use of a fantastic device—the *Wasserkabine* (water-cockpit). Although knowledge on the *Wasserkabine* is extremely limited, it seems to have been a kind of ejectable survival capsule. It was full of water during the critical phase of the flight, to protect the pilot (in prone-position and a *Druckanzug*—a full-pressure suit) from both the vibrations and the extreme physical conditions expected in case of ejection at high altitude.

Supposedly, there would have been a fast system to disconnect flying controls and no electronic equipment within the cockpit—except for the telephone wire to communicate with the launch airplane. The forward section of the water-cockpit should have allowed enough visibility for the pilot to see the instrument board located outside it and downwards. Thus, and combined with the characteristic raised angle-of-attack (AOA) of the delta plane, the pilot could not see the runway during landing.

To prevent discomfort and great reduction of visibility, it is possible that the water-cockpit was only partially filled before the launch, either by pumping water from the mother airplane or perhaps transferring it from some ballast tanks located in the Ho X.

An approximate estimation of the weight of the water is 400 kg, which, accumulating in the forward part of the airplane, would make the nose slightly heavy. This feature might be useful during dive flight but would make things very difficult at landing. It seems reasonable to assume that the water was evacuated outside to improve exterior visibility and reduce weight before landing. A similar procedure was used to drop the water ballast during the test flights of the *Reichenberg*, the piloted version of the V-1.

The speculative drawings showing the possible internal structure of the Ho X merely reflect the conjectures of the author. The Ho X project started with a series of test flights in Hornberg and Göttingen with scale models made of balsa wood. Afterwards, construction of a wooden glider (1/1 scale) was started to investigate subsonic handling and landing problems, but the work was not finished by the end of the war in Europe.

The plan was to install a conventional Argus engine pusher to make dive flying tests until reaching a maximum speed of 500 kph. The next phase of the project would have consisted of building the prototype (Ho X *Entwurf I*) equipped with a He S 011 turbojet and *Wasserkabine* for transonic flight testing. Prior studies made with the control system proved that the drag rods could not be extended or retracted fast enough during flight at high speed.

The *Entwurf II* variant, with a tailfin located over the turbojet, was then designed. Aerodynamic tests conducted in a wind tunnel proved that the engine had many possibilities to stop during landing at high Angle of Attack (AOA), because the air intake stayed within the aerodynamic shadow produced by the nose.

The *Entwurf III* configuration appeared at this point with a tailfin and the air intake in ventral position. Such precautions proved to be unfounded when the very similar British airplane Handley Page H.P. 115 flew in 1961, equipped with a dorsal air intake, without any stopping of the engine.

Published in 1998, *The Horten Brothers* by Dr David Myhra revealed, among other unknown projects, the existence of the Horten *Ho X-B*, on which only two pictures of a scale model have ever come into circulation. It seems to have been a combat version of the Ho X, somehow slower and more manoeuverable with a 60-degree delta wing and a *Strahlrudder* in the exhaust nozzle. The scale drawings pictured here, produced to speculatively recreate the interior, are solely based on the author's personal knowledge and the known data of other similar designs.

Jet Planes of the Third Reich, the Secret Projects by German historian Manfred Griehl was also published in 1998, and included a drawing of an airplane referred to as *Ho 13-C*. In the author's opinion, it is a third supersonic version of the Ho X, with a reheated HeS 011 B engine and expansive conical nozzle.

According to the hypothetical reconstruction of the inside shown in the drawings below, it ought to have been possible for the pilot to have been not in prone position, but in a semi-prone 'praying mantis' position, more suited to air combat and already adopted in the Ho IV sailplane. It is probably more accurate to refer to this project as *Ho X-C*, since it is clearly derived from the Ho X and without any structural relationship to the swept-winged Ho XIII interceptor.

Technical data *Volksjäger I*

Engine Type	BMW 003 E
Engine Power	900 kp
Usage	fighter
Stage	Model
Structure	steel and wood
Wingspan	14 m
Length	7.2 m
Height	2.3 m
Pilot	seated
Wing Area	35 sq. m
Sweep	43/60 degrees
Max. Weight	6,075 kg
Wing Loading	173.6 kg/sq. m
Armament	1 Mk 108/30 and 2 x MG 131

Technical data *Volksjäger II*

Engine Type	HeS 011
Engine Power	1,300 kp
Usage	fighter
Stage	drawing
Structure	steel and wood
Wingspan	14 m
Length	7.2 m
Height	2.3 m
Pilot	seated
Wing Area	35 sq. m
Sweep	43/60 degrees
Max. Weight 6	,000 kg
Wing Loading	171.4 kg/sq. m
Landing Speed	100 kph
Max. Speed Level	1,100 kph
Armament	1 Mk 213/30 and 2 x MG 131
Ceiling	49,200 feet
Range	2,000 km

Technical data Ho X Glider 1st

Usage	research
Stage	prototype
Structure	wood
Wingspan	7.2 m
Length	10 m
Height	2.38 m
Pilot	prone
Wing Area	37.8 sq. m
Sweep	70 degrees
Thickness	7 per cent
Empty Weight	300 kg
Max. Weight	400 kg
Wing Loading	10.5 kg/sq. m
Armament	none

Technical data Ho X Glider 2nd

Engine Type	As 10C
Engine Power	240 hp
Usage	research
Stage	project
Structure	wood
Wingspan	7.2 m
Length	10 m
Height	2.38 m
Pilot	prone
Wing Area	37.8 sq. m
Sweep	70 degrees
Thickness	7 per cent
Empty Weight	600 kg
Max. Weight	700 kg
Wing Loading	18.5 kg/sq. m
Stall Speed	56 kph
Landing Speed	88 kph
Max. Speed Dive	500 kph
Armament	none

Technical data Ho X—A

Engine Type	HeS 011
Engine Power	1,300 kp
Usage	research
Stage	project
Structure	steel and wood
Wingspan	7.2 m

Length	10 m
Height	2.38 m
Pilot	prone
Wing Area	37.8 sq. m
Sweep	70 degrees
Thickness	7 per cent
Max. Weight	7,000 kg
Wing Loading	185 kg/sq. m
Max. Speed Level	1,000 kph
Max. Speed Dive	1,200 kph
Armament	none
Ceiling	49,200 feet
Range	2,000 km

Technical data Ho X—B (probable)

Engine Type	HeS 011
Engine Power	1,300 kp
Usage	fighter
Stage	project
Structure	steel and wood
Wingspan	7.2 m
Length	9.8 m
Pilot	seated
Sweep	65 degrees
Armament	four Mk 213/30

Technical data Ho X—C (probable)

Engine Type	HeS 011B
Engine Power	1,500 kp
Usage	fighter
Stage	project
Structure	steel and wood
Wingspan	7.2 m
Length	12 m
Height	2.25 m
Pilot	semi prone
Wing Area	37.8 sq. m
Sweep	70 degrees
Thickness	7 per cent
Armament	four Mk 213/30

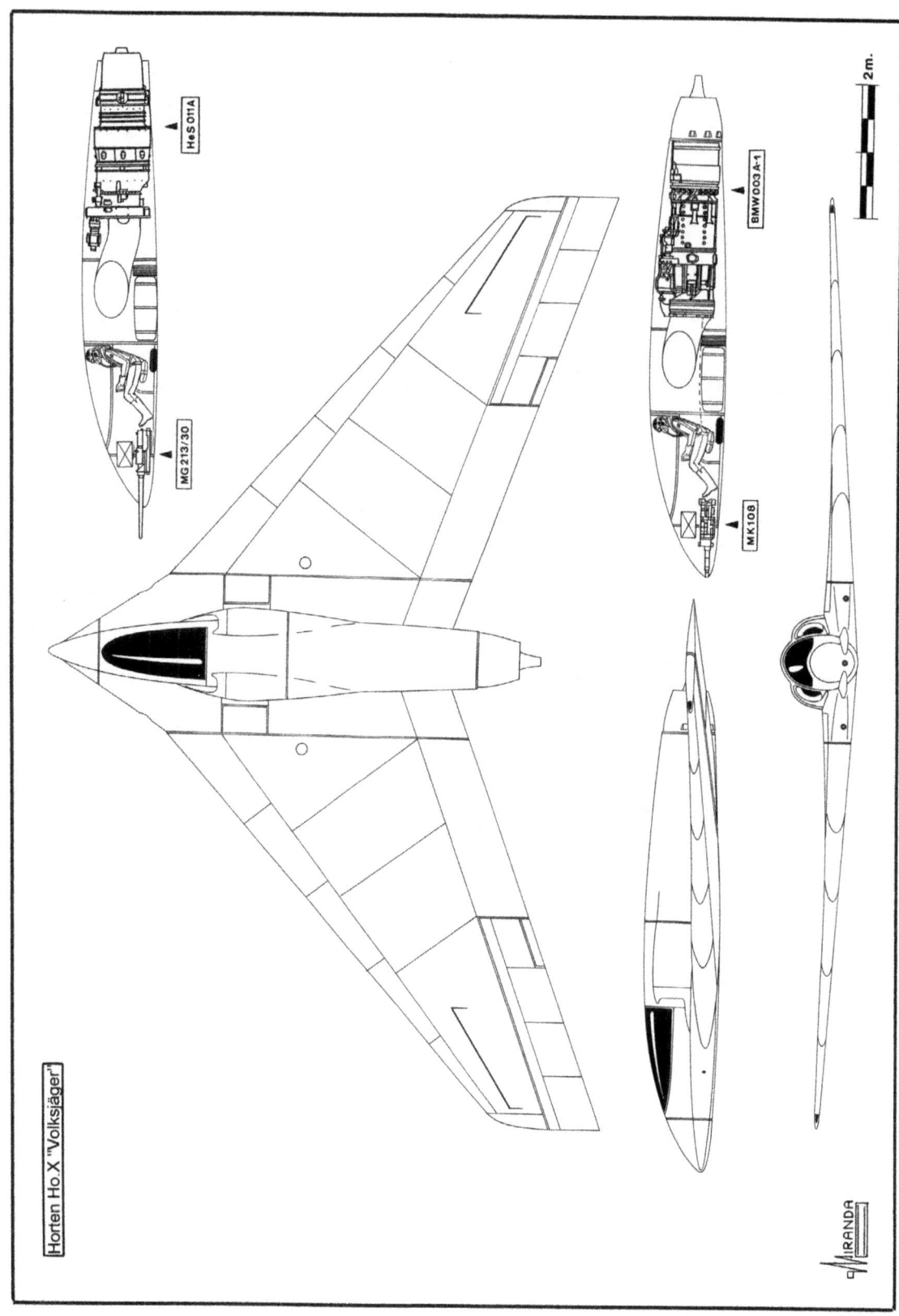

HeS 011A

MG 213/30

BMW 003 A-1

MK 108

2 m.

Horten Ho. X "Volksjäger"

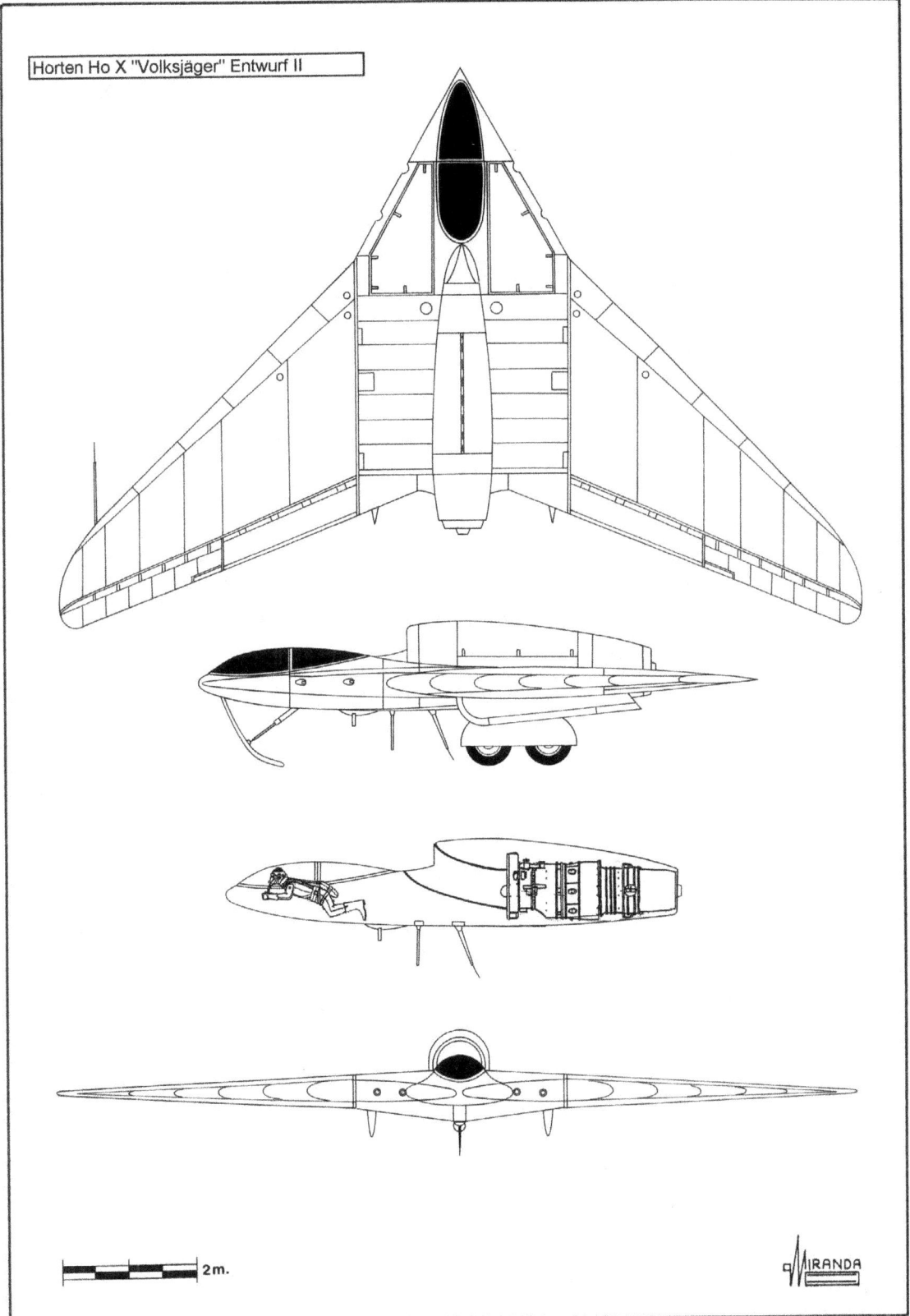

Horten Ho X "Volksjäger" Entwurf II

2m.

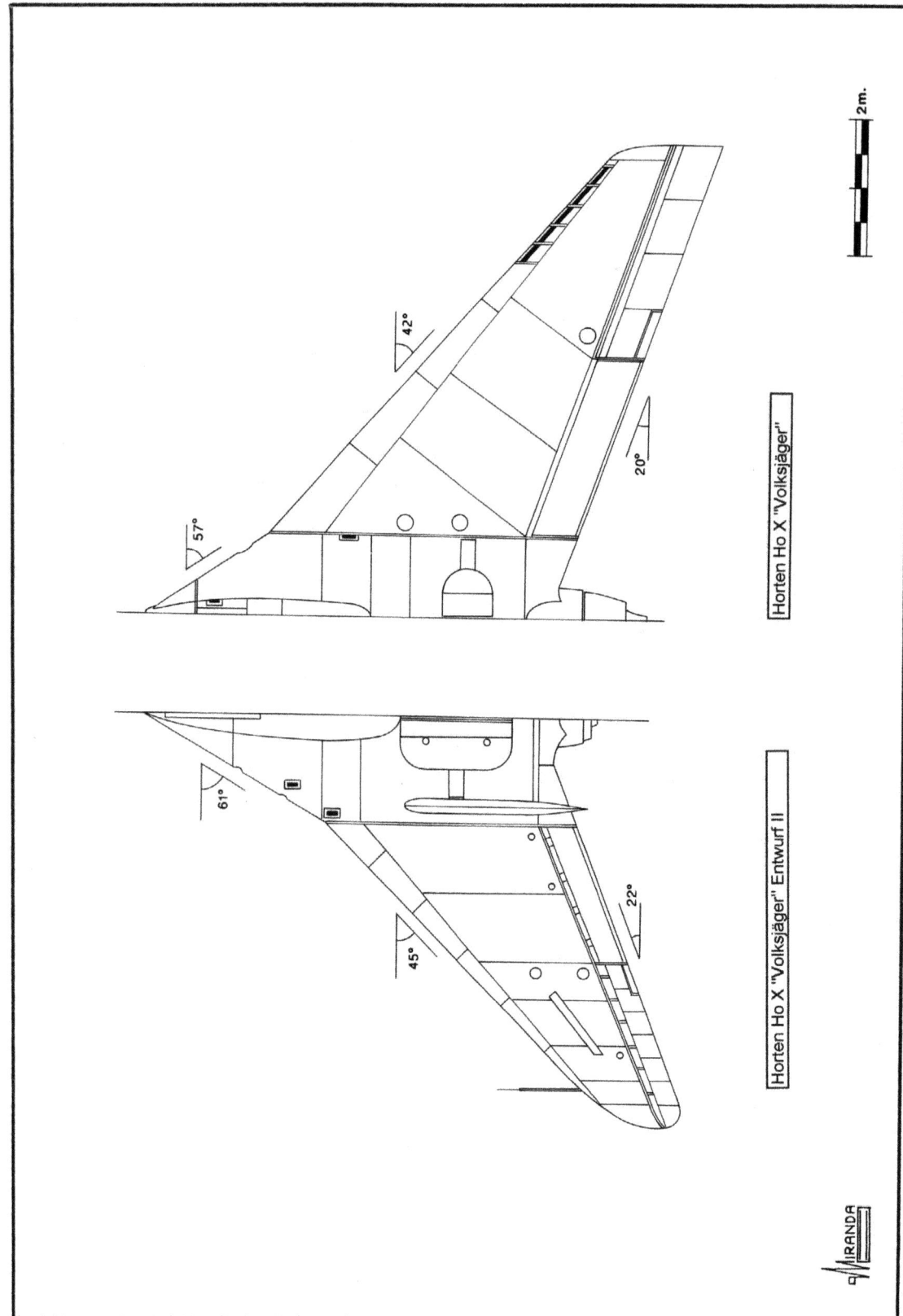

57°

42°

20°

Horten Ho X "Volksjäger"

2 m.

61°

45°

22°

Horten Ho X "Volksjäger" Entwurf II

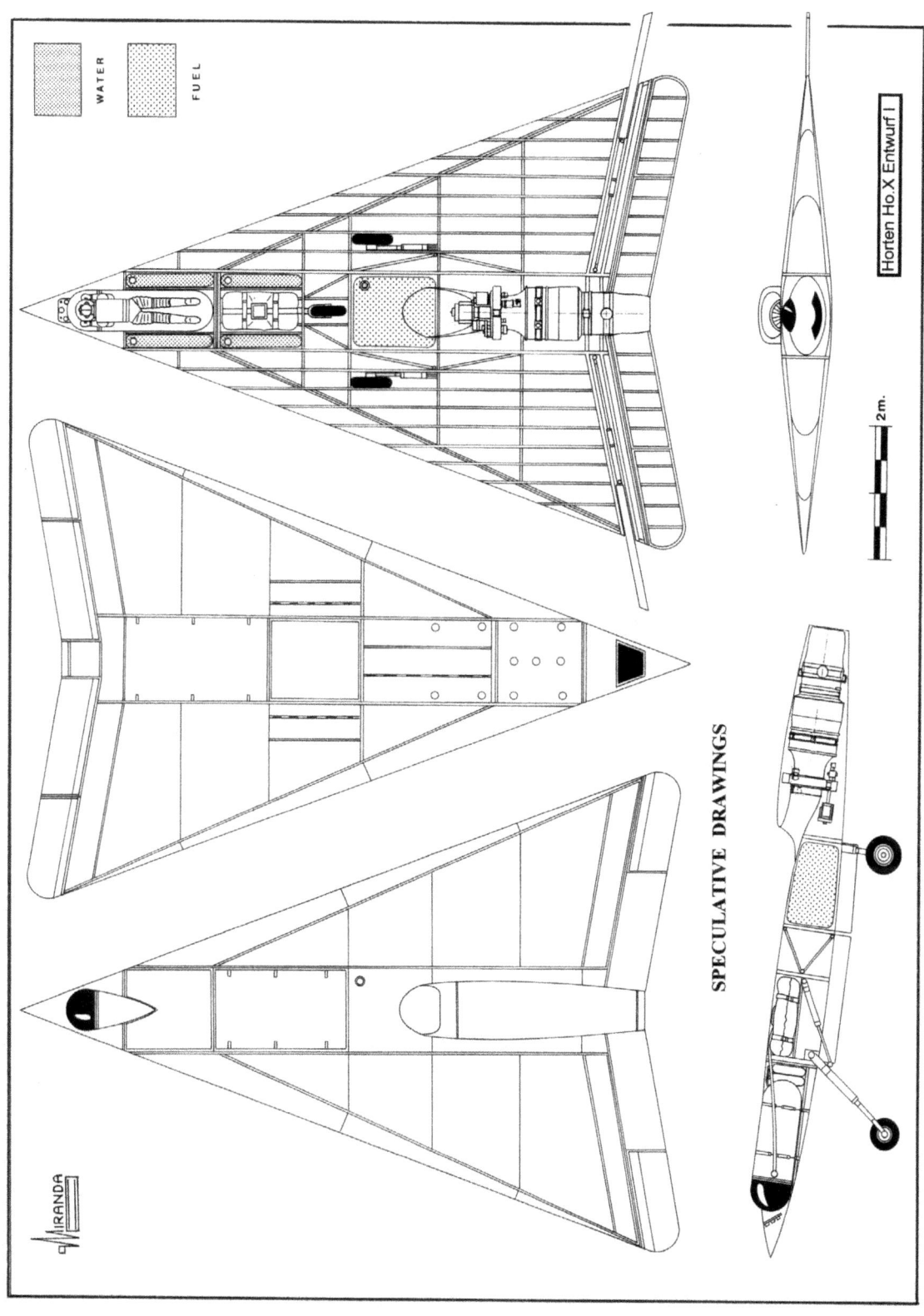

WATER

FUEL

Horten Ho X Entwurf I

2 m.

SPECULATIVE DRAWINGS

MIRANDA

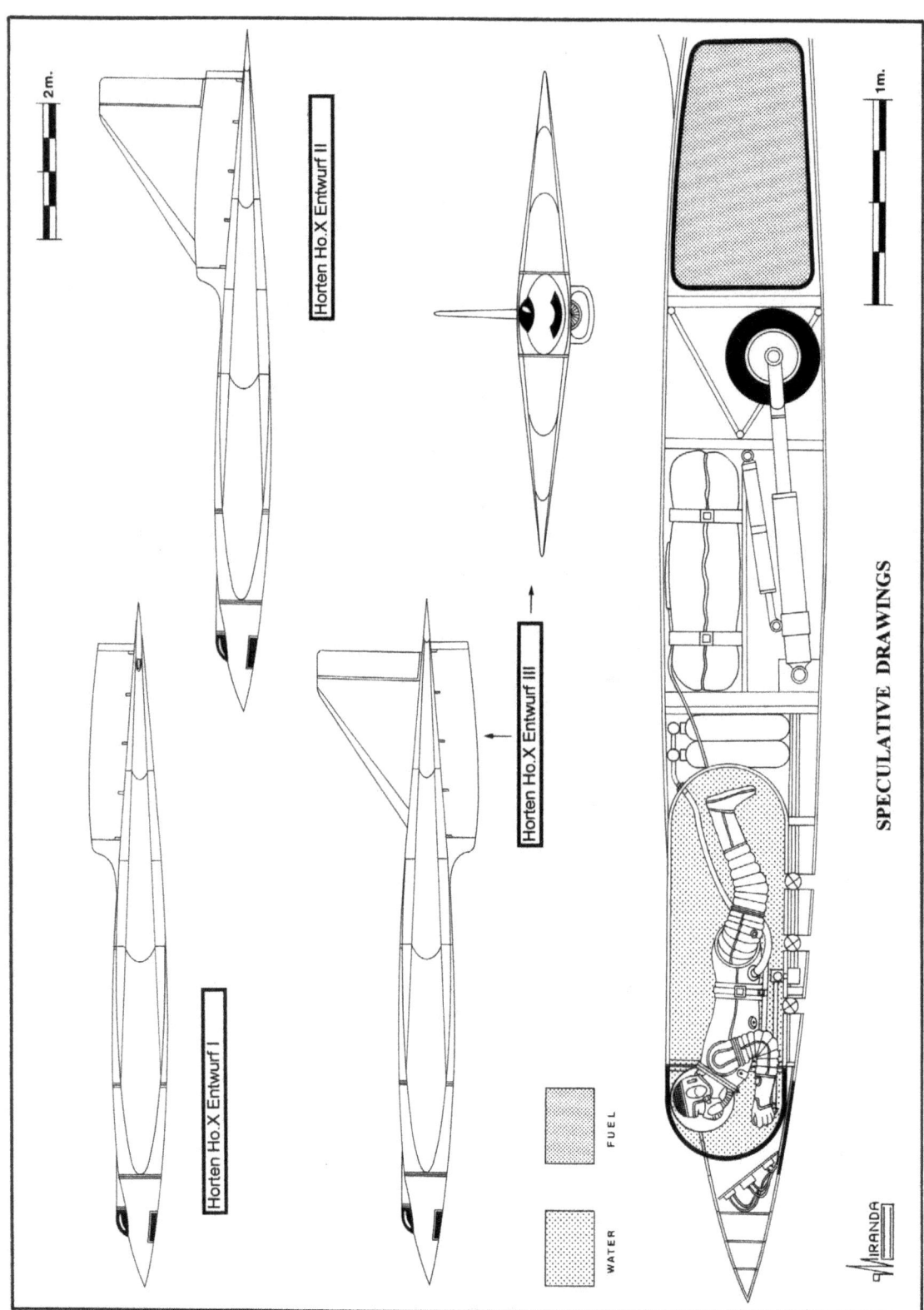

2 m.

Horten Ho.X Entwurf II

Horten Ho.X Entwurf III

Horten Ho.X Entwurf I

1 m.

SPECULATIVE DRAWINGS

FUEL

WATER

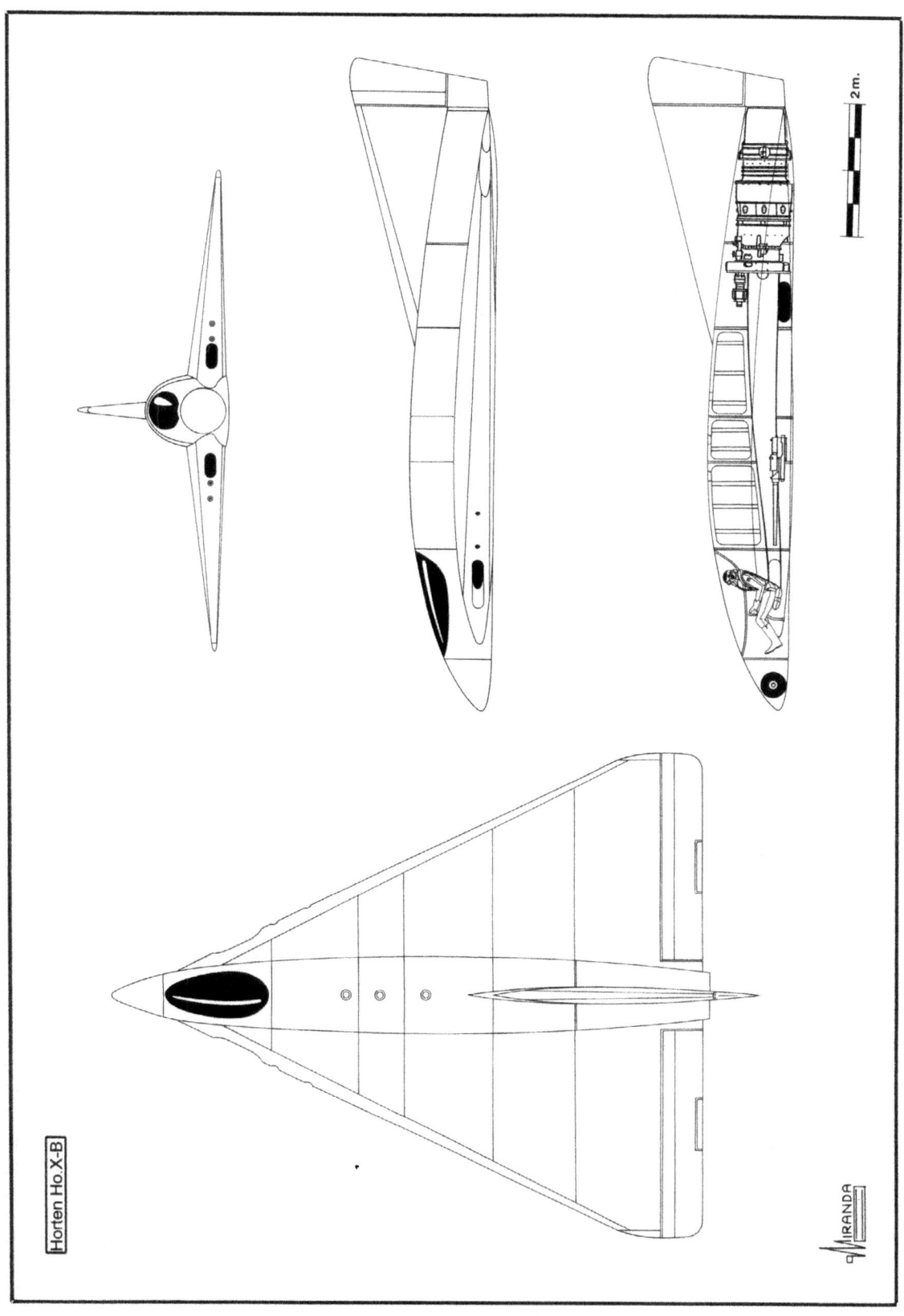

2 m.

Horten Ho.X-B

MIRANDA

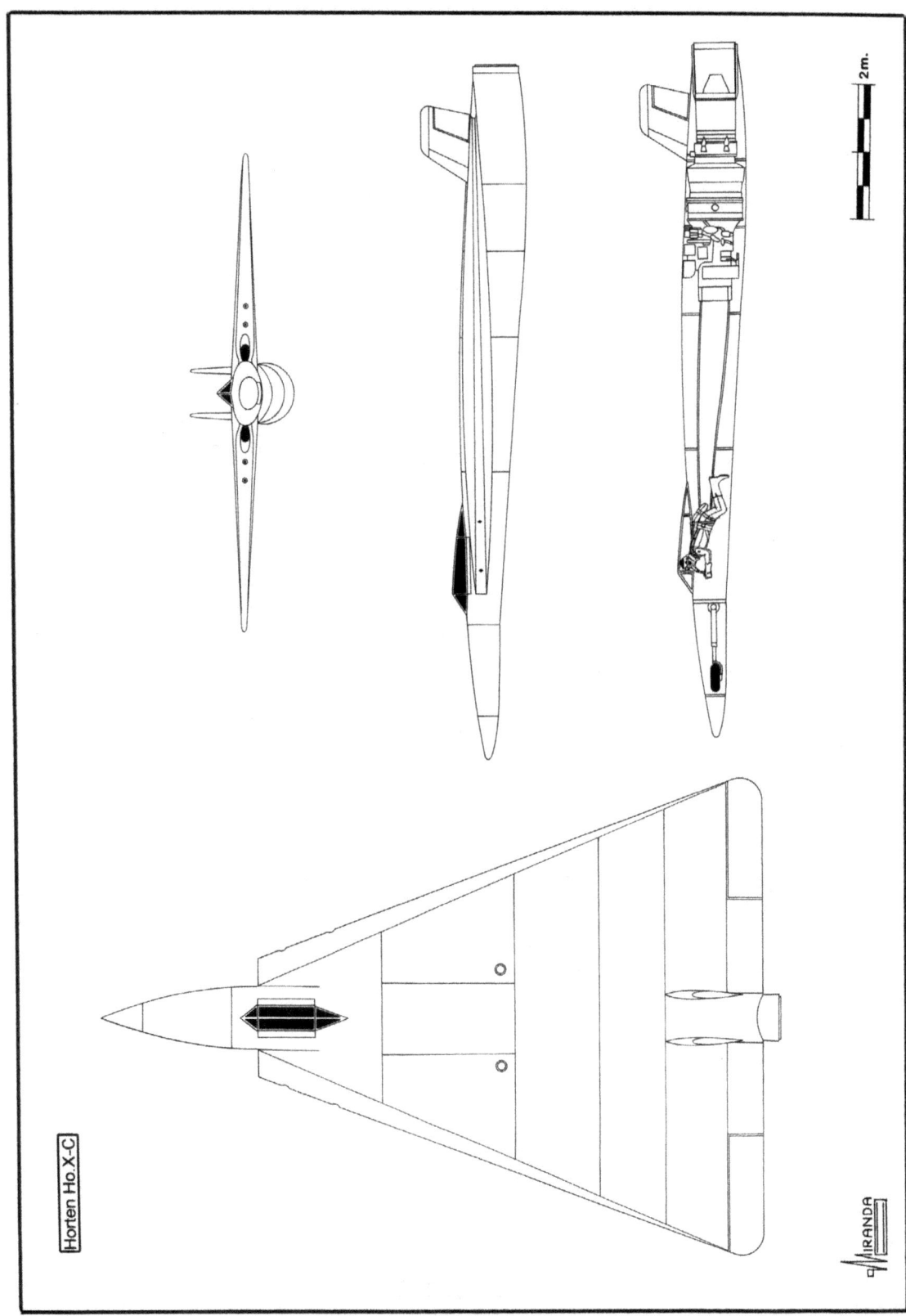

2 m.

Horten Ho.X-C

MIRANDA

Chapter 19

Horten Ho XIII B

The Ho XIII B was designed at the beginning of 1942 with a view to correcting the main defects of the first generation of German jet fighters. The Horten could fly 11,500 feet higher than the Me 262 A without suffering any compressibility problems during combat. It was also 240 kph faster and could use its rocket engine 5 minutes longer than the Me 163 B.

When the propellants were exhausted, the Horten was not rendered defenceless against enemy fighters like the *Komet*. It could continue combat using the turbojet. Its manoeuvrability at high altitude was excellent thanks to its wide wing area, and its performance at low altitude was as good as that of the *Komet*.

The great capacity of the propellants that it was able to carry within the wing allowed several rocket ignitions during flight, which provided great operational flexibility. As a target defence interceptor, it would have been able to hunt the future 'jet Mosquito' using both engines from take off. In CAP missions, its range was 950 km wider than the Me 262 As, and it could use the high speed of the rocket to reach any enemy airplane found by ground control. The location of the engines, ahead of the centre of gravity, gave stability during supersonic flight, thus reducing the effort required of the pilot to operate flight controls.

The main disadvantage of the Ho XIII B was the poor visibility during combat and landing, which was caused by the cockpit design within the tailfin. It was also very difficult to install the standard frontal armour against 12.7-mm ammunition. To face the new B-29 heavy bombers, the MG 213/20 guns could easily be replaced by the MG 213/30 ones. The structure of the wing's leading edge also allowed for the installation of R4M rockets within, without diminishing its aerodynamic qualities.

Technical data

Type	high-altitude interceptor.
Phase	wind-tunnel model.
Wings	delta with 60-degree leading edge and 7-per-cent profile thickness, wood structure, and Formholz cladding.
Fuselage	welded steel-tube framework, metallic cladding.
Landing gear	tricycle type, hydraulically retractable.

Engines	one Heinkel HeS 011 R turbojet rated at 1,300-kp static thrust coupled with an HWK 109-718 rocket with 1,000 kp of thrust.
Propellant tanks	two of R-Stoff of 570 litres each and two of SV-Stoff of 530 litres each in the wing roots.
Fuel tanks	two of K1 kerosene with 400 litres in the wing roots and two more of 120 litres in the leading edge.
Armament	one Mk 108/30 and two MG 213/20 cannons in the nose.
Equipment	pressurised cockpit, Heinkel-Kartusche ejector seat, EZ 42 gyroscopic gunsight, FuG 25a Erstling IFF, FuG 24 SE VHF R/T device, FuG 125a Hermine radio-beacon receiver.
Span	12 m
Length	12 m
Height	3.6 m
Wing area	53 sq. m
Max. weight	9,000 kg
Max. speed	1,200 kph (Mach 1.07) at 19,700 feet
Service	ceiling 49,200 feet
Range	2,000 km
Rocket	endurance 13 min

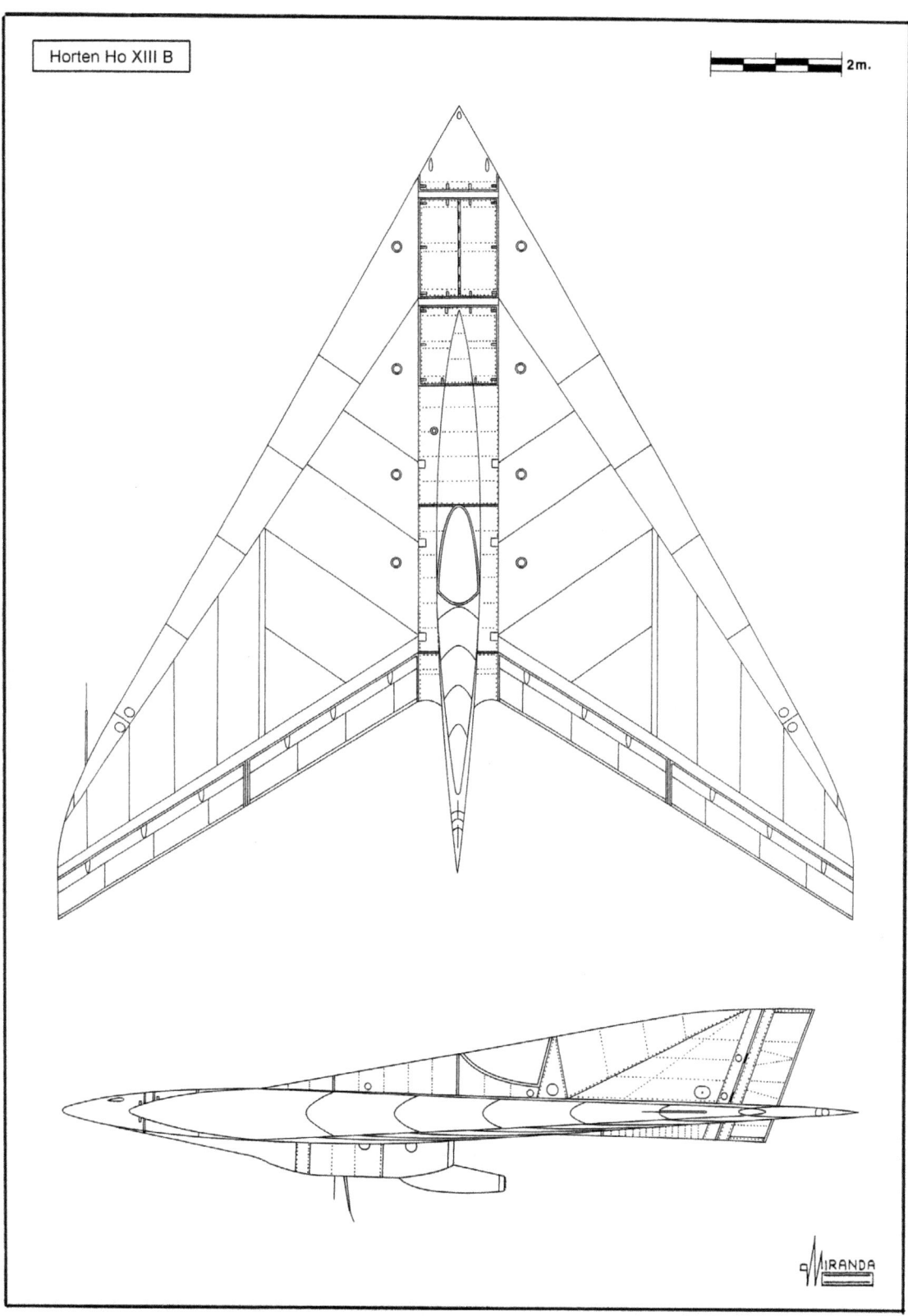

Horten Ho XIII B

2m.

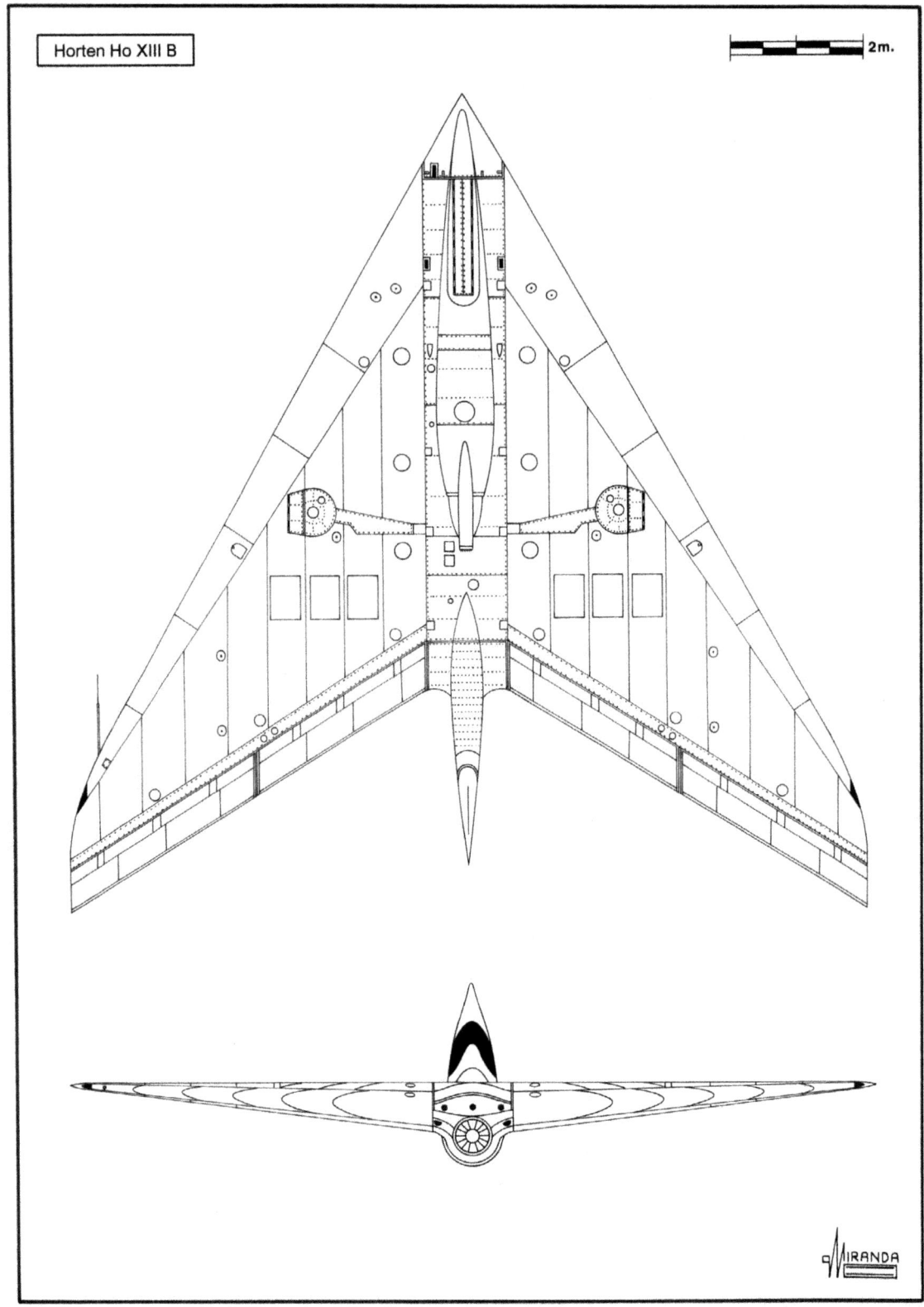

Horten Ho XIII B

2m.

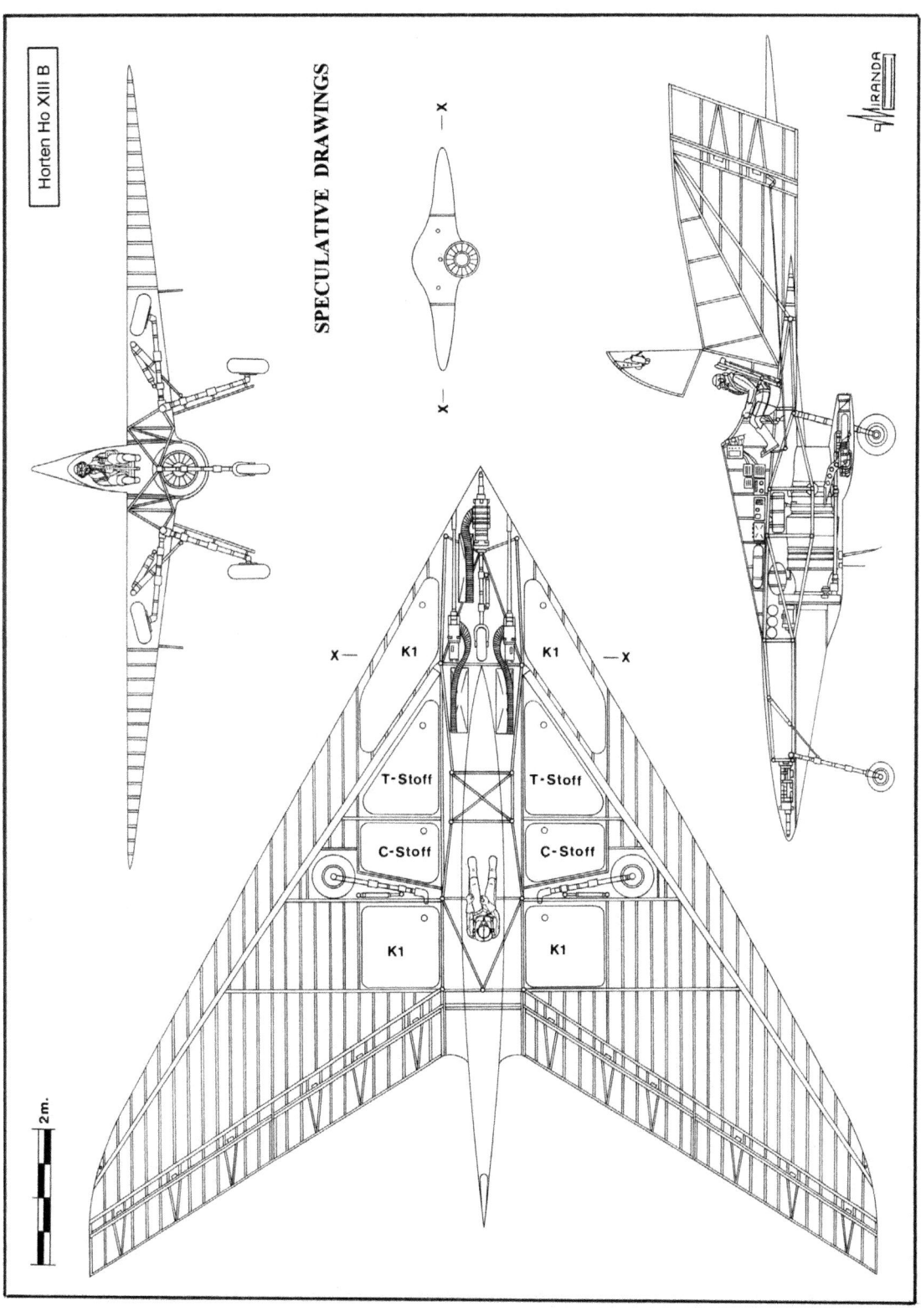

Horten Ho XIII B

SPECULATIVE DRAWINGS

2 m.

K1   K1

T-Stoff   T-Stoff

C-Stoff   C-Stoff

K1   K1

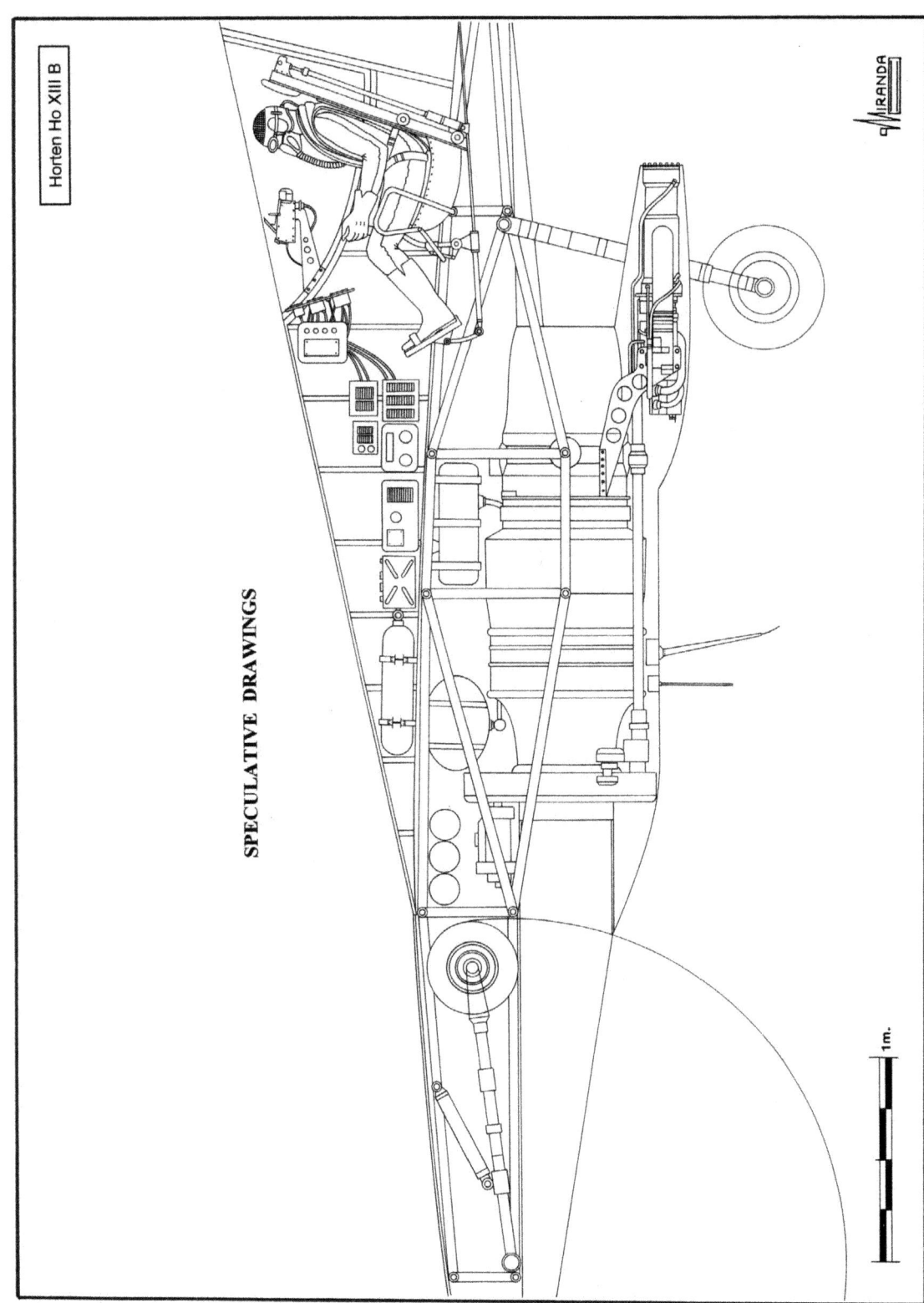

Horten Ho XIII B

SPECULATIVE DRAWINGS

1 m.

Chapter 20

Horten Ho XVIII *Amerikabomber*

On 8 July 1944, Reich Minister for Armaments Albert Speer ordered the cancellations of all the heavy bomber projects to save available resources for the manufacture of fighters. However, he permitted the test flights of the existing prototypes of the BV 238, Ju 390, and Me 264.

When the stealth properties of flying wings were discovered, the concept of an unstoppable bomber was born. Its manufacture did not require the use of strategic materials.

In the future, it would no longer be necessary to have great fleets of bombers like in 1940, built of aluminium to lead massive attacks at the cost of many lives. A reduced number of flying wings, equipped with the most advanced navigation devices, could do the work without losing dozens of well-trained crew members in each raid. Besides, the flying wings could bear the additional weight of weapons and fuel for a greater distance than conventional airplanes, given their large wing surface and low drag.

In autumn 1944, after a series of conferences organized by Göring between the representatives of the aeronautical industry, the Oberkommando der Luftwaffe published three specifications aimed at the construction of stealth bombers.

The first one requested a twin jet *Schnellbomber*, able to pass through the defences of the Chain Home with a bomb load of 1,000 kg, a range of 1,000 km, and a speed of 1,000 kph. The Arado Ar.I, the Focke Wulf 1000 x 1000 x 1000, the Horten *Schnellkampfflugzeug* and the Lippisch P.11 described in this book were the answer. All of them were flying wings that used composites and some kind of RAM in their construction.

The Focke Wulf project was considered the most efficient, being the rest of projects redesigned as night fighters or *Zerstörer*.

The second specification was a four-engine of the *Uralbomber* (extended range bomber) category, to replace the Ju 88 in strategic missions over the USSR at a time when the Russians started to equip night fighters with radar. The requirement was a range of 5,000 km, a maximum speed of 800/900 kph, and a payload of 4,000 kg. The models bidding for this contest were the Arado E-555, the BMW *Strahlbomber Projekt II* (jet bomber project II), the Junkers EF-130, the Horten *Projekt 18* (23 February 1945), and the Messerschmitt P.1108. By the end of March 1945, all of them had been cancelled, except the P.1108, which was the last project developed by Messerschmitt during the war.

The third specification was an intercontinental *Amerikabomber*, to bomb New York or Washington with impunity, operating from bases in Germany. This brushed the limits of the technology then available, and the design required the collaboration of several manufacturers. Horten provided the aerodynamic solutions already tested with the Ho IX, with the turbojets positioned within the wing, and the calculations for long range which had already been made for the Ho VIII reconnaissance airplane. Junkers contributed the Jumo 004 engines and the design of the pressurised cockpit developed for the Ju 388 and Ju 287. Messerschmitt brought his experience in long distance flights, obtained with the Me 261 and Me 264, to the ensemble. The result, Ho XIII B-1, was a pure flying wing spanning 40 m, powered by six turbojets and a crew of three, and was presented to the OKL on 25 February 1945.

Although the operational version would have been a heavy bomber with a 4,000-kg payload, defensive armament and an undercarriage, some authors suggest that the project would have been a simple technological demonstrator with just 1,000 kg of payload. It would have used a take off trolley powered by rockets and landing skids to reduce weight, which would have made most of the 27-hour flight possible with just four of its six turbojets.

It may be speculated that it would need an FuG 123 *Truhe* cartographic radar to locate the target in black-out conditions, an FuG 101a radio altimeter, an FuG 25a *Erstling* IFF device, and an FuG 125a/FuG 16Zy navigation system combined with a Peil G6/APZ6 radiogoniometer.

To communicate with the base, it would need a long-range R/T device of the FuG 10P MF/HF variety, and an FuG 16 to contact submarines and refuelling aircraft. The defensive armament (dorsal only) would be two MG 131 machine guns of 13 mm, installed in the FDL-131/z remotely controlled barbette with an RF1A/RF2B periscopic aiming system.

For high-altitude automatic bomb releasing, it would be necessary to have a computer integrated with the *Lofte 7H* visor, the *Patin PK S11* autopilot, and the FuG 123 radar. As for the type of bomb planned for these ultra-long-range raids, the reader may find some indications in the introduction of this book.

By the beginning of March 1945, Junkers AG received the order to manufacture the prototype. As it happened with the Gotha and the Horten 8-229, the manufacturer was not able to adapt either to the Horten construction system or to the refined aerodynamic requirements of its design.

The most criticised aspect was the absence of a tailfin, which was considered the cause of the crash of the Horten Ho 229 V2 in February. Junkers argued that the tailfin and rudder provided longitudinal stability in case of engine malfunction, as well as the capacity to quickly regain control after going through a barrier of explosives produced by the AA batteries.

The Ho XVIII was redesigned with a narrow cockpit for a crew of four, located at the base of the tailfin, and six turbojets hanging under the fuselage to facilitate maintenance. The bomb bay and main undercarriage positions were not changed, but a single nose leg was adopted.

Defensive armament consisted of two 20-mm cannons installed beneath the rudder in an HL-151/20 Rheinmetall-Borsig remotely controlled tail barbette. As the tailfin structure did not allow the use of a periscopic gunsight, it may be assumed that the aiming system consisted of a sophisticated television system of the Blaupunkt *Tonne* type, guided by a joystick and *Seedorf* TV screen from the cockpit. The installation of an unspecified in-flight refuelling device was planned in the extremity of the nose.

To compensate for the drag produced by these changes, it was decided to install the more powerful Jumo 004 H turbojets. The wider diameter of these engines forced them to be partially hidden in the fuselage in sets of two nacelles, in imitation of the solution already adopted in the design of the Horten Ho XIII b.

Technical data Horten XVIII (21/02/1945)

Type	heavy bomber.
Wings	wood and plastic with 35- and 45-degree sweep at the leading edge and 15-degree sweep at the trailing edge, housing the engines, fuel tanks, and undercarriage.
Fuselage	steel tubing and Formholz housing the pressurised cockpit and the bomb bay.
Engines	four Heinkel HeS 011 turbojets rated at 1,300-kp static thrust.
Armament	none
Payload	5,600 kg
Wingspan	30 m
Length	13 m
Height	3.40 m
Wing area	156 sq. m
Max. speed	860 kph
Max. weight	37,600 kg
Fuel	23,000 litres
Range	5,400 km
Ceiling	52,500 feet
Crew	four

Technical data Horten XVIII (25/02/1945)

Type	intercontinental bomber.
Wings	wood and plastic with 30-degree sweep at the leading edge and 15-degree sweep at the trailing edge, housing the engines, fuel tanks, and main undercarriage legs.
Fuselage	steel tubing and Formholz housing the pressurised cockpit, the nose legs, the bomb bay, and fuel tanks.
Engines	six Jumo 004 B turbojets rated at 900-kp static thrust.
Armament	one FDL-131/Z remotely controlled gun barbette, behind the cockpit.
Payload	4,000 kg
Wingspan	40 m
Length	13.40 m
Height	4 m
Wing	area 150 sq. m
Aspect	ratio 10.7:1
Max. speed	900 kph
Max. weight	32,000/38,000 kg

Fue	23,000/26,000 litres
Ceiling	52,500 feet
Range	11,000/13,000 km
Crew	three

Technical data Horten XVIII (23/03/1945)

Type	intercontinental bomber.
Wings	wood and plastic with 40-degree sweep at the leading edge and 26- to -5-degree sweep at the trailing edge, housing the fuel tanks.
Fuselage	steel tubing and Formholz housing the pressurised cockpit, engines, undercarriage, bomb bay, and tailfin.
Engines	six Jumo 004 H turbojets rated at 1,160-kp static thrust.
Armament	one HL-151/20 remotely controlled gun barbette, at the base of the tailfin.
Payload	4,000 kg
Wingspan	42.50 m
Length	19 m
Height	5.50 m
Max. speed	910 kph
Max. weight	44,000 kg
Range	12,000 km
Crew	four

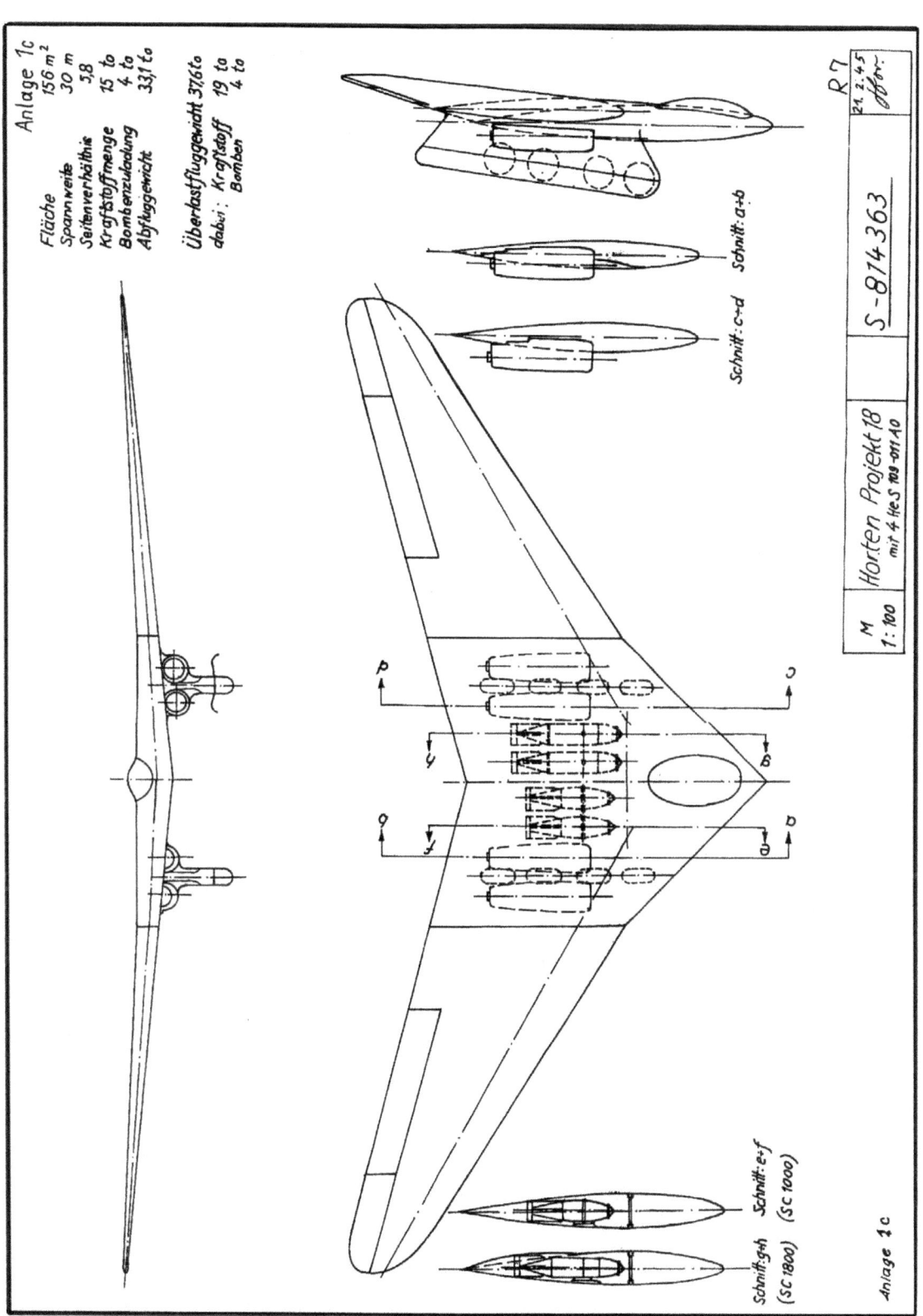

Anlage 1c

Fläche   156 m²
Spannweite   30 m
Seitenverhältnis   5,8
Kraftstoffmenge   15 to
Bombenzuladung   4 to
Abfluggewicht   33,1 to

Überlastfluggewicht 37,6 to
dabei: Kraftstoff 19 to
       Bomben   4 to

Schnitt: a-b

Schnitt: c-d

R 7

24.2.45

S - 814 363

M   Horten Projekt 18
1:100   mit 4 He S 109-011.A0

Schnitt: g-h   Schnitt: e-f
(SC 1800)   (SC 1000)

Anlage 1c

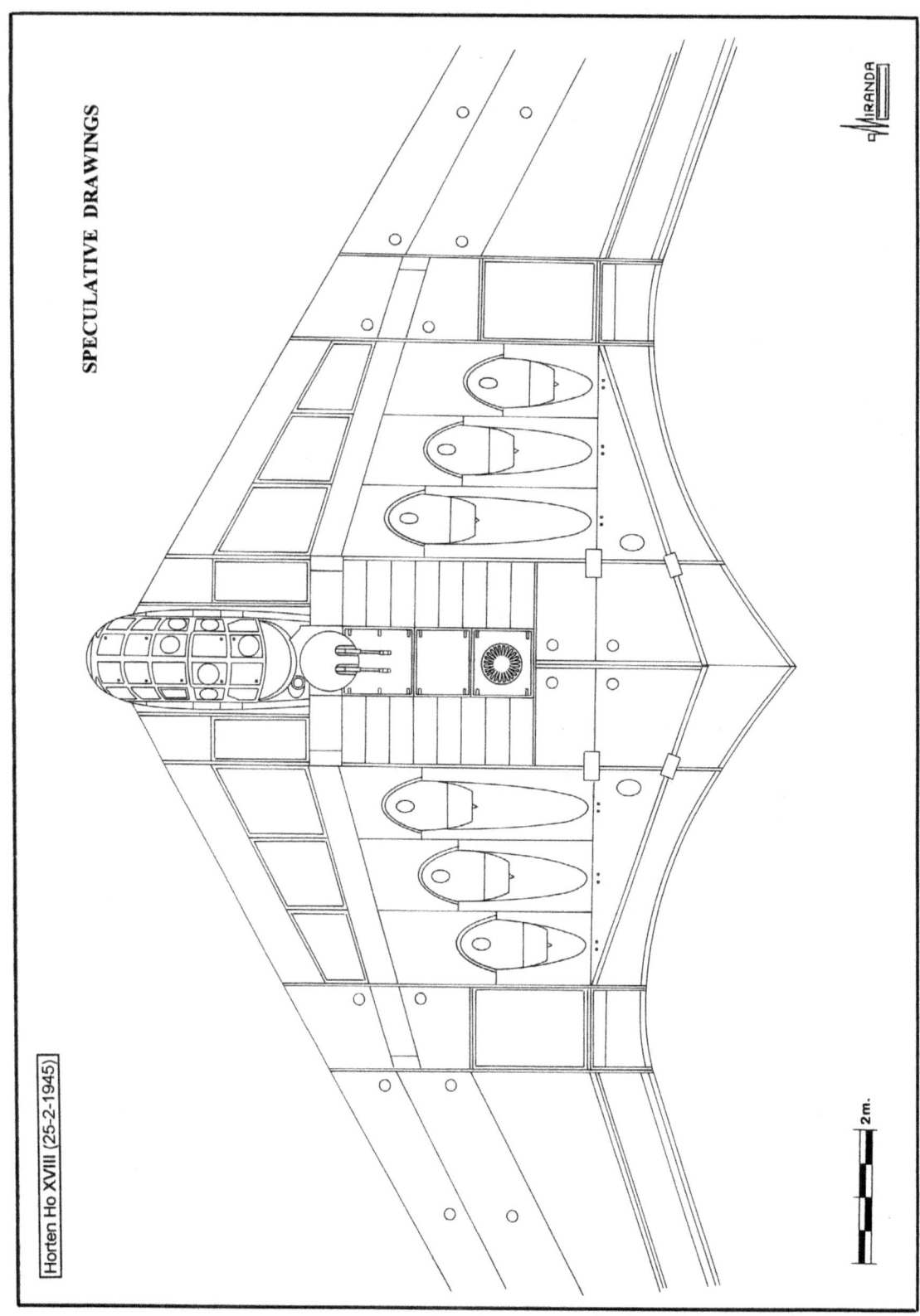

SPECULATIVE DRAWINGS

Horten Ho XVIII (25-2-1945)

2m.

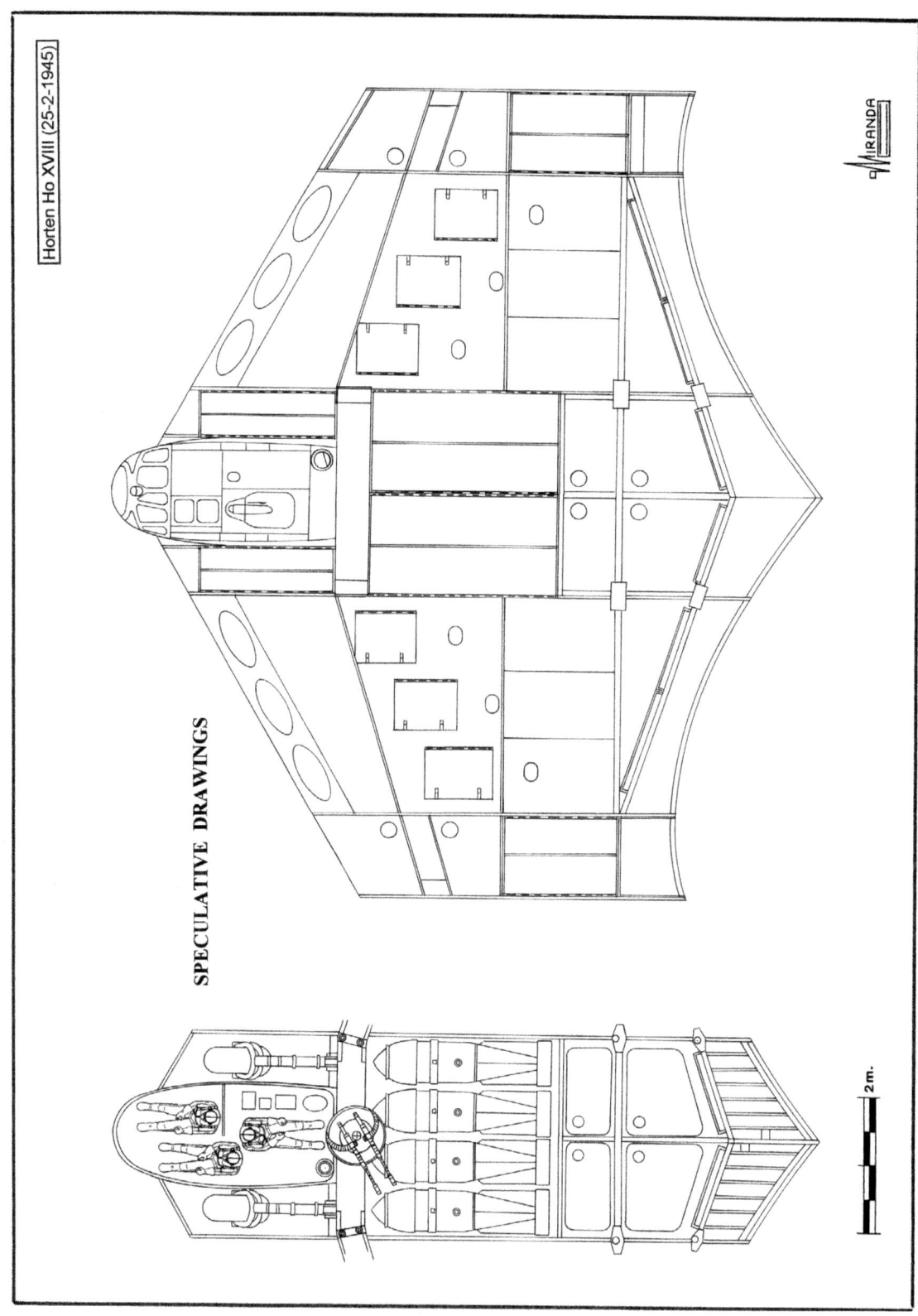

SPECULATIVE DRAWINGS

Horten Ho XVIII (25-2-1945)

2 m.

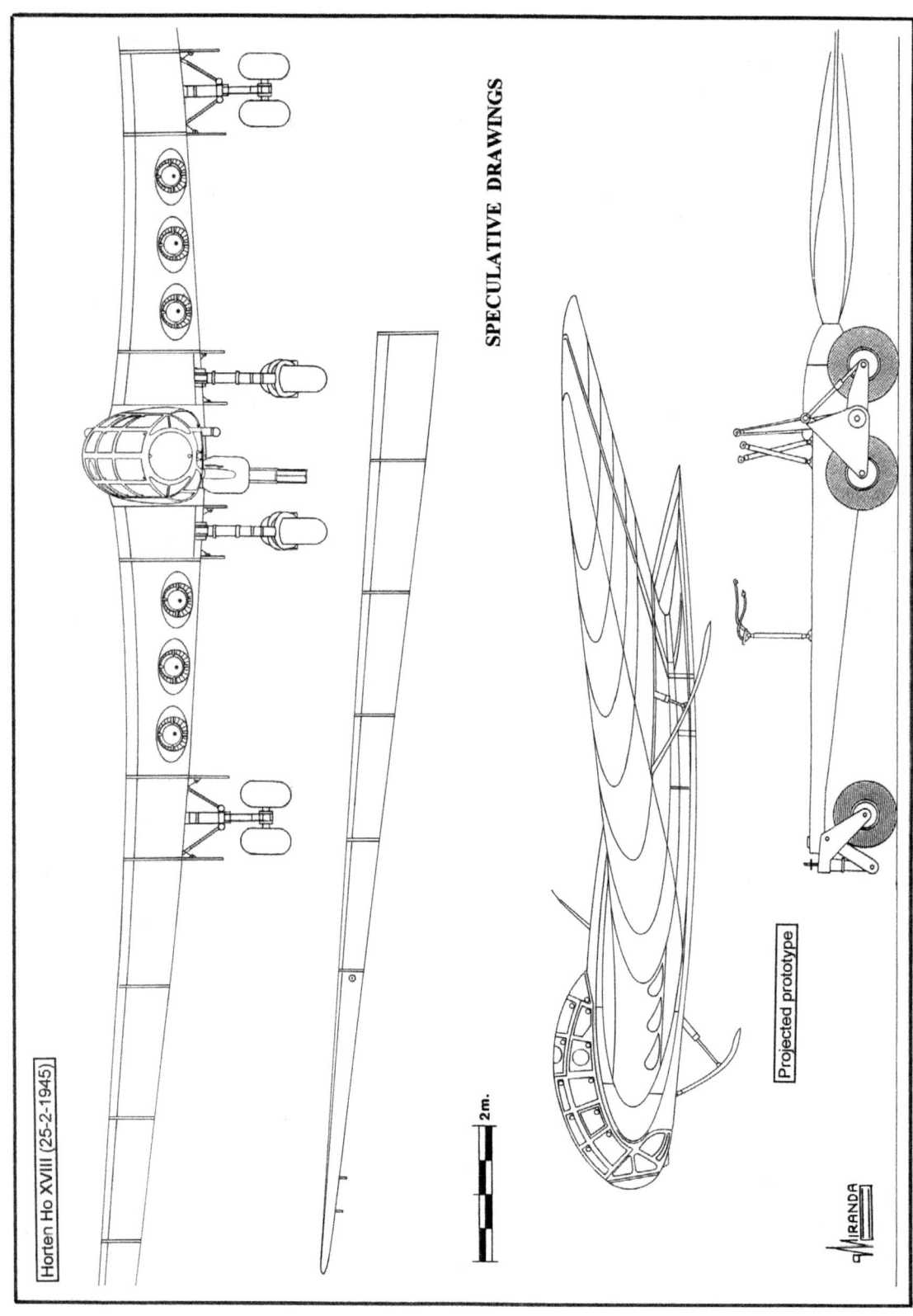

SPECULATIVE DRAWINGS

Horten Ho XVIII (25-2-1945)

2m.

Projected prototype

MIRANDA

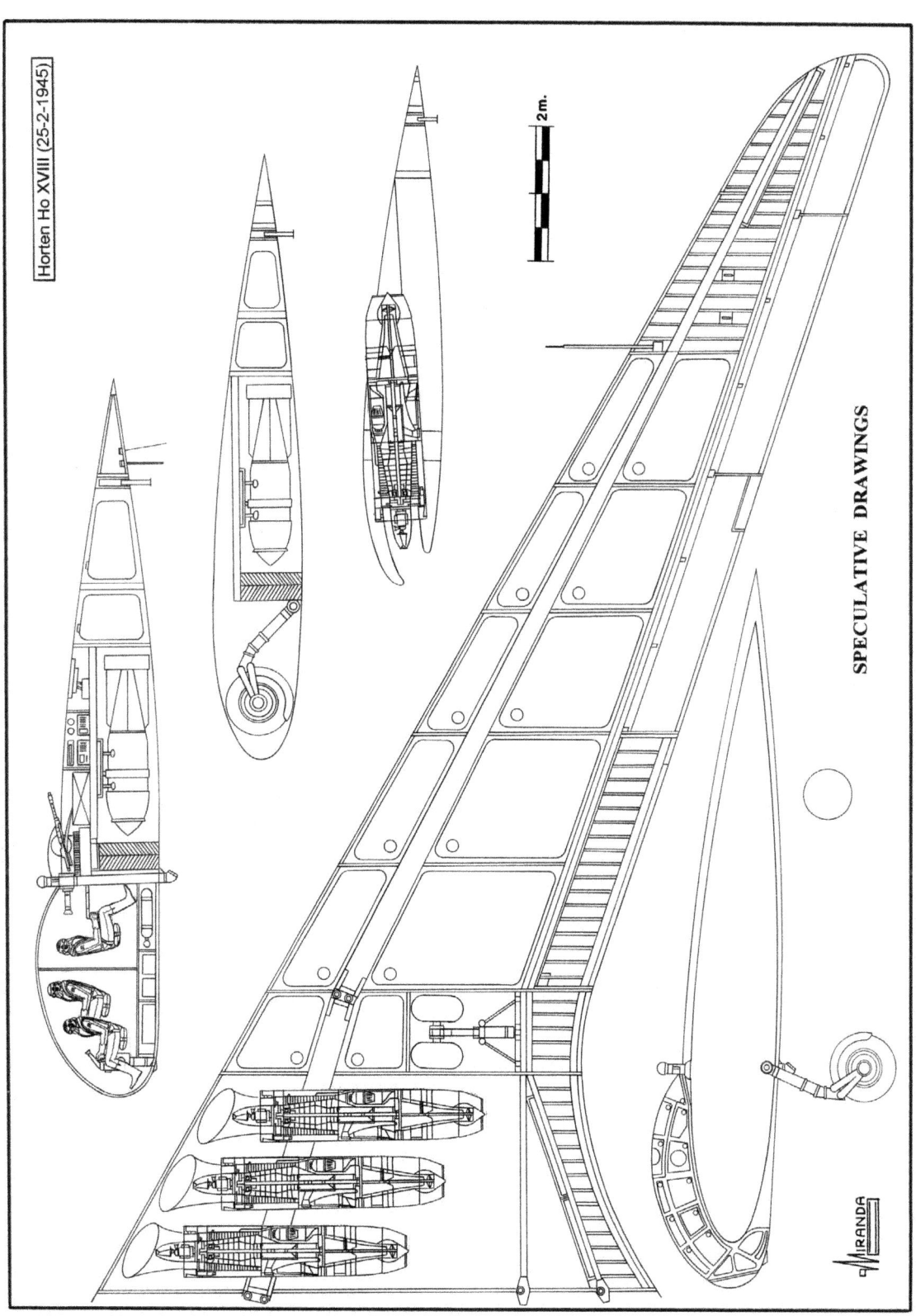

Horten Ho XVIII (25-2-1945)

2m.

SPECULATIVE DRAWINGS

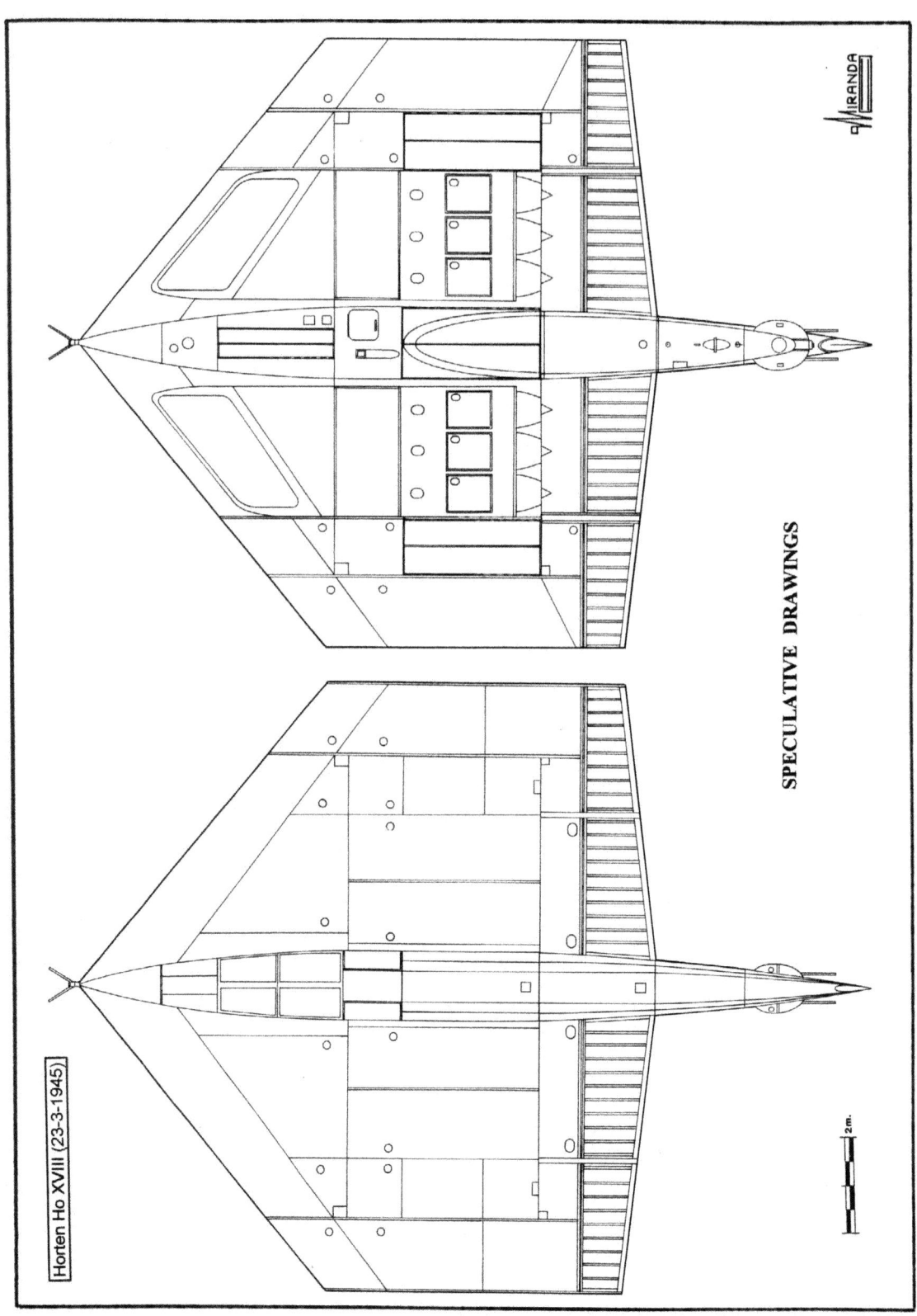

Horten Ho XVIII (23-3-1945)

SPECULATIVE DRAWINGS

2m.

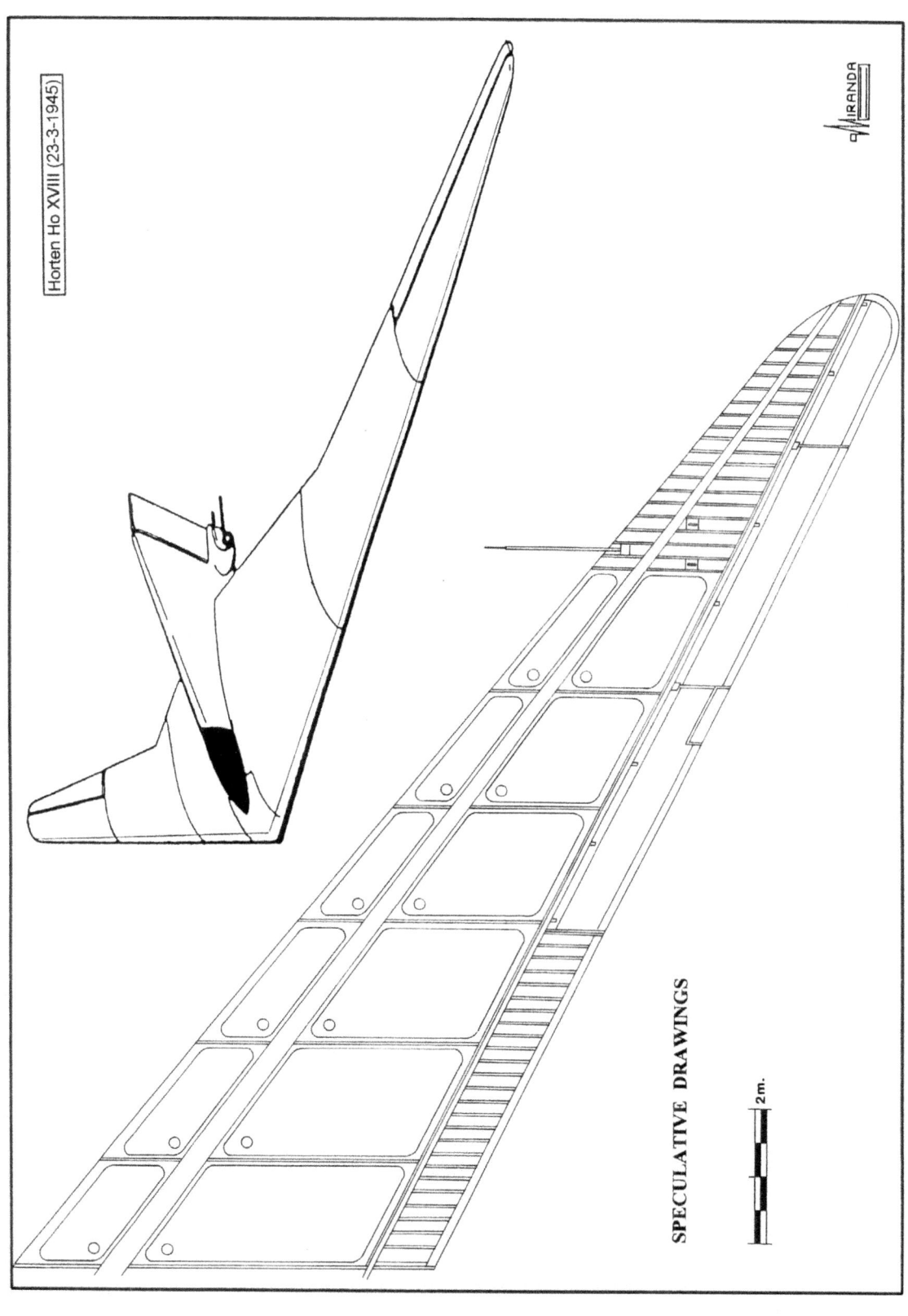

Horten Ho XVIII (23-3-1945)

SPECULATIVE DRAWINGS

2 m.

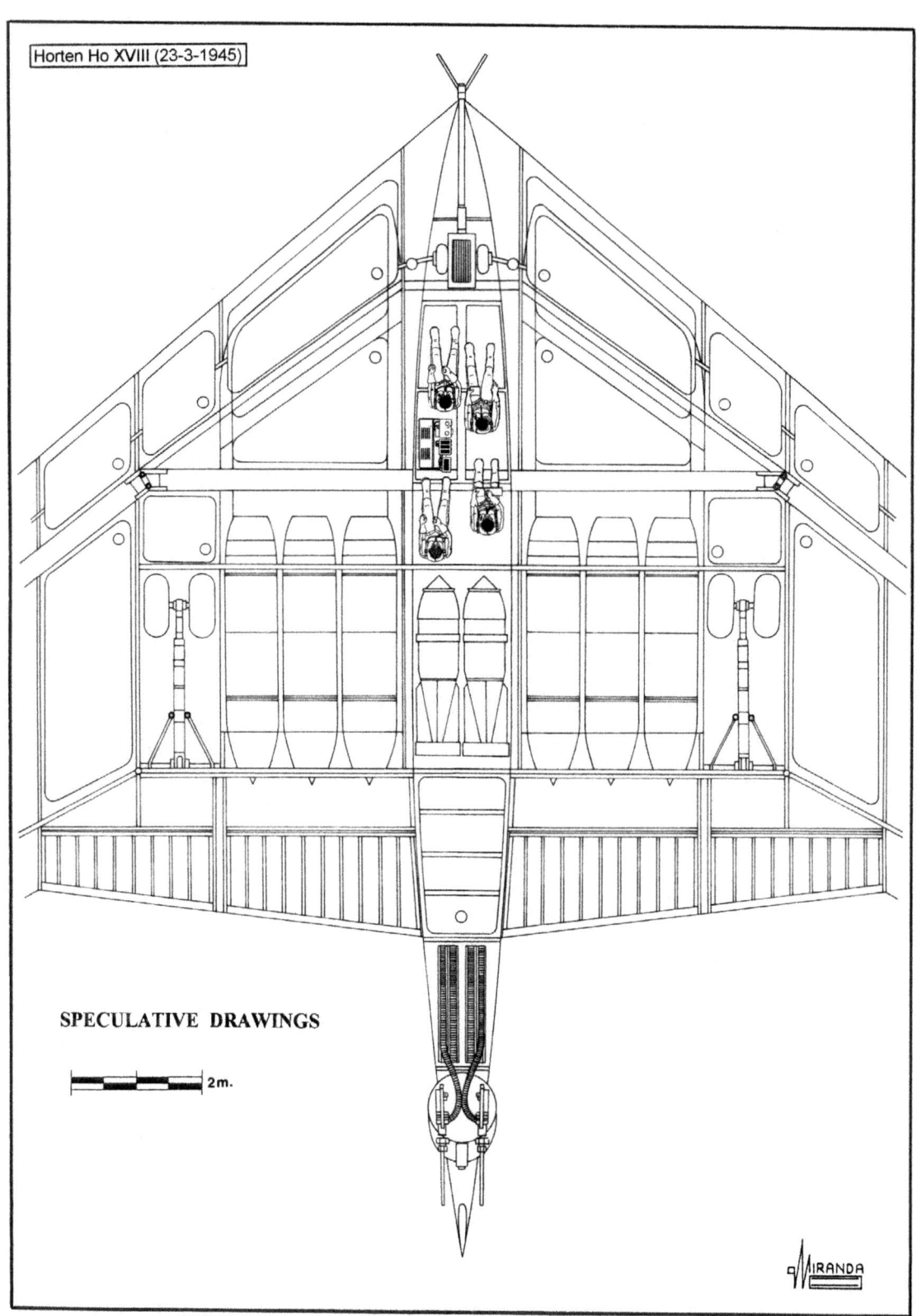

Horten Ho XVIII (23-3-1945)

SPECULATIVE DRAWINGS

2m.

MIRANDA

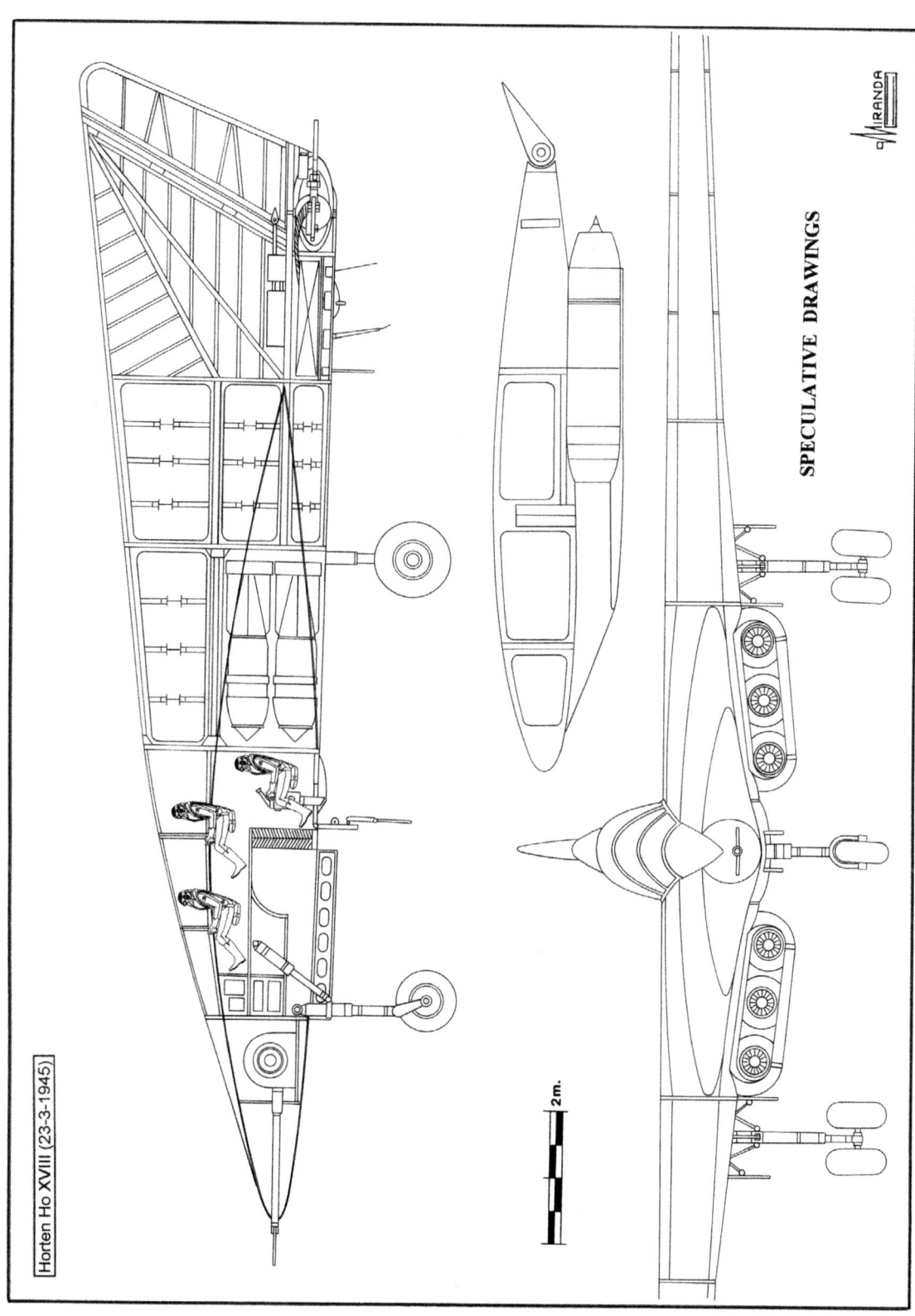

Horten Ho XVIII (23-3-1945)

SPECULATIVE DRAWINGS

2 m.

Chapter 21

Junkers/DFS EF-130

The Junkers/DFS EF-130 was a four-engine heavy bomber of the *Uralbomber* class designed in the autumn of 1944 to compete against the Arado E-555, the BMW *Strahlbomber Projekt II*, the Horten *Projekt 18* (23 February 1945), and the Messerschmitt P.1108.

It had a pressurised cockpit for a crew of three, originally designed for the Ju 388, and the undercarriage of a Junkers EF-131. The wing was a DFS design with leading-edge slats, flaps, and ailerons.

The system used to power the rotation manoeuvre during take off is unknown. It may stand to reason that the engines could swing with the help of a hydraulic mechanism, in order to change the thrust direction. That would explain the odd position in which they were located: in the aerodynamic shadow generated by the cockpit.

The project did not pass the wind-tunnel model phase, and was subsequently cancelled in March 1945.

Technical data Junkers/DFS EF-130	
Type	heavy bomber.
Wings	wood and plywood with 34-degree sweep at the leading edge and 13-degree sweep at the trailing edge, housing fuel tanks and undercarriage main legs.
Fuselage	light alloy, housing the pressurised cockpit, the bomb bay, the nose leg and the engines.
Engines	four BMW 109-003 C turbojets rated at 1,030-kp static thrust.
Armament	none
Payload	4,000 kg
Wingspan	24 m
Length	10.38 m
Height	4.32 m
Wing area	120 sq. m
Max. speed	950 kph
Max. weight	38,100 kg
Range	7,500 km
Ceiling	38,000 feet

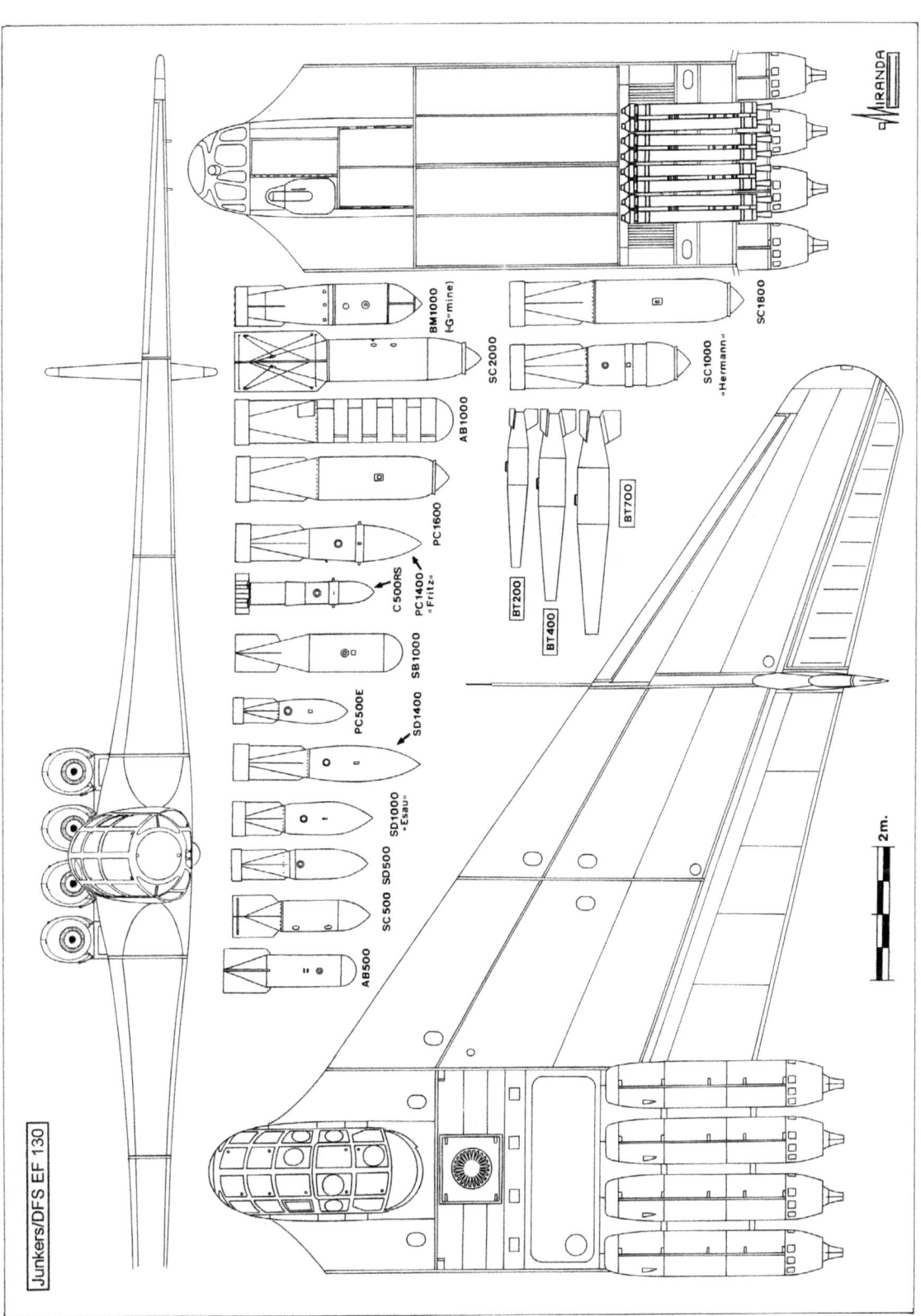

Junkers/DFS EF 130

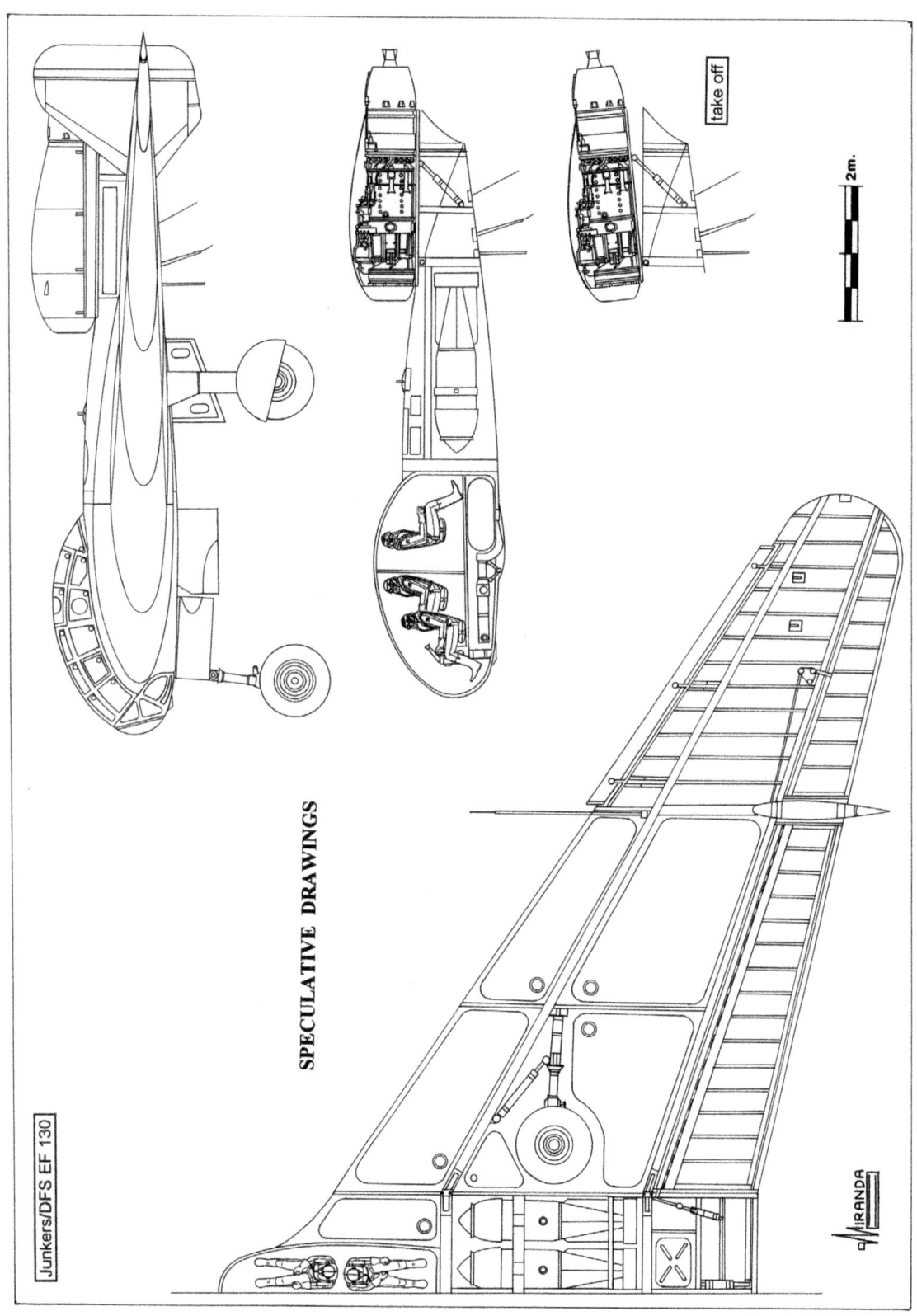

take off

2m.

SPECULATIVE DRAWINGS

Junkers/DFS EF 130

MIRANDA

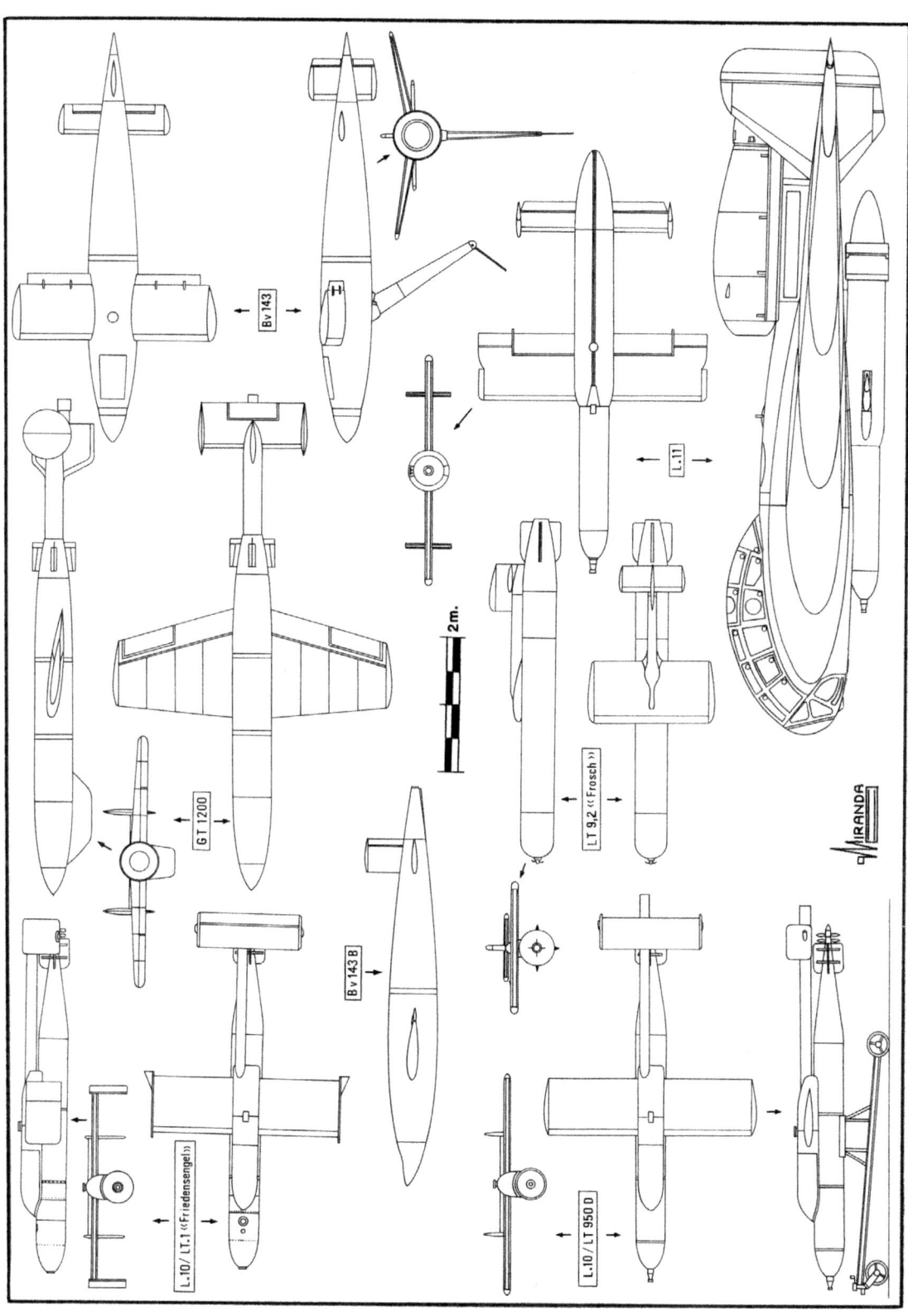

← Bv 143 →

← L.11 →

2 m.

← GT 1200 →

LT 9,2 «Frosch» →

Bv 143 B →

L.10 / LT.1 («Friedensengel»)

L.10 / LT 950 D

MIRANDA

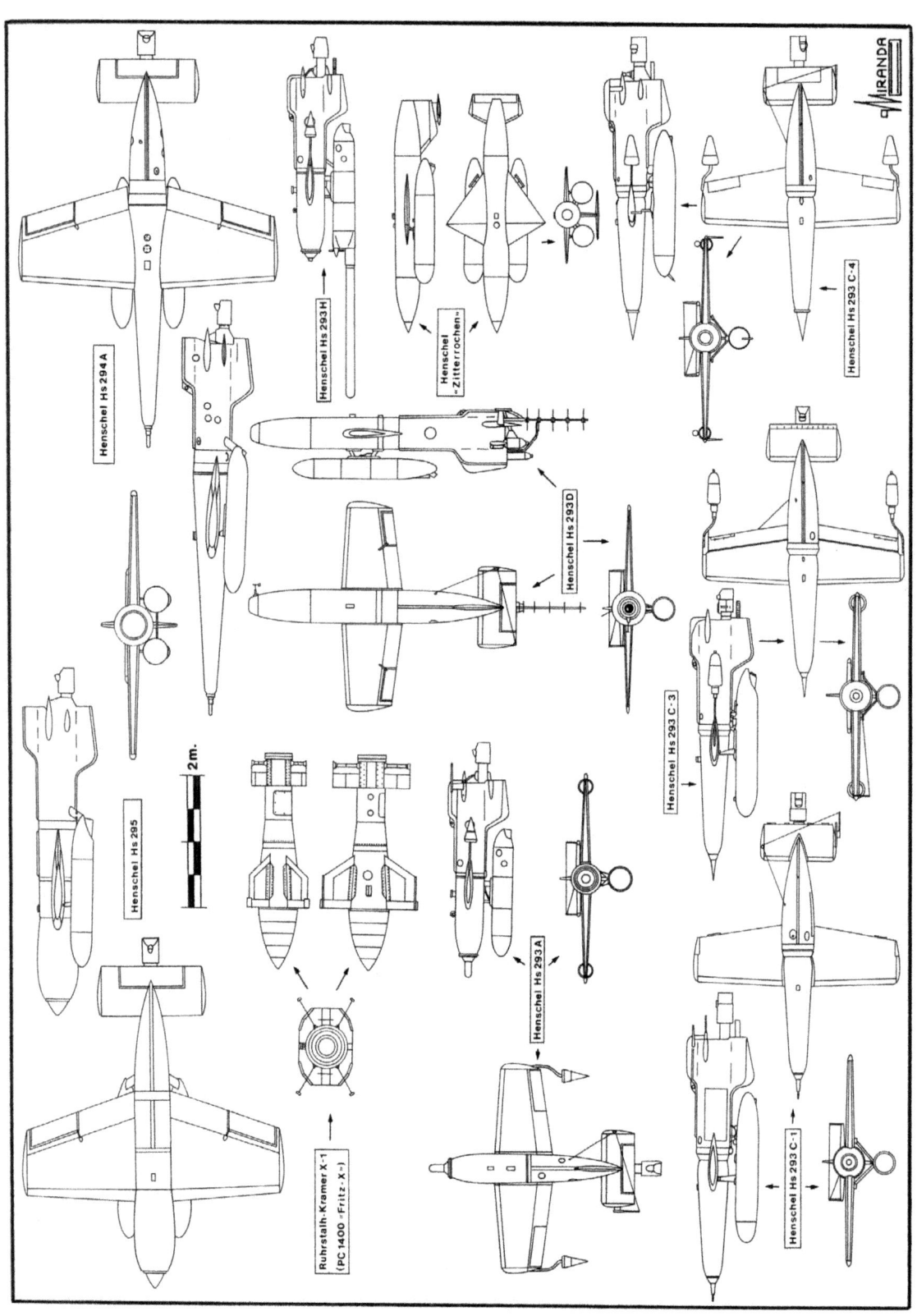

Henschel Hs 294 A

Henschel Hs 293H

Henschel "Zitterrochen"

Henschel Hs 293 C-4

Henschel Hs 293D

Henschel Hs 293 C-3

Henschel Hs 295

2 m.

Ruhrstahl-Kramer X-1 (PC 1400 -"Fritz-X-")

Henschel Hs 293A

Henschel Hs 293 C-1

Lippisch *Projekt X*

For many years, Alexander Lippisch was one of the most audacious aeronautical designers in the world. Always ahead of his time and seldom understood for his technological
innovation, he obtained some official support thanks only to the exceptional circumstances created during the Second World War.

During the 1920s and '30s, Lippisch methodically followed his dream to build a tailless
airplane that would be stable and safe enough for civil use. His working method consisted
of testing new ideas—first as a flying balsa model, then as a manned glider, and finally
as a powered airplane. The results achieved with his sports designs *Ente, Storch,* and
Delta were not very successful. They were difficult to fly, and required seasoned pilots.

In fact, the *Delta IV c*, developed in 1936 with the support of Deutsche Forschungsanstalt
für Segelflug (DFS), was the first Lippisch design to obtain a full certificate of airwor-
thines. It became the DFS 39. The development of liquid fuel rockets in Germany in
1936 had reached a point where results could be put into practice: Wernher von Braun
worked on a 300-kg thrust engine in Kummersdorf and Helmuth Walter on the 400-kg
HWK RI. In 1937, Heinkel performed some tests with both engines, which were still very
insecure and had a tendency to explode. The von Braun engine was promised to reach
900 kg, and Walter's intended to reach 600 kg within a year.

After the He 176 flight, the new power system could no longer be ignored, although it
attracted the RLM's attention in the worst possible sense. The Lutfwaffe had not forgotten
or forgiven the He 51 fiasco of the Spanish Civil War, and had already decided that the
main fighter provider from then onwards would be Messerschmitt, and that the new
rocket engine was ideal to power a high-altitude interceptor. The authorization to build
the He 176 V2 was denied and the V1 was sent to the Berlin Air Museum.

Dr Lorenz of the Technisches Amt (Research Department of the Air Ministry of the
Reich)—which was sponsoring the Walter developments—was convinced that conventional
airplanes were not fitted to use the new powering system, as confirmed with the He
176. In his opinion, the tailless swept wing design would be right to reach high speeds.

Lippisch was the German designer with the most experience in this field, so Dr Lorenz
contacted him to propose the development of a DFS 39 version—able to fly at 500 kph—as
technological demonstrator of the Walter HWK RI-203 rocket that promised enormous
power for its weight. The engine used compressed air to force a weak concentration of

hydrogen peroxide into a reaction chamber, lined with a paste catalyst, which instantly changed it into water and oxygen. The reaction would be so violent that the water would emerge as superheated steam, able to provide propulsion after accelerating in the venturi nozzle.

By the beginning of 1937, the RLM signed a contract with the DFS for the construction of the airplane, classified as *Projekt X*, under extensive security measures. Lippisch was only informed of the size, weight, and engine thrust, but he was not provided with blueprints. The first tests performed with wind-tunnel models in the AVA Göttingen proved that the DFS 39 airframe was not able to support the rocket thrust of the flight at high altitude.

To that end, a completely new airplane known as *Delta VI d* or DFS 194 was designed. Two different variants were considered: *Ausführung I*, with anhedral wingtips and reduced tailfin, and *Ausführung II*, with straight wingtips and a higher tailfin. On 7 July 1938, it was decided to proceed with the development of the *Ausführung II* rather than the *Ausführung I* because it was more stable at high speed. By the end of 1938, it was considered to build a wooden prototype powered by a conventional engine with pusher airscrew, to complement the theoretical work and test its behaviour at low speed.

The Oberkommando der Luftwaffe, troubled by Soviet research in this same field, vetoed its construction to avoid potential leaks, as well as any contact between DFS and Heinkel. This was problematic in that Lippisch had just discovered that the highly volatile rocket fuel could react with wood, causing fires. DFS lacked the technical means to build a metallic fuselage, and so Heinkel was contacted on the basis of their experience with the RI-203.

The official criterion was finally imposed and the whole *Projekt X* team moved to the Messerschmitt complex in Augsburg where it was integrated as *Abteilung L* on 1 January 1939. The DFS 194 fuselage with steel-tube and *Electron* magnesium sheet skinning was built there. *Projekt X* was then named Messerschmitt Me 163.

Using Messerschmitt facilities, it was possible to integrate a Walter RI-203 'cold' rocket engine with 400 kg thrust into the metallic fuselage. But the power plant assemblies were integrated with the aircraft airframe because only the fuel and compressed air lines were removable. As a result, all static tests had to be carried out in the airframe, and the wooden wings were not installed to avoid corrosion problems.

Problems of accessibility and low serviceability convinced the team to design the Me 163 A in such a way that the rocket would be easily removable. In August 1940, the DFS 194 made several test flights in Peenemünde, reaching the speed of 550 kph in one of them. After these good results, the construction of the Me 163 A prototype received the highest priority.

It was conceived as a transitional experimental model to obtain information applicable to a future fighter version. The Me 163 A had a wooden wing that was 78 cm shorter than the one in the DFS 194, and a trailing edge sweep increased from 7 to 10 degrees to improve the pitch moment arm of the elevons at 0.8 Mach. The airplane was aerodynamically very clean and had a tendency to float in ground effect, which caused some accidents during the first test flights.

To improve the stalling characteristics, Type C leading-edge slots designed by J. Hubert were installed in the 40-per-cent span, in addition to drag landing flaps beneath the inboard half of the wings. They had the hinge line well forward of the trailing edge, so that the pitching moment was not affected. The fuselage was modified to facilitate access to the engine, a cold HWK RII-203 with 750 kg pneumatic controllable thrust and an operational temperature of 500 °C. The canopy improved its aerodynamics and the tailfin increased its height by 22 cm.

The Me 163 A Vl made its first flight without an engine on 13 February 1941, reaching a speed of 850 kph in a dive during its test programme. On 13 August, a Me 163 A, powered by a variable-thrust Walter R II-203 b of 750 kg, flew for the first time. In a subsequent test, it reached 805 kph in level flight.

The fuel rocket burnt so fast during take off that the fuel tanks were empty before the end of the tests. To discover its limits, the Me 163 A V4 was towed up to 13,000 feet by a Me 110 over Peenemünde West with full load of fuel on 2 October. After the rockets' ignition, the airplane reached a critical number of 0.84 Mach before suffering the compressibility effects.

The shock wave caused the air flow over the outer wing to separate suddenly and the aircraft pitched nose down at 11 g, plunging into a shock stall dive. Shutting the engine, the pilot recovered control, landing normally. It was later ascertained that it had flown at 1,004.5 kph. The record was kept secret for security reasons and the construction of eight additional prototypes was ordered, to serve as trainers of the Me 163 B, the fighter version.

On 22 October, the OKL approved the construction of seventy airframes of the B series in the Regensburg plant. Production started on 1 December 1941. It was then that the delivery of the RII-211 engines began to suffer delays, putting the whole programme at risk. Officially known as HWK 109-509 A, it was in fact a 'hot' double-combustion engine, able to operate at 1,750 °C with 1,500-kg thrust in the A-0 version, 1,600 kg in the A-1, and 1,700 kg in the A-2.

Its mass production was slow because it represented an excessive technological jump for its time. It was not until August 1943 that the Me 163B V2 made its first flight, powered by the RII-211.

At the beginning of 1943, the OKL had serious doubts about the viability of the Me-163. To the various incidents that punctuated flight tests must be added the delay in the availability of the HWK RII-211 rocket engine, of which the first units approved for air service—though still far from being safe—only arrived in Peenemünde in July.

Allied bomber offensives increased every day. Their escort fighters repelled the Bf 109 and Fw 190, and more devastating incursions were expected with the improvement of the weather. The Me 262 did not seem to be the best solution. Its performance in dog fighting was not brilliant, its combat ceiling was insufficient, its engines were unsafe, and its airframe suffered from compressibility buffeting.

The *Komet*—of which the first seventy airframes were uselessly awaiting their engines at Regensburg factory—was urgently needed in combat. *Abteilung L* proposed the construction of two *Parallelenwürfe* (alternative versions) in April. The first project was named Lippisch P.20 on 16 April 1943. It basically was a Me 163 with a Jumo 004 turbojet installed beneath the pilot, a 36-degree swept wing, and tricycle type undercarriage. The second project, Lippisch 8-334, never received the RLM's official designation. Due to the strong personal disagreement between Lippisch and Messerschmit, *Abteilung L* was dissolved on 28 April and Lippisch himself left the company on 1 May.

The Lippisch 8-334 was to be powered by conventional 12-cylinder piston Daimler Benz DB 603 or 605 engines, located at the nose and driving a pusher propeller through an extension shaft.

Chapter 23

Lippisch P.15

The systematic bombing of the German industrial heartland forced the decentralisation of the aeronautical production in multitudes to small plants and workshops.

The chaos produced in the Reich transportation systems during the last months of the war broke up a previously well-ordered production schedule: some spare parts were scarce, others did not arrive at the assembly lines on time, and some were even overstocked.

In March 1945, the LFA-Wien decided to make the most of the situation by designing some *Frankenstein* airplanes, built with surplus parts—the same 'panic fighter' concept used in the design of the North American Fisher P.75 and the Commonwealth CA-12 Boomerang in Australia.

Conceived as a fighter cheap to manufacture in large quantities and easy to be operated by young inexperienced pilots, Heinkel's *Volksjäger* was to be a costly failure. The wooden wing was incorrectly designed; the landing speed was excessive; the twin tailfin generated too much drag, penalising performances; and the fuselage design did not allow for the installation of heavy guns.

On 4 March 1945, the Lippisch design team proposed to the OKL the creation of an assembly centre in the Wiener Neustadt Werke (WNF) that specifically catered to the manufacturing of the P.15 fighter *Diana*. It was an airplane easy to operate, as stable at low speed as the *Komet,* able to transport 30-mm guns and to fly faster and higher than the He 162, despite being powered by the same engine.

The P.15 used the frontal three quarters of the He 162 fuselage, for there was an excess in its production in the Khala subterranean complex. It also used the wooden wings from a Me 163 B—from which there were many spares—as well as the tailfin of a Junkers 248, the electronics of a Me 262, and the undercarriage of the *Salamander*. The WNF simply had to build the central section of the wing, the air intakes, and the internal air ducts. The installed engine could be a Jumo 004, a BMW 003, or one of the new HeS 011 turbojets.

Wind-tunnel tests made with a 1:25 scale model proved that the airplane was stable up to 0.84 Mach. This vindicated the effectiveness of the concept and Lippisch used it again for the design of the transonic version (P.15, 3 March 1945), which combined different elements used in the Messerschmitt projects on which Lippisch had cooperated.

The 52-degree swept wing was an adaptation of the Me P.1112 S/2 wing (3 March 1945);

the air intakes were based on the LP.13 and Me P.1092 designs (16 July 1943), whereas the tailfin and the canopy came from the LP.14 and LP.12 respectively. The air came from the turbojet through two S-shaped pipes that surrounded the cockpit, passing across the wing roots. The armament was reduced to just two Mk 108/30 cannons in the wing roots, and the electronic equipment was be the same as that of the Ju 248.

Technical data DFS 194

Type	single-seat research rocket-airplane.
Wings	wooden structure, plywood cladding with 20- and 29-degree swept at the leading edge and 7-degree swept at the trailing edge.
Fuselage	steel-tube and magnesium cladding.
Undercarriage	detachable twin wheels trolley and landing skid.
Engine	one Walter RI-203 cold rocket engine with 400-kp thrust.
Propellant	tanks in the fuselage, behind the pilot.
Armament	none
Electronics	none
Wingspan	10.40 m
Length	6.40 m
Height	2.13 m
Wing area	18 sq. m
Max. weight	2,100 kg
Max. speed	550 kph
Rate of climb	1,615 m/min

Technical data Me 163 A

Type	single-seat research rocket-airplane.
Wings	wooden structure, plywood cladding with 29- and 34-degree swept at the leading edge and 10-degree swept at the trailing edge, Type C slots in the 40-per-cent span, landing flaps, elevator, and ailerons.
Fuselage	light alloy structure and cladding.
Undercarriage	detachable twin wheels trolley and landing skid.
Engine	one Walter HWK RII 203 cold rocket engine with 750-kp pneumatic controllable thrust.
Propellant tanks	one of 530 litres in the fuselage, behind the pilot.
Armament	none
Electronics	none
Wingspan	8.85 m
Length	5.25 m
Height	2.16 m
Aspect ratio	1:4.4
Wing area	17.50 sq. m
Max. weight	2,400 kg
Max. speed	0.85 Mach
Endurance	4.5 min

Technical data Lippisch P.20

Type	single-seat interceptor fighter.
Wings	wooden structure, plywood cladding with 36-degree swept at the leading edge and 29-degree swept at the trailing edge.
Fuselage	light alloy structure and cladding.
Cockpit	pressurised, control heating, frontal armour against 12.7-mm shelling and from the rear against 20-mm shelling.
Tailfin	light alloy structure and cladding.
Undercarriage	tricycle type, the main legs retractable inwards and the front gear retractable to the rear after switching 90 degrees.
Engine	one Junkers Jumo 004C with 1,000-kp static thrust.
Fuel tank	behind the pilot.
Armament	two Mk 103/30 cannons in the wing roots and two Mk 108 in the nose.
Electronics	one EZ 42 gyrogunsight, FuG 16 Zy VHF transmitter/receiver, and one FuG 25a IFF radio set.
Wingspan	9.3 m
Length	5.73 m
Height	3.02 m
Aspect ratio	5.0:1
Wing area	17.30 sq. m
Max. weight	3,627 kg
Max. speed	905 kph
Service ceiling	38,000 feet

Technical data Lippisch 8-334 (Me 334)

Type	single-seat interceptor fighter.
Wings	wooden structure, plywood cladding.
Fuselage	light alloy structure and cladding.
Cockpit	pressurised, control heating, frontal armour against 12.7-mm shelling and from the rear against 20-mm shelling, Heinkel-Kartusche ejector seat.
Tailfin	light alloy structure and cladding with tail bumper.
Undercarriage	tricycle type, the main legs retractable inwards and the front gear retractable to the rear after switching 90 degrees to fold underneath the engine.
Engine	a Daimler Benz DB 605 of 1,475 hp or a DB 603 of 1,900 hp, both twelve-cylinder, inverted-V, liquid-cooled engines, driving a 3-m-diameter pusher propeller through an extension shaft.
Fuel tank	behind the pilot.
Armament	two Mk 108/30 cannons in the wing roots and two MG 131/13 machine guns on top of the engine cowl.
Electronics one	EZ 42 gyrogunsight, FuG 16 Zy VHF transmitter/receiver, and one FuG 25a IFF radio set.
Wingspan	9.3 m
Length	7 m
Height	3.72 m

Aspect ratio	5.0:1
Wing area	17.3 sq. m
Max. weight	3,000 kg
Max. speed	(with DB 605) slightly better than a Me 109 G.
Service ceiling	(with DB 605) slightly better than a Me 109 G.

Technical data Lippisch P.15 *Diana* (4 April 1945)

Type	single-seat jet fighter.
Wings	wood structure and cladding, 23-degree swept.
Fuselage	metallic structure and cladding, non-pressurised cockpit, Heinkel-Kartusche ejector seat.
Landing gear	tricycle type from the He 162.
Engine	one Junkers Jumo 004, or one BMW 003 rated at 800-kp static thrust, or one HeS 011 rated at 1,300-kp static thrust.
Fuel tanks	in the fuselage, behind the pilot.
Armament	two Mk 108/30 cannons in the wing roots and two MG 151/20 cannons in the nose.
Wingspan	10.08 m
Length	6.40 m
Wing area	20 sq. m
Aspect ratio	5:1
Max. speed	(with HeS 011) Mach 0.84
Endurance	(with HeS 011) 45 min

Technical data Lippisch P.15 (3 March 1945)

Type	transonic jet fighter.
Wings	52 degrees swept back and a 7-per-cent thickness/chord ratio, metallic structure and cladding.
Fuselage	integrated in the wing, pressurised cockpit, metallic structure and cladding.
Landing gear	tricycle type, based on the Messerschmitt P.1112 S/2 one.
Engine	one HeS 011 turbojet of 1,290-kp thrust.
Fuel tanks	two in the wings.
Armament	two Mk 108 cannons of 30 mm in the wing roots.
Wingspan	7.80 m
Length	8.10 m
Height	2.90 m
Wing area	22 sq. m
Max. speed	Mach 1

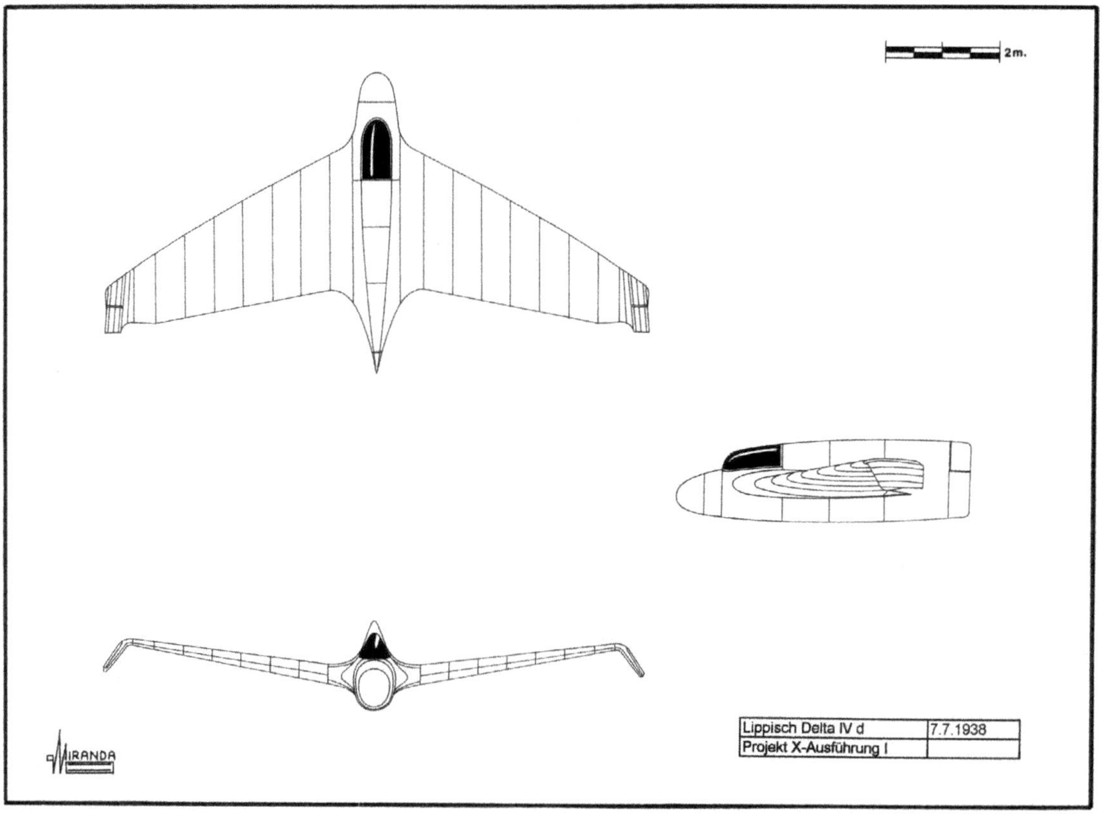

2m.

Lippisch Delta IV d	7.7.1938
Projekt X-Ausführung I	

MIRANDA

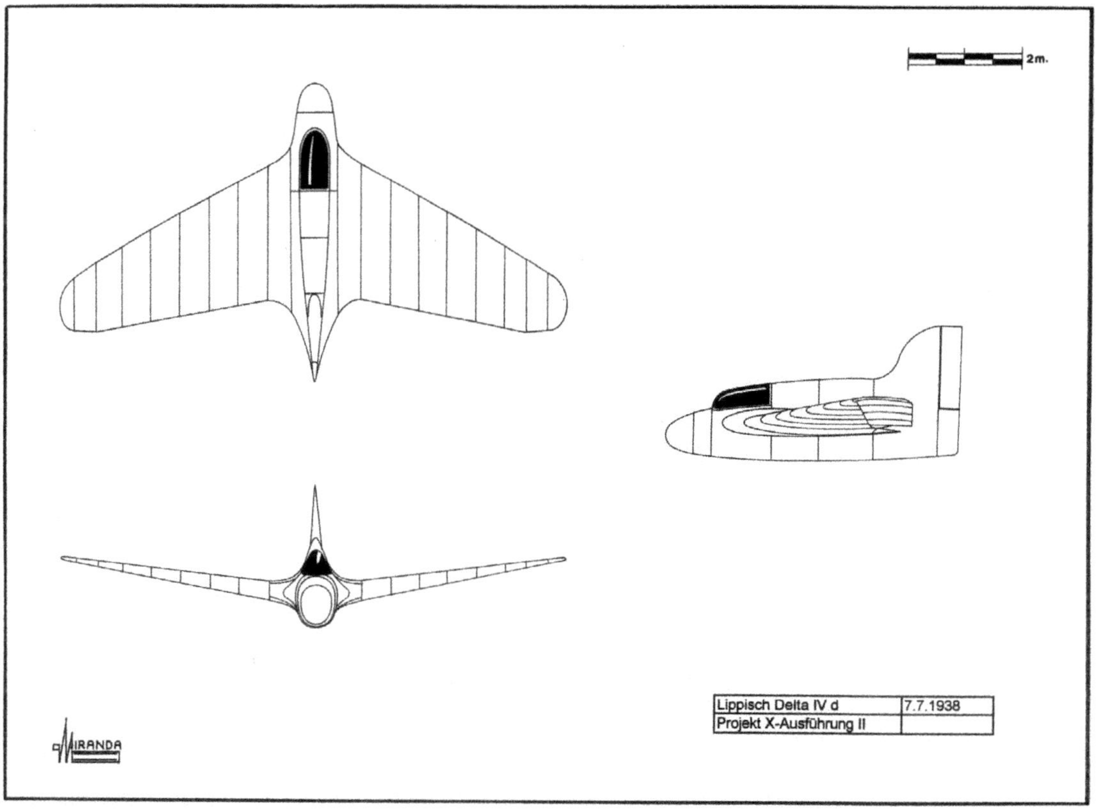

2m.

Lippisch Delta IV d	7.7.1938
Projekt X-Ausführung II	

MIRANDA

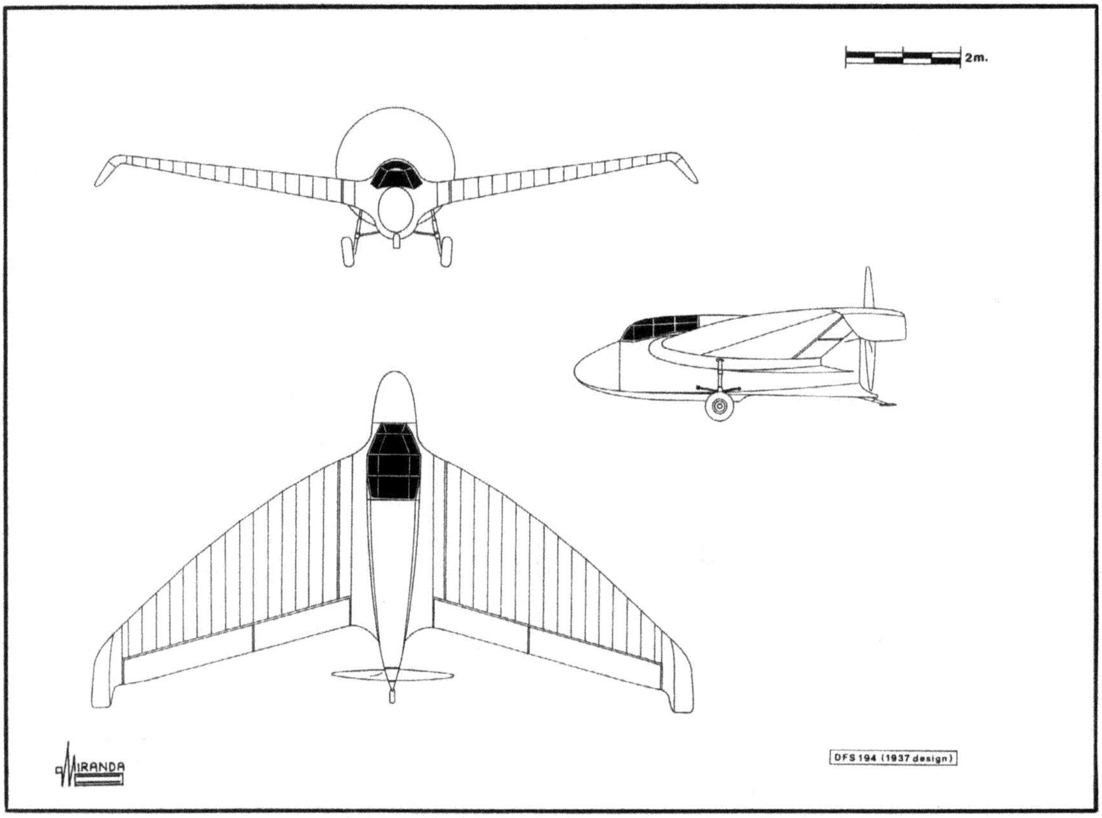
2m.
MIRANDA
DFS 194 (1937 design)

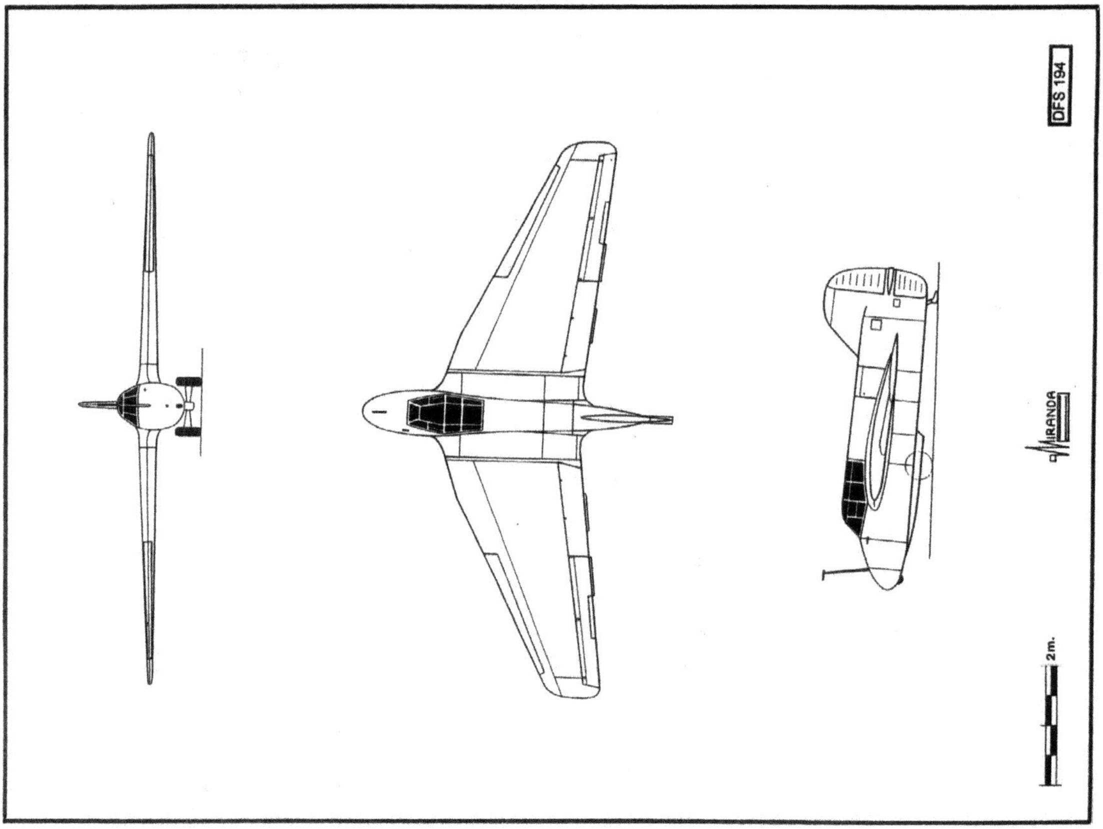
DFS 194
MIRANDA
2m.

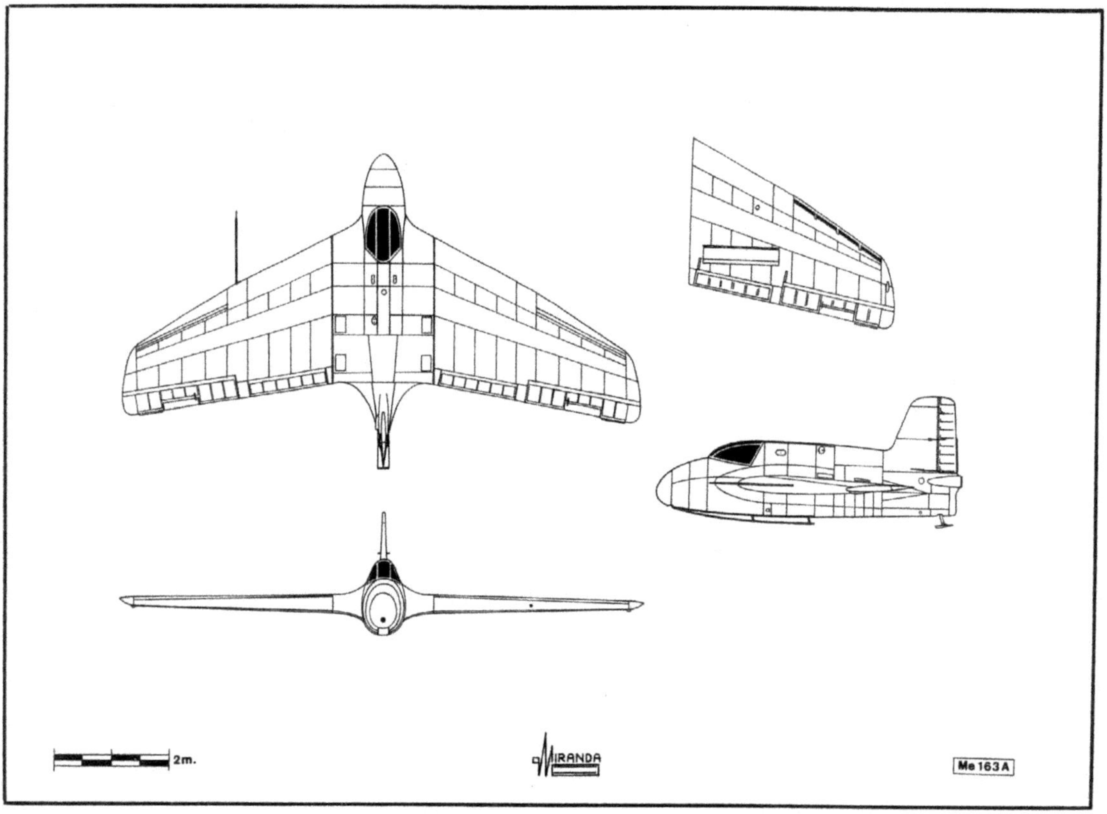

2m.   MIRANDA   Me 163 A

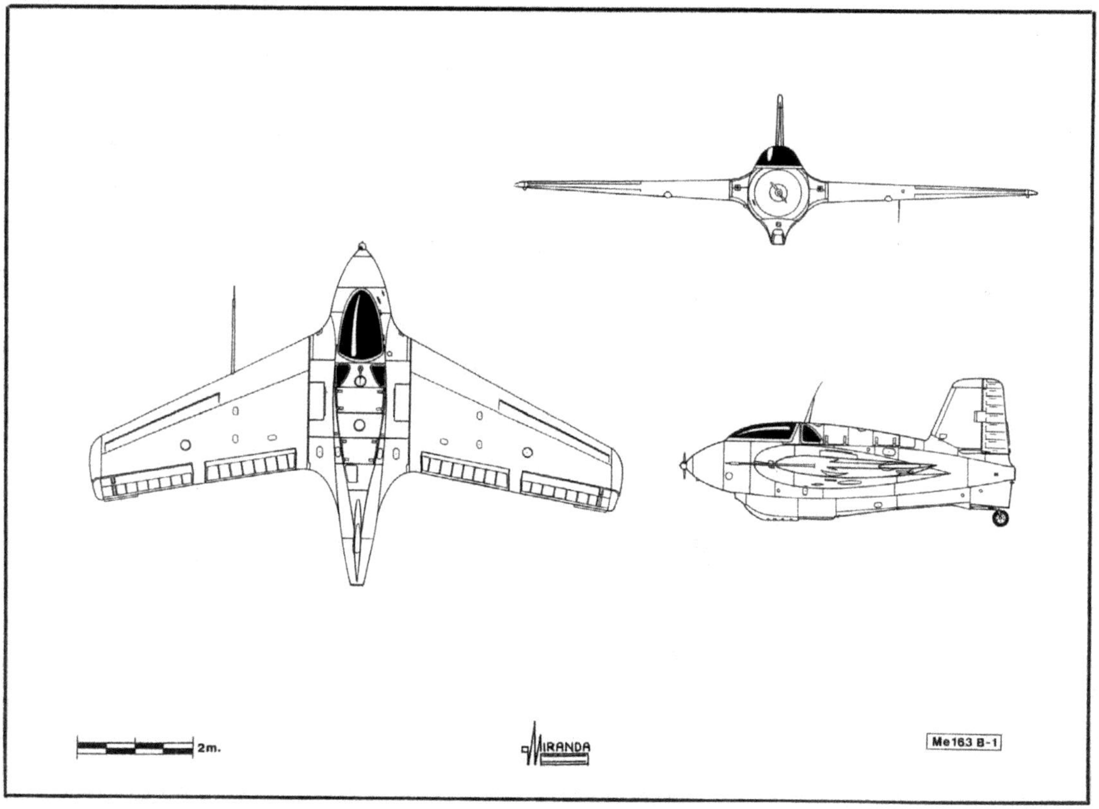

2m.   MIRANDA   Me 163 B-1

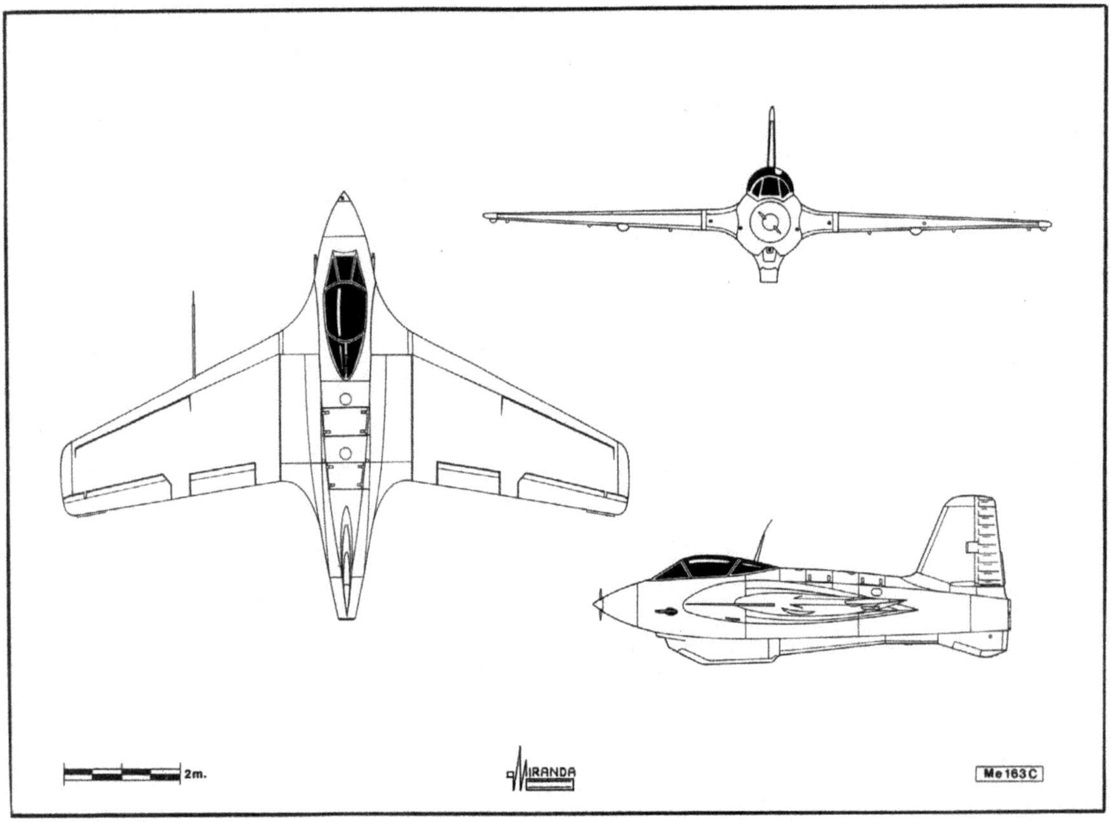

2m.

MIRANDA

Me 163 C

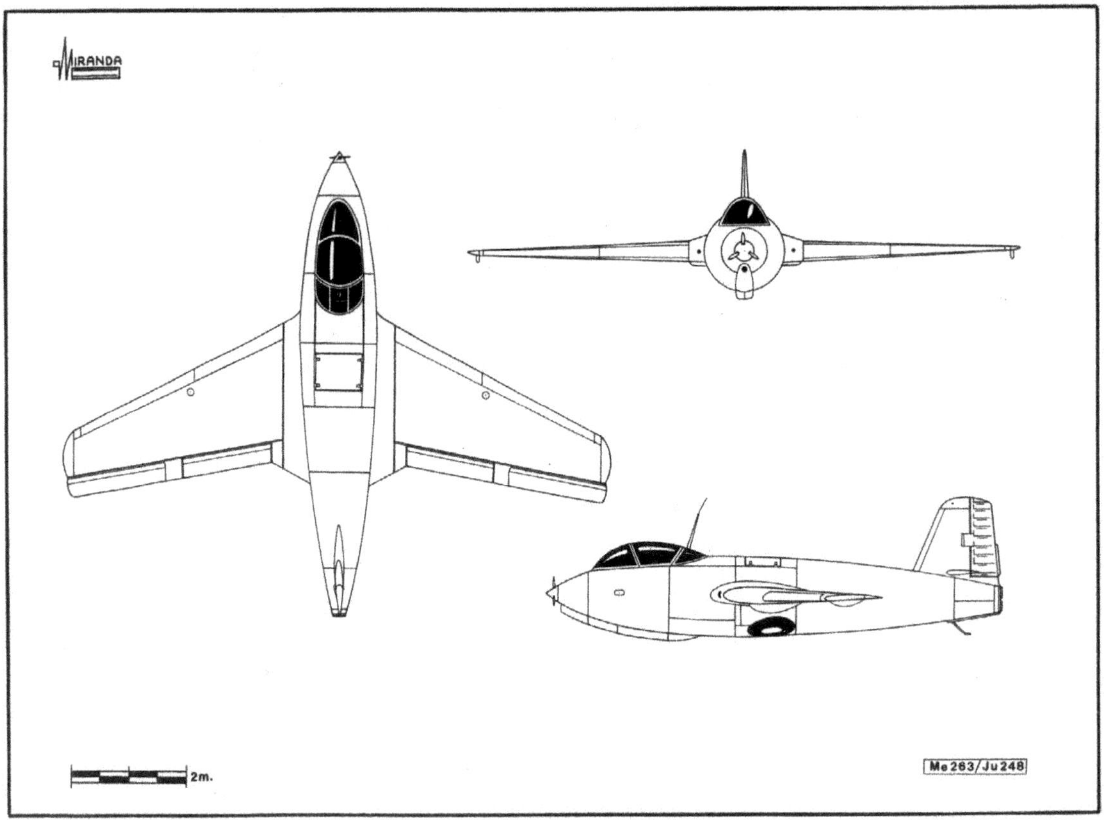

MIRANDA

2m.

Me 263 / Ju 248

Lippisch P.20

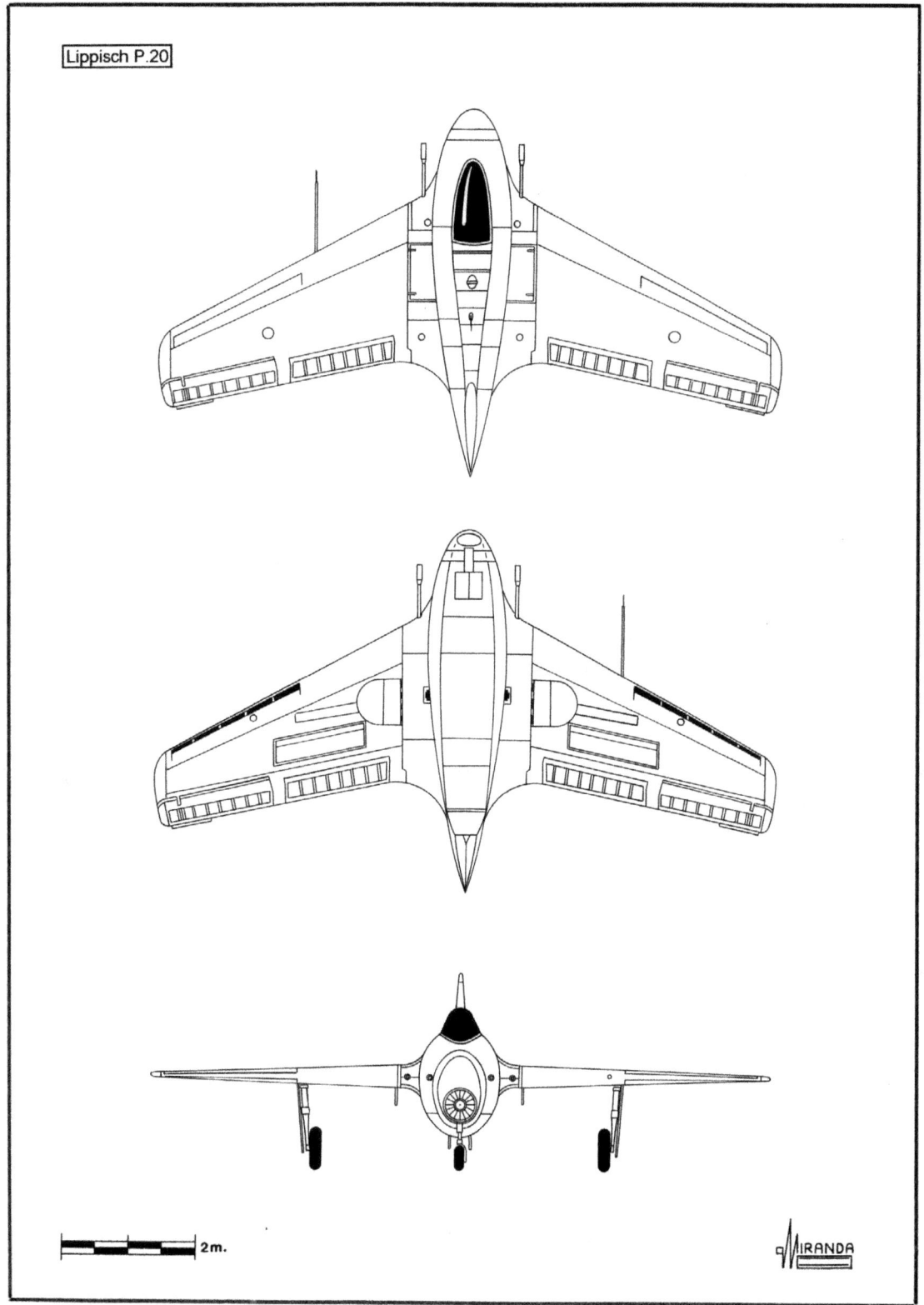

2m.

MIRANDA

Lippisch P.20

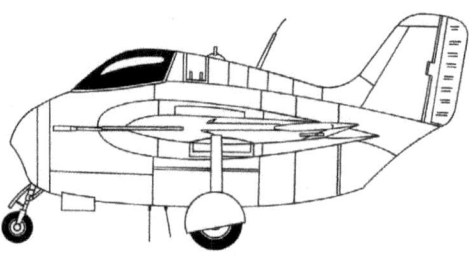

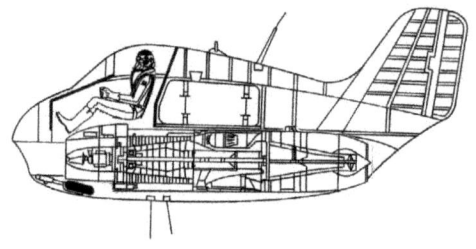

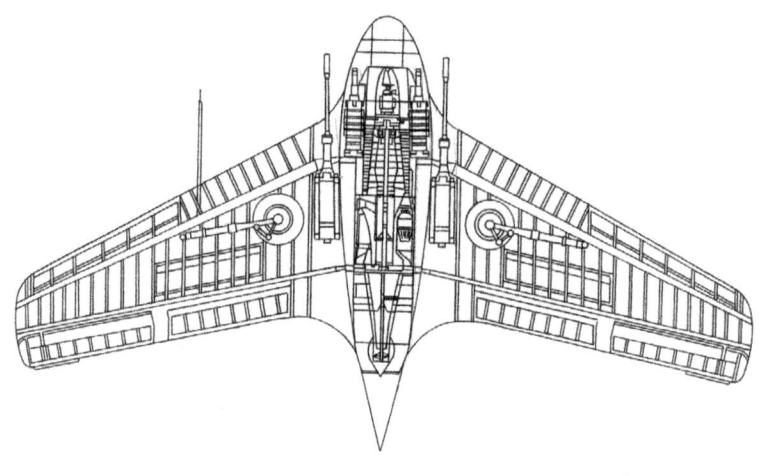

2m.

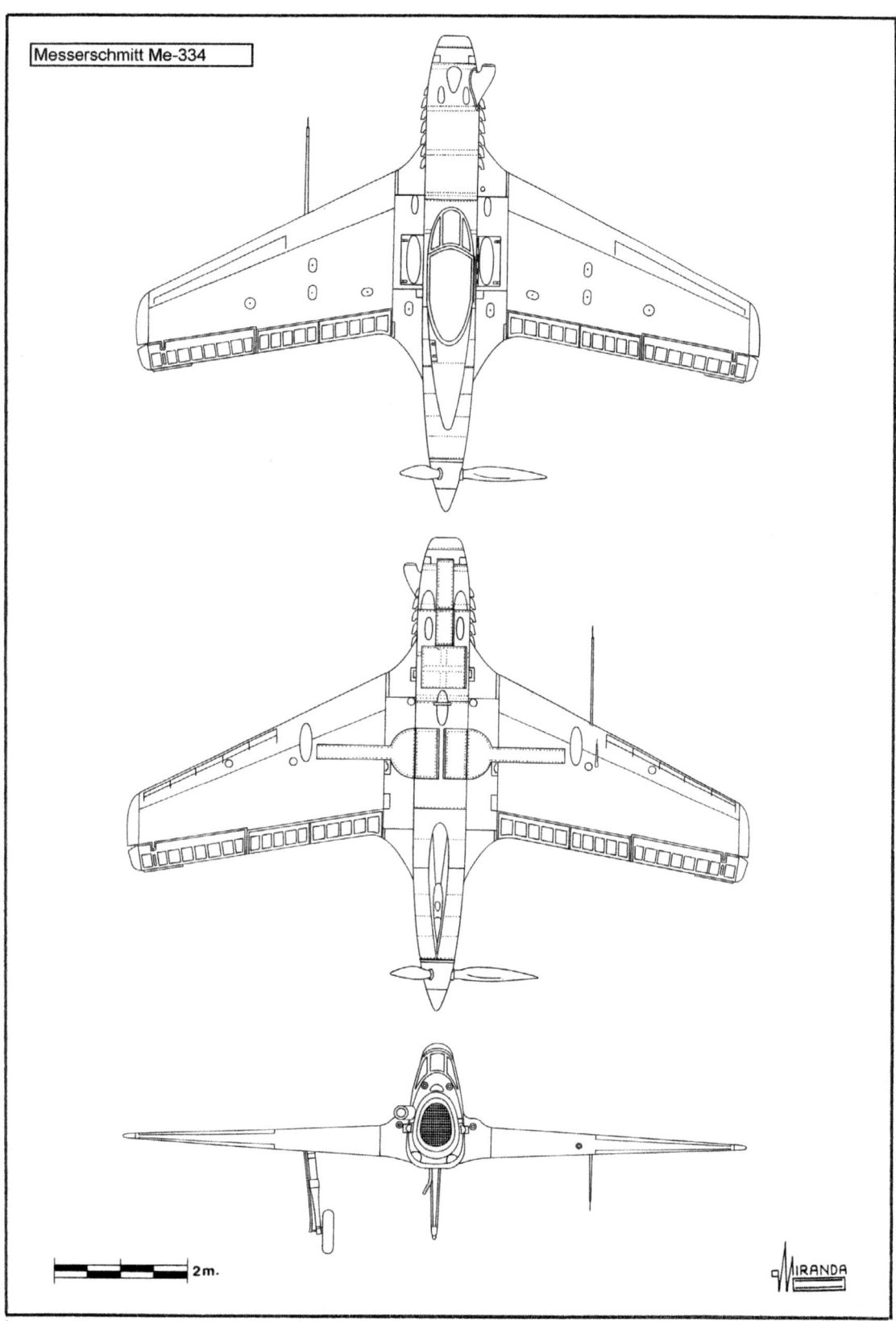

Messerschmitt Me-334

2m.

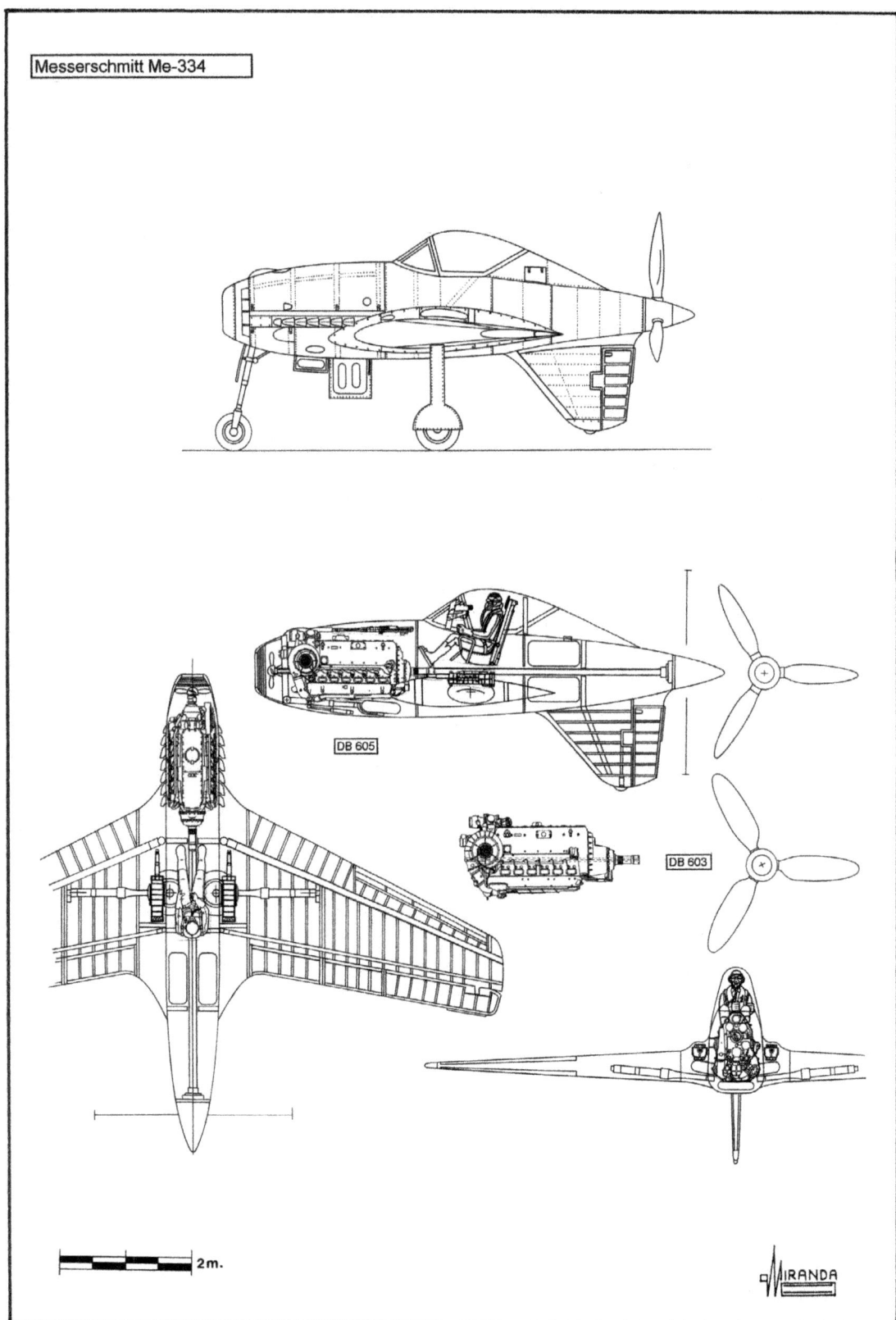

Messerschmitt Me-334

DB 605

DB 603

2 m.

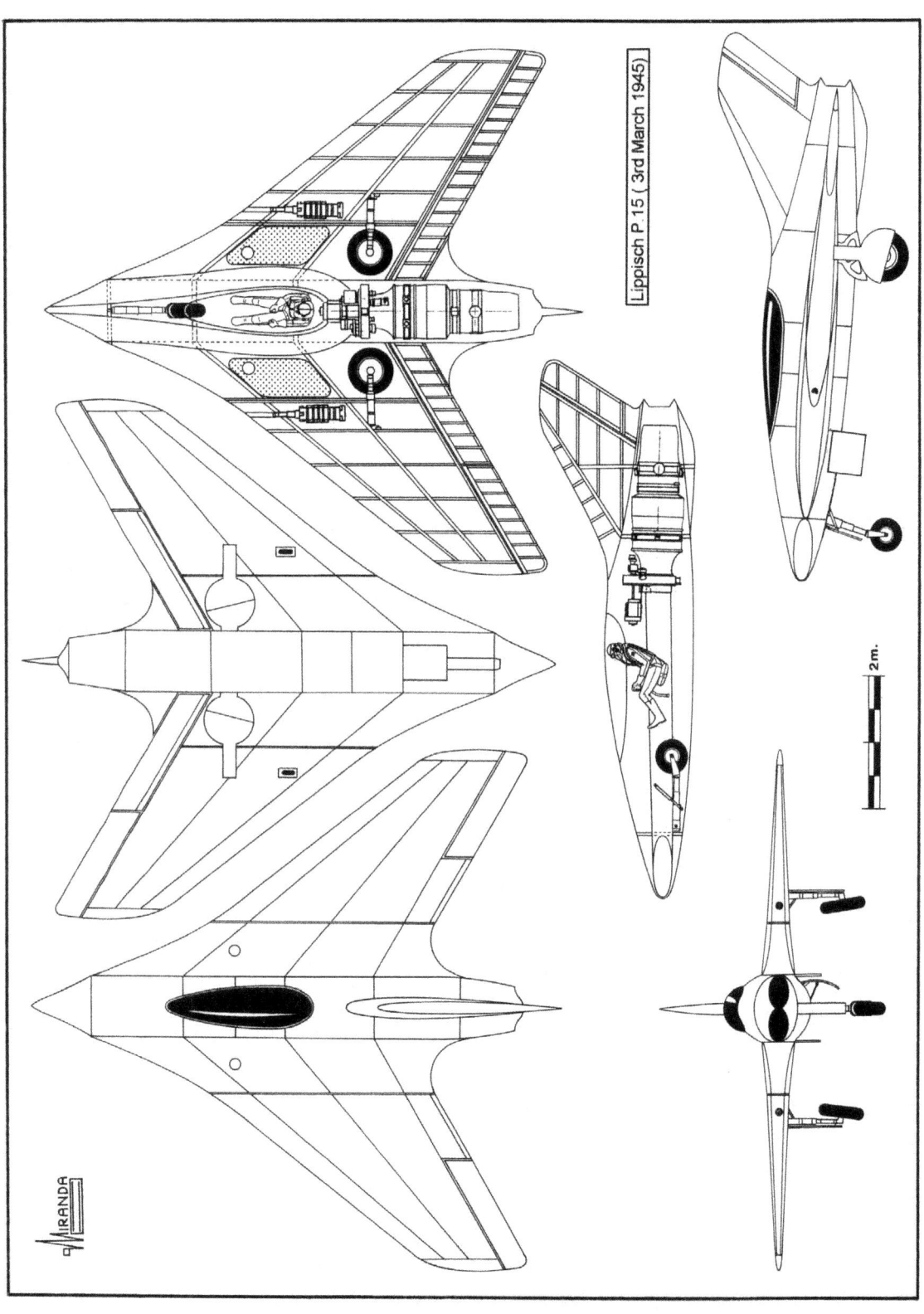

Lippisch P.15 (3rd March 1945)

2 m.

Lippisch P.15 (4th April 1945)

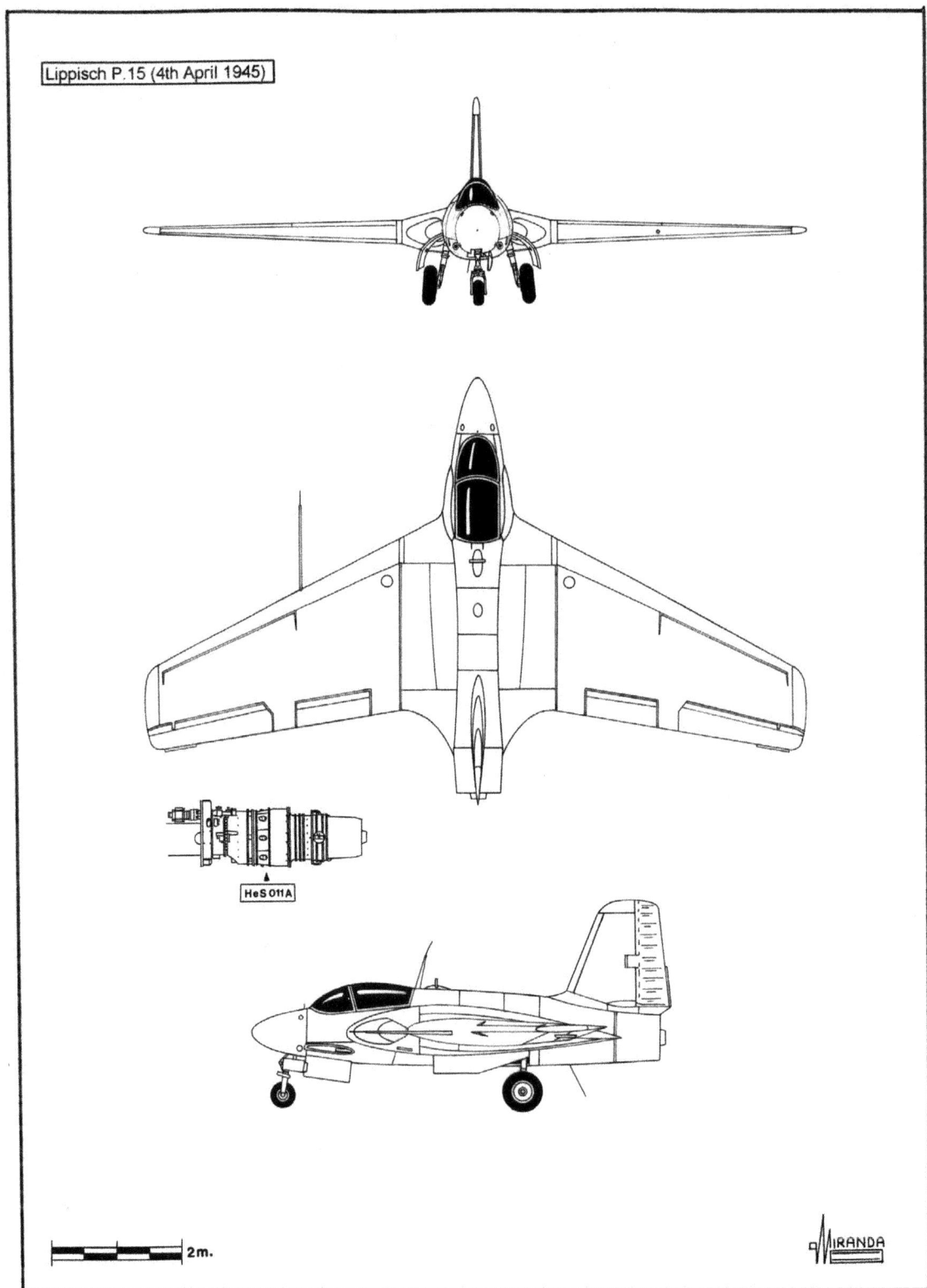

HeS 011A

2m.

Chapter 24

Lippisch P.11

In October 1941, it was evident that the rocket engines planned for the Me 163 B would not be available for some months or even years.

By the beginning of the month, the excellent aerodynamic features of the Me 163 A had allowed it to reach 1,000 kph (0.84 Mach), and Lippisch started to consider the possibilities of the new Junkers T1 turbojets that had been successfully tested some days after the record was broken.

They were too long for a *Komet* airframe, so had to be installed in a bigger airplane, a heavy fighter of 6 tons, equivalent to the Me 262 which, with the Me 163 aerodynamics, would have a better ceiling, climb rate, and maximum speed.

On 28 November 1941, it was presented to the Oberkommando der Luftwaffe as *Lippisch P.09*, a single heavy fighter armed with four 20-mm guns. It was too advanced for its time and the manufacturing of the Me 262 was preferred.

Lippisch decided to turn the basic design into a *Schnellbomber* by installing a second crew member, widening the wingspan 1.4 m, and reducing the sweep by 3 degrees. The fuselage contained two fuel tanks and a bomb bay underneath them had capacity for an SC 1000 L2.

The new project, known as *Lippisch P.11-92* (13 September 1942), was presented to the OKL as the answer to the specification published by the RLM's Technical Department on 20 October 1942. The latter required a bomber with a 1,000-kg payload, a 700-kph maximum speed, and a 1,046-km penetration depth.

It did not turn out well. Designers had not considered that the acceleration generated by the turbojet was much lower than the rockets on which the original project was based. It was estimated that a tailless bomber, when heavily loaded, would have difficulty in making the rotation during take off, due to the short distance between the elevators and the centre of gravity, even supported by the RATO auxiliary rockets. The P.11-92 was cancelled in November 1942.

On 2 December, the design team of *Abteilung L* tried again with an improved design (P.11-105), one which replaced the radio operator with new electronic equipment for fighters. The cockpit was installed in the nose to reduce the drag produced by the old canopy, and the climb rate and ceiling were improved, increasing the wing surface. A retractable tailplane, formed by two trapezoidal surfaces of 3 sq. m each, was installed to solve the problem at take off.

The P.11-105 could dive bomb using a *Revi C16* reflector gunsight or engage at high altitude in a flight levelled with the *Lofte 7* bombsight. The idea of the retractable tail-plane was not favoured by OKL, who cancelled the project at the beginning of 1943 out of concern for the aircraft's stability. Instead, production of Me 410 B-1 was initiated.

After Messerschmitt's *Abteilung L* was dissolved in April, the Lippisch design team moved to Vienna to form the Luftfahrtforschungsanstalt Wien (Aeronautical Research Institute). The work on the P.11 continued there, introducing for the first time the 'jet-exhaust deflection flaps' effect—aerodynamic surfaces located behind the engines which, by changing the angle of incidence by hydraulic actuators, helped to keep the tail low during take off.

The building of new monocoque structures for the wings based on *Tronal*—a composite material made of wood pulp fibre and the *Dynal Z5* phenolic resin developed by Dynamit Nobel Troisdorf—was also the subject of experimentation. The outer surface of the wings was covered by *Polystal V*, a phenolformaldehyde resin that considerably reduced drag.

On 1 May 1943, the construction of the P.11-121 was proposed to the OKL. It was a *Schnellbomber* with a 35-degree swept delta wing, thick enough to contain the engines and a great quantity of fuel. The wing surface was increased to 50 sq. m, and the wingspan reduced to gain speed.

Another innovation was the detachable 'cocoon' bomb bay, built of *Tronal*, which could contain extra fuel, recce cameras, one anti-ship SC 1000 bomb or a heavy recoilless cannon. The whole set could be detached in an emergency. The original single tailfin was replaced by a double one in the *Zerstörer* version (named *Delta VI Projekt*) based on the P.11-121 formula.

The construction of a wood/plywood experimental glider *Delta VI-1* was begun by the end of 1943, with the intention of testing the features of the new wing—built with non-strategic materials. It was 38 degrees swept, had ventral flaps in 'V', elevators with double joint, and ailerons and movable wingtips to increase lift and controllability. Both the length and the wingspan had been lightly increased (with reference to the P.11-121), and a new type of undercarriage was adopted, with double-tyre bogies and electrical operation.

The second prototype, *Delta VI-426*, would have had a metallic central section and two Jumo 004 B turbojets for the propulsion tests. The production version, presented to the OKL in February 1944, would be named *Delta VI-2* and would reach an estimated maximum speed of 1,040 kph. It might have transported different combinations of armament, with 20- and 30-mm guns and, in the *Delta VI-426* variant, even a 75-mm recoilless cannon in a ventral detachable container.

All versions shared the fixed armament of two Mk 213/30 cannons in the wing roots with a great amount of ammunition housed within the leading edge. The 75-mm cannon could be shot at a great distance, but it required the installation of a ZFR 4a telescopic gunsight.

There also existed the *Delta VI-3* version, with a 40-degree sweep and a new landing gear from which the nose leg would have been removed. This was going back to the classical configuration, with two tail wheels that allowed the nose to remain elevated, and the tail low, at take off.

The whole production of turbojets was absorbed by the assembly lines of the Me 262 and Ar 234. The Jumo 004 and BMW 003 were not very reliable and difficult to manufacture in great quantities; the fuel, the spare parts and the additives required to harden the special steel of the blades were scarce. The new HeS 011 was just an unfinished prototype.

Lippisch turned his attention towards a third type of jet engine, the Lorin ramjets, to power his future designs. His first try on 12 April 1944 projected the integration of a *Delta VI* airframe with a 20,000-hp Lorin *Strahlrohr* of oval section, with a wind-electric generator installed within the air intake.

These types of engines worked with liquid fuel carbon disulphide, self-igniting at the compression temperature of the air at the end of the Oswatitsch-type multiple-shock diffusers. Lippisch pursued his research with the P.12 and P.13, which already included ramjets designed by him.

Technical data *Lippisch P.11-105* (December 1942)

Type	single-seat fast bomber.
Wings	wooden structure, plywood cladding with 32-degree swept at the leading edge and 13- and 7-degree swept at the trailing edge, containing two fuel tanks of 810 litres and two of 600 litres, the main undercarriage legs (retracting outwards) with 840 x 300-mm-diameter tyres, leading-edge Type C slots (40-per-cent span), ailerons, flaps, and airbrakes.
Fuselage	light alloy structure and cladding, housing the engines, the cockpit (pressurised, control heating, rear armour against 20-mm shelling), the front undercarriage gear (retractable to the rear after switching 90 degrees) with one 500 x 180 tyre, one 480-litre fuel tank, two MG 151/20 cannon, and two RATO rockets.
Tailfins	light alloy structure and cladding with hydraulic retractable tailplane.
Engines	two Junkers Jumo 004B turbojets with 760-kp static thrust and two RATO Rheinmetall-Borsig 109-502 solid fuel rockets with 771-kp peak thrust.
Payload	one SC 1000 L2 anti-ship bomb of 1,027 kg.
Electronics	FuG 16Zy, FuG 25a, FuG 101, Revi C/12 D gunsight, and Lofte 7 bombsight.
Wingspan	12.65 m
Length	8.14 m
Height	4 m
Wide track	2 m
Wing area	37.30 sq. m
Max. weight	7,500 kg
Max. speed	900 kph

Technical data *Lippisch P.11-121* Bomber (1 May 1943)

Type	single-seat fast bomber.
Wings	35-degree swept at the leading edge, monocoque structure with stressed skin composite made of Tronal and Dynal Z5, covered by a smooth external layer of Polystal V, housing two fuel tanks of 1,800 litres each, the main undercarriage legs (retracting forwards) with 840 x 300-mm-diameter tyres, flaps, elevators, and ailerons.

Fuselage	light alloy structure and cladding, housing the engines, the bomb bay, two Mk 103/30 cannons, the nose leg (retracting forwards) with one 500 x 180 tyre, the cockpit (pressurised, control heating, rear armour against 20-mm shelling), tailfin, and two jet exhaust deflection flaps.
Engines	two Junkers Jumo 004 C turbojets with 1,015-kp static thrust.
Payload	one SC 1000 L2 anti-ship bomb of 1,027 kg.
Electronics	FuG 16Zy, FuG 25a, FuG 101, Revi C/12 D gunsight, and Lofte 7 bombsight.
Wingspan	10.60 m
Length	6.80 m
Height	2.70 m
Wide track	2.44 m
Wing area	50 sq. m
Max. weight	7,260 kg

LIPPISCH P.11-121 ZERSTÖRER (DECEMBER 1943)

Double tailfin, no bomb bay, armed with four Mk 103/30 located in the wing roots and on the underbelly fairing, and another MG 151/20 cannon shooting backwards with some type of periscopic gunsight.

Technical data *Lippisch Delta VI-2* (February 1944)	
Type	single-seat *Zerstörer*.
Wings	38-degree swept at the leading edge, aspect ratio 2.33:1, 17-per-cent-thickness profile at the wing root and 9 per cent at the wingtip. Monocoque structure of *Tronal/Dynal Z5/Polystal V* composites, housing four fuel tanks with a total capacity of 3,600 litres, the main undercarriage legs with double tyre bogies, electrical operation (retracting forwards) flaps, ailerons, movable wingtips, and two ammunition tanks for the Mk 213/30 cannons.
Fuselage	light alloy structure and cladding housing the engines, two Mk 213/30 cannons, the nose leg (retracting backwards), the cockpit (pressurised, control heating, frontal armour against 12.7-mm shelling and at rear against 20-mm shelling), and double tailfins.
Engines	two Junkers Jumo 004 B turbojets with 890-kp static thrust, two RATO Schmidding 109-553 solid fuel rockets with 1,750-kp peak thrust, and four Schmidding 109-543 with 150-kp peak thrust.
Armament	two Mk 213/30 cannons in the wing roots and one-shot recoilless cannon Rhein-metall-Borsig *Düka 75*, with two nozzles diverging by 30 degrees, each in a *Tronal* aerodynamic container suspended under the airplane belly.
Electronics	FuG 16Zy, FuG 25a, ZFR 4a telescopic gunsight.
Wingspan	10.80 m
Length	7.48 m
Height	2.76 m
Wide track	2.90 m

Wing area	50 sq. m
Aspect ratio	2.33:1
Max. speed	1,040 kph in clean configuration
Range	3,000 km
Max. weight	8,000 kg

Technical data *Lippisch Delta VI-3*

Type	single-seat heavy fighter.
Wings	40-degree swept at the leading edge, same structure as the VI-2 but with the main undercarriage retracting backwards. Tyres of 700 x 195.
Fuselage	same structure as the VI-2 but with twin tail wheels with (465 x 165) tyres retracting backwards.
Engines	two Junkers Jumo 004 B turbojets with 890-kp static thrust, and two RATO Schmidding 109-553 solid fuel rockets with 1,750-kp peak thrust.
Armament	*Delta VI-441*, 4 x Mk 103/30
	Delta VI-412, 5 x Mk 103/30
	Delta VI-483, 4 x Mk 108/30
	Delta VI-470, 5 x Mk 108/30
	Delta VI-486, 2 x Mk 103/30 + 2 x MG 213/30
Electronics	FuG 16Zy, FuG 25a, Revi C/12 gunsight.
Wingspan	10.80 m
Length	7.39 m
Height	2.29 m
Wide track	3 m
Max. weight	7,260 kg

Technical data *Lippisch Delta VI mit Lorin Strahlrohr* (12/04/1944)

Type	single-seat transonic experimental airplane.
Wings	same structure and undercarriage as the VI-2.
Fuselage	light alloy structure and cladding housing the engine, the cockpit, the nose leg (retracting backwards) and twin tailfins.
Engine	one liquid-fuel Lorin ramjet with 20,000-hp thrust.
Wingspan	10.62 m
Length	9.36 m
Height	2.54 m

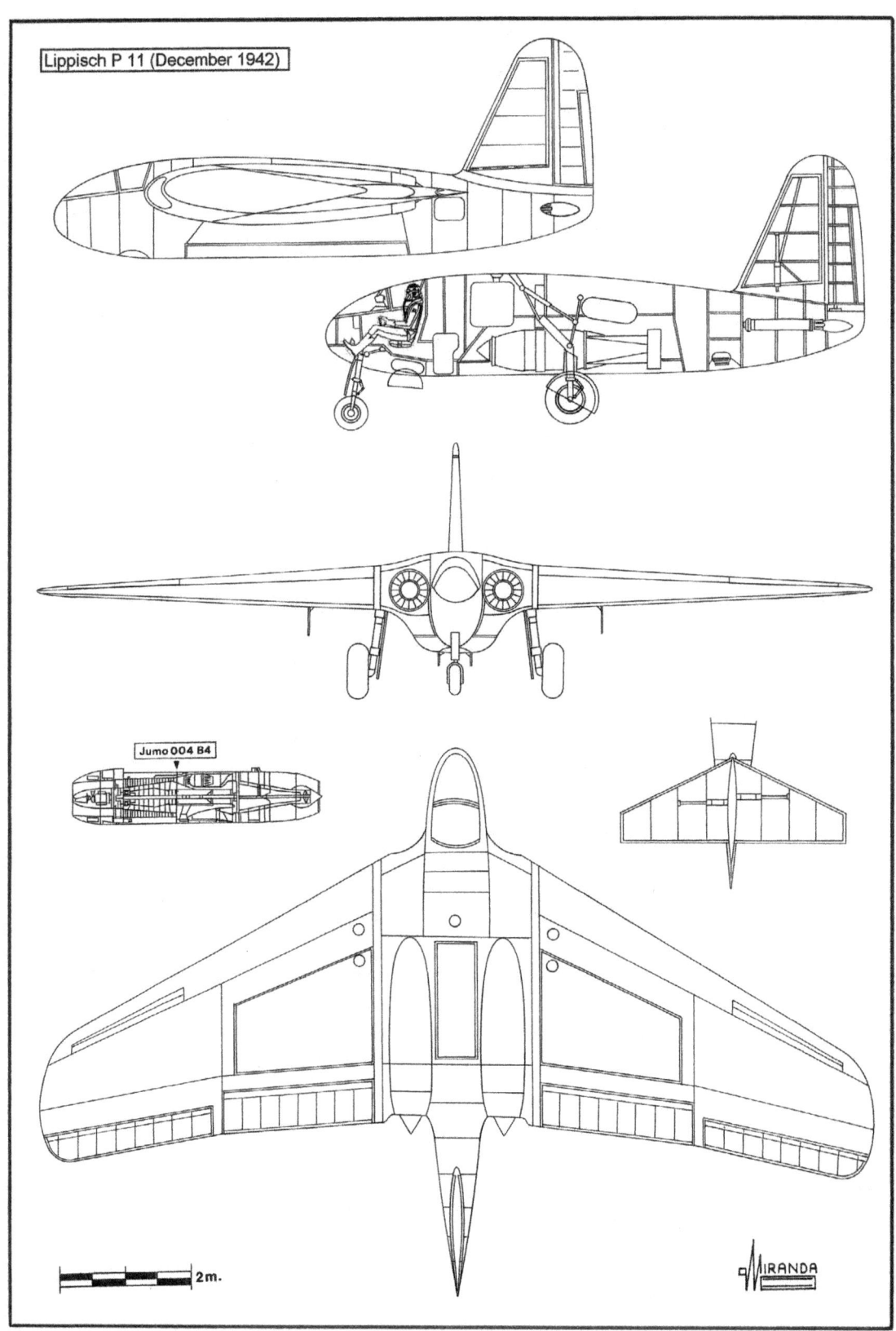

Lippisch P 11 (December 1942)

Jumo 004 B4

2m.

MIRANDA

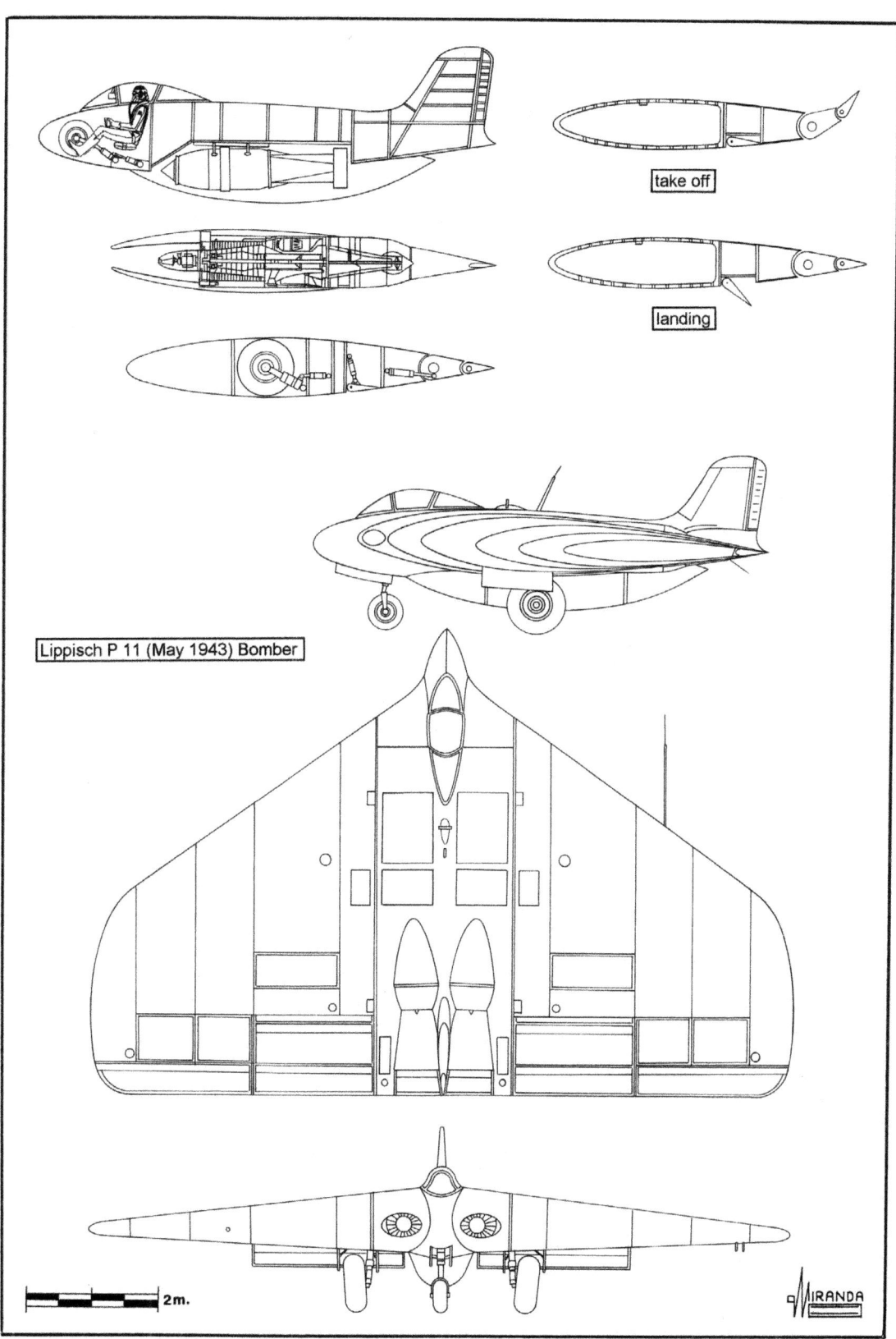

take off

landing

Lippisch P 11 (May 1943) Bomber

2m.

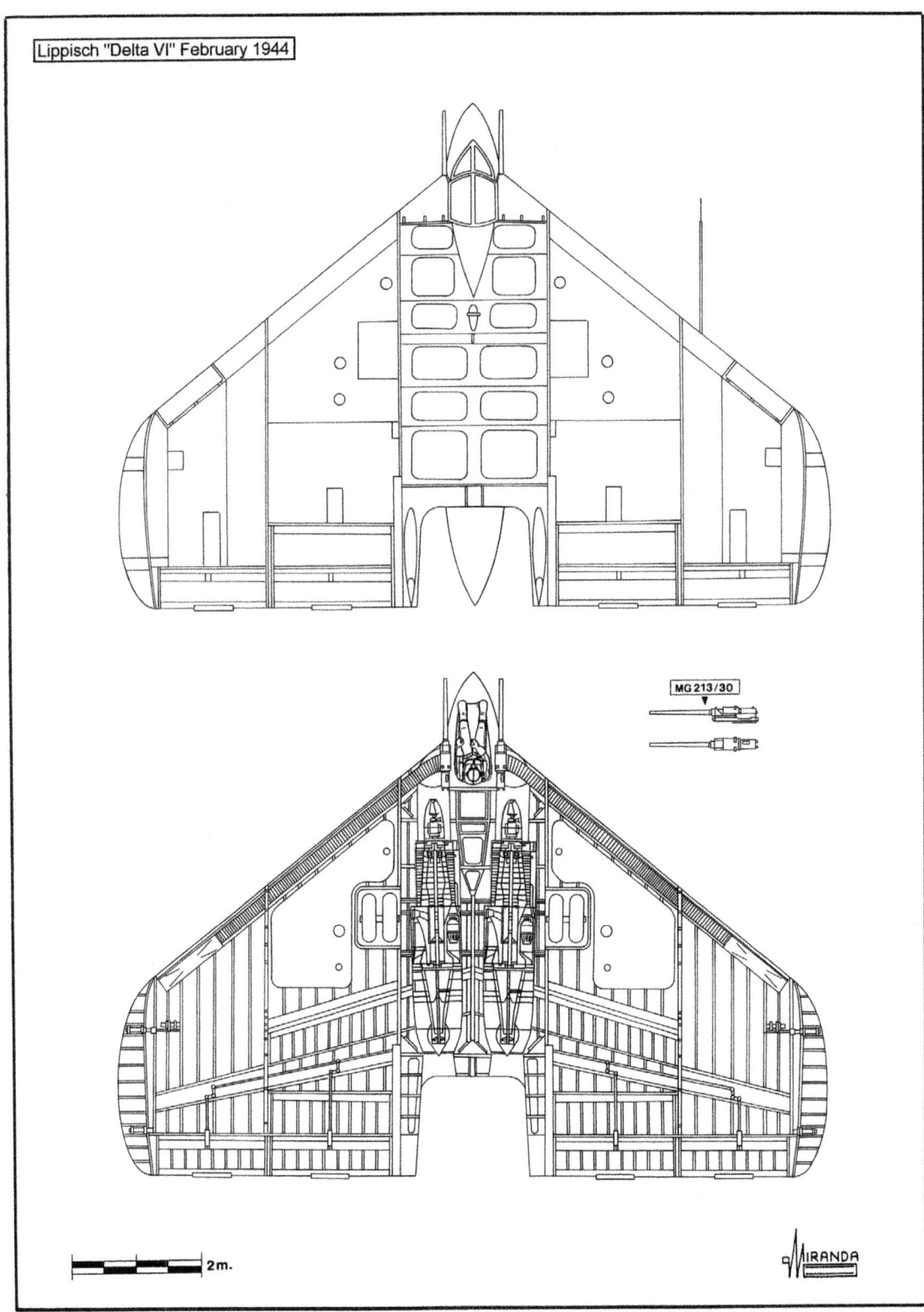

Lippisch "Delta VI" February 1944

MG 213/30

2m.

MIRANDA

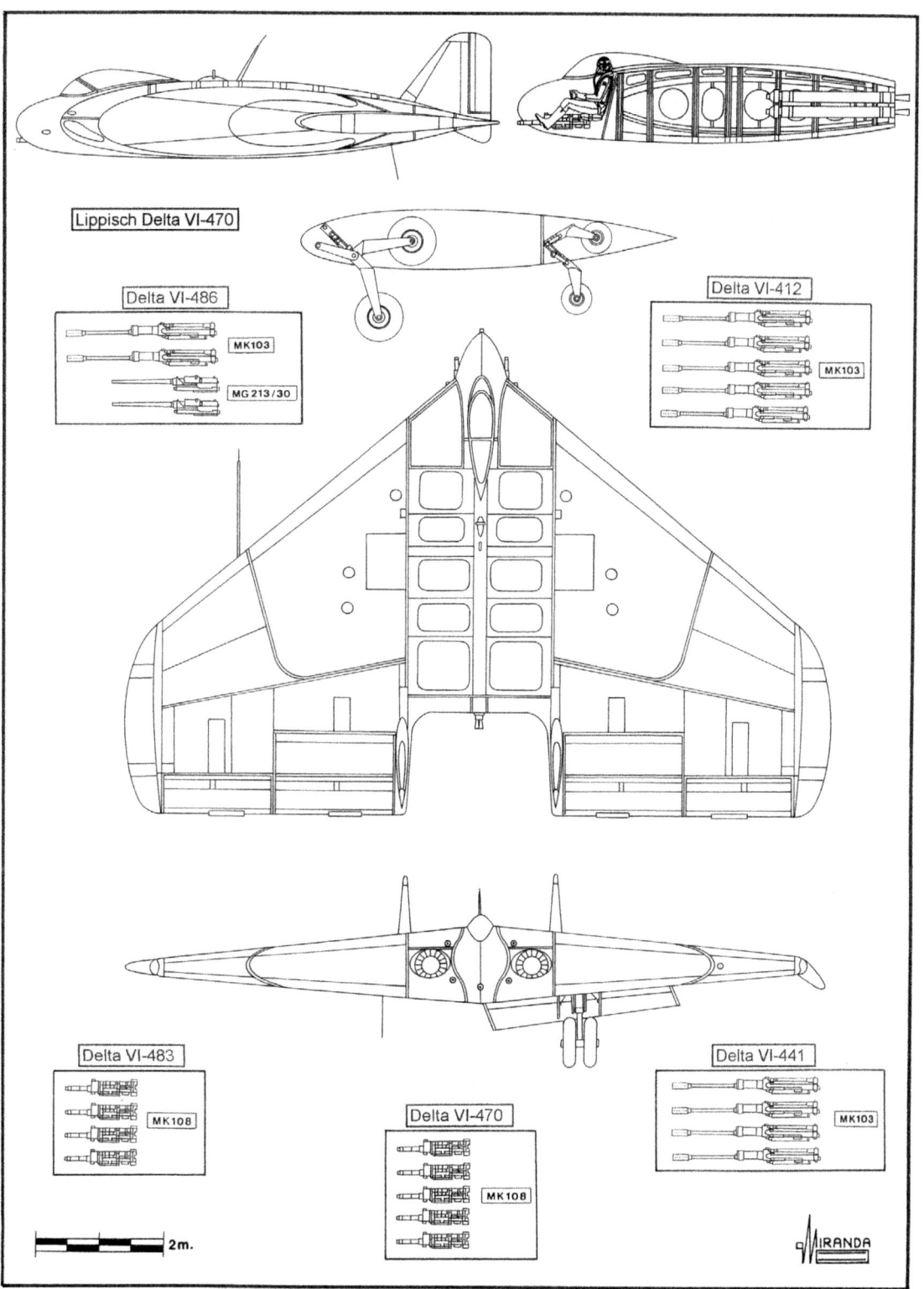

Lippisch Delta VI-470

Delta VI-486

MK103

MG 213/30

Delta VI-412

MK103

Delta VI-483

MK108

Delta VI-470

MK108

Delta VI-441

MK103

2m.

MIRANDA

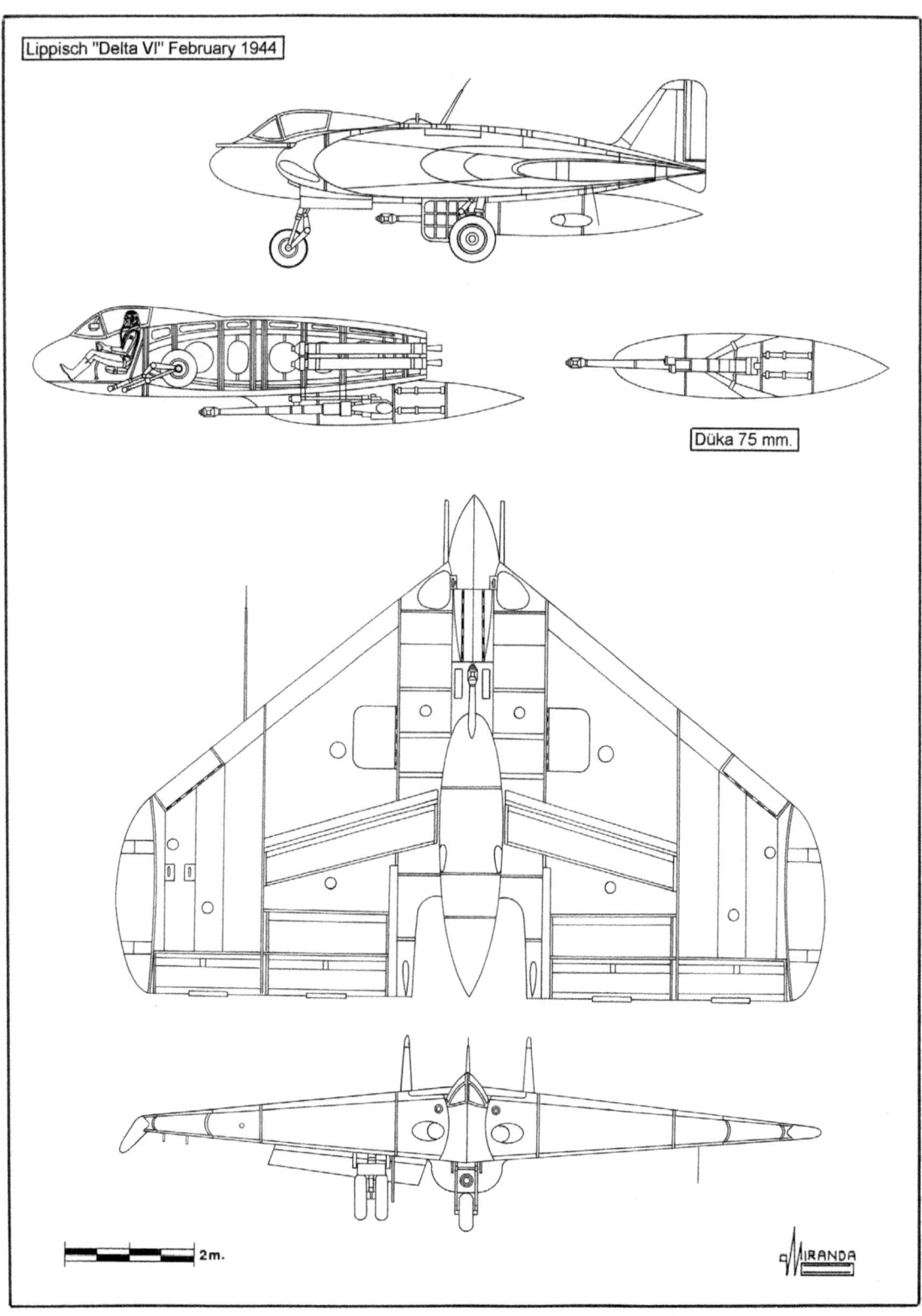

Lippisch "Delta VI" February 1944

Düka 75 mm.

2m.

ORIGINAL DRAWINGS

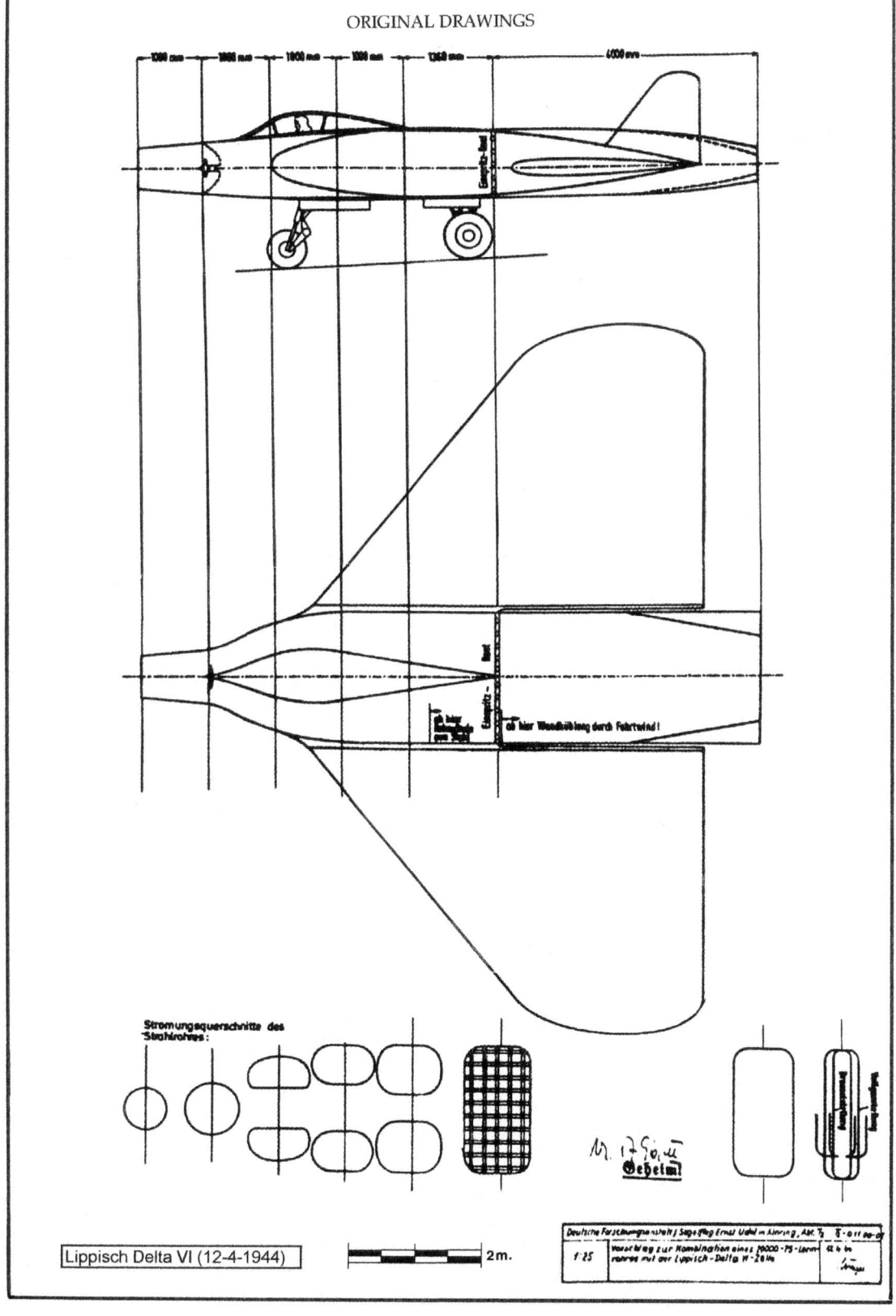

Lippisch Delta VI (12-4-1944)

2m.

Chapter 25

Lippisch P.12/13

In spite of appearances, the short range of airplanes powered by rockets seriously hindered their capacity for military use. The logical alternative was to favour the development of the turbo jet to achieve more reliable and powerful engines. Unfortunately, German industry was not able to produce the required metallic alloys, which were especially resistant to heat and stress. They lacked metals, like chromium and molybdenum, which were essential to harden the steel.

Chemists produced silicones to replace the rubber, and synthetic oil of low quality from coal. But the ceramic materials for the compressor blades of the turbojets would not be ready on time, and everyone was aware of it. The pulsejet of the V-1 did not have enough power, and though different variants of the He 162, Me 262, and Me 328 were designed—powered by two, four, and even six pulsejets—it was soon evident that they were a dead end. The vibrations they generated threatened to destroy the airplane structure.

The only solution left was the ramjet, and a high-speed version of the Me 262 powered by two athodyd ramjets was soon designed. Henschel designed the P.1080, Focke Wulf the Ta 283, and Skoda-Kauba the P.14. All of them were of the Lorin type and were based on the engine developed by Dr Eugen Sänger's team in the DFS. They had a circular section and worked from 20,000 to 60,000 hp, using any type of fuel.

Lippisch was also interested by the idea of powering his radio-guided glider bomb GB 3/L. A 1:50 scale wind-tunnel model was built and tests offered such good results that it was decided to build a research airplane to study the possibilities of the new power plant in transonic flight.

The new design, LP.12 *Entwurf I* (Configuration I), consisted of a set of triangular wings and tailfin fitted to the ramjet tube that acted as fuselage. The pilot went in the tailfin and the fuel tanks in the wing. The ramjet, like the pulsejet, needed to move at a great speed before being started. To achieve this, it was proposed in August 1944 that the PL12 be carried up to 26,000 feet over a Focke Wulf Fw 58, in a Mistel configuration, and launched from there.

But tests performed in April that year on a ramjet for the heavy fighter project P.11 *Delta VI* proved that they could generate more power by increasing the number of sprinkles in the grid of the fuel injection system and the volume of the combustion chamber. The new airframe *Entwurf II* was designed around a bigger ramjet to adapt the new power plant to the LP.12. *Entwurf II* kept the circular intake. A dividing wall within this intake split the air into two 'D'-shaped ducts to either side of the pilot cockpit. After passing through the two sprinkling grids, the fuel mixed in the air ducts that converged in a hexagonal combustion chamber, located behind the cockpit that stretched towards the exhaust nozzle. The wind-tunnel tests proved that the model had too much drag.

Entwurf III had added internal aerodynamic refinements like an elliptical section along the whole ramjet. As for the outer parts, the wing and tail surfaces were redesigned and the landing gear given a unique retractable wheel. Even so, the model still generated a great degree of drag due to its complex system of inner ducts, and had no transonic capacity.

Entwurf IV simplified the air intake by removing the bifurcation. To that end, the pilot had to be in prone position, lying over the air intake and within a clear aerodynamic canopy. To reduce aerodynamic drag, the vertical tailfin was reduced to a minimum area and no rudder was installed. The whole control was achieved with the elevons. The rear swept angle of the wing increased to 64.2 degrees on the leading edge, and the trailing edge changed to a forward swept angle of 15 degrees. The air intake had an elliptical section, but with a flatter axis relation of 2.8:1, ending in an elliptical sprinkler grid that led to a hexagonal combustion chamber. The nozzle, equipped with four hydraulically operated flaps, had a rectangular section of variable geometry. The ventral wheel and the 'L'-shaped wingtips of the *Entwurf III* were replaced by a retractable skid underneath the air intakes and two smaller ones at the wing roots.

The fuel tanks for all the P.12 configurations were located at the outward sections of the wings, between the spars. *Entwurf IV* was considered a transonic project and it is known in specialised literature as the 'Lippisch Supersonic Flying Wing'.

Chapter 26

Lippisch P.13

During the last year of the war, Germany's oil shortages induced scientists and engineers to experiment with alternative fuels.

The most refined oil types were used for conventional piston engines. The BMW 003 turbojets worked with B.4 (87-octane petrol). The J2 and K1 fuel types, burnt by the Jumo 004 and Heinkel HeS 011 turbojets, were heavy kerosene. The Argus pulsejet of the V-1 worked with crude oil. Peenemünde engineers designed a V-2 that worked with diesel oil and *S-Stoff*—mixture of nitric acid (96 per cent) and ferrous chloride (4 per cent). Dr Pabst, from the Gas Dynamics section of the Focke Wulf Company, suggested that the ramjets of the future *Triebflügel* fighter burned even less volatile fuels, such as pitch oil or lignite tar. To that end, they had to design a compact evaporating plant that could be installed onboard.

What about coal? An airplane is certainly not a locomotive, nor can it carry the weight of a steam boiler. But it is common knowledge among coal miners that air saturated with coal dust is a powerful explosive.

In the Speer Ministry research division near Lofer, Dr Zippermeyer built the vortex gun *Wirbelkanone* and the atmospheric whirlwind gun *Luftwirbelkanone*, both of them based on this type of combustion. The prototype was satisfactory.

Dr K. Wahl of the Kirchheim Technische Institut made a Lorin ramjet work with coal dust fuel. The idea was adopted by Lippisch for the powering of his P.13 project. They built a burner prototype of rectangular section which burnt a brown coal tablet in the middle of a strong wind flow. The tablet was made of suspending coal dust in pressurised inflammable oil foam which needed to be carried to the air stream in a wire mesh container and set in the duct at a small angle of 6 degrees. It was 265 x 200 x 15 cm and weighed 670 kg.

The first configuration of the P.13 was named P.13a *Entwurf I*. The P.13b would be a scaled-up reconnaissance version. It would have triangular wings based on the ones of P.12 *Entwurf IV*, and a tailfin housing the cockpit for the pilot, similar to the one in the P.12 *Entwurf I*, but with pointed instead of rounded tips. The air came into the combustion chamber through two oblique air intakes fitted with deflector vanes. It was then guided by a hydraulically operated flap towards the upper part of the carbon tablet, already burning thanks to a gas burner. The air was forced to run through the whole surface of the tablet, spreading the combustion, thus increasing its volume and temperature and converting it into carbon dioxide. Afterwards, it went to an expansion chamber and was expelled through a rectangular nozzle fitted with hydraulically operated flaps. The burning speed (320 kph) was achieved by means of a Walter rocket located at the base of the tailfin.

As had happened with the LP.12, the wind-tunnel tests proved that the deflectors and the flap located within the air duct produced too much drag. This conclusion led to the PP 13a *Entwurf II*, equipped with an air intake based on that of the *Entwurf I*, rounded wingtips and tailfin tips, and a cockpit with improved visibility.

A reduced-scale air model named LP.12/13 was also built to test the new ramjet in flight. It was discovered that the slope of the tablet generated too much drag and that the combustion geometry was incorrect. To make up for these defects, the LP.13a *Entwurf II* was equipped with a new type of burner—which was hoped to be the production version—and renamed LP.13a *Entwurf III*.

This modification consisted of replacing the tablet with an 800-kg block of oval section, housed in a wire mesh circular basket that, powered by an electric engine, rotated around its vertical axis at 60 rpm. The combustion was initiated by a gas burner and liquid fuel could be employed to facilitate starting up. The coal now used was formed of small granules and not irregular lumps—as had previously been the case—since granules produced a more controlled, even burning.

The system was tested in the *Luftfahrtforschungsanstalt* (LFW) in Vienna, before the end of the war in Europe, with success. It was expected that the new engine would have a power superior to the 60,000 hp reached by the Sänger ramjets of liquid fuel, and a range of 45 minutes of powered flight.

The operational routine of the LP.13 was very similar to that of the Komet. A jettisonable trolley and a Walter rocket working for 3 minutes helped during take off. The ramjet automatic start up happened at 320 kph. Then the plane went upwards in an angle of 45 degrees until reaching an operational altitude of 98,400 feet, at which point it surpassed Mach 2. When the airplane approached enemy bombers, it came down to 32,800 feet and reduced speed, opening the nozzle flaps—acting as airbrakes—to their maximum.

Although some authors refer to the onboard installation of two Mk 108 cannons, their use in combat would have been problematic due to the high approaching speed that was already excessive in the *Komet*. A better option would have been to install two MG 213/20 high-rate firing guns as defensive armament against escort fighters. The main armament, developed during the operational tests of the *Komet*, would be a combination of the R4M *Orkan* rockets—fired in salvos with intervals of 0.07 seconds—and the EZ 42 gyroscopic gunsight.

Another possibility was the installation of a *Sondergerät Jägerfaust* armament system, based on recoilless vertical guns automatically fired by a photoelectric cell when passing between 20 and 90 m below the bomber. The *Sondergerät* SG116 fired the 30-mm rounds of the Mk 103 and the *Sondergerät* SG 500 the 50-mm rounds of the BK 5. The Opta-radio automatic firing system was activated by the diminishing intensity of the light—captured by the *Fotozellenfühler* (photoelectric cell)—which was caused by the shadow produced by the attacked bomber. The guns were installed with a 2-degree divergence between them, so that the projectiles reached the same target area in spite of the speed of the attacking airplane.

Although the power of the engine could be regulated by opening or closing the nozzle flaps, it could not be stopped at will by the pilot. As with the Komet, the LP.13 was meant to fly patiently in a defensive circle until it had run out of fuel, and then glide down to land over its three retractable skids. After landing, the airplanes were fully exposed to the fighter's mercy until the arrival of the *Scheuschlepper* recovery vehicles which carried the airplanes to the base.

Readiness for a new flight required a huge effort for ground crews. Besides all the essential measures required to reload the Walter rocket with its dangerous fuel, one of the wings had to be taken apart so that the new charge of solid fuel could be introduced through the lateral gap. It was also necessary to recharge the battery and to refill the oxygen and gas tanks. The rockets and the Jägerfaust had to be reloaded and the electric firing connections reviewed one by one.

Even though the LP.13's dog-fighting capacity was almost non-existent, all of the issues mentioned above were likely balanced out by the fact that this airplane could not be intercepted.

Technical data *Lippisch LP.13a Entwurf III*

Type	supersonic ramjet-powered interceptor.
Wings	60-degree swept at the leading edge and 15-negative-degree sweep at the trailing edge, 12 per cent thickness at root, delta planform with elevons. Wooden structure and cladding.
Tailfin	66-degree swept, 17.5 per cent thickness at root, housing the pressurised cockpit, the *T-Stoff* tanks, and the Walter rocket.
Landing gear	formed by a central skid and another two at the wing roots, all of them hydraulically retractable.
Engine	one solid fuel ramjet with more than 60,000 hp of power and a bifuel Walter HWK 109-509 S2 rocket with 1,993-kp static thrust.
Propellants tanks	one of *T-Stoff*—hydrogen peroxide (80 per cent) oxyquinoline or phosphate (20 per cent)—with 170 litres in the tailfin and another two of *C-Stoff*—mixture of *M-Stoff* (57 per cent), *B-Stoff* (30 per cent), a watery solution (100 cc/litre) of potasium cuprocyanide (13 per cent)—with 155 litres in the wings.
Armament	two MG 213/20 guns in the wings and twenty-four R4M *Orkan* rockets of 55 m, or two SG 500 *Jägerfaust* devices with twelve guns of 50 mm each.
Wingspan	6 m
Length	6.70 m
Height	3.25 m
Wing area	20 sq. m
Empty weight	1,800 kg
Take off weight	3,000 kg
Max. speed	Mach 2
Service ceiling	98,400 feet
Range	(Max. powered endurance) 45 min.

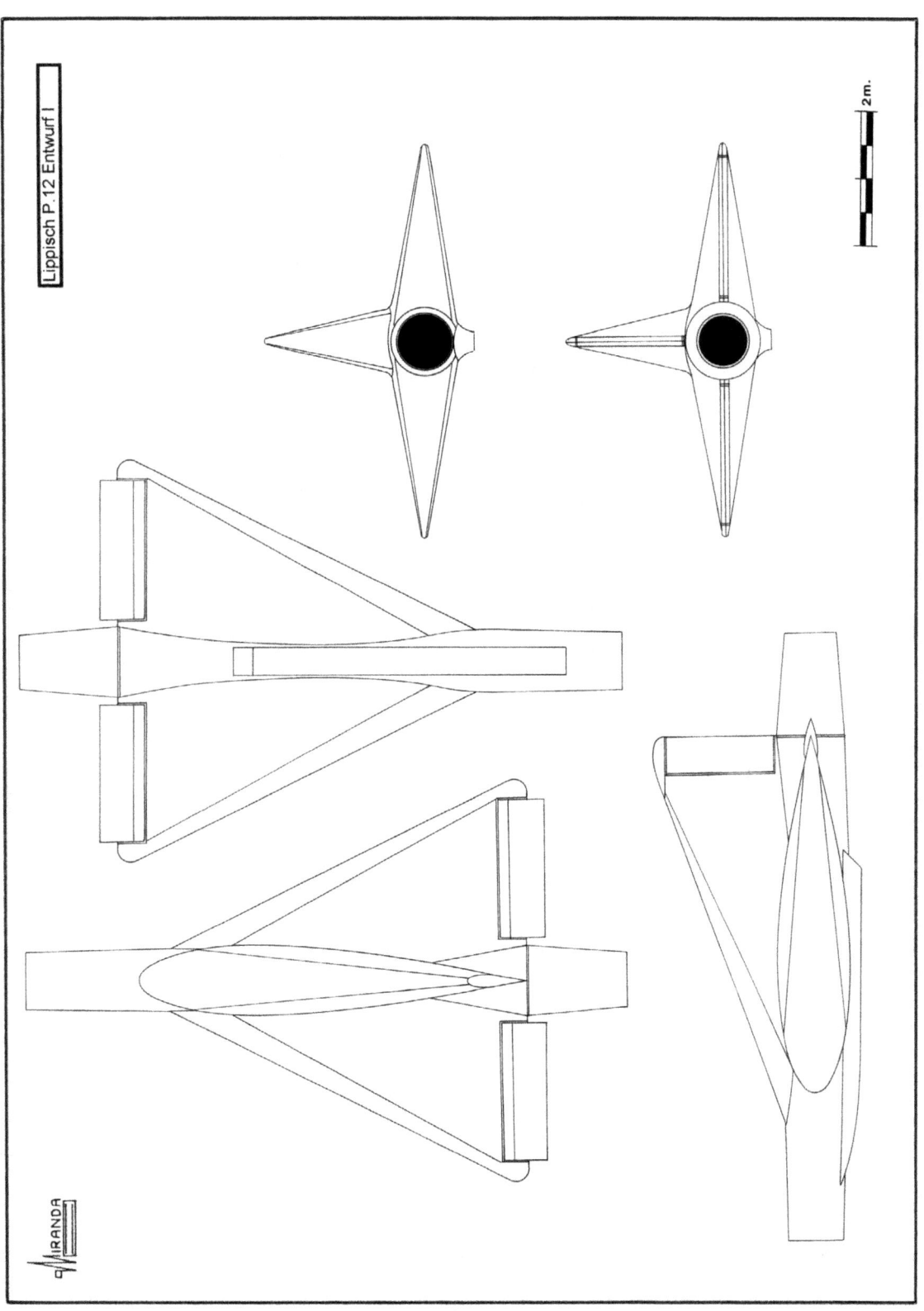

Lippisch P.12 Entwurf I

2 m.

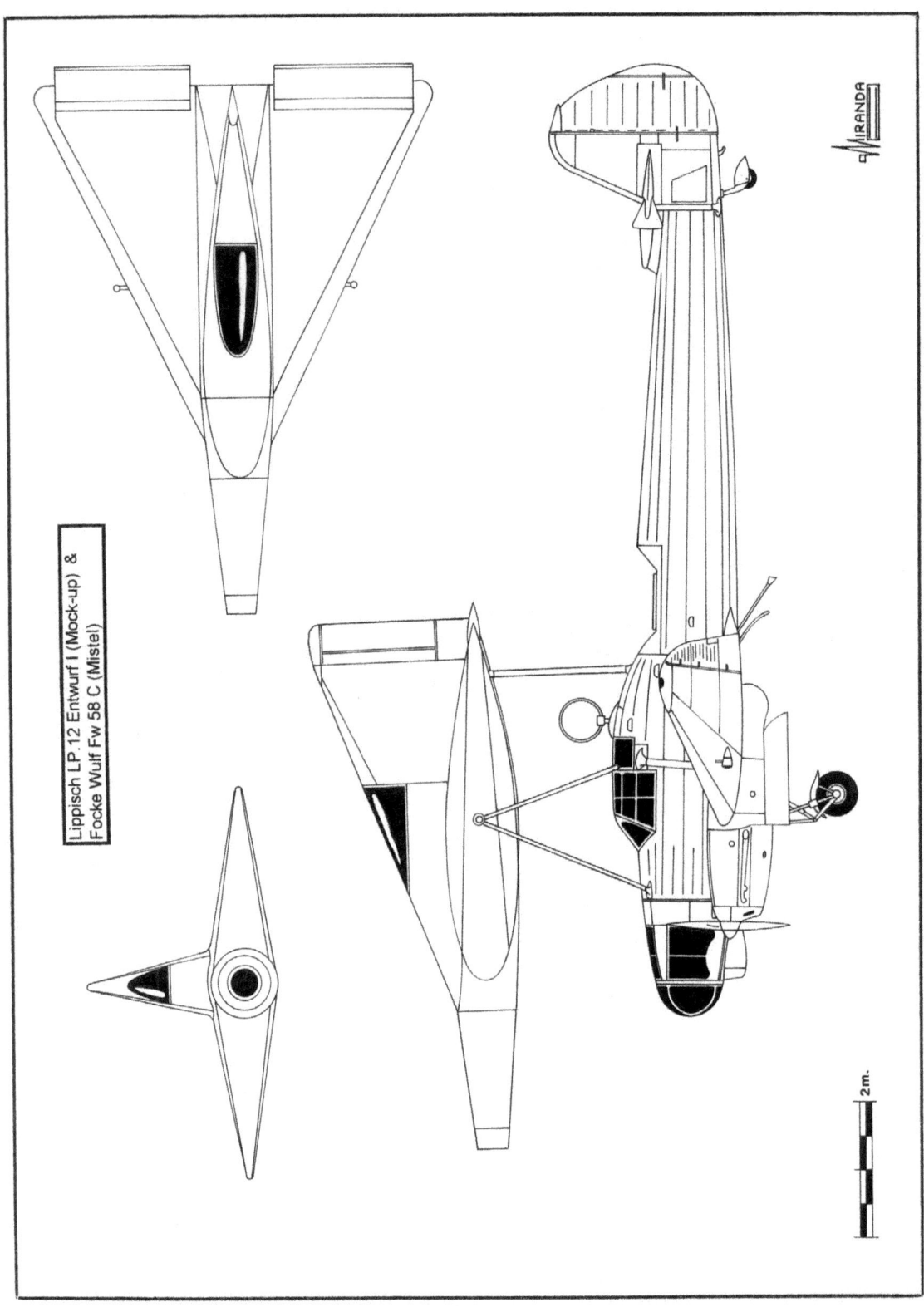

Lippisch LP.12 Entwurf I (Mock-up) &
Focke Wulf Fw 58 C (Mistel)

2 m.

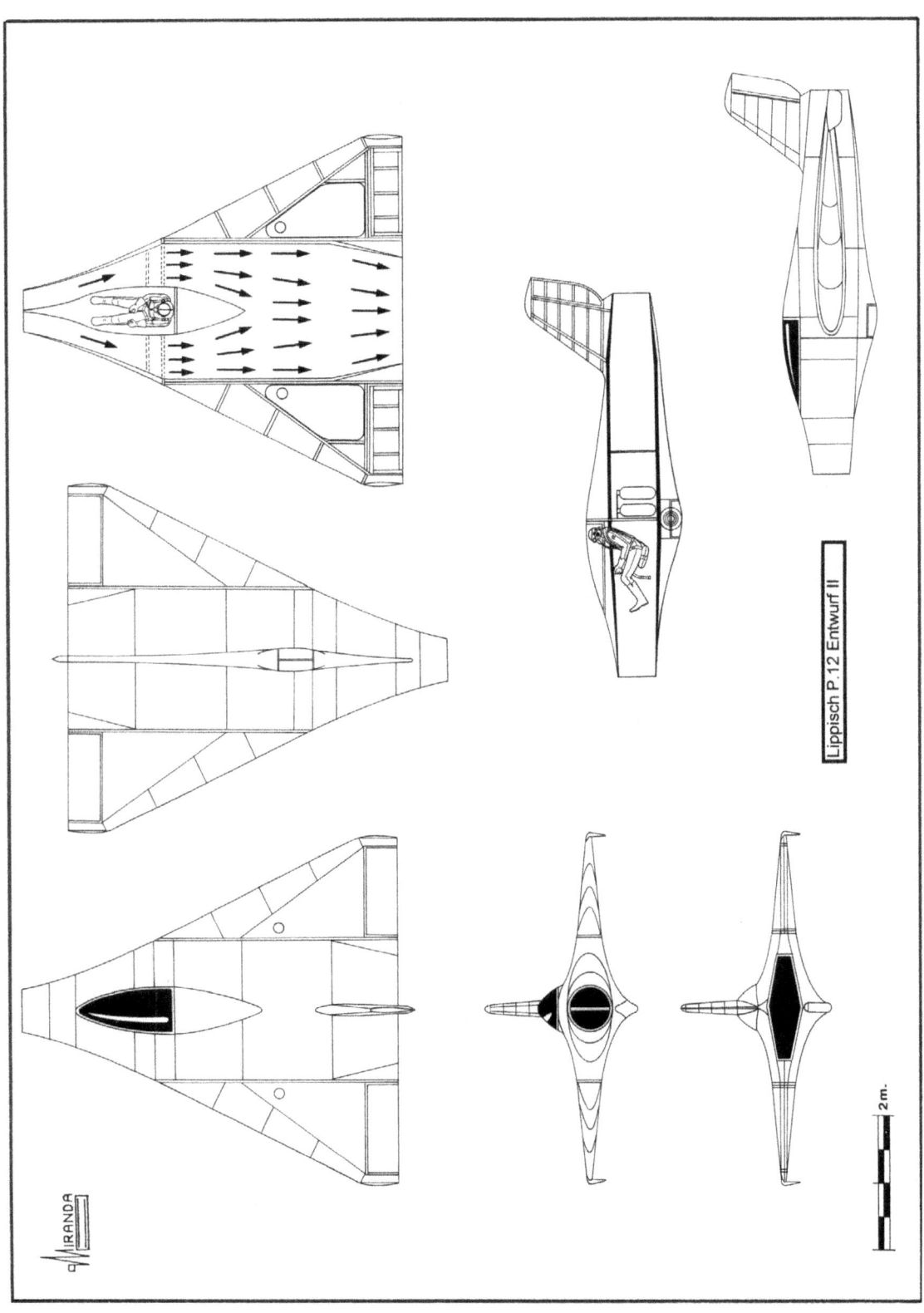

Lippisch P.12 Entwurf II

2 m.

MIRANDA

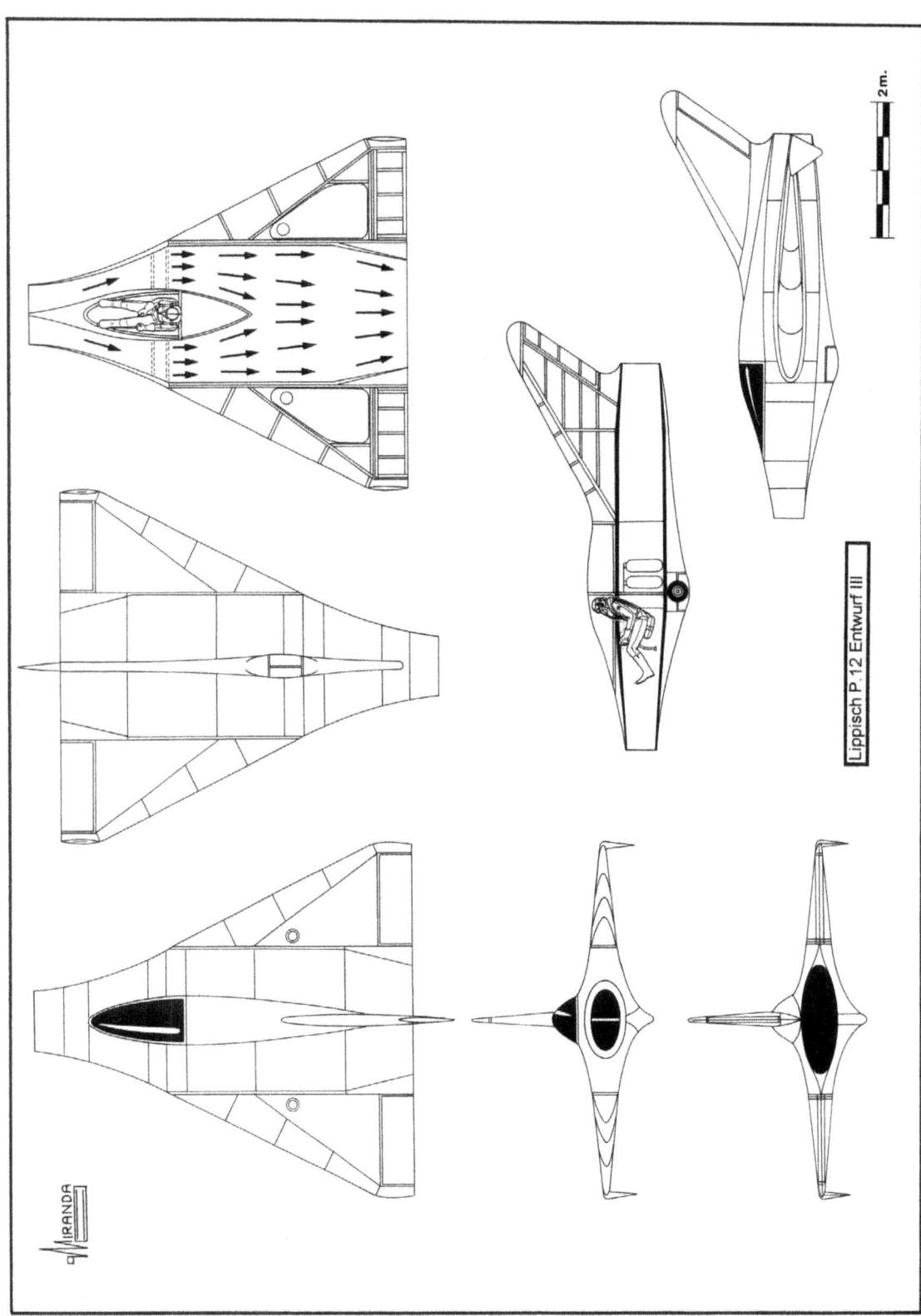

2 m.

Lippisch P.12 Entwurf III

MIRANDA

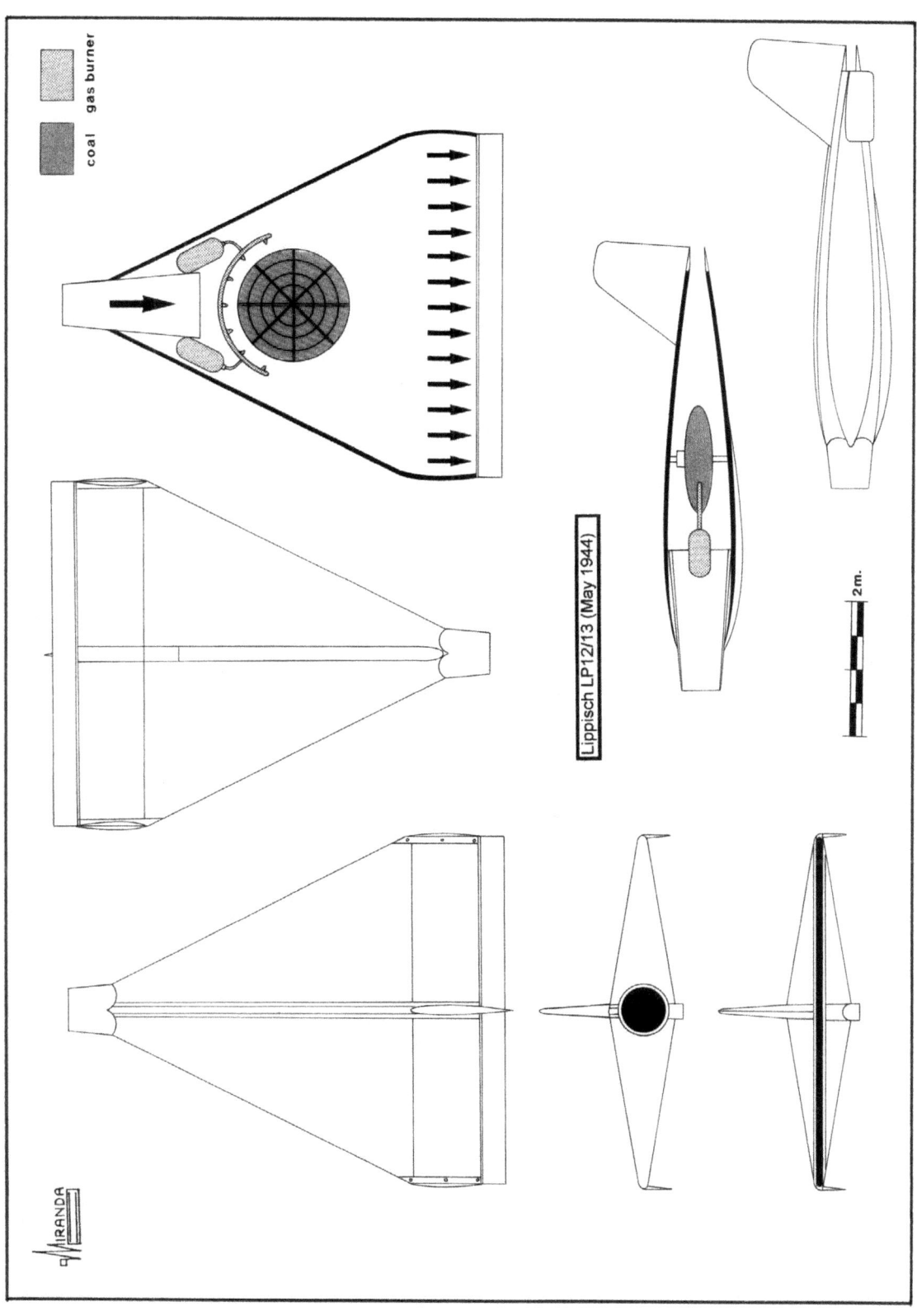

coal   gas burner

Lippisch LP12/13 (May 1944)

2 m.

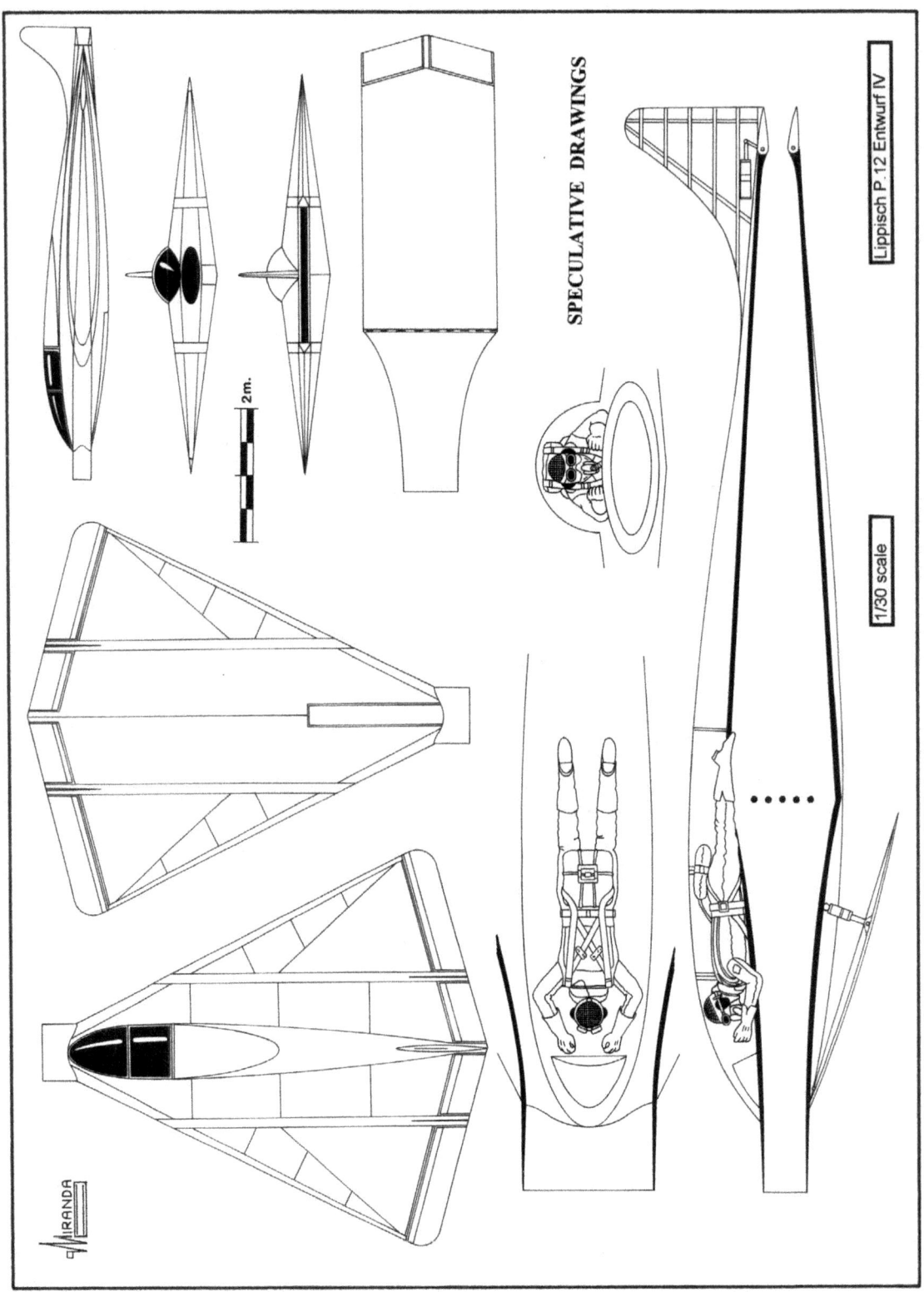

SPECULATIVE DRAWINGS

Lippisch P .12 Entwurf IV

1/30 scale

2m.

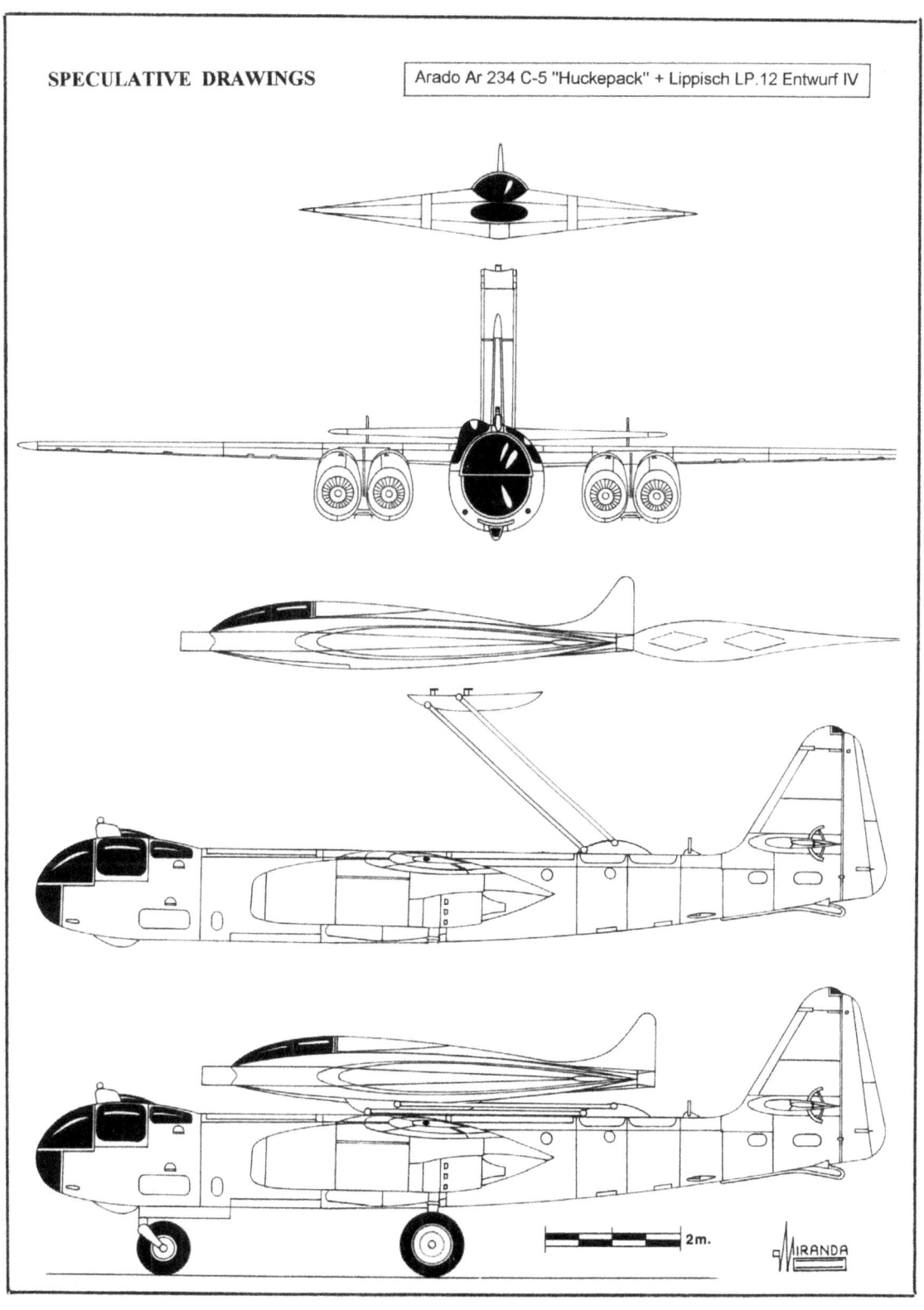

SPECULATIVE DRAWINGS

Arado Ar 234 C-5 "Huckepack" + Lippisch LP.12 Entwurf IV

2m.

MIRANDA

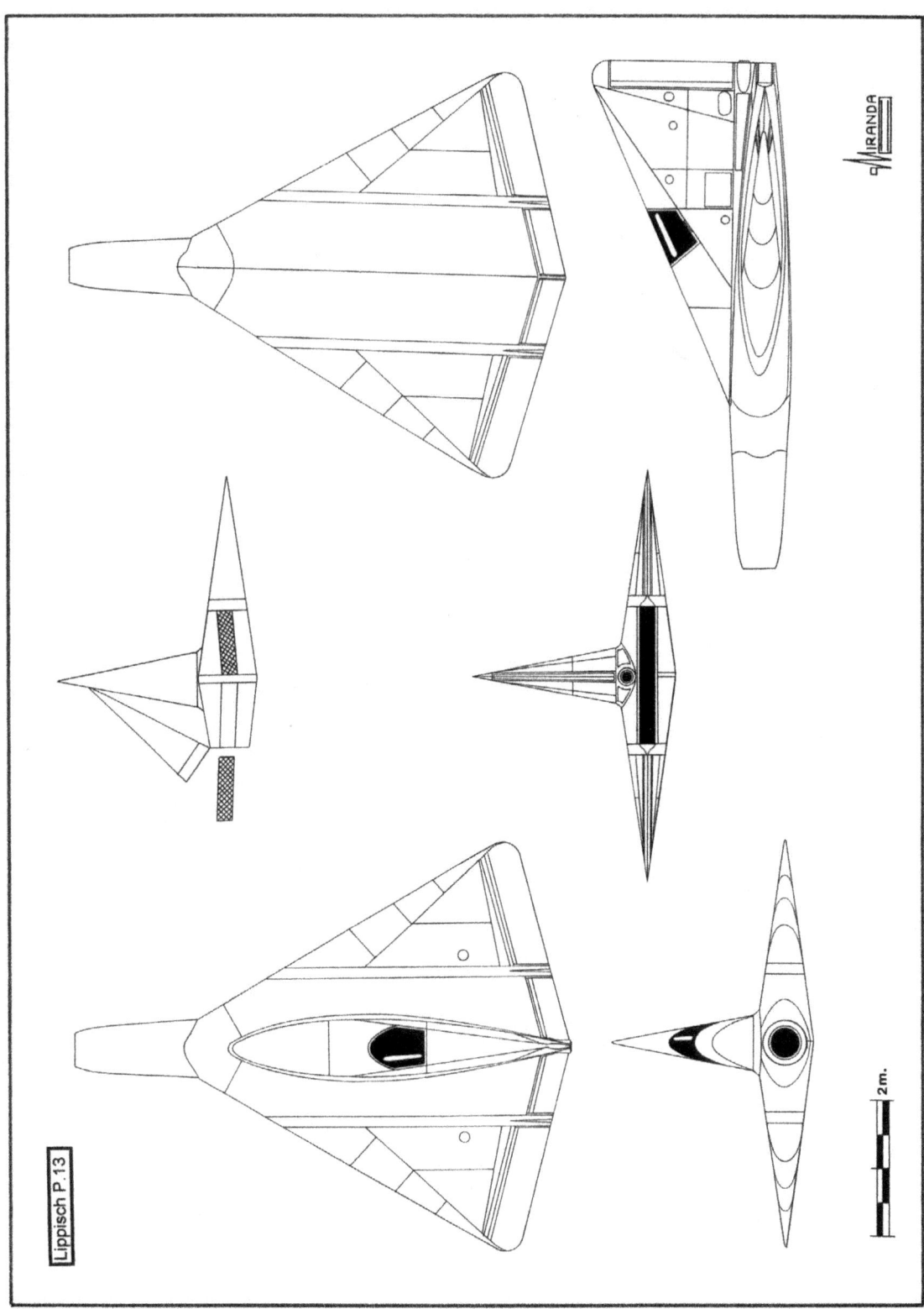

Lippisch P.13

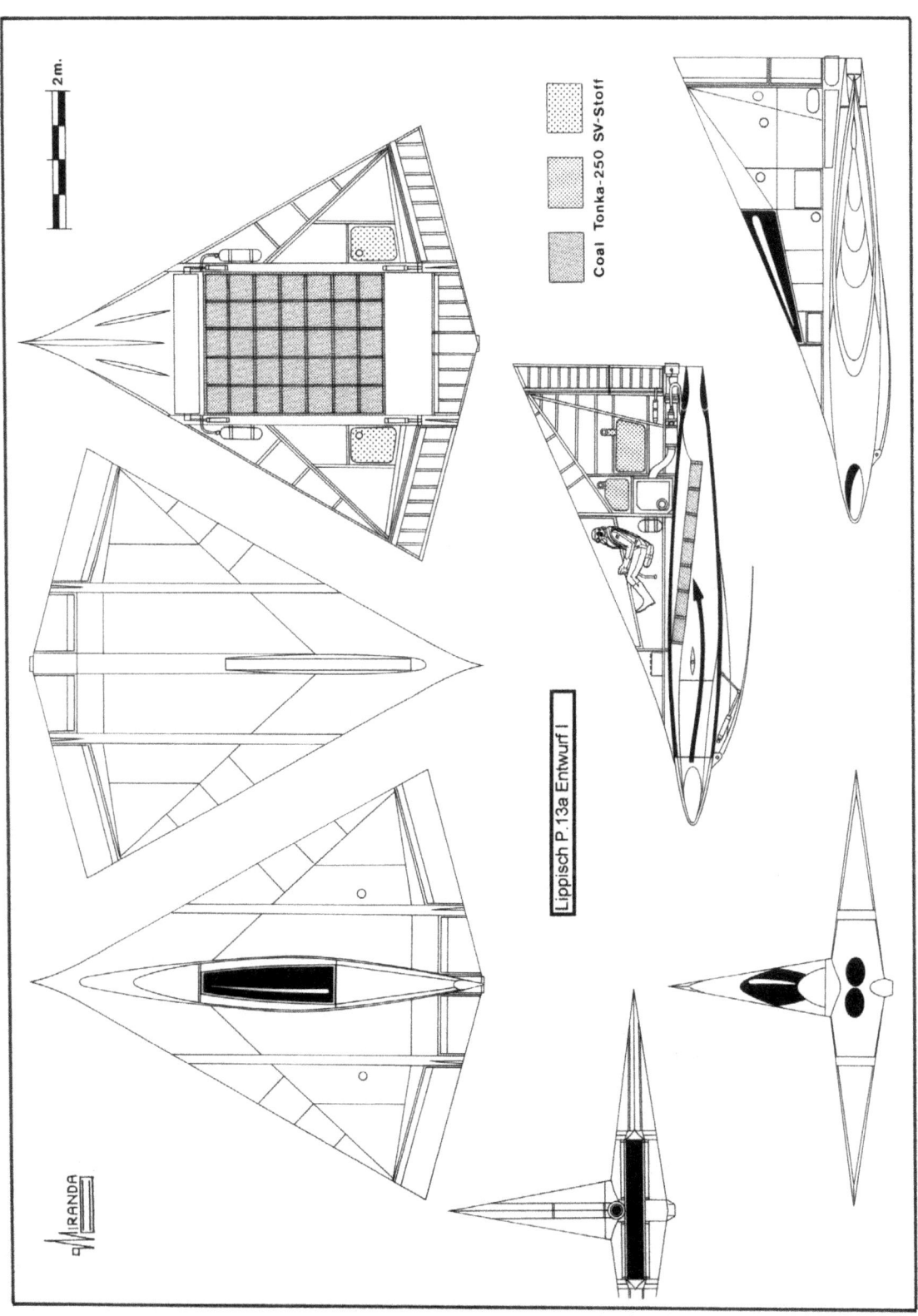

Coal Tonka-250 SV-Stoff

Lippisch P.13a Entwurf I

2 m.

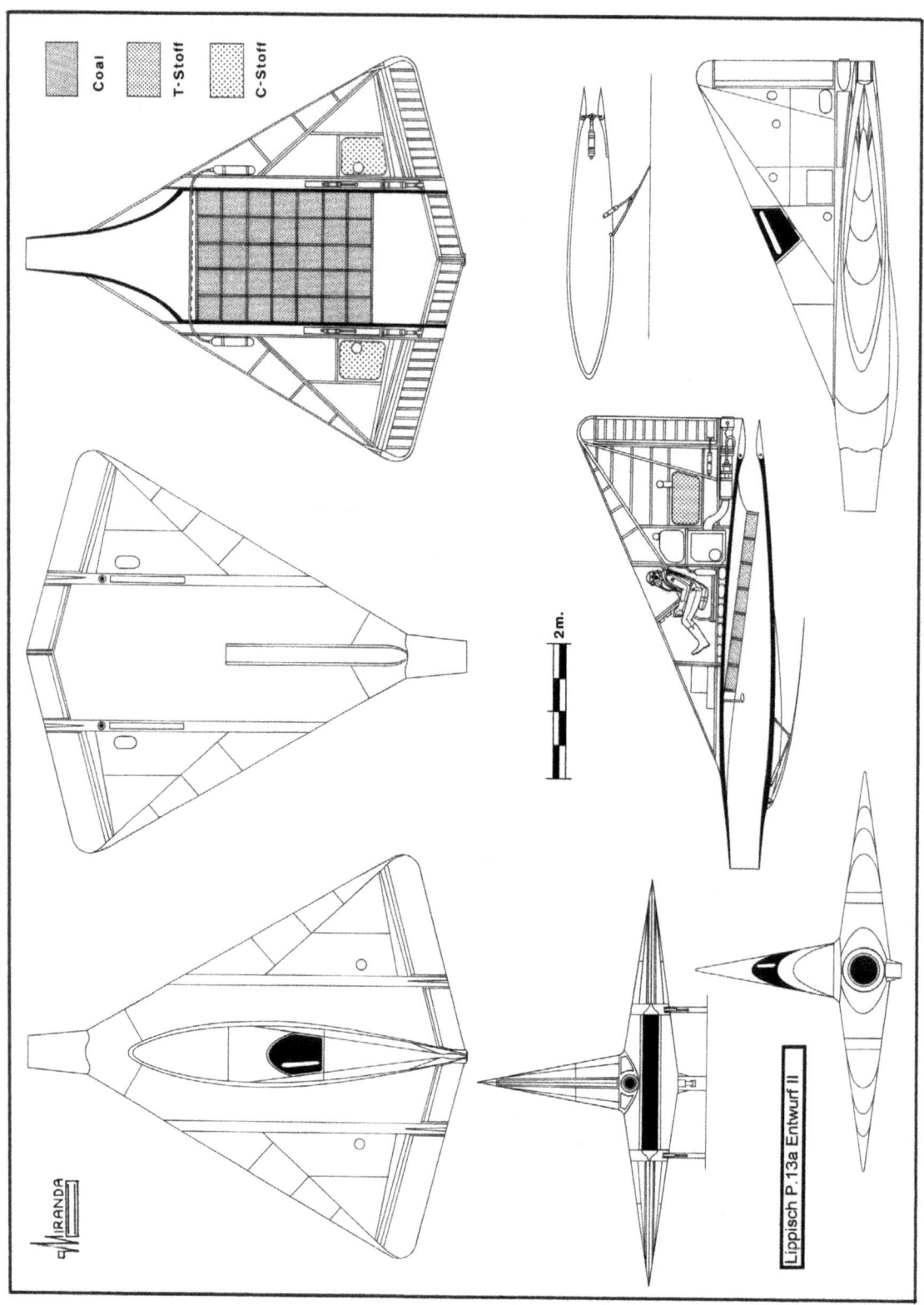

Coal

T-Stoff

C-Stoff

2m.

MIRANDA

Lippisch P.13a Entwurf II

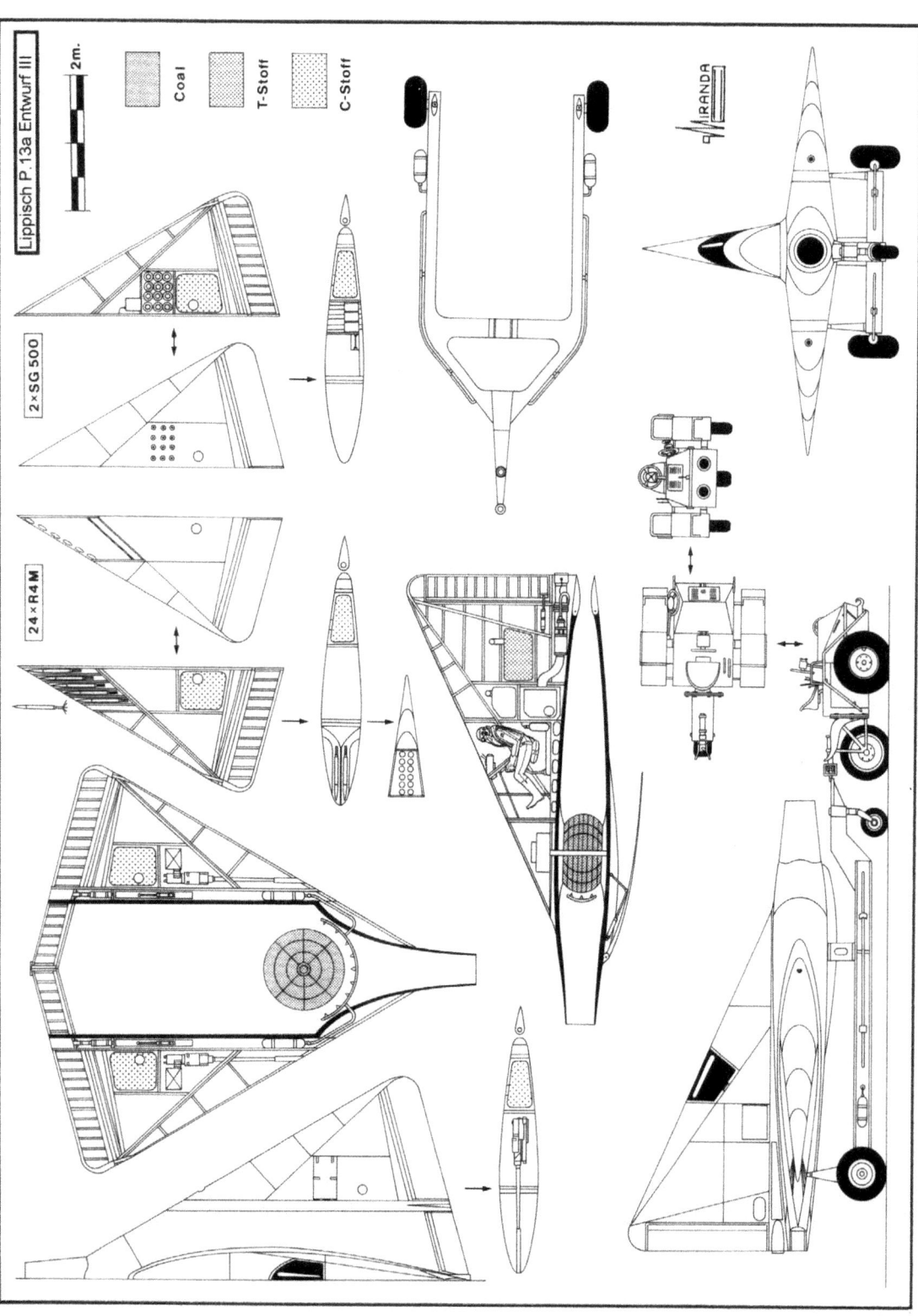

Chapter 27

Lippisch GB 3/L

The Lippisch GB 3/L was a glide bomb based on the aerodynamic solutions developed for the Lippisch LP.12 by Deutsche Forschungsanstalt für Segelflug (DFS).

Designed in July 1944 to compete against the anti-ship missile Henschel Hs 293D, it could transport a warhead of 250 kg at 800 kph and reach a mobile target located 5 km away, with an error margin of just 6 m. This could be achieved thanks to its TV guidance system, developed by Fernseh GmbH/Blaupunkt. The TV transmitter *Tonne* worked on a frequency of 400 Mhz, with an operating range of 150 km. Its measurements were 40 x 17 x 17 cm and it had a Zeiss *Biogon* lens of 35-mm focal length, a scan of 441 (vertical) lines at 25 pictures per second, and of 20 watts.

Together with the DEAG battery and the yagi antenna, the whole installation weighed 150 kg.

The missile was guided by a joystick and a *Seedorf* TV screen from the launch airplane, a Dornier Do 217 E.

The glide range was of 5 km when the bomb was launched from an altitude of 3,300 feet and of 15 km from 24,600 feet. The bomb was AGL released with speeds of between 235 and 486 KTAS (Knots True Airspeed).

The tests for the *Tonne/Seedorf* system, performed with Hs 293 D missiles between January and August 1944, proved the equipment to be unreliable and its manufacturing was cancelled.

Technical data

Wingspan	2.2 m
Overall length	4.6 m
Height	1.3 m
Wing area	2.25 sq. m
Launch	weight 550 kg
Engine one	Rheinmetall-Borsig 109-502 *Diglykol* solid fuel rockets with 771-kp peak thrust.
Warhead	one SC 250 *Minenbombe* with 130 kg of *Trialen-105* on 100 kg of *Nipolit* without metal casing.
Fuse	ELAZ (38) B electrical impact.
Airframe	wood/plywood with 100-kg structural weight.

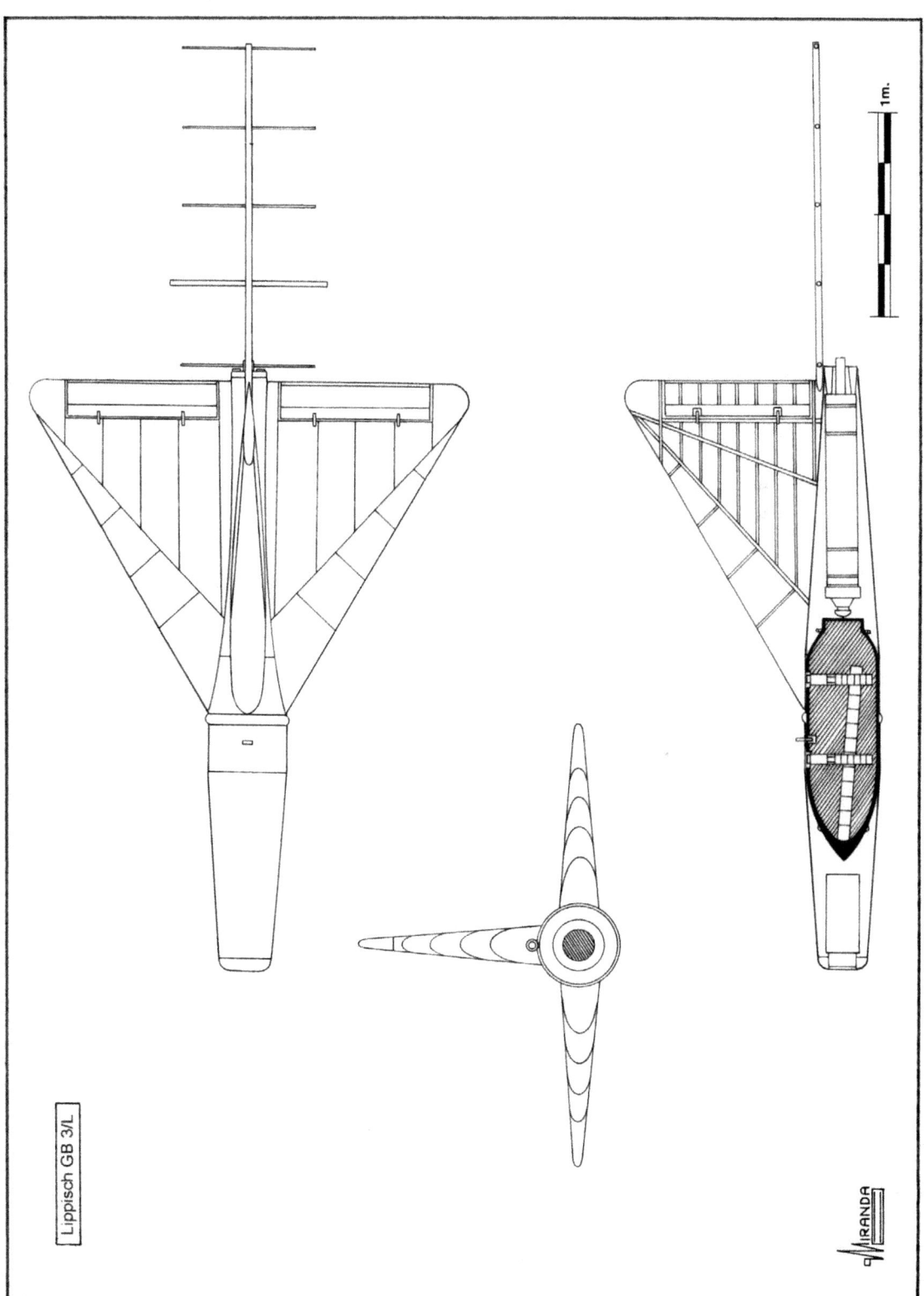

Lippisch GB 3/L

Chapter 28

Lippisch DM Series

The spindle is the perfect aerodynamic shape, but at speeds below Mach 5, this type of body does not produce enough lift to keep it flying. Any attempt to add a wing collides with the problem known as 'area rule' during supersonic flight, which consists of a proportional increase of drag.

In 1942, the technical team of aerodynamics at the Aerodynamische Versuchsanstalt (AVA), led by Dr Ing. Alexander Lippisch, built a heart-shaped scale model with a 60-degree swept delta wing that proved to be an ideal supersonic body. Tests performed in the Göttingen wind tunnel showed that the body offered minimal drag at over Mach 1, using less power than any of the other tested models. This configuration—known as *Überschall Delta*—was unstable in flight, given the technology available in the mid-1940s, and therefore could not be considered as a base to build a supersonic airplane.

Most of the research work done by Lippisch for the rest of the war was devoted to the creation of a delta wing suitable for stable supersonic flight. This meant that they had to reach and surpass Mach 1 in horizontal flight using very powerful engines, and also had to have a great swept.

At the time, designers were afraid that this type of wing would make it dangerous to land at low speed. A test glider named DM-1 was built to analyse this question, with the cooperation of FFG Darmstadt and FFG München in 1945. It was a delta wing with 60-degree swept on the leading edge and -15-degree sweep on the trailing edge, and with the cockpit built within the tailfin. It had to be carried in Mistel configuration over a Siebel Si 204A and taken to an altitude of 26,200 feet. The plan was to reach 800 kph, powered by two Rheinmetall-Borsig 109-502 rockets, with 771-kp peak thrust each and 560 kph in unpowered flight. The landing speed was to be of 72 kph at 35 degrees of AOA (angle of attack).

After the war, the DM-1 was moved to the USA, where its development was pursued by the Scientific Advisory Group of the United States Airforce under the direction of Professor Theodore Von Kármán in the National Advisory Committee for Aeronautics (NACA), and in the Langley wind tunnel. The static tests employed different configurations of cockpit and tailfin and several types of new leading edges. They were trying to find out why the Reynolds coefficient—which measured the relative viscosity of the air flow at high speed—was too high.

The final version was named NACA #8. It had a new leading edge with sharp edges and 64.2-degree sweep, a bubble cockpit, and a triangular tailfin with 15 per cent thickness and 35-degree sweep. It was declared stable at supersonic speed, but due to its small size, it would not have been able to carry enough propellants if a rocket engine had been installed to reach Mach 1.

The real transonic project was the DM-2. It was 150 per cent bigger than the DM-1 and had twice the fuel capacity of the *Komet*. The design of February 1945 was an airplane with an HWK 509 A-1 rocket able to work for 17 minutes with a static thrust of 1,600 kp. It was expected that this would be enough to study its behaviour during flight, in the range between Mach 0.8 and 1.2. When fully loaded, the airplane was too heavy to take off using the frail landing gear that appears in the designs. It was possibly carried up to 26,000 feet by an airplane of the Ju 390 or He 274 type and launched from there to save rocket propellants.

The Ho X was designed for the same purpose and also had a delta wing, although it was powered by an HeS 011 turbojet.

Designed at the same time as the Lippisch DM-2, the DM-3 was an airplane powered by two Walter 509 rockets with a pressurised cockpit. The rest was identical to the DM-2. They intended to launch it from a bomber at an altitude of 26,000 feet, in a similar way to the American Bell X-1; after firing both rockets, the airplane should surpass 65,000 feet very quickly. It stayed there until reaching a speed of Mach 2.5, using the remaining fuel for 8 minutes of powered flight.

A very similar project was the two-engine version of the DFS 346, with swept wings and tail surfaces.

Lippisch DM-2/DM-3 technical data (DM-3 between brackets)

Type	transonic (supersonic) rocket plane.
Wings	64.2-degree sweep at the leading edge and 3-negative-degree sweep at the trailing edge, 12 per cent thickness at root, delta planform with elevons. Metallic structure and cladding.
Tailfin	36-degree sweep, 12 per cent thickness, metallic structure and cladding.
Fuselage	housing the (pressurised) cockpit, with the pilot in a prone position, the forward landing gear and the rocket engine. Metallic structure and cladding.
Landing gear	tricycle type, similar to the DM-1 model.
Engine	one (two) Walter HWK 509 A1 with a static thrust of 1,600 kp.
Fuel tanks	Two *T-Stoff* of 765 litres and another two of 430 litres in the wings, behind the main spar. Two *C-Stoff* of 435 litres and another two of 200 litres in the wings ahead of the main spar.
Armament	none
Wingspan	8.25 m
Length	8.94 m (8.85 m)
Height	4.12 m
Wing area	38 sq. m
Empty weight	3,700 kg (3,870 kg)
Take off weight	11,500 kg (11,670 kg)
Max. speed	Mach 1.2 (Mach 2.5)
Service ceiling	39,300 feet (more than 98,500 feet)
Range	(Max. powered endurance) 17 min. (8 min.)

Chapter 29

Lippisch LP.14

The DM-3 model's tests in the wind tunnel produced such good results that it was decided to design a two-engine fighter based on this formula, as an alternative to the Me 262 HG III.

Initially known as *DM-4* and *LP.14* in January 1945, this was a supersonic heavy fighter that benefited from different technologies, already tested with previous Lippisch models. The delta wing was 63 degrees swept back and 6 per cent thick. It was based on the *DM-2* wing but with more rounded wingtips and a straight trailing edge to make combat manoeuvres easier. The pressurised cockpit, based on the *DM-3* model, housed the pilot in prone position to allow him to withstand the severe acceleration in the vertical plane, so that a sustained 7 G could be endured without losing consciousness.

The engines were two HeS 011 turbojets. The air came to them through air intakes and curved ducts, developed for the high-speed Me 262 HG III and Me P.1111. The position of the engines and the design of the landing gear were based on those of the P.11 project (May to December 1943). Therefore, it is possible that the P.14 would have had two solid fuel Schmidding rockets at the tailfin base to help at take off.

Rounded and large, the tailfin shape came from the P 01-117 project (a high-altitude interceptor with pressurised cockpit and pilot in prone position) of July 1941.

Technical data	
Type	single-seat heavy jet fighter
Wingspan	8 m
Length	8.42 m
Height	3.74 m
Wing area	30 sq. m
Empty weight	5,500 kg
Max. speed	Mach 1.5

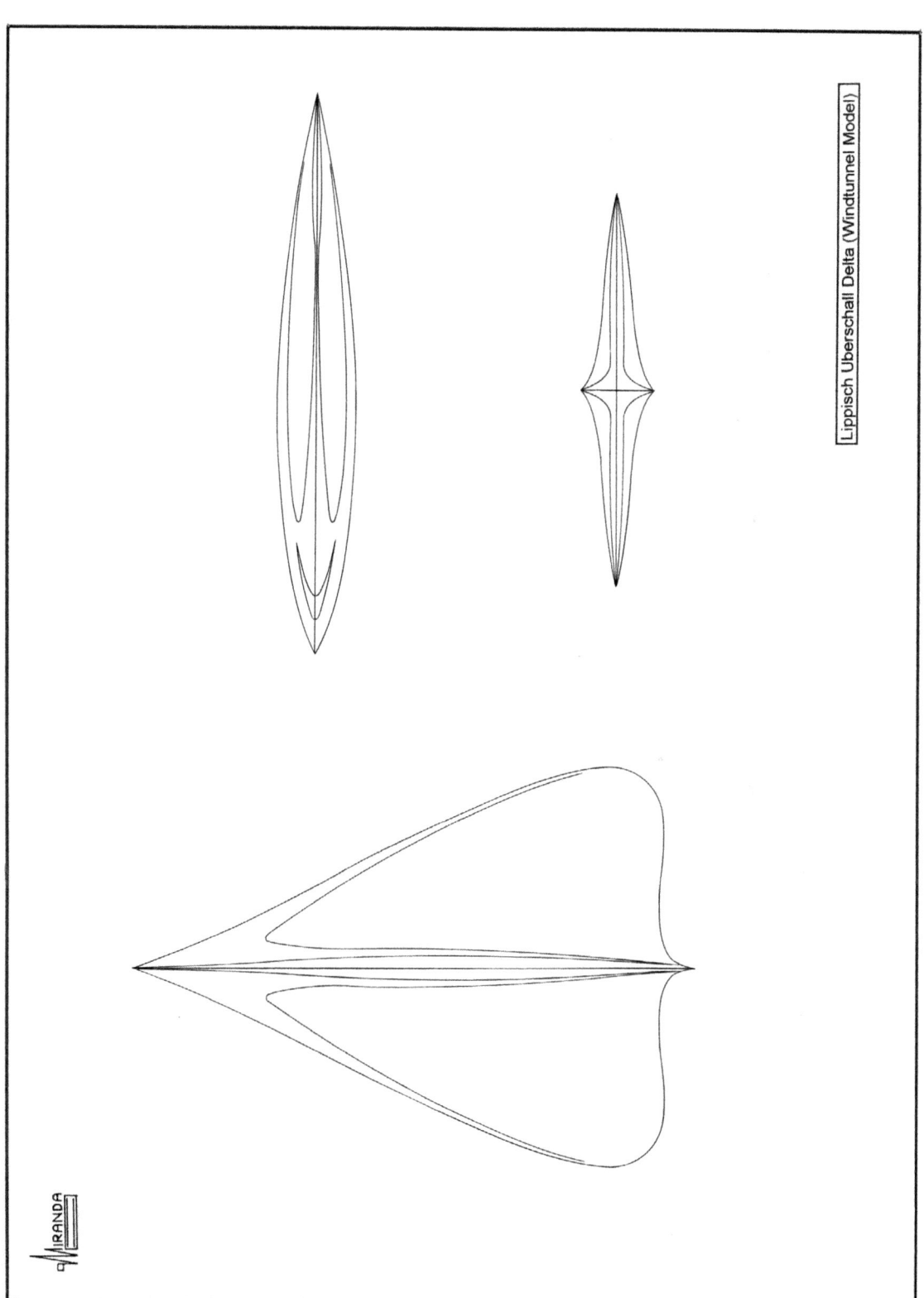

Lippisch Überschall Delta (Windtunnel Model)

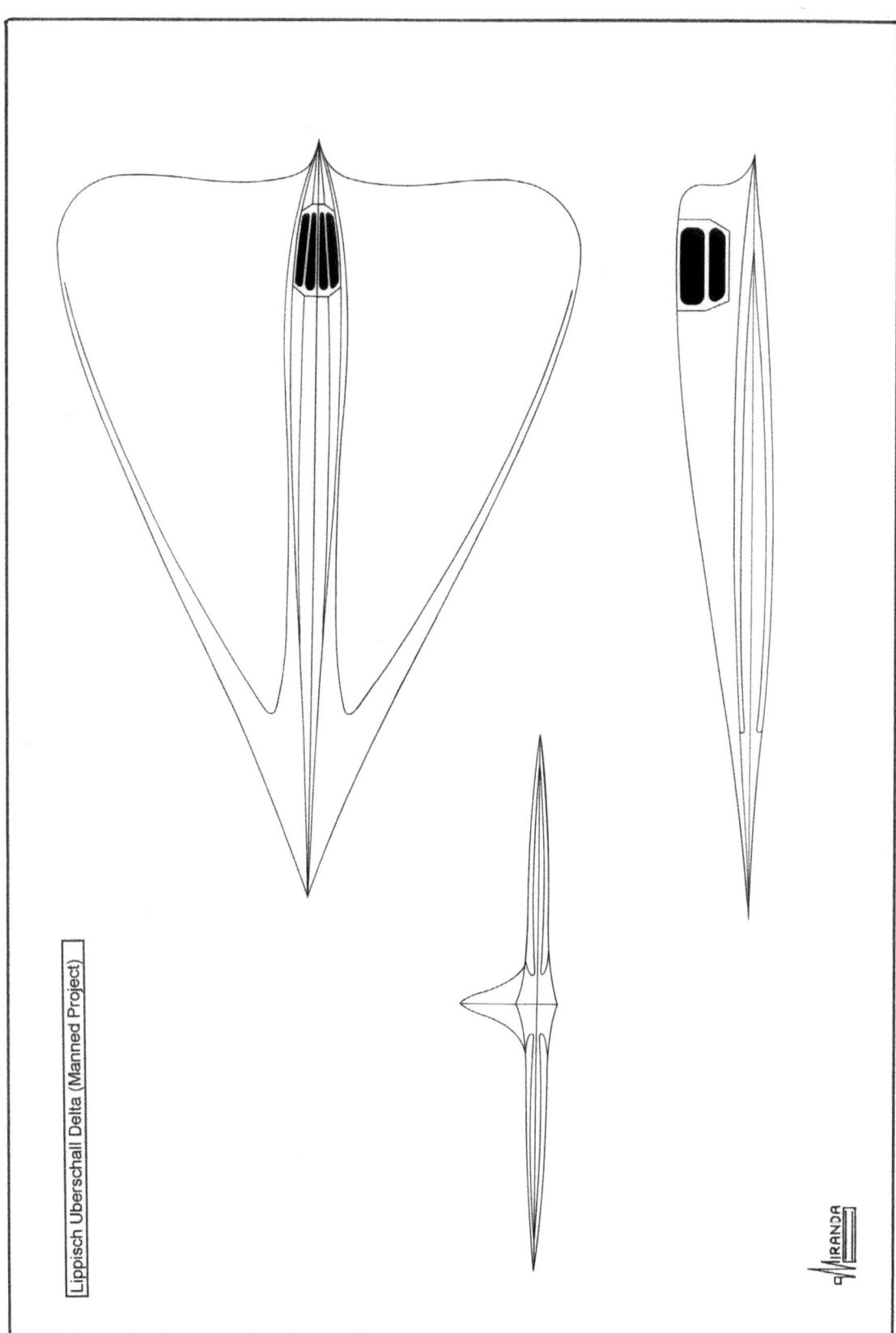

Lippisch Überschall Delta (Manned Project)

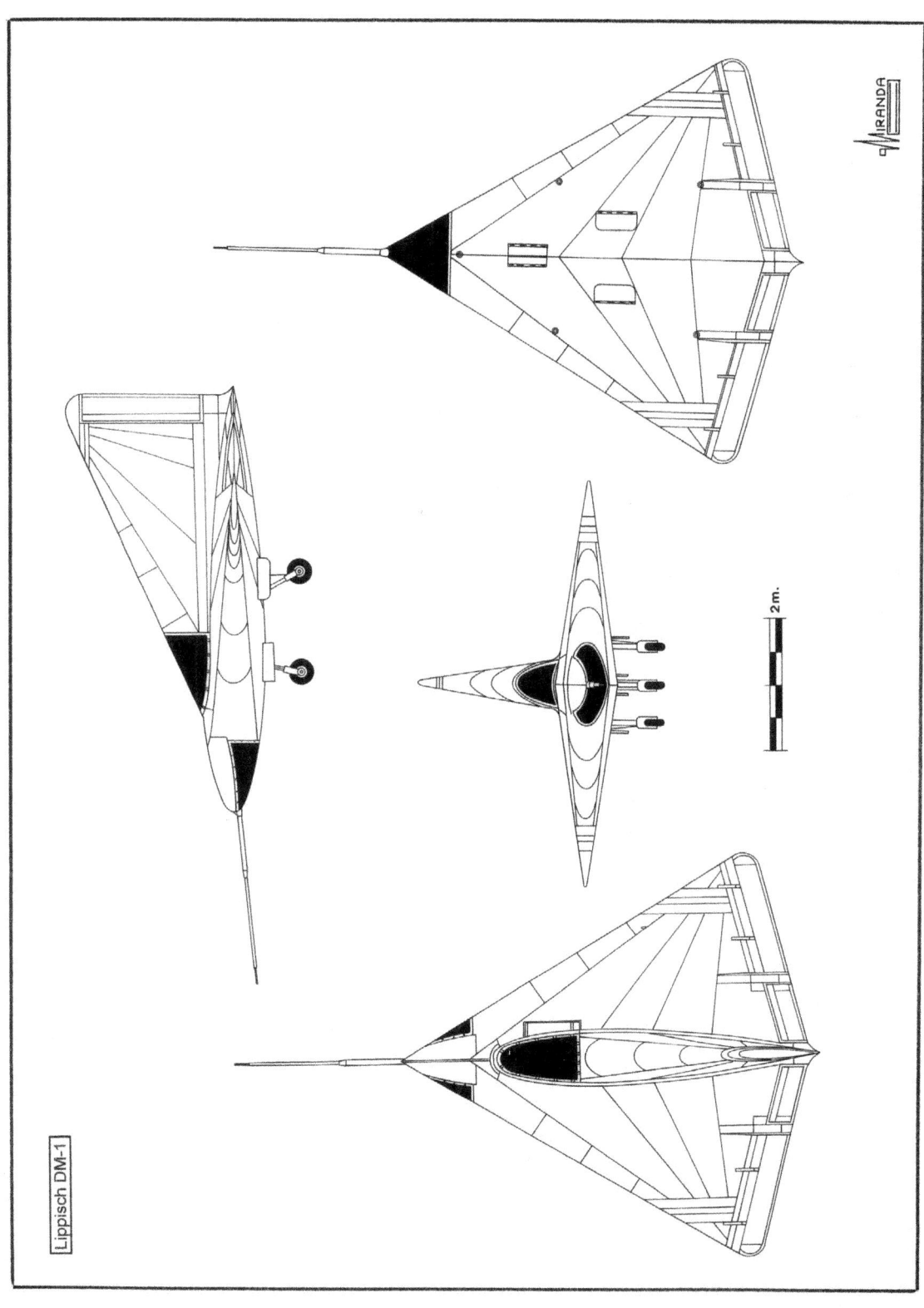

Lippisch DM-1

2 m.

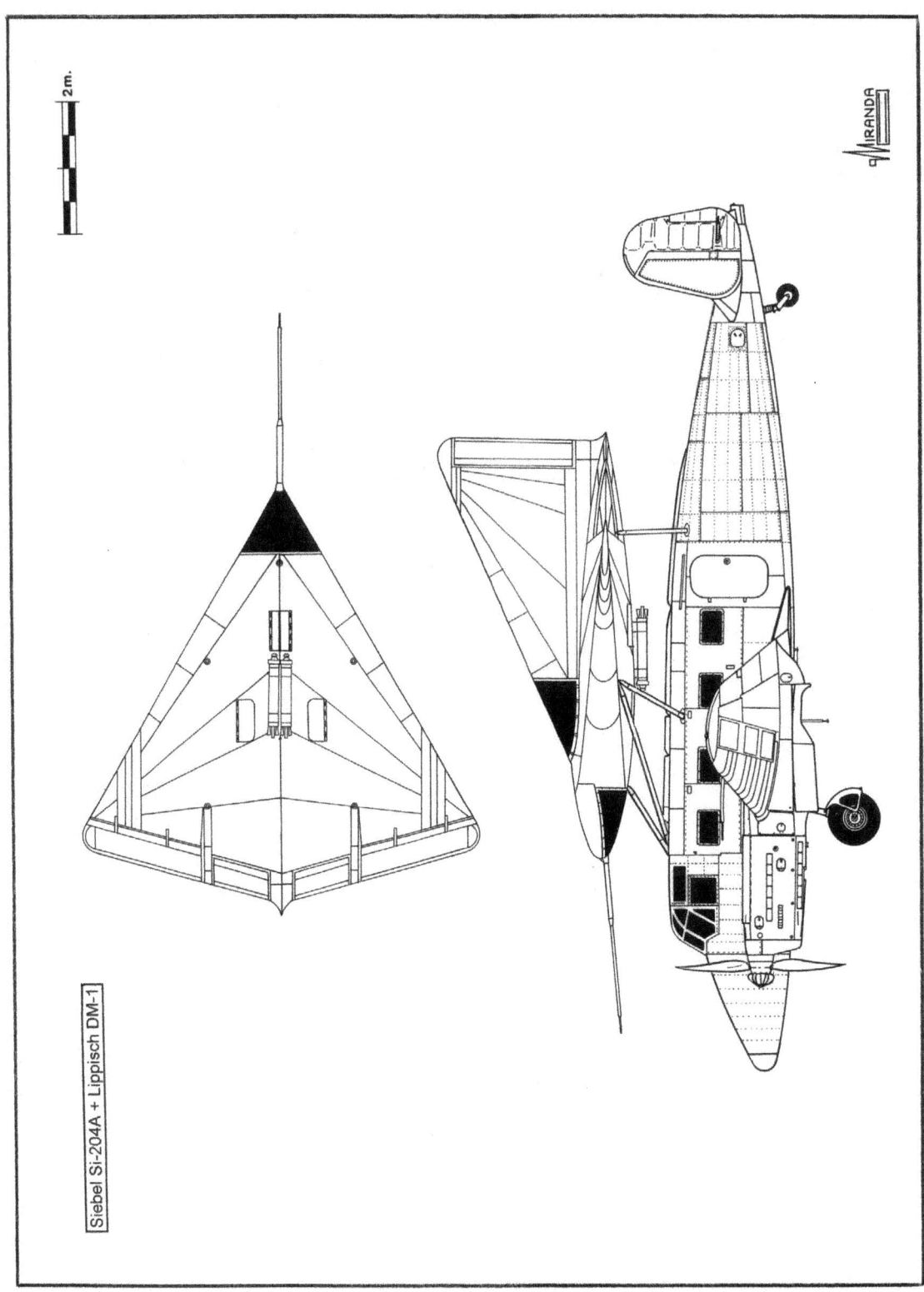

Siebel Si-204A + Lippisch DM-1

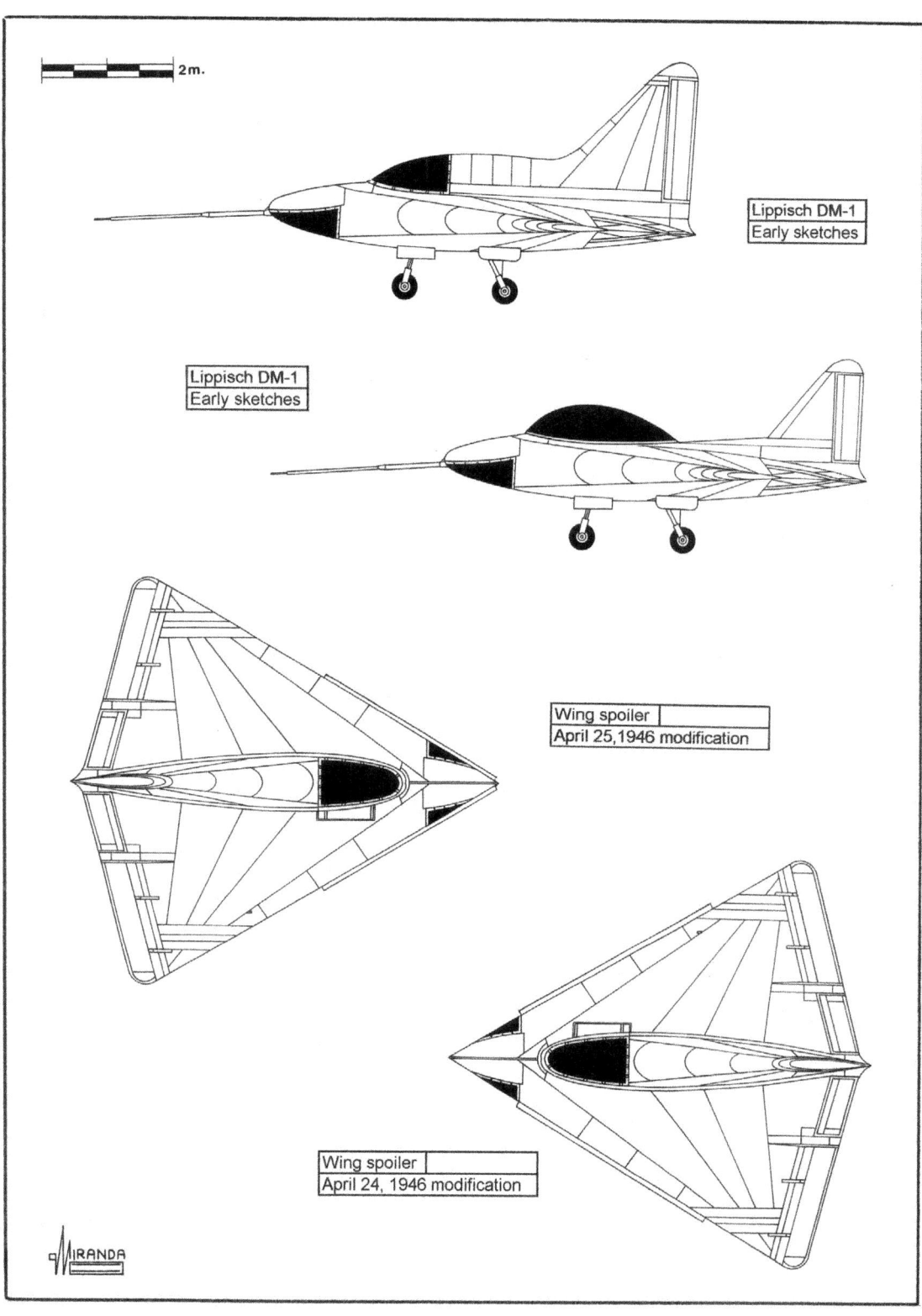

2m.

Lippisch DM-1
Early sketches

Lippisch DM-1
Early sketches

Wing spoiler
April 25,1946 modification

Wing spoiler
April 24, 1946 modification

MIRANDA

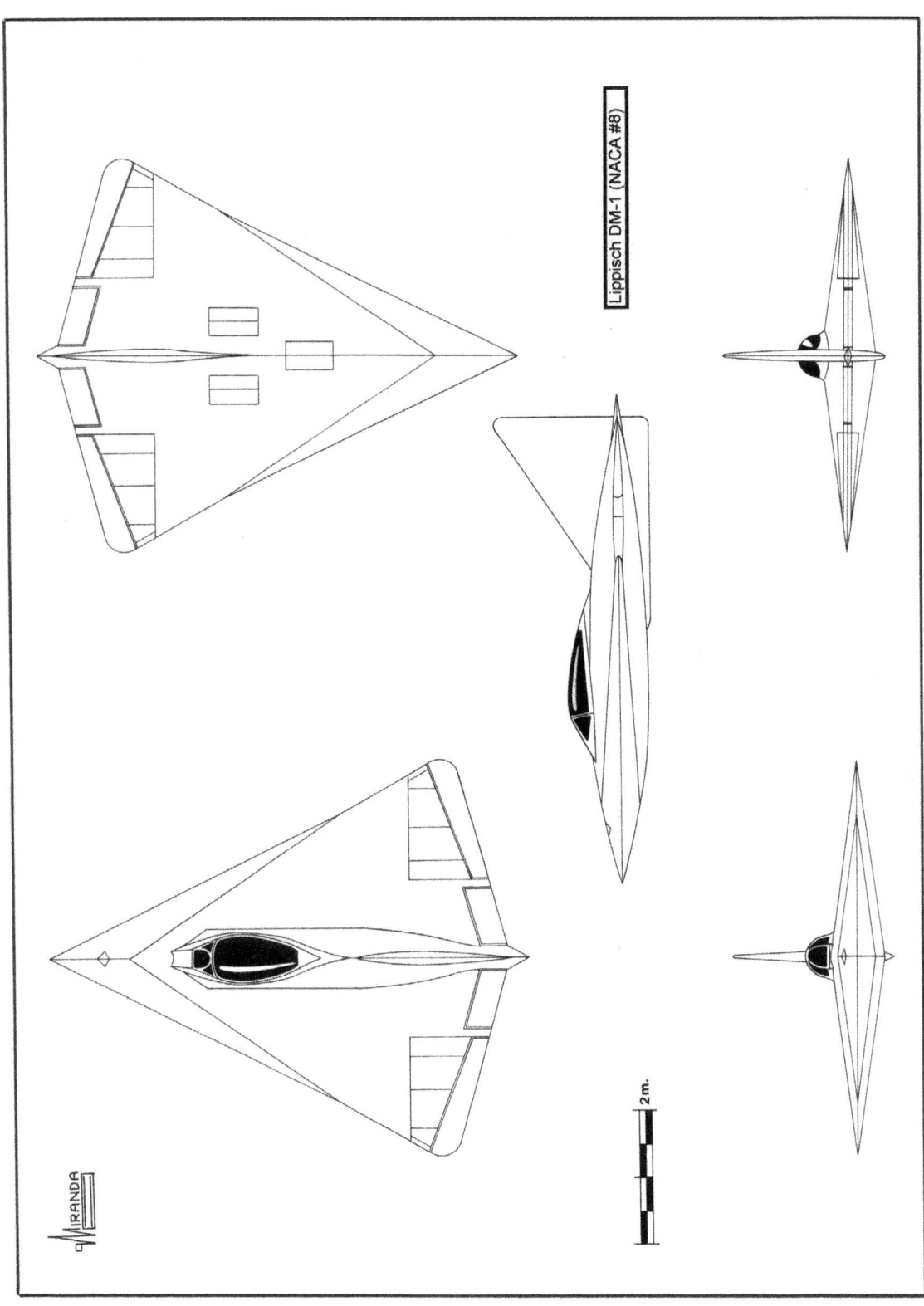

Lippisch DM-1 (NACA #8)

2 m.

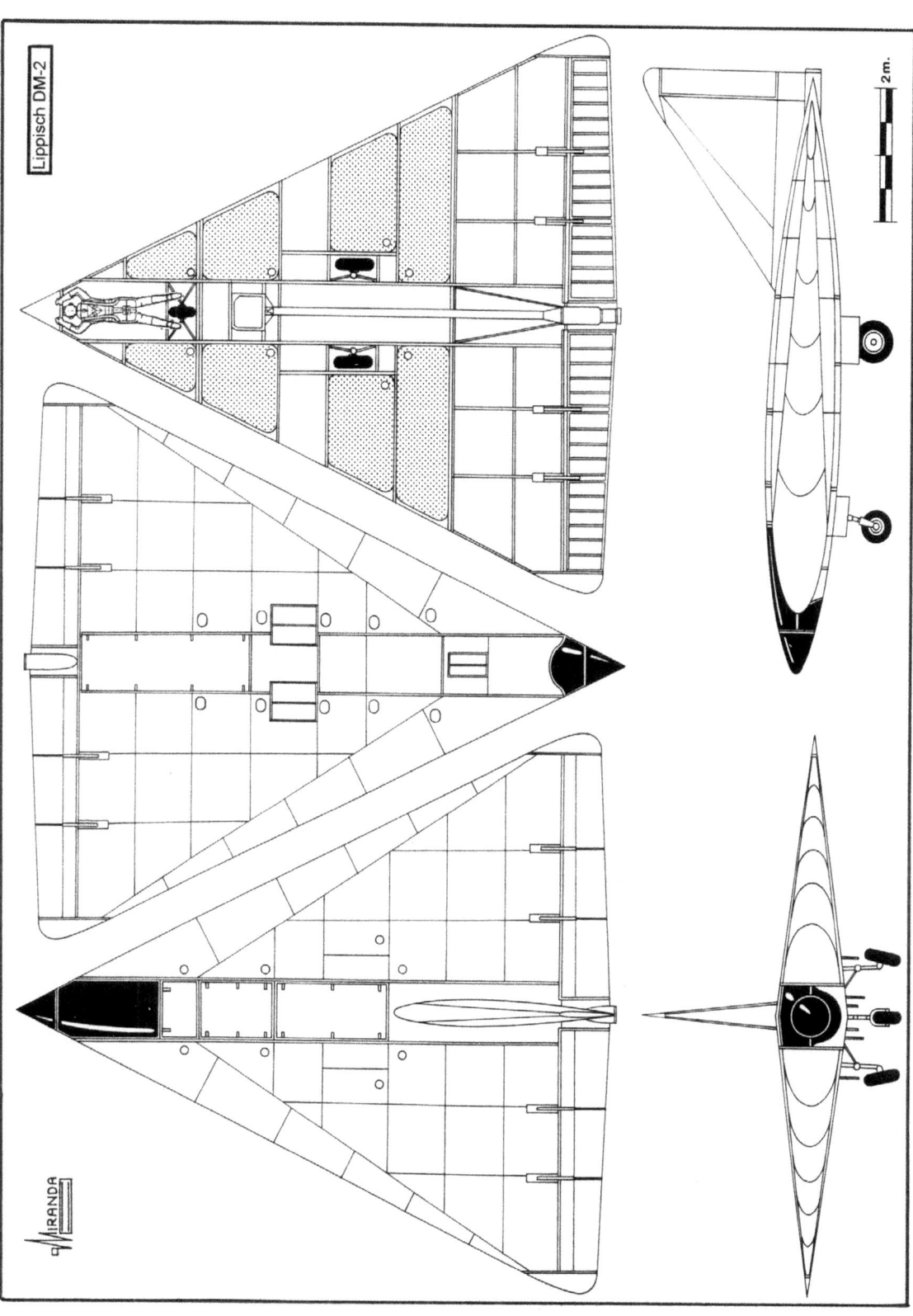

Lippisch DM-2

2 m.

MIRANDA

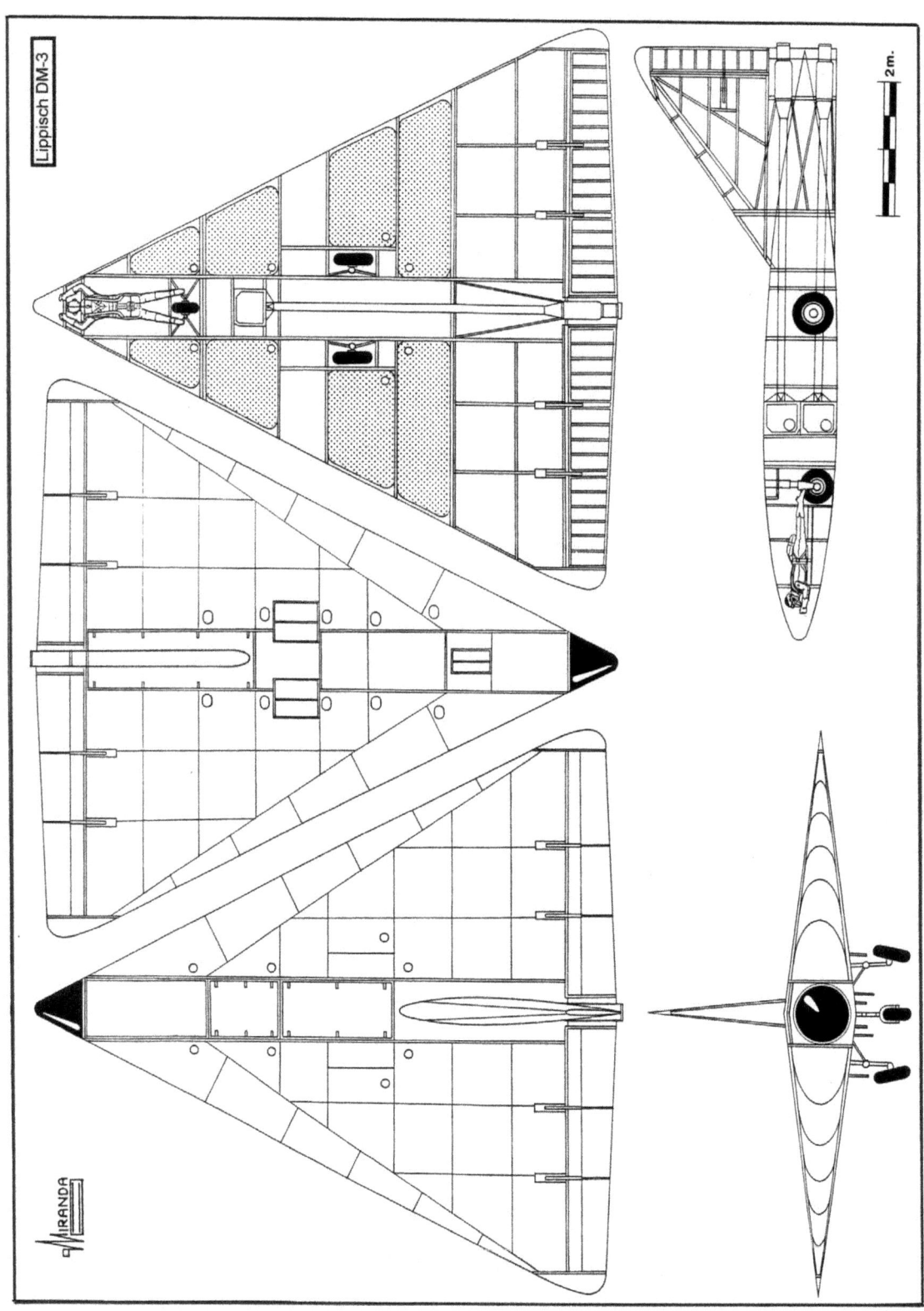

Lippisch DM-3

2 m.

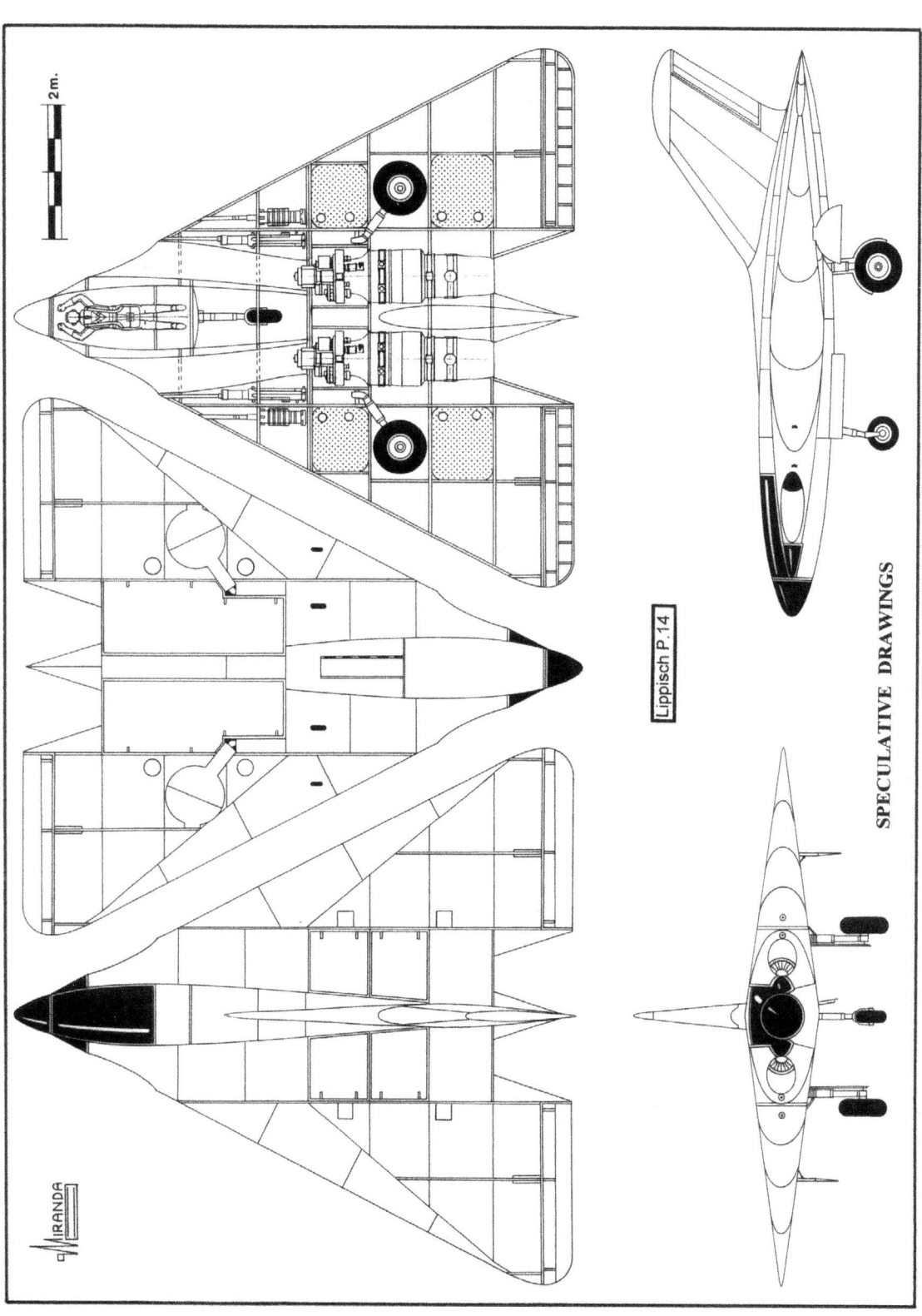

2 m.

Lippisch P.14

SPECULATIVE DRAWINGS

MIRANDA

Chapter 30

Messerschmitt Transonic Combat Airplanes (Mach 0.8 to 1.2)

Twin-engine fighters like the Me 210 and Me 262, designed before 1942, were not suitable for high-altitude combat. The reasons for this were their great mass and the turbulence they generated at high altitude between the lower face of the wing and the engine nacelles.

During flight tests of the Me 262 C-1a *Heimatschützer I* (Home Protector I), it transpired that the excess of power provided by the Walter 509 rocket had to be counterbalanced by flying with the nose tilted slightly upwards to avoid the airplane reaching the critical Mach figure. The designers tried another solution: they gave the Me 262 a more stream-lined shape, which delayed the generation of the turbulence.

The *Hochgeschwindigkeit* (HG) programme started in 1944. Through gradual developments, the sweeping of the wing and tail surfaces was increased to up to 45 degrees and the new HeS 011 engines—with a special cowling and oval air intakes at the leading edge—were installed within the wing.

The wind-tunnel tests proved that this was the right way to proceed. The final version, named 'HG III *Überschall-Turbinenjäger*', was a 1,000-kph design with transonic capabilities when fighting at high altitude without losing control.

The Luftwaffe considered the Me 262 within the *Zerstörer* category, and from their viewpoint, it was an expensive airplane, since it required a great deal of fuel, ammunition, and engine power. As quoted in the *Jägernotprogramm 226/2* specifications of 15 July 1944, the Oberkommando der Luftwaffe wanted a single-engine machine worthy of replacing the Bf 109. The requirements were that it should need neither rocket propellants—difficult to handle—nor any special support vehicles—as was the case with the *Komet*—nor any complicated take off techniques, as those foreseen by the new designs powered by ramjets.

The new airplane was only to be powered by a Heinkel-Hirth 109-011 A turbojet of 1,300 kp, giving it a range equivalent to that of the Me 262 and manoeuvrability between 36,000 and 46,000 feet. Its maximum speed at horizontal flight was to be 1,000 kph at 23,000 feet and it had to have capacity for four 30-mm guns and either twenty-four R4M rockets, two R100 BS rockets, or two X-4 missiles. The estimated monthly rate of production was 5,000 fighters, which demanded a very simple airframe and an extensive usage of non-strategic materials, such as wood, steel, and plastics. The limited power available encouraged the design of a small airplane.

The Blohm & Voss P.213.03, Heinkel P.1078 C, Henschel P.135, Junkers EF 128, and Focke Wulf Ta 183 were good designs that adapted to the specification. However, Messerschmitt wanted to go further, building an airplane able to reach transonic speed during combat diving, without losing manoeuvrability.

To that end, he pursued two lines of research: on the one hand, the Me 163 powered by a HeS 011; on the other, a single-engine development of the Me 262 HGIII, with the new 40-degree swept wing of the 'A' type, originally developed for the P.1101.

During the autumn of 1944, the P.1101 model tests in the wind tunnel proved that the maximum speed would still be lower than expected. The reason was the turbulence generated in the joint of the rear fuselage with the engine nacelle that had an '8' shaped section. It appeared that the airplane generated a triple shock wave at transonic speed. The first one was formed around the cockpit, the second over the wing, and the third over the tailplane. These shock waves overlapped each other, causing a braking effect on the airplane akin to an arrow piercing three disks of felt in the air.

As an alternative to all these fast airplanes with high wing loads, the Luftwaffe insisted on building a fighter able to fly as well as the *Komet* did, but with a conventional landing gear and a HeS 011 turbojet engine.

Messerschmitt's answer in January 1945 was the P.1111 design. It combined the reduced frontal section of the P.1110 and the air intakes of the Me 262 HG III with a new 52-degree swept wing and 9.16-m wingspan, based on that of the Me 163. The airplane had everything: it was fast, climbed very rapidly and highly, manoeuvred exceedingly well at low speed, had enough room to transport a lot of fuel and armament, could be built in wood, and was surprisingly small and attractive.

However, the design contained a fatal flaw. The airplane was very unstable at transonic speed, at which point the centre of pressure displaced itself rearwards and outwards from its usual location, following the wing axis. The consequences had already been noticed during the July 1944 tests of the Me 163 B V18. There were violent oscillations in the vertical axis, followed by a prolonged nose-down pitch with a 60- to 80-degree dive and total loss of control. Meanwhile, the Mach number increased rapidly until it became impossible to hold the aircraft, which took over and steepened the dive to vertical.

The P.1112/S2 of 3 March 1945 was an attempt to resolve this problem. It had a broader and shorter wing that was supposed to delay displacement of the centre of pressure. The cockpit was integrated into the fuselage curvature and located almost 2 m further than in the P.1111, to prevent the shock wave generated interfering with the air intakes. The design proved to be more stable, with 6 sq. m of wing surface less, but on the other hand, it had diminished performance at low speed and could no longer carry most of the fuel in the unarmoured fuel tanks in the wings.

Lippisch also worked on this problem, designing another variant of the P.1111 named *LP.15* on 3 March 1945. To him, the solution was to increase the wing chord, moving forwards the centre of gravity and positioning the air intakes in the nose. This design bears no relation to the *LP.15 Diana* of 4 April 1945.

The Northrop X-4 was specifically built to test the performances of this type of wing during the experiments conducted between 1949 and 1951. They proved that this type of airplane was unstable in transonic regime (higher than 0.92 Mach) and that the migration of the centre of pressure could not be resolved with the technology of the day.

The British also built the De Havilland DH.108, an experimental tailless airplane based on the same aerodynamic solution. The designer, no doubt worried by the lack of experience with swept wings and fearing that the airplane could be unstable at low speed, built a wing of extended (12 m) rather than reduced span like Messerschmitt did with the P.1112/S2 (7.80 m) or Northrop with the X-4 (8.18 m). Centre of pressure migration was aggravated under these conditions, producing an additional problem of aileron reversal, due to the twisting of the wing.

The DH.108 proved to be a very unstable airplane from Mach 0.91 upwards. Unfortunately, the three prototypes built crashed for various reasons, killing their pilots, and deemed unfit by the g-forces. Nevertheless, the DH.108 has the distinction of being the first British airplane to reach Mach 1.04 (during an uncontrolled dive) on 6 September 1948.

Chapter 31

Messerschmitt Me P.1112 IV/156
(25 February 1945)

Designed as an alternative to the Me 262 B-2a (12 Febraury 1945), the Me P.1112 IV/156 had the same electronics and armament, but a better climb rate, ceiling, and manoeuvrability at high altitude.

From an aerodynamic viewpoint, it was a 64-per-cent scaled-down version of the P.1107 heavy bomber (drawing IX/117 of 12 January 1945), but the wing structure, the slats, the elevators, the ailerons, the fuel tanks, and the main undercarriage legs were identical to those of the P.1111. The wing sweep had, however, been reduced to improve manoeuvrability at low speed during night landings.

However, the design did not comply with the Oberkommando der Luftwaffe 24 January 1945 specification to include a third crew member. The Messerschmitt design team preferred to develop an extended-wingspan version of the Me 262, with an elongated fuselage of 12.59 m and the turbojets within the wing roots (Me 262 B-2U, 17 March 1945).

The delta design was never presented to the OKL; the P.1112 denomination was used for an improved version of the P.1111.

Technical data P.1111 and P.1112/S2 (3 March 1945) (P.1112/S2 between brackets)	
Type	single-seat turbojet fighter.
Wings	52-degree (52-degree) swept, 8 per cent (8 per cent) relative thickness, wooden structure and cladding with automatic slot on the leading edge and air intakes located in the wing root extensions.
Fuselage	circular section, metallic structure and cladding. Pressurised cockpit with armoured plates for the pilot against rounds of 12.7 mm from the front and 20 mm from the rear. Ejection seat available.
Landing gear	tricycle type. The main wheels were housed in the wing roots, behind the pilot.
Engine	one HeS 011 A-0 turbojet with 1,300-kp static thrust (it was planned to install a HeS 011 B-0 of 1,500 kp in the P.1112/S2).
Fuel tanks	two of 750 litres (600 litres) each in the wings (and two armoured ones of 500 litres and 200 litres in the fuselage). The P.1111 could carry an additional two tanks of 50 litres within the wing, behind the main spar, and the P.1112/S2 two detachable tanks of 250 litres each.

Armament	two Mk 108 in the nose and two more in the wing roots, with 100 rounds per gun (an Mk 214 of 50 mm or an Mk 112 of 55 mm might also be installed in the P.1112/S2 in the place of the four Mk 108 of 30 mm).
Electronics	FuG 15, FuG 25, FuG 125, EZ 42.
Wingspan	9.16 m (7.80 m)
Length	8.92 m (8.20 m)
Height	3.06 m (3.05 m)
Wing area	28 sq. m (22 sq. m)
Empty weight	2,740 kg (2,290 kg)
Take off weight	4,282 kg (4,673 kg)
Max. speed	995 kph at 7,000 m (more than 1,000 kph)
Service ceiling	more than 46,000 feet (36,000 feet)
Range	1,500 km at an altitude of 32,800 feet

Technical data P.1112 IV/156

Type	two-seat night fighter.
Wings	built of wood and plywood with 45-degree sweep at the leading edge and 15-degree sweep at the trailing edge. Housing the engines, four unprotected fuel tanks, slots, elevators, ailerons, and main undercarriage legs.
Fuselage	built of light alloy, housing the radar, the nose leg, the armament, the cockpit (pressurised, control heating, armoured windshield against 12.7 mm shelling, ejectable seats), and the tailfin.
Engines	two HeS 109-011 turbojets rated at 1,300-kp static thrust.
Armament	four Mk 108/30 cannons in the nose and two Mk 108/30 cannons in 80-degree upwards Schräge Musik configuration to either side of the radar operator.
Wingspan	12.70 m
Length	10.30 m
Height	3.40 m
Wing area	38 sq. m
Electronics	EZ 42 gryro-gunsight, *Revi C16 A-N Schräge Musik* gunsight. EiV7 crew intercom, FuG 244 *Bremen 0* radar, FuG 24 radio transmitter, FuG 101a radio altimeter, FuG 350 Zc *Naxos Z* radar passive receiver, FuG 120 *Bernhardine* radio beacon teleprinter, FuG 25a *Erstling* IFF.

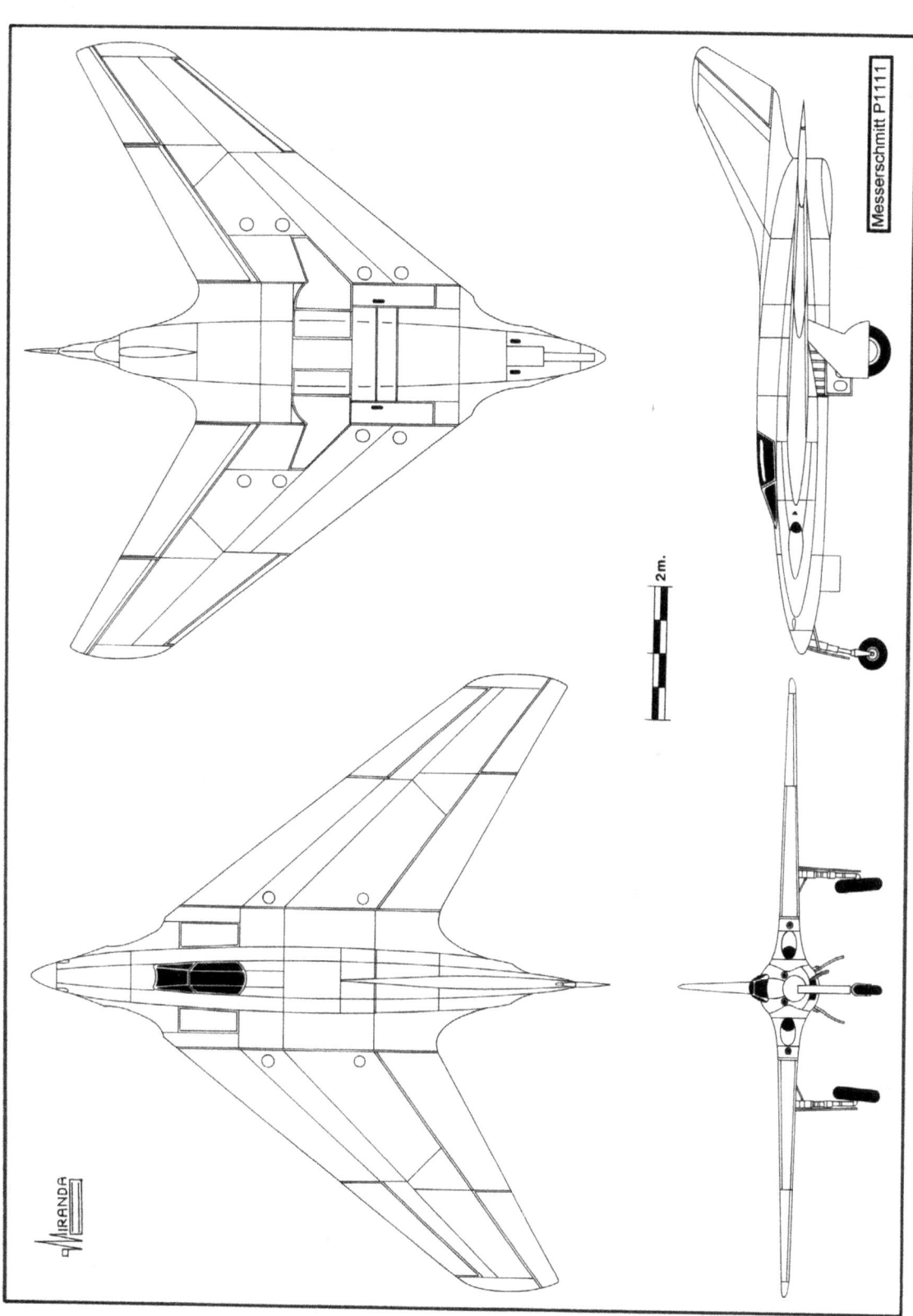

Messerschmitt P1111

2m.

2 m.

Messerschmitt P1111

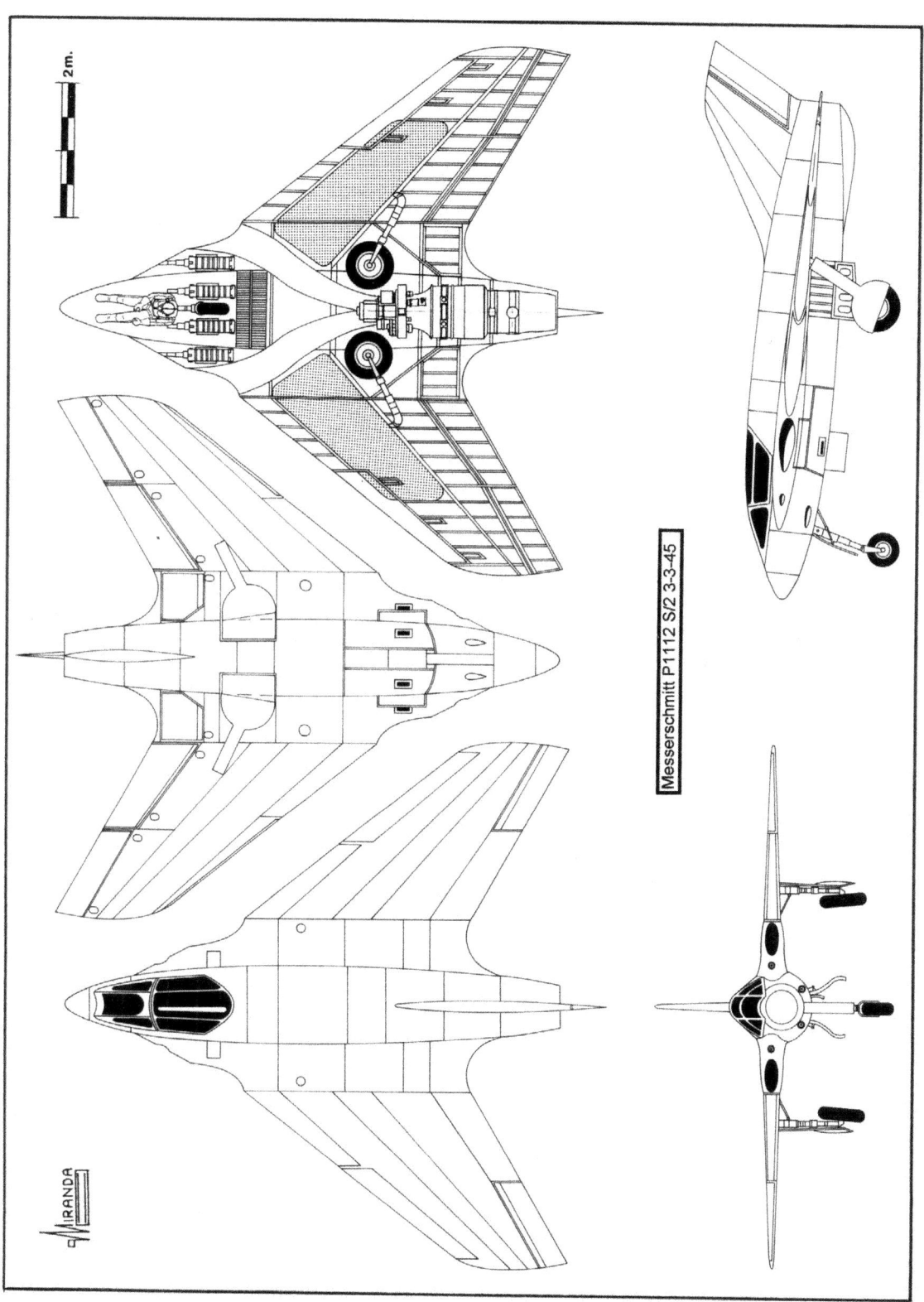

Messerschmitt P1112 S/2 3-3-45

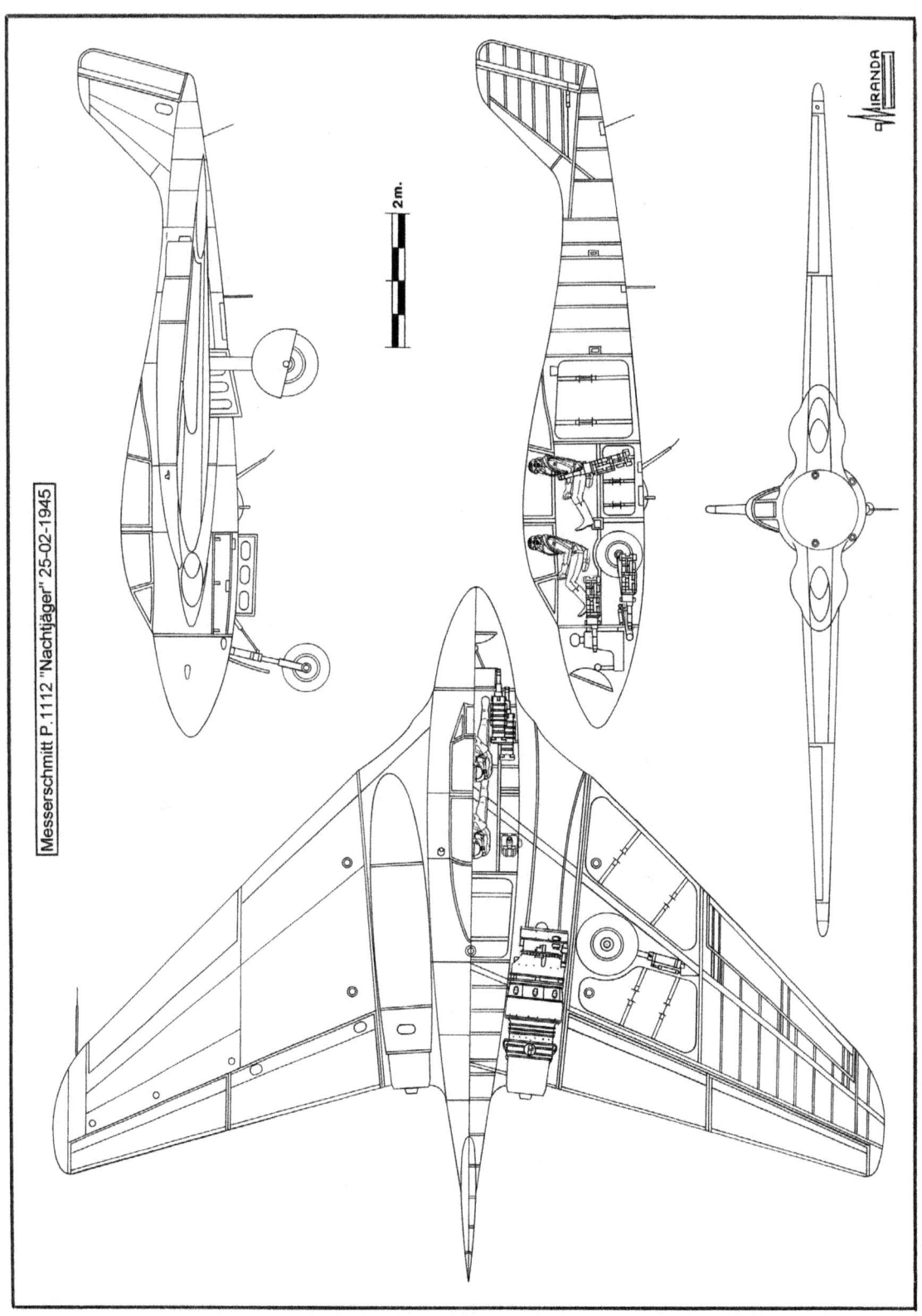

2 m.

Messerschmitt P.1112 "Nachtjäger" 25-02-1945

Conclusion

Flying Wings—The Next Chapter

In the wreckage of a British Stirling shot down over Rotterdam in February 1943, a Luftwaffe research team discovered a radar device that was able to operate in centimetric wavelengths—something the scientists of the Reich had considered impossible. Understanding that they had lost the technological race in the field of radar, the Germans focused their efforts on neutralizing the efficiency of Allied electronic equipment. To that end they built radar passive receiver devices for the U-boats, sophisticated infra-red telescopes for the night fighters, and interfering electronic equipment to counteract the radio navigation and communication systems of the Allies. They also made huge advances in the research of radar-absorbent materials (RAM) to hamper the detection of the U-boats, a special 'anti-radar' painting for the airplanes, and their own version of the Allied 'Window' system named *Düppelstreifen*.

The shape and the synthetic materials used for the building of some flying wings led to the casual discovery of their 'stealth' properties—a finding that made some of the desperate generals of the Luftwaffe believe they had finally found the ultimate weapon to use against radar. The status of 'flying wings' therefore changed from curiosity to high-priority secret weapon.

At the beginning of 1945 there were three programmes to manufacture stealth bombers in Germany, specifically designed to launch attacks on London, Moscow, and New York with special bombs of an unspecified type. Fortunately for the Allies, the war in Europe ended before the first prototypes being built at the underground workshops of the Kahla-Thuringia complex were ready.

Apparently the Germans were able to preserve their secret after surrender; the Allies considered the flying wings captured in the Gothaer-Friedrichroda manufacturing plant as aeronautical rarities. At that time, the best Allied scientists were fascinated by the German research on rockets, aerodynamics, and the problems associated with transonic flight.

The British conducted a very thorough study of some Horten flying wings at the Royal Aircraft Establishment in Farnborough, Hampshire, but they were mainly interested in finding out how the control surfaces worked. Perhaps they were looking for the causes in the instability of their own failed flying wing designs.

In the USA, Northrop engineers looked for the same answers when they were authorized to examine some captured German and Japanese flying wings. The Horten brothers,

Alexander Lippisch, and Günther Bock had extensive knowledge on RAM techniques and materials, but they did not reveal it for different reasons.

When the test flight of the gigantic Northrop YB-49 flying wing bombers started in 1947, civil and military radar operators reported sudden losses of the blip signal on their screens every time the bomber changed direction. Northrop engineers were incredulous and decided to carry out detailed tests on the stealth features of the YB-49. To that purpose they performed a series of flights, during which a P-61 C night fighter used its APS-720 radar to scan the YB-49 from different angles. The conclusive results of the experiment caused great concern among the US political and military leadership as huge sums had already been invested in the creation of the LASHUP radar system of air defence.

It was known that the Soviets had captured some flying wings in Germany, together with scientists and engineers of the Gothaer Waggonfabrik Flugzeugbau firm. The fear of losing technological superiority to the Soviets in the field of radar, and the possibility of Soviet-built stealth bombers, generated significant disagreements regarding defence strategy between the Department of Defense and the Northrop firm at the beginning of the Cold War. Great investment had already been made in the Northrop bomber programme and the manufacture of a pre-series had been initiated.

The engineers argued that the flying wings were to change the future of aviation as this type of airframe could transport a greater load of bombs at a higher altitude and with lower fuel consumption than conventional airplanes, while operating beyond the capabilities of enemy radar detection. Politicians were doubtful and the military preferred to keep their radars. They finally solved the issue by ordering the destruction of all the flying wings that had already been built. The idea was circulated that this type of airplane suffered from unsolvable control problems; several disinformation tactics were employed, including conspiracy theories and the creation of the 'Flying Saucers' myth, still considered a pseudo-religion by many people nowadays.

The strategy worked and when the Soviets manufactured their first A-bomb, it was so large that they were forced to manufacture a copied version of the Boeing B-29 to transport it. All subsequent developments of strategic bombers were of conventional design. When the Cold War was over, Northrop started to manufacture flying wing bombers anew.

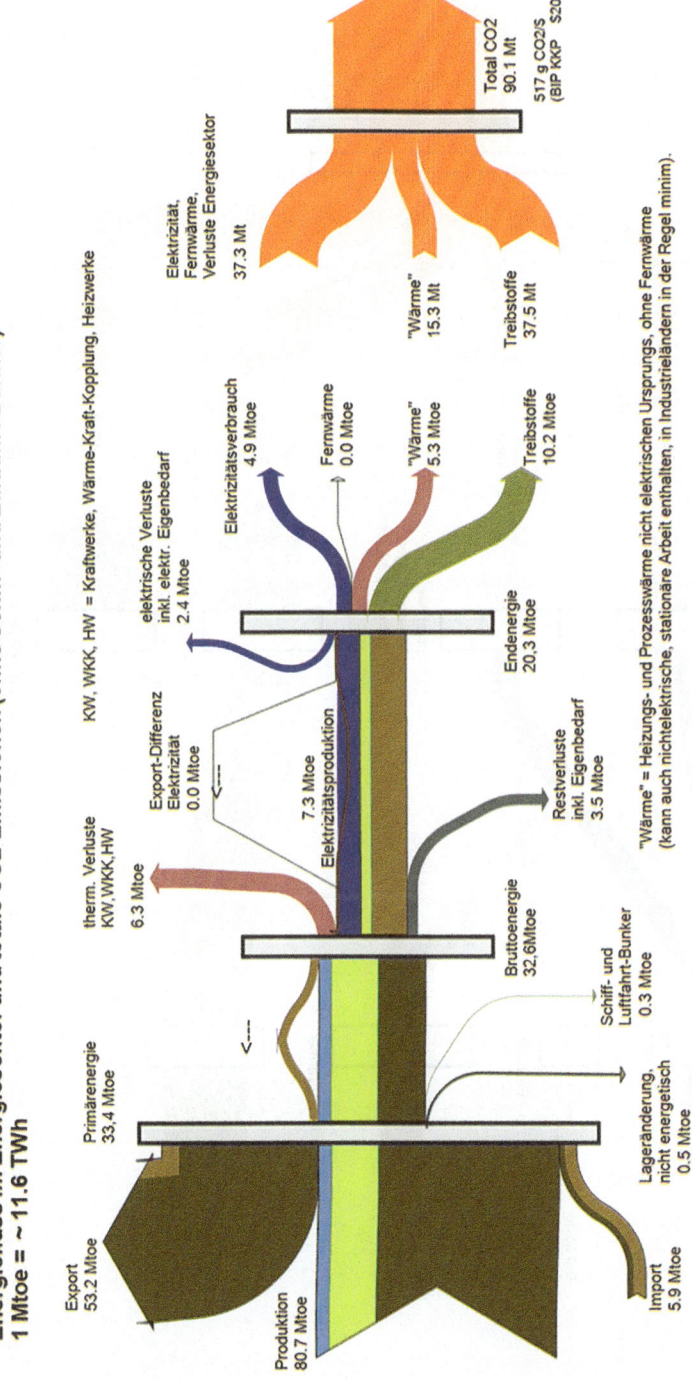

Abb. 4.7 Venezuela: Energiefluss im Energiesektor von der Primärenergie zur Endenergie und CO_2-Ausstoss. Die Energieträgerfarben sind wie in Abb. 2.8 und 2.10 (Erdöl dunkelbraun, Erdölprodukte hellbraun)

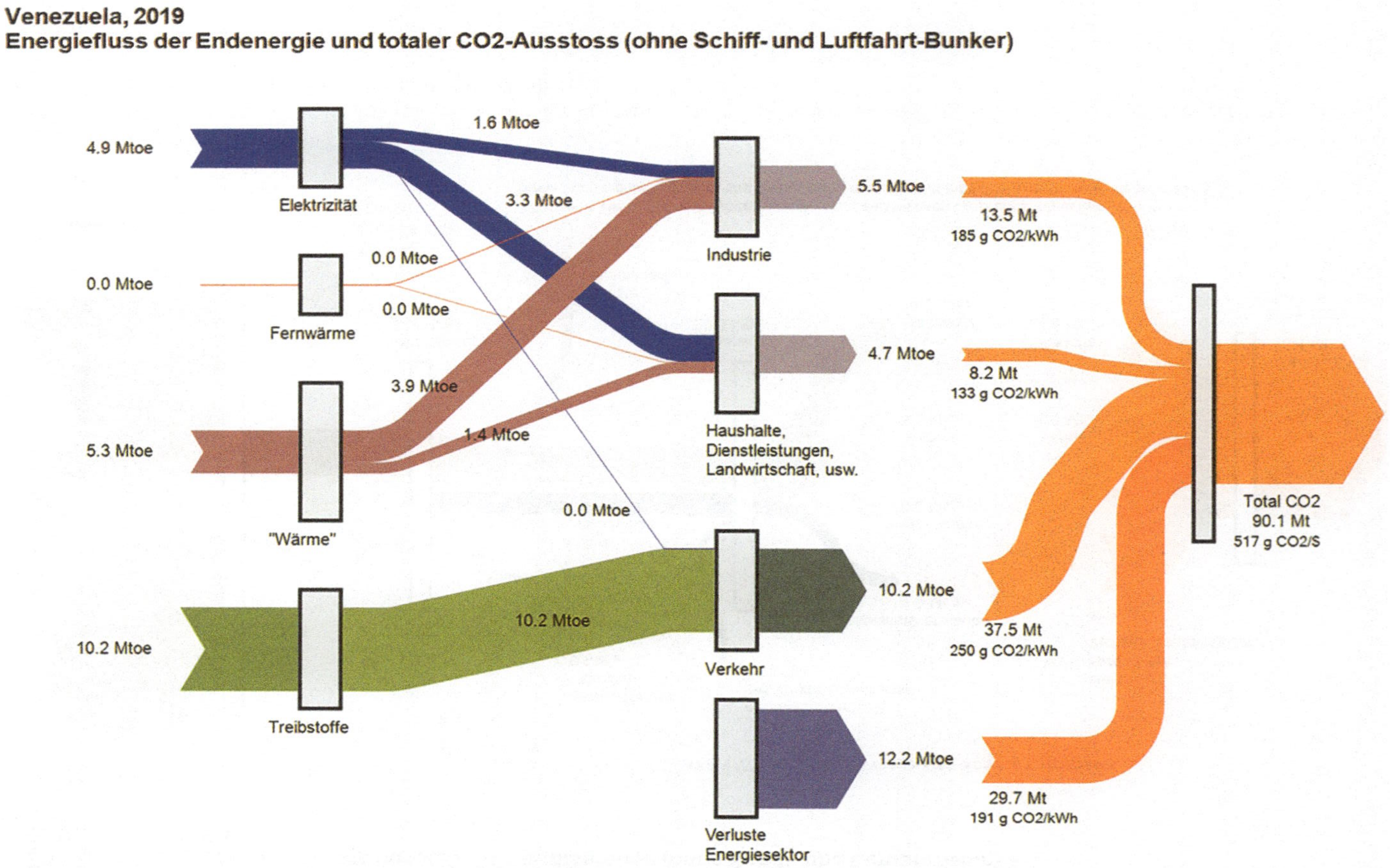

Venezuela, 2019
Energiefluss der Endenergie und totaler CO2-Ausstoss (ohne Schiff- und Luftfahrt-Bunker)

Abb. 4.8 Venezuela: Energiefluss der Endenergie zu den Endverbrauchern und zugeordnete CO$_2$-Emissionen

Südamerikas (Abb. 2.31), dies trotz der relativ CO_2-armen stark auf Wasserkraft basierenden Elektrizitätsproduktion (Abb. 4.2). Hauptgrund ist der Einbruch der Wirtschaft durch die politische Instabilität und die Abwanderung. Dies hatte eine starke Verschlechterung der **Energieeffizienz** (s. auch Tab. 4.8) und auch der CO_2-Intensität der Wirtschaft zur Folge. Eine weitere verstärkte Elektrifizierung des Landes könnte bei politischer Stabilität Fortschritt bringen, mit mehr erneuerbaren Energien zur Elektrizitätsproduktion und für den Export (Wind und Sonne, auch Geothermie hat ein grosses Potential).

4.3 Tabellen und Kommentare zu Indikatoren und CO$_2$-Intensitäten gewichtiger Länder des Kontinents

Die Tab. 4.2 bis 4.8 geben die *Energieintensität* und die *Emissionen pro Kopf* sowie die detaillierten Werte der *CO$_2$-Intensitäten der Endenergien und der Endverbraucher* für die demographisch gewichtigsten Länder (2019 zusammen 79 % der Bevölkerung Amerikas). Dazu folgende Kommentare:

- Die **CO$_2$-Intensität des Energiesektors** wird stark vom Grad der *CO$_2$-Freiheit der Elektrizitätserzeugung* beeinflusst. Beste Werte (<160 g CO_2/kWh) in Brasilien und Kolumbien. Eine CO_2-arme Elektrizitätserzeugung ist die beste und dringendste

Tab. 4.2 USA, 2019 (Energieintensität 1,31 kWh/\$, Emissionen 14,4 t CO$_2$/Kopf)

Energieart (Abb. 1.11)	g CO$_2$/kWh	Verbraucher (Abb. 1.12)	g CO$_2$/kWh
Wärme (ohne Elektr.)	188	Industrie	176
Treibstoffe	242	Haushalte etc.	177
Energiesektor	176	Verkehr	243
Total	**199**	Verluste Energiesektor	184

Tab. 4.3 Kanada, 2019 (Energieintensität 2,02 kWh/\$, Emissionen 15,2 t CO$_2$/Kopf)

Energieart (Abb. 1.13)	g CO$_2$/kWh	Verbraucher (Abb. 1.14)	g CO$_2$/kWh
Wärme (ohne Elektr.)	196	Industrie	141
Treibstoffe	253	Haushalte etc.	138
Energiesektor	123	Verkehr	251
Total	**172**	Verluste Energiesektor	158

Massnahme, neben der Verminderung der Energieintensität, zur Verbesserung der CO_2-Nachhaltigkeit und Erreichung der Klimaziele.

- In Brasilien und Kanada liegt die *CO$_2$-Intensität des Energiesektors* (weitgehend von derjenigen der Elektrizität bestimmt) bei weniger als 50 % derjenigen des **Verkehrssektors**. Eine verbreitete *Elektrifizierung* des Verkehrs (Bahnen, Elektro- und Hybridautos) würde dann stark zur Verbesserung der CO_2-Nachhaltigkeit beitragen.
- Der Einsatz von **Wärmepumpen** ist allgemein sehr sinnvoll, da der Anteil an CO_2-freier Umweltenergie meistens bei etwa 75 % liegt. Somit helfen Wärmepumpen die CO_2-Intensität des Wärmebereichs selbst dann zu reduzieren, wenn die CO_2-Intensität des Energiesektors sogar über derjenigen des Wärmesektors liegt (wie in Kolumbien und Mexiko).
- Die **Energieintensität** ist ein weiterer wichtiger Indikator. Er hängt von *der Effizienz des Energieeinsatzes* ab. Vor allem in Kanada und Venezuela (>2 kWh/$), aber auch in Venezuela und den USA (>1,3 kWh/$), muss die Energieintensität deutlich vermindert werden, Amerika sollte insgesamt einen Wert unter 1,0 kWh/$ BIP (KKP in $ von 2010) anpeilen (Abschn. 2.6).
- Der **Indikator der CO_2-Nachhaltigkeit** (g CO_2/$) ist das Produkt von Energieintensität und CO_2-Intensität der Energie.

In den *USA*, als gewichtigstes Land Amerikas, hat die CO_2-Nachhaltigkeit in 2019 mit 1,31 kWh/$ * 199 g CO_2/kWh = 260 g CO_2/$ einen erheblichen Nachholbedarf. (als Vergleich Westeuropa in 2018: 0,87 kWh/$ * 169 g CO_2/kWh = 147 g CO_2/$, ([10], Band 1 der Reihe). Die *Emissionen pro Kopf* in t CO_2/Kopf und Jahr ergeben sich als Produkt von Index der CO_2-Nachhaltigkeit und Wohlstandsindikator ($/Kopf und Jahr):

$$t\,CO_2 / Kopf,\ a = g\,CO_2 / \$ * \$ / Kopf, a / 10^6.$$

Im Jahr 2019 waren, in USA + Kanada, das mittlere kaufkraftbereinigte Bruttoinlandprodukt *54 200 $/Kopf* und die CO_2-Emissionen *14,5 t/Kopf*, entsprechend einem Index der CO_2-Nachhaltigkeit von *267 g CO_2/$*. Um bis 2050 eine für die Klimaziele notwendige Reduktion der CO_2-Emissionen auf *3 t/Kopf* zu erzielen (s. Abschn. 3.1 und 3.2), muss, bei einer Zunahme des BIP (KKP) auf z. B. *60 000 $/Kopf*, der Index der CO_2-Nachhaltigkeit auf etwa *50 g CO_2/$* gesenkt werden.

In Lateinamerika (Mittel- + Südamerika, inklusive Mexiko) waren 2019: das mittlere BIP (KKP) etwa *13 200 $/Kopf* und die CO_2-Emissionen *2,24 t/Kopf*, entsprechend einem Index der CO_2-Nachhaltigkeit von *169 g CO_2/$*. Um bis 2050 eine für die Klimaziele notwendige Reduktion der CO_2-Emissionen auf *1,0 t/Kopf* zu erzielen (s. Abschn. 2.3 bis 2.6), muss, bei einer Zunahme des BIP (KKP) auf z. B. *20 000 $/Kopf*, der Index der CO_2-Nachhaltigkeit ebenfalls auf *50 g CO_2/$* vermindert werden.

Tab. 4.4 Mexiko, 2019 (Energieintensität 0,93 kWh/$, Emissionen 3,3 t CO_2/Kopf)

Energieart (Abb. 1.15)	g CO_2/kWh	Verbraucher (Abb. 1.16)	g CO_2/kWh
Wärme (ohne Elektr.)	181	Industrie	188
Treibstoffe	243	Haushalte etc.	155
Energiesektor	187	Verkehr	243
Total	**202**	Verluste Energiesektor	107

Tab. 4.5 Brasilien, 2019 (Energieintensität 1,17 kWh/$, Emissionen 2,0 t CO_2/Kopf)

Energieart (Abb. 1.19)	g CO_2/kWh	Verbraucher (Abb. 1.20)	g CO_2/kWh
Wärme (ohne Elektr.)	123	Industrie	99
Treibstoffe	192	Haushalte etc.	85
Energiesektor	78	Verkehr	193
Total	**127**	Verluste Energiesektor	107

Tab. 4.6 Argentinien, 2019 (Energieintensität 1,00 kWh/$, Emissionen 3,6 t CO_2/Kopf)

Energieart (Abb. 3.3)	g CO_2/kWh	Verbraucher (Abb. 3.4)	g CO_2/kWh
Wärme (ohne Elektr.)	195	Industrie	164
Treibstoffe	218	Haushalte etc.	183
Energiesektor	159	Verkehr	218
Total	**185**	Verluste Energiesektor	171

Tab. 4.7 Kolumbien, 2019 (Energieintensität 0,74 kWh/$, Emissionen 1,5 t CO_2/Kopf)

Energieart (Abb. 3.5)	g CO_2/kWh	Verbraucher (Abb. 3.6)	g CO_2/kWh
Wärme (ohne Elektr.)	136	Industrie	142
Treibstoffe	194	Haushalte etc.	88
Energiesektor	140	Verkehr	194
Total	**153**	Verluste Energiesektor	175

Tab. 4.8 Venezuela, 2019
(Energieintensität 2,17 kWh/\$,
Emissionen 3,2 t CO_2/Kopf)

Energieart (Abb. 3.7)	g CO_2/kWh	Verbraucher (Abb. 3.8)	g CO_2/kWh
Wärme (ohne Elektr.)	251	Industrie	213
Treibstoffe	317	Haushalte etc.	152
Energiesektor	188	Verkehr	317
Total	**239**	Verluste Energiesektor	218

Teil II
Naher Osten und Südasien

Energiewirtschaftliche Analyse 5

5.1 Einführung

In Teil II dieses zweiten Bandes der Reihe „Kennzahlen zur Erreichung der weltweiten Klimaziele" werden der *Nahe Osten und Südasien* analysiert. Zusammen bilden sie ein Erdteil mit reichem kulturellen Erbe, demographisch wird er von Indien dominiert. Das wirtschaftliche Potenzial ist riesig und dürfte die Zukunft des Planeten erheblich beeinflussen.

Nach der Analyse in Kap. 5 der Entwicklung aller maßgebenden Größen wie Bevölkerung, Bruttoinlandprodukt, detaillierter Energieverbrauch und CO_2-Emissionen bis 2019, wird dann in Kap. 6 eine künftige Evolution der wichtigsten Indikatoren der einzelnen Regionen und Länder dargelegt, welche die Klimaziele respektiert.

5.2 Bevölkerung und Bruttoinlandprodukt

Wir unterteilen *Nah- und Süd-Asien* in drei Regionen die folgendermaßen definiert sind (Abb. 5.1 und 5.2)

- *Naher Osten* (Israel, Iran, Irak, Syrien, Libanon, Jordanien, Saudi Arabien, Jemen, Oman, Vereinigte Arabische Emirate, Katar, Bahrain, Kuwait)
- *Indien*
- *Restliches Südasien* (an Indien angrenzende Länder: Pakistan, Sri-Lanka, Bangladesch, Nepal, Myanmar). Über Afghanistan und Bhutan sind keine IEA-Daten verfügbar.

© Springer Fachmedien Wiesbaden GmbH, ein Teil von Springer Nature 2023
V. Crastan, *Kennzahlen zur Erreichung der weltweiten Klimaziele*,
https://doi.org/10.1007/978-3-658-40073-6_5

Abb. 5.1 Länder des Nahen Ostens (arabische Halbinsel + Iran)

Der *Nahe Osten und Südasien* weisen zusammen in 2019 mit 2 Mrd. Einwohner (Abb. 5.3) ein kaufkraftbereinigtes Bruttoinlandprodukt BIP (KKP) von 14.900 Mrd. US$ ($ von 2010) auf. Indien dominiert mit 65 % der Bevölkerung und 55 % des BIP.

Das BIP (KKP) pro Kopf von Nahost und Süd-Asien beträgt zusammen im Mittel 7300 $/a, was etwa der Hälfte des weltweiten Durchschnitts (14.900 $/a) entspricht.

Die Verteilung des BIP (KKP) pro Kopf in *Südasien* (Indien + Rest-Südasien) zeigt Abb. 5.4. In *Indien* beträgt das BIP (KKP) pro Kopf in 2019 rund 6000 $/a, ist immer noch unterdurchschnittlich hat sich aber seit 2010 um gut 40 % erhöht. Jenes von Bangladesch hat sich um mehr als 70 %, jenes von Pakistan lediglich um 3 % erhöht.

Die Verteilung des BIP/Kopf im *Nahen Osten* zeigt Abb. 5.5. Durchschnittlich ist es, trotz Abnahme in den letzten 9 Jahren, insgesamt mit 18.000 $/a mehr als das Dreifache von jenem von Südasien und auch weltweit gesehen überdurchschnittlich, wobei aber lokal enorme Unterschiede festzustellen sind. Die gegenwärtigen kriegerischen Auseinandersetzungen vertiefen diesen Graben. Zu beachten ist die starke Bevölkerungszunahme

Abb. 5.2 Länder von Südasien

seit dem Jahr 2000 auf der arabischen Halbinsel (+64 %). In den Vereinigten Emiraten z. B., hat sich die Wohnbevölkerung von 2000 bis 2019 von 3,1 auf 9,8 Mio. mehr als verdreifacht. Dies erklärt die starke Abnahme des BIP's/Kopf seit 2000. Ähnliches gilt seit 2010 auch für Katar, Kuwait und Oman.

5.3 Bruttoenergie, Endenergie, Verluste des Energiesektors und entsprechende CO_2-Emissionen

Die **Endenergie** setzt sich zusammen aus Wärmebedarf (aus Brennstoffen, ohne Elektrizität und Fernwärme), Treibstoffen, Elektrizität (alle Anwendungen) und Fernwärme.

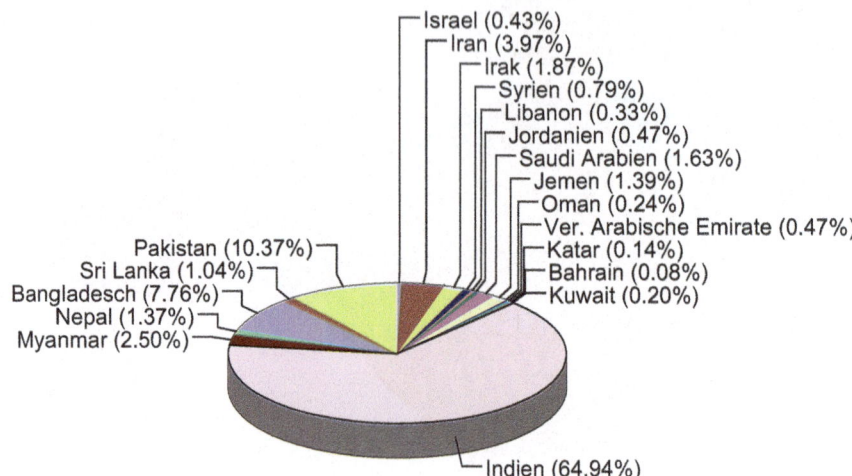

Bevölkerung von Nah- und Süd-Asien
2019, Total 2'092 Mio.

Israel (0.43%)
Iran (3.97%)
Irak (1.87%)
Syrien (0.79%)
Libanon (0.33%)
Jordanien (0.47%)
Saudi Arabien (1.63%)
Jemen (1.39%)
Oman (0.24%)
Ver. Arabische Emirate (0.47%)
Katar (0.14%)
Bahrain (0.08%)
Kuwait (0.20%)

Pakistan (10.37%)
Sri Lanka (1.04%)
Bangladesch (7.76%)
Nepal (1.37%)
Myanmar (2.50%)

Indien (64.94%)

Abb. 5.3 Prozentuale Aufteilung der Bevölkerung von Nahost und Südasien

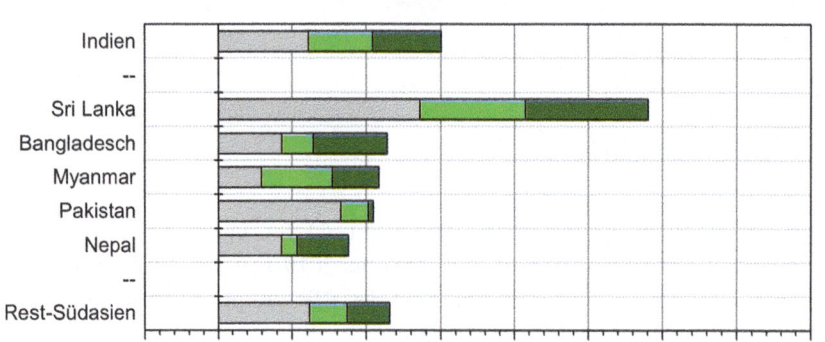

BIP/Kopf (KKP) in 10'000 $/Kopf
Indien und Rest-Südasien, 2019

in 10'000 $/a ($ von 2010)

Abnahme von 2010 bis 2019   Zunahme von 2010 bis 2019
Abnahme von 2000 bis 2010   Zunahme von 2000 bis 2010

Abb. 5.4 BIP (KKP) pro Kopf von Indien und vom restliches Südasien und Fortschritte seit 2000

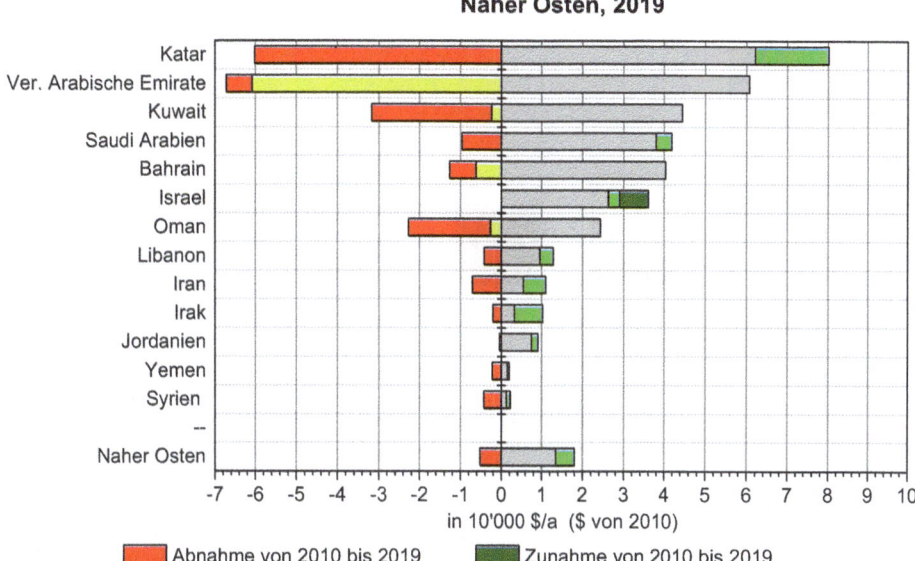

Abb. 5.5 BIP (KKP) pro Kopf der Länder des Nahen Ostens und Änderungen seit 2000

Die **Bruttoenergie** ist die Summe von Endenergie und aller im *Energiesektor* entstehenden Verluste. Der Energiesektor dient in erster Linie der Umwandlung von Bruttoenergie in Endenergie, wobei die Elektrizitätserzeugung die Hauptrolle spielt.

Die Energiestruktur ist in den drei Regionen stark unterschiedlich wie Abb. 5.6 veranschaulicht. Der *Nahe Osten* ist stark auf Erdöl und Erdgas ausgerichtet, während *Indien* neben Biomasse einen sehr hohen Kohleanteil aufweist. Im *restlichen Südasien* ist sie durch einen sehr hohen Anteil an Biomasse für die Wärmeanwendungen gekennzeichnet, der gut 40 % der Endenergie ausmacht. Ebenso grosse Unterschiede sind im Energiesektor (der in entwickelten Ländern in erster Linie der Produktion von Elektrizität dient) festzustellen: nur Öl und Erdgas im *Nahen Osten*, vorwiegend Öl und Gas auch in *Rest-Südasien* und vor allem Kohle in *Indien*. Der Elektrifizierungsgrad ist in Rest-Südasien noch gering.

Die **Verluste des Energiesektors** in Prozent der verwendeten Bruttoenergie betragen 35 % im *Nahen Osten*, 35 % in *Indien* und nur 18 % in *Rest-Südasien* was dem hohen Anteil an Hydroelektrizität und an Biomasse für die Wärmeanwendungen zu verdanken ist.

Die **Elektrizitätsproduktion** der drei Regionen ist in Abb. 5.7 veranschaulicht.

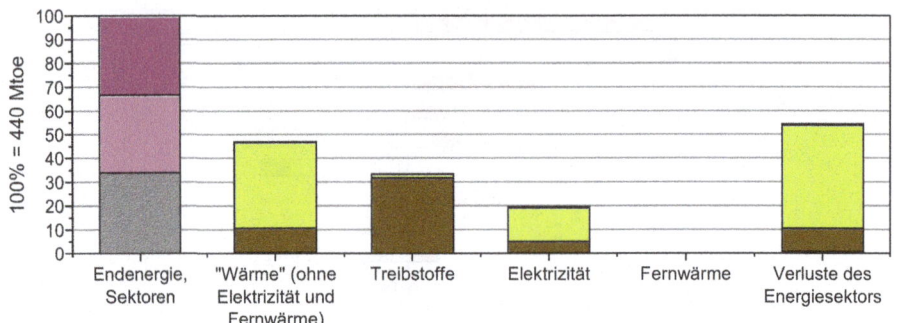

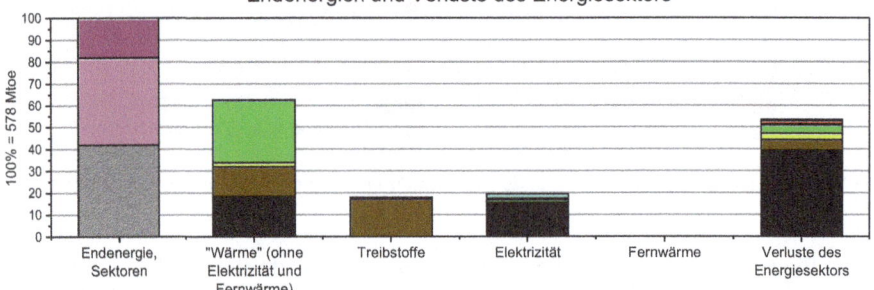

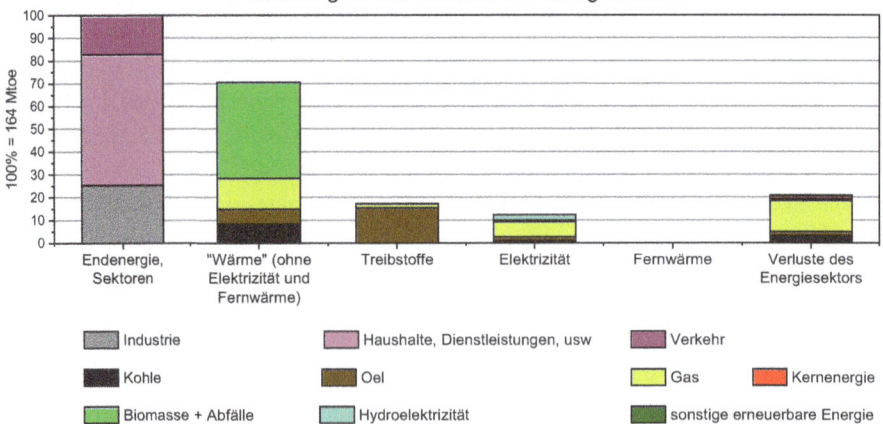

Abb. 5.6 Bruttoenergie = Endenergie + Verluste des Energiesektors, der drei Regionen von Nah- und Süd-Asien in 2019. Die Endenergie setzt sich zusammen aus Wärme, Treibstoffe und Elektrizität

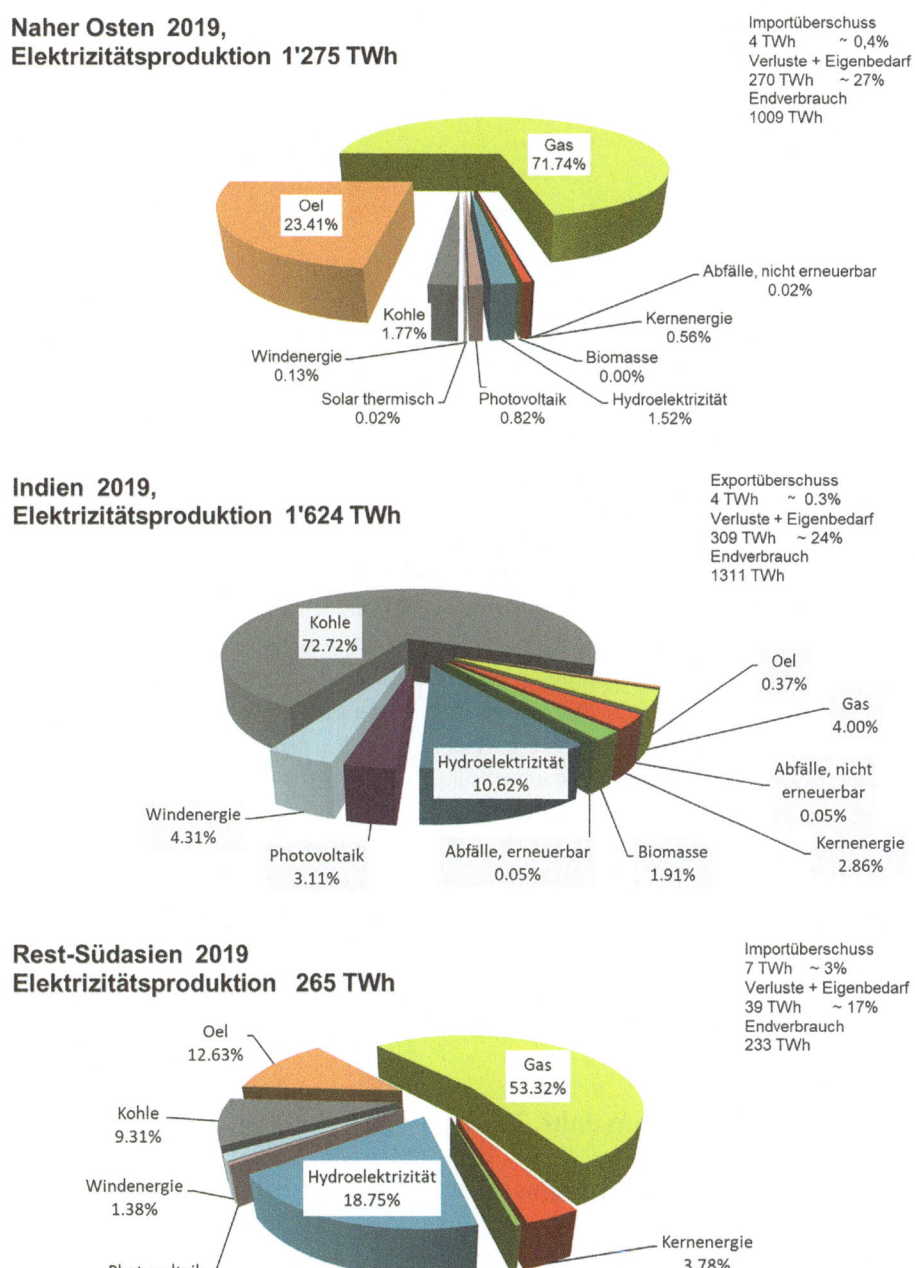

Naher Osten 2019,
Elektrizitätsproduktion 1'275 TWh

Importüberschuss
4 TWh   ~ 0,4%
Verluste + Eigenbedarf
270 TWh   ~ 27%
Endverbrauch
1009 TWh

Gas
71.74%

Oel
23.41%

Abfälle, nicht erneuerbar
0.02%

Kohle
1.77%

Kernenergie
0.56%

Windenergie
0.13%

Biomasse
0.00%

Solar thermisch
0.02%

Photovoltaik
0.82%

Hydroelektrizität
1.52%

Indien 2019,
Elektrizitätsproduktion 1'624 TWh

Exportüberschuss
4 TWh   ~ 0.3%
Verluste + Eigenbedarf
309 TWh   ~ 24%
Endverbrauch
1311 TWh

Kohle
72.72%

Oel
0.37%

Gas
4.00%

Hydroelektrizität
10.62%

Abfälle, nicht
erneuerbar
0.05%

Windenergie
4.31%

Photovoltaik
3.11%

Abfälle, erneuerbar
0.05%

Biomasse
1.91%

Kernenergie
2.86%

Rest-Südasien 2019
Elektrizitätsproduktion   265 TWh

Importüberschuss
7 TWh   ~ 3%
Verluste + Eigenbedarf
39 TWh   ~ 17%
Endverbrauch
233 TWh

Oel
12.63%

Gas
53.32%

Kohle
9.31%

Windenergie
1.38%

Hydroelektrizität
18.75%

Photovoltaik
0.44%

Kernenergie
3.78%

Abfälle, erneuerbar
0.00%

Biomasse
0.38%

Abb. 5.7 Elektrizitätsproduktion in 2019 der drei Regionen und entsprechende Energieträgeranteile. Importüberschuss und Verluste + Eigenbedarf in % des Endverbrauchs

Tab. 5.1 Erneuerbare und
CO_2-arme Energien sowie
Elektrifizierungsgrad

	Erneuerbar	CO_2-arm	Elektrifizierung
Naher Osten	2,5 %	3,1 %	20 %
Indien	20 %	23 %	19 %
Restliches Südasien	21 %	25 %	12 %
Nahost und Südasien	13 %	15 %	19 %

Die erneuerbaren Energien (Wasserkraft, Windenergie, Photovoltaik, Biomasse, Abfälle, Geothermie) bzw. die CO_2-armen Energien (erneuerbare Energien + Kernenergie) tragen zur Elektrizitätsproduktion gemäß Tab. 5.1 bei. Die Tabelle gibt auch den Elektrifizierungsgrad der drei Regionen (Elektrizitätsanteil der Endenergie: ist ein guter Index der Entwicklung).

Aus der Energiestruktur ergeben sich für 2019 die in Abb. 5.8 dargestellten **CO2-Emissionen:** Gesamtwert in *Mt*, Gesamtwert in *Gramm/$ BIP (KKP)* sowie Gesamtwert und detaillierte Verteilung in *Tonnen/Kopf* für die Verbrauchssektoren.

In der Industrie und im Haushalt-/Dienstleitungs-/Landwirtschaftssektor sind die Emissionen durch den Elektrizitäts- und Wärmebedarf aus fossilen Energien bestimmt, im Verkehrsbereich im Wesentlichen durch die Treibstoffe.

Die Emissionen, die durch die Verluste im Energiesektor entstehen, sind in erster Linie der Elektrizitätsproduktion zuzuschreiben. In *Indien* herrscht weiterhin die Kohle und die spezifischen Gesamt-Emissionen sind mit 283 g CO_2/$ immer noch hoch, in den vergangenen drei Jahren hat der Anteil an CO_2-armen Energien nur leicht zugenommen (Abb. 5.7); im *Nahen Osten*, wo Öl und Gas den Ton angeben, sind sie mit 401 g CO_2/$ deutlich am höchsten. In *Rest-Südasien* sind sie hingegen mit 148 g CO_2/$ vorerst noch gering, wegen Unterentwicklung, aber auch dank dem relativ hohen Beitrag der Wasserkraft, haben aber leicht steigende Tendenz.

Die Pro-Kopf Emissionen sind je nach Entwicklungsstand stark unterschiedlich, in Rest-Südasien weniger als ein Zehntel von jenen des Nahen Ostens (Abb. 5.8).

5.4   Energieflüsse im Jahr 2019

5.4.1   Energiefluss im Energiesektor

Nachfolgende Flussdiagramme (z. B. Abb. 5.9) beschreiben den Energiefluss im Energiesektor von der Primärenergie über die Bruttoenergie (oder Bruttoinlandverbrauch) zur Endenergie. Primärenergie und Bruttoenergie werden durch die verwendeten **Energieträger** veranschaulicht. Alle Energien werden in Mtoe (Megatonnen Öläquivalente, 1 Mtoe = 11,6 TWh) angegeben.

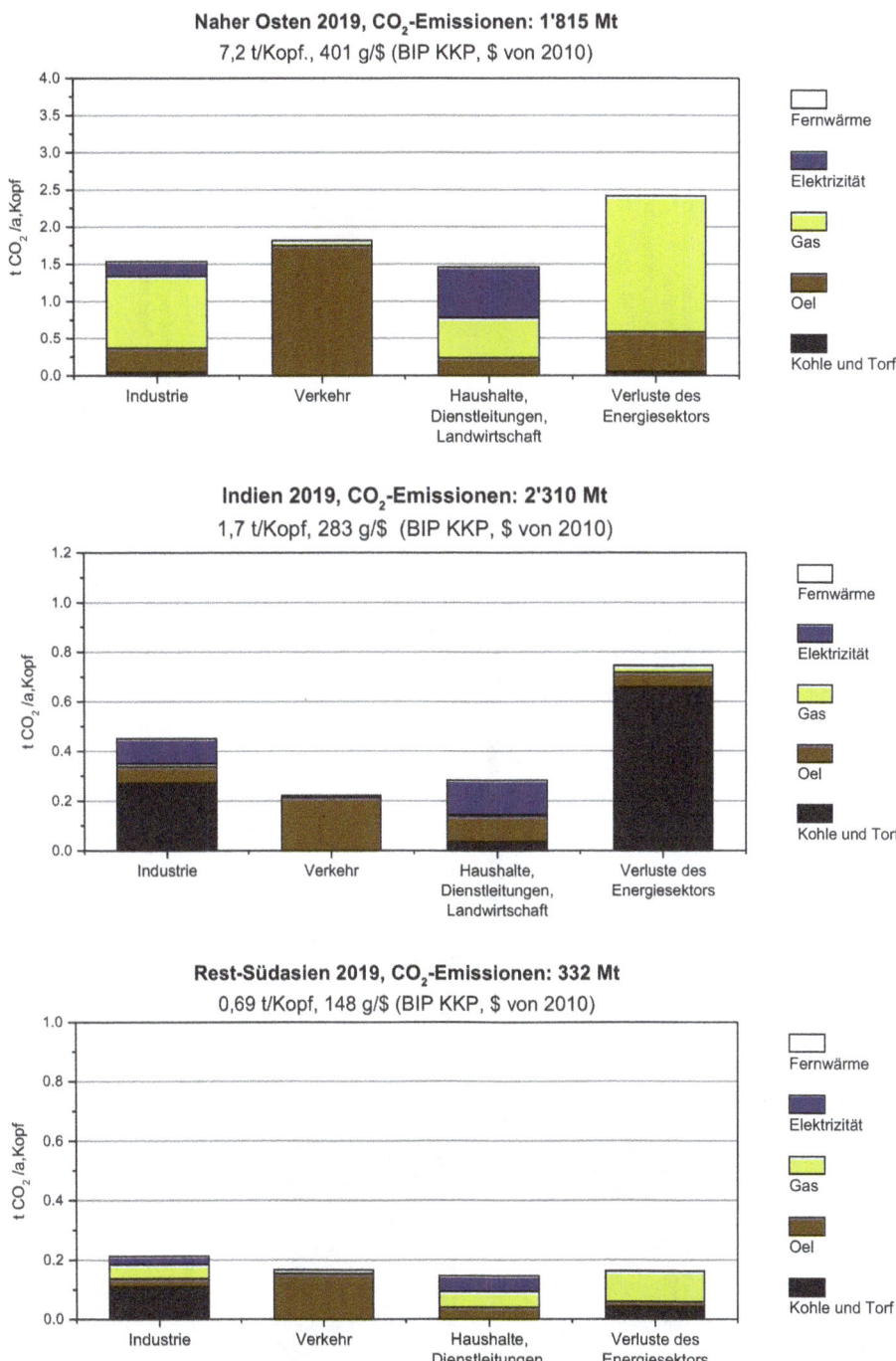

Abb. 5.8 CO_2-Ausstoss pro Kopf der drei Regionen nach Verbrauchssektor und Energieträger

Naher Osten, 2019
Energiefluss im Energiesektor und totale CO2-Emissionen (ohne Schiff- und Luftfahrt-Bunker)

KW, WKK, HW = Kraftwerke, Wärme-Kraft-Kopplung, Heizwerke

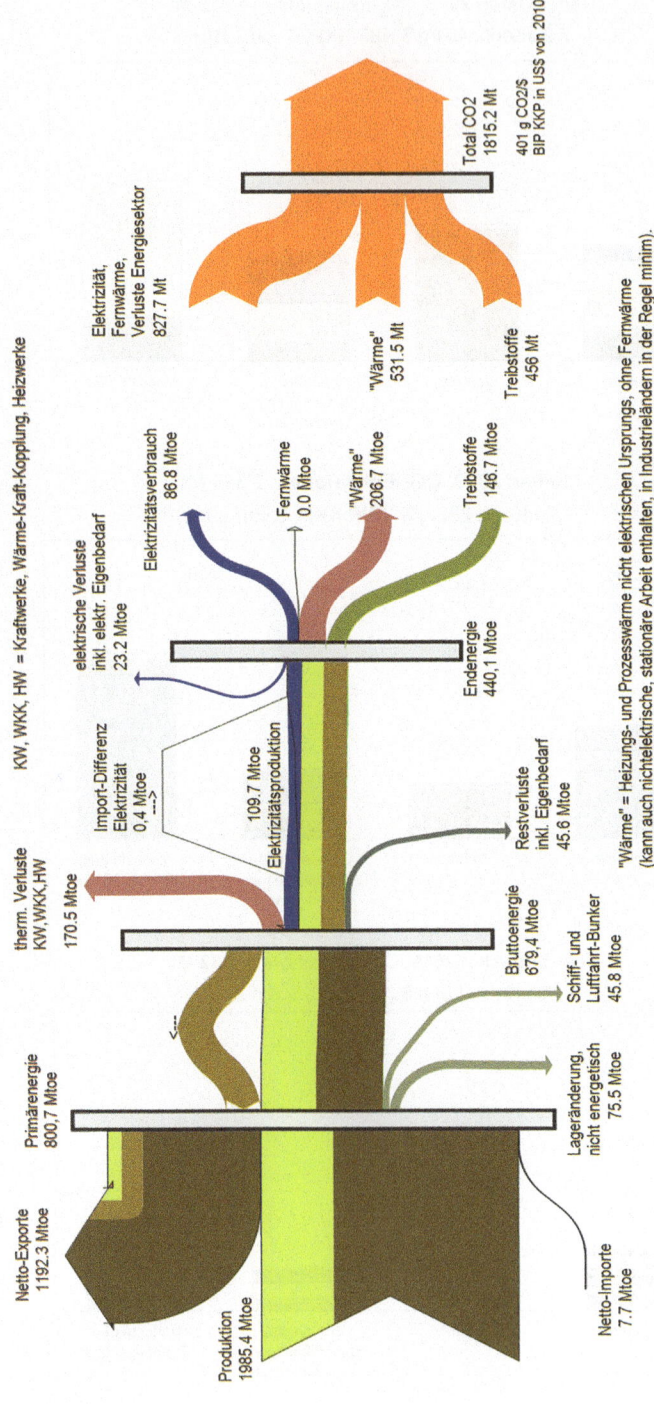

Abb. 5.9 Naher Osten: Energiefluss im Energiesektor von der Primärenergie zur Endenergie und CO$_2$-Ausstoss. Die Energieträgerfarben sind wie in Abb. 5.6 und 5.8 (aber Erdöl dunkelbraun, Erdölprodukte hellbraun).

Die **Primärenergie** ist die Summe aus einheimischer Produktion und, für Regionen, Netto-Importe abzüglich Netto-Exporte von Energieträgern (für Länder effektive Importe/Exporte statt nur Netto-Importe/Exporte pro Energieträger).

Die **Bruttoenergie** ergibt sich aus der Primärenergie nach Abzug des nichtenergetischen Bedarfs (z. B. für die chemische Industrie) und eventueller Lagerveränderungen. Abgezogen werden die für die internationale Schiff- und Luftfahrt-Bunker benötigten Energiemengen. Die entsprechenden CO_2-Emissionen werden nur weltweit erfasst.

Es ist die **Aufgabe des Energiesektors,** den Verbrauchern Energie in Form von *Endenergie* zur Verfügung zu stellen. Wir unterscheiden in diesem Diagramm 4 Formen von Endenergie: *Elektrizität, Fernwärme, Treibstoffe* und *„Wärme".* Letztere besteht hauptsächlich aus nichtelektrischer Heizungs- und Prozesswärme (aus fossilen oder erneuerbaren Energien) und ohne Fernwärme. Stationäre Arbeit nichtelektrischen Ursprungs kann ebenfalls enthalten sein (z. B. stationäre Gas- Benzin- oder Dieselmotoren sowie Pumpen); zumindest in Industrieländern ist dieser Anteil jedoch minim. Mit der Umwandlung von Bruttoenergie in Endenergie sind Verluste verbunden.

Diese **Verluste des Energiesektors** setzen sich zusammen aus den *thermischen Verlusten* in Kraftwerken (thermodynamisch bedingt) sowie in Wärme-Kraft-Kopplungsanlagen und in Heizwerken, ferner aus den *elektrischen Verlusten* im Transport- und Verteilungsnetz, elektrischer Eigenbedarf des Energiesektors und schliesslich aus den *Restverlusten* des Energiesektors (in Raffinerien, Verflüssigungs- und Vergasungsanlagen, durch Wärmeübertragung, Wärme-Eigenbedarf usw.)

Das Schema zeigt ferner die mit den Verlusten des Energiesektors und dem Verbrauch der Endenergien verbundenen, also vom Bruttoinlandverbrauch verursachten *CO_2-Emissionen in Mt.* Der grösste Teil der Verluste des Energiesektors ist in der Regel mit der Elektrizitäts- und Fernwärmeproduktion gekoppelt, weshalb die CO_2-Emissionen dieser drei Faktoren zusammengefasst werden. Eine Trennung kann mithilfe der nachfolgenden Diagramme (z. B. Abb. 5.10) oder auch von Abb. 5.8 vorgenommen werden.

5.4.2 Energiefluss der Endenergie zu den Endverbrauchern

Die weiteren Flussdiagramme (z. B. Abb. 5.10) zeigen wie sich die 4 Endenergiearten auf die drei Endverbraucherkategorien verteilen. Ebenso werden die CO_2-Emissionen diesen Verbrauchergruppen zugeordnet.

Die Endverbraucher sind (gemäss IEA-Statistik)

- Industrie
- Haushalt, Dienstleistungen, Landwirtschaft etc.
- Verkehr

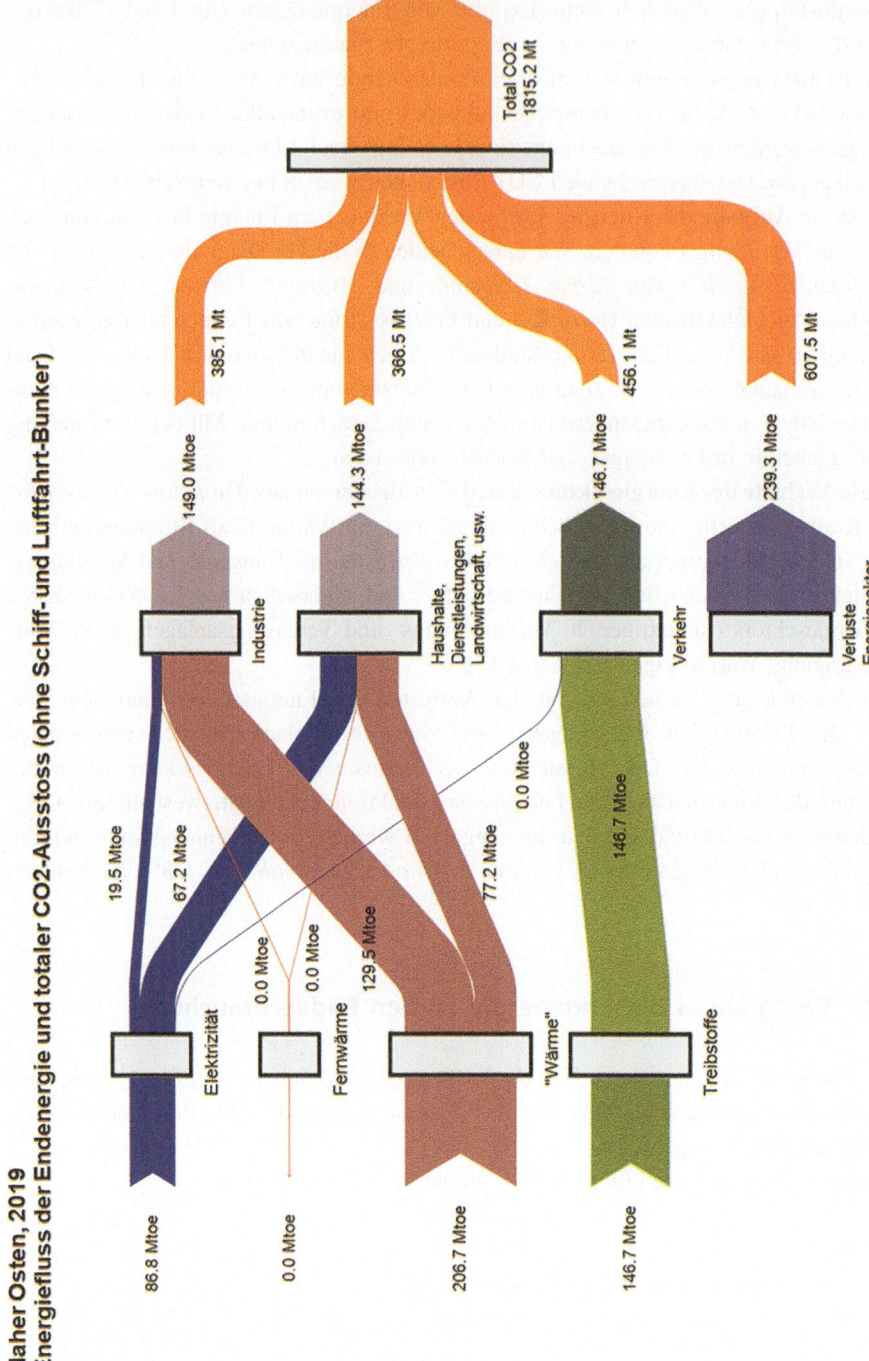

Abb. 5.10 Naher Osten: Energiefluss der Endenergie zu den Endverbrauchern und zugeordnete CO₂-Emissionen

Zur Bildung der Gesamt-Emissionen werden noch die CO_2-Emissionen der im Energie-sektor entstehenden Verluste hinzugefügt.

Die Flussdiagramme werden für den Nahen Osten, sowie für Indien und das restliche Südasien gegeben.

5.4.3   Naher Osten

Der Energiefluss im Energiesektor von der Primärenergie zur Endenergie und die sich ergebenden totalen CO_2-Emissionen sind in Abb. 5.9 dargestellt. In Abb. 5.10 wird der Energiefluss der Endenergie zu den Endverbrauchern veranschaulicht und die entspre-chenden CO_2-Emissionen sind den Verbrauchersektoren zugeordnet. Der Nahe Osten ist ein starker Energieträgerproduzent und Energieträgerexporteur (Öl und Gas). Details sind für *Iran* und *Saudi Arabien* in Kap. 3 gegeben.

5.4.4   Indien

Die entsprechenden Diagramme für Indien, für den Energiefluss im Energiesektor und der Endenergie zu den Verbrauchssektoren, findet man in den Abb. 5.11 und 5.12. Indien ist auf Energieimporte angewiesen und die Energiewirtschaft stark kohle-lastig. Die Klima-ziele lassen sich nur durch eine starke Abkehr der Elektrizitätsproduktion von der Kohle erreichen.

5.4.5   Restliches Südasien

Die Abb. 5.13 und 5.14 zeigen die Energieflüsse des restlichen Südasiens. Rest-Südasien exportiert zwar Gas (Myanmar, s. Kap. 7) ist aber insgesamt auf Energieimporte angewiesen. Details weiterer Länder in Kap. 7.

5.4.6   Naher Osten und Südasien insgesamt

Die Abb. 5.15 und 5.16. ergeben sich durch Aufsummierung der Energieflüsse der drei Regionen. Für den Wärmebereich sind Biomasse und Erdöl/Erdgas vorherrschend. Für die Elektrizitätserzeugung, aufgrund des starken Gewichts Indiens, hat die Kohle einen erheblichen Anteil. Insgesamt ist Nah- und Südasien dank dem Nahen Osten ein Energieexporteur.

Tab. 5.2 vergleicht die Indikatoren der drei Regionen.

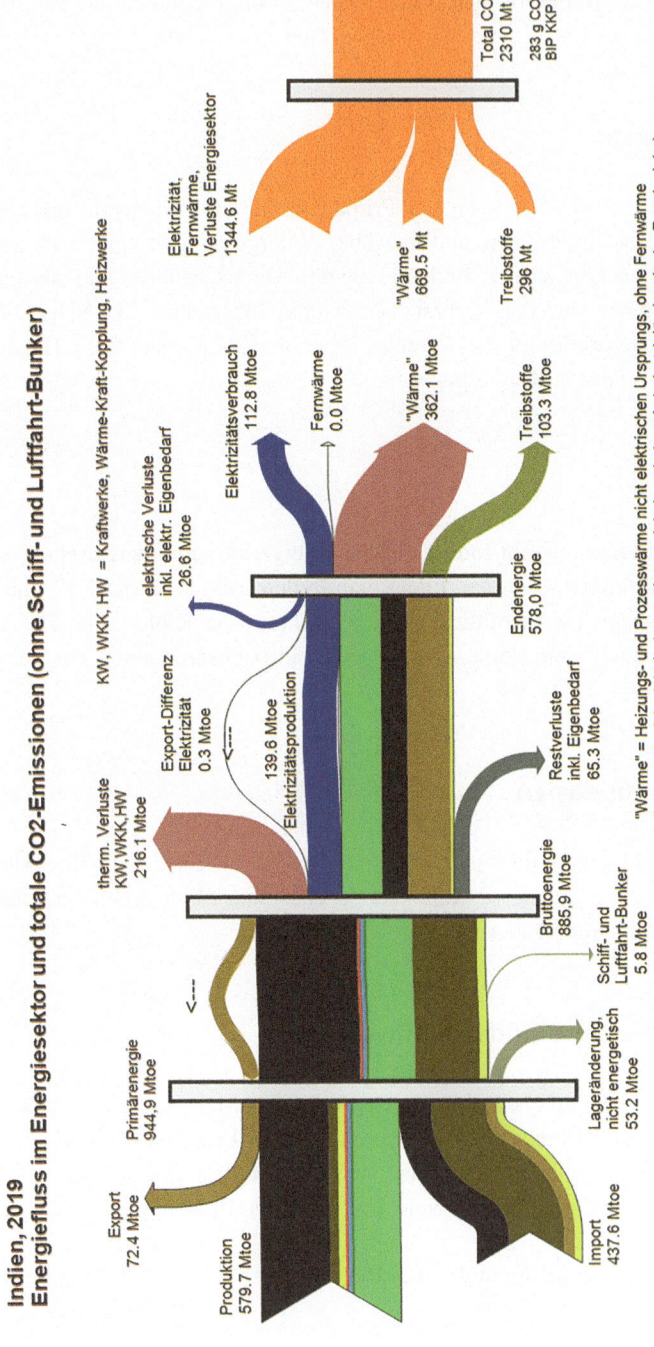

Abb. 5.11 Indien: Energiefluss im Energiesektor von der Primärenergie zur Endenergie und CO_2-Ausstoss. Die Energieträgerfarben sind wie in Abb. 1.6 und 1.8 (aber Erdöl dunkelbraun, Erdölprodukte hellbraun)

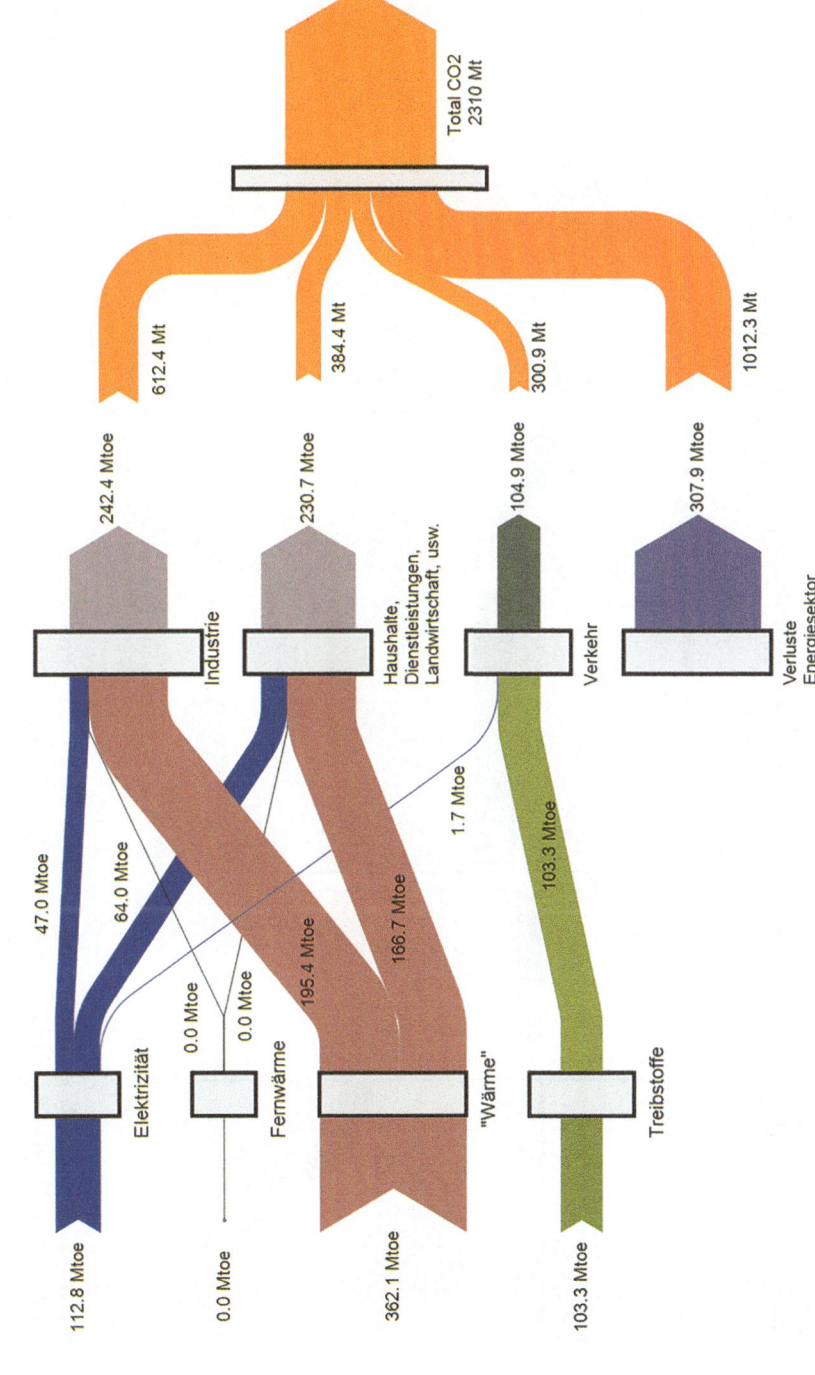

Abb. 5.12 Indien: Energiefluss der Endenergie zu den Endverbrauchern und zugeordnete CO_2-Emissionen

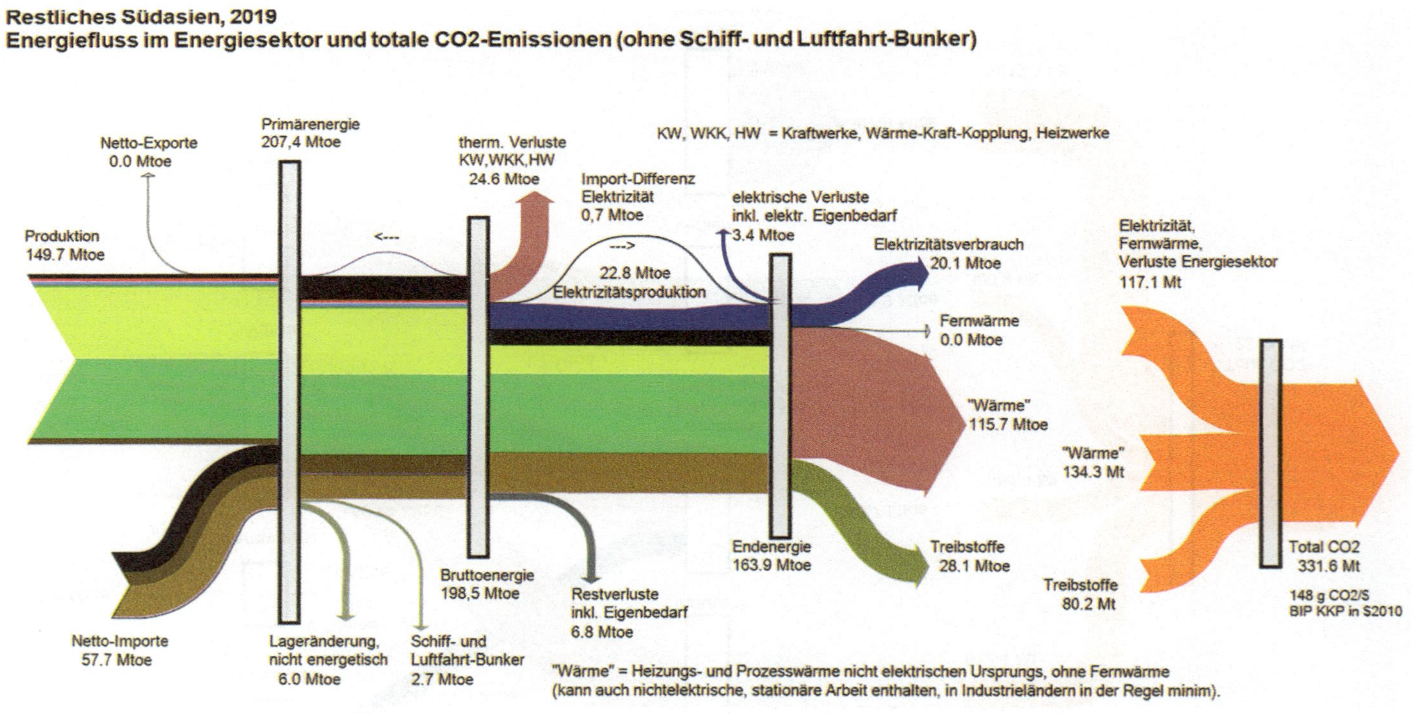

Restliches Südasien, 2019
Energiefluss im Energiesektor und totale CO2-Emissionen (ohne Schiff- und Luftfahrt-Bunker)

KW, WKK, HW = Kraftwerke, Wärme-Kraft-Kopplung, Heizwerke

Total CO2
331.6 Mt

148 g CO2/$
BIP KKP in $2010

Elektrizität,
Fernwärme,
Verluste Energiesektor
117.1 Mt

"Wärme"
134.3 Mt

Treibstoffe
80.2 Mt

Elektrizitätsverbrauch
20.1 Mtoe

Fernwärme
0.0 Mtoe

"Wärme"
115.7 Mtoe

Treibstoffe
28.1 Mtoe

elektrische Verluste
inkl. elektr. Eigenbedarf
3.4 Mtoe

Endenergie
163.9 Mtoe

Import-Differenz
Elektrizität
0.7 Mtoe

22.8 Mtoe
Elektrizitätsproduktion

Restverluste
inkl. Eigenbedarf
6.8 Mtoe

"Wärme" = Heizungs- und Prozesswärme nicht elektrischen Ursprungs, ohne Fernwärme
(kann auch nichtelektrische, stationäre Arbeit enthalten, in Industrieländern in der Regel minim).

therm. Verluste
KW, WKK, HW
24.6 Mtoe

Primärenergie
207.4 Mtoe

Bruttoenergie
198.5 Mtoe

Schiff- und
Luftfahrt-Bunker
2.7 Mtoe

Netto-Exporte
0.0 Mtoe

Lageränderung,
nicht energetisch
6.0 Mtoe

Produktion
149.7 Mtoe

Netto-Importe
57.7 Mtoe

Abb. 5.13 Restliches Südasien: Energiefluss im Energiesektor von der Primärenergie zur Endenergie und CO$_2$-Ausstoss. Die Energieträgerfarben sind wie in Abb. 5.6 und 5.8 (Erdöl dunkelbraun, Erdölprodukte hellbraun)

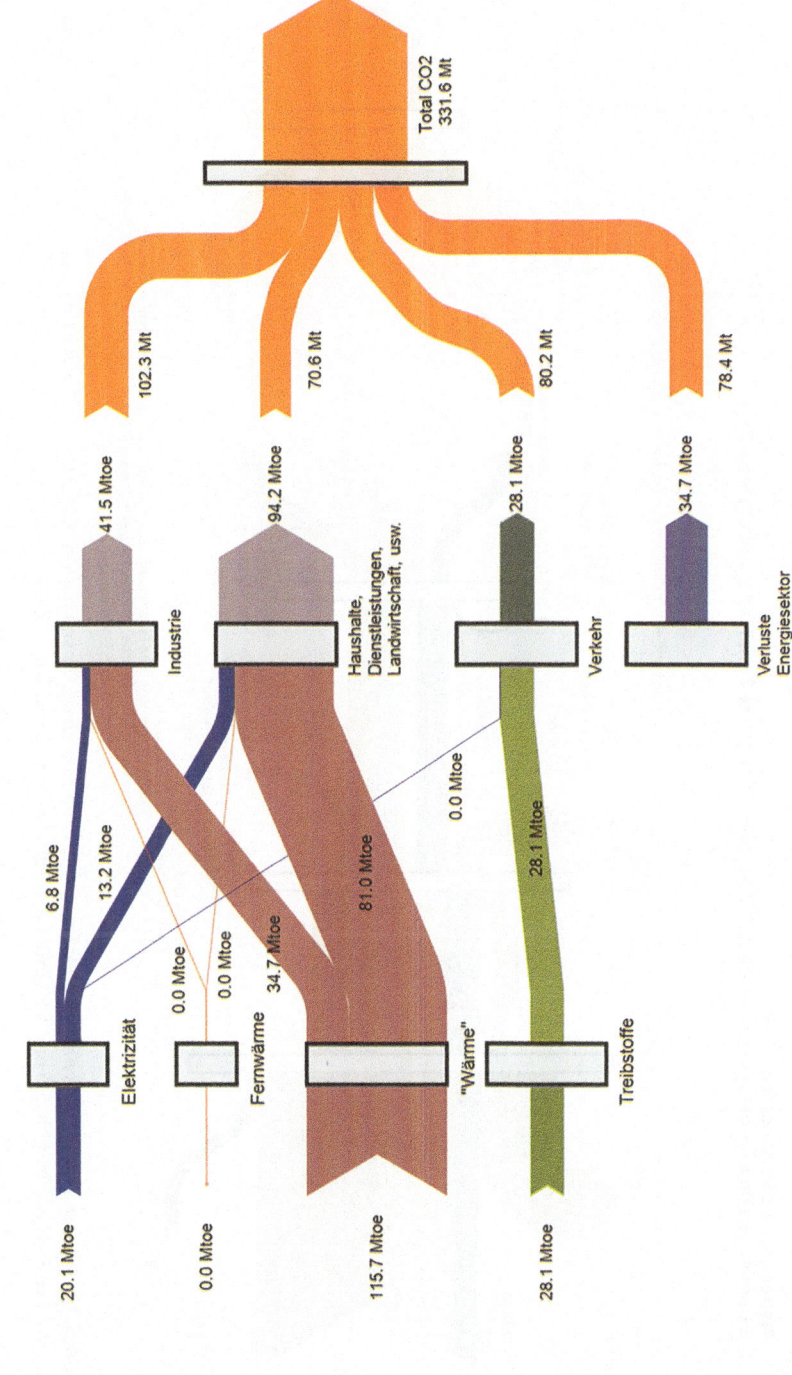

Restliches Südasien, 2019
Energiefluss der Endenergie und totaler CO2-Ausstoss (ohne Schiff- und Luftfahrt-Bunker)

Abb. 5.14 Restliches Südasien: Energiefluss der Endenergie zu den Endverbrauchern und zugeordnete CO$_2$-Emissionen

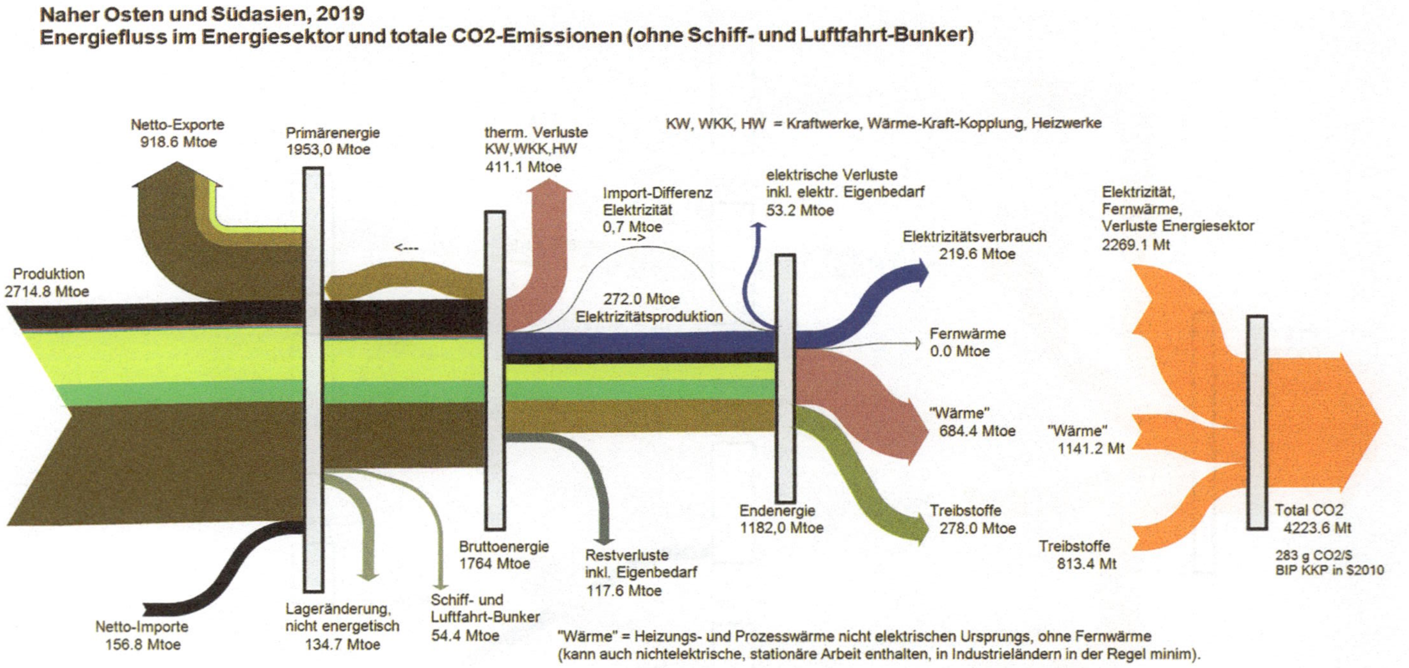

Naher Osten und Südasien, 2019
Energiefluss im Energiesektor und totale CO2-Emissionen (ohne Schiff- und Lufffahrt-Bunker)

KW, WKK, HW = Kraftwerke, Wärme-Kraft-Kopplung, Heizwerke

Primärenergie
1953,0 Mtoe

Netto-Exporte
918.6 Mtoe

Produktion
2714.8 Mtoe

Lageränderung,
nicht energetisch
134.7 Mtoe

Netto-Importe
156.8 Mtoe

therm. Verluste
KW,WKK,HW
411.1 Mtoe

elektrische Verluste
inkl. elektr. Eigenbedarf
53.2 Mtoe

Import-Differenz
Elektrizität
0.7 Mtoe
--->

272.0 Mtoe
Elektrizitätsproduktion

Elektrizität,
Fernwärme,
Verluste Energiesektor
2269.1 Mt

Elektrizitätsverbrauch
219.6 Mtoe

Fernwärme
0.0 Mtoe

"Wärme"
684.4 Mtoe

Treibstoffe
278.0 Mtoe

Endenergie
1182,0 Mtoe

Restverluste
inkl. Eigenbedarf
117.6 Mtoe

Bruttoenergie
1764 Mtoe

Schiff- und
Lufffahrt-Bunker
54.4 Mtoe

Total CO2
4223.6 Mt

283 g CO2/S
BIP KKP in S2010

"Wärme"
1141.2 Mt

Treibstoffe
813.4 Mt

"Wärme" = Heizungs- und Prozesswärme nicht elektrischen Ursprungs, ohne Fernwärme
(kann auch nichtelektrische, stationäre Arbeit enthalten, in Industrieländern in der Regel minim).

Abb. 5.15 Nahost und Süd-Asien insgesamt: Energiefluss im Energiesektor von der Primärenergie zur Endenergie und CO_2-Ausstoss. Die Energie-trägerfarben sind wie in Abb. 5.6 und 5.8 (Erdöl dunkelbraun, Erdölprodukte hellbraun)

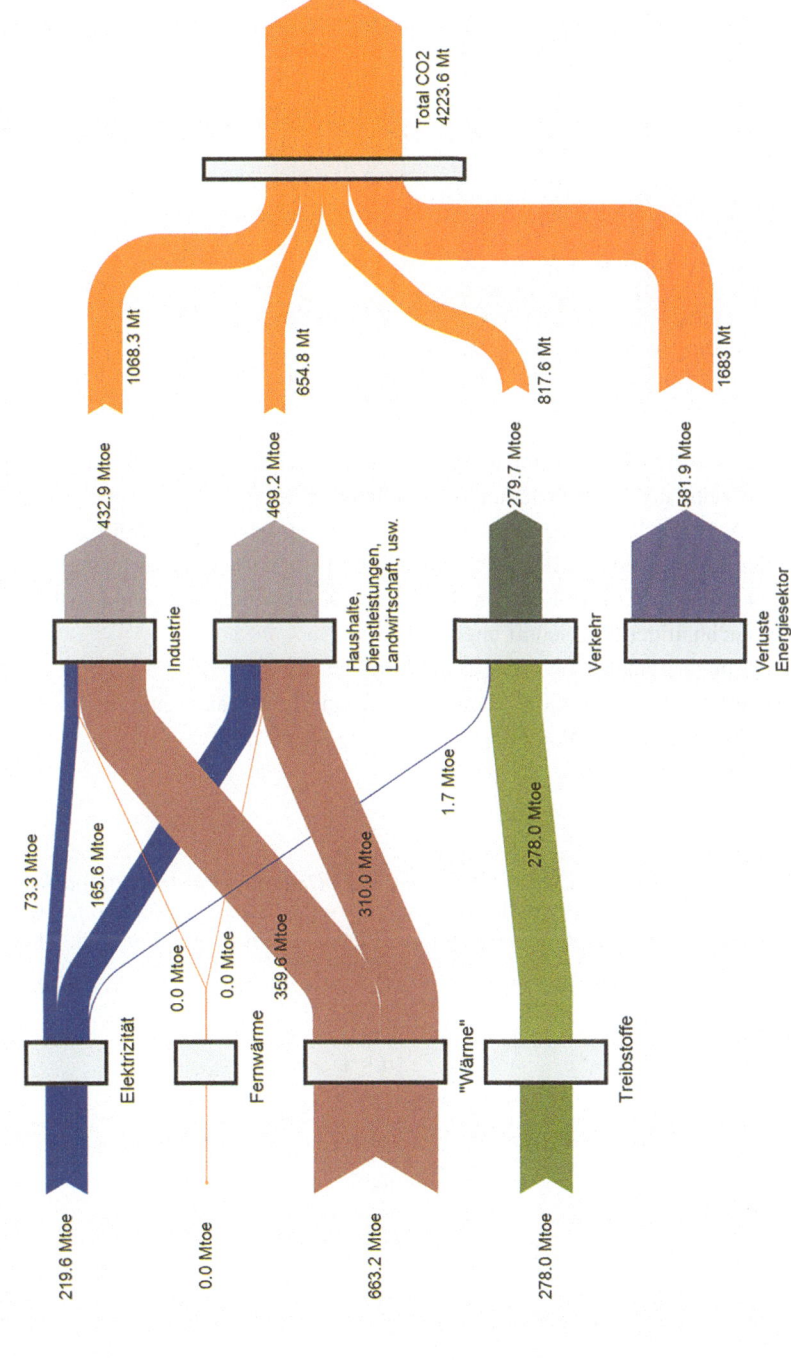

Naher Osten und Südasien, 2019
Energiefluss der Endenergie und totaler CO2-Ausstoss (ohne Schiff- und Luftfahrt-Bunker)

Abb. 5.16 Nahost und Südasien insgesamt: Energiefluss der Endenergie zu den Endverbrauchern und zugeordnete CO_2-Emissionen

Tab. 5.2 Vergleich der Indikatoren in 2019 ($ von 2010)

	Naher Osten	Indien	Rest-Südasien	Nahost und Südasien
kWh/$	1,74	1,26	1,03	1,32
g CO_2/kWh	230	224	144	205
g CO_2/$	401	283	148	270
BIP (KKP) $ pro Kopf, a	18.000	6000	4600	7600
t CO_2/Kopf, a	7,2	1,7	0,7	2,1

kWh/$ = Energieintensität
g CO_2/kWh = CO_2-Intensität der Energie
g CO_2/$ = Maßstab für die Nachhaltigkeit der Wirtschaft bezüglich CO_2-
Emissionen (kurz: Indikator der CO_2-Nachhaltigkeit)
(Vergleichswerte in $ von 2010: EU 140 g CO_2/$, USA 240 g CO_2/$)

Der Indikator g CO_2/$ ergibt sich als Produkt von Energieintensität (abhängig von der Energieeffizienz der Wirtschaft) und CO_2-Intensität der Energie.

Die CO_2-Emissonen steigen bei zunehmender Entwicklung der Wirtschaft wegen des steigenden Energiebedarfs, da meist zunehmend fossile Energieträger eingesetzt werden. Eine Entkopplung wird im Rahmen der für den Klimaschutz notwendigen Umgestaltung zu einer nachhaltigen Wirtschaft angestrebt.

Werte einiger Länder von Nahost und Südasien in Tab. 5.3.

Hauptsünder bezüglich CO_2-Nachhaltigkeit sind Iran, Irak, Saudi Arabien und Indien *(Indikator deutlich über 250 g CO_2/$)*.

Tab. 5.3 Prozentualer Anteil der *erneuerbaren* und *CO_2-armen Elektrizitätsproduktion*, im Jahr 2019, in den bevölkerungsreichsten Ländern von Nahost und Südasien (>30 Mio.), sowie *Indikator der CO_2-Nachhaltigkeit in g CO_2/$*. CO_2-arme Energien = erneuerbare Energien + Kernenergie

	Erneuerbare Energien	CO_2-arme Energien	g CO_2/$ (BIP KKP)
Iran	5 %	7,5 %	639
Saudi-Arabien	0,1 %	0,1 %	346
Irak	2 %	2 %	346
Indien	20 %	23 %	262
Pakistan	24 %	42 %	192
Myanmar	44 %	44 %	154
Bangladesch	1 %	1 %	130

5.5 Energieintensität

Bevölkerungsreichster Staat von Südasien ist *Indien* und dessen Entwicklung deshalb für die Region von grundlegender Bedeutung. Die Energieintensität Indiens ist in 2019 mit 1,26 kWh/$ (Abb. 5.17) angesichts der Unterentwicklung eher hoch, aber tiefer als der Weltdurchschnitt von 1,37 kWh/$. Die gute Entwicklung seit 2000 ist als positives Signal zu werten.

Unter den Ländern *Rest-Südasiens* (Abb. 5.17) hat sich die hohe Energieintensität Nepals seit 2016 (s. auch 2. Auflage von Band II) deutlich verbessert und ist bezüglich Klimaschutz tragbar, da Nepal eine sehr niedrige CO_2-Intensität der Energie aufweist (Verwendung vor allem von Biomasse und Wasserkraft). Die bis 2010 positive Entwicklung von Myanmar hat ab 2016 eine Kehrtwende erfahren, ebenso jene Pakistans, Gut bleibt die Entwicklung in Sri-Lanka und Bangladesch.

Der Öl- und Gasreiche *Nahe Osten,* hat den Durchschnittswert von 1,44 kWh/$ in 2016 auf 1,74 in 2019 erhöht (Abb. 5.18), was weit über dem Weltdurchschnitt liegt. Die seit 2000 insgesamt festzustellende Zunahme hat sich seit 2010 und vor allem in den letzten Jahren stark verstärkt, was z. T. auf die kriegerischen Ereignissen und entsprechenden Migrationsbewegungen zurückzuführen ist. Syrien ist davon stark betroffen, ebenso Iran. Eine positive Entwicklung bezüglich Energieeffizienz ist nur in Israel und den Vereinigten Arabischen Emiraten festzustellen.

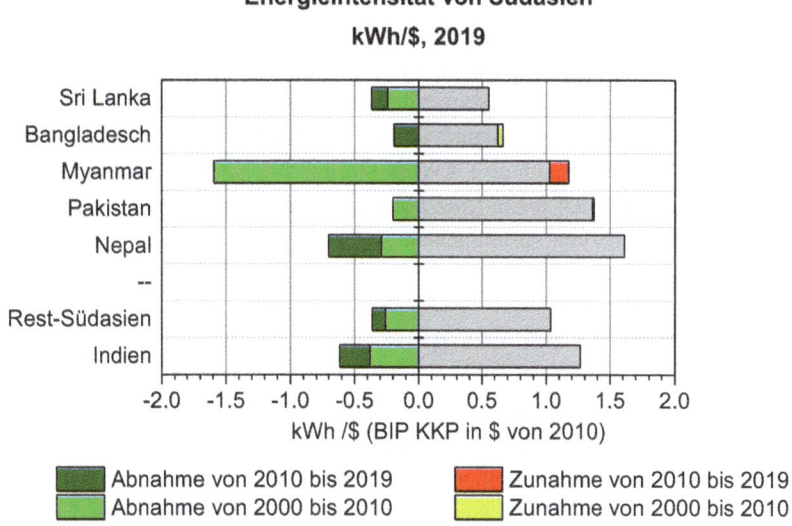

Abb. 5.17 Energieintensität der Länder Südasiens und Änderungen seit 2000

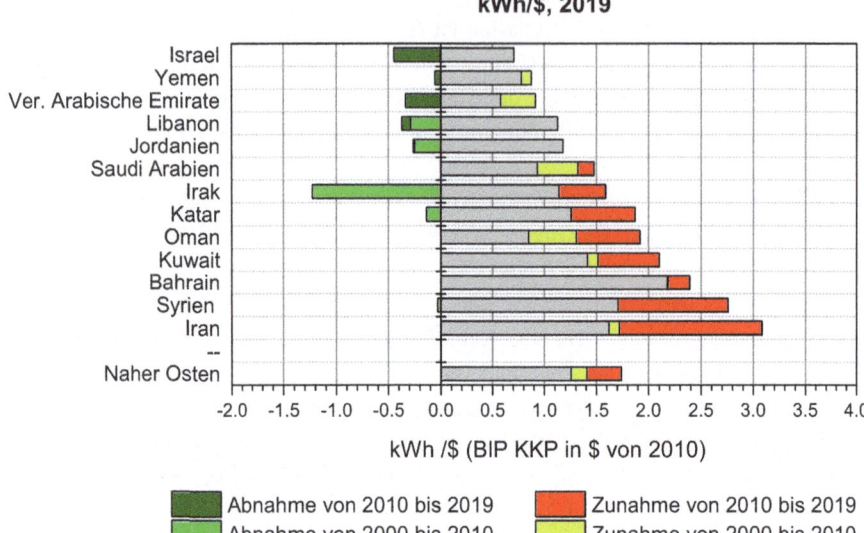

Abb. 5.18 Energieintensität der Länder des Nahen Ostens und Änderungen seit 2000

In Abb. 5.19 wird schließlich für *Nahost und Südasien* der Zusammenhang zwischen Energieintensität und Bruttoinlandprodukt pro Kopf dargestellt. Bei schwacher Entwicklung (BIP < 15.000 $/a) ist weltweit allgemein eine starke Streuung der Energieintensität feststellbar. Diese hängt stark von den lokalen Verhältnissen ab (verfügbare Energieträger). Bei zunehmendem Wohlstand konvergiert sie, weltweit gesehen, meistens auf Werte zwischen 1 und 1,5 kWh/$. In Zukunft müsste die Energieintensität aus Umwelt- und Klimaschutzgründen deutlich unter 1 kWh/$ sinken. Im Nahen Osten ist sie in vielen Ländern überdurchschnittlich hoch, trotz hohem mittlerem BIP, was mit der hohen (und billigen) Energieverfügbarkeit zusammenhängt.

5.6 CO$_2$-Intensität der Energie

Die CO$_2$-Intensität des Nahen Ostens und Südasiens liegt insgesamt dank Rest-Südasien mit 217 g CO$_2$/kWh knapp über dem Weltdurchschnitt von 213 g CO$_2$/kWh. Die Werte sind je nach Land stark unterschiedlich (Abb. 5.20). Anders als bei der Energieintensität ist bei Unterentwicklung in der Regel ein niedriger Wert der CO$_2$-Intensität der Energie zu erwarten, entsprechend dem stark auf Biomasse ausgerichteten Energieverbrauch (CO$_2$-Neutralität der Biomasse wird angenommen). Zunehmende Entwicklung führt zunächst

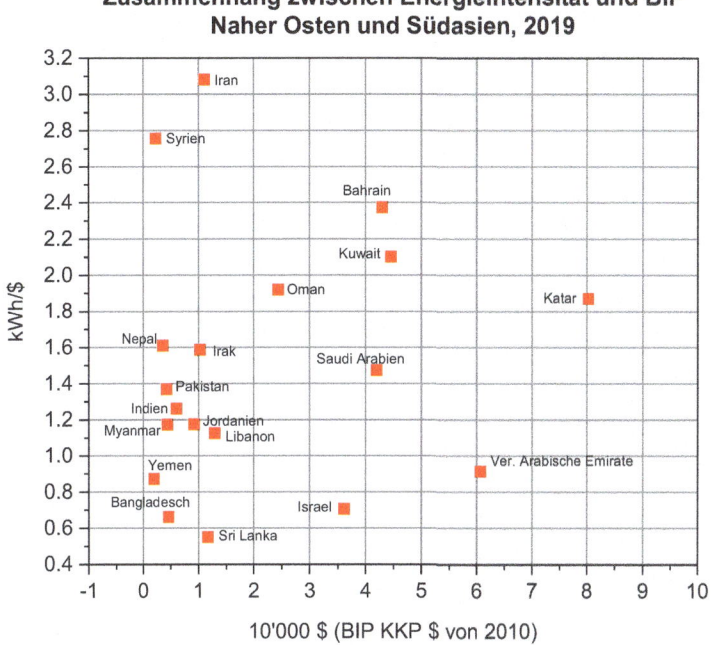

Abb. 5.19 Energieintensität der Länder des Nahen Ostens und Süd-Asiens in Abhängigkeit vom BIP KKP pro Kopf ($ von 2010), in 2019

zum vermehrten Verbrauch fossiler Brennstoffe und somit zu einer Erhöhung der CO$_2$-Intensität der Energie.

Dies zeigt sich in *Indien* wo diese CO$_2$-Intensität 200 g CO$_2$/kWh deutlich überschritten hat und weiter zunimmt (Abb. 5.21). Die restlichen Länder *Südasiens* sind ebenso betroffen, obwohl eher Öl und Gas als Kohle verwendet werden oder, wie in Nepal und Myanmar, Wasserkraft eine größere Rolle spielt. Die steigende Tendenz ist, vor allem seit 2010, trotzdem deutlich. Im *Nahen Osten* insgesamt (Abb. 5.22) stagniert der Index auf etwa 230 g CO$_2$/kWh. Auffallend ist die starke Zunahme in Oman und den Vereinigten Arabischen Emiraten.

Für den Klimaschutz wäre es angebracht, vor allem in *Indien* und im *Nahen Osten,* diesen Indikator bis 2030 auf etwa 200 g CO$_2$/kWh oder weniger zu stabilisieren und dann durch stärkere Gewichtung erneuerbarer Energien bei der Elektrizitätsproduktion (Wasser, Wind und Sonne), evtl. auch durch Kernenergie, empfindlich weiter zu reduzieren, siehe dazu Kap. 6. Im restlichen Südasien muss die mit der wirtschaftlichen Entwicklung zunehmende CO$_2$-Intensität der Energie mit Hilfe erneuerbarer Energien möglichst rasch gebremst werden.

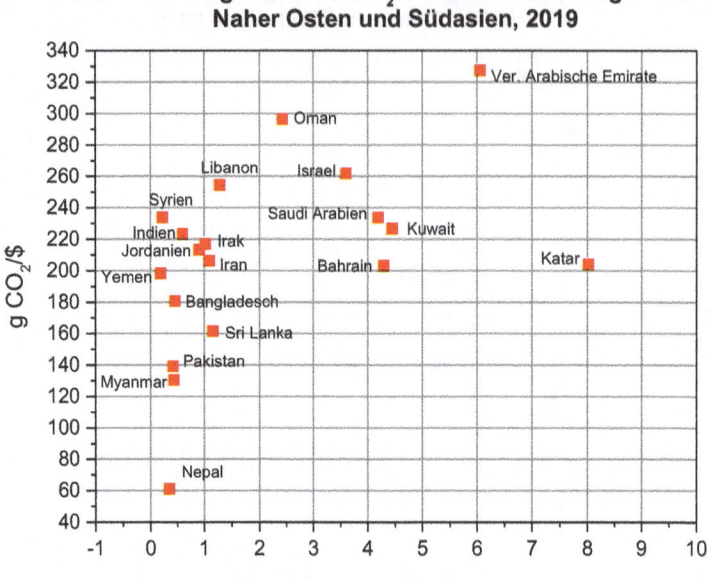

Abb. 5.20 CO_2-Intensität der Energie im Nahen Osten und Südasien in Abhängigkeit vom BIP KKP pro Kopf (in \$ von 2010), Weltdurchschnitt 213 g CO_2/kWh

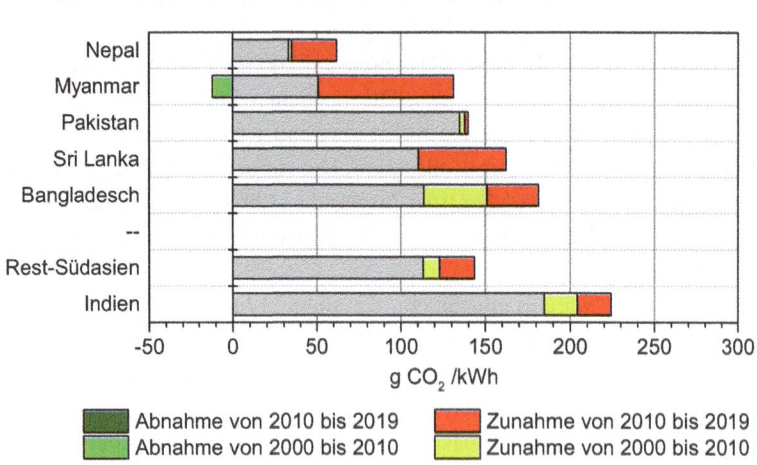

Abb. 5.21 CO_2-Intensität der Energie der Länder Südasiens und Änderungen seit 2000

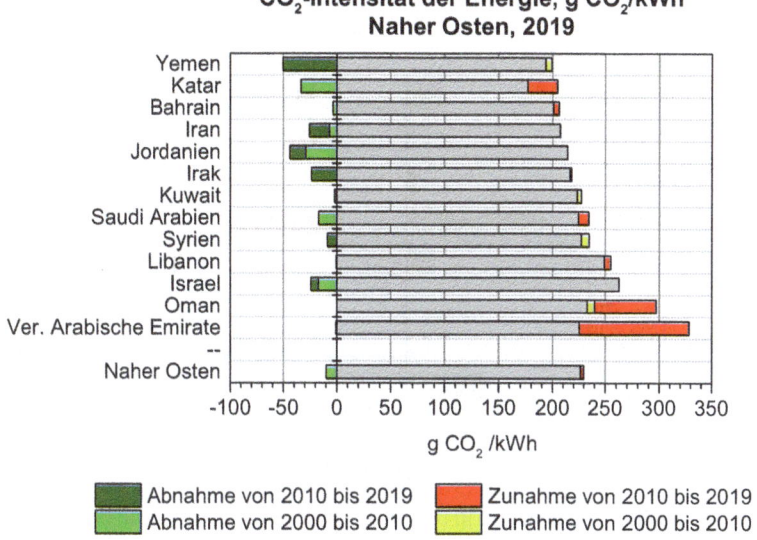

Abb. 5.22 CO$_2$-Intensität der Energie der Länder des Nahen Ostens und Änderungen seit 2000

5.7 Indikator der CO$_2$-Nachhaltigkeit

Die Nachhaltigkeit der Energieversorgung bezüglich CO$_2$-Ausstoss wird durch das Produkt von Energieintensität und CO$_2$-Intensität der Energie bestimmt und somit durch den **Indikator g CO$_2$/$.**

In 2019 ist der Durchschnittswert *Südasiens* mit 270 g CO$_2$/$ immerhin niedriger als der Weltdurchschnitt von 292 g CO$_2$/$ [1]. Trotz erfreulicher Fortschritte seit 2000, ist der Wert von *Indien* immer noch zu hoch, in Relation zum niedrigen Entwicklungsstand (Abb. 5.23). *Rest-Südasien* weist im Mittel seit 2010 keine Fortschritte auf. Besonders Myanmar fällt negativ auf. Alle Länder sollten versuchen zur Erreichung der Klimaziele Werte von 100 g CO$_2$/$ oder weniger anzupeilen.

Deutlich weniger nachhaltig ist der *Nahe Osten* (Abb. 5.24) dessen Indikator im Mittel 400 g CO$_2$/$ erreicht hat. Lediglich Israel und Jordanien haben sich Klimaschutzkonform entwickelt. Dies ist der in den meisten Staaten seit 2010 zunehmenden Energieintensität als auch der stagnierenden CO$_2$-Intensität der Energie zuzuschreiben. Bis 2030 müsste man, um die Klimaschutz-Bedingungen zu erfüllen, einen Wert von 250 g CO$_2$/$ unterschreiten (Kap. 6).

Die Abb. 5.25 veranschaulicht für Nahost und Südasien insgesamt den statistischen Zusammenhang zwischen CO$_2$-Nachhaltigkeit und Bruttoinlandprodukt pro Kopf. Schwach entwickelte Länder sind zwar mehrheitlich, dank Biomasse oder Wasserkraft, bezüglich CO$_2$-Ausstoss unter 200 g CO$_2$/$ und somit vorerst noch relativ nachhaltig.

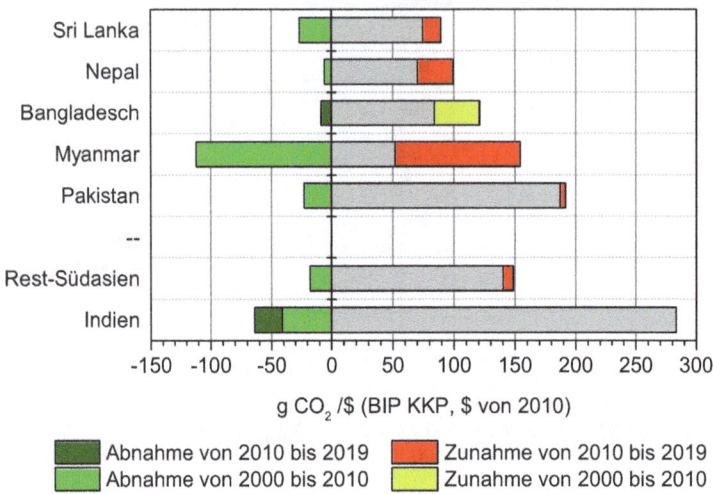

Abb. 5.23 Indikator der CO_2-Nachhaltigkeit der Länder Südasiens in 2019 und Fortschritte bzw. Rückschritte seit 2000

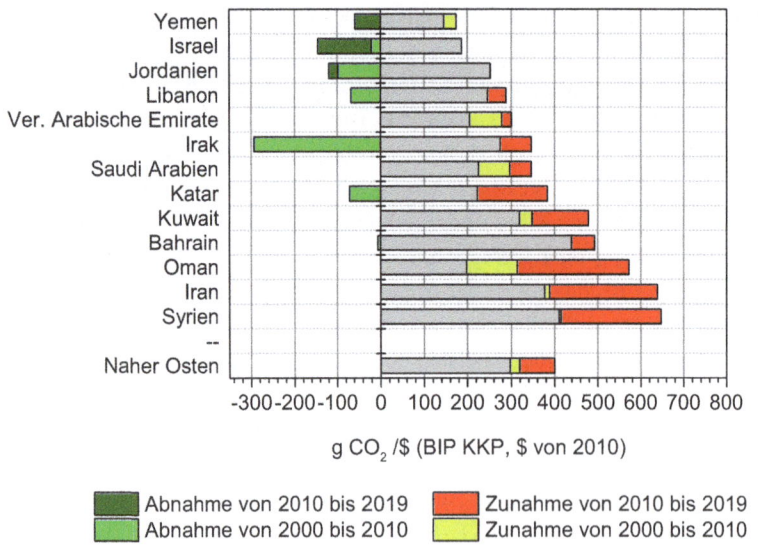

Abb. 5.24 Indikator der CO_2-Nachhaltigkeit der Länder des Nahen Ostens in 2016 und Änderungen seit 2000

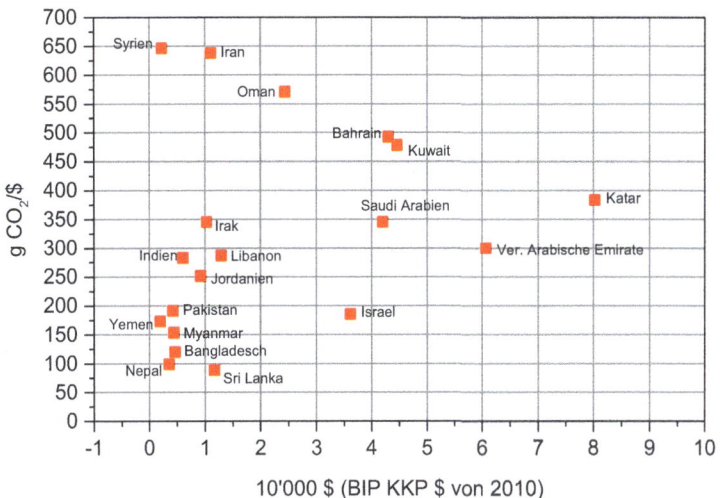

Abb. 5.25 CO$_2$-Nachhaltigkeit der Länder von Nahost und Südasien in Abhängigkeit vom BIP KKP pro Kopf

Ausnahmen sind Indien, wegen starkem Kohleanteil bei der Stromerzeugung, und Iran, wegen schlechter Energieeffizienz. Trotz fortschreitender wirtschaftlicher Entwicklung wäre es angebracht, entsprechend den Klimaschutz-Vorgaben, bis 2030 Werte unter 200 g CO$_2$/\$ anzupeilen. Dies gilt wie schon erwähnt auch für alle heute stark entwickelten Nahost-Länder, durch.

- stärkere Förderung erneuerbarer Energien,
- durch Kernenergie oder CCS (Carbon Capture and Storage),
- Erzeugung von CO$_2$ neutralen Brenn- und Treibstoffen aus Solarenergie.

CO$_2$-Emissionen und Indikatoren bis 2019 und notwendiges Szenario zur Einhaltung des 2-Grad- bzw. 1,5 Grad-Ziels

6

6.1 Naher Osten

Mit dem 2-Grad- und 1,5-Grad-Ziel (s. Kap. 1) kompatible Szenarien bis 2050 für den Nahen Osten zeigt die Abb. 6.1. Der entsprechende Verlauf der Indikatoren ist in Abb. 6.2 wiedergegeben. Ab dem Jahr 2020 ist sowohl eine Verbesserung der Energieeffizienz notwendig, als auch eine Reduktion der CO$_2$.-Intensität der Energie durch Förderung erneuerbarer Energien oder Kernenergie evtl. CCS, sowie Erzeugung CO$_2$-neutraler Treibstoffe.

Seit 2015 ist die Tendenz der Indikatoren zumindest stagnierend. Entsprechend den Vorgaben der Klimawissenschaft ist vor allem das 1,5-Grad-Ziel anzustreben, mit weniger als 250 g CO$_2$/\$ bis 2030. Die dazu notwendigen *prozentualen jährlichen Änderungen* für die beiden Varianten sind detaillierter in Abb. 6.3 wiedergegeben.

Der zugehörige Verlauf der *pro Kopf Indikatoren* für das kaufkraftbereinigte Bruttoinlandprodukt, die Bruttoenergie und den CO$_2$-Ausstoss ist schliesslich in Abb. 6.4 dargestellt, für 1980 bis 2019 und entsprechend den beiden Klimaszenarien. Der BIP/Kopf Wert von 2026 entspricht den Prognosen des IMF.

6.2 Indien

Mit dem 2-Grad- und dem 1,5-Grad-Ziel kompatible Szenarien bis 2050 für Indien zeigt Abb. 6.5. Der entsprechende Verlauf der Indikatoren ist in Abb. 6.6 wiedergegeben. Indien hat insgesamt gute Aussichten die Klimaziele einzuhalten.

Indien hat 2019 mit 1,26 kWh/\$ eine für ein Entwicklungsland immer noch hohe **Energieintensität,** was auf eine verbreitete Ineffizienz des Energieeinsatzes hinweist. Die im Mittel gute Tendenz seit 2000 muss fortgesetzt werden.

© Springer Fachmedien Wiesbaden GmbH, ein Teil von Springer Nature 2023
V. Crastan, *Kennzahlen zur Erreichung der weltweiten Klimaziele*,
https://doi.org/10.1007/978-3-658-40073-6_6

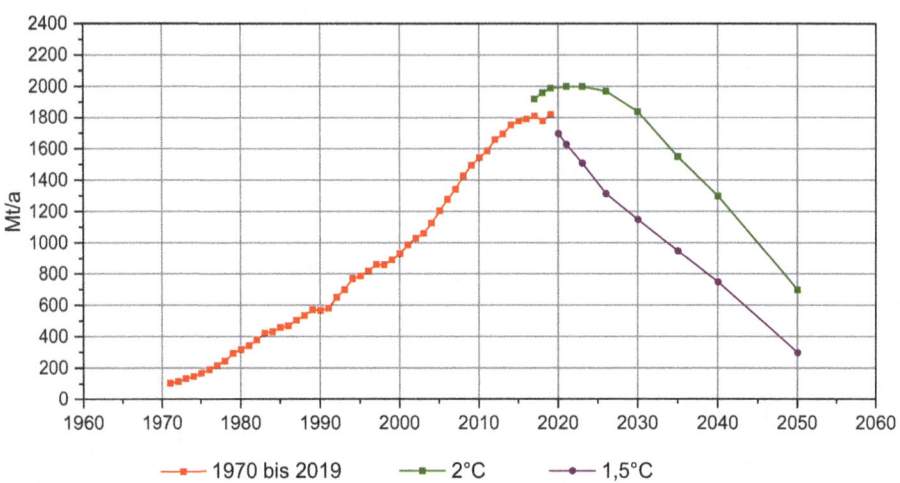

Abb. 6.1 Mit dem 2-Grad- und 1,5-Grad-Ziel kompatible Szenarien für den Nahen Osten

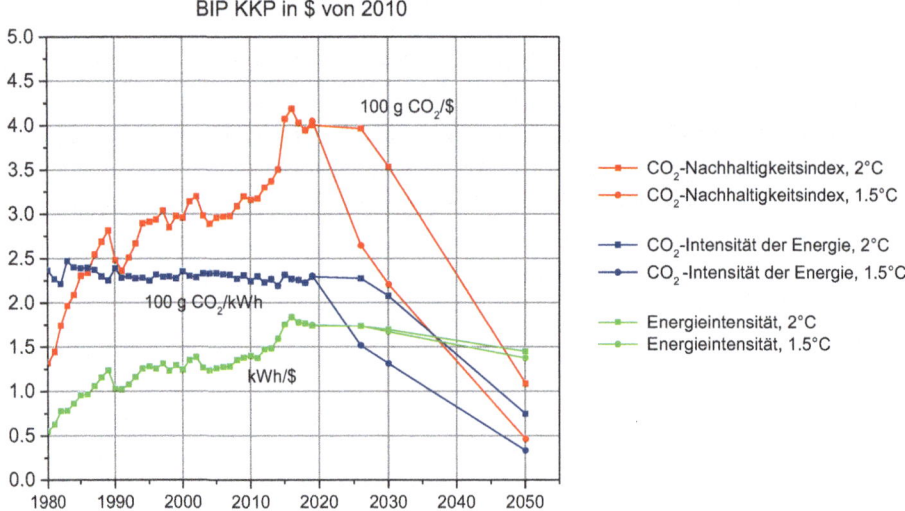

Abb. 6.2 Indikatoren-Verlauf von 1980 bis 2019 und mit dem 2-Grad- bzw. 1,5-Grad-Ziel kompatibler Verlauf bis 2050

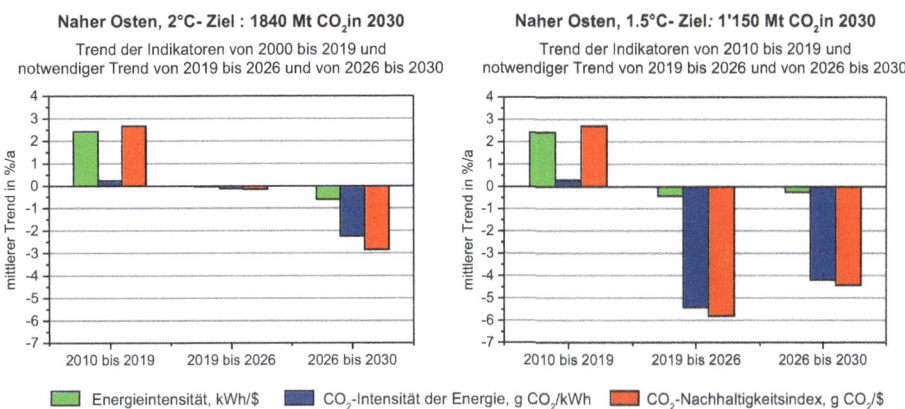

Abb. 6.3 Indikatoren-Trend in %/a von 2000 bis 2019 und notwendige Trendänderung ab 2019 bis 2030 zur Einhaltung des 2- Grad- bzw. des 1,5-Grad-Ziels

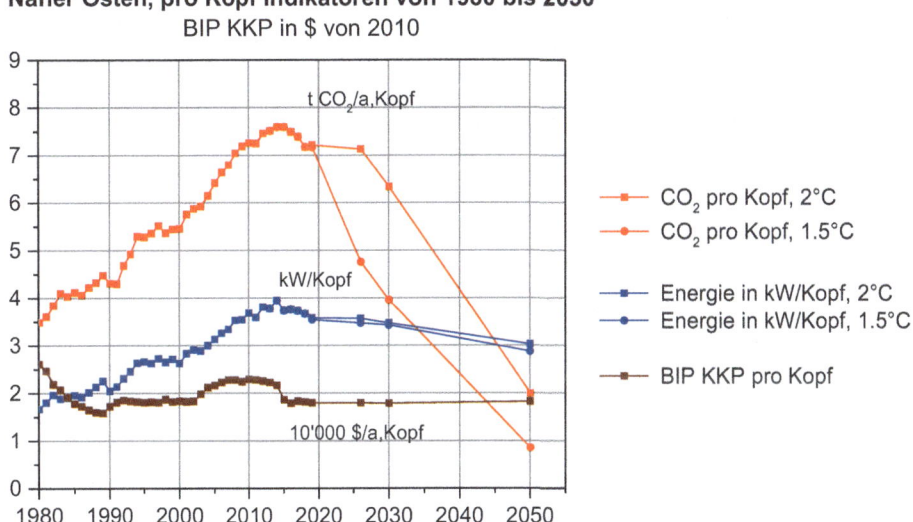

Abb. 6.4 Pro Kopf Indikatoren-Verlauf von 1980 bis 2019 und notwendiger Verlauf bis 2050 für das 2-Grad- und das 1,5-Grad-Ziel

Die **CO_2-Intensität der Energie** von etwa 224 g CO_2/\$ in 2019 ist bis 2030 durch Reduktion des Kohleeinsatzes, durch Kernenergie und erneuerbare Energien und evtl. durch CCS auf deutlich unter 200 g CO_2/\$ zu vermindern. Das 2-Grad-Ziel verlangt bis 2050 eine Reduktion auf 120 g CO_2/\$, das 1,5-Grad-Ziel gar auf 50 g CO_2/\$

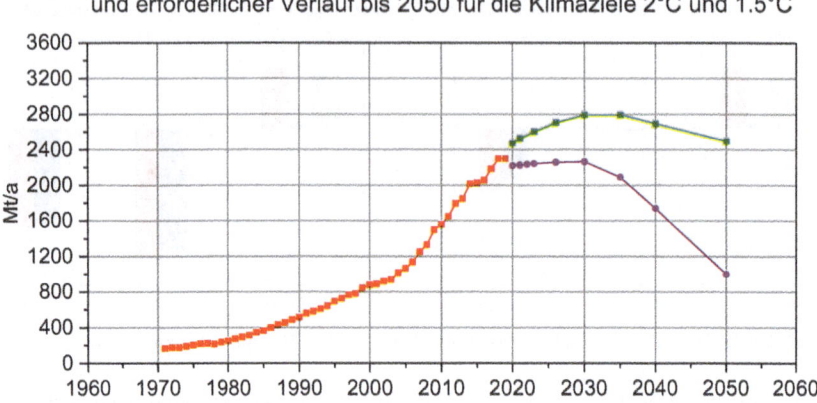

Abb. 6.5 Mit dem 2-Grad- bzw. 1,5-Grad-Ziel kompatible Emissions-Szenarien für Indien

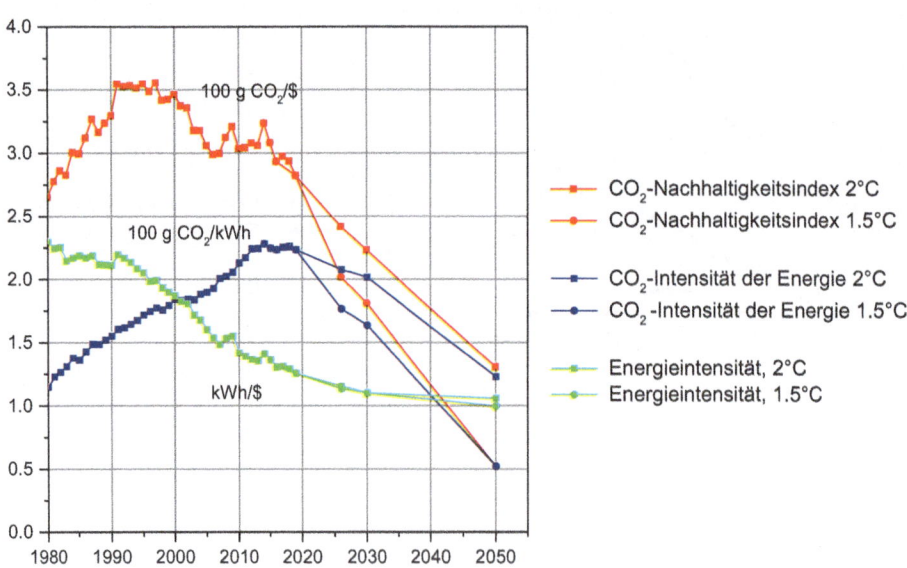

Abb. 6.6 Indikatoren-Verlauf von 1980 bis 2019 und mit den Klimazielen kompatibler Verlauf bis 2050

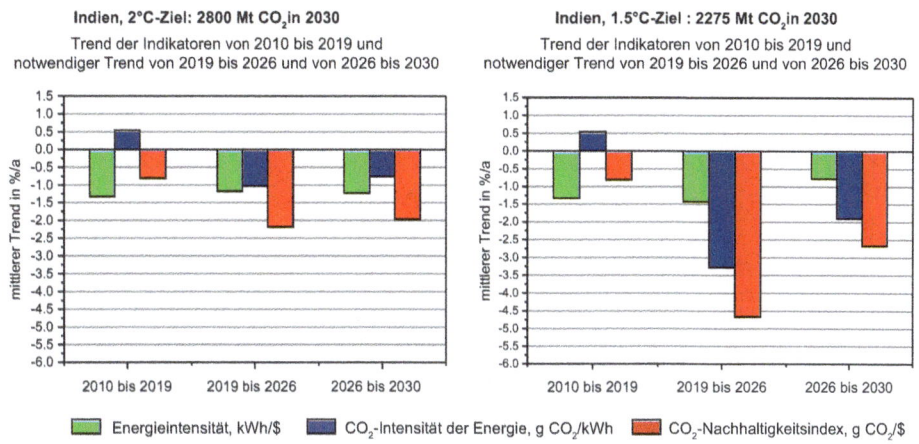

Abb. 6.7 Indikatoren-Trend in %/a von 2000 bis 2019 und notwendige Trendänderung ab 2019 bis 2030 zur Einhaltung des 2-Grad- bzw. 1,5-Grad-Ziels

Die dazu notwendigen *prozentualen jährlichen Änderungen* bis 2030 für das 2-Grad- und das 1,5-Grad-Ziel sind detaillierter in Abb. 6.7 wiedergegeben.

Der zugehörige Verlauf der *pro Kopf Indikatoren* für das kaufkraftbereinigte Bruttoinlandprodukt, die Bruttoenergie und den CO_2-Ausstoss sind schliesslich in Abb. 6.8 dargestellt, für 1980 bis 2019 und entsprechend den Klimaszenarien.

6.3 Rest-Südasien

Mit dem 2-Grad- bzw. 1,5-Grad-Ziel kompatible Emissions-Szenarien bis 2050 für das insgesamt eher unterentwickelte Rest-Südasien zeigt Abb. 6.9. Der entsprechende Verlauf der Indikatoren ist in Abb. 6.10 wiedergegeben. Notwendig ist die Beibehaltung der Tendenz zur Reduktion der **Energieintensität** und eine Stabilisierung und dann Inversion der Tendenz der in den letzten Jahren stark steigenden **CO_2-Intensität der Energie,** mithilfe erneuerbarer Energien.

Die dazu notwendigen prozentualen jährlichen Änderungen bis 2030 für das 2-Grad- und das 1.5-Grad-Ziel sind detaillierter in Abb. 6.11 wiedergegeben.

Der zugehörige Verlauf der *pro Kopf Indikatoren* für das kaufkraftbereinigte Bruttoinlandprodukt, die Bruttoenergie und den CO_2-Ausstoss sind schliesslich in Abb. 6.12 dargestellt, für 1980 bis 2019 und entsprechend den Klimaszenarien.

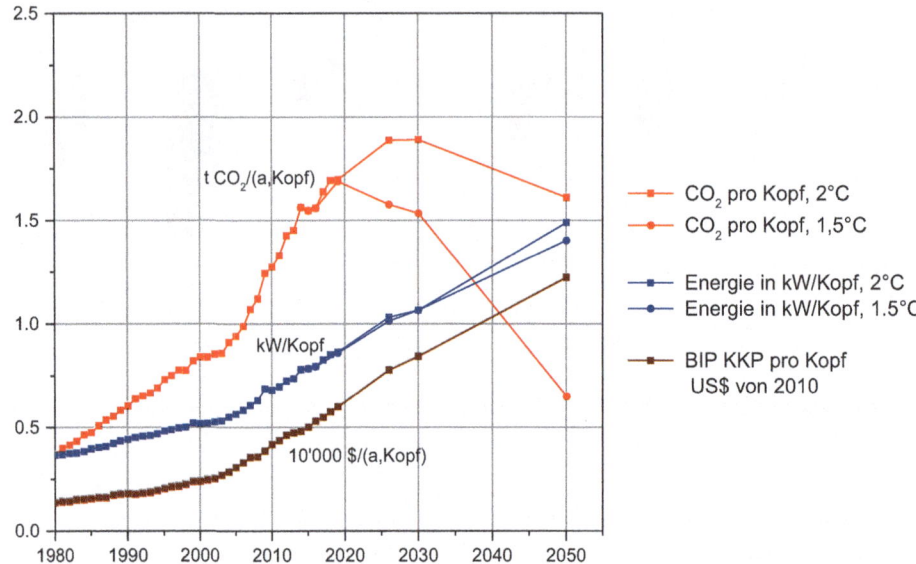

Abb. 6.8 Pro Kopf Indikatoren Indiens von 1980 bis 2019 sowie 2-Grad-Szenario und 1,5-Grad-Szenario bis 2050. Das BIP-Szenario entspricht bis 2026 den Prognosen des IMF

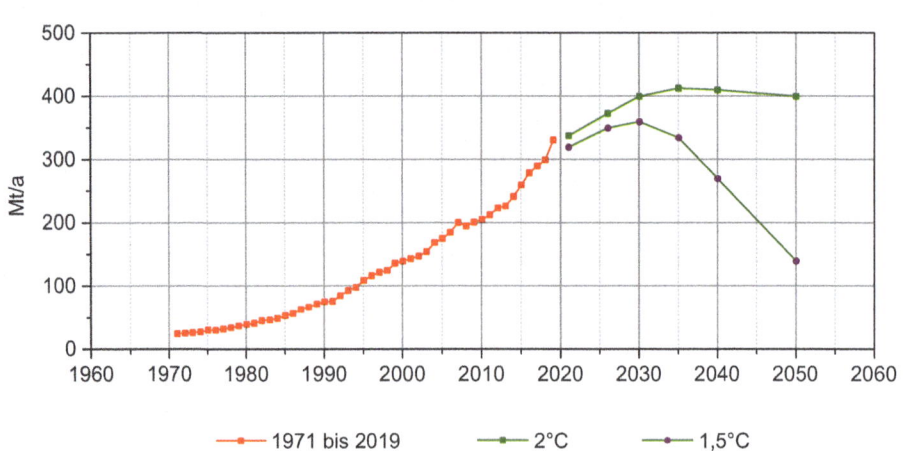

Abb. 6.9 Mit dem 2-Grad- bzw. 1,5-Grad-Ziel kompatible Emissionen für Rest-Südasien

Rest - Südasien, Indikatoren 1980 bis 2019 (BIP KKP in $ von 2010)
und erforderlicher Verlauf bis 2050 für das 2°C- bzw. 1.5°C-Ziel

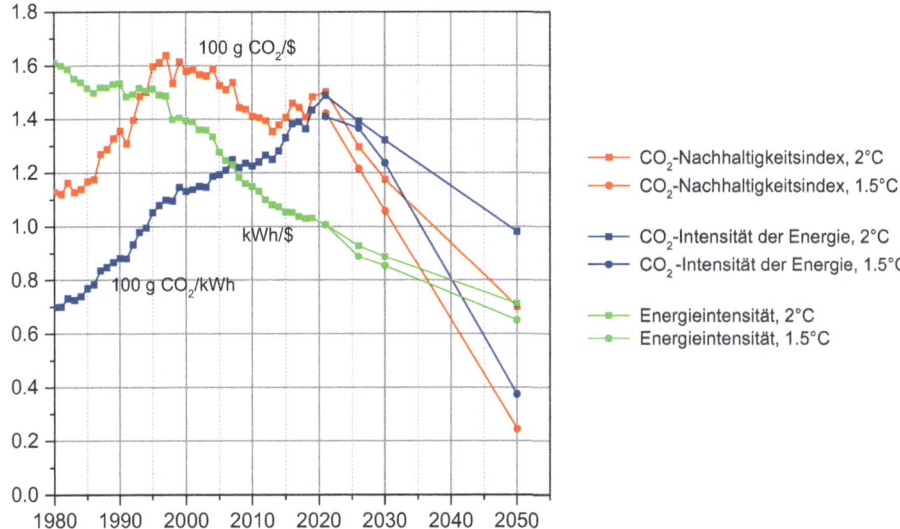

Abb. 6.10 Indikatoren-Verlauf von 1980 bis 2019 und mit den Klimazielen kompatibler Verlauf bis 2050 für Rest-Südasien

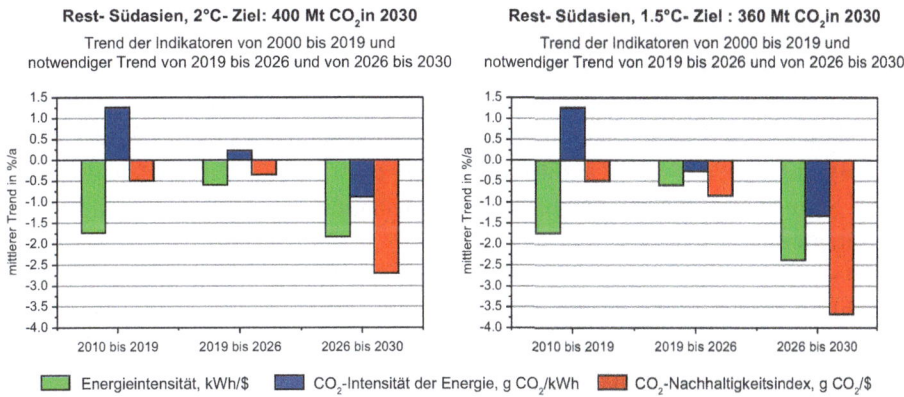

Abb. 6.11 Indikatoren-Trend in %/a von 2000 bis 2019 und notwendige Trendänderung ab 2019 bis 2030 zur Einhaltung des 2-Grad- bzw. 1,5-Grad-Ziels

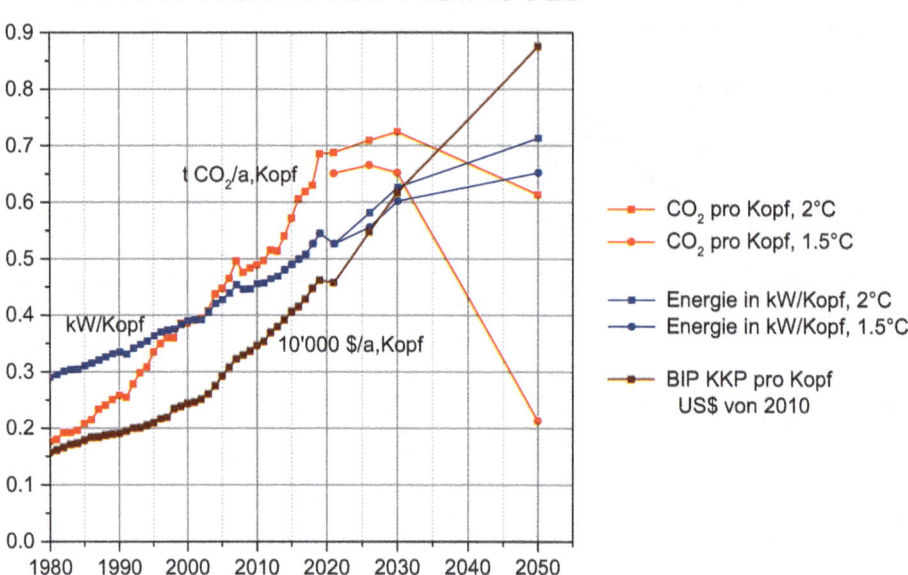

Abb. 6.12 Pro Kopf Indikatoren Rest-Südasiens von 1980 bis 2019 sowie 2-Grad- und 1,5-Grad-Szenario bis 2050. Das BIP-Szenario bis 2026 entspricht den Prognosen des IMF

6.4   Zusammenfassung

Die Abb. 6.13 und 6.14 geben die notwendige Änderung in % des Indikators g CO$_2$/$, von 2019 bis 2030, um das 2-Grad-Klimaziel bzw. das 1,5-Grad-Klimaziel zu erreichen.

Die *grüne Linie* entspricht der für die beiden Klimaziele im **Mittel weltweit notwendigen Reduktion** des Indikators.

Die *roten Werte* geben, in Übereinstimmung mit der vorangehenden Analyse, die **empfohlene Änderung** für die drei Regionen sowie für Nah- und Süd-Asien insgesamt.

Die **Marge relativ zum weltweit notwendigen Mittel** ist ein Bonus für die Entwicklungs- und Schwellenländer. Sie wird ermöglicht und kompensiert durch die stärkere Anstrengung der Industriewelt (siehe, was Europa betrifft, Band I und für Amerika Teil I dieses zweiten Bandes).

Der *Nahe Osten* wurde etwas geschont angesichts der gegenwärtigen Tendenzen und der Instabilität. *Rest-Südasien* hat bei entsprechender Unterstützung beste Voraussetzungen für den Aufbau einer nachhaltigen Energiewirtschaft. Aber *Indien* spielt, in diesem Erdteil, die für die Erreichung der Ziele entscheidende Rolle.

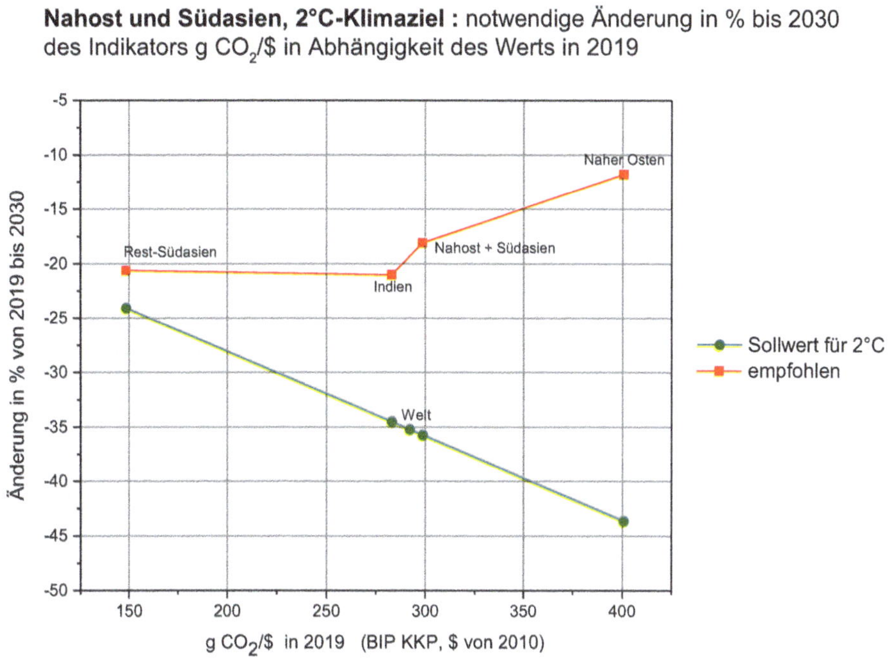

Nahost und Südasien, 2°C-Klimaziel : notwendige Änderung in % bis 2030 des Indikators g CO_2/\$ in Abhängigkeit des Werts in 2019

Abb. 6.13 Notwendige Änderung des Indikators g CO_2/\$ von 2019 bis 2030, um das 2-Grad-Klimaziel zu erreichen

Ziele unter 2 °C

Ausgehend von der 2-Grad- Variante sind Ziele unter 2 °C, mit verstärkten Anstrengungen ab 2030 ebenfalls möglich, sogar 1,5 °C, falls es dann gelingt bis 2050 die CO_2-Emissionen zu annullieren. Für das 1,5-Grad Ziel dürfen bis 2100 die kumulierten Emissionen seit 1820 weltweit höchstens 550 Gt C betragen (siehe Einleitung Kap. 1).

Ein **sanftes Erreichen des 1,5-Grd-Ziels** ist im diesem Kapitel detailliert besprochen worden und eher möglich.

Die rasche und starke Verbesserung der CO_2-Nachhaltigkeit zur Gewährleistung mindestens der Klimaziele erfordert (wobei diese Forderungen teilweise nur in entwickelten Länder oder durch Ablasshandel kurz- bis mittelfristig bezahlbar sein dürften):

- Bei **Heizwärme- und Kühlung:** bessere Gebäudeisolation, Ersatz von Ölheizungen durch Gasheizungen und vor allem durch Wärmepumpenheizungen (s. dazu auch Kap. 3 und [1]), sowie durch möglichst CO_2-frei erzeugte Fernwärme sowie Solar-Warmwasser, Kühlung mit Erdsonden und CO_2-arm erzeugte Elektrizität.
- Bei **Prozesswärme:** Ersatz fossiler Energieträger soweit möglich durch CO_2-arm erzeugte Elektrizität und Solarwärme.

Nahost und Südasien, 1.5°C-Klimaziel : notwendige Änderung in % bis 2030
des Indikators g CO2/$ in Abhängigkeit des Werts in 2019

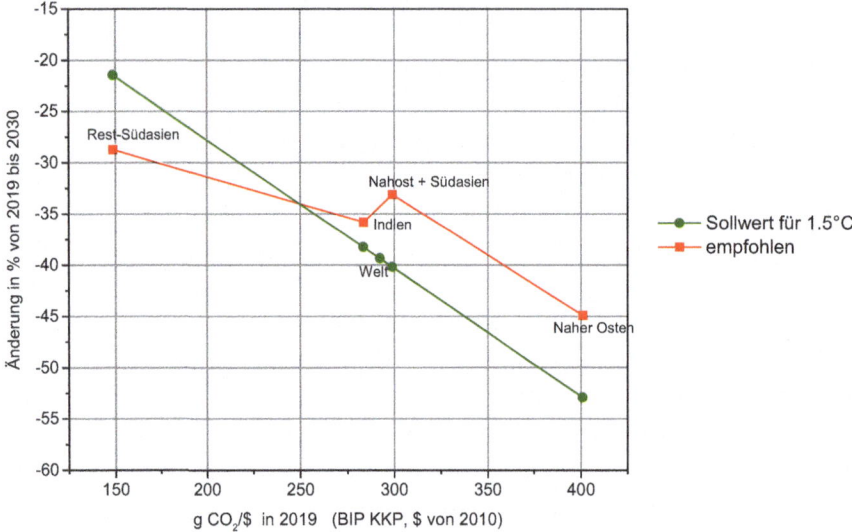

Abb. 6.14 Notwendige Änderung des Indikators g CO_2/$ von 2019 bis 2030, um das 1,5-Grad-Klimaziel zu erreichen

- Im **Verkehr**: *effizientere* Motoren und fortschreitende *Elektrifizierung*: Bahnverkehr, Elektro- und Hybridfahrzeuge für den Privat- und Warenverkehr. Letztere sind sehr sinnvoll bei einer *CO_2-armen* Elektrizitätsproduktion von mindestens 50 % (s. dazu Tab. 1.3). Die Produktion mittels Photovoltaik von *CO_2-neutralen* Treibstoffen dürfte ebenfalls einen wichtigen Beitrag leisten.

Dazugehörende und für alle wichtigste Massnahme ist eine rasch fortschreitende Entwicklung zu einer möglichst **CO_2-freien Elektrizitätsproduktion.** Diese kann in erster Linie durch erneuerbare Energien insbesondere auch mit Geothermie, aber auch durch Kernenergie oder CCS erreicht werden. Ebenso notwendig ist die Anpassung der Netze und Speicherungstechniken an die hohe Variabilität von Solar– und Windenergie.

Weitere Daten von Ländern des Nahen Ostens und Südasiens

7.1 Naher Osten: Iran und Saudi Arabien

7.1.1 Energieflüsse in Iran (Abb. 7.1 und 7.2)

7.1.2 Energieflüsse in Saudi Arabien (Abb. 7.3 und 7.4)

7.1.3 Elektrizitätsproduktion und -verbrauch in Iran und Saudi Arabien (Abb. 7.5)

7.2 Südasien: Pakistan, Bangladesch, Myanmar

Indien ist in den Abschn. 5.3, 5.44 und 6.2 behandelt worden.

7.2.1 Energieflüsse in Pakistan

Hierzu siehe die Abb. 7.6 und 7.7.

7.2.2 Energieflüsse in Bangladesch

Die Energieflüsse von Bangladesch sind in den Abb. 7.8 und 7.9 dargestellt.

© Springer Fachmedien Wiesbaden GmbH, ein Teil von Springer Nature 2023
V. Crastan, *Kennzahlen zur Erreichung der weltweiten Klimaziele*,
https://doi.org/10.1007/978-3-658-40073-6_7

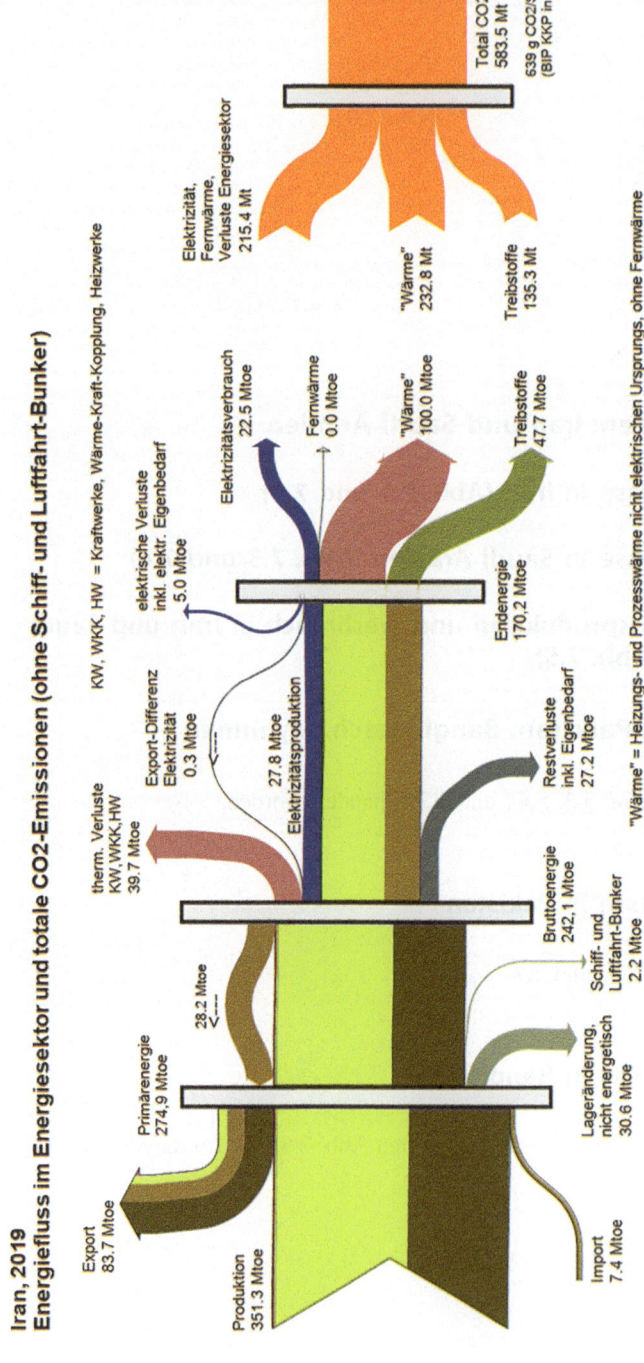

Abb. 7.1 Iran: Energiefluss im Energiesektor von der Primärenergie zur Endenergie und CO_2-Ausstoss. Die Energieträgerfarben sind wie in Abb. 5.6 und 5.8 (aber Erdöl dunkelbraun, Erdölprodukte hellbraun)

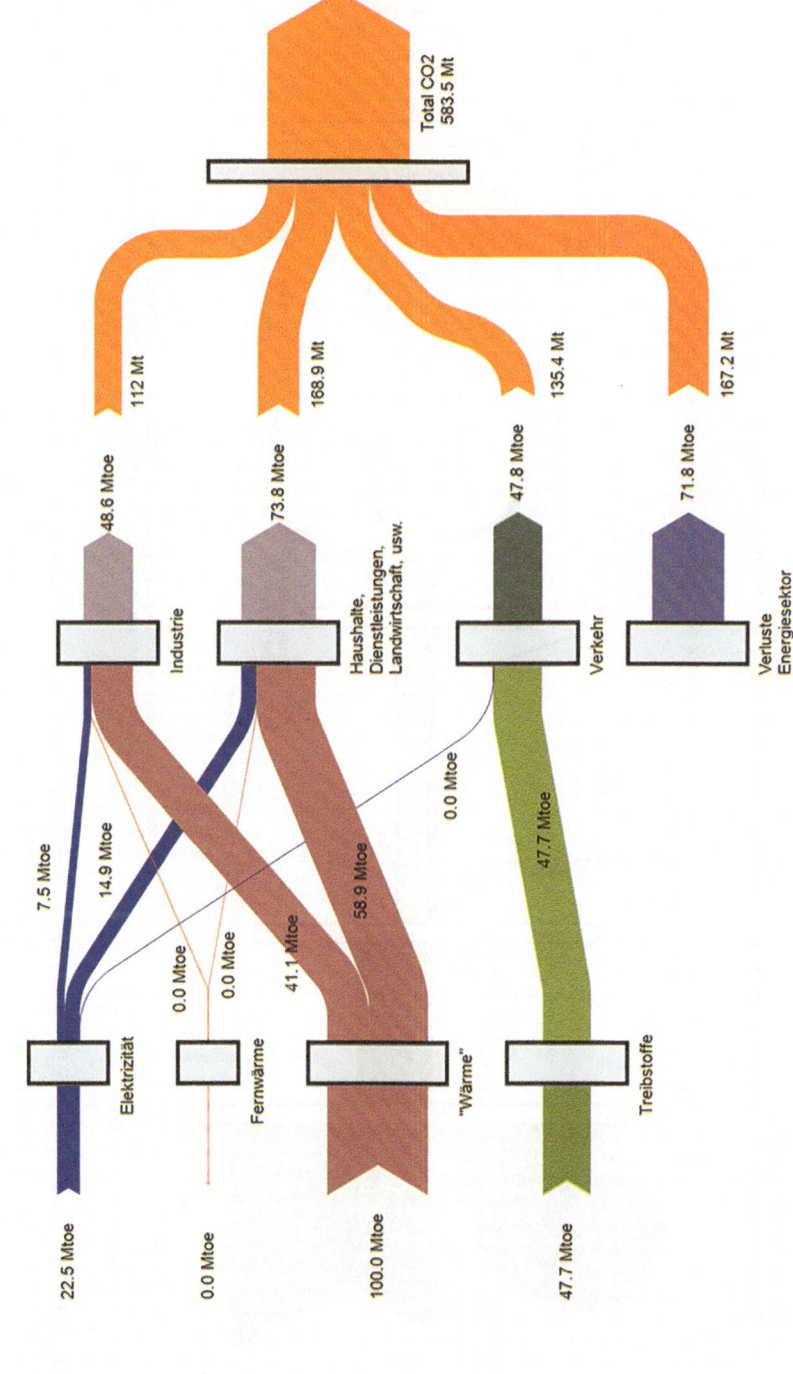

Iran, 2019
Energiefluss der Endenergie und totaler CO2-Ausstoss (ohne Schiff- und Luftfahrt-Bunker)

Abb. 7.2   Iran: Energiefluss der Endenergie zu den Endverbrauchern und zugeordnete CO$_2$-Emissionen

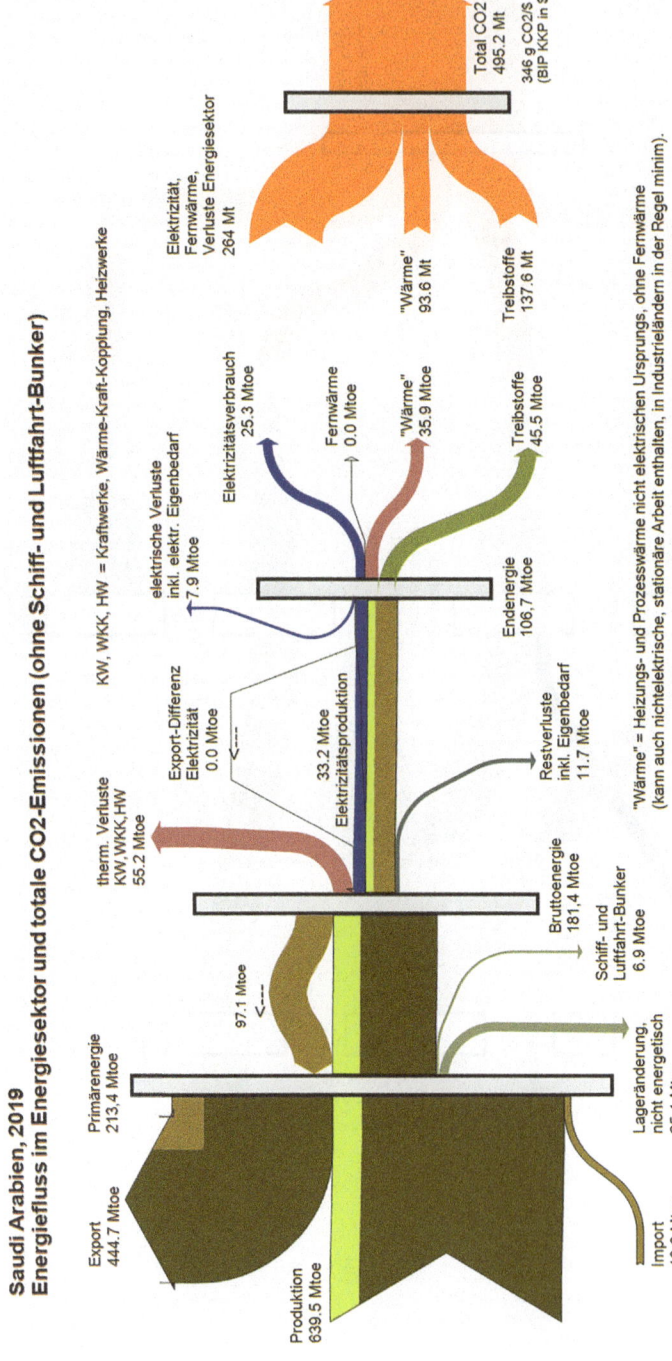

Saudi Arabien, 2019
Energiefluss im Energiesektor und totale CO2-Emissionen (ohne Schiff- und Luftfahrt-Bunker)

KW, WKK, HW = Kraftwerke, Wärme-Kraft-Kopplung, Heizwerke

Primärenergie 213,4 Mtoe

Export 444.7 Mtoe

Produktion 639.5 Mtoe

Import 18.6 Mtoe

Lageränderung, nicht energetisch 25.1 Mtoe

97.1 Mtoe

Bruttoenergie 181,4 Mtoe

Schiff- und Luftfahrt-Bunker 6.9 Mtoe

therm. Verluste KW,WKK,HW 55.2 Mtoe

Export-Differenz Elektrizität 0.0 Mtoe

33.2 Mtoe Elektrizitätsproduktion

elektrische Verluste inkl. elektr. Eigenbedarf 7.9 Mtoe

Restverluste inkl. Eigenbedarf 11.7 Mtoe

Elektrizitätsverbrauch 25.3 Mtoe

Fernwärme 0.0 Mtoe

"Wärme" 35.9 Mtoe

Treibstoffe 45.5 Mtoe

Endenergie 106,7 Mtoe

Elektrizität, Fernwärme, Verluste Energiesektor 264 Mt

"Wärme" 93.6 Mt

Treibstoffe 137.6 Mt

Total CO2 495.2 Mt

346 g CO2/$ (BIP KKP in $2010)

"Wärme" = Heizungs- und Prozesswärme nicht elektrischen Ursprungs, ohne Fernwärme (kann auch nichtelektrische, stationäre Arbeit enthalten, in Industrieländern in der Regel minim).

Abb. 7.3 Saudi Arabien: Energiefluss im Energiesektor von der Primärenergie zur Endenergie und CO_2-Ausstoss. Die Energieträgerfarben sind wie in Abb. 5.6 und 5.8 (aber Erdöl dunkelbraun, Erdölprodukte hellbraun)

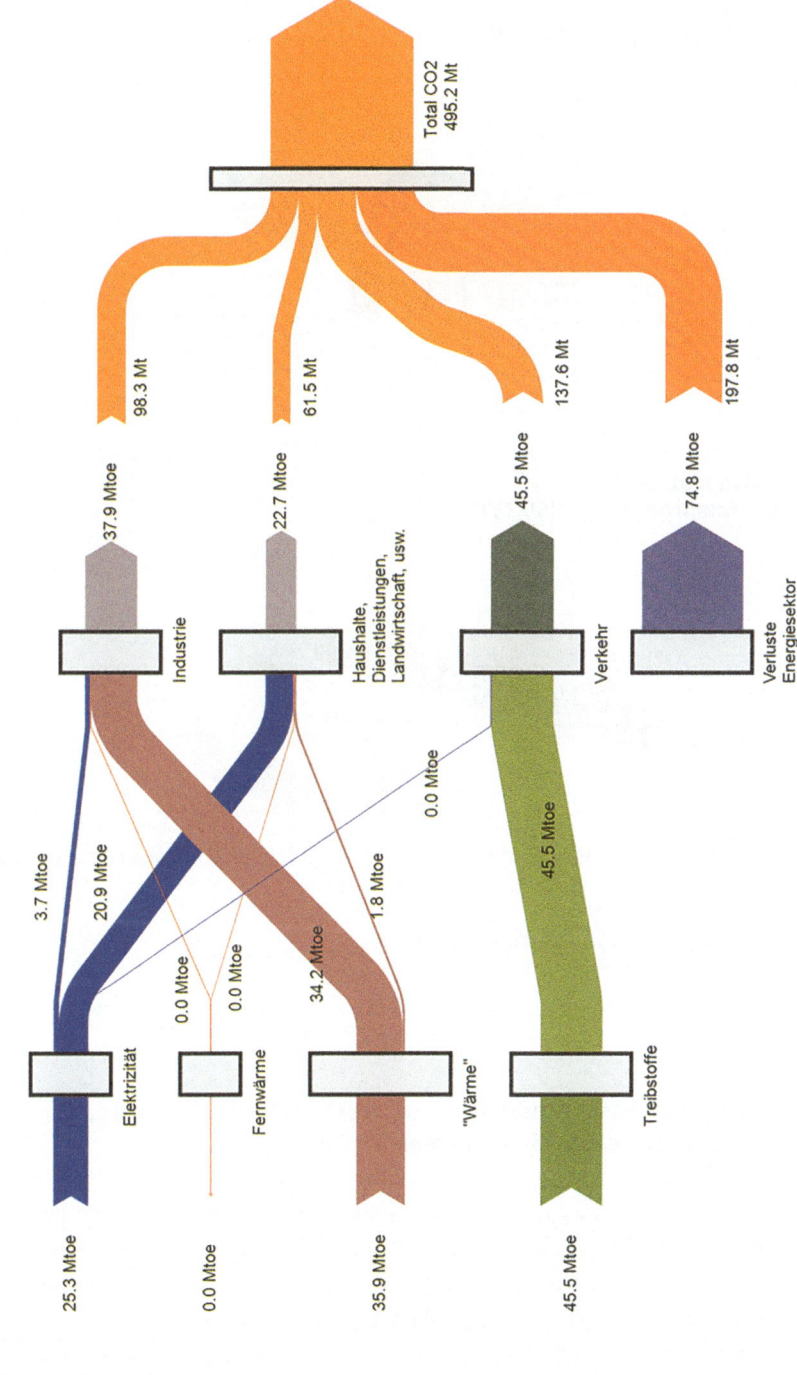

Abb. 7.4 Saudi Arabien: Energiefluss der Endenergie zu den Endverbrauchern und zugeordnete CO_2-Emissionen

Iran 2019,
Elektrizitätsproduktion 323 TWh

Endverbrauch
261 TWh
Verluste + Eigenbedarf
58 TWh   ~ 22%
Exportüberschuss
4 TWh   ~1%

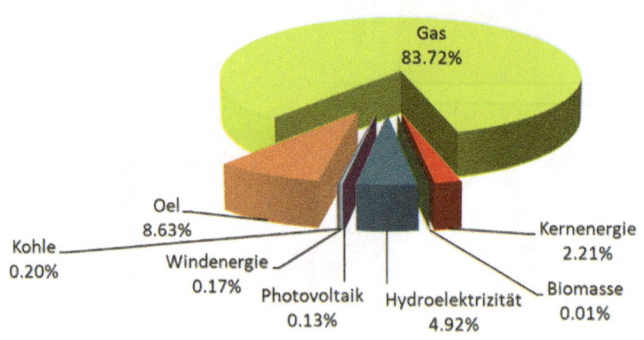

Saudi Arabien 2019,
Elektrizitätsproduktion 386 TWh

Endverbrauch
294 TWh
Verluste + Eigenbedarf
92 TWh   ~ 31%
Importüberschuss
0 TWh   ~0%

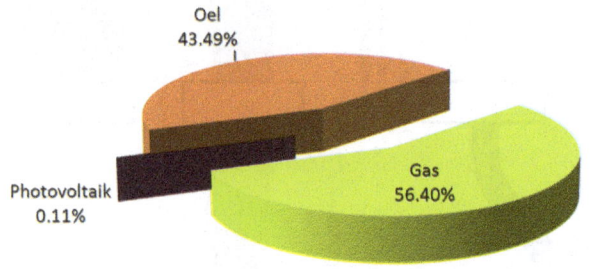

Abb. 7.5 Anteile der Energieträger an der Elektrizitätsproduktion von Iran und Saudi Arabien

7.2.3 Energieflüsse in Myanmar

Die Energieflüsse von Myanmar sind in den Abb. 7.10 und 7.11 wiedergegeben.

7.2.4 Elektrizitätsproduktion und -verbrauch in Pakistan, Bangladesch und Myanmar

Die Zusammensetzung der Elektrizitätsproduktion (einschliesslich Verbrauchsanteil) in den Staaten Pakistan, Bangladesch sowie Myanmar ist in Abb. 7.12 veranschaulicht.

Kommentar zu Iran, Einwohnerzahl: 83 Mio.
Iran ist vorwiegend Ölexporteur. Gas wird für die Elektrizitätsproduktion verwendet (Abb 7.1) und deckt weitgehend den Wärmebedarf für Haushalte und Industrie. (Abb. 7.2).

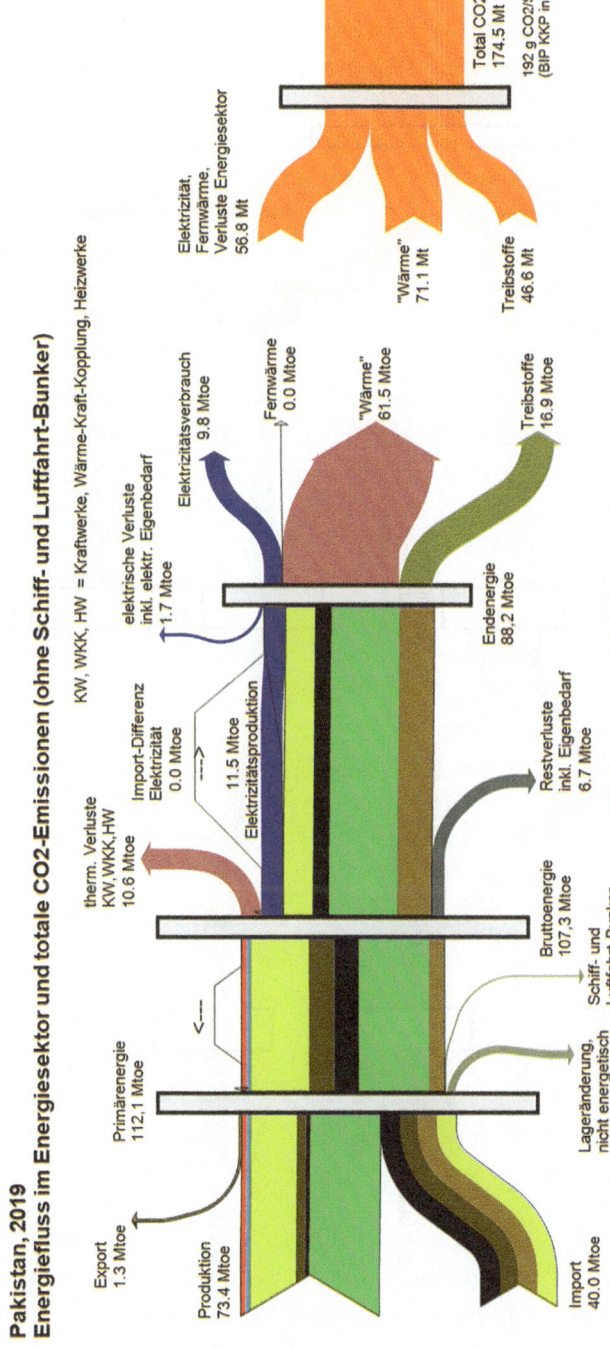

Pakistan, 2019
Energiefluss im Energiesektor und totale CO2-Emissionen (ohne Schiff- und Luftfahrt-Bunker)

KW, WKK, HW = Kraftwerke, Wärme-Kraft-Kopplung, Heizwerke

Total CO2
174.5 Mt

192 g CO2/S
(BiP KKP in S2010)

Elektrizität,
Fernwärme,
Verluste Energiesektor
56.8 Mt

"Wärme"
71.1 Mt

Treibstoffe
46.6 Mt

Elektrizitätsverbrauch
9.8 Mtoe

Fernwärme
0.0 Mtoe

elektrische Verluste
inkl. elektr. Eigenbedarf
1.7 Mtoe

"Wärme"
61.5 Mtoe

Treibstoffe
16.9 Mtoe

Endenergie
88.2 Mtoe

Import-Differenz
Elektrizität
0.0 Mtoe

11.5 Mtoe

Elektrizitätsproduktion

Restverluste
inkl. Eigenbedarf
6.7 Mtoe

therm. Verluste
KW,WKK,HW
10.6 Mtoe

Bruttoenergie
107.3 Mtoe

Schiff- und
Luftfahrt-Bunker
0.8 Mtoe

Primärenergie
112.1 Mtoe

Lageränderung,
nicht energetisch
4.0 Mtoe

Export
1.3 Mtoe

Produktion
73.4 Mtoe

Import
40.0 Mtoe

"Wärme" = Heizungs- und Prozesswärme nicht elektrischen Ursprungs, ohne Fernwärme
(kann auch nichtelektrische, stationäre Arbeit enthalten, in Industrieländern in der Regel minim).

Abb. 7.6 Pakistan: Energiefluss im Energiesektor von der Primärenergie zur Endenergie und CO2-Ausstoss. Die Energieträgerfarben sind wie in Abb. 5.6 und 5.8 (aber Erdöl dunkelbraun, Erdölprodukte hellbraun)

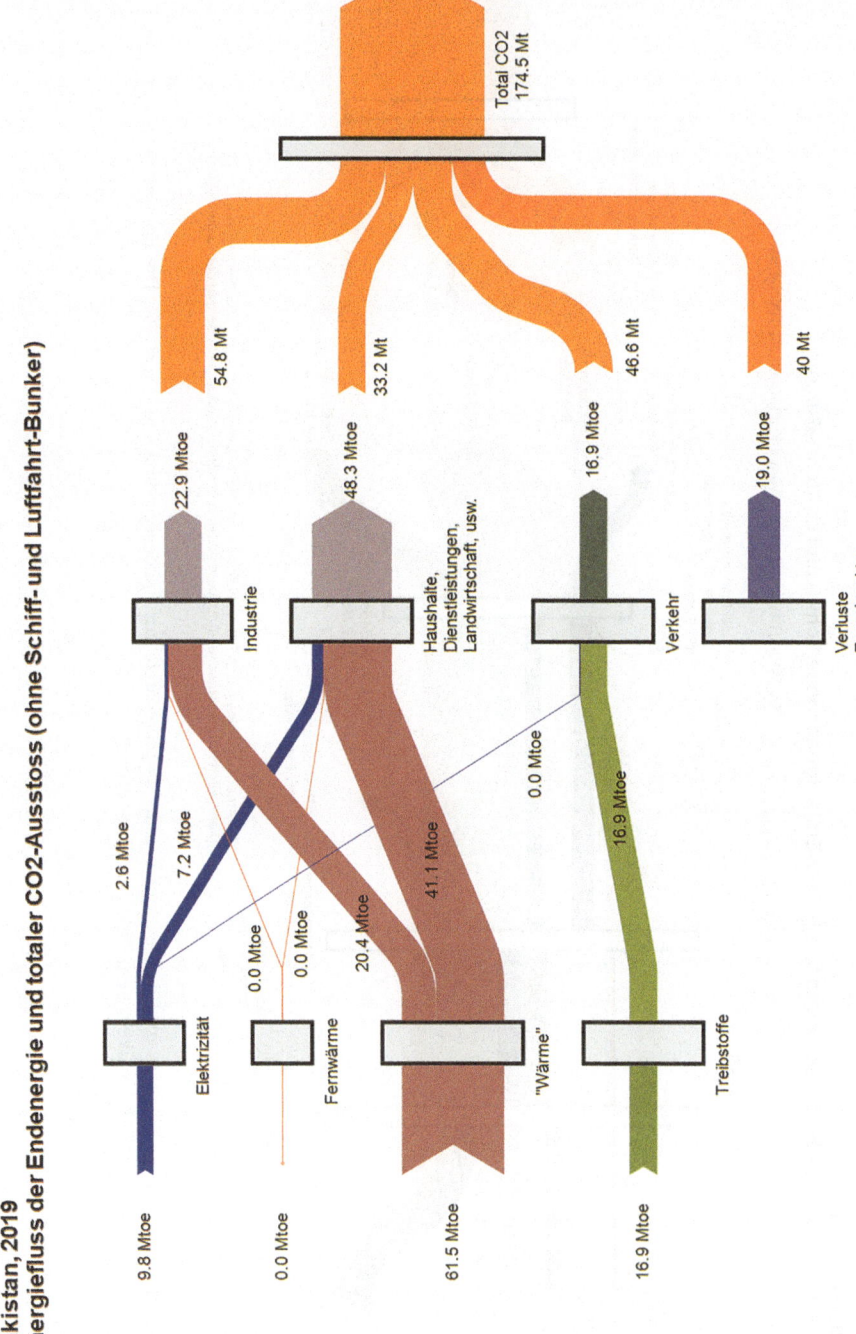

Pakistan, 2019
Energiefluss der Endenergie und totaler CO2-Ausstoss (ohne Schiff- und Luftfahrt-Bunker)

Abb. 7.7   Pakistan: Energiefluss der Endenergie zu den Endverbrauchern und zugeordnete CO_2-Emissionen

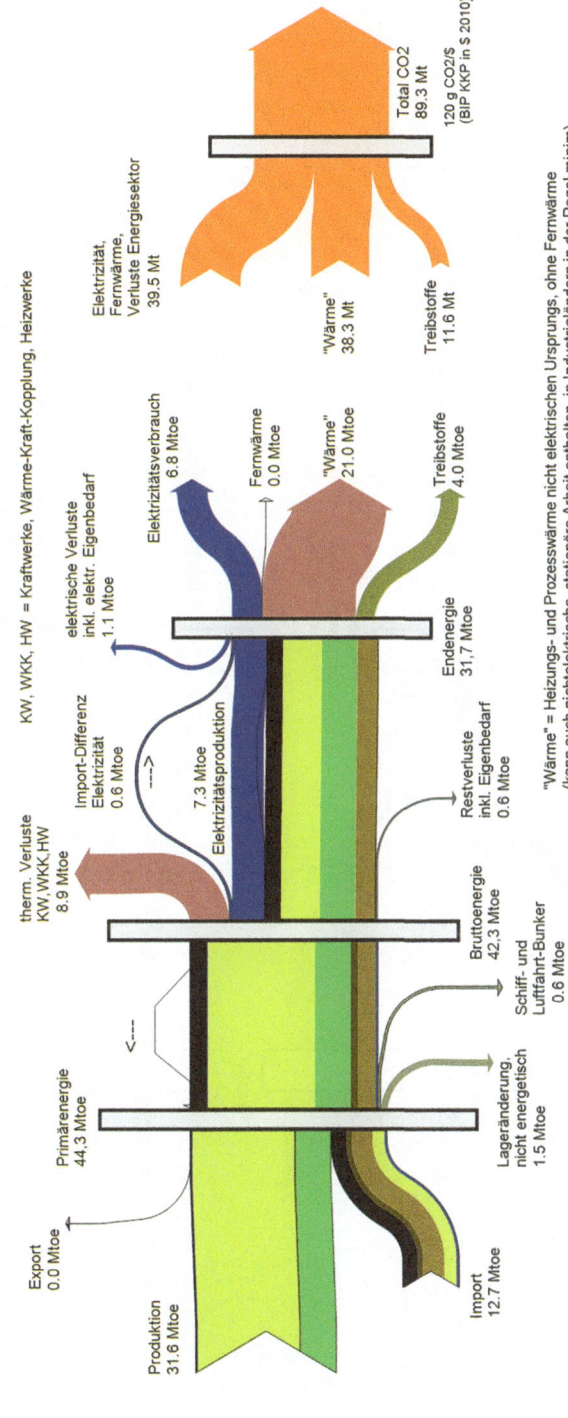

Abb. 7.8 Bangladesch: Energiefluss im Energiesektor von der Primärenergie zur Endenergie und CO_2-Ausstoss. Die Energieträgerfarben sind wie in Abb. 5.6 und 5.8 (aber Erdöl dunkelbraun, Erdölprodukte hellbraun)

Bangladesch, 2019
Energiefluss der Endenergie und totaler CO2-Ausstoss (ohne Schiff- und Luftfahrt-Bunker)

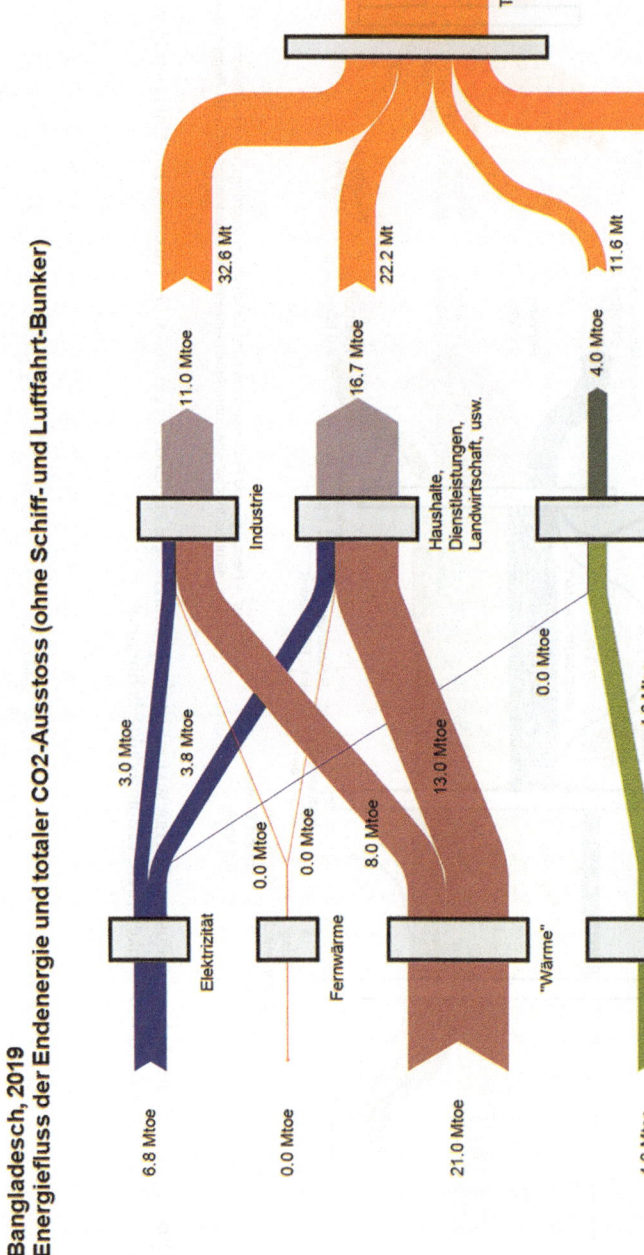

Abb. 7.9   Bangladesch: Energiefluss der Endenergie zu den Endverbrauchern und zugeordnete CO_2-Emissionen

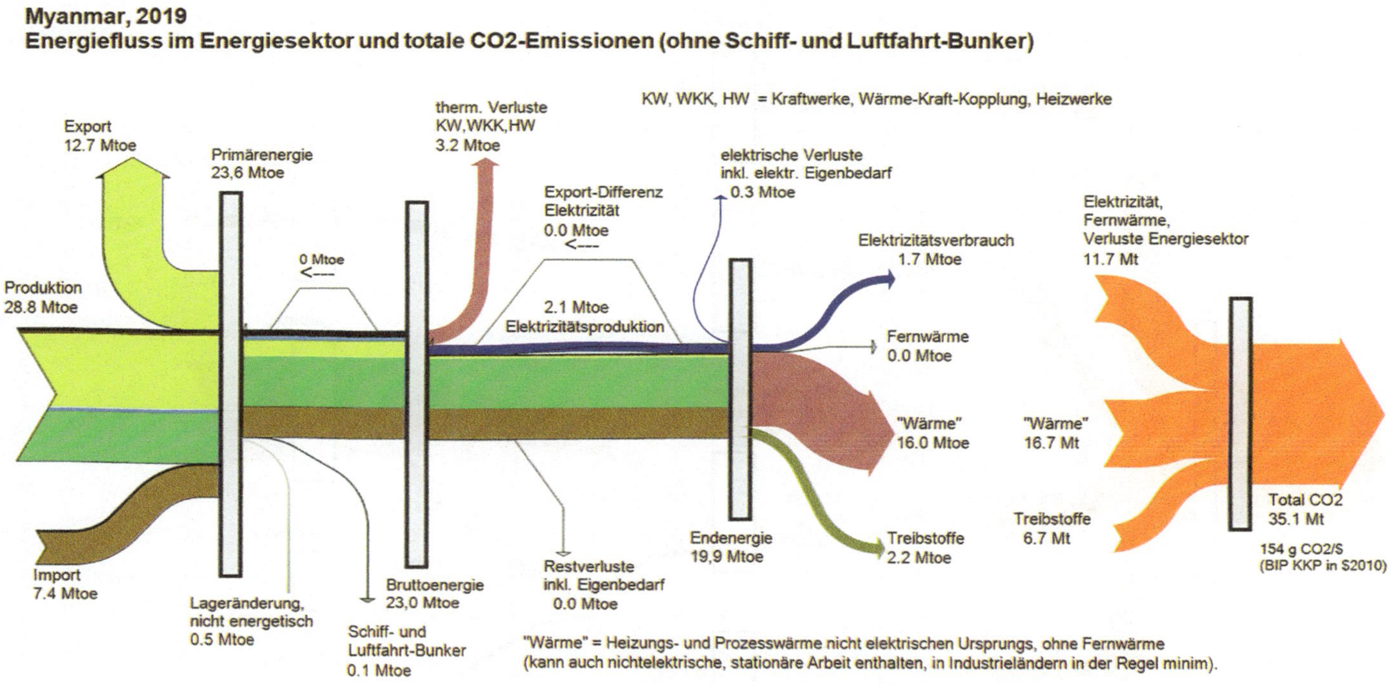

Myanmar, 2019
Energiefluss im Energiesektor (ohne Schiff- und Luftfahrt-Bunker)

KW, WKK, HW = Kraftwerke, Wärme-Kraft-Kopplung, Heizwerke

Total CO2
35.1 Mt

154 g CO2/$
(BIP KKP in $2010)

Elektrizität,
Fernwärme,
Verluste Energiesektor
11.7 Mt

"Wärme"
16.7 Mt

Treibstoffe
6.7 Mt

Elektrizitätsverbrauch
1.7 Mtoe

Fernwärme
0.0 Mtoe

"Wärme"
16.0 Mtoe

Treibstoffe
2.2 Mtoe

Endenergie
19.9 Mtoe

elektrische Verluste
inkl. elektr. Eigenbedarf
0.3 Mtoe

Export-Differenz
Elektrizität
0.0 Mtoe

2.1 Mtoe
Elektrizitätsproduktion

Restverluste
inkl. Eigenbedarf
0.0 Mtoe

therm. Verluste
KW, WKK, HW
3.2 Mtoe

Primärenergie
23.6 Mtoe

0 Mtoe

Bruttoenergie
23.0 Mtoe

Schiff- und
Luftfahrt-Bunker
0.1 Mtoe

Export
12.7 Mtoe

Produktion
28.8 Mtoe

Lageränderung,
nicht energetisch
0.5 Mtoe

Import
7.4 Mtoe

"Wärme" = Heizungs- und Prozesswärme nicht elektrischen Ursprungs, ohne Fernwärme
(kann auch nichtelektrische, stationäre Arbeit enthalten, in Industrieländern in der Regel minim).

Abb. 7.10 Myanmar: Energiefluss im Energiesektor von der Primärenergie zur Endenergie und CO_2-Ausstoss. Die Energieträgerfarben sind wie in Abb. 5.6 und 5.8 (aber Erdöl dunkelbraun, Erdölprodukte hellbraun)

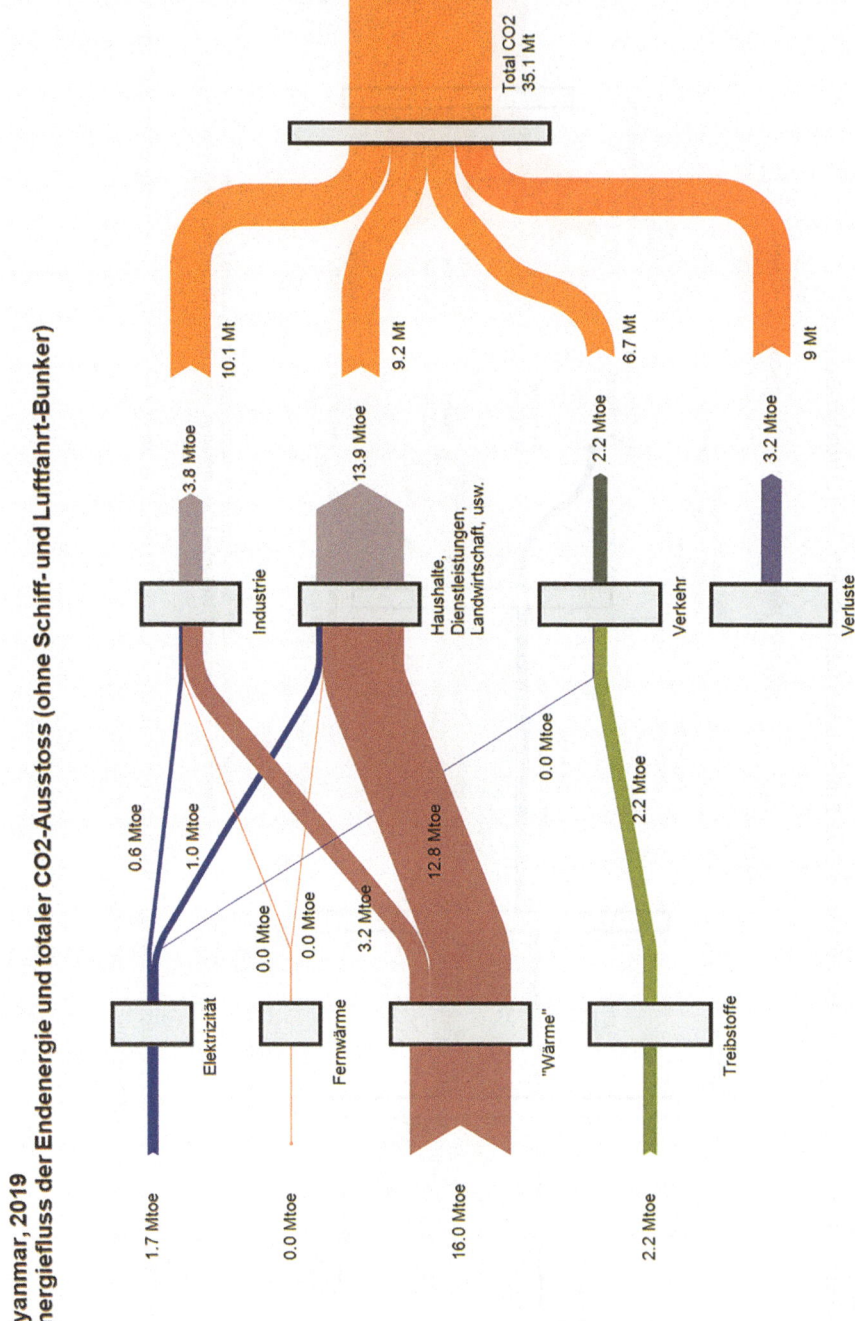

Myanmar, 2019
Energiefluss der Endenergie und totaler CO2-Ausstoss (ohne Schiff- und Luftfahrt-Bunker)

Abb. 7.11 Myanmar: Energiefluss der Endenergie zu den Endverbrauchern und zugeordnete CO_2-Emissionen

Pakistan 2019,
Elektrizitätsproduktion 133 TWh

Endverbrauch
114 TWh
Verluste + Eigenbedarf
20.TWh   ~ 18%
Importüberschuss
0.5 TWh   ~ 0.5%

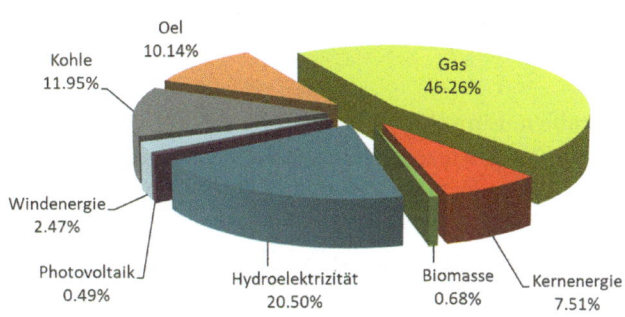

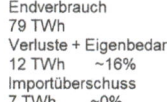

Bangladesch 2019,
Elektrizitätsproduktion 85 TWh

Endverbrauch
79 TWh
Verluste + Eigenbedarf
12 TWh   ~16%
Importüberschuss
7 TWh   ~0%

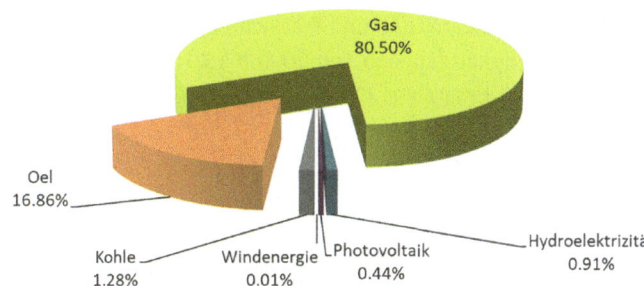

Myanmar 2019,
Elektrizitätsproduktion 24,3 TWh

Endverbrauch
19.7 TWh
Verluste + Eigenbedarf
3.6 TWh   ~ 18%
Exportüberschuss
1 TWh   ~ 5%

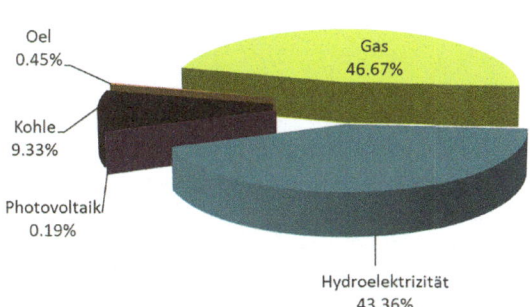

Abb. 7.12 Anteile der Energieträger an der Elektrizitätsproduktion in Pakistan, Bangladesch und Myanmar

Die CO_2-Nachhaltigkeit ist mit 639 g CO_2/$ extrem schlecht (zweitletzter Rang, Abb. 5.24). Eine wesentliche Trendwende ist für den Klimaschutz notwendig mit verstärktem Einsatz von CO_2-armen Energien für die Elektrizitätsproduktion (erneuerbare Energieträger und Kernenergie) und deutliche Verbesserung der Energieeffizienz, s. dazu auch die Tab. 7.1 in Abschn. 7.3.

Kommentar zu Saudi-Arabien, Einwohnerzahl: 34 Mio.
Saudi-Arabien ist ein wichtiger Ölproduzent und -exporteur. Gas wird für Elektrizitätsproduktion und Industriewärme verwendet (Abb. 7.3 und 7.4). Die CO_2-Nachhaltigkeit hat sich seit dem Jahr 2000 sowie seit 2010 weiter verschlechtert und liegt 2019 bei 346 g CO_2/$ (Abb. 5.24). Eine starke Verbesserung ist notwendig durch Einsatz CO_2-armer Energien (evtl. auch Kernenergie) und evtl. CCS, für die Elektrizitätsproduktion, sowie Verbesserung der Energieeffizienz und mittelfristig Elektrifizierung des Verkehrs, s. dazu auch die Tab. 7.2 in Abschn. 7.3.

Kommentar zu Pakistan, Einwohnerzahl: 217 Mio.
Pakistan ist auf Importe von Erdöl und Erdölprodukte angewiesen. Selber produziert es Erdgas, das aber im Inland für die Elektrizität- und Wärmeproduktion verwendet wird (Abb. 7.6 und 7.7). Die CO_2-Nachhaltigkeit hat sich von 2000 bis 2010 trotz guter wirtschaftlicher Entwicklung verbessert (dank Ersatz von Öl durch Gas). Ab 2010 ist sie mit 192 g CO_2/$

Tab. 7.1 Iran (Energieintensität 3,08 kWh/$, Emissionen 7,0 t CO_2/Kopf), El-G = 13,2 %

Energieart (Abb. 7.1)	g CO_2/ kWh	Verbraucher (Abb. 7.2)	g CO_2/kWh
Wärme (ohne Elektr.)	201	Industrie	199
Treibstoffe	244	Haushalte etc.	197
Energiesektor	197	Verkehr	244
Total	**208**	Verluste Energiesektor	201

Tab. 7.2 Saudi-Arabien (Energieintensität 1,47 kWh/$, Emissionen 14,5 t CO_2/Kopf), El-G = 23,7 %

Energieart (Abb. 7.3)	g CO_2/ kWh	Verbraucher (Abb. 7.4)	g CO_2/kWh
Wärme (ohne Elektr.)	227	Industrie	224
Treibstoffe	201	Haushalte etc.	233
Energiesektor	239	Verkehr	261
Total	**236**	Verluste Energiesektor	228

Tab. 7.3 Indien
(Energieintensität 1,26 kWh/$,
Emissionen 1,7 t CO_2/Kopf),
El-G = 19,5 %

Energieart (Abb. 5.11)	g CO_2/ kWh	Verbraucher (Abb. 5.12)	g CO_2/kWh
Wärme (ohne Elektr.)	159	Industrie	218
Treibstoffe	247	Haushalte etc.	144
Energiesektor	276	Verkehr	247
Total	**225**	Verluste Energiesektor	283

Tab. 7.4 Pakistan
(Energieintensität 1,37 kWh/$,
Emissionen 0,8 t CO_2/Kopf),
El-G = 11,1 %

Energieart (Abb. 7.6)	g CO_2/ kWh	Verbraucher (Abb. 7.7)	g CO_2/kWh
Wärme (ohne Elektr.)	100	Industrie	206
Treibstoffe	237	Haushalte etc.	59
Energiesektor	170	Verkehr	237
Total	**140**	Verluste Energiesektor	181

in 2019 recht stabil geblieben (Abb. 5.23). Eine stärkere Senkung auf etwa 110 g CO_2/$ bis 2030 ist aber zur Einhaltung der Klimaziele notwendig, dies durch weitere Elektrifizierung und Deckung des steigenden Bedarfs möglichst nicht, wie in den letzten Jahren leider geschehen, durch Kohleimporte (als Öl-Ersatz) sondern durch Wasserkraft, Wind, Photovoltaik und evtl. Kernenergie (Abb. 7.12). Das Potenzial an erneuerbaren Energien ist erheblich. Der Elektrifizierungsgrad beträgt lediglich 11 % und müsste gesteigert werden. Die Energieeffizienz ist weiterhin zu verbessern und auf Werte deutlich unter 1 kWh/$ zu senken (Abb. 5.17 und 6.10), s dazu auch die Tab. 7.4 in Abschn. 7.3.

Kommentar zu Bangladesch, Einwohnerzahl: 162 Mio.
Bangladesch produziert Gas für den Eigenbedarf, vorwiegend für die Elektrizitätsproduktion (Abb. 3.8 und 3.9). Die CO_2-Nachhaltigkeit hat sich von 2000 bis 2010 wegen des Kohleeinsatzes stark verschlechtert ist aber mit 120 g CO_2/$ im Vergleich noch akzeptabel und seit 2010 stabil (Abb. 5.23). Die schwache Energieintensität ist typisch für Unterentwicklung (Abb. 5.19). Der Elektrifizierungsgrad von 21 % ist für ein Entwicklungsland sehr gut. Eine noch stärkere Elektrifizierung von Landwirtschaft, Haushalte und Industrie würde zur Überwindung der Unterentwicklung des Landes beitragen. Eine weiter zuverlässig funktionierende Elektrizitätsversorgung ist für den wirtschaftlichen Fortschritt essentiell, Kohle und auch Gas müssten aber rasch ersetzt werden durch erneuerbare Energien (Wasserkraft, Windenergie und Photovoltaik, Abb. 7.12).

Tab. 7.5 Bangladesch (Energieintensität 0,66 kWh/\$, Emissionen 0,55 t CO_2/Kopf), El-G $= 21,3$ %

Energieart (Abb. 7.8)	g CO_2/ kWh	Verbraucher (Abb. 7.9)	g CO_2/kWh
Wärme (ohne Elektr.)	158	Industrie	256
Treibstoffe	247	Haushalte etc.	114
Energiesektor	197	Verkehr	247
Total	**182**	Verluste Energiesektor	188

Tab. 7.6 Myanmar (Energieintensität 1,18 kWh/\$, Emissionen 0,7 t CO_2/Kopf), El-G $= 8,5$ %

Energieart (Abb. 7.10)	g CO_2/ kWh	Verbraucher (Abb. 7.11)	g CO_2/kWh
Wärme (ohne Elektr.)	90	Industrie	228
Treibstoffe	268	Haushalte etc.	57
Energiesektor	206	Verkehr	268
Total	**111**	Verluste Energiesektor	246

Kommentar zu Myanmar, Einwohnerzahl: 53 Mio.

Neben Biomasse ist Erdgas die wichtigste eigene Energiequelle (Abb. 7.10 und 7.11). Der Elektrifizierungsgrad beträgt nur 9 %. Die Entwicklung Myanmars erfordert eine starke Elektrifizierung. Myanmar war 2016 bezüglich CO_2-Nachhaltigkeit in Südasien noch rangbestes Land, ist aber 2019 auf den zweitletzten Platz zurückgefallen (Abb. 5.23) da der verstärkte Energiebedarf durch Kohle statt durch Wasserkraft, Solarenergie und Geothermie gedeckt wurde (Abb. 7.12). Durch erneuerbare Energien könnte Myanmar einen weiteren starken Anstieg des Indikators der CO_2-Intensität der Energie vermeiden (hat sich seit 2010 wesentlich erhöht, s. Abb. 5.21, s. dazu auch die Tab. 7.6 in Abschn. 7.3.

7.3 Tabellen zu Indikatoren und CO_2-Intensitäten gewichtiger Länder des Nahen Ostens und Südasiens

Die Tab. 7.1 bis 7.6 geben die *Energieintensität* und die *Emissionen pro Kopf* sowie *CO_2-Intensitäten der Endenergien und der Endverbraucher* für einige der gewichtigsten Länder von Nah- und Süd-Asien (Die Werte folgen aus den Energiefluss-Diagrammen).

Dazu folgende Bemerkungen:

- Die **CO_2-Intensität des Energiesektors** wird stark vom Grad der CO_2-Freiheit der Elektrizitätserzeugung beeinflusst. Einzig Myanmar weist dank Wasserkraft einen Wert unter 120 g CO_2/kWh. Der Nahe Osten und Südasien müssen ihre stark auf fossile Energien basierende Elektrizitätserzeugung progressiv auf CO_2-ärmere Energien umstellen, wobei neben Wasserkraft, Wind- und Solarenergie auch *Geothermie* und evtl. Kernenergie eine grössere Rolle spielen könnten. Umwandlung von Kohle in Gas, CCS und Erzeugung CO_2-neutraler Treibstoffe, könnten ebenfalls mithelfen. Eine CO_2-arme Elektrizitätserzeugung ist der beste Weg, neben der Verminderung der Energieintensität, zur Verbesserung der CO_2-Nachhaltigkeit und Erreichung der Klimaziele.
- In den meisten Ländern liegt die CO_2-Intensität des Energiesektors vorerst über oder auf ähnlichem Niveau wie diejenige des **Verkehrssektors.** Eine verbreitete *Elektrifizierung* des Verkehrs ist deshalb erst mittelfristig sinnvoll. Ausnahme ist Pakistan (s. Abb. 7.1 bis 7.6).
- Der Einsatz von *Wärmepumpen ist* allgemein sinnvoll, da der Anteil an CO_2-freier Umweltenergie meistens bei etwa 75 % liegt. Somit würden Wärmepumpen, zumindest in den Ländern des Nahen Ostens, die CO_2-Intensität des **Wärmebereichs** reduzieren, auch wenn die CO_2-Intensität des Energiesektors (wie in Indien und Saudi Arabien) etwa gleich oder sogar über derjenigen des Wärmesektors liegt.
- Die **Energieintensität** ist ein weiterer wichtiger Indikator. Er hängt von der *Effizienz des Energieeinsatzes* ab. Bei Unterentwicklung ist er hoch, nimmt normalerweise bei zunehmender Entwicklung ab und sollte bis 2050 für Nah- und Süd-Asien insgesamt auf Werte unter 1,0 kWh/\$ stabilisiert werden (Abb. 6.14).
- Der **Indikator der CO_2-Nachhaltigkeit** (g CO_2/\$) ist das Produkt von Energieintensität und CO_2-Intensität der Energie.
- Die **Emissionen pro Kopf** in t CO_2/Kopf und Jahr ergeben sich als Produkt von Index der CO_2-Nachhaltigkeit und Wohlstandsindikator (\$/Kopf und Jahr):

$$tCO_2/Kopf, a = g\ CO_2/\$ * \$/Kopf, a/10^6$$

Im Jahr 2019 ist im **Nahen Osten** das mittlere jährliche kaufkraftbereinigte Bruttoinlandprodukt *18.800 \$/Kopf* und die CO_2-Emission betragen *7.2 t/Kopf,* entsprechend einem Index der CO_2-Nachhaltigkeit von *401 g CO_2/\$.* Um bis zu 2050, nach Stabilisierung und anschliessender Reduktion auf einen für das Klimaziel von 2 °C zulässigen Wert von *2.0 t/Kopf* zu kommen (s. Abschn. 6.1), muss, bei einer Zunahme des BIP (KKP) auf z.B. *20.000 \$/Kopf,* der Index der CO_2-Nachhaltigkeit auf rund *110 g CO_2/\$* vermindert werden. Für das Klimaziel Begrenzung des Temperaturanstiegs auf 1.5 °C müssten gar *50 g CO_2/\$* angestrebt werden.

In **Indien** waren in 2019 das mittlere BIP (KKP) *6000 \$/Kopf* und die CO_2-Emissionen *1,7 t/Kopf,* entsprechend einem Index der CO_2-Nachhaltigkeit von *283 g CO_2/\$.* Um bis

2050 die CO_2-Emissionen auf einen für das Klimaziel von 2 °C noch zulässigen Wert von *1,6 t/Kopf* zu stabilisieren (s. Abschn. 6.2), muss, bei einer Zunahme des BIP (KKP) auf z. B. *12.500 \$/Kopf,* der Index der CO_2-Nachhaltigkeit auf maximal *130 g CO_2/\$* begrenzt werden. Für das 1,5-Grad-Klimaziel müssten *50 g CO_2/\$* angestrebt werden.

Die Tab. 7.1, 7.2, 7.3, 7.4, 7.5 und 7.6 **zeigen:** Energieintensität, Emissionen pro Kopf und CO_2-Intensitäten der Energie (letztere detailliert pro Endenergie und Endverbraucher) *im Jahr 2019* für einige der die bevölkerungsreichsten Länder des Nahen Ostens und Südasiens. El-G = Elektrifizierungsgrad (Anteil Elektrizität an der Endenergie, z. Vergleich: Westeuropa 25 %, USA: 24 %).

Energiewirtschaftliche Analyse

8

8.1 Einführung

In **Teil III** dieses zweiten Bandes der Reihe „Kennzahlen zur Erreichung der weltweiten Klimaziele" wird **Ostasien/Ozeanien** analysiert. Dieser Erdteil ist demographisch weltweit bestimmend und wird es in Zukunft auch wirtschaftlich sein.

Nach der Analyse in Kap. 8 der Entwicklung aller maßgebenden Größen wie Bevölkerung, Bruttoinlandprodukt, detaillierter Energieverbrauch und CO_2-Emissionen bis 2019, wird anschließend in Kap. 9 die künftige Evolution der wichtigsten Indikatoren der einzelnen Regionen und Länder, welche die Klimaziele respektieren, dargelegt.

8.2 Bevölkerung und Bruttoinlandprodukt

Wir unterteilen Ostasien/Ozeanien in drei Regionen die folgendermaßen definiert sind (siehe dazu Abb. 8.1):

- **OECD Ostasien/Ozeanien** (Japan, Südkorea, Australien, Neuseeland)
- **China** (mit Hongkong)
- **Restliches Ostasien/Ozeanien** (Indonesien, Brunei, Kambodscha, Nordkorea, Malaysia, Mongolei, Philippinen, Singapur, Taiwan, Thailand, Vietnam, restliche Länder).

© Springer Fachmedien Wiesbaden GmbH, ein Teil von Springer Nature 2023
V. Crastan, *Kennzahlen zur Erreichung der weltweiten Klimaziele*,
https://doi.org/10.1007/978-3-658-40073-6_8

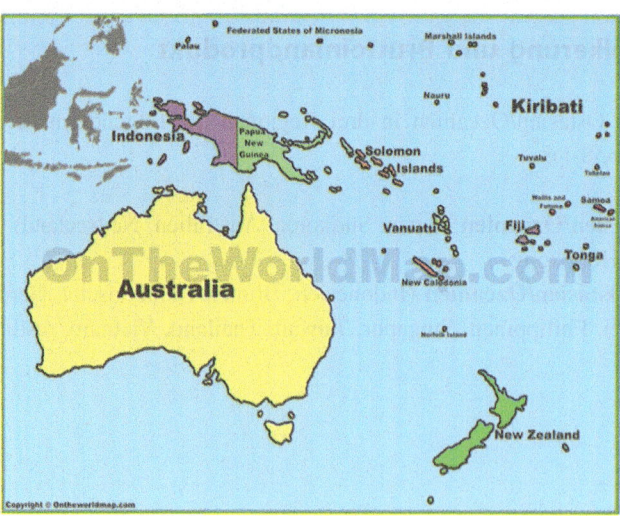

Abb. 8.1 Ostasien und Ozeanien

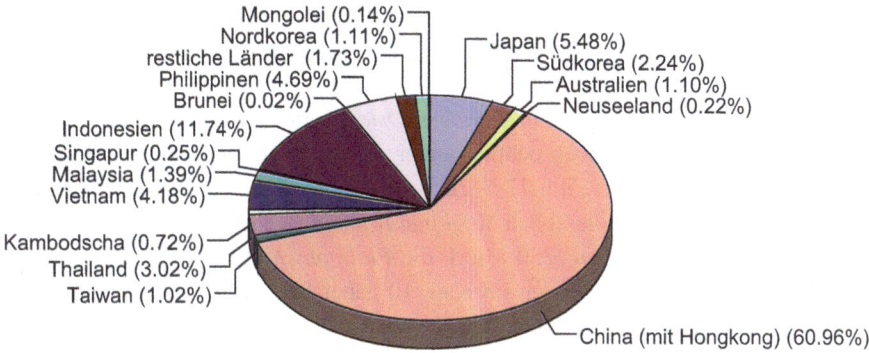

Abb. 8.2 Prozentuale Aufteilung der Bevölkerung von Ostasien/Ozeanien

Ostasien/Ozeanien weist 2019, mit 2,31 Mrd. Einwohner (Abb. 8.2) ein kaufkraftberei-nigtes Bruttoinlandprodukt BIP (KKP) von 36.200 Mrd. US\$ (von 2010). Dominierend ist China mit 61 % der Bevölkerung und 55 % des BIP KKP.

Das BIP (KKP) pro Kopf der *OECD-Länder* von Ostasien/Ozeanien, sowie von *China* und *Indonesien* (als demographisch bedeutendstes Land vom Rest-Ostasien) zeigt Abb. 8.3

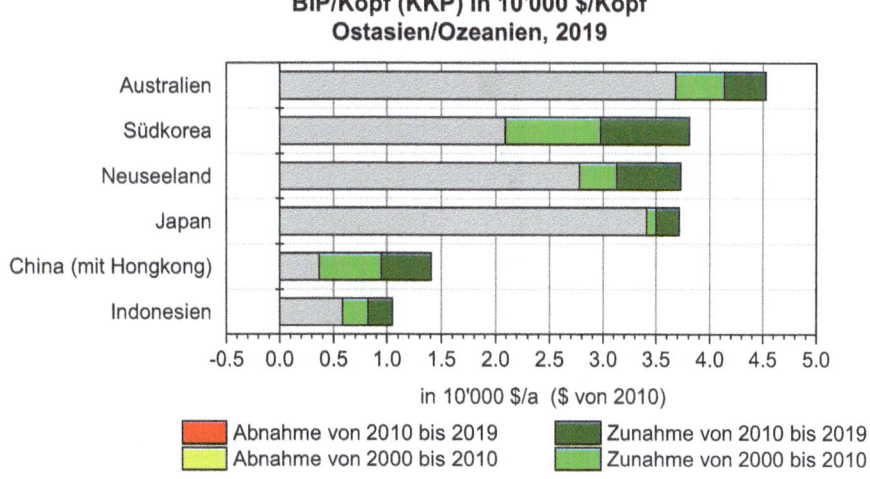

Abb. 8.3 BIP (KKP) pro Kopf in Ostasien/Ozeanien und Fortschritte seit 2000

Das BIP (KKP) pro Kopf von *Ostasien/Ozeanien insgesamt,* betrug in 2019 im Mittel 15.700 $/a, und lag somit leicht über dem weltweiten Durchschnitts von 14.900 $/a [4, 5].

Die *OECD-Länder* sind bezüglich BIP mit den Industrieländern Europas und Nord-amerikas vergleichbar. *China* hat seit 2000 sein BIP (KKP) pro Kopf nahezu vervierfacht und *Indonesien* um gut 80 % erhöht.

Die Verteilung des BIP/Kopf im *restlichen Ostasien* zeigt Abb 8.4. Durchschnittlich ist es mit 12.200 $/a immer noch deutlich unter dem Weltdurchschnitt. Insgesamt ist im Mittel seit 2000 eine Zunahme um 77 % zu verzeichnen. Hohe Bruttoinlandprodukte pro Kopf über 30.000 $/a weisen lediglich *Singapur, Brunei und Taiwan* auf. Demographische Hauptgewichte sind *Indonesien* (280 Mio.), die *Philippinen* (108 Mio.) und *Vietnam* (je 96 Mio.). Diese drei Länder werden im Kap. 10 näher betrachtet. Einige Angaben über *Thailand* (70 Mio. Einwohner) findet man in Abschn. 10.3.

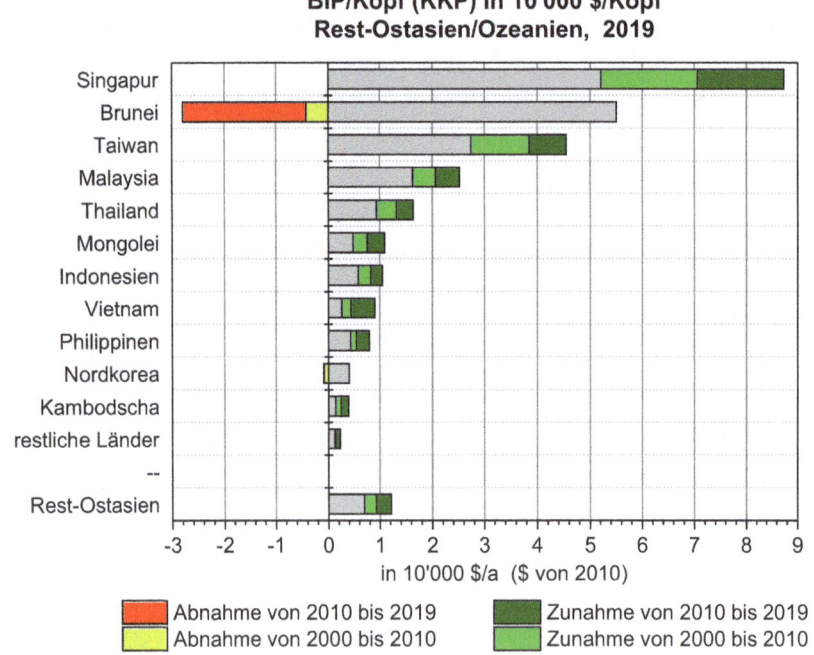

Abb. 8.4 BIP (KKP) pro Kopf der Länder des restlichen Ostasens und Änderungen seit 2000

8.3 Bruttoenergie, Endenergie, Verluste des Energiesektors und entsprechende CO_2-Emissionen, 2019

Die *Endenergie* setzt sich zusammen aus dem Wärmebedarf (aus Brennstoffen, ohne Elektrizität und Fernwärme), den Treibstoffen, der Elektrizität (alle Anwendungen) und der Fernwärme. Die *Bruttoenergie* ist die Summe von Endenergie und *aller im Energiesektor entstehenden Verluste*. Der Energiesektor dient der Umwandlung von Bruttoenergie in Endenergie, wobei die Elektrizitätserzeugung die Hauptrolle spielt.

Die *Energiestruktur* ist in den drei Regionen stark unterschiedlich wie Abb. 8.5 veranschaulicht. Im *industrialisierten OECD-Raum* ist die Endenergie, neben einem hohen Elektrizitäts-Anteil, stark auf Erdöl und Erdgas ausgerichtet. *China* hat, entsprechend ihrem Entwicklungsstand, einen niedrigeren Elektrizitätsanteil und setzt neben Biomasse vor allem auf Kohle. Auch der Mobilitätsbereich ist noch unterentwickelt. Im *restlichen Ostasien* hat sich in den letzten 3 Jahren die Rolle der Biomasse für die Wärmeanwendungen stark reduziert, zu Gunsten der Kohle. Für Industrie und Haushalte spielen hier neben Kohle auch Öl und Erdgas eine wichtiger werdende Rolle.

Die *Verluste des Energiesektors* in Prozent der verwendeten Bruttoenergie betragen 38 % im OECD-Raum, 40 % in China und 36 % im restlichen Ostasien/Ozeanien (als Vergleich: Westeuropa 32 %, Russland 40 %, USA 32 %, Kanada 31 %).

Die **Elektrizitätsproduktion** der drei Regionen ist in Abb. 8.6 veranschaulicht. Vor allem China ist trotz Fortschritte noch sehr einseitig auf Kohle (mit 65 %) ausgerichtet.

Die erneuerbaren Energien (Wasserkraft, Windenergie, Photovoltaik, Biomasse, Abfälle, Geothermie) bzw. die CO_2-armen Energien (erneuerbare Energien + Kernenergie) tragen zur Elektrizitätsproduktion gemäß Tab. 8.1 bei. Die Tabelle gibt auch den Elektrifizierungsgrad der drei Regionen (Elektrizitätsanteil der Endenergie: ist ein guter Index der Entwicklung).

Aus der Energiestruktur ergeben sich für 2019 die in Abb. 8.7 *dargestellten CO_2-Emissionen:*

Gesamtwert *in Mt,* Gesamtwert in *Gramm pro $ BIP KKP* sowie Gesamtwert und detaillierte Verteilung in *Tonnen/Kopf* für die Verbrauchssektoren.

In der Industrie und im Haushalt-/Dienstleitungs-/Landwirtschaftssektor sind die Emissionen durch den Elektrizitäts- und Wärmebedarf aus fossilen Energien bestimmt, im Verkehrsbereich im Wesentlichen durch die auf Erdöl basierenden Treibstoffe. Die Emissionen, die durch die Verluste im Energiesektor entstehen sind in erster Linie der Elektrizitätsproduktion zuzurechnen. In *China* sind die spezifischen Emissionen mit 488 g CO_2/\$ sehr hoch, aber auch der *OECD-Raum* ist mit 9,9 t CO_2/Kopf nicht besonders nachhaltig.

In Kap. 9 findet man nähere Angaben über Japan, Südkorea und Australien sowie über Indonesien, die Philippinen, Vietnam und Thailand.

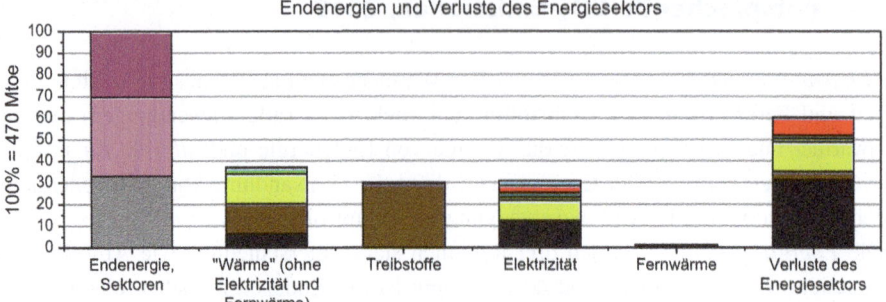

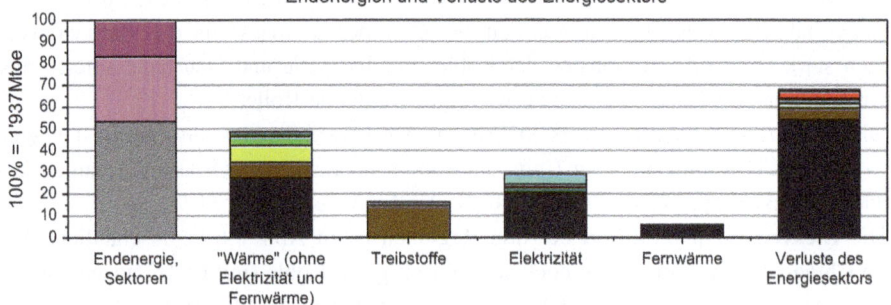

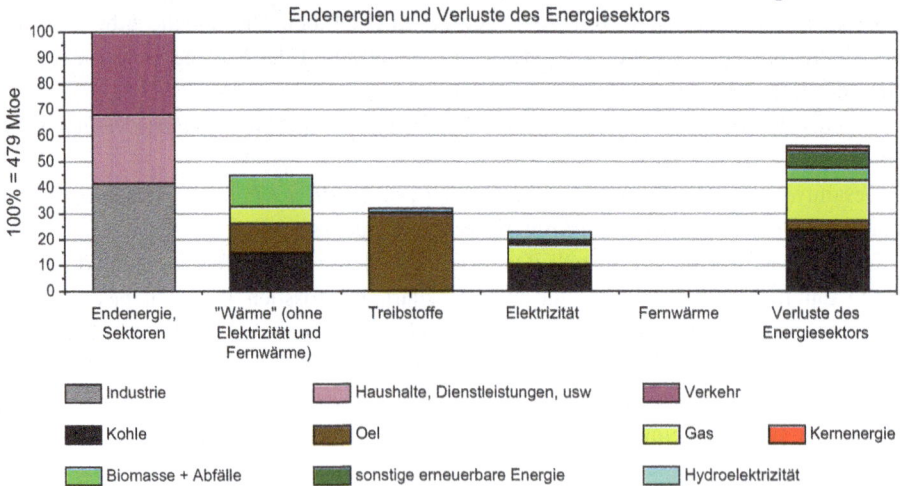

Abb. 8.5 Bruttoenergie = Endenergie + Verluste des Energiesektors, der drei Regionen von Ostasien/Ozeanien in 2019. Die Endenergie setzt sich zusammen aus Wärme, Treibstoffe und Elektrizität

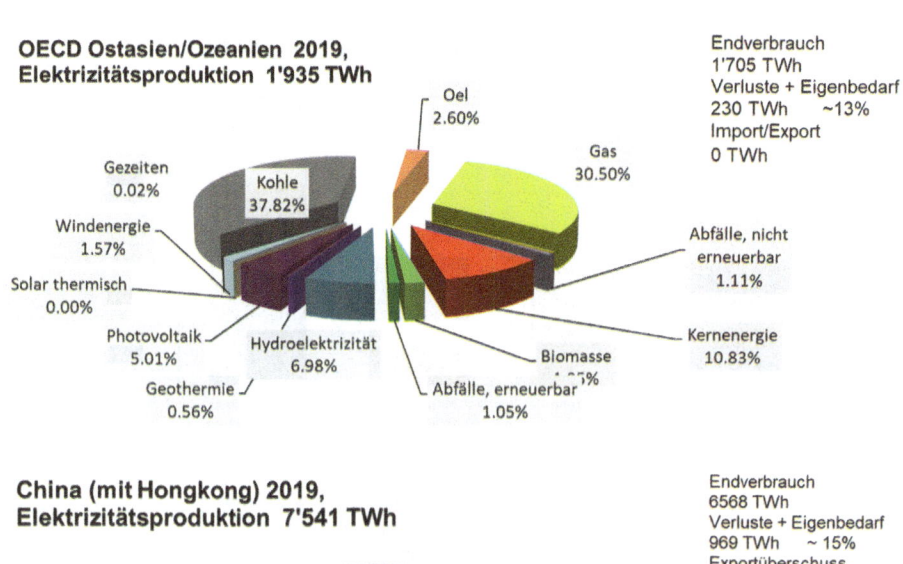

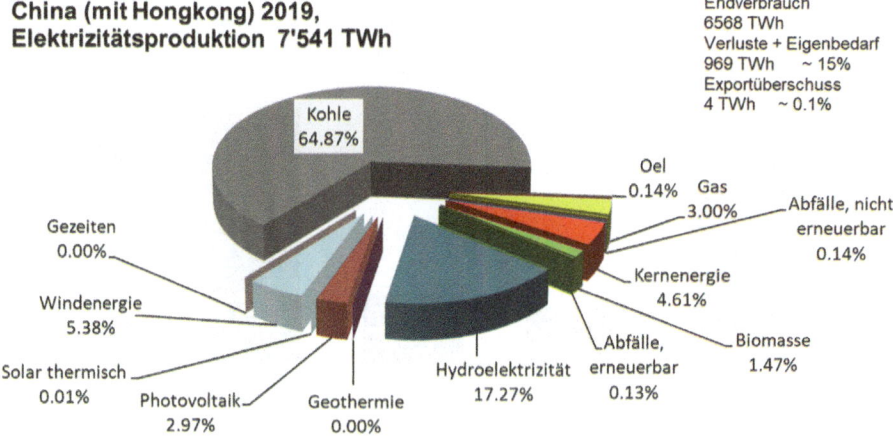

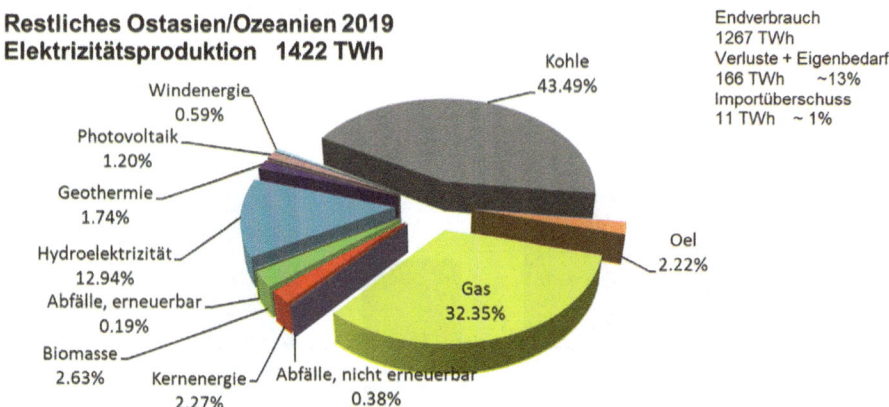

Abb. 8.6 Elektrizitätsproduktion in 2019 der drei Regionen und entsprechende Energieträgeranteile Importüberschuss und Verluste + Eigenbedarf in % des Endverbrauchs

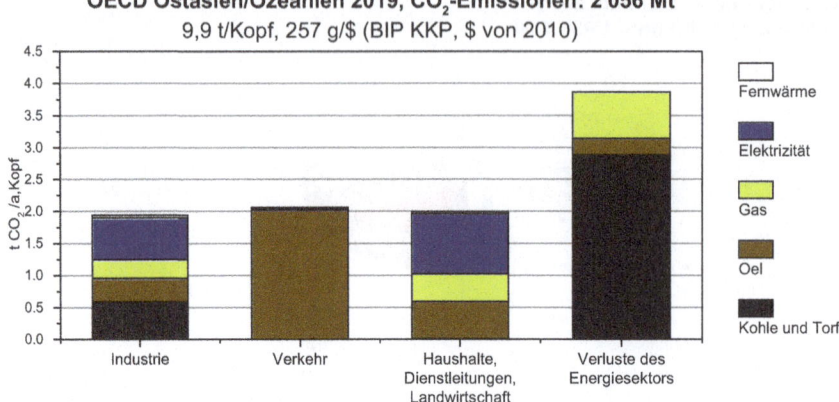

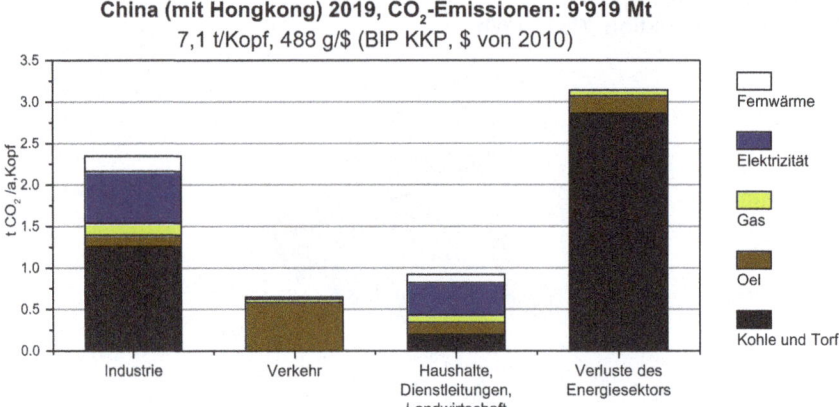

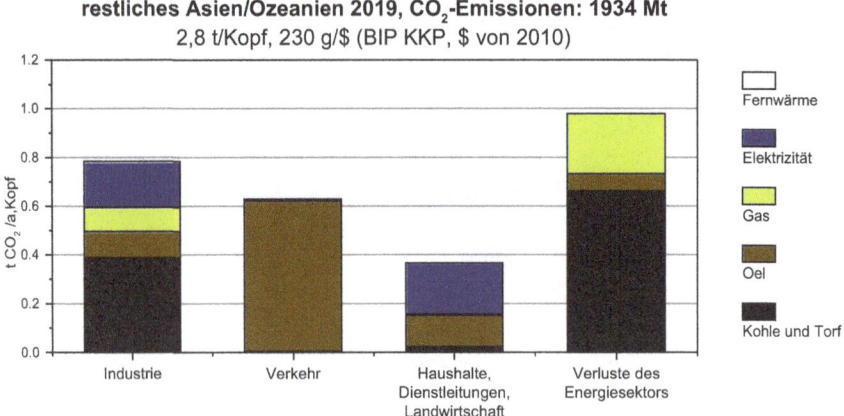

Abb. 8.7 CO_2-Ausstosspro Kopf der drei Regionen nach Verbrauchssektor und Energieträger

Tab. 8.1 Anteil erneuerbarer und CO_2-arme Energien, Elektrifizierungsgrad, in 2019

	Erneuerbar	CO_2-arm	Elektrifizierung
OECD-Ostasien/Ozeanien	17 %	28 %	31 %
China	27 %	32 %	29 %
Restliches Ostasien	19 %	22 %	23 %

8.4 Energieflüsse im Jahr 2019

8.4.1 Energiefluss im Energiesektor

Die entsprechenden Abbildungen für die drei Regionen beschreiben den Energiefluss im Energiesektor von der Primärenergie über die Bruttoenergie (oder Bruttoinlandverbrauch) zur Endenergie. Primärenergie und Bruttoenergie werden durch die verwendeten *Energieträger* veranschaulicht. Alle Energien werden in Mtoe angegeben.

Die **Primärenergie** ist die Summe aus einheimischer Produktion und, für Regionen, Netto-Importe abzüglich Netto-Exporte von Energieträgern (für Länder effektive Importe/Exporte statt nur Netto-Importe/Exporte pro Energieträger).

Die **Bruttoenergie** ergibt sich aus der Primärenergie nach Abzug des nichtenergetischen Bedarfs (z. B. für die chemische Industrie) und eventueller Lagerveränderungen. Abgezogen werden die für die internationale Schiff- und Luftfahrt-Bunker benötigten Energiemengen. Die entsprechenden CO_2-Emissionen werden nur weltweit erfasst.

Es ist die Aufgabe des *Energiesektors*, den Verbrauchern Energie in Form von *Endenergie* zur Verfügung zu stellen. Wir unterscheiden in diesem Diagramm 4 Formen von Endenergie: *Elektrizität, Fernwärme, Treibstoffe* und „*Wärme*". Letztere besteht hauptsächlich aus nichtelektrischer Heizungs- und Prozesswärme (aus fossilen oder erneuerbaren Energien) und ohne Fernwärme. Stationäre Arbeit nichtelektrischen Ursprungs kann ebenfalls enthalten sein (z. B. stationäre Gas- Benzin- oder Dieselmotoren sowie Pumpen); zumindest in Industrieländern ist dieser Anteil jedoch minim. Mit der Umwandlung von Bruttoenergie in Endenergie sind Verluste verbunden, die wir gesamthaft als **Verluste des Energiesektors** bezeichnen.

Diese Verluste setzen sich zusammen aus den *thermischen Verlusten* in Kraftwerken (thermodynamisch bedingt) sowie in Wärme-Kraft-Kopplungsanlagen und in Heizwerken, ferner aus den *elektrischen Verlusten* im Transport- und Verteilungsnetz, einschliesslich elektrischer Eigenbedarf des Energiesektors und schliesslich aus den *Restverlusten* des Energiesektors (in Raffinerien, Verflüssigungs- und Vergasungsanlagen, durch Wärmeübertragung, Wärme-Eigenbedarf usw.).

Das Schema zeigt ferner die mit den Verlusten des Energiesektors und dem Verbrauch der Endenergien verbundenen, also vom Bruttoinlandverbrauch verursachten *CO_2-Emissionen in Mt.* Der grösste Teil der Verluste des Energiesektors ist in der

Regel mit der Elektrizitäts- und Fernwärmeproduktion gekoppelt, weshalb die CO_2-Emissionen dieser drei Faktoren zusammengefasst werden. Eine Trennung kann mithilfe der nachfolgenden Diagramme oder auch von Abb. 8.6 vorgenommen werden.

8.4.2 Energiefluss der Endenergie zu den Endverbrauchern

Die entsprechenden Diagramme zeigen wie sich die 4 Endenergiearten auf die drei Endverbraucherkategorien verteilen. Ebenso werden die CO_2-Emissionen diesen Verbrauchergruppen zugeordnet.

Die Endverbraucher sind (gemäss IEA-Statistik)

- Industrie
- Haushalt, Dienstleistungen, Landwirtschaft etc.
- Verkehr

Zur Bildung der Gesamt-Emissionen werden noch die CO_2-Emissionen der im Energiesektor entstehenden Verluste hinzugefügt.

8.4.3 OECD Ostasien/Ozeanien

Der Energiefluss im Energiesektor von der Primärenergie zur Endenergie und die sich ergebenden totalen CO_2-Emissionen sind in Abb. 8.8 für OECD Ostasien/Ozeanien dargestellt. In Abb. 8.9 wird der Energiefluss der Endenergie zu den Endverbrauchern veranschaulicht und die entsprechenden CO_2-Emissionen sind den Verbrauchersektoren zugeordnet. Insgesamt ist der OECD-Raum ein starker Energieimporteur.

Indikatoren wichtiger Länder von Ostasien/Ozeanien sind in Tab. 8.2 und 8.3 gegeben.

Für Änderungen seit 2016 vergleiche mit Daten in der 2. Auflage dieses Buches.

(weitere Vergleiche g CO_2/$: Westeuropa 130 g CO_2/$, USA 240 g CO_2/$).

Der Indikator g CO_2/$ ergibt sich als Produkt von Energieintensität (abhängig von der Energieeffizienz der Wirtschaft) und CO_2-Intensität der Energie. Hauptsünder bezüglich CO_2-Nachhaltigkeit ist vor allem China mit *über 450 g CO_2/$)* aber auch Australien, Vietnam und Südkorea mit nahezu oder *mehr als 300 g CO_2/$.*

8.4.4 China (mit Hongkong)

Die Diagramme für China, für den Energiefluss im Energiesektor und für den Fluss der Endenergie zu den Verbrauchssektoren, sind in den Abb. 8.10 und 8.11 dargestellt. China

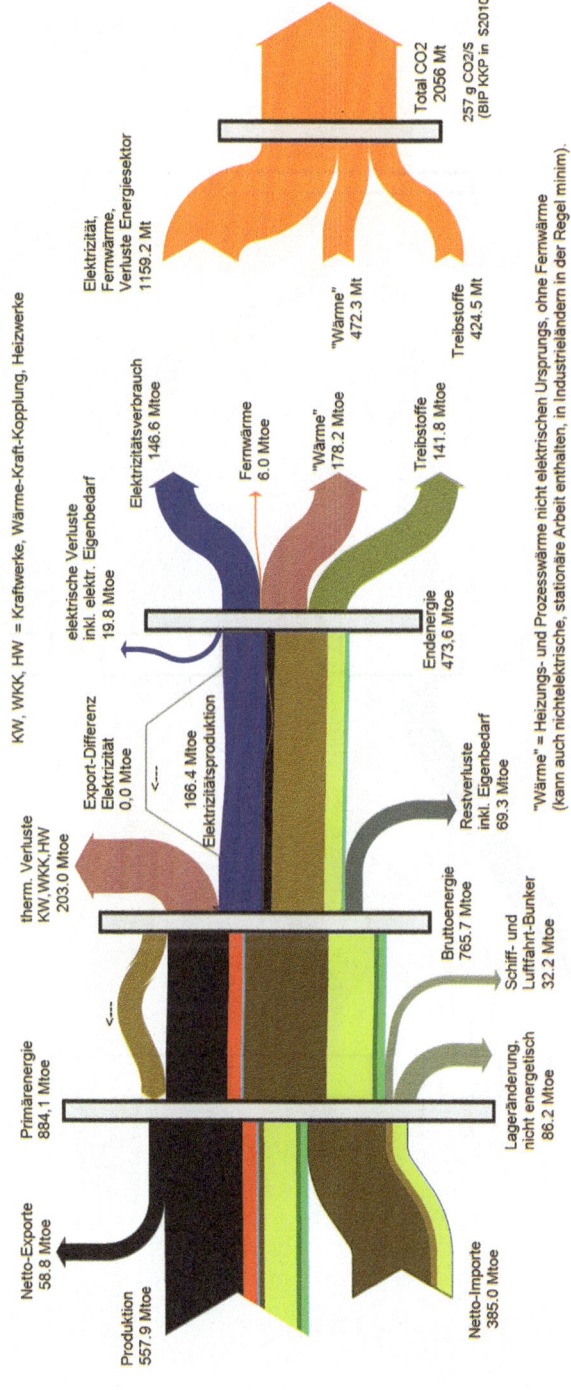

Abb. 8.8 OECD Ostasien/Ozeanien: Energiefluss im Energiesektor von der Primärenergie zur Endenergie und CO_2-Ausstoss. Die Energieträgerfarben sind wie in Abb. 8.5 und 8.7 (aber Erdöl dunkelbraun, Erdölprodukte hellbraun)

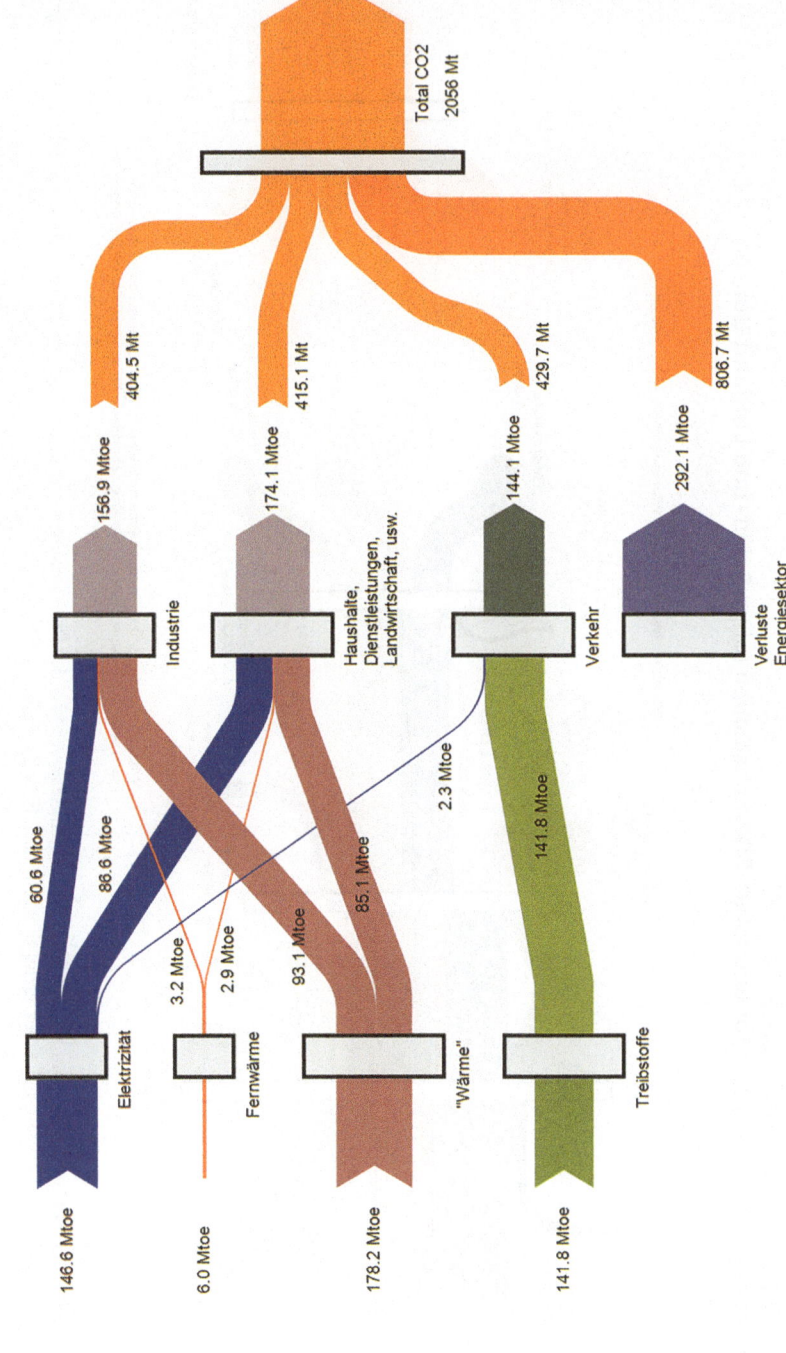

OECD Ostasien/Ozeanien, 2019
Energiefluss der Endenergie und totaler CO2-Ausstoss (ohne Schiff- und Luftfahrt-Bunker)

Abb. 8.9   OECD Ostasien/Ozeanien: Energiefluss der Endenergie zu den Endverbrauchern und zugeordnete CO_2-Emissionen

Tab. 8.2 Vergleich der Indikatoren in 2019 ($ von 2010),

	OECD-Länder	China	Rest-Ostasien	Ostasien/Ozeanien insgesamt
kWh/$	1,09	1,84	1,02	1,49
g CO_2/kWh	235	266	224	254
g CO_2/$	257	488	230	379
BIP (KKP) $ pro Kopf,a	38.400	14.500	12.200	15.900
t CO_2/Kopf,a	9,9	7,1	2,8	6,0

kWh/$ = Energieintensität

g CO_2/kWh = CO_2-Intensität der Energie

g CO_2/$ = Maßstab für die Nachhaltigkeit der Wirtschaft bezüglich CO_2-Emissionen (kurz: Indikator der CO_2-Nachhaltigkeit)

Tab. 8.3 Prozentualer Anteil der *erneuerbaren* und *CO_2-armen Elektrizitätsproduktion,* im Jahr 2019, in den bevölkerungsreichsten Ländern von Ostasien und Ozeanien, sowie *Indikator der CO_2-Nachhaltigkeit in g CO_2/$*

	Erneuerbare Energien	CO_2-arme Energien	g CO_2/$ (BIP KKP)
China	27 %	32 %	488
Australien	20 %	20 %	332
Vietnam	31 %	31 %	325
Südkorea	5 %	30 %	297
Thailand	18 %	18 %	251
Japan	19 %	25 %	225
Indonesien	17 %	17 %	205
Philippinen	21 %	21 %	158

CO_2-arme Energien = erneuerbare Energien + Kernenergie

produziert Kohle für den Eigenbedarf, ist insgesamt 2019 aber auf Öl- und Gasimporte angewiesen.

8.4.5 Restliches Ostasien/Ozeanien

Dasselbe gilt auch für die in den Abb. 8.12 und 8.13 dargestellten Diagramme der Energieflüsse des restlichen Ostasiens. Importe und Exporte sind insgesamt hier nahezu ausgeglichen, Ölimporte sind notwendig.

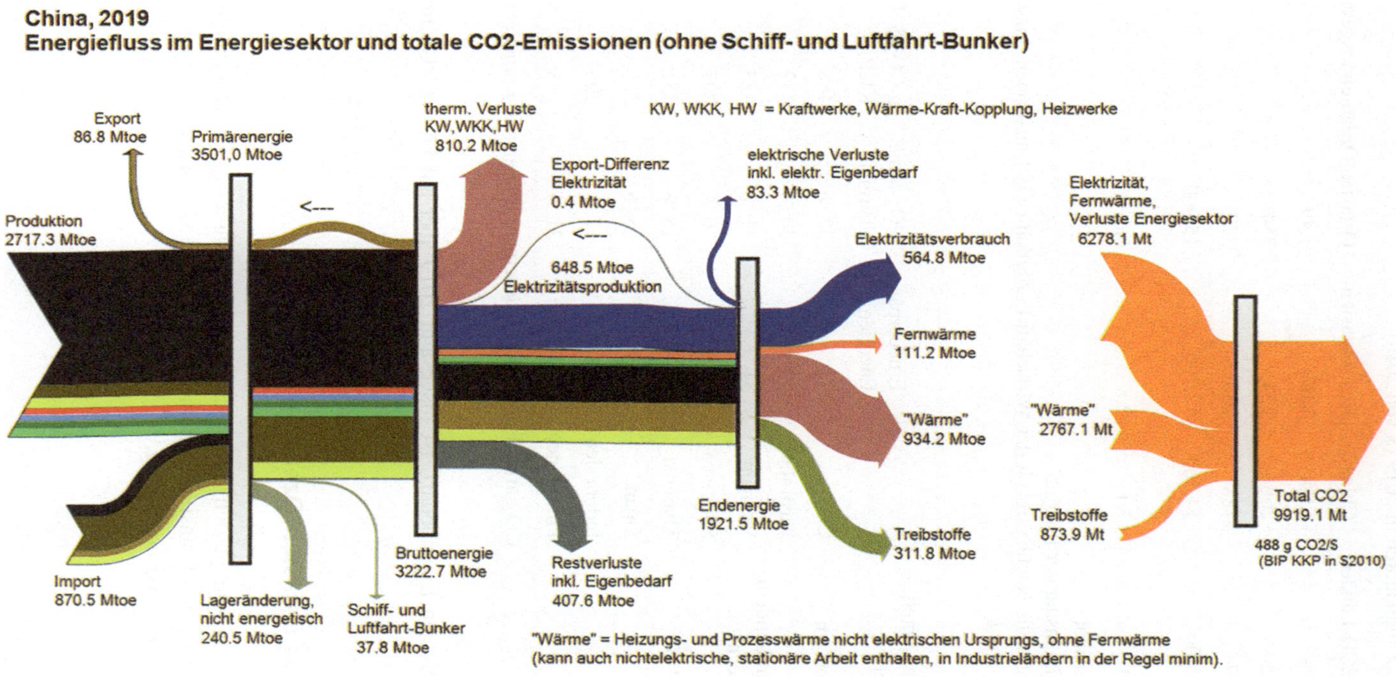

Abb. 8.10 China (mit Hongkong): Energiefluss im Energiesektor von der Primärenergie zur Endenergie und CO_2-Ausstoss. Die Energieträgerfarben sind wie in Abb. 8.5 und 8.7 (Erdöl dunkelbraun, Erdölprodukte hellbraun)

China, 2019
Energiefluss im Energiesektor und totale CO2-Emissionen (ohne Schiff- und Luftfahrt-Bunker)

KW, WKK, HW = Kraftwerke, Wärme-Kraft-Kopplung, Heizwerke

elektrische Verluste
inkl. elektr. Eigenbedarf
83.3 Mtoe

Elektrizität,
Fernwärme,
Verluste Energiesektor
6278.1 Mt

Total CO2
9919.1 Mt

488 g CO2/S
(BIP KKP in $2010)

"Wärme"
2767.1 Mt

Treibstoffe
873.9 Mt

Elektrizitätsverbrauch
564.8 Mtoe

Fernwärme
111.2 Mtoe

"Wärme"
934.2 Mtoe

Treibstoffe
311.8 Mtoe

Endenergie
1921.5 Mtoe

Export-Differenz
Elektrizität
0.4 Mtoe

648.5 Mtoe
Elektrizitätsproduktion

therm. Verluste
KW,WKK,HW
810.2 Mtoe

Restverluste
inkl. Eigenbedarf
407.6 Mtoe

Bruttoenergie
3222.7 Mtoe

Primärenergie
3501.0 Mtoe

Export
86.8 Mtoe

Schiff- und
Luftfahrt-Bunker
37.8 Mtoe

Lageränderung,
nicht energetisch
240.5 Mtoe

Import
870.5 Mtoe

Produktion
2717.3 Mtoe

"Wärme" = Heizungs- und Prozesswärme nicht elektrischen Ursprungs, ohne Fernwärme
(kann auch nichtelektrische, stationäre Arbeit enthalten, in Industrieländern in der Regel minim).

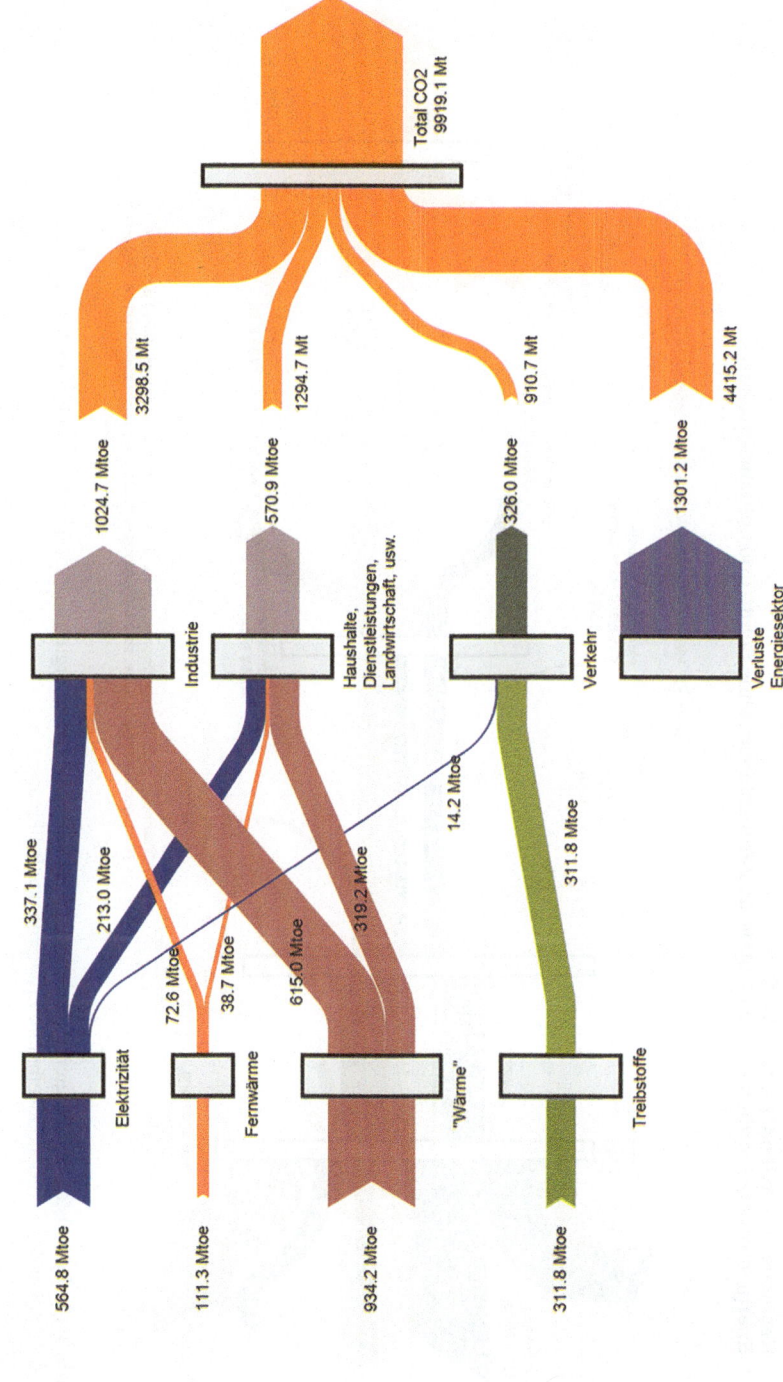

China, 2019
Energiefluss der Endenergie und totaler CO2-Ausstoss (ohne Schiff- und Luftfahrt-Bunker)

Abb. 8.11 China (mit Hongkong): Energiefluss der Endenergie zu den Endverbrauchern und zugeordnete CO$_2$-Emissionen

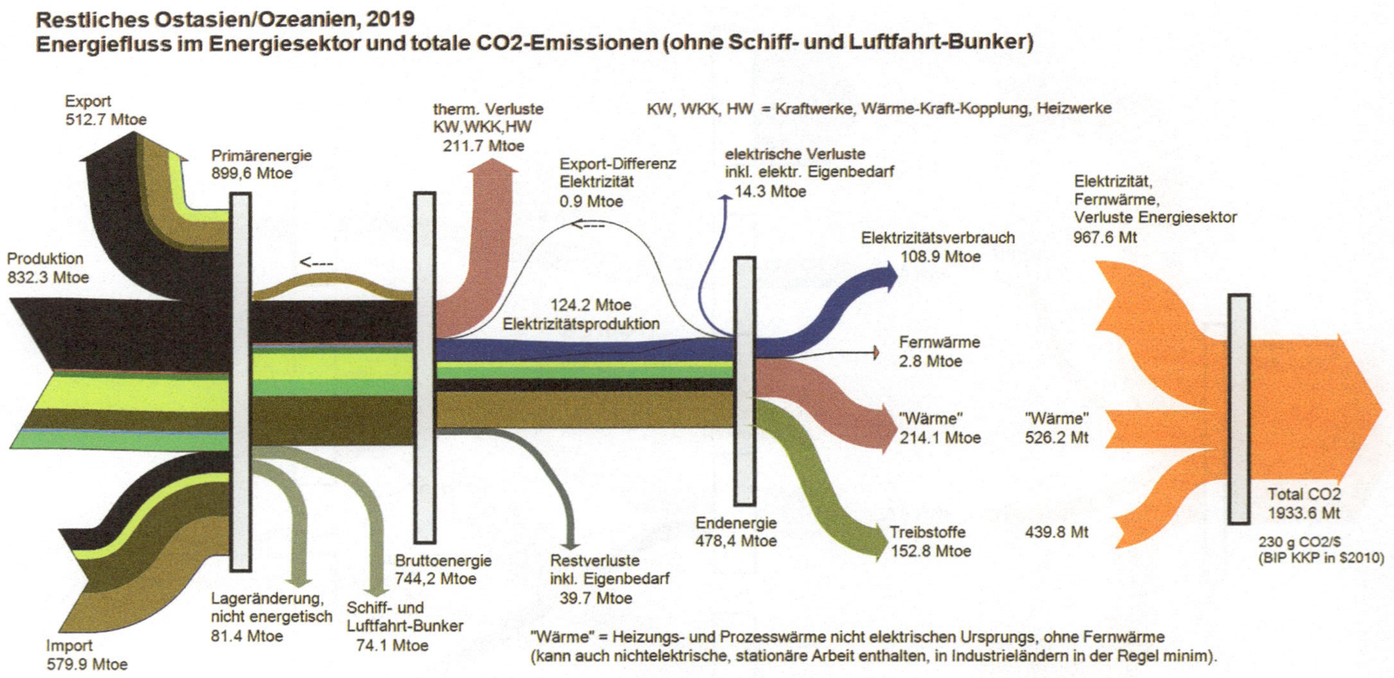

Restliches Ostasien/Ozeanien, 2019
Energiefluss im Energiesektor und totale CO2-Emissionen (ohne Schiff- und Luftfahrt-Bunker)

KW, WKK, HW = Kraftwerke, Wärme-Kraft-Kopplung, Heizwerke

Export
512.7 Mtoe

Produktion
832.3 Mtoe

Primärenergie
899.6 Mtoe

therm. Verluste
KW,WKK,HW
211.7 Mtoe

Export-Differenz
Elektrizität
0.9 Mtoe

124.2 Mtoe
Elektrizitätsproduktion

Bruttoenergie
744.2 Mtoe

Schiff- und
Lufffahrt-Bunker
74.1 Mtoe

Lageränderung,
nicht energetisch
81.4 Mtoe

Import
579.9 Mtoe

elektrische Verluste
inkl. elektr. Eigenbedarf
14.3 Mtoe

Elektrizitätsverbrauch
108.9 Mtoe

Fernwärme
2.8 Mtoe

"Wärme"
214.1 Mtoe

Treibstoffe
152.8 Mtoe

Endenergie
478.4 Mtoe

Restverluste
inkl. Eigenbedarf
39.7 Mtoe

Elektrizität,
Fernwärme,
Verluste Energiesektor
967.6 Mt

"Wärme"
526.2 Mt

439.8 Mt

Total CO2
1933.6 Mt

230 g CO2/$
(BIP KKP in $2010)

"Wärme" = Heizungs- und Prozesswärme nicht elektrischen Ursprungs, ohne Fernwärme
(kann auch nichtelektrische, stationäre Arbeit enthalten, in Industrieländern in der Regel minim).

Abb. 8.12 Rest-Ostasien: Energiefluss im Energiesektor von der Primärenergie zur Endenergie und CO₂-Ausstoss. Die Energieträgerfarben sind wie in Abb. 8.5 und 8.7 (Erdöl dunkelbraun, Erdölprodukte hellbraun)

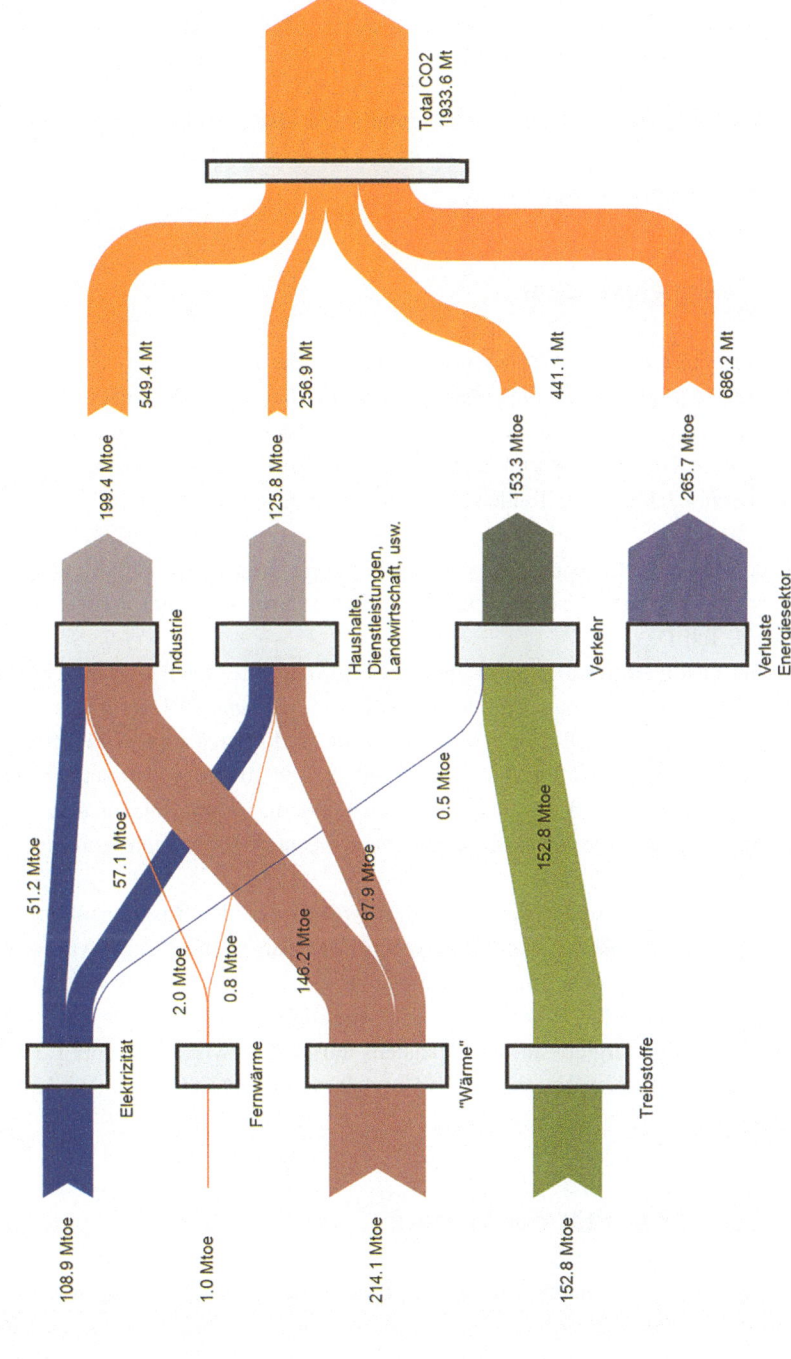

Restliches Ostasien/Ozeanien, 2019
Energiefluss der Endenergie und totaler CO2-Ausstoss (ohne Schiff- und Luftfahrt-Bunker)

Abb. 8.13 Rest-Ostasien/Ozeanien: Energiefluss der Endenergie zu den Endverbrauchern und zugeordnete CO_2-Emissionen

8.4.6   Ostasien/Ozeanien insgesamt

Die Abb. 8.14 und 8.15 erhält man durch Aufsummierung der Flüsse der drei Regionen. Für die Elektrizitätserzeugung und den Wärmebereich, unter anderem wegen des starken Gewichts Chinas, hat die Kohle einen erheblichen Anteil. Die Handelsbilanz von Ostasien/Ozeanien weist insgesamt Energieimporte auf (vor allem Öl). Tab. 8.2 vergleicht die Indikatoren der drei Regionen.

8.5   Energieintensität

Bevölkerungsreichster Staat von Fern-Asien ist *China* und dessen Entwicklung deshalb für die Region von grundlegender Bedeutung. Die Energieintensität Chinas ist mit 1,84 kWh/\$ (Abb. 8.16) angesichts des Entwicklungsstandes immer noch sehr hoch. Die ausgezeichnete Effizienz-Entwicklung von 2000 bis 2010 hat seit 2010 nachgelassen und in den letzten 4 Jahren eine Tendenzinversion erfahren.

Auch *Australien, Neuseeland und Südkorea* weisen, trotz Fortschritte, eine für Industrieländer noch ungenügende Effizienz des Energieeinsatzes auf (Westeuropa deutlich weniger als 1 kWh/\$). Sie entspricht eher den nordamerikanischen Verhältnissen (USA 1,4 kWh/\$, Teil I).

Die vier bevölkerungsreichsten Länder des *restlichen Ostasien* (Abb. 8.17) sind Indonesien, die Philippinen, Thailand und Vietnam, die *zusammen 79 % der Bevölkerung* der Region ausmachen und 68 % des BIP erbringen. Indonesien und die Philippinen weisen ein gute Effizienz und gute Fortschritte auf. Seit 2010 haben sich auch Thailand und Vietnam verbessert. Von den industrialisierten Ländern, weist Singapur eine gute Effizienz aus und Taiwan gute Fortschritte auf. Verschlechtert haben sich Nordkorea und vor allem Brunei.

In Abb. 8.18 wird schließlich für *Ostasien/Ozeanien* der Zusammenhang zwischen *Energieintensität und Bruttoinlandprodukt pro Kopf* dargestellt. Bei schwacher Entwicklung ist weltweit allgemein eine starke Streuung der Energieintensität feststellbar. Diese hängt stark von den lokalen Verhältnissen ab (verfügbare Energieträger). Bei zunehmendem Wohlstand konvergiert sie dann meistens auf Werte zwischen 1 und 1,5 kWh/\$. In Zukunft müsste die Energieintensität aus Umwelt- und Klimaschutzgründen deutlich unter 1 kWh/\$ sinken.

8.6 CO_2-Intensität der Energie

Anders als bei der Energieintensität ist bei Unterentwicklung in der Regel ein eher niedriger Wert der CO_2-Intensität der Energie zu erwarten, was mit dem stark auf Biomasse ausgerichteten Energieverbrauch zusammenhängt (Abb. 8.19). Zunehmende Entwicklung

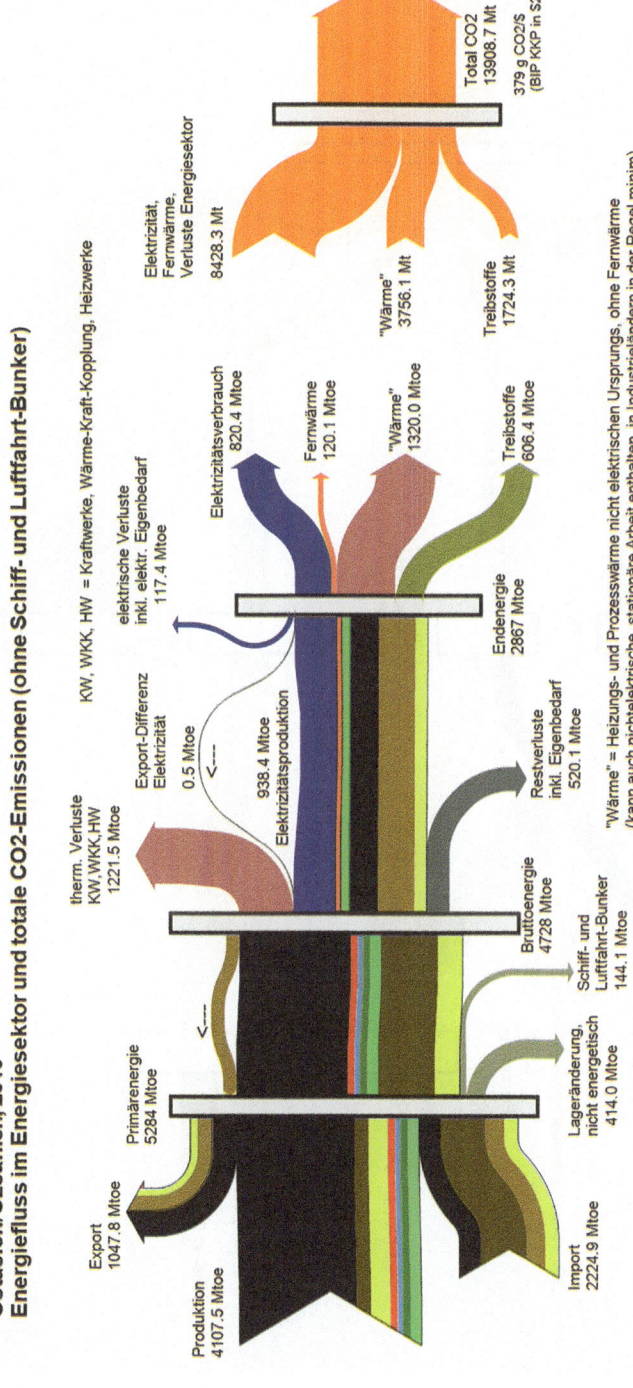

Abb. 8.14 Ostasien/Ozeanien: Energiefluss im Energiesektor von der Primärenergie zur Endenergie und CO₂-Ausstoss. Die Energieträgerfarben sind wie in Abb. 8.5 und 8.7 (Erdöl dunkelbraun, Erdölprodukte hellbraun)

Ostasien/Ozeanien, 2019
Energiefluss im Energiesektor und totale CO2-Emissionen (ohne Schiff- und Lufffahrt-Bunker)

KW, WKK, HW = Kraftwerke, Wärme-Kraft-Kopplung, Heizwerke

Export
1047.8 Mtoe

Produktion
4107.5 Mtoe

Primärenergie
5284 Mtoe

therm. Verluste
KW,WKK,HW
1221.5 Mtoe

Export-Differenz
Elektrizität
0.5 Mtoe

938.4 Mtoe
Elektrizitätsproduktion

elektrische Verluste
inkl. elektr. Eigenbedarf
117.4 Mtoe

Elektrizitätsverbrauch
820.4 Mtoe

Fernwärme
120.1 Mtoe

"Wärme"
1320.0 Mtoe

Treibstoffe
606.4 Mtoe

Bruttoenergie
4728 Mtoe

Schiff- und
Lufffahrt-Bunker 144.1 Mtoe

Lageränderung,
nicht energetisch
414.0 Mtoe

Import
2224.9 Mtoe

Restverluste
inkl. Eigenbedarf
520.1 Mtoe

Endenergie
2867 Mtoe

Elektrizität,
Fernwärme,
Verluste Energiesektor
8428.3 Mt

"Wärme"
3756.1 Mt

Treibstoffe
1724.3 Mt

Total CO2
13908.7 Mt

379 g CO2/$
(BIP KKP in $2010)

"Wärme" = Heizungs- und Prozesswärme nicht elektrischen Ursprungs, ohne Fernwärme
(kann auch nichtelektrische, stationäre Arbeit enthalten, in Industrieländern in der Regel minim).

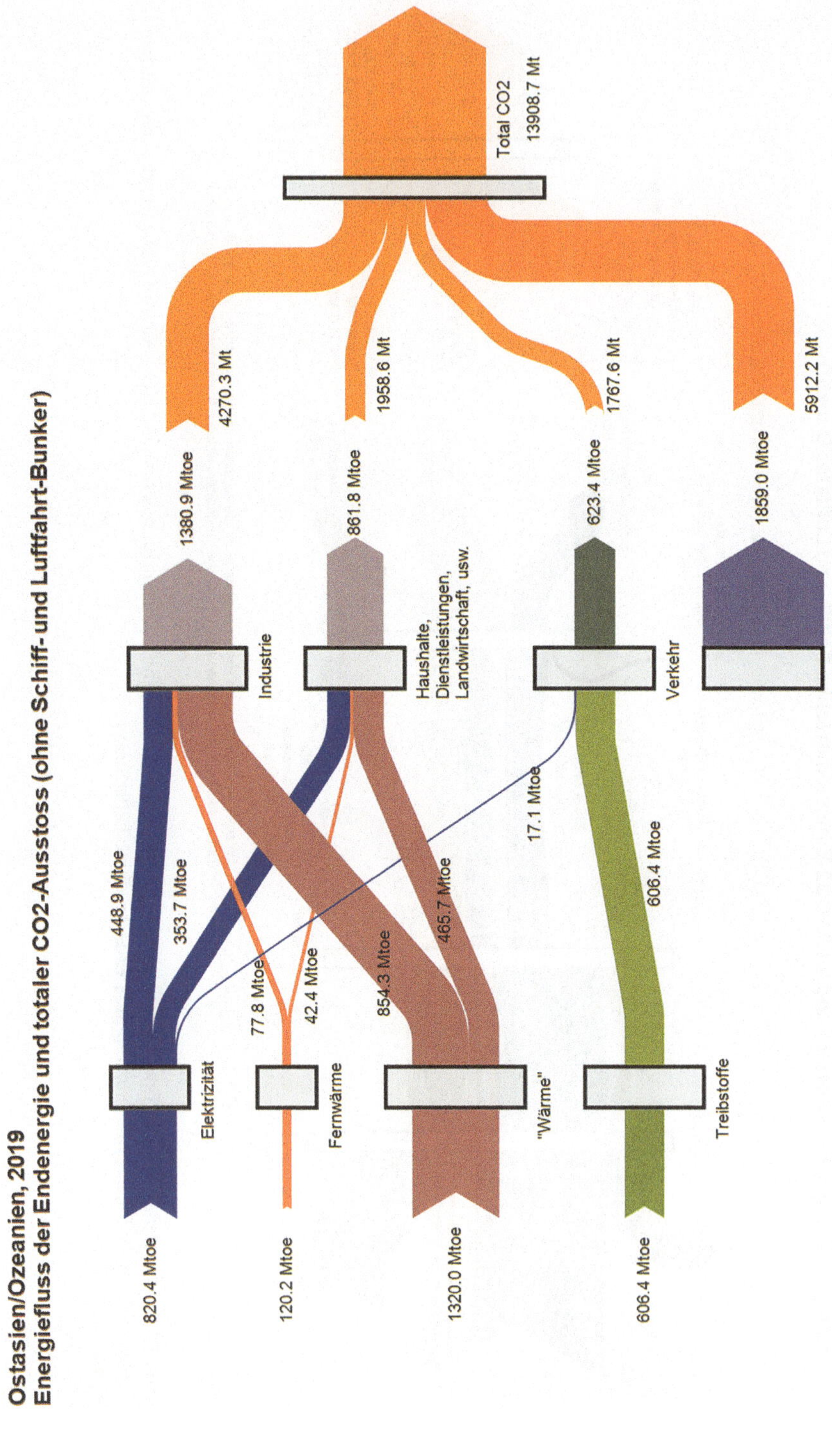

Abb. 8.15 Ostasien/Ozeanien: Energiefluss der Endenergie zu den Endverbrauchern und zugeordnete CO_2-Emissionen

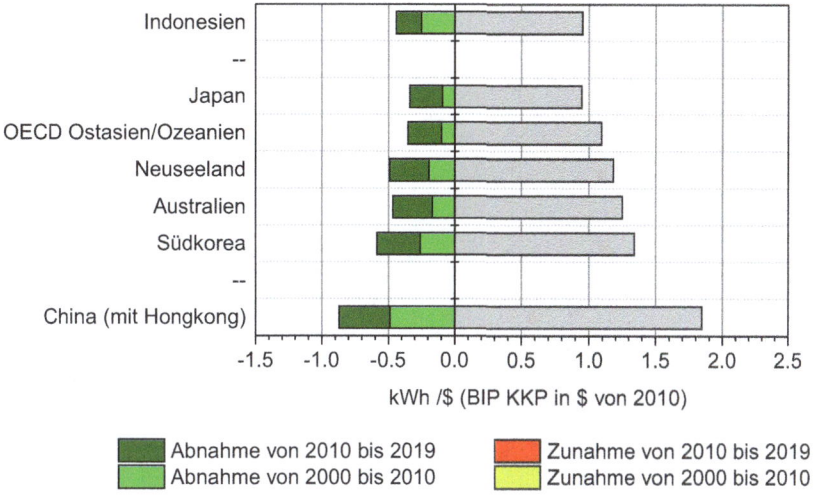

Abb. 8.16   Energieintensität von OECD Ostasien/Ozeanien, China und Indonesien, Fortschritte seit 2000

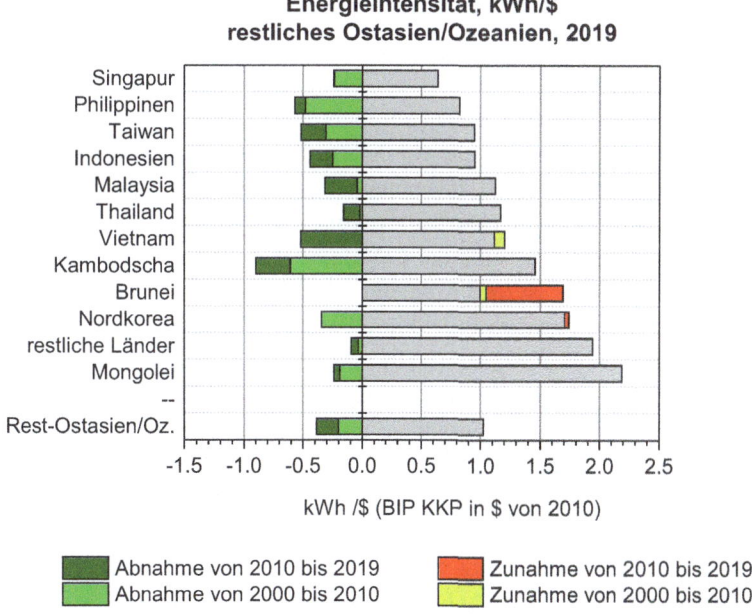

Abb. 8.17   Energieintensität der Länder von Rest-Ostasien und Änderungen seit 2000

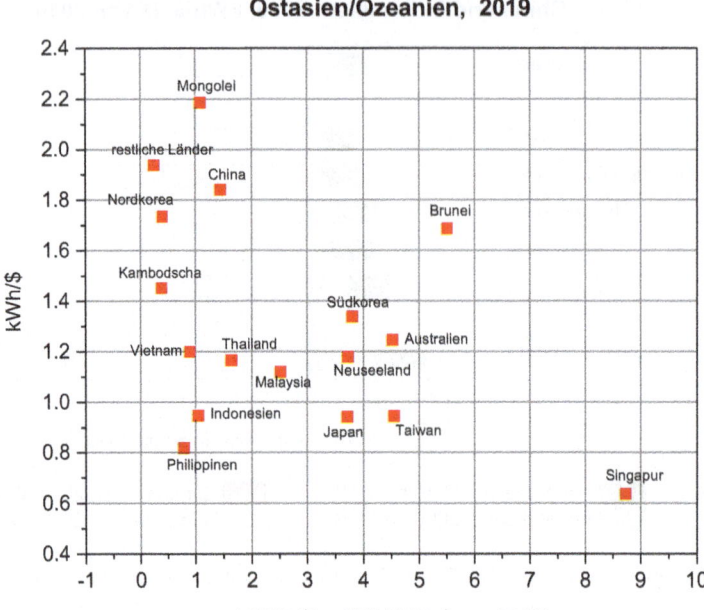

Abb. 8.18 Energieintensität der Länder Ostasien/Ozeaniens in Abhängigkeit vom BIP KKP pro Kopf ($ von 2010), in 2019

führt zunächst zum vermehrten Verbrauch fossiler Brennstoffe und somit zu einer Erhöhung der CO_2-Intensität der Energie (s. Indonesien). Dies zeigt sich auch in *China* wo diese CO_2-Intensität seit 2000 zugenommen hat (Abb. 8.20) und 250 g CO_2/kWh deutlich überschritten hat. Die leichte Verbesserung seit 2010 ist ein hoffnungsvolles Zeichen. Bei höherem Wohlstand sollte die CO_2 Intensität wieder abnehmen, wie dies im *OECD-Raum* leicht der Fall ist (mit Ausnahme des gewichtigen Japan). Die Zunahme in Japan (Abb. 8.20) hängt mit dem Fukushima-Unfall und nachfolgender Abstellung von Kernkraftwerken zusammen.

Die meisten Länder des *restlichen Ostasien* verhalten sich mehr oder weniger nach diesem Schema und befinden sich insgesamt noch in der Zunahme-Phase wie Abb. 8.21 zeigt. Insgesamt steigt die CO_2-Intensität der Energie deutlich über 200 g CO_2/kWh. Von 2010 bis 2019 fallen insbesondere Vietnam, Indonesien und Kambodscha negativ auf. Positiv ist die Entwicklung in Singapur und Brunei.

Im Hinblick auf den Klimaschutz wäre es angebracht zu versuchen, diesen Indikator in Rest-Ostasien bis 2030 auf etwa 200 g CO_2/kWh oder weniger zu stabilisieren und

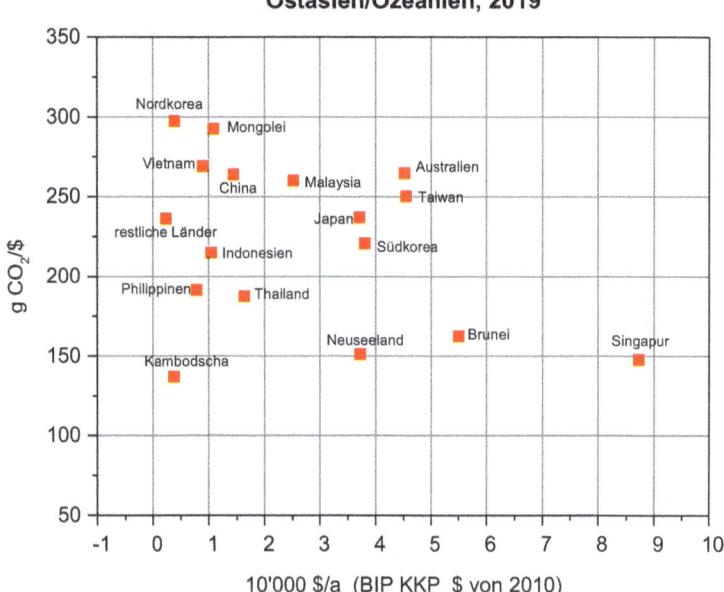

Abb. 8.19 CO_2-Intensität der Energie in Ostasien/Ozeanien in Abhängigkeit vom BIP KKP pro Kopf (in $ von 2010)

dann durch stärkere Gewichtung erneuerbarer Energien vor allem bei der Elektrizitäts-produktion (Geothermie, Wasser, Wind und Sonne evtl. auch von Kernenergie) bis 2050 empfindlich zu reduzieren (s. Kap. 9).

8.7 Indikator der CO$_2$-Nachhaltigkeit

Die Nachhaltigkeit der Energieversorgung bezüglich CO$_2$-Ausstoss wird durch das Produkt von Energieintensität und CO$_2$-Intensität der Energie gut charakterisiert und somit durch den *Indikator g CO$_2$/$*.

In 2019 ist der Durchschnittswert von Gesamt-Ostasien/Ozeanien mit rund 380 g CO$_2$/$, wesentlich höher als der Weltdurchschnitt von 290 g CO$_2$/$. Bedingt ist er durch den extrem hohen Wert von *China* (Abb. 8.22). In China sind in den letzten Jahren, nach erfreulichen Fortschritten bis 2016, wieder Rückschritte festzustellen. Auch *Australien* und *Südkorea* müssen weiterhin empfindlich nachbessern. Auch das gewichtige *Indonesien* sollte die Tendenz umkehren.

Etwas nachhaltiger ist insgesamt das *restliche Ostasien* (Abb. 8.23) mit im Mittel 215 g CO$_2$/$, in erster Linie dank der abnehmenden Tendenz der Energieintensität (Abb. 8.17).

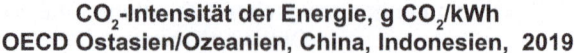

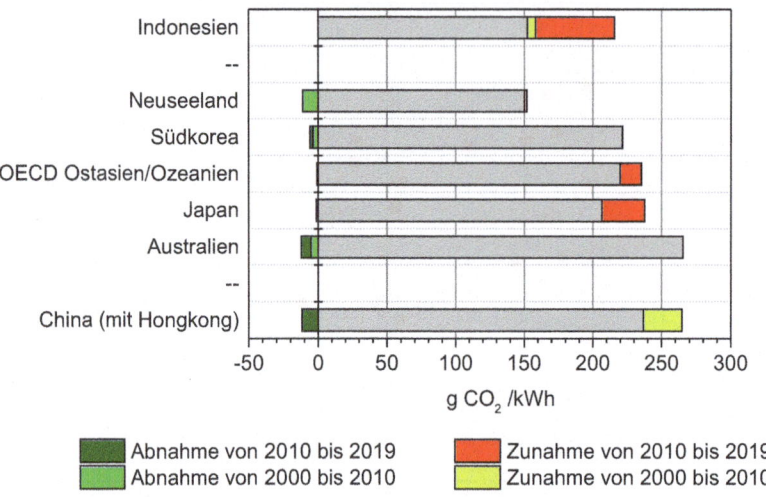

Abb. 8.20 CO_2-Intensität der Energie von OECD Ostasien/Ozeanien, China und Indonesien, Änderungen seit 2000

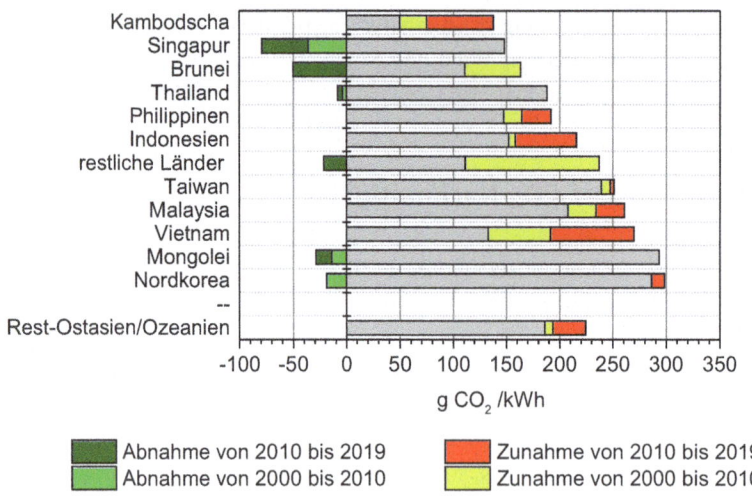

Abb. 8.21 CO_2-Intensität der Energie der Länder des restlichen Ostasien/Ozeanien und Änderungen seit 2000

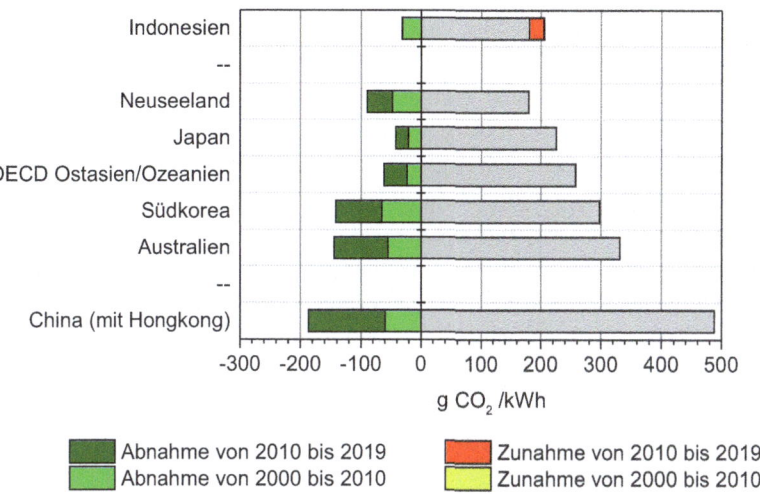

Abb. 8.22 Indikator der CO_2-Nachhaltigkeit von OECD Ostasien/Ozeanien, China und Indonesien, Änderungen seit 2000

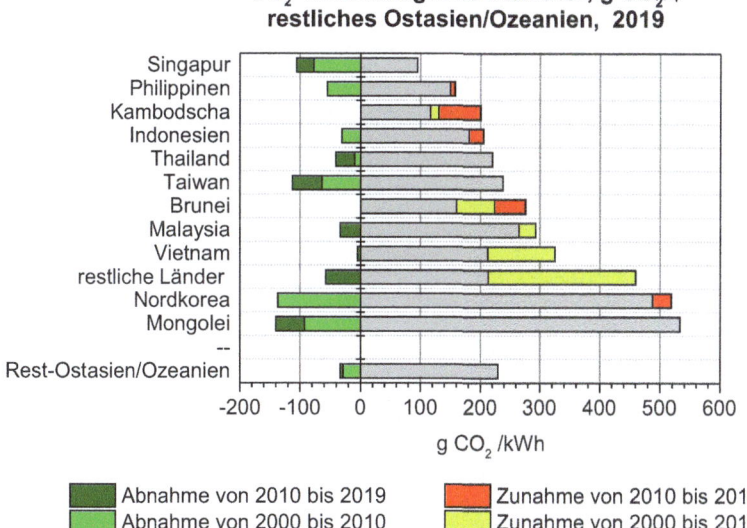

Abb. 8.22 Indikator der CO_2-Nachhaltigkeit des restlichen Ostasien in 2019 und Änderungen seit 2000

Umkehren muss die Tendenz der CO_2-Intensität der Energie (Abb. 8.21). Eine maßgebende Rolle spielt hier Indonesien. Bis 2030 sollte man, um die Klimaschutz-Bedingungen zu erfüllen, einen Wert von höchstens 140 g CO_2/$ anpeilen (Kap. 9).

Schließlich veranschaulicht die Abb. 8.24 für *Ostasien/Ozeanien* den statistischen Zusammenhang zwischen CO_2-Nachhaltigkeit und Bruttoinlandprodukt pro Kopf. Schwach entwickelte Länder sind zwar mehrheitlich, dank Biomasse oder Wasserkraft, bezüglich CO_2-Ausstoss unter 200 g CO_2/$ und somit vorerst noch relativ nachhaltig. Ausnahmen sind Länder mit starkem Kohleanteil bei der Stromerzeugung (wie China, Nordkorea, Vietnam und die Mongolei) und/oder mit schlechter Energieeffizienz. Trotz fortschreitender wirtschaftlicher Entwicklung wäre es angebracht, entsprechend den Klimaschutz-Vorgaben, bis 2030 Werte deutlich unter 250 g CO_2/$ anzupeilen (Kap. 9). Dies gilt auch für alle heute schon stark entwickelten OECD-Länder, durch stärkere Förderung erneuerbarer Energien und gegebenenfalls durch Kernenergie oder CCS (Carbon Capture and Storage).

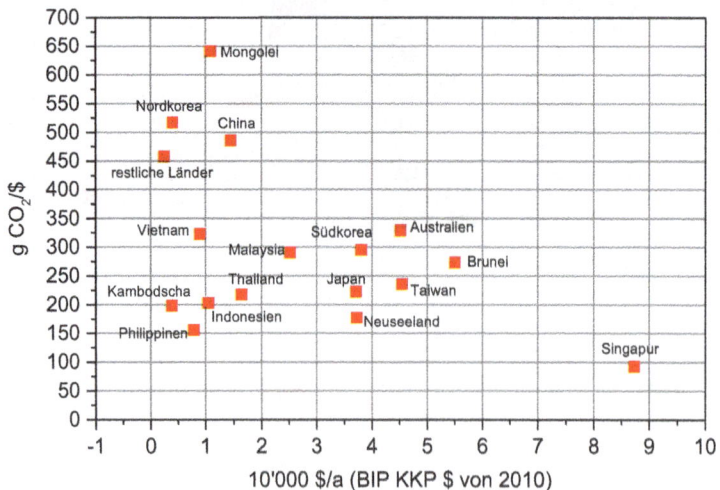

Abb. 8.24 CO_2-Nachhaltigkeit der Länder Ostasien/Ozeaniens in Abhängigkeit vom BIP KKP pro Kopf

CO$_2$-Emissionen und Indikatoren von 1980 bis 2019 und notwendige Szenarien zur Einhaltung des 2-Grad- bzw. 1,5-Grad-Ziels

9

9.1 Ostasien/Ozeanien

Mit dem 2-Grad- und 1,5-Grad-Ziel (s. Kap. 1) kompatible Szenarien bis 2050 für den OECD-Raum von Ostasien/Ozeanien zeigt die Abb. 9.1. Der entsprechende Verlauf der Indikatoren ist in Abb. 9.2 wiedergegeben. Der OECD-Raum schliesst ein: Japan, Südkorea, Australien und Neuseeland.

Eine weitere Abnahme der Energieintensität ist notwendig, aber vor allem eine Reduktion der eher stagnierenden oder gar zunehmenden CO$_2$-Intensität der Energie, durch Förderung erneuerbarer Energien und Reduktion der starken Kohle-Anteile bei der Elektrizitätsproduktion.

Die dazu notwendigen prozentualen jährlichen Änderungen bis 2030 für die beiden Varianten sind detaillierter in Abb. 9.3 wiedergegeben. Die Zunahme der CO$_2$-Intensität seit 2011 ist eine Folge des Fukushima-Unfalls (Abstellung von Kernkraftwerken in Japan).

Der zugehörige Verlauf der pro Kopf Indikatoren für das kaufkraftbereinigte Bruttoinlandprodukt, die Bruttoenergie und den CO$_2$-Ausstoss ist schliesslich in Abb. 9.4 dargestellt, für 1980 bis 2019 und entsprechend dem beiden Klimaschutz-Szenarien.

9.2 China (mit Hongkong)

Mit dem 2-Grad- und 1,5-Grad-Ziel (s. Kap. 1) kompatible Szenarien bis 2050 für China zeigt Abb. 9.5. Der entsprechende Verlauf der Indikatoren ist in Abb. 9.6 wiedergegeben.

China hat mit 488 g CO$_2$/\$ den weltweit schlechtesten *CO$_2$-Nachhaltigkeitsindikator*. Um bis 2030 auf Werte unter 200 g CO/\$ zu gelangen (Abb. 9.6) müsste die abnehmende Tendenz seit 2005 verschärft werden. Dies durch weitere Verbesserung der

© Springer Fachmedien Wiesbaden GmbH, ein Teil von Springer Nature 2023
V. Crastan, *Kennzahlen zur Erreichung der weltweiten Klimaziele*,
https://doi.org/10.1007/978-3-658-40073-6_9

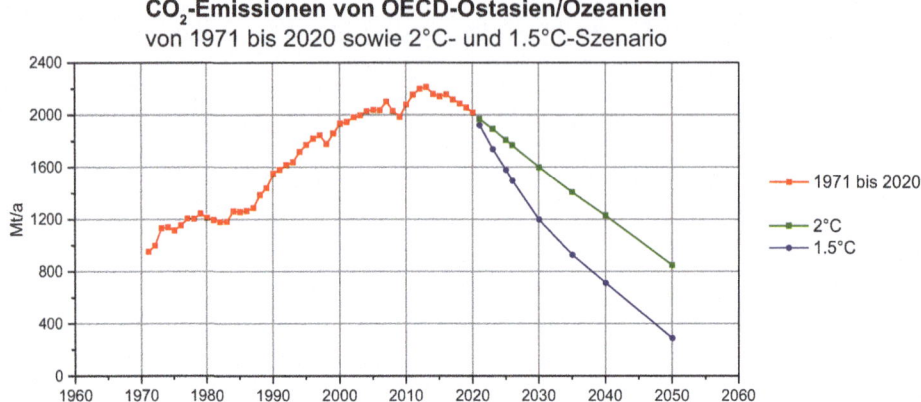

Abb. 9.1 Mit dem 2-Grad- und 1,5-Grad-Ziel kompatible Szenarien für OECD Ostasien/Ozeanien

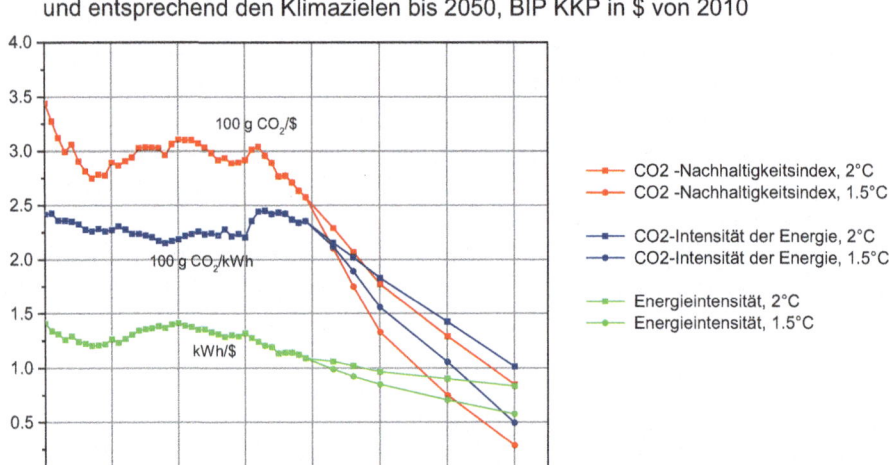

Abb. 9.2 Indikatoren-Verlauf von 1980 bis 2019 und mit dem 2-Grad bzw. 1,5-Grad-Ziel kompatiblen Verlauf bis 2050

Energieeffizienz und Reduktion der *CO_2-Intensität der Energie.* Letztere sollte bis 2030 durch Umstellung von Kohle auf Gas, durch Kernenergie und erneuerbare Energien und evtl. durch CCS möglichst auf Werte unter 200 g CO_2/kWh vermindert und dann bis 2050 auf weniger als 100 g CO_2/kWh reduziert werden. China ist weltweit entscheidend für die Einhaltung der Klimaziele.

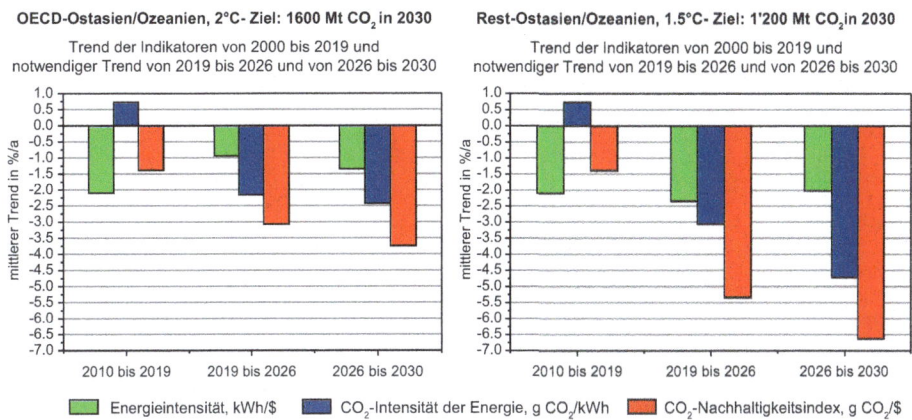

Abb. 9.3 Indikatoren-Trend in %/a von 2000 bis 2019 und notwendige Trendänderung ab 2019 zur Einhaltung des 2-Grad- und 1,5-Grad-Ziels

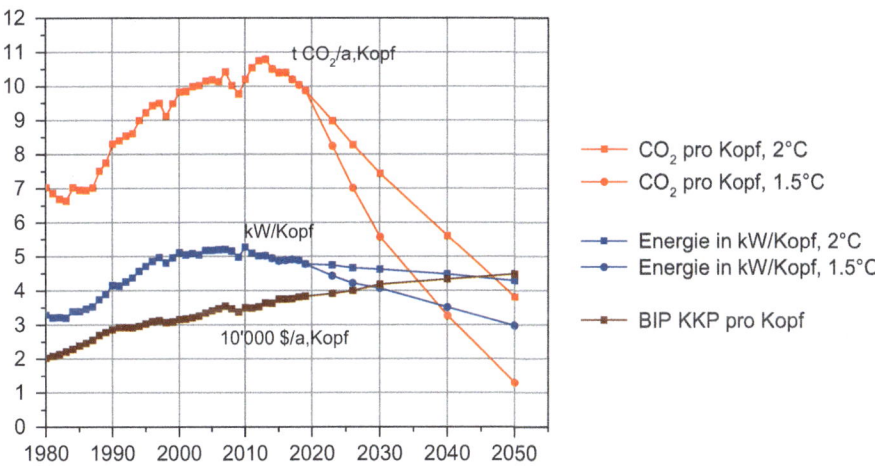

Abb. 9.4 Pro Kopf Indikatoren vom OECD Ostasien/Ozeanien von 1980 bis 2019 und 2-Grad- bzw. 1,5-Grad-Szenario bis 2050

Die dazu notwendigen prozentualen jährlichen Änderungen bis 2030 für das 2-Grad- und 1,5-Grad-Ziel sind detaillierter in Abb. 9.7 wiedergegeben.

Der zugehörige Verlauf der *pro Kopf Indikatoren* für das kaufkraftbereinigte Bruttoinlandprodukt, die Bruttoenergie und den CO_2-Ausstoss ist schliesslich in Abb. 9.8 dargestellt, für 1980 bis 2019 und entsprechend den beiden Klimaszenarien.

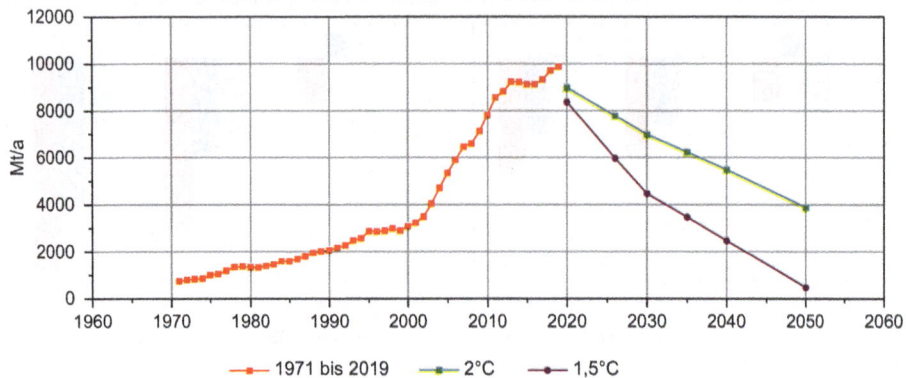

Abb. 9.5 Mit dem 2-Grad- und 1,5-Grad-Ziel kompatible Szenarien für China

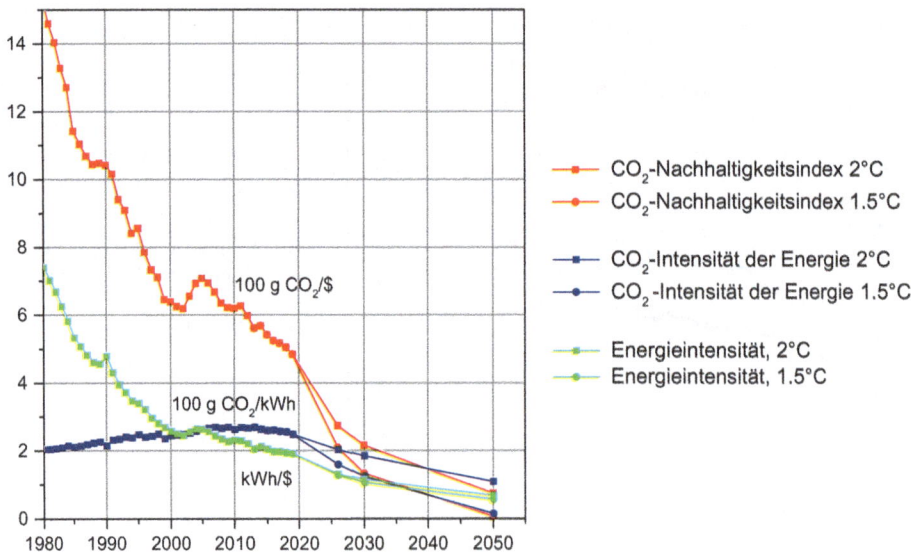

Abb. 9.6 Indikatoren-Verlauf von 1990 bis 2019 und mit dem 2-Grad- bzw. 1,5-Grad-Ziel kompatiblen Verlauf bis 2050

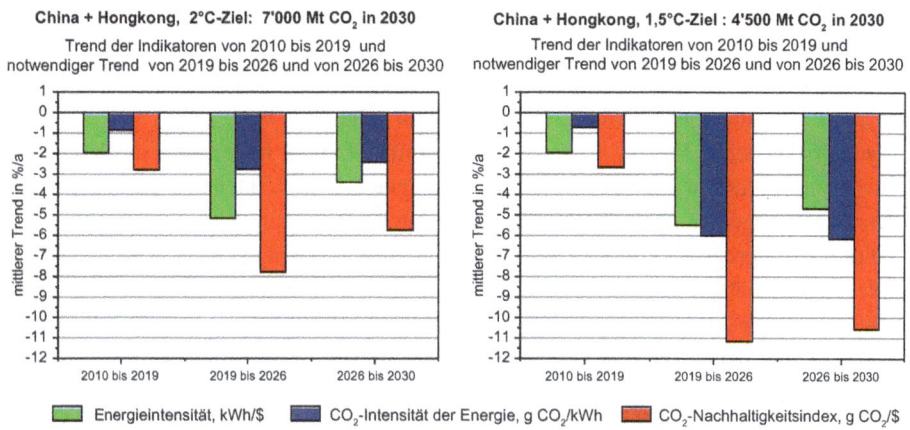

Abb. 9.7 Indikatoren-Trend in %/a von 2000 bis 2019 und notwendige Trendänderung ab 2019 zur Einhaltung des 2- Grad- bzw. 1,5-Grad-Ziels

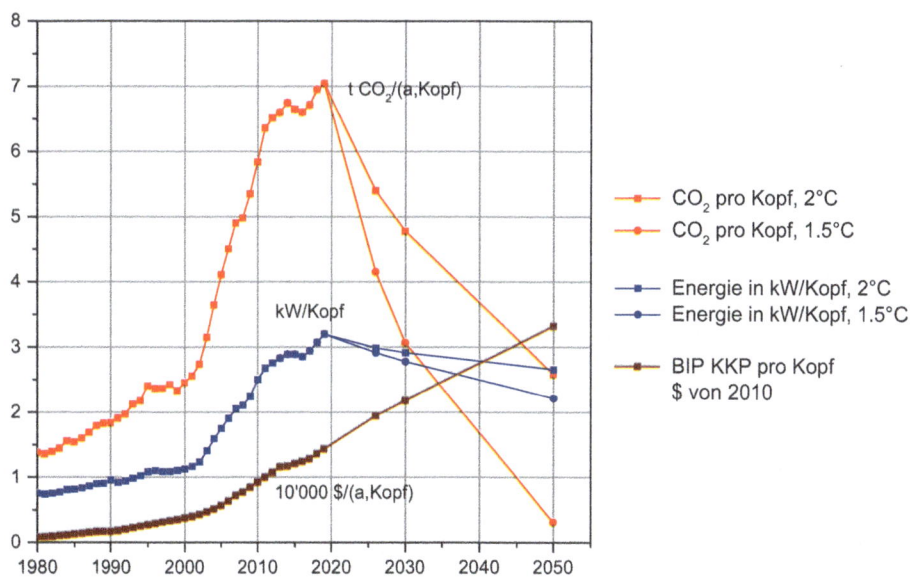

Abb. 9.8 Pro Kopf Indikatoren Chinas von 1980 bis 2019 und Klimaszenarien bis 2050

9.3   Restliches Ostasien/Ozeanien

Mit dem 2-Grad- und 1,5-Grad-Ziel kompatible Emissions-Szenarien bis 2050 für das insgesamt eher unterentwickelte restliche Ostasien zeigt Abb. 9.9.

Der entsprechende Verlauf der Indikatoren ist in Abb. 9.10 wiedergegeben. Notwendig ist die weitere Verminderung der bereits relativ guten Energieintensität und eine rasche Inversion der gegenwärtigen Tendenz der CO$_2$-Intensität der Energie.

Dies durch Förderung erneuerbarer Energien und Reduktion der starken Kohle-Anteile bei der Elektrizitätsproduktion.

Die dazu notwendigen prozentualen jährlichen Änderungen bis 2030 für die beiden Klimaziele sind detaillierter in Abb. 9.11 wiedergegeben.

Der zugehörige Verlauf der pro Kopf Indikatoren für das kaufkraftbereinigte Bruttoinlandprodukt, die Bruttoenergie und den CO$_2$-Ausstoss ist schliesslich in Abb. 9.12 dargestellt, für 1980 bis 2019 und entsprechend den beiden Klimaschutz-Szenarien.

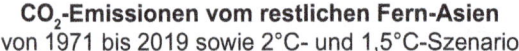

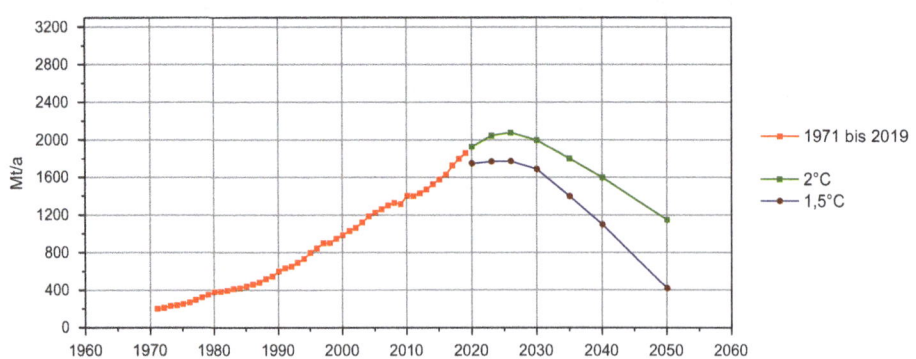

Abb. 9.9 Mit dem 2-Grad- und 1,5-Grad-Ziel kompatible Szenarien für Rest-Ostasien/Ozean

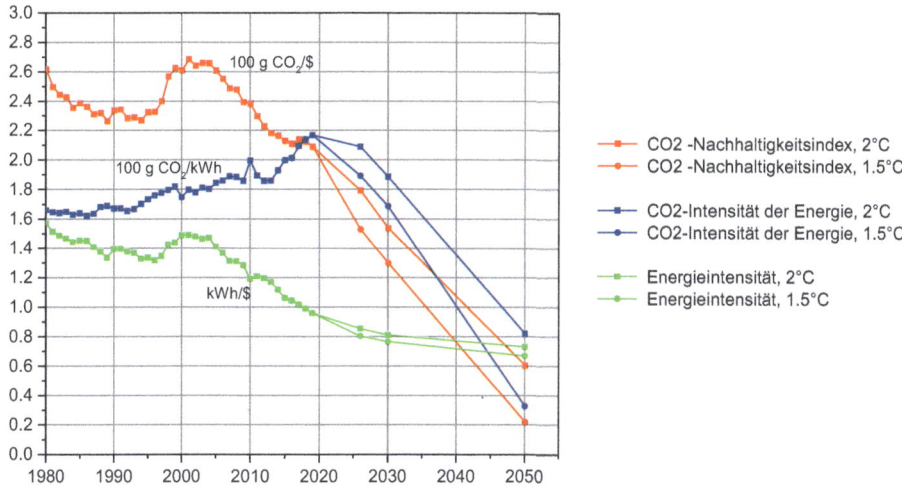

Abb. 9.10 Indikatoren-Verlauf von 1980 bis 2019 und mit dem 2-Grad- bzw. 1,5-Grad-Ziel kompatiblen Verlauf bis 2050

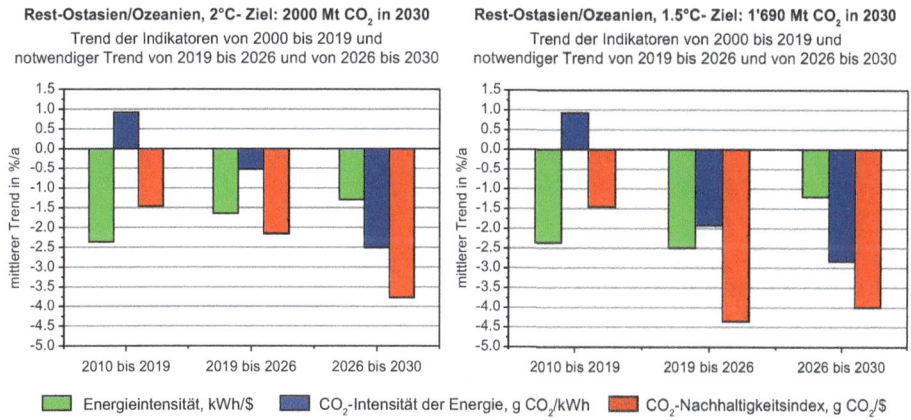

Abb. 9.11 Indikatoren-Trend in %/a von 2000 bis 2019 und notwendige Trendänderung ab 2019 zur Einhaltung des 2- Grad- bzw. 1,5-Grad-Ziels

9.4   Ostasien/Ozeanien insgesamt

Die entsprechenden Diagramme für Ostasien/Ozeanien insgesamt, ergeben sich durch Aufsummierung der Diagramme der drei Regionen.

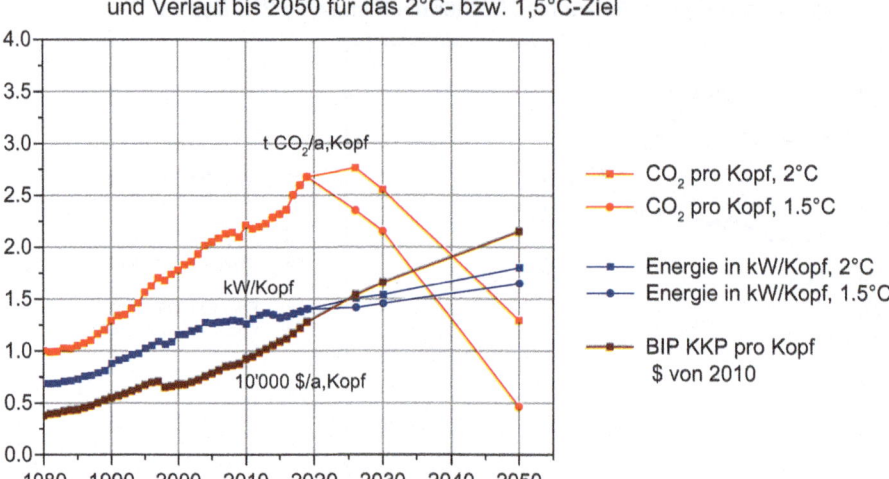

Abb. 9.12 Pro Kopf Indikatoren von Rest-Ostasien/Ozeanien Chinas von 1980 bis 2019 und Klimaschutz-Szenarien bis 2050

Die Abb. 9.13 und 9.14 veranschaulichen die CO$_2$-Emissionen und die entsprechenden Indikatoren bis 2050 für die beiden Klimaziele.

Der entsprechende Verlauf der pro Kopf Indikatoren für das kaufkraftbereinigte Bruttoinlandprodukt, die Bruttoenergie und den CO$_2$-Ausstoss ist in Abb. 9.15 dargestellt.

Die bis 2030 notwendigen prozentualen jährlichen Änderungen der Indikatoren für die 2-Grad- und 1,5-Grad- Varianten sind schliesslich detaillierter in Abb. 9.16 wiedergegeben.

9.5   Zusammenfassung

Die Abb. 9.17 und 9.18 geben die notwendige Änderung in % des Indikators g CO$_2$/$, von 2019 bis 2030, um das 2-Grad- bzw. das 1,5-Grad-Klimaziel zu erreichen.

Die *grüne Kurve* entspricht der *im Mittel weltweit notwendigen Reduktion* des Indikators.

Die *rote Kurve* gibt, in Übereinstimmung mit der vorangehenden Analyse, die *empfohlene Änderung* für die einzelnen Regionen und für Fernasien/Ozeanien insgesamt. Die Marge relativ zum weltweiten Mittel ist ein Bonus, der in der Regel Entwicklungs- und Schwellenländer zugestanden wird. Diese Marge wird ermöglicht und kompensiert durch eine entsprechend stärkere Anstrengung der stark industrialisierten Welt (siehe z. B., was

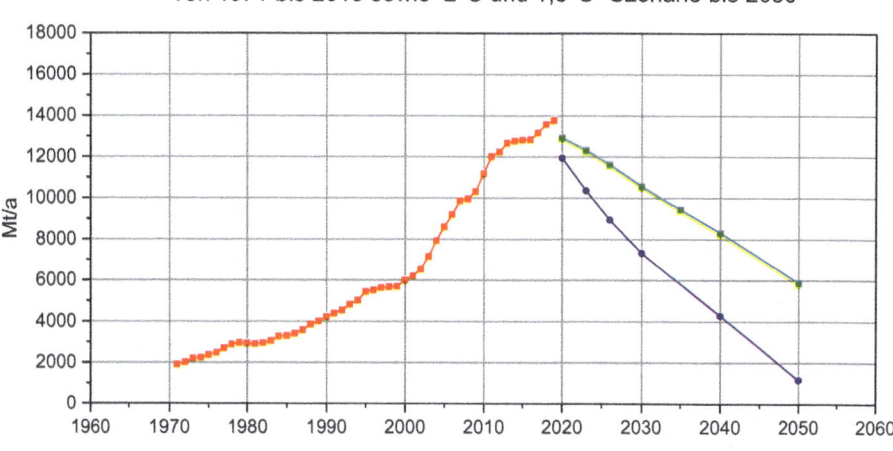

Abb. 9.13 Mit dem 2-Grad- bzw. 1,5-Grad-Ziel kompatibles Szenario für Ostasien/Ozeanien

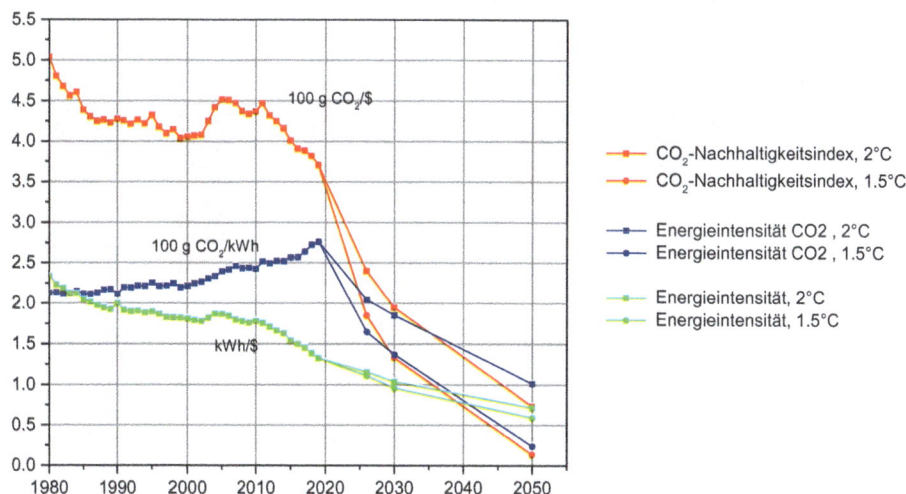

Abb. 9.14 Indikatoren-Verlauf von 1980 bis 2019 und mit dem 2-Grad- bzw. 1,5-Grad-Ziel kompatibler Verlauf bis 2050

Ostasien/Ozeanien, pro Kopf Indikatoren von 1980 bis 2019
und Verlauf bis 2050 für das 2°C- bzw. 1,5 °C-Ziel

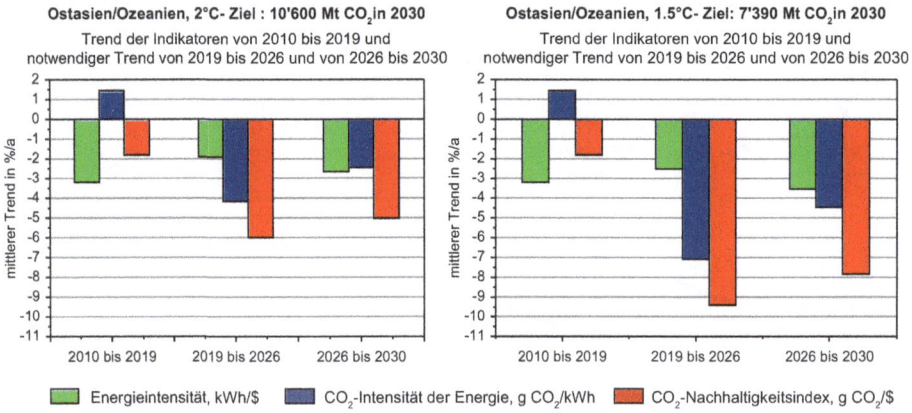

Abb. 9.15 Pro Kopf Indikatoren Ostasien/Ozeaniens von 1980 bis 2019 und 2-Grad- bzw. 1,5-Grad-Szenario bis 2050

Abb. 9.16 Indikatoren-Trend in %/a von 2010 bis 2019 und notwendige Trendänderung ab 2019 für beide Klimaziele

Europa betrifft, Band 1 [11] und für Amerika, Teil I dieses Bandes. Für das sanftere 2-Grad-Ziel kann man *China* (wesentlichstes Land für Fernasien) als relativ entwickeltes Land betrachten und entsprechend mehr Anstrengung verlangen.

Fern-Asien/Ozeanien 2°C-Klimaziel: notwendige Änderung in % bis 2030
des Indikators g CO_2/\$ in Abhängigkeit des Werts in 2019

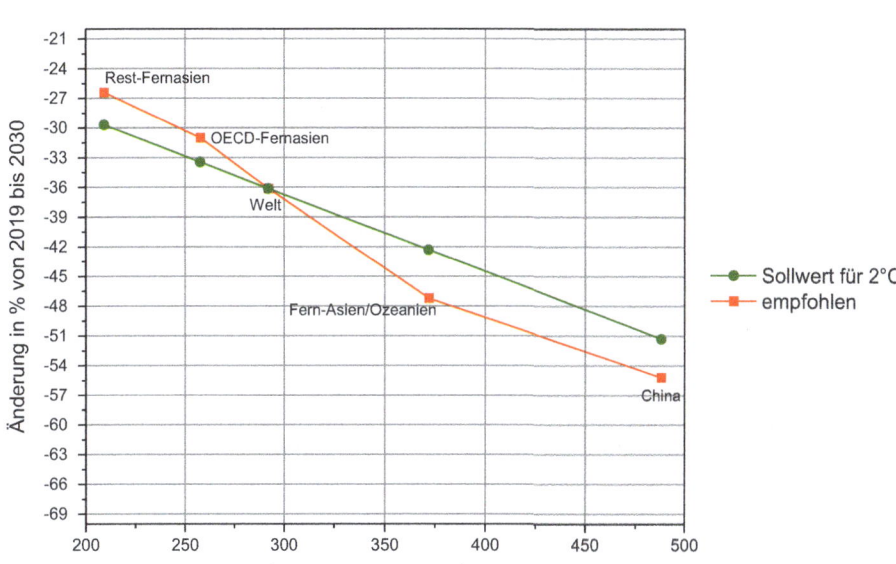

Abb. 9.17 Notwendige Änderung des Indikators g CO_2/\$, um das 2-Grad-Zziel zu erreichen

Ein sanftes Erreichen des 1,5-Grad-Ziels ist im diesem Kapitel für die drei Regionen detailliert besprochen worden. Die entsprechenden notwendigen Reduktionen des Indikators g CO_2/\$ sind in Abb. 9.18 zusammengefasst. Verlaufen die Emissionen entsprechend der für das 2-Grad-Ziel gegebenen Kurven, ist theoretisch das Erreichen des 1,5-Grad-Ziel immer noch möglich (s. Einleitung Kap. 1). Dazu dürfte zusätzlich die Hilfe „negativer Emissionen" [8, 10] erforderlich sein.

Die rasche und starke Verbesserung der CO_2-Nachhaltigkeit zur Gewährleistung der Klima-Ziele (mindestens 2 °C und wenn möglich 1,5 °C) erfordert:

- Bei **Heizwärme- und Kühlung:** bessere *Gebäudeisolation,* Ersatz von Ölheizungen durch Gasheizungen aber allem durch *Wärmepumpenheizungen* (s. dazu auch Kap. 3 und [1]), sowie durch möglichst *CO_2-frei erzeugte Fernwärme* sowie *Solar-Warmwasser.* Kühlung mit *Erdsonden und CO_2-arm erzeugte Elektrizität.*
- Bei **Prozesswärme:** Ersatz fossiler Energieträger soweit möglich durch *CO_2-arm erzeugte Elektrizität* und *Solarwärme.*
- Im **Verkehr:** *effizientere* Motoren und fortschreitende *Elektrifizierung:* Bahnverkehr, sowieElektro- und Hybridfahrzeuge für den Privat- und Warenverkehr. Letztere sind

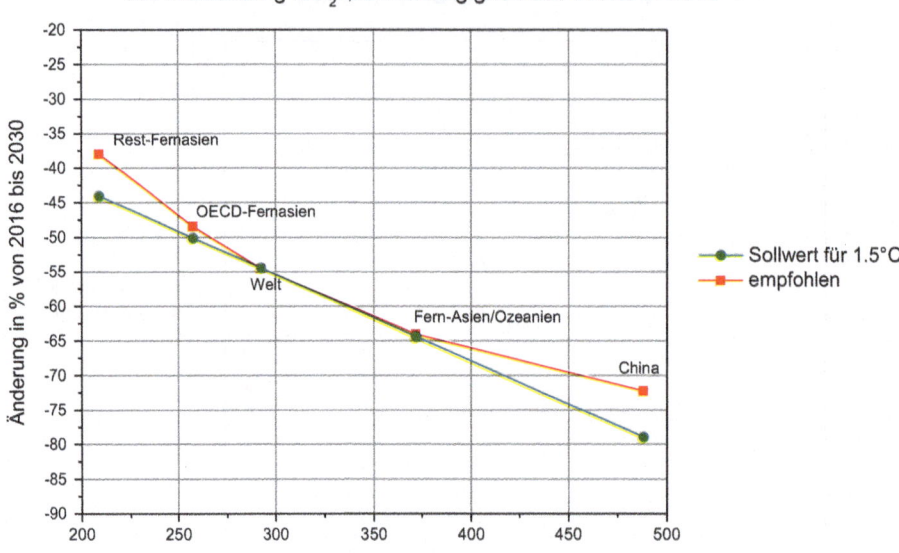

Abb. 9.18 Notwendige Änderung des Indikators g CO$_2$/$, um das 1,5-Grad°-Klimaziel sanft zu erreichen,

sehr sinnvoll ab einer *CO$_2$-armen Elektrizitätsproduktion* von mindestens 50 % (s. dazu Tab. 8.3). Ebenso wichtig sind *CO$_2$-neutrale Treibstoffe* für Luft -und Seeverkehr.

Für unterentwickelte Länder dürften diese Forderungen nur mit gezielter Unterstützung der industrialisierten Welt bezahlbar sein.

Dazugehörende und für alle **wichtigste Massnahme,** ist die rasch fortschreitende Entwicklung zu einer möglichst *CO$_2$-freien Elektrizitätsproduktion*. Diese kann in erster Linie durch erneuerbare Energien insbesondere auch mit Geothermie, aber auch durch Kernenergie oder CCS erreicht werden. Ebenso wichtig ist die Anpassung der Netze und Speicherungstechniken an die hohe Variabilität der Solar- und Windenergie.

Weitere Daten der Länder von Ostasien/Ozeanien

10.1 Japan, Südkorea, Australien

10.1.1 Energieflüsse in Japan (Abb. 10.1 und 10.2)

10.1.2 Energieflüsse in Südkorea (Abb. 10.3 und 10.4)

10.1.3 Energieflüsse in Australien (Abb. 10.5 und 10.6)

10.1.4 Elektrizitätsproduktion und -verbrauch in Japan, Südkorea und Australien (Abb. 10.7)

10.2 Indonesien, Philippinen, Vietnam, Thailand

10.2.1 Energieflüsse in Indonesien (Abb. 10.8 und 10.9)

10.2.2 Energieflüsse in den Philippinen (Abb. 10.10 und 10.11)

10.2.3 Energieflüsse in Vietnam (Abb. 10.12 und 10.13)

10.2.4 Energieflüsse in Thailand (Abb. 10.14 und 10.15)

10.2.5 Elektrizitätsproduktion und -verbrauch in Indonesien, in den Philippinen, Vietnam und Thailand (Abb. 10.16 und 10.17)

© Springer Fachmedien Wiesbaden GmbH, ein Teil von Springer Nature 2023
V. Crastan, *Kennzahlen zur Erreichung der weltweiten Klimaziele*,
https://doi.org/10.1007/978-3-658-40073-6_10

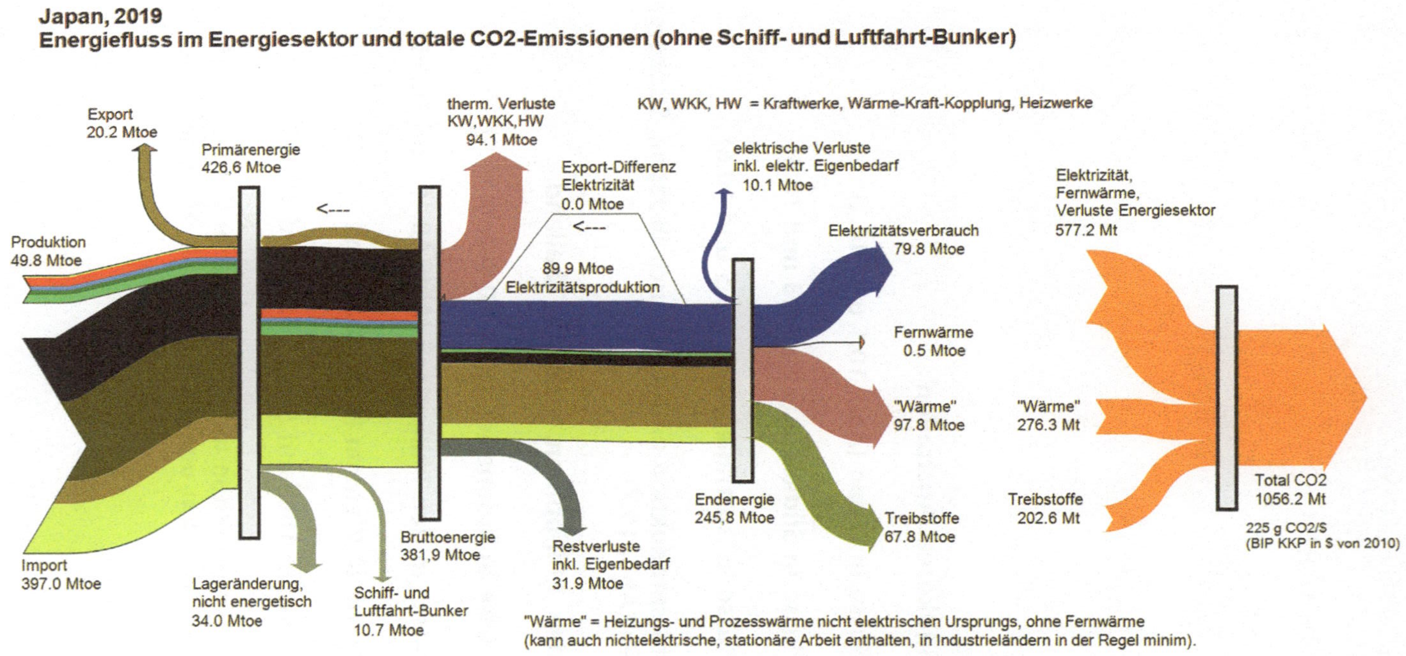

Japan, 2019
Energiefluss im Energiesektor und totale CO2-Emissionen (ohne Schiff- und Luftfahrt-Bunker)

KW, WKK, HW = Kraftwerke, Wärme-Kraft-Kopplung, Heizwerke

Export 20.2 Mtoe

Primärenergie 426.6 Mtoe

Produktion 49.8 Mtoe

therm. Verluste KW,WKK,HW 94.1 Mtoe

elektrische Verluste inkl. elektr. Eigenbedarf 10.1 Mtoe

Elektrizitätsverbrauch 79.8 Mtoe

Export-Differenz Elektrizität 0.0 Mtoe

89.9 Mtoe Elektrizitätsproduktion

Fernwärme 0.5 Mtoe

"Wärme" 97.8 Mtoe

Treibstoffe 67.8 Mtoe

Bruttoenergie 381.9 Mtoe

Schiff- und Luftfahrt-Bunker 10.7 Mtoe

Lageränderung, nicht energetisch 34.0 Mtoe

Endenergie 245.8 Mtoe

Restverluste inkl. Eigenbedarf 31.9 Mtoe

Import 397.0 Mtoe

Elektrizität, Fernwärme, Verluste Energiesektor 577.2 Mt

"Wärme" 276.3 Mt

Treibstoffe 202.6 Mt

Total CO2 1056.2 Mt

225 g CO2/$ (BIP KKP in $ von 2010)

"Wärme" = Heizungs- und Prozesswärme nicht elektrischen Ursprungs, ohne Fernwärme (kann auch nichtelektrische, stationäre Arbeit enthalten, in Industrieländern in der Regel minim).

Abb. 10.1 Japan: Energiefluss im Energiesektor von der Primärenergie zur Endenergie und CO2-Ausstoss. Die Energieträgerfarben sind wie in Abb. 8.5 und 8.7 (Erdöl dunkelbraun, Erdölprodukte hellbraun)

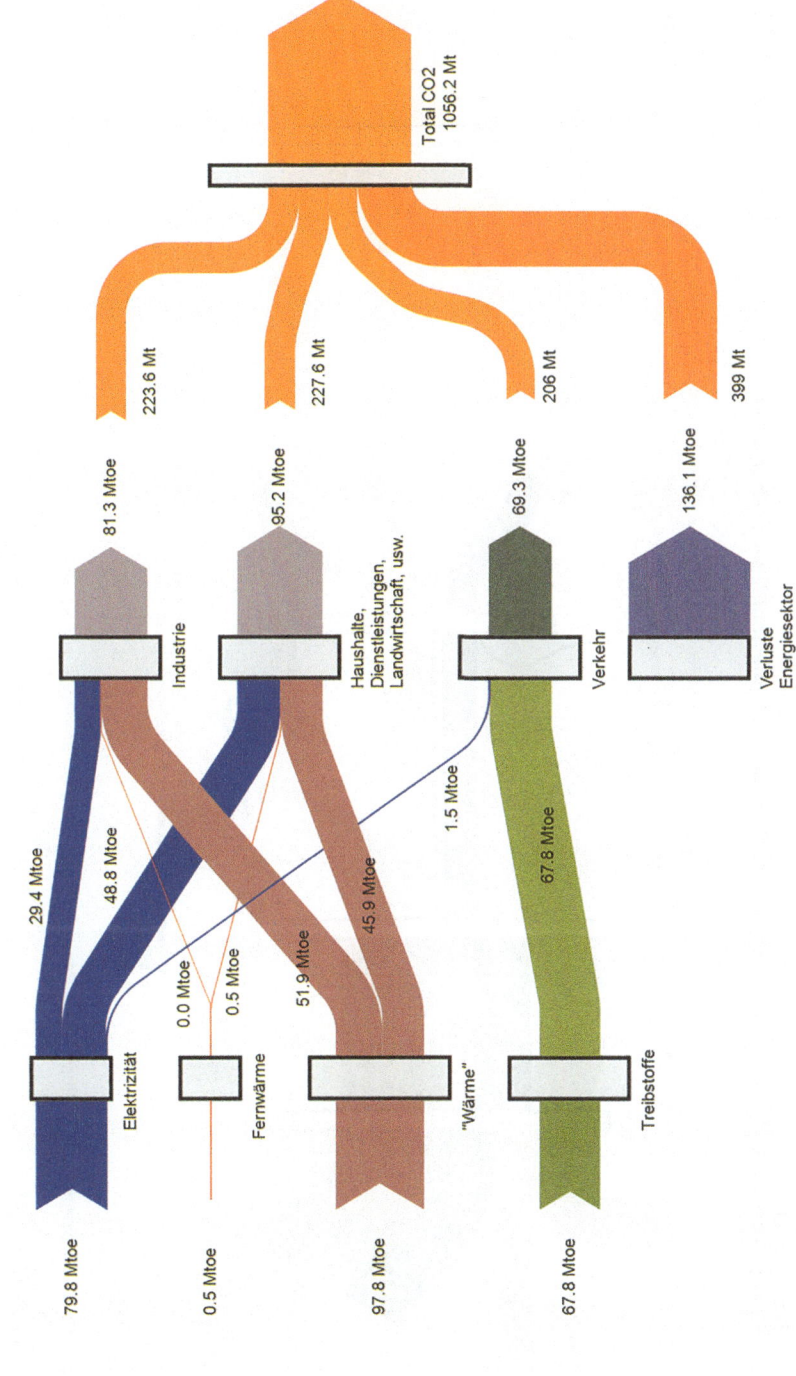

Japan, 2019
Energiefluss der Endenergie und totaler CO2-Ausstoss (ohne Schiff- und Luftfahrt-Bunker)

Abb. 10.2   Japan: Energiefluss der Endenergie zu den Endverbrauchern und zugeordnete CO_2-Emissionen

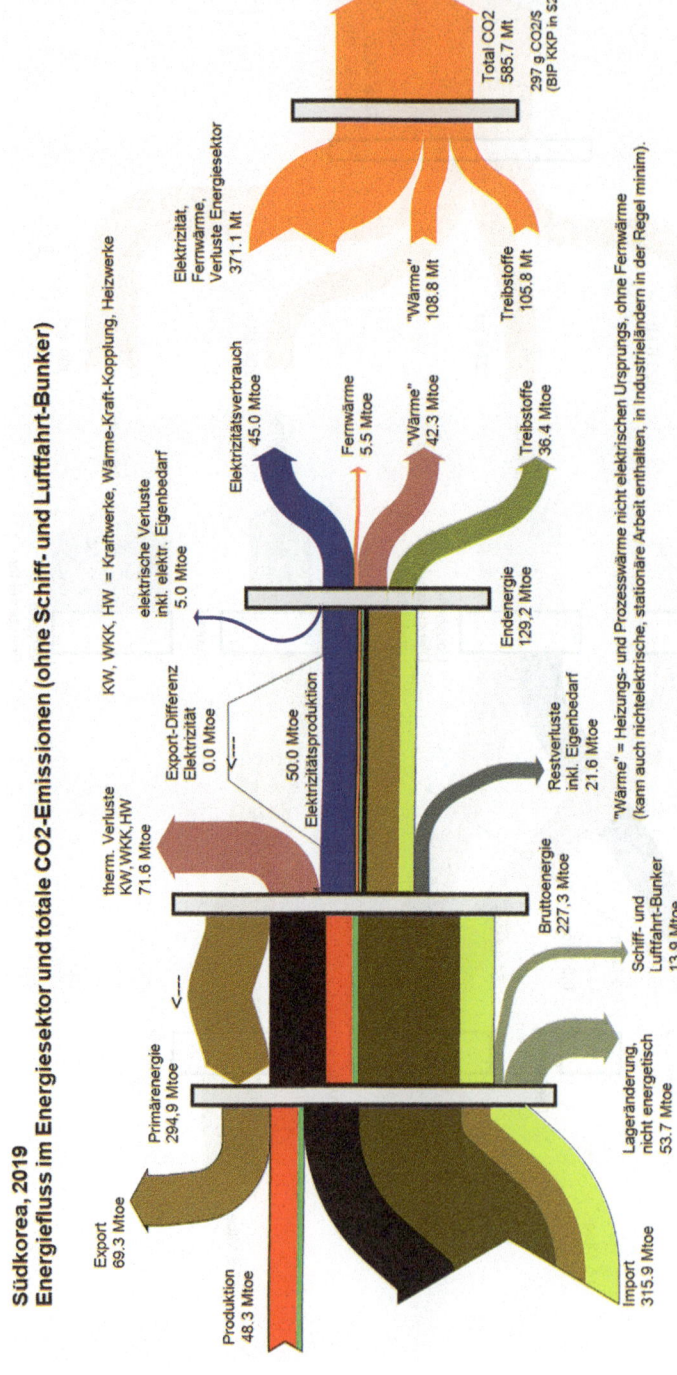

Südkorea, 2019
Energiefluss im Energiesektor und totale CO2-Emissionen (ohne Schiff- und Luftfahrt-Bunker)

Abb. 10.3 Südkorea: Energiefluss im Energiesektor von der Primärenergie zur Endenergie und CO2-Ausstoss. Die Energieträgerfarben sind wie in Abb. 8.5 und 8.7 (Erdöl dunkelbraun, Erdölprodukte hellbraun)

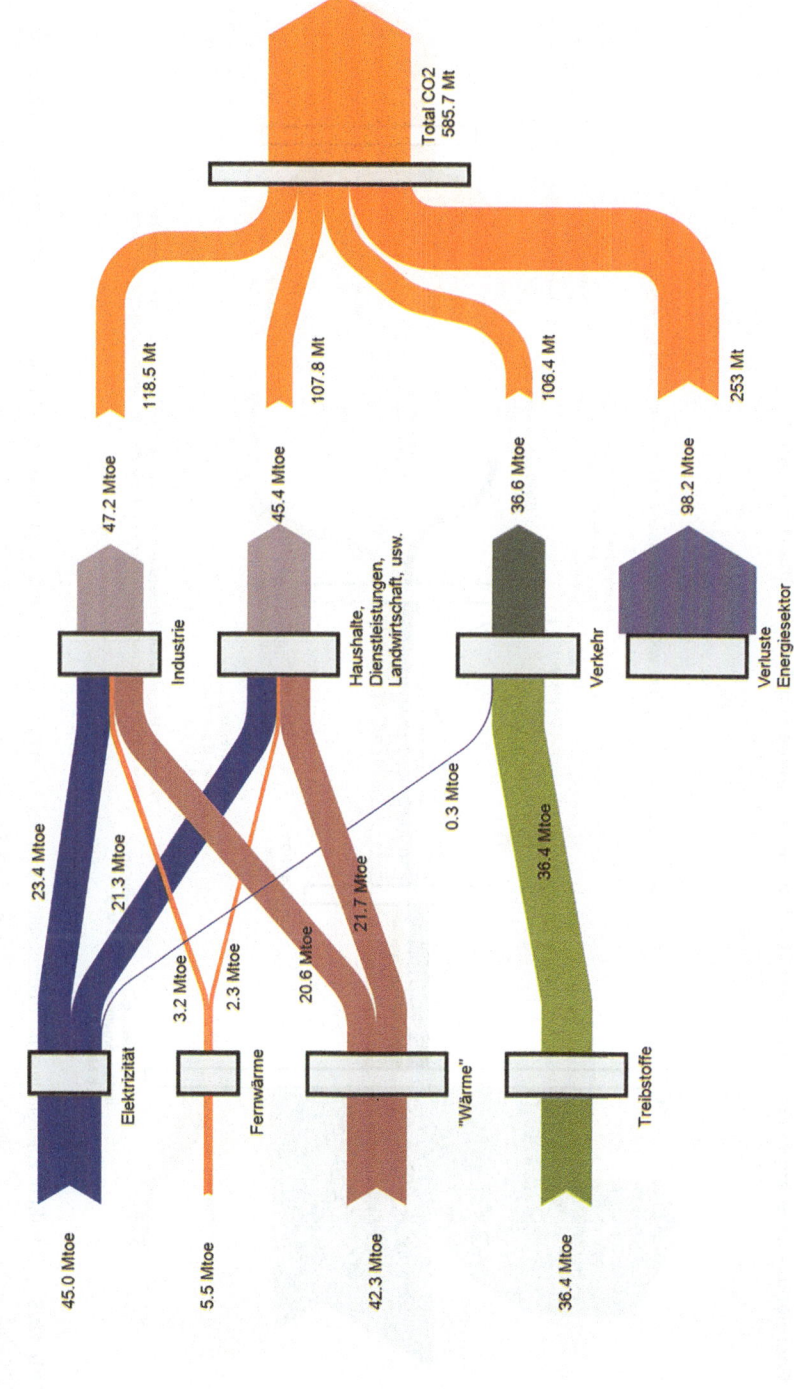

Südkorea, 2019
Energiefluss der Endenergie und totaler CO2-Ausstoss (ohne Schiff- und Luftfahrt-Bunker)

Abb. 10.4   Südkorea: Energiefluss der Endenergie zu den Endverbrauchern und zugeordnete CO_2-Emissionen

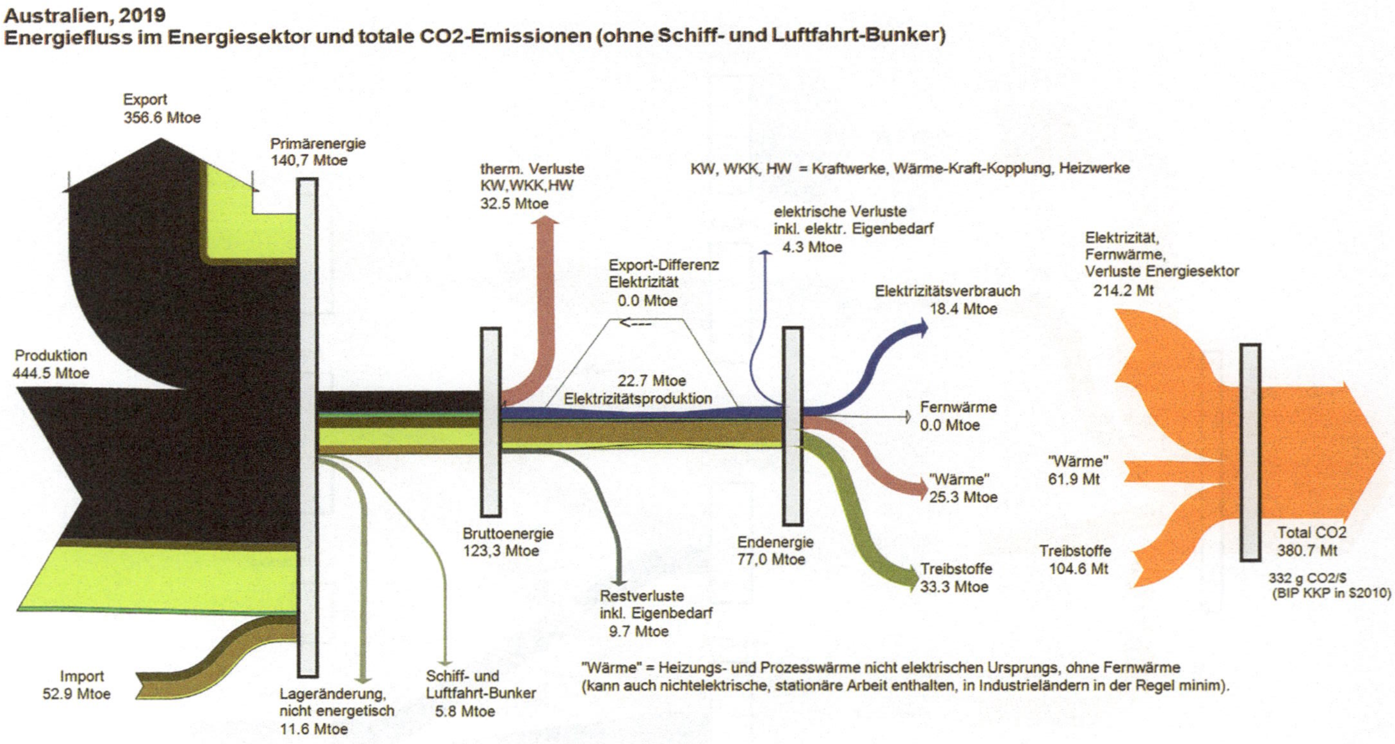

Australien, 2019
Energiefluss im Energiesektor und totale CO2-Emissionen (ohne Schiff- und Luftfahrt-Bunker)

KW, WKK, HW = Kraftwerke, Wärme-Kraft-Kopplung, Heizwerke

Primärenergie
140.7 Mtoe

Export
356.6 Mtoe

Produktion
444.5 Mtoe

Import
52.9 Mtoe

Lageränderung,
nicht energetisch
11.6 Mtoe

Schiff- und
Lufffahrt-Bunker
5.8 Mtoe

Bruttoenergie
123.3 Mtoe

therm. Verluste
KW,WKK,HW
32.5 Mtoe

Export-Differenz
Elektrizität
0.0 Mtoe

Elektrizitätsproduktion
22.7 Mtoe

elektrische Verluste
inkl. elektr. Eigenbedarf
4.3 Mtoe

Restverluste
inkl. Eigenbedarf
9.7 Mtoe

Endenergie
77.0 Mtoe

Elektrizitätsverbrauch
18.4 Mtoe

Fernwärme
0.0 Mtoe

"Wärme"
25.3 Mtoe

Treibstoffe
33.3 Mtoe

Elektrizität,
Fernwärme,
Verluste Energiesektor
214.2 Mt

"Wärme"
61.9 Mt

Treibstoffe
104.6 Mt

Total CO2
380.7 Mt

332 g CO2/$
(BIP KKP in $2010)

"Wärme" = Heizungs- und Prozesswärme nicht elektrischen Ursprungs, ohne Fernwärme
(kann auch nichtelektrische, stationäre Arbeit enthalten, in Industrieländern in der Regel minim).

Abb. 10.5 Australien: Energiefluss im Energiesektor von der Primärenergie zur Endenergie und CO₂-Ausstoss. Die Energieträgerfarben sind wie in Abb. 8.5 und 8.7 (Erdöl dunkelbraun, Erdölprodukte hellbraun)

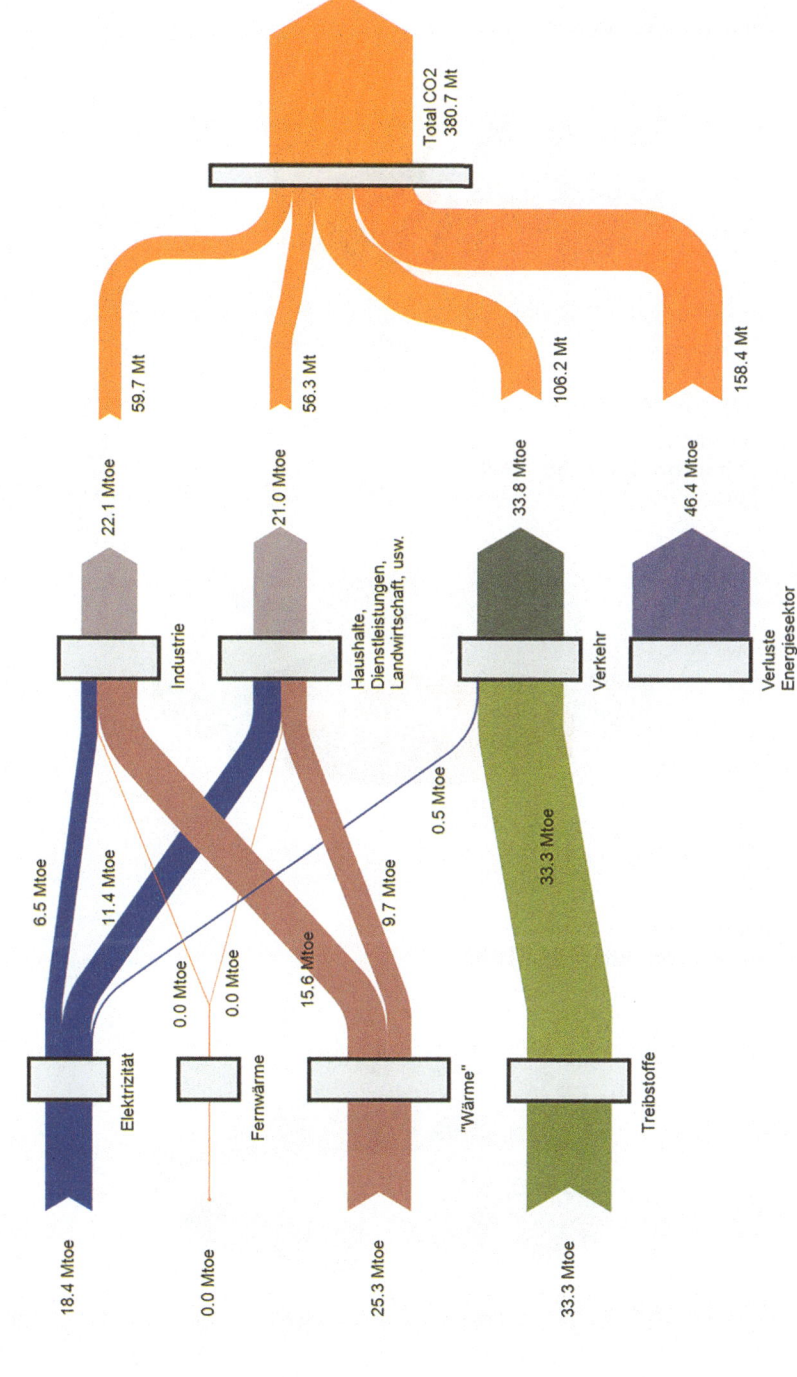

Australien, 2019
Energiefluss der Endenergie und totaler CO2-Ausstoss (ohne Schiff- und Luftfahrt-Bunker)

Abb. 10.6   Australien: Energiefluss der Endenergie zu den Endverbrauchern und zugeordnete CO_2-Emissionen

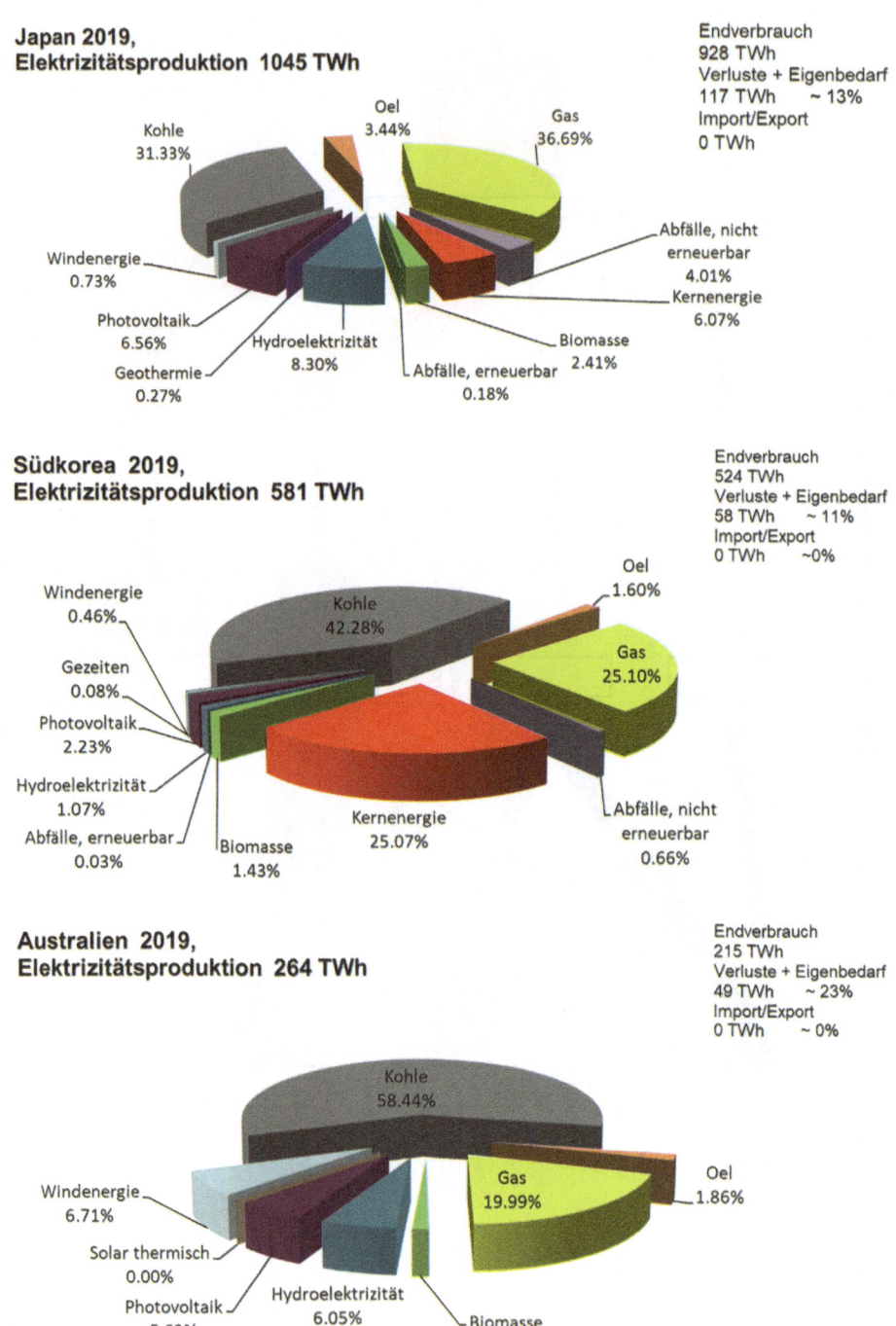

Abb. 10.7 Anteile der Energieträger an der Elektrizitätsproduktion in Japan, Südkorea und Australien

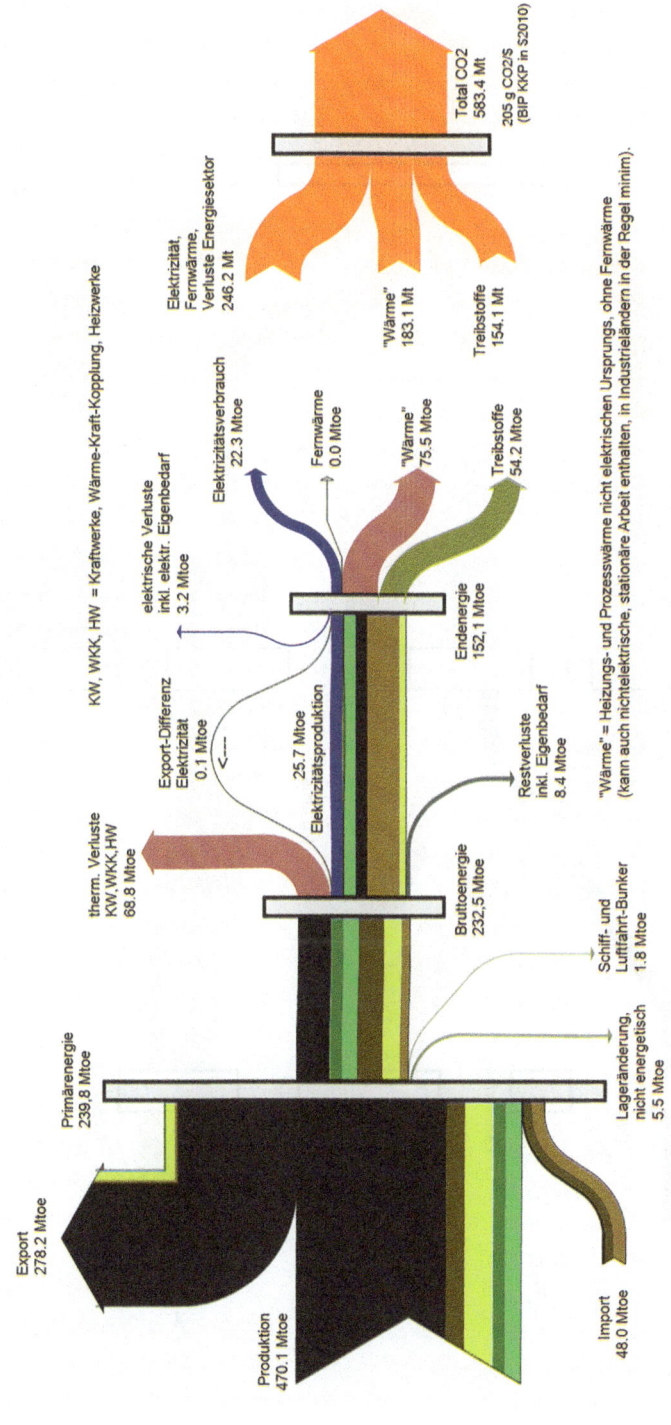

Abb. 10.8 Indonesien: Energiefluss im Energiesektor von der Primärenergie zur Endenergie und CO_2-Ausstoss. Die Energieträgerfarben sind wie in Abb. 8.5 und 8.7 (Erdöl dunkelbraun, Erdölprodukte hellbraun)

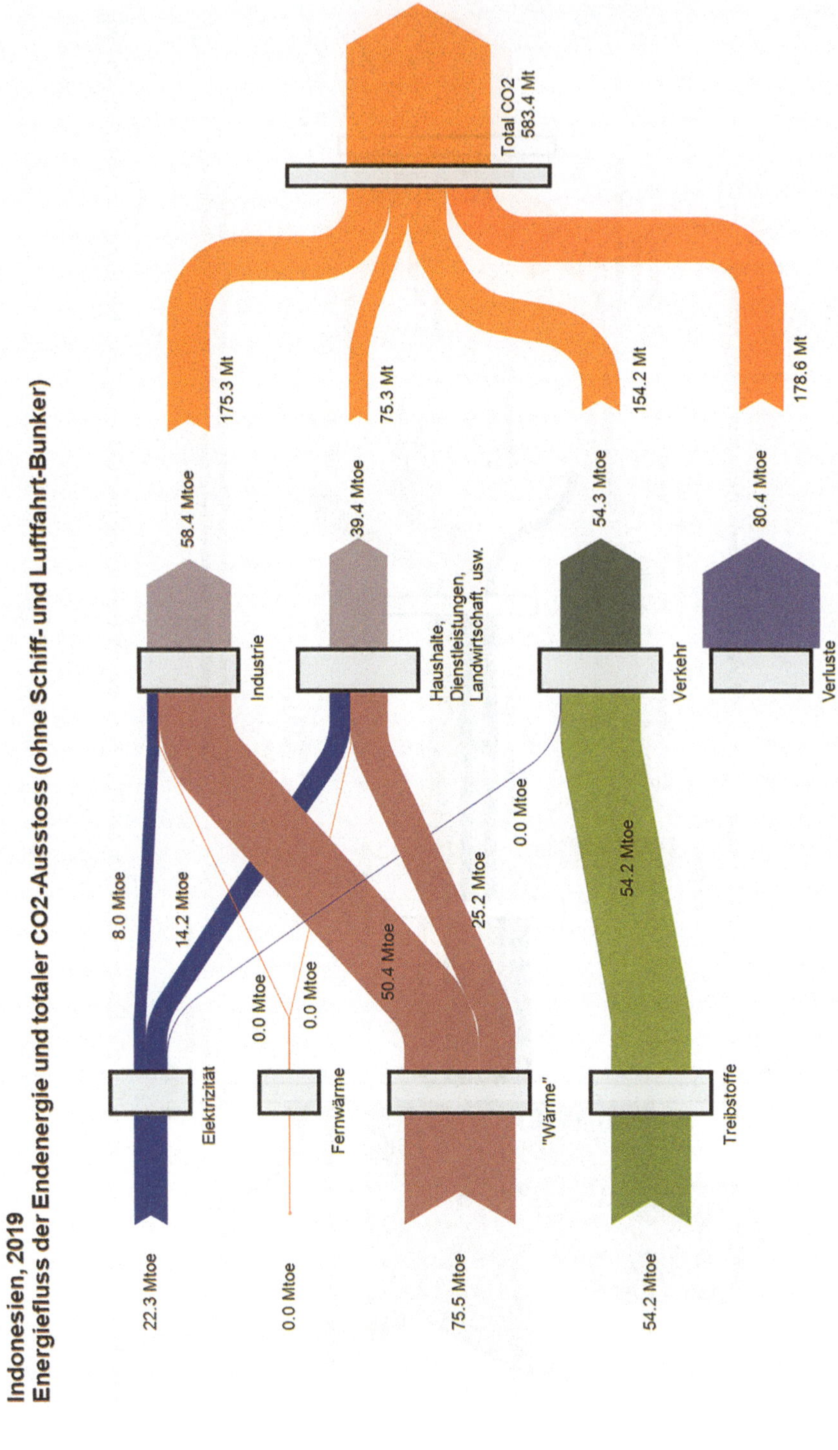

Indonesien, 2019
Energiefluss der Endenergie und totaler CO2-Ausstoss (ohne Schiff- und Luftfahrt-Bunker)

Total CO2
583.4 Mt

175.3 Mt

75.3 Mt

154.2 Mt

178.6 Mt

58.4 Mtoe

39.4 Mtoe

54.3 Mtoe

80.4 Mtoe

Industrie

Haushalte,
Dienstleistungen,
Landwirtschaft, usw.

Verkehr

Verluste
Energiesektor

8.0 Mtoe

14.2 Mtoe

0.0 Mtoe

0.0 Mtoe

50.4 Mtoe

25.2 Mtoe

0.0 Mtoe

54.2 Mtoe

Elektrizität

Fernwärme

"Wärme"

Treibstoffe

22.3 Mtoe

0.0 Mtoe

75.5 Mtoe

54.2 Mtoe

Abb. 10.9   Indonesien: Energiefluss der Endenergie zu den Endverbrauchern und zugeordnete CO$_2$-Emissionen

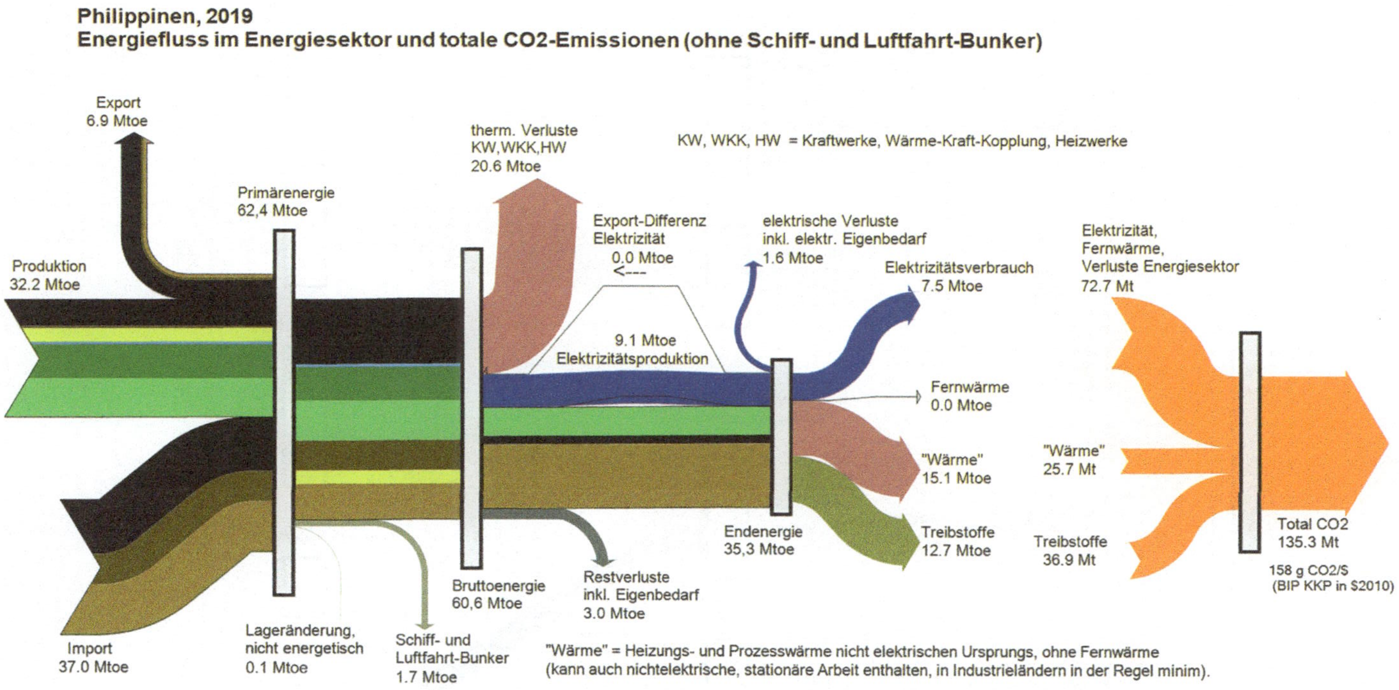

Philippinen, 2019
Energiefluss im Energiesektor und totale CO2-Emissionen (ohne Schiff- und Luftfahrt-Bunker)

KW, WKK, HW = Kraftwerke, Wärme-Kraft-Kopplung, Heizwerke

Total CO2
135.3 Mt

158 g CO2/$
(BIP KKP in $2010)

Elektrizität,
Fernwärme,
Verluste Energiesektor
72.7 Mt

"Wärme"
25.7 Mt

Treibstoffe
36.9 Mt

Elektrizität,
Fernwärme,
Verluste Energiesektor

elektrische Verluste
inkl. elektr. Eigenbedarf

Elektrizitätsverbrauch
7.5 Mtoe

Fernwärme
0.0 Mtoe

"Wärme"
15.1 Mtoe

Treibstoffe
12.7 Mtoe

elektrische Verluste
inkl. elektr. Eigenbedarf
1.6 Mtoe

therm. Verluste
KW,WKK,HW
20.6 Mtoe

Export-Differenz
Elektrizität
0.0 Mtoe

9.1 Mtoe
Elektrizitätsproduktion

Endenergie
35,3 Mtoe

Restverluste
inkl. Eigenbedarf
3.0 Mtoe

Bruttoenergie
60,6 Mtoe

Schiff- und
Luftfahrt-Bunker
1.7 Mtoe

Primärenergie
62,4 Mtoe

Lageränderung,
nicht energetisch
0.1 Mtoe

Export
6.9 Mtoe

Produktion
32.2 Mtoe

Import
37.0 Mtoe

"Wärme" = Heizungs- und Prozesswärme nicht elektrischen Ursprungs, ohne Fernwärme
(kann auch nichtelektrische, stationäre Arbeit enthalten, in Industrieländern in der Regel minim).

Abb. 10.10 Philippinen: Energiefluss im Energiesektor von der Primärenergie zur Endenergie und CO2-Ausstoss. Die Energieträgerfarben sind wie in Abb. 8.5 und 8.7 (Erdöl dunkelbraun, Erdölprodukte hellbraun)

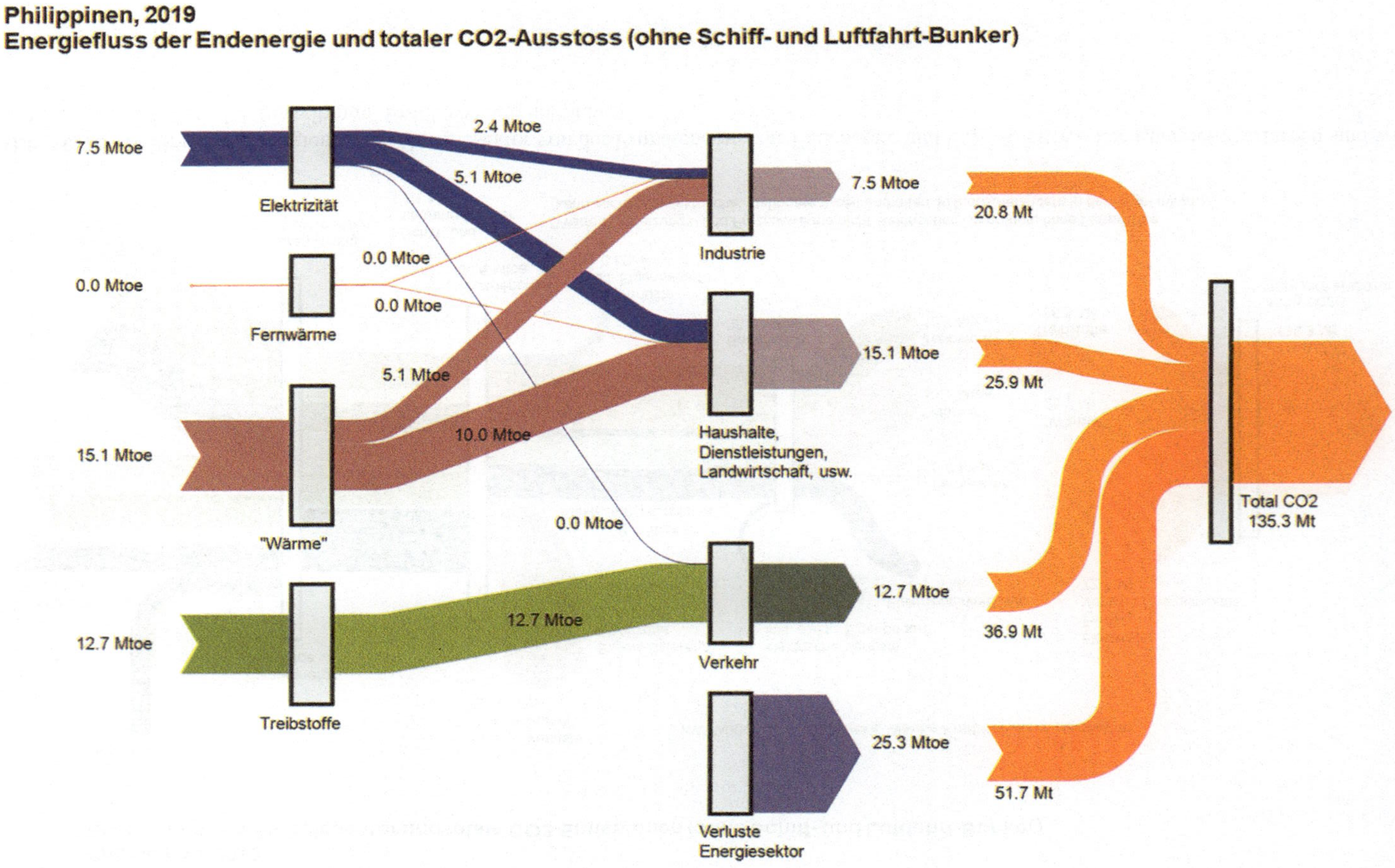

Philippinen, 2019
Energiefluss der Endenergie und totaler CO2-Ausstoss (ohne Schiff- und Luftfahrt-Bunker)

Total CO2
135.3 Mt

20.8 Mt

25.9 Mt

36.9 Mt

51.7 Mt

7.5 Mtoe

15.1 Mtoe

12.7 Mtoe

25.3 Mtoe

Industrie

Haushalte,
Dienstleistungen,
Landwirtschaft, usw.

Verkehr

Verluste
Energiesektor

2.4 Mtoe

5.1 Mtoe

0.0 Mtoe

0.0 Mtoe

5.1 Mtoe

10.0 Mtoe

0.0 Mtoe

12.7 Mtoe

Elektrizität

Fernwärme

"Wärme"

Treibstoffe

7.5 Mtoe

0.0 Mtoe

15.1 Mtoe

12.7 Mtoe

Abb. 10.11 Philippinen: Energiefluss der Endenergie zu den Endverbrauchern und zugeordnete CO_2-Emissionen

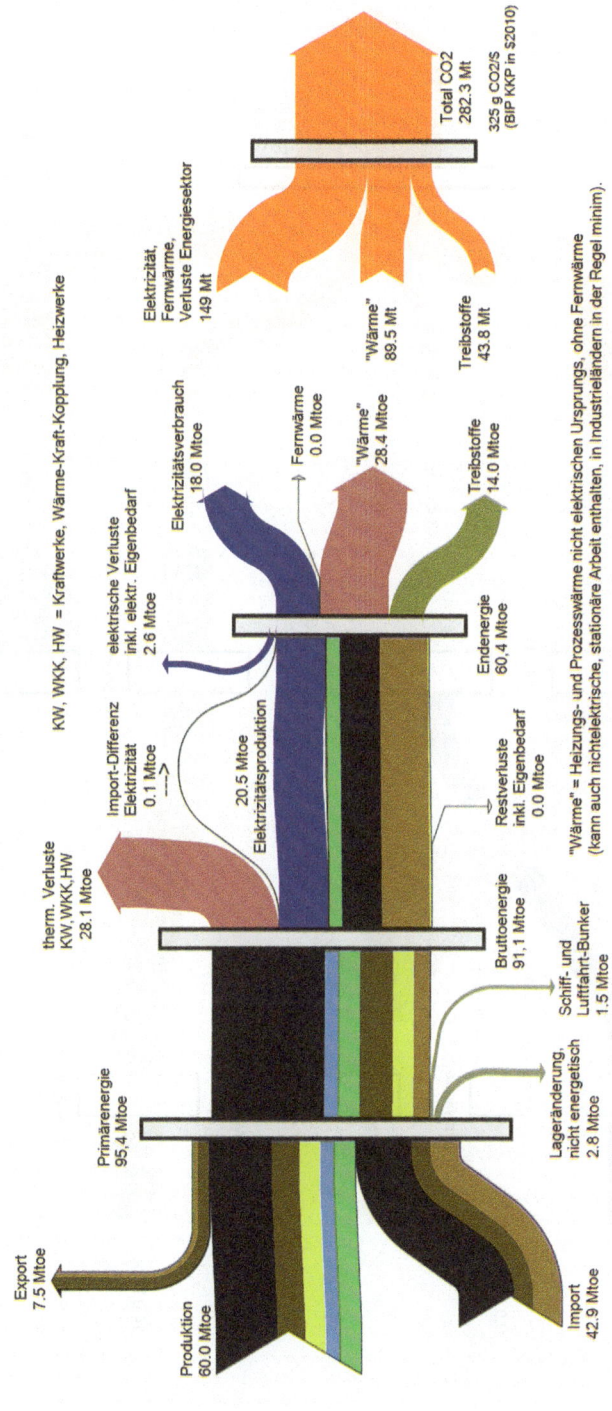

Vietnam, 2019
Energiefluss im Energiesektor und totale CO2-Emissionen (ohne Schiff- und Lufffahrt-Bunker)

KW, WKK, HW = Kraftwerke, Wärme-Kraft-Kopplung, Heizwerke

Export
7.5 Mtoe

Produktion
60.0 Mtoe

Primärenergie
95.4 Mtoe

therm. Verluste
KW,WKK,HW
28.1 Mtoe

Import-Differenz
Elektrizität
0.1 Mtoe

20.5 Mtoe
Elektrizitätsproduktion

elektrische Verluste
inkl. elektr. Eigenbedarf
2.6 Mtoe

Elektrizitätsverbrauch
18.0 Mtoe

Fernwärme
0.0 Mtoe

"Wärme"
28.4 Mtoe

Treibstoffe
14.0 Mtoe

Elektrizität,
Fernwärme,
Verluste Energiesektor
149 Mt

Total CO2
282.3 Mt

325 g CO2/S
(BIP KKP in $2010)

"Wärme"
89.5 Mt

Treibstoffe
43.8 Mt

Endenergie
60.4 Mtoe

Bruttoenergie
91.1 Mtoe

Restverluste
inkl. Eigenbedarf
0.0 Mtoe

Lageränderung,
nicht energetisch
2.8 Mtoe

Schiff- und
Lufffahrt-Bunker
1.5 Mtoe

Import
42.9 Mtoe

"Wärme" = Heizungs- und Prozesswärme nicht elektrischen Ursprungs, ohne Fernwärme
(kann auch nichtelektrische, stationäre Arbeit enthalten, in Industrieländern in der Regel minim).

Abb. 10.12 Vietnam: Energiefluss im Energiesektor von der Primärenergie zur Endenergie und CO_2-Ausstoss. Die Energieträgerfarben sind wie in Abb. 8.5 und 8.7 (Erdöl dunkelbraun, Erdölprodukte hellbraun)

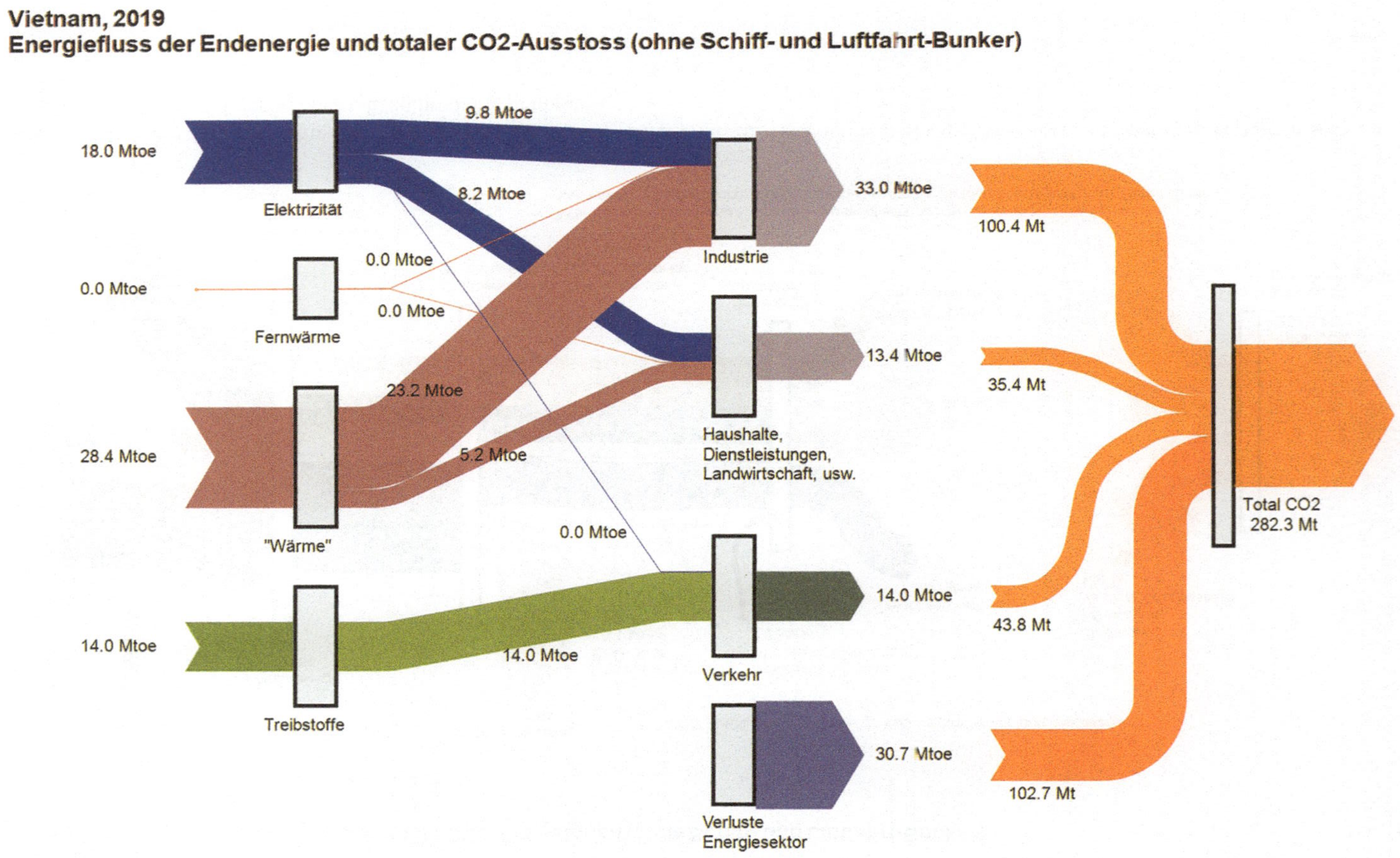

Vietnam, 2019
Energiefluss der Endenergie und totaler CO2-Ausstoss (ohne Schiff- und Luftfahrt-Bunker)

Total CO2 282.3 Mt

100.4 Mt

35.4 Mt

43.8 Mt

102.7 Mt

33.0 Mtoe — Industrie

13.4 Mtoe — Haushalte, Dienstleistungen, Landwirtschaft, usw.

14.0 Mtoe — Verkehr

30.7 Mtoe — Verluste Energiesektor

9.8 Mtoe

8.2 Mtoe

0.0 Mtoe

0.0 Mtoe

23.2 Mtoe

5.2 Mtoe

0.0 Mtoe

14.0 Mtoe

Elektrizität

Fernwärme

"Wärme"

Treibstoffe

18.0 Mtoe

0.0 Mtoe

28.4 Mtoe

14.0 Mtoe

Abb. 10.13 Vietnam: Energiefluss der Endenergie zu den Endverbrauchern und zugeordnete CO_2-Emissionen

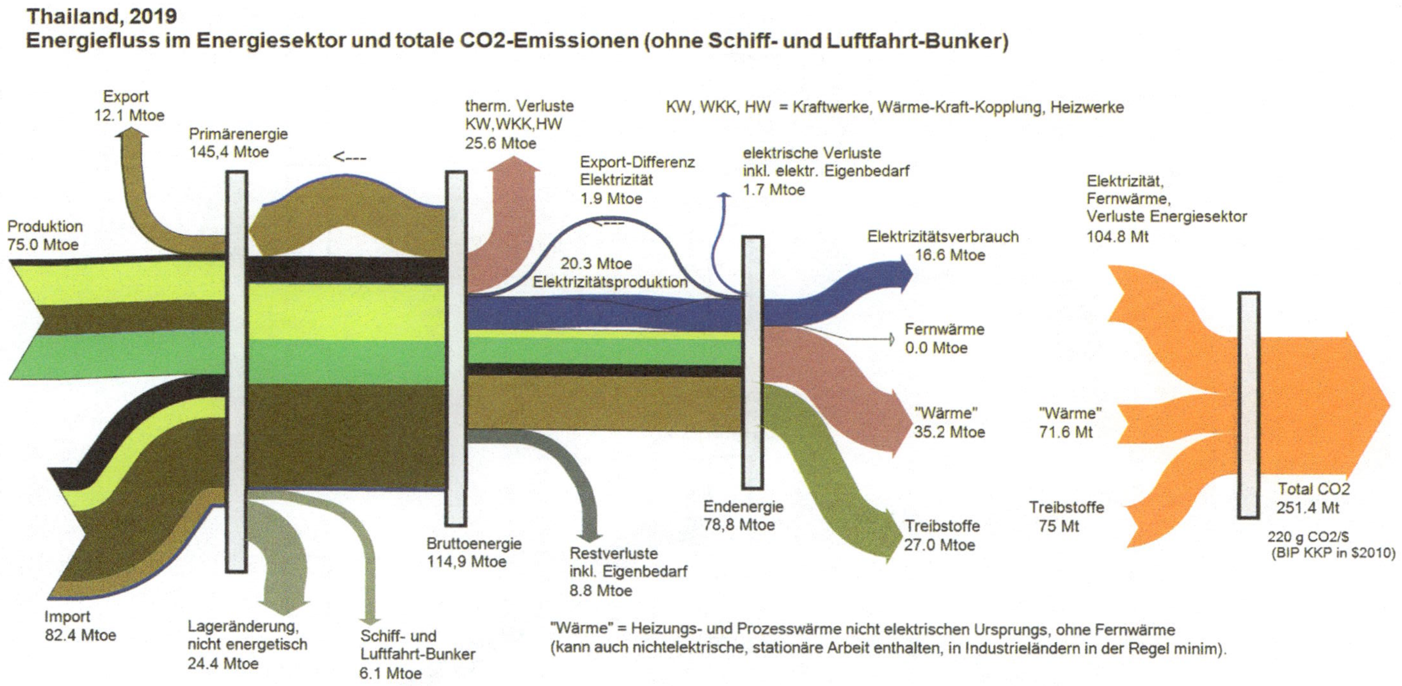

Thailand, 2019
Energiefluss im Energiesektor und totale CO2-Emissionen (ohne Schiff- und Luftfahrt-Bunker)

KW, WKK, HW = Kraftwerke, Wärme-Kraft-Kopplung, Heizwerke

therm. Verluste
KW,WKK,HW
25.6 Mtoe

Export-Differenz
Elektrizität
1.9 Mtoe

elektrische Verluste
inkl. elektr. Eigenbedarf
1.7 Mtoe

Elektrizitätsverbrauch
16.6 Mtoe

Fernwärme
0.0 Mtoe

"Wärme"
35.2 Mtoe

Treibstoffe
27.0 Mtoe

Elektrizität,
Fernwärme,
Verluste Energiesektor
104.8 Mt

Total CO2
251.4 Mt

220 g CO2/$
(BIP KKP in $2010)

"Wärme"
71.6 Mt

Treibstoffe
75 Mt

Endenergie
78.8 Mtoe

Restverluste
inkl. Eigenbedarf
8.8 Mtoe

20.3 Mtoe
Elektrizitätsproduktion

Bruttoenergie
114.9 Mtoe

Export
12.1 Mtoe

Primärenergie
145.4 Mtoe

Lageränderung,
nicht energetisch
24.4 Mtoe

Schiff- und
Luftfahrt-Bunker
6.1 Mtoe

Produktion
75.0 Mtoe

Import
82.4 Mtoe

"Wärme" = Heizungs- und Prozesswärme nicht elektrischen Ursprungs, ohne Fernwärme
(kann auch nichtelektrische, stationäre Arbeit enthalten, in Industrieländern in der Regel minim).

Abb. 10.14 Thailand: Energiefluss im Energiesektor von der Primärenergie zur Endenergie und CO_2-Ausstoss. Die Energieträgerfarben sind wie in Abb. 8.5 und 8.7 (Erdöl dunkelbraun, Erdölprodukte hellbraun)

Thailand, 2019
Energiefluss der Endenergie und totaler CO2-Ausstoss (ohne Schiff- und Luftfahrt-Bunker)

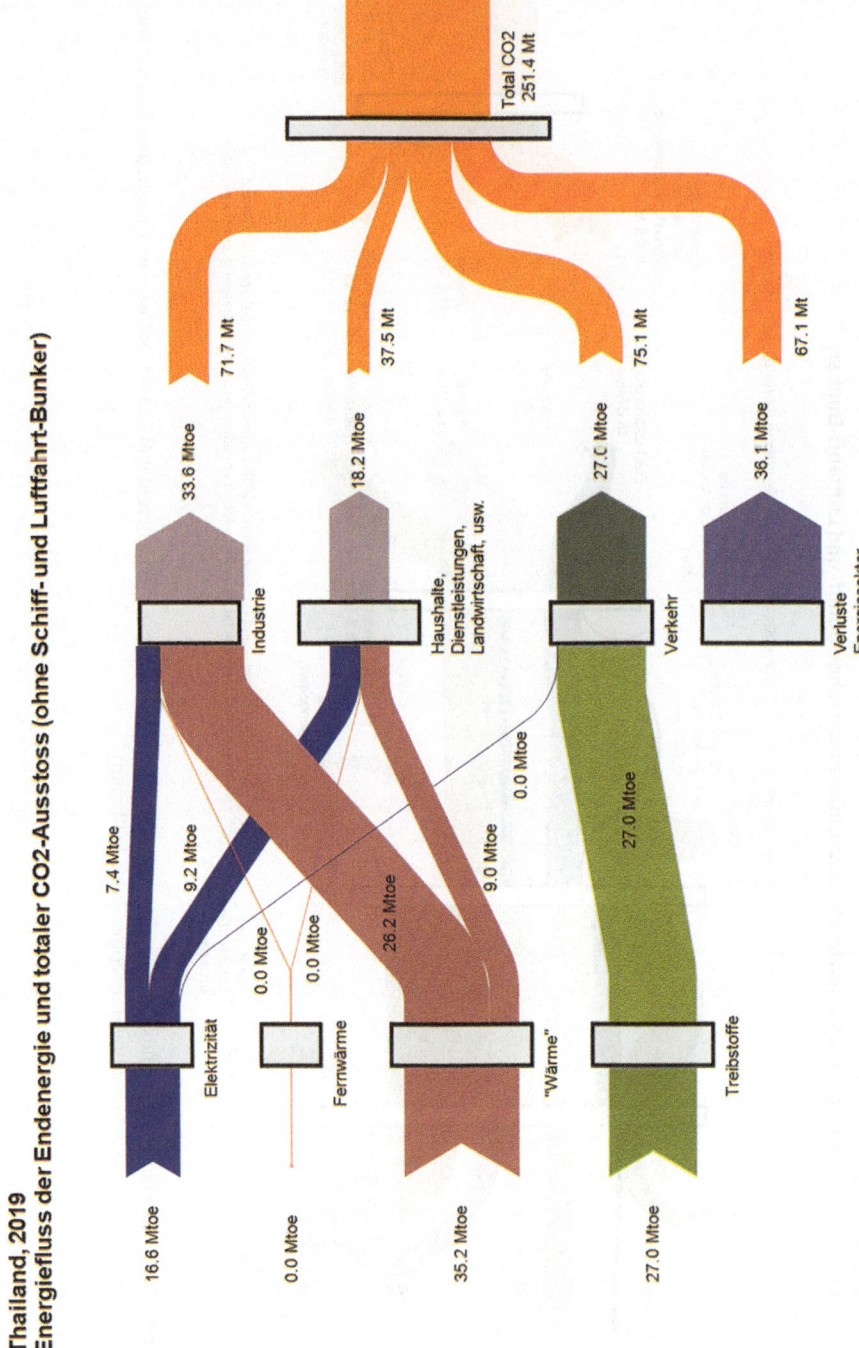

Abb. 10.15 Thailand: Energiefluss der Endenergie zu den Endverbrauchern und zugeordnete CO_2-Emissionen

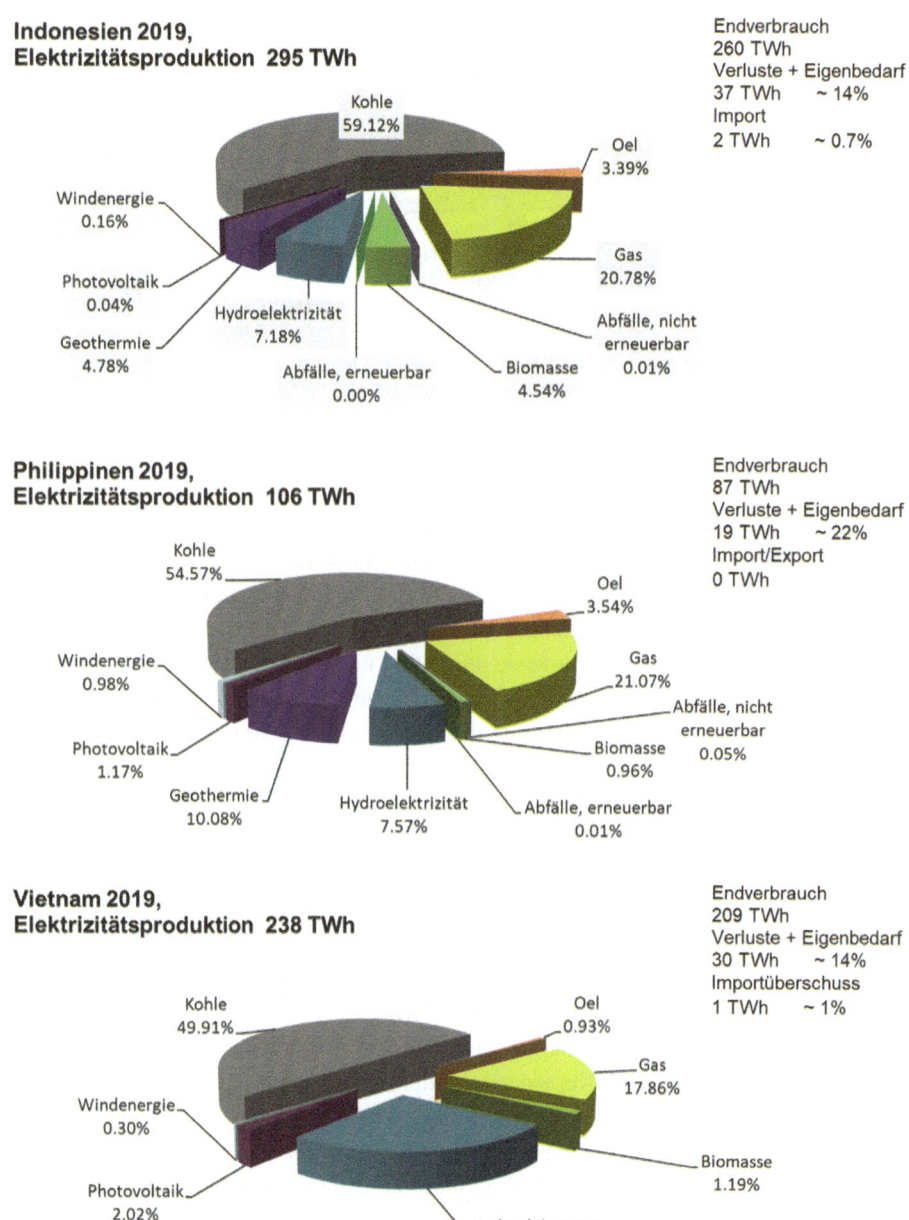

Indonesien 2019, Elektrizitätsproduktion 295 TWh

Endverbrauch
260 TWh
Verluste + Eigenbedarf
37 TWh   ~ 14%
Import
2 TWh   ~ 0.7%

Kohle
59.12%

Oel
3.39%

Windenergie
0.16%

Gas
20.78%

Photovoltaik
0.04%

Hydroelektrizität
7.18%

Abfälle, nicht
erneuerbar
0.01%

Geothermie
4.78%

Abfälle, erneuerbar
0.00%

Biomasse
4.54%

Philippinen 2019, Elektrizitätsproduktion 106 TWh

Endverbrauch
87 TWh
Verluste + Eigenbedarf
19 TWh   ~ 22%
Import/Export
0 TWh

Kohle
54.57%

Oel
3.54%

Windenergie
0.98%

Gas
21.07%

Photovoltaik
1.17%

Abfälle, nicht
erneuerbar
0.05%

Biomasse
0.96%

Geothermie
10.08%

Hydroelektrizität
7.57%

Abfälle, erneuerbar
0.01%

Vietnam 2019, Elektrizitätsproduktion 238 TWh

Endverbrauch
209 TWh
Verluste + Eigenbedarf
30 TWh   ~ 14%
Importüberschuss
1 TWh   ~ 1%

Kohle
49.91%

Oel
0.93%

Gas
17.86%

Windenergie
0.30%

Biomasse
1.19%

Photovoltaik
2.02%

Hydroelektrizität
27.78%

Abb. 10.16 Anteile der Energieträger an der Elektrizitätsproduktion in Indonesien, in den Philippinen und in Vietnam

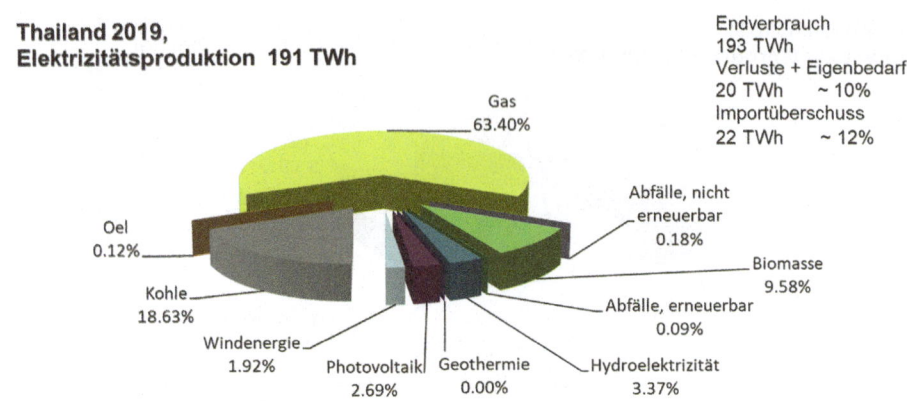

Abb. 10.17 Anteile der Energieträger an der Elektrizitätsproduktion in Thailand

Kommentar zu Japan, Einwohnerzahl: 126 Mio.

Gegenwärtig ist Japan ein nahezu reiner Energieimporteur (Abb. 10.1). Nach dem Fukushima-Unfall im Jahr 2011 wurde bis 2014 die Elektrizitätsproduktion aus Kernenergie, die einen Anteil von rund 25 % hatte, annulliert und dann bis 2019 wieder auf 6 % angefahren (Abb. 10.7). In erster Linie wurde sie durch Gas und Kohle ersetzt. Dementsprechend hat sich die CO_2-Intensität der Energie seit 2010 deutlich erhöht (Abb. 8.20). Die CO_2-Nachhaltigkeit konnte dank Verbesserung der Energieeffizienz trotzdem auf 225 g CO_2/$ (BIP KKP) leicht reduziert werden (Abb. 8.22). Um die Klimaziele zu erreichen sollten die OECD-Mitglieder Ostasiens bis 2030 unter 180 g CO_2/$ bleiben und bis 2050 maximal 80 g CO_2/$ zulassen (Abb. 9.2). In Japan ist dies durch Verstärkung der Elektrizitätsproduktion aus erneuerbaren Energien, Wiedereinschaltung mehrerer Kernkraftwerke und Elektrifizierung des Verkehrs erreichbar. Die Energieintensität muss gleichzeitig deutlich unter 1 kWh/$ gesenkt werden.

Kommentar zu Südkorea, Einwohnerzahl: 52 Mio.

Die Situation Südkoreas ist als Energieimporteur ähnlich derjenigen Japans (Abb. 10.3), aber selbst mit einem Anteil der Kernenergie an der Elektrizitätsproduktion von 25 % ist die Energieversorgung, trotz erheblicher Fortschritte seit 2000 (Abb. 8.21), mit 297 g CO_2/$ alles andere als nachhaltig. Zur Erzielung der Klimaziele muss die Elektrizitätsversorgung den Kohleanteil stark reduzieren (Abb. 10.7) zu Gunsten von Gas und erneuerbaren Energien. Auch die Energieeffizienz muss verbessert werden, d. h. die Energieintensität, die mit mehr als 1,3 kWh/$ deutlich über derjenigen Japans liegt, ist stark zu reduzieren.

Kommentar zu Australien, Einwohnerzahl: 25 Mio.

Als grosser Kohleproduzent und Exporteur (Abb 10.5) basiert auch die Elektrizitätsproduktion Australiens zu nahezu 60 % auf Kohle (Abb. 10.7). Dementsprechend ist die Nachhaltigkeit der Energiewirtschaft mit 332 g CO_2/$ die schlechteste im asiatischen OECD-Raum. Die Erreichung der Klimaziele im Rahmen der OECD-Gruppe Ostasien/Ozeanien (s. Abschn. 9.1) erfordert erhebliche Anstrengungen seitens Australiens. Neben starker Förderung erneuerbarer Energien (Sonne, Wind und Geothermie) könnten auch CCS und evtl. Kernenergie (Australien als grosses Uranförderland) einen Beitrag leisten. Die Energieintensität ist seit 2000 deutlich verbessert worden, muss aber bis 2050 signifikant unter 1 kWh/$ sinken (Abb. 9.2).

Kommentar zu Indonesien, Einwohnerzahl: 271 Mio.
Indonesien ist nach China der bevölkerungsreichste Staat Ostasiens und demzufolge für die Erreichung der Klimaziele von grosser Bedeutung. Indonesien ist ein grosser Kohleproduzent und Exporteur (Abb. 10.8) und auch die eigene Elektrizitätserzeugung basiert zu knapp 60 % auf Kohle (Abb. 10.16), in den letzten Jahren mit steigender Tendenz (in 2016 waren es 54 %). Dementsprechend hat die CO_2-Intensität der Energie stark zugenommen (Abb. 8.20). Auch der Nachhaltigkeitsindikator stieg seit 2010 auf 205 g CO_2/$, trotz Verbesserung der Effizienz, auch wegen der Substitution von Biomasse durch Kohle im Wärmebereich (Abb. 10.8). Zur Erreichung der Klimaziele ist eine *Trendumkehr* bei der CO_2-Intensität der Energie dringend notwendig durch stärkere Förderung der erneuerbaren Energien, insbesondere durch Geothermie, Wind- und Solarenergie sowie Wasserkraft. Die immer noch relativ schwache Elektrifizierung des Landes (15 %) muss für die Entwicklung überwunden werden. Zur Erreichung der Klimaziele sollte der Indikator der CO_2-Nachhaltikeit gemäss Abb. 9.10, für das 2-Grad-Ziel, bis 2030 um 27 % und bis 2050 um 70 % vermindert werden. Für das 1,5-Grad-Ziel lauten die entsprechenden Zahlen minus 40 % und minus 90 %.

Kommentar zu den Philippinen, Einwohnerzahl: 108 Mio.
Die Elektrizitätsproduktion basiert in steigendem Masse zu 55 % auf Kohle (Abb. 10.16), die importiert werden muss, sowie auf einer eigenen Gasproduktion (Abb. 10.10 und 10.11). Die CO_2-Nachhaltigkeit hat sich seit 2010 leicht verschlechtert auf 158 g CO_2/$ (Abb. 8.23), trotz Verbesserung der Effizienz und hohem Biomasse-Anteil bei der Wärmeversorgung. Zur Erreichung der Klimaziele muss auf den Kohleimport verzichtet und der Kohleanteil durch den weiteren Ausbau erneuerbarer Energien (Geothermie, Wasser, Wind und Photovoltaik) ersetzt werden. Die fortgeschrittene Elektrifizierung (21 %) bietet, falls konsequent mit erneuerbaren Energien weitergeführt, gute Voraussetzungen für die Elektromobilität.

Kommentar zu Vietnam, Einwohnerzahl: 96 Mio.
Der Anteil der Wasserkraft an der Elektrizitätsproduktion hat sich seit 2016 von 39 % auf 28 % verschlechtert, dafür ist der Kohleanteil auf 50 % gestiegen. Dementsprechend weist Vietnam eine *starke Verschlechterung* der CO_2-Intensität der Energie auf. Der Indikator der CO_2-Nachhaltigkeit hat sich auf 325 g CO_2/$ etwa gehalten dank deutliche Verbesserung der Energieeffizienz auf 1,2 kWh/$. Ein Grund ist auch die starke Kohleabhängigkeit der Wärmeversorgung im Industriebereich (Abb. 10.12 und 10.13). Die beträchtliche Kohleproduktion

des Landes genügt nicht ganz der Deckung der eigenen Bedürfnisse. Auf Kohleimporte sollte aber verzichtet werden. Zur Erreichung der Klimaziele (s. Abb. 9.9 und 9.10) ist eine Trendwende zugunsten der in Vietnam reichlich vorhandenen erneuerbaren Energien aus Wind und Sonne notwendig. Geothermie und evtl. Kernenergie könnten ebenfalls einen Beitrag leisten.

Kommentar zu Thailand, Einwohnerzahl: 70 Mio.
Thailand ist heute auf Importe fossiler Energieträger (Kohle und Erdöl) angewiesen. Lediglich Erdgas stammt mehrheitlich aus eigener Produktion. (Abb. 10.14). Nur 17 % der Elektrizitätsproduktion wird, trotz Fortschritte, von erneuerbaren Energien (vorwiegend Wasserkraft und Biomasse, Abb. 10.17) geliefert. Dementsprechend ist Thailand mit 220 g CO_2/\$ nicht besonders nachhaltig. Um die Klimaziele zu respektieren (Abb. 9.10), muss die recht starke Elektrizitätsproduktion weg von der Kohle und vorwiegend durch erneuerbare Energien (Wind, Sonne und Wasser) gedeckt werden. Auch die Energieintensität muss bis 2030 durch Effizienzverbesserungen von heute 1,17 kWh/\$ auf weniger als 1 kWh/\$ sinken (Abb. 8.17 und 10.10).

10.3 Tabellen zu Indikatoren und CO_2-Intensitäten gewichtiger Länder von Ostasien/Ozeanien

Die Tab. 10.1 10.2, 10.3, 10.4, 10.5, 10.6, 10.7 und 10.8 geben **für 2019** die *Energieintensität* und die *Emissionen pro Kopf, die CO_2-Intensitäten der Endenergien und der Endverbraucher* sowie den *Elektrifizierungsgrad El-G* für einige der gewichtigsten Länder von Ostasien/Ozeanien (die Werte folgen aus den Energiefluss-Diagrammen). Für Fortschritte bzw. Rückschritte relativ zu 2016 vergleiche mit 2. Auflage dieses Buches.
   Vergleichswerte:

	Westeuropa 2018	USA 2018
Energieintensität kWh/\$	0,87	1,35
Emissionen/Kopf t CO_2/Kopf	6,0	15,0

Tab. 10.1 China
(Energieintensität 1,84 kWh/\$, Emissionen 7,1 t CO_2/Kopf)
El-G: 29,4 %

Energieart (Abb. 8.10)	g CO_2/kWh	Verbraucher (Abb. 8.11)	g CO_2/kWh
Wärme (ohne Elektr.)	255	Industrie	277
	242	Haushalte etc.	196
Treibstoffe	274	Verkehr	241
Energiesektor	**265**	Verluste	292
Total		Energiesektor	

| CO$_2$-Intensität der Energie g CO$_2$/kWh (Total) | 169 | 203 |
| El-G % | 24,5 | 23,2 |

Dazu folgende Bemerkungen:

- **Die CO$_2$-Intensität** des *Energiesektors* wird stark vom *Grad der CO$_2$-Freiheit der Elektrizitätserzeugung* beeinflusst. Eine CO$_2$-arme Elektrizitätserzeugung ist der beste Weg, neben der Verminderung der Energieintensität, zur Verbesserung der CO$_2$-Nachhaltigkeit und Erreichung der Klimaziele. Kein gewichtiges Land in Ostasien erreicht 2019 Werte unter 170 g CO$_2$/$ (beste Werte mit rund 190 g CO$_2$/$ in Thailand und den Philippinen); entsprechende Anstrengungen sind notwendig.
- Eine verbreitete **Elektrifizierung des Verkehrs** (Bahnen, Elektro- und Hybridautos) ist erst dann auf die CO$_2$-Bilanz wirksam, wenn die *CO$_2$-Intensität des Energiesektors* (weitgehend von derjenigen der Elektrizität bestimmt) bei weniger als 60 % derjenigen des *Verkehrssektors* liegt; erst dann trägt sie wesentlich zur Verbesserung der CO$_2$-Nachhaltigkeit bei. Am nächsten zu dieser Grenze liegen Thailand mit 71 % und die Philippinen: mit 76 %, (Tab. 10.6 und 10.8), Japan und Südkorea hingegen liegen bei etwa 90 %.
- Der **Einsatz von Wärmepumpen** ist allgemein sehr sinnvoll, da der Anteil an CO$_2$-freier Umweltenergie meistens bei etwa 75 % liegt. Somit helfen Wärmepumpen die CO$_2$-Intensität des Wärmebereichs selbst dann zu reduzieren, wenn die CO$_2$-Intensität des Energiesektors sogar über derjenigen des Wärmesektors liegt (wie in fast allen Ländern ausser Japan, Südkorea und Thailand).
- Die **Energieintensität** ist ein weiterer wichtiger Indikator. Er hängt von *der Effizienz des Energieeinsatzes* ab. Vor allem in China (1,84 kWh/$), aber auch in Südkorea (>1,3 kWh/$) muss sie deutlich vermindert werden, Ostasien sollte bis 2030 insgesamt einen Wert von 1,0 kWh/$ BIP(KKP) anpeilen (Abb. 9.14).
- Der **Indikator der CO$_2$-Nachhaltigkeit** (g CO$_2$/$) ist das Produkt von Energieintensität und CO$_2$-Intensität der Energie.
- In **China,** als gewichtigster Land Ostasiens, hat die CO$_2$-Nachhaltigkeit mit 1,84 kWh/$ * 265 g CO$_2$/kWh = 488 g CO$_2$/$ einen erheblichen Nachholbedarf. (als Vergleich Westeuropa 2018: 0.87 kWh/$ * 169 g CO$_2$/kWh = 147 g CO$_2$/$, Band 1 der Reihe [16])
- Die **Emissionen pro Kopf** in t CO$_2$/Kopf und Jahr ergeben sich als Produkt von Index der CO$_2$-Nachhaltigkeit und Wohlstandsindikator ($/Kopf und Jahr):

$$t\,CO_2 \big/ Kopf, \; a = g\,CO_2 \big/ \$ * \$ \big/ Kopf, a \big/ 10^6.$$

Tab. 10.2 Japan
(Energieintensität 0,95 kWh/$,
Emissionen 8,4 t CO_2/Kopf)
El-G: 32,4 %

Energieart (Abb. 10.1)	g CO_2/kWh	Verbraucher (Abb. 10.2)	g CO_2/kWh
Wärme (ohne	244	Industrie	237
Elektr.)	258	Haushalte etc.	206
Treibstoffe	230	Verkehr	256
Energiesektor	**238**	Verluste	253
Total		Energiesektor	

Tab. 10.3 Südkorea
(Energieintensität 1,34 kWh/$,
Emissionen 11,3 t CO_2/Kopf)
El-G: 34,9 %

Energieart (Abb. 10.3)	g CO_2/kWh	Verbraucher (Abb. 10.4)	g CO_2/kWh
Wärme (ohne	222	Industrie	217
Elektr.)	251	Haushalte etc.	205
Treibstoffe	215	Verkehr	250
Energiesektor	**222**	Verluste	222
Total		Energiesektor	

Tab. 10.4 Australien
(Energieintensität 1,25 kWh/$,
Emissionen 15,0 t CO_2/Kopf)
El-G: 23,9 %

Energieart (Abb. 10.5)	g CO_2/kWh	Verbraucher (Abb. 10.6)	g CO_2/kWh
Wärme (ohne	211	Industrie	233
Elektr.)	271	Haushalte etc.	231
Treibstoffe	285	Verkehr	271
Energiesektor	**266**	Verluste	295
Total		Energiesektor	

Tab. 10.5 Indonesien
(Energieintensität 0,95 kWh/$,
Emissionen 2,2 t CO_2/Kopf)
El-G: 14,6 %

Energieart (Abb. 10.8)	g CO_2/kWh	Verbraucher (Abb. 10.9)	g CO_2/kWh
Wärme (ohne	209	Industrie	259
Elektr.)	245	Haushalte etc.	165
Treibstoffe	207	Verkehr	245
Energiesektor	**216**	Verluste	191
Total		Energiesektor	

Tab. 10.6 Philippinen
(Energieintensität 0,82 kWh/$,
Emissionen 1,25 t CO_2/Kopf)
El-G: 21,2 %

Energieart (Abb. 10.10)	g CO_2/kWh	Verbraucher (Abb. 10.11)	g CO_2/kWh
Wärme (ohne	147	Industrie	239
Elektr.)	250	Haushalte etc.	148
Treibstoffe	191	Verkehr	250
Energiesektor	**193**	Verluste	176
Total		Energiesektor	

Tab. 10.7 Vietnam (Energieintensität 1,20 kWh/\$, Emissionen 2,9 t CO_2/Kopf) El-G: 29,8 %

Energieart (Abb. 10.12)	g CO_2/kWh	Verbraucher (Abb. 10.13)	g CO_2/kWh
Wärme (ohne Elektr.)	272	Industrie	263
Treibstoffe	269	Haushalte etc.	228
Energiesektor	270	Verkehr	269
Total	**271**	Verluste Energiesektor	299

Tab. 10.8 Thailand (Energieintensität 1,17 kWh/\$, Emissionen 3,6 t CO_2/Kopf) El-G: 21,1 %

Energieart (Abb. 10.14)	g CO_2/ kWh	Verbraucher (Abb. 10.15)	g CO_2/kWh
Wärme (ohne Elektr.)	175	Industrie	184
Treibstoffe	240	Haushalte etc.	178
Energiesektor	171	Verkehr	240
Total	**189**	Verluste Energiesektor	160

In **China** lagen im Jahr 2019 das mittlere kaufkraftbereinigte Bruttoinlandprodukt bei *14.000 \$/Kopf* und die CO_2-Emissionen bei *7,06 t/Kopf*, entsprechend einem Index der CO_2-Nachhaltigkeit von *488 g CO_2/\$*. Um *bis 2050* eine für das 2-Grad-Klimaziel notwendige Reduktion der CO_2-Emissionen auf *2,6 t/Kopf* zu erzielen (s. Abschn. 2.2), muss, bei einer Zunahme des BIP (KKP) auf z. B. *33.000 \$/Kopf*, der Index der CO_2-Nachhaltigkeit auf *80 g CO_2/\$* gesenkt werden. Für das 1.5-Grad-Ziel lauten die Zahlen *0,33 t/Kopf* und *10 g CO_2/\$*.

Im **OECD-Raum Ostasiens** war im Jahr 2019 das mittlere BIP (KKP) etwa *38.400 \$/Kopf* und die CO_2-Emissionen *9,9 t/Kopf*, entsprechend einem Index der CO_2-Nachhaltigkeit von *258 g CO_2/\$*. Um bis 2050 eine für das 2-Grad Klimaziel notwendige Begrenzung der CO_2-Emissionen auf *3,5 t/Kopf* zu erreichen (s. Abschn. 2.1), muss, bei einer Zunahme des BIP (KKP) auf z. B. *44.000 \$/Kopf*, der Index der CO_2-Nachhaltigkeit auf *85 g CO_2/\$* vermindert werden. Für das 1.5-Grad-Ziel lauten die Zahlen *1,1 t/Kopf* und *30 g CO_2/\$*.

Im **restlichen Ostasien** war 2019: das mittlere BIP (KKP) etwa *20.900 \$/Kopf* und die CO_2-Emissionen rund *2,7 t/Kopf*, entsprechend einem Index der CO_2-Nachhaltigkeit von *210 g CO_2/\$*. Um bis 2050 eine für das 2-Grad-Klimaziel notwendige Begrenzung der CO_2-Emissionen auf *1,3 t/Kopf* zu erreichen (s. Abschn. 2.3), muss, bei einer Zunahme des BIP (KKP) auf z. B. *19.000 \$/Kopf*, der Index der CO_2-Nachhaltigkeit auf rund *60 g CO_2/\$* vermindert werden. Für das 1.5-Grad-Ziel lauten die Zahlen *0,5 t/Kopf* und *20 g CO_2/\$*.

Literatur

1. Crastan V.: Elektrische Energieversorgung 2, 5. Auflage, Springer-Verlag, 2022
2. Crastan V.: Weltweiter Energiebedarf und 2-Grad-Klimaziel, Analyse und Handlungsempfehlungen, Springer- Verlag, 2016
3. Crastan V.: Weltweite Energiewirtschaft und Klimaschutz, 2016, Springer-Verlag
4. IEA, International Energy Agency. Statistics & Balances, www.iea.org, October 2019
5. IMF, WEO Databases www.imf.org, October (2019)
6. IPCC (Intergovernmental Panels on Climate Change): 5. Bericht, Working Group I, September 2013
7. IPCC, 5. Bericht, Working Group II, März 2014
8. IPCC, 5. Bericht, Working Group III, April 2014
9. Steinacher M., Joos F., Stocker T.F. Allowable carbon emissions lowered by multiple climate targets. Nature 499, 2013
10. Oliver Geden, SWP-Studie, Berlin, Die Modifikation des 2-Grad-Ziels, 2012
11. Crastan V.: Klimawirksame Kennzahlen Band I – Europa + Eurasien und Afrika (3. Auflage), Springer Fachmedien Wiesbaden 2020
12. Crastan V.: Klimawirksame Kennzahlen Band II – Amerika, Nahost und Südasien, Ostasien und Ozeanien (2. Auflage), Springer Fachmedien Wiesbaden 2018

© Springer Fachmedien Wiesbaden GmbH, ein Teil von Springer Nature 2023
V. Crastan, *Kennzahlen zur Erreichung der weltweiten Klimaziele*,
https://doi.org/10.1007/978-3-658-40073-6

The manufacturer's authorised representative in the EU is Springer
Nature Customer Service Centre GmbH, Europaplatz 3, 69115 Heidelberg,
Germany. If you have any concerns regarding our products, please
contact ProductSafety@springernature.com

Printed and bound by CPI Group (UK) Ltd, Croydon, CR0 4YY
28/04/2026
02098500-0003